# SAS Component Language: Reference, Version 8

*The Power to Know*™

 SAS Publishing

The correct bibliographic citation for this manual is as follows: SAS Institute Inc., *SAS®
Component Language: Reference, Version 8*, Cary, NC: SAS Institute Inc., 1999. 812 pp.

**SAS® Component Language: Reference, Version 8**

Copyright © 1999 by SAS Institute Inc., Cary, NC, USA.

ISBN 1–58025–495–0

SAS Institute Inc., SAS Campus Drive, Cary, North Carolina 27513.

1st printing, October 1999

# Contents

# Changes and Enhancements

## Introduction

This section describes the features of SAS Component Language that have been implemented or enhanced since Release 6.12. Information about changes and enhancements that were implemented in Version 8 is preceded by **V8**. All other changes and enhancements described in this section were implemented in Version 7. In other words, if your site upgraded from Version 7 to Version 8, then only the items preceded by **V8** are new to you.

## Name Change to SAS Component Language

SAS Component Language is the new name of what was known in Version 6 as SAS Screen Control Language. A component is a self-contained, reusable object with specific properties that include a set of public attributes, public methods, event handlers that execute in response to various types of events, and a set of supported interfaces.

## Long Names

Names (except for libref and fileref names) can contain up to 32 characters. This includes names of SCL variables, arrays, SCL lists, SAS tables, views, indexes, catalogs, catalog entries, macros, and macro variables.

## Scope of Variables

SCL variables can have the local scope of a DO or SELECT block.

## Shortcut for Invoking Methods

A new feature called dot notation provides a shortcut for invoking methods and for setting or querying attribute values. Using dot notation reduces typing and makes SCL programs easier to read.

Dot notation cannot be used within DATA step INPUT or PUT functions.

## New Data Types

SCL provides the new data types NUM, CHAR, and LIST, as well as new object types. NUM and CHAR are new as named data types, although these data types have been available in previous versions as unnamed data types (for example, $). LIST and object types store identifiers for SCL lists and components, respectively. The object types can be specific (CLASS or INTERFACE) or generic (OBJECT).

**V8** Version 8 introduces another specific object type, CLASSPKG.

You declare a variable to have a specific object type by specifying a class name or interface name as the variable type. For example:

```
dcl sashelp.fsp.object.class object1;
```

If the object type of the variable cannot be determined at compile time, you can declare a variable to have a generic object type by using the named type OBJECT. For example:

```
dcl object object2;
```

## Terminology Change

To be more consistent with database management terminology, SAS Component Language now uses the terms *table*, *row*, and *column* in place of *data set*, *observation*, and *variable*. However, you may still encounter the old terms in some SAS products and documentation.

## Integrity Constraints for SAS Tables

SCL provides a set of functions that enable you to work with integrity constraints (IC). Integrity constraints are a Version 7 feature of SAS software for preserving the consistency and correctness of data that is stored in SAS tables. When integrity constraints are assigned to a table, they are automatically enforced for each addition, update, and deletion action on that table.

The new IC functions are ICCREATE, ICDELETE, ICTYPE, and ICVALUE.

## SCL Debugger

The SCL debuggerincludes new functionality that enables you

☐ to execute SCL functions through the CALC command

☐ to use dot notation in any debugger command that takes an expression or variable as an argument.

# Image Functions

The SCL functions that control Image objects in the Image Extensions to SAS/ GRAPH software are now documented in Appendix 1, "Commands Used with the IMGCTRL, IMGOP and PICFILL Functions," on page 735. New Image commands for the IMGOP function are

FILTER
>   allows user-provided Convolution Filters. This support is available in the Image Editor, in the SAS/AF Frame Image Data Object, and in Image SCL functions.

GET-BARCODE
>   decodes a bar code in an image and returns the value of the bar code. It can be used with the Image data object.

**V8** PRINT
>   prints an image. This command is available for the Frame Image Data Object and the Image SCL functions.

**V8** The READ command now supports TWAIN scanners and cameras in the Windows operating environments.

# New Language Elements

For details about these new language elements, see Chapter 16, "SAS Component Language Dictionary," on page 249.

**V8** CATCH statement
>   defines the actions that SCL takes when a specific exception is raised.

CLASS statement
>   enables you to use SCL to create a SAS/AF class and to define all the properties for the class, including attributes, methods, events, and interfaces.

**V8** COMPAREARRAY function
>   enables you to compare two arrays for size and data equality.

COMPARELIST function
>   compares two SCL lists. This comparison can include item names, values, or both.

**V8** COPYARRAY function
>   enables you to copy data from one array into another array.

CREATESCL function
>   writes a class definition from a CLASS or INTERFACE catalog entry to a CLASS or INTERFACE statement in an SCL entry.
>       **V8** CREATESCL will also write a class package definition from a CLASSPKG entry to a PACKAGE statement in an SCL entry and generate proxy classes.

DCREATE function
>   creates a directory on the user's host operating system.

DECLARE statement
>   declares a variable of any type, including the new CHAR, NUM, LIST and OBJECT types. (By contrast, the LENGTH statement can declare only unnamed numeric and character variables.)

**V8** DELARRAY function
>   deletes a dynamic array.

DIALOG function
: runs a FRAME entry and disables all other windows when the FRAME window opens.

**V8** GETVARF function
: assigns the formatted value of a SAS table column to an SCL character variable.

IMPORT statement
: defines a search path for references to CLASS entries in an SCL program so that you can refer to a class by its one- or two-level name instead of having to specify the four-level name each time.

INITROW function
: initializes the table data vector (TDV) to missing values. This prevents bad data from being written to a row of a SAS table when values are not explicitly assigned to columns and you use the APPEND function with the NOINIT option.

INTERFACE statement
: specifies the design of an interface.

**V8** ITEM statement
: specifies a class on the server that can be accessed by applications on the client.

**V8** MAKEARRAY function
: creates an array of the given size and initializes all of the elements in the array either to missing (for numeric elements) or blank (for character elements).

MESSAGEBOX function
: displays a host message box that can contain an icon, buttons, and message text. MESSAGEBOX returns the user's selection.

NAMEDIVIDE function
: returns the number of parts in a two- to four-level compound name as well as the values of each part.

NAMEMERGE function
: merges two to four name parts into a compound name.

_NEO_ operator
: provides a faster and more direct way to create an object. This operator combines the actions of loading a class (using LOADCLASS) and initializing the object with the _new method, which invokes the object's _init method.

_NEW_ operator
: creates an object and runs the associated class constructor.

OPENENTRYDIALOG function
: displays a list of entries in SAS catalogs and returns the user's selection.

OPENSASFILEDIALOG function
: displays a list of SAS files and returns the user's selection.

**V8** PACKAGE statement
: defines a group of classes whose metadata must be recognized by objects that are defined on the client.

**V8** REDIM function
: resizes a dynamic array.

SAVEENTRYDIALOG function
: enables you to implement a **Save As** choice by displaying a dialog box that lists entries in SAS catalogs and returns the selected catalog name.

SAVESASFILEDIALOG function
> enables you to implement a **Save As** choice by displaying a dialog box that lists SAS files and returning the selected filename.

SELECTICON function
> displays a selection list of icons and returns the number that identifies the selected icon.

**V8** SUBMITCLEAR function
> aborts a pending submit transaction.

**V8** THROW statement
> raises an exception.

UNIQUENUM function
> returns a number that is unique for each call to the function during a SAS session.

USECLASS statement
> binds methods that are implemented within it to the specified class definition.

# Enhanced SCL Elements

For details about these new language elements, see Chapter 16, "SAS Component Language Dictionary," on page 249.

ATTRN function
> now provides the NLOBSF option, which returns the number of logical rows (those not marked for deletion) in a SAS table when an active WHERE clause is applied. Also, the new ICONST option provides information about integrity constraints for generation data sets, and the GENMAX and GENNEXT options provide information about generation numbers.

CONTROL statement
> now provides a new option, HALTONDOTATTRIBUTE, which enables you to specify whether your application halts execution if SCL detects an error in the dot notation.

DELETE function
> now provides the FILE type for deleting external files or directories.

ENTRY statement
> now enables you to specify the parameter modifiers INPUT, UPDATE, and OUTPUT. In Version 6, all parameters were treated as if they were UPDATE parameters.

FILEDIALOG function
> now provides a DESCRIPTION option for each filter that you specify so that you can provide a description of each filter.

FONTSEL function
> can now open the portable font selector for hardware fonts, using the new 'H' font-selector option.

GETLATTR function
> can now return the value of the HONORCASE|IGNORECASE attribute, which specifies whether character values are stored in the case in which they are entered or whether they are stored in uppercase.

METHOD statement
> now enables you to specify an access scope for methods. You can specify PUBLIC, PRIVATE, or PROTECTED. All Version 6 methods were treated as PUBLIC

methods. Also, you can specify the parameter modifiers INPUT, UPDATE, or OUTPUT in the argument list. All Version 6 parameters were treated as UPDATE parameters.

NAMEDITEM function
now enables you to specify whether a search is case sensitive.

RENAME function
now provides the FILE option for renaming external files or directories.

SETLATTR function
now provides the HONORCASE|IGNORECASE attribute, which specifies whether character values are stored in the case in which they are entered or whether they are stored in uppercase.

In addition, most data set functions that take a data set name as a parameter have been enhanced to support generation data sets. *Generation data sets* enable you to keep multiple copies of a SAS data set. Refer to *SAS Language Reference: Concepts* for more information on generation data sets.

# Compatibility Issues

ACCESS routine
The functionality of ACCESS is available through the CALL BUILD routine. Both ACCESS and BUILD now open the Explorer window. Old programs that use ACCESS will still work, although the TYPE and MODE parameters are not supported from the Explorer window. Using BUILD for new programs is recommended because it provides additional functionality.

CALC routine
The CALL CALC routine is not supported in Version 7.

CARDS statement
The DATA step statement DATALINES replaces the CARDS statement.

CATALOG function
The functionality of CATALOG is now available through the CALL BUILD routine. Like CATALOG, BUILD opens the Explorer window when a catalog is specified as the first parameter. Old programs with the CATALOG function will still run, although the SHOWTYPE and PMENU parameters are not supported from the Explorer window. Using BUILD for new programs is recommended because it provides additional functionality.

CATLIST, DIRLIST, and FILELIST, and IVARLIST functions
Version 7 tables may contain mixed-case names. If any existing application relies on one of these functions to return an uppercased name, you may need to modify the application. See Chapter 16, "SAS Component Language Dictionary," on page 249 for more information.

CATLIST, DIRLIST, FILELIST, and LIBLIST windows
These windows have been replaced with host selector windows in which the AUTOCLOSE option will now be ignored.

P A R T *1*

# SCL Fundamentals

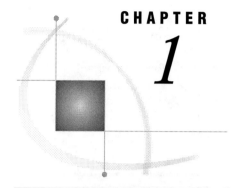

**CHAPTER**

*1*

# Introduction to SCL

## Introduction

SAS Component Language (SCL)* is a programming language that enables you to develop many different types of applications, from simple programs that accomplish a few tasks to sophisticated, interactive applications that use procedures available in other SAS software products. For example, you can use SCL with other SAS software to create data entry applications, to display tables and menus, and to generate and submit SAS source code. SAS/ASSIST software is an example of the powerful applications that you can build with SCL.

## SAS Component Language Elements

SAS Component Language has statements, functions, CALL routines, operators, expressions, and variables—elements that are common to the base SAS language and to many other programming languages. If you have experience writing DATA or PROC steps in the base SAS language, the basic elements of SCL are familiar to you. For example, in SCL programs, you can use DO loops, IF-THEN/ELSE statements, comparison operators such as EQ and LT, and SAS macros.

SCL provides additional statements, functions, and other features that make it easy to create object-oriented, interactive applications. For example, SCL provides CLASS

---

\* In earlier releases of SAS software, SCL was called SAS Screen Control Language. Version 7 introduced several new features that enable you to design object-oriented applications. The new name, SAS Component Language, reflects the object-oriented capabilities of the new SCL.

and INTERFACE statements that enable you to define classes and interfaces to those classes. You can use dot notation to access an object's attributes directly and to invoke methods instead of using the SEND and NOTIFY routines.

Chapter 2, "The Structure of SCL Programs," on page 9 describes the organization of an SCL application. Chapter 3, "SCL Fundamentals," on page 17 describes the basic elements of SCL and the rules that you must follow to put these elements together in a program. Chapter 6, "Controlling Program Flow," on page 65 describes the statements and other features that you can use to control the flow of your application.

# Entering SCL Code

You can enter your SCL code in four ways:

☐ In the SAS Explorer, select the catalog where you want to store your SCL code, and select

 File ▶ New... ▶ SCL Program

☐ Issue the BUILD command followed by the name of the entry that you want to edit:

   BUILD *libref.catalog.entry*.SCL

☐ In the Build window for the frame, select

 View ▶ Frame SCL

☐ In the Build window for the program screen, select

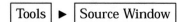 Tools ▶ Source Window

# Compiling SCL Programs

You must compile SCL programs before testing or executing an application. The SCL compiler translates your SCL application into an intermediate form that can be executed by the SCL interpreter. In the process of translating your application, the compiler identifies any syntax errors that are present. You should correct these errors and compile the code again until the program compiles without errors. If there are errors in the program, then no intermediate code is produced, and running the entry produces a message stating that the entry has no code.

The compiler produces a list of errors, warnings, and notes in the Log window. A program that compiles with no errors or warnings produces a message like the following in the message line of the Source window:

```
NOTE:
Code generated for SALES.FRAME. Code size=2649.
```

## Compiling Your Program Interactively

*Note:* You must save frames before you can compile them. △

You can compile frames, program screens, and SCL programs by issuing the COMPILE command in the Build window or by selecting **Compile** from the pull-down menus. In the Build window for frames or SCL programs, select

Build ► Compile

In the Build window for program screens, select

Run ► Compile

You can also compile FRAME, PROGRAM, and SCL entries from the SAS Explorer. If your SCL code is associated with a frame or a program screen, then you must compile the FRAME or PROGRAM entry in order for the associated code to be compiled correctly. The SCL code is compiled when you compile the FRAME or PROGRAM entry. If your SCL code is not associated with a FRAME or PROGRAM entry, then you compile the SCL entry. To compile an entry from the Explorer, select the entry, then select **Compile** from the pop-up menu.

If you compile a FRAME or PROGRAM entry that does not have any associated SCL code, the SCL compiler displays an error message.

## Compiling Your Program in Batch

To compile your SCL application in batch, run PROC BUILD with the COMPILE option:

**PROC BUILD** CATALOG=*libref.catalog* BATCH;

COMPILE < ENTRYTYPE=*entry-type*>;

RUN;

The default entry type is PROGRAM. If you do not specify an *entry-type*, then all PROGRAM, FRAME, and SCL entries in the catalog are compiled. All PROGRAM, FRAME, and SCL entries in an application must be compiled before the application can be executed.

If you compile a frame in batch, and the compiler cannot find the associated SCL source, the frame will not compile.

## The SCL Data Vector

Compiling an SCL program opens a temporary storage area called the SCL data vector (SDV). The SDV holds the values of all window, nonwindow, and system variables that are used in the application.* Areas in the SDV are created automatically for system variables as well as for window variables for all controls in the application window, even if the variables are not used in the SCL program. Figure 1.1 on page 6 shows the SDV for an application that uses the window variables NAME, HEIGHT, AGE, and WEIGHT and the nonwindow variables HFACTOR and WFACTOR.

---

\* The SDV is similar to the program data vector (PDV) that is created by base SAS software when it compiles a DATA step. The program data vector holds the values of the variables that are defined in the DATA step.

**Figure 1.1**  SCL Data Vector for a Typical Application

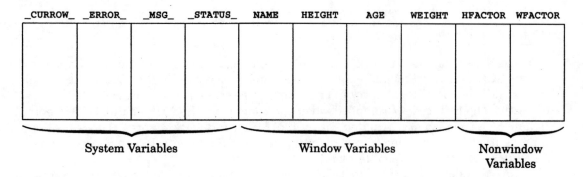

## Testing Applications

After an SCL program compiles successfully, you can test it. For catalog entries that use the TESTAF, AF, or AFA command, you can issue the command from either the Source window or the Display window. You must use the AF or AFA command if a program contains SUBMIT statements, or if you are testing a FRAME entry that is in a library accessed with SAS/SHARE software. It is recommended that you issue the SAVE command before issuing the AF or AFA command.

SCL programs for FSEDIT and FSVIEW applications run when you return to the FSEDIT or FSVIEW window.

## Debugging Programs

SCL includes an interactive debugger for monitoring the execution of SCL programs. The debugger enables you to locate logical errors while a program is executing. To use the debugger, issue the DEBUG ON command before compiling. Then either use the TESTAF command or use the AF or AFA command with the DEBUG=YES option to run the entry under the debugger. To deactivate the SCL debugger, issue the DEBUG OFF command followed by the COMPILE command. For more information about the SCL debugger, see Chapter 13, "The SCL Debugger," on page 191.

## Saving Programs

After you create an SCL program, use the SAVE command to save it. You should also use SAVE /ALL to save the entry before issuing a TESTAF command if the entry uses CALL DISPLAY to call itself. Also be sure to save all other open entries before issuing a TESTAF command so that CALL DISPLAY and method calls will execute the most recent versions of your SAS/AF entries.

## Optimizing the Performance of SCL Code

You can optimize the performance of SCL programs in your applications with the SCL analysis tools.

The following table lists the available tools and provides information about when you might want to use each tool.

| Use the... | when you want to... |
|---|---|
| Coverage Analyzer | monitor an executing application and access a report that shows which lines of SCL code are not executed during testing. |
| List Diagnostic Utility | monitor an executing application and access reports on the use of SCL lists, including any lists that are left undeleted. |
| Performance Analyzer | monitor an executing application and identify any bottlenecks in the application's SCL code. |
| Static Analyzer | access reports that detail SCL code complexity; variable, function, method and I/O usage; and error and warning messages. |

To display a menu of the SCL analysis tools, enter **sclprof** at the command prompt. For detailed information about using these tools, see the SAS/AF online Help.

# Using Other SAS Software Features in SCL Programs

SCL supports most of the features of the base SAS language. Some base SAS features are directly supported by SCL. Other base SAS features have equivalent features in SCL, although there may be small differences in functionality. For example, the IN operator in SCL, returns the index of the element if a match is found rather than a 1 (true).

Chapter 16, "SAS Component Language Dictionary," on page 249 provides entries for elements that have different functionality in SCL programs. The differences are summarized in "Using SAS DATA Step Features in SCL" on page 78.

Although SCL does not provide an equivalent for every command that is available under your operating system, it does provide features that interact directly with SAS software and with host operating systems. For example, you can use the SUBMIT statement to access other features of SAS software, and you can use the SYSTEM function to issue host operating system commands. SCL also supports the SAS macro facility. For more information about these features, see Chapter 7, "Using Other SAS Software Products," on page 77.

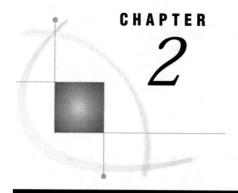

**CHAPTER**

*2*

# The Structure of SCL Programs

## Introduction

An SCL application consists of one or more SCL entries. These SCL entries can contain the following types of modules:

- □ labeled sections
- □ CLASS blocks
- □ METHOD blocks
- □ USECLASS blocks
- □ INTERFACE blocks
- □ macros.

For example, an SCL program may consist of only one labeled section, or it may contain two labeled sections, a METHOD block, and a couple of macros. A complex program may contain several CLASS, METHOD, USECLASS, and INTERFACE blocks.

Some types of modules can be stored together in one SCL entry, but others cannot. One SCL entry may contain any one of the following:

- □ one or more labeled sections and/or one or more macros
- □ one CLASS block, which may also contain one or more METHOD blocks
- □ one INTERFACE block
- □ one or more USECLASS blocks, each of which may contain one or more METHOD blocks
- □ one or more METHOD blocks (that are not contained within a CLASS or USECLASS block).

In strictly object-oriented applications, METHOD blocks are contained within CLASS or USECLASS blocks. If your application is not a strictly object-oriented application, you can save METHOD blocks by themselves in SCL entries.

Object-oriented applications use CLASS, METHOD, USECLASS, and INTERFACE blocks extensively. For information about designing and implementing object-oriented applications see *SAS Guide to Applications Development* in addition to the information contained in this documentation.

# Using Labeled Sections

SCL programs execute in phases, such as the initialization phase and the termination phase. During each phase, control of the entry can pass to a different segment of an SCL program. The segments of the program are identified by labels; that is, the SCL program is divided into labeled sections.

Labeled sections are program segments that are designed to be called only within the program in which they are defined. Labeled sections begin with a label and end with a RETURN statement. A label may be one of the reserved labels such as INIT or MAIN; it may correspond to a field name, window-variable name, or object name in your application; or it may simply identify a module that is called repetitively, such as a module that sorts data.

Labeled sections are a good solution when you are working within one SCL program because they can help divide the program into smaller, simpler pieces.

For example, the following SCL program contains an INIT section that is executed before the application window is displayed; two sections that correspond to window variables, NAME and ADDRESS; and a MAIN section that is executed each time the user updates a field in the window.

```
init:
    ...some SCL statements...
    return;

name:
    ...some SCL statements...
    return;

address:
    ...some SCL statements...
    return;

main:
    ...some SCL statements...
    return;
```

## Reserved Labels

There are five reserved labels:

FSEINIT

An FSEINIT section, which is valid in FSEDIT and FSBROWSE applications only, contains any statements that are needed to initialize the application. These statements are executed one time only when the user invokes the FSEDIT or FSBROWSE procedure and before the first row is displayed.

INIT

> The INIT section is executed before the application window is displayed to the user. Typically, you use the INIT section to initialize variables, to import values through macro variables, to open tables, and to define initial messages to display when the window is opened. In FSEDIT and FSBROWSE applications, as well as Data Table and Data Form controls, the INIT section is executed before each SAS table row is displayed.

MAIN

> The MAIN section is executed each time the user modifies a field in the window and presses ENTER.

TERM

> The TERM section is executed when the user issues the END command. You might use the TERM section to close tables, to export values of macro variables, and to construct and submit statements for execution. In FSEDIT applications, Data Table controls, and Data Form controls, the TERM section is executed after each SAS table row is displayed, provided that the MAIN section has been executed for the row.

FSETERM

> The FSETERM section is valid in FSEDIT applications only. This section executes once after the user issues the END command and terminates the FSEDIT procedure.

In FSVIEW applications, you write individual formulas consisting of one or more lines of SCL code for each computed variable, rather than complete SCL programs. These formulas are stored in FORMULA entries. The FSVIEW procedure automatically adds a label before the formula and a RETURN statement after the formula. The label is the same as the name of the variable whose value you are calculating.

An SCL program for FSEDIT or FSBROWSE applications must contain at least one of the following reserved labels: INIT, MAIN, or TERM. If a program does not include at least one of these three reserved labels, the procedure never passes control to your SCL program. If a program does not contain all three of these reserved labels, you get one or more warning messages when you compile the program.

The FSEINIT and FSETERM labels are optional. The compiler does not issue any warnings if these labels are not present.

Neither SCL programs for FRAME entries nor programs in SCL entries that contain method block definitions require any reserved sections.

For more information about the FSVIEW, FSEDIT, and FSBROWSE procedures, see *SAS/FSP Software Procedures Guide*. For more information about FRAME applications, see *SAS Guide to Applications Development*.

# Window Variable Sections

SCL provides a special type of labeled section, called a window variable section, that automatically executes when a user takes an action in a particular control or field. For example, window variable sections might be used to verify values that users enter in controls or fields. An SCL program can include labeled sections for any number of window variables.

The sequence for executing window variable sections is determined by the physical position of the window element. Window variable sections execute sequentially for each window element, from left to right and from top to bottom. A window variable section must be labeled with the name of the associated window variable. For more information about window variables, see *SAS Guide to Applications Development*.

## Correcting Errors in Window Variables

To correct an error in a window variable, you can allow users to correct the error in the window, or you can include a CONTROL ERROR statement along with statements in the window variable section that make a correction, as shown in the following example:

```
INIT:
     control error;
return;


Name:
    if error(Name) then do;
        erroroff Name;
        Name=default-value-assigned-elsewhere;
        _msg_=
            'Value was invalid and has been reset.';
    end;
return;
```

Using a window variable section in this manner reduces overhead because the program's MAIN section executes only after the window variable sections for all modified window variables have executed correctly.

If a program also uses CONTROL ERROR, CONTROL ALWAYS, or CONTROL ALLCMDS, then the MAIN section executes after the window variable sections even if an error has been introduced. For more information about the CONTROL statement, see "CONTROL" on page 302.

# Defining Classes

Classes define data and the operations that you can perform on that data. You define classes with the CLASS statement. For example, the following code defines a class, Simple, that defines an attribute named **total** and implements a method named addNums:

**Example Code 2.1**   Example Class Definition

```
class Simple;
  public num total;

  addNums: public method n1:num n2:num return=num;
      total=n1+n2;
      return(total);
  endmethod;

endclass;
```

The CLASS statement does not have to implement the methods. The methods may be only declared. For example:

```
class Simple;
  public num total;

  addNums: public method n1:num n2:num return=num
      / (scl=work.a.simMeth.scl');
endclass;
```

The code to implement the method is contained in **work.a.simMeth.scl** (see Example Code 2.2 on page 14).

For more information about defining and using classes, see Chapter 8, "SAS Object-Oriented Programming Concepts," on page 93; Chapter 9, "Example: Creating An Object-Oriented Application," on page 137; and "CLASS" on page 277.

# Defining and Using Methods

Methods define operations that you can perform on data. Methods are defined with the METHOD statement. Methods can be implemented in CLASS blocks or in USECLASS blocks. In addition, if you are not designing a strictly object-oriented application, they can be stored in separate SCL entries.

Storing method implementations in SCL entries enables you to write methods that perform operations that are common to or shared by other applications. You can call the methods from any SAS/AF application.

For more information about defining and using methods in CLASS and USECLASS blocks, see Chapter 8, "SAS Object-Oriented Programming Concepts," on page 93 and Chapter 9, "Example: Creating An Object-Oriented Application," on page 137.

## Defining Method Blocks

To define a method, use the METHOD statement. For example, the METHOD statement in Example Code 2.1 on page 12 defines the public method addNums, which takes two numeric parameters, adds them, and returns the total.

*Note:*   Do not include window-specific statements or functions (for example, the PROTECT and CURSOR statements and the FIELD and MODIFIED functions) in method blocks that are stored in independent SCL entries. SCL entries that contain window-specific statements or functions will not compile independently. They must be compiled in conjunction with the associated FRAME entry. △

When you want to pass parameters between an SCL program and a method block, you use the same principles as when you are passing parameters between a CALL DISPLAY statement and an ENTRY statement. Unless the REST=, ARGLIST=, or OPTIONAL= option is used in the METHOD statement, the parameter list for the METHOD statement and the argument list for the associated ENTRY statement must agree in the following respects:

- ☐ The number of parameters passed by the METHOD statement must equal the number of arguments received by the ENTRY statement.
- ☐ The position of each parameter in the METHOD statement must be the same as the position of the corresponding argument in the ENTRY statement.
- ☐ Each parameter in the METHOD statement and its corresponding argument in the ENTRY statement must have the same data type.

The parameters and arguments do not have to agree in name. For more information, see "METHOD" on page 540 and "ENTRY" on page 369.

## Calling a Method That Is Stored in an SCL Entry

If the method module is stored in a PROGRAM entry or SCREEN entry, then you must use a LINK or GOTO statement to call it. Although parameters cannot be passed with LINK or GOTO statements, you can reference global values in those statements.

If the module is an SCL entry, then call the method module with a CALL METHOD routine. The CALL METHOD routine enables you to pass parameters to the method. For example, a program that needs to validate an amount can call the AMOUNT method, which is stored in METHDLIB.METHODS.VALIDATE.SCL:

```
call method('methdlib.methods.validate.scl',
            'amount',amount,controlid);
```

After the method module performs its operations, it can return modified values to the calling routine.

If the method module is stored in the SCL entry that is associated with the FRAME entry, then you must compile the SCL entry as a separate entity from the FRAME entry in addition to compiling the FRAME entry.

For more information about the CALL METHOD routine, see "METHOD" on page 539.

# USECLASS Blocks

USECLASS blocks contain method blocks. A USECLASS block binds the methods that are implemented within it to a class definition. This binding enables you to use the attributes and methods of the class within the methods that are implemented in your USECLASS block. However, your USECLASS block does not have to implement all of the methods defined in the class.

For example, the USECLASS block for the class defined in "Defining Classes" on page 12 would be stored in **work.a.simMeth.scl** and would contain the following code:

**Example Code 2.2**   USECLASS Block for the addNums Method

```
useclass simple.class;
  addNums: public method n1:num n2:num return=num;
      total=n1+n2;
      return(total);
  endmethod;
enduseclass;
```

Using USECLASS blocks to separate the class definition from the method implementations enables multiple programmers to work on method implementations simultaneously.

For more information, see Chapter 8, "SAS Object-Oriented Programming Concepts," on page 93; "USECLASS — Level One" on page 150; and "USECLASS" on page 698.

# Defining Interfaces

Interfaces are groups of method declarations that enable classes to possess a common set of methods even if the classes are not related hierarchically. Interfaces are especially useful when you have several unrelated classes that perform a similar set of actions. These actions can be declared as methods in an interface, and each associated class can provide its own implementation for each of the methods. In this way, interfaces provide a form of multiple inheritance.

For more information about defining and using interfaces, see Chapter 8, "SAS Object-Oriented Programming Concepts," on page 93; Chapter 9, "Example: Creating An Object-Oriented Application," on page 137; and "INTERFACE" on page 486.

# Using Macros

You can use the SAS macro facility to define macros and macro variables for your SCL program. That is, you can use SAS macros and SAS macro variables that have been defined elsewhere in the SAS session or in autocall libraries. You can then pass parameters between macros and the rest of your program. In addition, macros can be used by more than one program. However, macros can be more complicated to maintain than the original program segment because of the symbols and quoting that are required.

If a macro is used by more than one program, you must keep track of all the programs that use the macro so that you can recompile all of them each time the macro is updated. Because SCL is compiled (rather than interpreted like the SAS language), each SCL program that calls a macro must be recompiled whenever that macro is updated in order to update the program with the new macro code.

Macros and macro variables in SCL programs are resolved when you compile the SCL program, not when a user executes the application. However, you can use the SYMGET and SYMGETN functions to retrieve the value of a macro variable or to store a value in a macro variable at execution time, and you can use the SYMPUT and SYMPUTN functions to create a macro variable at execution time. For more information, see "Using Macro Variables" on page 87.

*Note:* Macros and macro variables within submit blocks are not resolved when you compile the SCL program. Instead, they are passed with the rest of the submit block to SAS software when the block is submitted. For more information about submit blocks, see "Submitting SAS Statements and SQL Statements" on page 80. △

*Note:* Using macros does not reduce the size of the compiled SCL code. Program statements that are generated by a macro are added to the compiled code as if those lines existed at that location in the program. △

## Example

The following SCL program uses macros to validate an amount and a rate:

```
%macro valamnt;
  if amount < 0 or amount > 500 then do;
    erroron amount;
    _msg_='Amount must be between $0 and $500.';
    stop;
  end;
  else erroroff amount;
%mend;
%macro rateamnt;
  if rate<0 or rate>1 then do;
    erroron rate;
    _msg_='Rate must be between 0 and 1.';
    stop;
  end;
  else erroroff rate;
%mend;

INIT:
  control error;
  amount=0;
```

```
      rate=.5;
return;

MAIN:
  payment=amount*rate;
return;

TERM:
return;

AMOUNT:
  %valamnt
return;

RATE:
  %rateamnt
return;
```

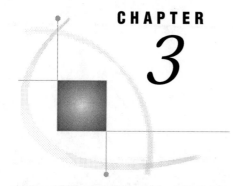

CHAPTER

*3*

# SCL Fundamentals

# Introduction

Like any language, SAS Component Language has its own vocabulary and syntax. An SCL program consists of one or more SCL statements, which can include keywords, expressions, constants, and operators.

# SCL Data Types

SCL has the following data types:

- □ NUM
- □ CHAR
- □ LIST
- □ generic OBJECT
- □ specific object (CLASS or INTERFACE).

## Declaring Data Types

You can use the DECLARE statement for declaring any type of SCL variable. You can use the LENGTH statement for declaring numeric and character variables.

You can also declare data types when you use the ENTRY and METHOD statements. In these statements, you must specify a colon before a named data type; with an unnamed data type, (for example, $), the colon is optional. For example:

```
ENTRY: name :$20
       location $20
       zipcode :num
       mybutton :mylib.mycat.button.class
       return=char;
```

For details, see "DECLARE" on page 330, "LENGTH" on page 510, "ENTRY" on page 369, and "METHOD" on page 540.

## Numeric (NUM) Variables

Numeric variables contain numbers and are stored as doubles. They are declared with the keyword NUM.

```
    /* declare a numeric variable AGE          */
  declare num age;

    /* declare the numeric variables AGE and YEARS*/
```

```
declare num age, years;

    /* declare numeric variables X and Y.     */
    /* Initialize X to 1 and Y to 20 plus the  */
    /* value of X.                             */
declare num x, y=20+x;
```

## Character (CHAR) Variables

Character variables can contain up to 32,767 characters and are declared with the keyword CHAR. A variable that is declared as CHAR without a specified length is assigned a default length of 200.

```
    /* declare a character variable NAME and  */
    /* assign the value ABC to it             */
declare char name='abc';

    /* declare a character variable NAME      */
    /* with a length of 20                    */
declare char(20) name;
```

## Lists

SCL lists are ordered collections of data. Lists are dynamic; they grow and shrink to accommodate the number or size of the items that you store in them. Lists can contain items of different data types.

To declare an SCL list, use the keyword LIST. The following example declares the list MYLIST:

```
declare list mylist;
```

The function that creates the list (for example, MAKELIST) assigns the identifier for the list to the variable, as shown below.

```
declare list mylist;
    ...more SCL statements...
mylist=makelist();
```

*Note:*  To maintain compatibility with previous releases, the SCL compiler does not generate error messages if a list is not declared or if it is declared as a numeric variable. However, it is recommended that you declare lists so that the compiler can identify errors. A list must be declared as type List when it is passed to a method that requires an argument of type List. See "Overloading and List, Object, and Numeric Types" on page 111.  △

For information about using lists, see Chapter 5, "SCL Lists," on page 47.

## Objects

Objects can be declared in either of two ways:
- as a specific object of type Class or Interface. When an object is declared with the name of the class, the compiler can validate attributes and methods for the object and can return error messages if incorrect attributes or methods are used.

□ as a generic object of type Object. The specific object class that is associated with the generic object cannot be resolved until run time. The compiler reserves space in the SAS Data Vector (SDV) for the object, but it cannot validate attributes or methods for the object, because it does not know the names of classes. Instead, this validation is deferred until program execution. Consequently, you should use the OBJECT keyword to declare an object only when necessary, so that you can obtain optimal run-time performance.

You can use dot notation for accessing attributes and methods for both specific objects and generic objects.

*Note:*   If you want to use dot notation to access the attributes or methods of a Version 6 widget, then you need to declare its widget ID of OBJECT type, and you must obtain its widget ID with the _getWidget method. For example, Text is a Version 6 text entry widget. To access its methods or attributes with dot notation, you should use code that looks like this:

```
dcl object obj;
/* dcl sashelp.fsp.efield.class obj; */
call notify ( 'Text', '_getWidget', obj );
obj.backgroundColor = 'blue';
```

See "Accessing Object Attributes and Methods With Dot Notation" on page 119 for more information.  △

## Specific Objects (CLASS and INTERFACE)

The following example declares an object named DataHolder as an instance of the Collection class, which is provided with SAS software:

```
declare sashelp.fsp.collection.class DataHolder;
```

When you declare a class, you can also use the IMPORT statement to reference the class and then use an abbreviated form of the class name in the DECLARE statement. For example:

```
import sashelp.fsp.collection.class;
declare collection DataHolder;
```

## Generic OBJECTs

In the following example, MyObject is recognized by the compiler as an object, but the compiler has no information about the type of class instance that the object will actually be:

```
declare object MyObject;
```

## Specifying the Object Type at Run Time

The following example declares an object named PgmObj2 and then specifies one condition under which PgmObj2 will be a collection object and another condition under which PgmObj2 will be an object that is created from a class named Foo. The _NEW_ operator creates the object.

```
declare object PgmObj2,
        num    x;
if x=1 then
   PgmObj2=_new_ sashelp.fsp.collection.class;
else
```

```
    PgmObj2=_new_ sashelp.fsp.foo.class;
```

As described above, you can use the IMPORT statement to reference a class definition and then use an abbreviated class name when you create the class.

```
import sashelp.fsp.collection.class;
import sashelp.fsp.foo.class;
declare object PgmObj2,
        num     x;
if x=1 then
   PgmObj2=_new_ collection();
   end;
else
   PgmObj2=_new_ foo();
```

Any errors that result from using incorrect methods or attributes for PgmObj2 and Foo will cause the program to halt.

# Names in SCL

In SCL, the rules for names are

1 Librefs and filerefs can have a maximum length of 8 characters. Other names — including names of SCL variables, arrays, SCL lists, SAS tables, views, indexes, catalogs, catalog entries, macros, and macro variables — can be 32 characters long.

2 The first character must be a letter (A, B, C, . . . , Z) or an underscore (_). Subsequent characters can be letters, numeric digits (0, 1, . . . , 9), or underscores.

3 Names are stored in the case in which they are entered, which can be lower case, mixed case, or upper case.

4 Names cannot contain blanks.

5 SCL honors the names that are reserved by SAS software for automatic variables, lists of variables, SAS tables, and librefs. Thus, you cannot use these names in your SCL programs.

   a When creating variables, do not use the names of special SAS automatic variables (for example, _N_ and _ERROR_) nor the names of lists of variables (for example, _CHARACTER_, _NUMERIC_, and _ALL_).

   b Do not use any of the following names as a libref:
      □ SASCAT
      □ SASHELP
      □ SASMSG
      □ SASUSER
      □ USER
      □ WORK

   Use LIBRARY only as the libref to point to a SAS data library containing a FORMATS catalog that was created with PROC FORMAT.

   c Do not assign any of the following names to a SAS table:
      □ _NULL_
      □ _DATA_
      □ _LAST_

Just as SCL recognizes keywords from position and context, it also recognizes names in the same way. If SCL sees a word that meets the requirements for a user-supplied

SAS name and that is not used in a syntax that defines it as anything else, it interprets the word as a variable name.

# SCL Keywords

An SCL keyword is a word or symbol in an SCL statement that defines the statement type to SAS software. Keywords are a fixed part of the SCL, and their form and meaning are also fixed. Generally, keywords define the function or CALL routine that you are using in an SCL program statement. For example, OPEN is the keyword in

```
table-id=OPEN('MYLIB.HOUSES');
```

# Variables

SCL variables have most of the same attributes as variables in the base SAS language:

□ name

□ data type

□ length.

However, SCL variables do not have labels.
SCL provides three categories of variables:

window variables
   are linked to a control (widget) or field in a window. They pass values between an SCL program and the associated window.

nonwindow variables
   are defined in an SCL program. They hold temporary values that users do not need to see.

system variables
   are provided by SCL. They hold information about the status of an application.

As in the base SAS language, you can group variables into arrays to make it easier to apply the same process to all the variables in a group. Arrays in SCL are described in Chapter 4, "SCL Arrays," on page 37.

## Window Variables

Most SCL programs are associated with a window for interacting with users. An SCL program for a window has variables that are associated with the controls and fields in the window. These variables are called window variables, and they are the means by which users and SCL programs communicate with each other. You can use these variables in the SCL program without explicitly declaring them.

### Name

The name of a window variable is the same as the name that is assigned to the control or field. The SCL program for the window cannot change that name.

## Data Type

A window variable also has a data type, which can be character, numeric, or an object data type. The type is determined by the value of the **Type** attribute, which is displayed in the Properties window (for a control) or in the Attributes window (for a field). For more information about data types that are used in SAS/AF applications, see the SAS/AF online Help and *SAS Guide to Applications Development.*

## Length

Lengths of window variables are determined as follows:

- ☐ Numeric and object variables are stored internally as doubles.
- ☐ Character variables have a maximum length that equals the width of the corresponding field in the application window. For example, if a field occupies 20 columns in the window, then the maximum length of the associated window variable is 20.

SCL programs can use methods to alter the lengths of window variables for some FRAME entry controls. Otherwise, you cannot alter the length of a window variable in an SCL program. Specifying a length for a window variable in a DECLARE or LENGTH statement produces an error message when you compile the program.

---

# Nonwindow Variables

SCL programs can define and use variables that do not have associated controls or fields in the window. These variables are called nonwindow variables, and they are used to hold values that users do not need to see. SCL programs that do not have an associated window use only nonwindow variables. Nonwindow variables are also referred to as program variables. Because nonwindow variables are used only within an SCL program, they have no informat or format.

## Name

The name of a nonwindow variable is determined by the first assignment statement that uses the variable, unless the variable is explicitly defined with a DECLARE or LENGTH statement. Names of nonwindow variables can be up to 32 characters long.

## Data Type

Nonwindow variables are numeric unless they are explicitly declared as a different data type.

## Length

Lengths of nonwindow variables are determined as follows:

- ☐ Numeric and object variables are stored as doubles.
- ☐ Character variables have a default length of 200. However, you can use the DECLARE statement to change the length from a minimum length of 1 to a maximum of 32K.

You can use the DECLARE or LENGTH statement to specify a different maximum length for nonwindow character variables. This can significantly reduce memory requirements if your program uses many nonwindow variables.

## Scope

The scope of a variable determines when a value can be assigned to it and when its value is available for use. In general, variables in an SCL program have program scope. That is, their scope is local to the program. They are available for use within the SCL program but not to other parts of SAS software. When the program finishes, the variables no longer exist, so their values are no longer available.

SCL provides a feature for defining variables as local to a DO or SELECT block. To define a variable with this type of scope, use a DECLARE statement inside a DO or SELECT block. Any variable that you declare in this way exists only for the duration of that DO or SELECT block, and its value is available only during that time. For example, the following program uses two variables named SECOND. One variable is numeric by virtue of the first assignment statement. The other is a character variable that is local to the DO block. After the DO block ends, only the numeric SECOND variable is available.

```
INIT:
   first=10;
   second=5;
   put 'Before the DO block: ' first= second=;
   do;
           /* Declare variable THIRD and new      */
           /* variable SECOND, which is local to  */
           /* the DO block and is CHAR data type  */
      declare char(3) second third;
      second='Jan';
      third ='Mar';
         /* FIRST is available because   */
         /* it comes from parent scope.  */
      put 'Inside the DO block: '
          first= second= third=;
   end;
      /* THIRD is not available because   */
      /* it ended when the DO block ended. */
   put 'After the DO block:   '
       first= second= third=;
return;
```

The example produces the following output:

```
Before the DO block: first=10 second=5
Inside the DO block: first=10 second=Jan third=Mar
After the DO block:  first=10 second=5 third=.
```

Although program variables are available only while an SCL program is running, SCL provides features for passing variables to other programs and also for receiving returned values. For more information, see "ENTRY" on page 369 and "METHOD" on page 539.

You can also use global macro variables to make variables available outside the SCL program. See "Using Macro Variables" on page 87 for details.

## System Variables

System variables are created automatically when an SCL program compiles. These variables communicate information between an SCL program and an application, and you can use them in programs. System variables can be Character, Numeric, or Object data type variables. The Object data type facilitates compile-time checking for SCL programs that use dot notation to invoke methods and to access attributes for objects. Although the system variables _CFRAME_, _FRAME_, and _SELF_ are designated as object variables in Version 8 of SAS software, applications that were built with earlier releases and that use these variables will continue to work with Version 8.

Do not declare the _SELF_, _FRAME_, _CFRAME_, _METHOD_, or _EVENT_ system variables inside a CLASS or USECLASS block. SCL automatically sets these values when it is running methods that are defined in CLASS or USECLASS blocks. Redefining any of these system variables can introduce unexpected behavior.

With the exceptions of _EVENT_, _METHOD_, and _VALUE_, you can simply reference a system variable in an SCL program without explicitly declaring it.

**_BLANK_**

> reports whether a window variable contains a value or sets a variable value to blank.
>
> > Type: Character

**_CFRAME_**

> contains the identifier of the FRAME entry that is currently executing, when a control is executing a method. Otherwise, it stores the identifier of the FRAME entry that is executing.
>
> > Type: Object

**_CURCOL_**

> contains the value of the first column on the left in an extended table object in a FRAME entry. It is used to control horizontal scrolling.
>
> > Type: Numeric

**_CURROW_**

> contains the number of the current row in an extended table.
>
> > Type: Numeric

**_ERROR_**

> contains a code for the application's error status.
>
> > Type: Numeric

**_EVENT_**

> returns the type of event that occurred on a control. It is useful only during a _select method. At other times, it may not exist as an attribute or it is blank. _EVENT_ can have one of the following values:

| | |
|---|---|
| ' ' | modification or selection |
| C | command |
| D | double click |
| P | pop-up menu request |
| S | selection or single click. |

> _EVENT_ must be explicitly declared in an SCL program. For example:

```
declare char(1) _event_;
```

> > Type: Character.

**_FRAME_**

> contains the identifier of the FRAME entry that contains a control, when the object is a FRAME entry control. Otherwise, it contains the identifier of the FRAME entry that is currently executing. You can use this variable to send

methods to a FRAME entry from a control's method. For example, a control method can send a _refresh method to the FRAME entry, causing the FRAME entry to refresh its display.
Type: Object

**_METHOD_**
contains the name of the method that is currently executing.

_METHOD_ must be explicitly declared in an SCL program. In the declaration statement, specify the maximum length for the name of a method. For example:

```
declare char(40) _method_;
```

Type: Character.

**_MSG_**
assigns text to display on the message line, or contains the text to be displayed on the window's message line the next time the window is refreshed.
Type: Character

**_SELF_**
contains the identifier of the object that is currently executing a method.
Type: Object

**_STATUS_**
contains a code for the status of program execution. You can check for the value of _STATUS_, and you can also set its value.
Type: Character

**_VALUE_**
contains the value of a control.

When _VALUE_ contains the value of a character control, it must be explicitly declared in an SCL program. In the declaration statement, specify the maximum length for a character window control. For example:

```
declare char(80) _value_;
```

Type: Character or Numeric.

# Constants

In SCL, a constant (or literal) is a fixed value that can be either a number or a character string. Constants can be used in many SCL statements, including assignment and IF-THEN statements. They can also be used as values for certain options.

## Numeric Constants

A numeric constant is a number that appears in a SAS statement, and it can be presented in the following forms:

□ standard syntax, in which numeric constants are expressed as integers, can be specified with or without a plus or minus sign, and can include decimal places.

□ scientific (E) syntax, in which the number that precedes the E is multiplied by the power of ten indicated by the number that follows the E.

□ hexadecimal syntax, in which a numeric hex constant starts with a numeric digit (usually 0), can be followed by more hexadecimal digits, and ends with the letter X. The constant can contain up to 16 hexadecimal digits (0 to 9, A to F).

&#9633; special SAS date and time values, in which the date or time is enclosed in single or double quotation marks, followed by a D (date), T (time), or DT (datetime) to indicate the type of value (for example, '15jan99'd).

## Character Constants

A character constant can consist of 1 to 32,767 characters and must be enclosed in quotation marks. Character constants can be represented in the following forms:

&#9633; hexadecimal form, in which a string of an even number of hex characters is enclosed in single or double quotation marks, followed immediately by an X, as in this example:

```
'534153'x
```

&#9633; bit form, in which a string of 0s, 1s, and periods is surrounded by quotation marks and is immediately followed by a B. Zero tests whether a bit is off, 1 tests whether a bit is on, and a period ignores a bit. Commas and blanks can be inserted in the bit mask for readability without affecting its meaning.

In the following example, if the third bit of A (counting from the left) is on, and the fifth through eighth bits are off, then the comparison is true and the expression results in 1. Otherwise, the comparison is false and the expression results in 0.

```
if a='..1.0000'b then do;
```

Bit constants cannot be used as literals in assignment statements. For example, the following statement is not valid:

```
x='0101'b;   /* incorrect */
```

If a character constant includes a single quotation mark, then either write the quotation mark as two consecutive single quotation marks or surround the entire value with double quotation marks, as shown in the following examples:

```
possession='Your''s';
company="Your's and Mine"
company="Your""s and Mine"
```

To use a null character value as an argument to a function in SCL, either use ''(without a space) or use a blank value with ' '(with a space).

## Numeric-to-Character Conversion

If a value is inconsistent with the variable's data type, SCL attempts to convert the value to the expected type. SCL automatically converts character variables to numeric variables and numeric variables to character variables, according to the following rules:

&#9633; A character variable is converted to numeric when the character variable is used

&#9633; with an operator that requires numeric operands (for example, the plus sign)

&#9633; with a comparison operator (for example, the equal sign) to compare a character variable and a numeric variable

&#9633; on the right side of an assignment statement, when a numeric variable is on the left side.

&#9633; A numeric variable is converted to character when the numeric variable is used

&#9633; with an operator that requires a character value (for example, the concatenation operator)

&#9633;  on the right side of an assignment statement, when a character variable is on the left side.

When a variable is converted automatically, a message in the LOG window warns you that the conversion took place. If a conversion from character to numeric produces invalid numeric values, then a missing value is assigned to the result, an error message appears in the LOG window, and the value of the automatic variable _ERROR_ is set to 1.

# Operators

Operators are symbols that request an arithmetic calculation, a comparison, or a logical operation. SCL includes the same operators that are provided in the base SAS language. The only restrictions on operators in SCL are for the minimum and maximum value operators. For these SAS operators, you must use the operator symbols (> < and < >, respectively) rather than the mnemonic equivalents (MIN and MAX, respectively).

## Arithmetic Operators

The arithmetic operators, which designate that an arithmetic calculation is performed, are shown here:

| Symbol | Definition |
| --- | --- |
| + | addition |
| / | division |
| ** | exponentiation |
| * | multiplication |
| - | subtraction |

## Comparison Operators

Comparison operators propose a relationship between two quantities and ask whether that relationship is true. Comparison operators can be expressed as symbols or written with letters. An operator that is written with letters, such as EQ for =, is called a mnemonic operator. The symbols for comparison operators and their mnemonic equivalents are shown in the following table:

| Symbol | Mnemonic Equivalent | Definition |
| --- | --- | --- |
| = | EQ | equal to |
| ^= * | NE | not equal to |
| ¬= * | NE | not equal to |
| > | GT | greater than |
| < | LT | less than |
| >= ** | GE | greater than or equal to |

| Symbol | Mnemonic Equivalent | Definition |
|---|---|---|
| <= ** | LE | less than or equal to |
| <> |  | maximum |
| >< |  | minimum |
| \|\| |  | concatenation |
|  | IN | equal to one item in a list |

\* The symbol that you use for NE depends on your keyboard.

\*\* The symbols =< and => are also accepted for compatibility with previous releases of SAS.

## Colon Modifier

You can add a colon (:) modifier after any operator to compare only a specified prefix of a character string. For example, the following code produces the message **pen found**, because the string **pen** occurs at the beginning (as a prefix) of **pencil**:

```
var='pen';
if var =: 'pencil'
    then put var 'found';
else
    put var 'not found';
```

The following code produces the message **phone not found** because **phone** occurs at the end (as a suffix) of **telephone**:

```
var='phone';
if var =: 'telephone';
    then put var 'found';
else put var 'not found';
```

The code produces these messages:

```
pen found
phone not found
```

## IN Operator

The IN operator compares a value produced by an expression on the left side of the operator to a list of values on the right. For example:

```
if age in (16, 21, 25);
```

If the IN operator returns 0 if the value on the left does not match a value in the list. The result is 1 if the value on the left matches a value in the list. In the case of arrays, the IN operator returns the index of the element if it finds a match.

The form of the comparison is

*expression* IN <*value-1*<, . . . ,*value-n*>)

The elements of the comparison are

*expression*
   can be any valid SAS expression, but it is usually a variable name when used with the IN operator.

*value*
   must be a SAS constant. *Value* can be an array of constants.

Suppose you have the following program section:

```
init:
declare a[5] = (2 4 6 8 10);
b = 6;
if b in a then put 'B is in array A';
c=b in a;
put c=;
return;
```

This code produces the following output:

```
B in in array A
c=3
```

---

## Logical (Boolean) Operators

Logical operators (also called Boolean operators) are usually used in expressions to link sequences of comparisons. The logical operators are shown in the following table:

| Symbol | Mnemonic Equivalent | Definition |
|---|---|---|
| & | AND | AND comparison |
| \| | OR | OR comparison |
| ¬ * | NOT | NOT comparison |
| ^ * | NOT | NOT comparison |
| ~ * | NOT | NOT comparison |

* The symbol that you use for NOT depends on your keyboard.

### AND Operator

If both conditions compared by an AND operator are true, then the result of the AND operation is true. Two comparisons with a common variable linked by AND can be condensed with an implied AND. For example, the following two subsetting IF statements produce the same result:

```
if 16<=age and age<=65;
if 16<=age<=65;
```

### OR Operator

If either condition compared by an OR operator is true, then the result of the OR operation is true.

Be careful when using the OR operator with a series of comparisons (in an IF, SELECT, or WHERE statement, for example). Remember that only one comparison in a series of OR comparisons needs to be true in order to make a condition true. Also, any nonzero, nonmissing constant is always evaluated as true. Therefore, the following subsetting IF statement is always true:

```
if x=1 or 2;
```

Although X=1 may be either true or false, the 2 is evaluated as nonzero and nonmissing, so the entire expression is true. In the following statement, however, the condition is not necessarily true, because either comparison can evaluate as true or false:

```
if x=1 or x=2;
```

You can also use the IN operator with a series of comparisons. The following statements are equivalent:

```
if x in (2, 4, 6);
if x=2 or x=4 or x=6;
```

## NOT Operator

Putting NOT in front of a quantity whose value is false makes that condition true. That is, negating a false statement makes the statement true. Putting NOT in front of a quantity whose value is missing is also true. Putting NOT in front of a quantity that has a nonzero, nonmissing value produces a false condition. That is, the result of negating a true statement is false.

# Expressions

An SCL expression can be a sequence of operands and operators forming a set of instructions that are performed to produce a result value, or it can be a single variable name, constant, or function. Operands can be variable names or constants, and they can be numeric, character, or both. Operators can be symbols that request a comparison, a logical operation, or an arithmetic calculation. Operators can also be SAS functions and grouping parentheses.

Expressions are used for calculating and assigning new values, for conditional processing, and for transforming variables. These examples show SAS expressions:

□ 3

□ x

□ age<100

□ (abc)/2

□ min(2,-3,1)

SCL expressions can resolve to numeric, character, or Boolean values. In addition, a numeric expression that contains no logical operators can serve as a Boolean expression.

## Boolean Numeric Expressions

In SCL programs, any numeric value other than 0 or missing is true, whereas a value of 0 or missing is false. Therefore, a numeric variable or expression can stand alone in a condition. If the value is a number other than 0 or missing, then the condition is true; if the value is 0 or missing, then the condition is false.

A numeric expression can be simply a numeric constant, as follows:

```
if 5 then do;
```

The numeric value returned by a function is also a valid numeric expression:

```
if index(address,'Avenue') then do;
```

## Using Functions in Expressions

You can use functions almost any place in an SCL program statement where you can use variable names or literal values. For example, the following example shows a way to perform an operation (in this case, the FETCH function) and take an action, based on the value of the return code from the function:

```
rc=fetch(dsid);
     /* The return code -1 means the  */
     /* end of the file was reached.  */
  if (rc=-1) then
     do;
     ...SCL statements to handle the
     end-of-file condition...
     end;
```

To eliminate the variable for the return code, you can use the function directly in the IF statement's expression, as shown in the following example:

```
if (fetch(dsid)=-1) then
     do;
     ...SCL statements to handle the
     end-of-file condition...
     end;
```

In this case, the FETCH function is executed, and then the IF expression evaluates the return code to determine whether to perform the conditional action.

As long as you do not need the value of the function's return code for any other processing, the latter form is more efficient because it eliminates the unnecessary variable assignment.

# SCL Statements

SCL provides all of the program control statements of the base SAS language. However, many base SAS language statements that relate to the creation and manipulation of SAS tables and external files are absent in SCL. In their place, SCL provides an extensive set of language elements for manipulating SAS tables and external files. These elements are described in Chapter 11, "Using SAS Tables," on page 165 and in Chapter 12, "Using External Files," on page 179.

SCL also provides CLASS and INTERFACE statements, which enable you to design and build true object-oriented applications. CLASS statements enable you to define classes from which you can create new objects. The INTERFACE statement enables you to define how applications can communicate with these objects.

## Executable and Declarative Statements

As in the base SAS language, SCL statements are either executable or declarative.

executable statements
   are compiled into intermediate code and result in some action when the SCL program is executed. (Examples of executable statements are the CURSOR, IF-THEN/ELSE, and assignment statements.)

declarative statements
> provide information to the SCL compiler but do not result in executable code unless initial values are assigned to the declared variables. (Examples of declarative statements are the DECLARE, LENGTH, and ARRAY statements.)

You can place declarative statements anywhere in an SCL program, but they typically appear at the beginning of the program before the first labeled section.

***CAUTION:***
> **Do not place executable statements outside the program modules.** Executable statements outside a program module (labeled section, class definition file, method implementation file, and so on) are never executed. See Chapter 2, "The Structure of SCL Programs," on page 9 for more information about program modules. △

## The Assignment Statement

The assignment statement in SCL works like the assignment statement in base SAS except:

- □ You can specify an array name (without the subscript) in the left side of the assignment statement. See "Using Assignment Statements" on page 42 and "Returning Arrays From Methods" on page 45 for more information.

- □ You can use the assignment statement to initialize the values of an SCL list. See "Initializing the Values in a List" on page 51 for more information.

# Program Comments

You can include comments anywhere in your SCL programs. Comments provide information to the programmer, but they are ignored by the compiler, and they produce no executable code.

SCL allows the following two forms of comments:

- □ /* *comment* */

```
      /* sort the data set and */
      /* then do something else */
   sysrc=sort(dsid,'year month');
```

- □ * *comment* ;

```
      * sort the data set and  ;
      * then do something else ;
   sysrc=sort(dsid,'year month');
```

# SCL Functions

Like the functions in the base SAS language, each SCL function returns a value that is based on one or more arguments that are supplied with the function. Most of the special features of SCL are implemented as functions. In addition, SCL provides all of the functions of the base SAS language except for the DIF and LAG functions. (The DIF and LAG functions require a queue of previously processed rows that only the DATA step maintains.)

SCL functions can be divided into the following groups according to the type of information they return:

☐ functions that return a value representing the result of a manipulation of the argument values. For example, the MLENGTH function returns the maximum length of a variable.

☐ functions that perform an action and return a value indicating the success or failure of that action. For these functions, the value that the function returns is called a *return code*. For example, the LIBNAME function returns the value 0 if it successfully assigns a libref to a SAS data library or directory. If the function cannot assign the libref, it returns a nonzero value that reports the failure of the operation. The SYSMSG function returns the text of the error message that is associated with the return code.

*Note:* Some functions use a return code value of 0 to indicate that the requested operation was successful, whereas other functions use a return code of 0 to indicate that the operation failed. △

# SCL CALL Routines

Like functions, CALL routines perform actions, based on the values of arguments that are supplied with the routine name. However, unlike functions, CALL routines do not return values. Many halt the program if the call is unsuccessful. Use CALL routines to implement features that do not require return codes.

SCL has a variety of CALL routines of its own. It also supports all of the CALL routines that are provided by the base SAS language.

# Passing Arguments to SCL Functions and CALL Routines

Some additional restrictions apply to the values that you pass as arguments to SCL functions and CALL routines. Some SCL functions and CALL routines accept only names of variables as arguments, but for most arguments you can specify either a literal value or the name of a variable that contains the desired value.

*Note:* For some functions, passing missing values for certain arguments causes the SCL program to stop executing and to display an error message. Restrictions on argument values are described in the entries in Chapter 16, "SAS Component Language Dictionary," on page 249. △

## Input, Output, and Update Parameters

Parameters to functions and methods can be one of three types:

input
   The value of the parameter is passed into the function, but even if the function modifies the value, it cannot pass the new value out to the calling function.

output
   Output parameters are used to return a value from a function.

update
   Update parameters can be used to pass a value into a function, and the function can modify its value and return the new value out to the calling function.

*Note:* If you use dot notation to specify a parameter to a method, then the parameter is treated as an update parameter if the method does not have a signature or if the object is declared as a generic object. SCL executes the _setAttributeValue method for all update parameters, which could cause unwanted effects. See "What Happens When Attribute Values Are Set or Queried" on page 122 for complete information. △

If you do not use dot notation to pass parameters to the functions and routines documented in Chapter 16, "SAS Component Language Dictionary," on page 249, then all parameters are input parameters except for those listed in Table 3.1 on page 35.

**Table 3.1** Functions With Update Parameters

| Function Name | Update Parameters |
|---|---|
| DELNITEM | *index* |
| DIALOG | all *parameters* other than *entry* |
| DISPLAY | all *parameters* other than *entry* |
| FGET | *cval* |
| FILEDIALOG | *filename* |
| FILLIST | *description* |
| LVARLEVEL | *n-level* |
| CALL METHOD | all *parameters* except *entry* and *label* |
| NAMEDIVIDE | all parameters except *name* |
| NOTIFY | all *parameters* except *control-name* and *method-name* |
| RGBDM | *RGB-color* |
| SAVEENTRYDIALOG | *description* |
| SEND | all *parameters* except *object-id* and *method-name* |
| SETNITEMC | *index* |
| SETNITEML | *index* |
| SETNITEMN | *index* |
| SETNITEMO | *index* |
| SUPER | all *parameters* except *object-id* and *method-name* |
| VARLEVEL | *n-level* |
| VARSTAT | *varlist-2* |

*Note:* The *argument* parameter of the DATA step SUBSTR (left of =) function is also an update parameter. △

For all methods that you define with the METHOD statement, all parameters are assumed to be update parameters unless either you specify input or output when you define the method or you invoke the method with SEND, NOTIFY, SUPER, or CALL METHOD. If you invoke the method with SEND, NOTIFY, SUPER, or CALL METHOD, then the first two parameters (listed in Table 3.1 on page 35) are assumed to be input parameters.

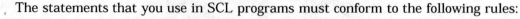

# Combining Language Elements into Program Statements

The statements that you use in SCL programs must conform to the following rules:

□ You must end each SCL program statement with a semicolon.

□ You can place any number of SCL program statements on a single line as long as you separate the individual statements with semicolons. If you plan to use the SCL debugger, it is helpful to begin each statement on a separate line.

□ You can continue an SCL program statement from one line to the next as long as no keyword is split.

□ You can begin SCL program statements in any column.

□ You must separate words in SCL program statements with blanks or with special characters such as the equal sign (=) or another operator.

□ You must place arguments for SCL functions and CALL routines within parentheses.

□ If a function or CALL routine takes more than one argument, you must separate the arguments with commas.

□ Character arguments that are literal values must be enclosed in either single or double quotation marks (for example, **'Y'** or **''N''**).

□ Numeric arguments cannot be enclosed in quotation marks.

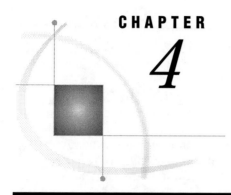

CHAPTER

*4*

# SCL Arrays

## Introduction

   SCL supports two types of arrays: static and dynamic. The size of a static array is set when you declare the array and cannot be changed at runtime. With dynamic arrays, you do not specify a size when you declare the array, but you can use any one of several different SCL functions to define the size of the array. With a dynamic array, you can create an array of a specfied size and resize the array as needed in your program.

   The differences between ARRAY statement execution in SCL and ARRAY statement execution in the DATA step are described in Chapter 7, "Using Other SAS Software Products," on page 77.

## Declaring Arrays

   You can use the DECLARE statement to declare static or dynamic arrays. Arrays that are declared with the DECLARE statement are all temporary arrays. That is, they default to the _TEMPORARY_ option. (See "Using Temporary Arrays to Conserve Memory" on page 46 for more information.) For example, the following statement declares an array named MONTH that contains five character variables that are each up to three characters in length:

```
declare char(3) month[5];
```

To declare a dynamic array, you must specify an asterisk (*) for the array dimensions:

```
declare char students[*];
```

This statement declares a one-dimensional array of type character. The DECLARE statement does not set the array bounds or create any elements. Dynamic arrays are only accessible within the scope in which they are declared.

You can use the ARRAY statement to declare indirect or non-temporary arrays. You can declare only static arrays with the ARRAY statement. You can declare temporary arrays by specifying the _TEMPORARY argument in the ARRAY statement. For example:

```
array month[5] $;
```

The ARRAY statement (but not the DECLARE statement) enables you to assign names to individual array elements. For example, the following statement assigns the names JAN, FEB, MAR, APR, and MAY to the five elements in the MONTH array.:

```
array month[5] $ jan feb mar apr may;
```

You can use these names to refer to the array elements in your SCL program.

In contrast to the ARRAY statement, you cannot use the DECLARE statement to assign names to individual array elements. The following DECLARE statement declares an array named MONTH plus five more character variables named JAN, FEB, MAR, APR, and MAY:

```
declare char month[5] jan feb mar apr may;
```

# Referencing Array Elements

To reference array elements, you can use the form *array-name*[*position*], where *position* is the index position of the variable in the array. This form of array reference is called *subscripting*. Subscripting is the only way to refer to array elements that were declared with the DECLARE statement. For example, FACTOR[4] is the only way to reference the fourth element of array FACTOR if it is created with the statement

```
declare num Factor[5];
```

This DECLARE statement also produces variables FACTOR[1] through FACTOR[5].

Because you must use the DECLARE statement to declare dynamic arrays, the only way to reference the elements of a dynamic array is with subscripting. However, you cannot reference the elements of a dynamic array until you have created the array. See "Creating and Initializing Dynamic Arrays" on page 40 for more information.

You can also use subscripting to refer to elements of an array that is declared with the ARRAY statement. For example, you can use MONTH[1] and MONTH[4] to refer to the first and fourth elements of an array that is declared with the following statement:

```
array month[5] $;
```

If the array is declared with an ARRAY statement that does not assign individual names to the array elements (as shown in this example), then you can also refer to these array elements as MONTH1 and MONTH4.

If the ARRAY statement assigns names to the individual array elements, then you can also use those names to refer to the array elements. For example, if you declare your array with the following statement, then you can refer to the elements in the array using the names JAN, FEB, and MAR:

```
array month[3] $ jan feb mar;
```

## Grouping Variables That Have Sequential Names

If an application program or window has a series of variables whose names end in sequential numbers (for example, SCORE1, SCORE2, SCORE3, and so on), then you can use an array to group these variables. For example, the following ARRAY statement groups the variables SCORE1, SCORE2, SCORE3, and SCORE4 into the array SCORE:

```
array score[4];
```

*Note:* If the variables do not already exist as window variables, then SCL defines new, nonwindow, numeric variables with those names. △

Grouping the variables into an array is useful when your program needs to apply the same operations to all of the variables. See "Repeating an Action for Variables in an Array" on page 44 for more information.

# Initializing The Elements of A Static Array

By default, all elements in a numeric array are initialized to numeric missing values if the array elements did not previously exist.

You can define initial values for the elements of a static array by listing the initial values in parentheses following the list of element names in the DECLARE or ARRAY statements. Commas are optional between variable values. For example, the following ARRAY statement creates a two-item array named COUNT, assigns the value 1 to the first element, and assigns the value 2 to the second element:

```
array count[2] (1 2);
```

You can also initialize array elements with the DECLARE statement. For example, the following program declares an array named MONTH, which contains five elements that can each contain three characters, and it assigns initial values to the array elements:

```
declare char(3) month[5]=('jan' 'feb' 'mar'
                          'apr' 'may');
INIT:
   put month;
return;
```

The example produces the following output:

```
month[1] = 'jan'
month[2] = 'feb'
month[3] = 'mar'
month[4] = 'apr'
month[5] = 'may'
```

## Assigning the Same Value to Multiple Elements

You can use repetition factors to initialize static arrays. Repetition factors specify how many times the values are assigned in the array. They have the following form:

```
5 * (2 3 4)
```

In this example, **5** is the repetition factor and **(2  3  4)** is the list of initial values for the array elements. If the list consists of only a single item, then you can omit the parentheses.

For example, the following ARRAY and DECLARE statements both use repetition factors to initialize the values of the array REPEAT:

```
array repeat[17] (0,3*1,4*(2,3,4),0);
declare num repeat[17]=(0,3*1,4*(2,3,4),0);
```

This example repeats the value 1 three times and the sequence 2, 3, 4 four times. The following values are assigned to the elements of the array REPEAT:

```
0, 1, 1, 1, 2, 3, 4, 2, 3, 4, 2, 3, 4, 2, 3, 4, 0
```

## Initializing Static Multidimensional Arrays

To initialize a static multidimensional array, use the ARRAY or DECLARE statement to list values for the first row of the array, followed by values for the second row, and so on. The following examples both initialize a two-dimensional array named COUNT with two rows and three columns:

```
array count[2,3] (1 2 3 4 5 6);
```

```
dcl num count[2,3]=(1 2 3 4 5 6);
```

Figure 4.1 on page 40 shows the values of the elements of this array.

**Figure 4.1**  Elements of the COUNT Array

| | Columns | | |
|---|---|---|---|
| | column 1 | column 2 | column 3 |
| row 1 | 1 | 2 | 3 |
| row 2 | 4 | 5 | 6 |

Rows

For more information about arrays, see "ARRAY" on page 254 and "DECLARE" on page 330.

## Creating and Initializing Dynamic Arrays

Dynamic arrays can be created and initialized in five ways:

- □ with the COPYARRAY function. See "Using The COPYARRAY Function" on page 43 for more information.
- □ using simple assignment statements that copy the values of one array into another array. For more information, see "Using Assignment Statements" on page 42.
- □ by a method that returns an array. See "Returning Arrays From Methods" on page 45 for more information.
- □ with the REDIM function. See "Resizing Dynamic Arrays" on page 41 for more information.
- □ with the MAKEARRAY function.

After you have declared a dynamic array, you can create the array with the MAKEARRAY function. The MAKEARRAY function creates an array of the given size with all elements in the array initialized to missing for numerics or blank for characters. The number of dimensions must be the same as what was specified in the DECLARE statement. The low bound for all dynamic arrays is 1, and the high bound is determined at runtime by the values that you specify with the MAKEARRAY (or REDIM) function. For example, the following statements create a one-dimensional dynamic array named STUDENTS that has three elements and initializes these array elements to **Mary**, **Johnny**, and **Bobby**:

**Example Code 4.1** Dynamic STUDENTS Array

```
declare char students[*];
students = MAKEARRAY(3);
students[1] = 'Mary';
students[2] = 'Johnny';
students[3] = 'Bobby';
put students;
```

The low bound for STUDENTS is 1, and the high bound 3. The output for this example is

```
students[1] = 'Mary'
students[2] = 'Johnny'
students[3] = 'Bobby'
```

## Resizing Dynamic Arrays

You can use the REDIM function to change the high bound of any dimension of a dynamic array at runtime. You cannot change the number of dimensions or type of the array, only the bounds. The REDIM function will also preserve the data in the array unless you resize the array to a smaller size. If you reduce the size of an array, you will lose the data in the eliminated elements.

For example, suppose that you have declared and initialized the STUDENTS array as shown in Example Code 4.1 on page 41. To add another student, you must resize the array. The following statements increase the high bound by 1 element, add the new variable STUDENTS[4], and initialize this new element to **Alice**.

```
declare num rc;
rc = REDIM(students, DIM(students) + 1);
students[DIM(students) + 1] = 'Alice';
put students;
```

All of the existing data is preserved. The low bound for the array STUDENTS is 1, and the new high bound is 4. The output for this example would be:

```
students[1] = 'Mary'
students[2] = 'Johnny'
students[3] = 'Bobby'
students[4] = 'Alice'
```

You can also use the REDIM function to create and initialize an array that has been declared but not yet created by other means. For example, the following statements declare, create, and initialize an array of five elements to numeric missing values:

```
dcl num rc;
dcl num a[*];
```

```
rc = redim(a,5);
```

There is no limit to the number of times that you can resize an array.

*Note:*  You can use the MAKEARRAY function to resize an array, but all the data will be lost. The MAKEARRAY function will reinitialize the elements to missing numeric values or to blank character values.  △

# Using Array Functions with Dynamic Arrays

You can use dynamic arrays with the other existing array functions (DIM, HBOUND, LBOUND) as long as the array has been created with MAKEARRAY or REDIM. If your program references a dynamic array before it has been created, a program halt will occur. If you pass a dynamic array to a method by reference (that is, as an input parameter), you cannot resize the array using MAKEARRAY, REDIM, or DELARRAY within the method.

# Copying Elements From One Array To Another

There are two ways to copy an array:

- □ using an assignment statement. When assigning the values of one array to another array, the two arrays must have the same size.
- □ using the COPYARRAY function. When using the COPYARRAY function, the arrays do not have to be the same size.

## Using Assignment Statements

You can assign values to an array from another array in an assignment statement. For example, the following code copies the values of array A into array B:

```
declare num a[3] = (1 3 5);
declare num b[3];
b = a;
put b;
```

These statements produce the following output:

```
b[1] = 1
b[2] = 3
b[3] = 5
```

When you use the assignment statement to copy an array, the two arrays must have the same type, dimensions, and size; otherwise, an error condition will occur.

You can use an assignment statement to create and initialize a dynamic array that has been declared but not yet created. If you specify a newly declared dynamic array as the array to which values are to be assigned, then SCL will create the dynamic array and copy the values of the existing array into the new array.

For example, the following statements create dynamic array B to the same size as A and then copies the values of array A into dynamic array B.

```
declare num a[3] = (1 3 5);
declare num b[*];
b = a;
```

```
put b;
```

These statements produce the following output:

```
b[1] = 1
b[2] = 3
b[3] = 5
```

## Using The COPYARRAY Function

You can also use the COPYARRAY function to copy elements from one array to another. By default, the COPYARRAY function produces the same result as the assignment statement and requires that the arrays be of the same type, dimension, and size. For example, the following statements copy the array A into arrays B and C:

```
declare num a[3] = (1 3 5);
declare num b[3] c[3];
rc = COPYARRAY(a,b);
put b;
c = a;
put c;
```

The output for this code would be:

```
b[1] = 1
b[2] = 3
b[3] = 5
c[1] = 1
c[2] = 3
c[3] = 5
```

However, with the COPYARRAY function, you can copy an array to an array of a different size if you set the IGNORESIZE parameter to **Y** in the call to COPYARRAY:

```
rc = COPYARRAY(array1,array2,'Y');
```

The type and dimensions of the arrays must still match. For example, the following statements will copy array A, which has three elements, into array B, which has five elements.

```
declare num a[3] = (1 3 5);
declare num b[5];
rc = COPYARRAY(a,b,'Y');
put b;
```

This code produces the following output:

```
b[1] = 1
b[2] = 3
b[3] = 5
b[4] = .
b[5] = .
```

The COPYARRAY can also be used to create dynamic arrays, just as you can create them using assignment statements. For example, the following statements create and initialize dynamic array B:

```
declare num a[3] = (1 3 5);
declare num b[*];
```

```
rc = COPYARRAY(a,b);
put b;
```

The output for this code would be:

```
b[1] = 1
b[2] = 3
b[3] = 5
```

*Note:* When you use the COPYARRAY function to create a new dynamic array, it is good practice to delete the newly created array using the DELARRAY function. However, if you do not delete the array with the DELARRAY function, SCL will delete the array at the end of the routine like all other dynamic arrays. See "Deleting Dynamic Arrays" on page 46 for more information. △

# Repeating an Action for Variables in an Array

To perform an action on variables in an array, you can use an iterative DO statement, using the index variable for the array subscript. A DO block is especially convenient when arrays contain many elements. For example, you could use a program like the following to sum the values of the array variables and to display the total in the SUM field:

```
array month[5] jan feb mar apr may (1,2,3,4,5);
INIT:
   do i=1 to 5;
      sum+month[i];
   end;
   put month;
   put sum=;
return;
```

The example produces the following output:

```
month[1] = 1
month[2] = 2
month[3] = 3
month[4] = 4
month[5] = 5
sum=15
```

The preceding DO block has the same effect as any one of the following assignment statements:

```
sum1=jan+feb+mar+apr+may;
sum2=sum(of month[*]);
sum3=sum(of jan--may);
put sum1= sum2= sum3= ;
```

This example produces the following output:

```
sum1=15 sum2=15 sum3=15
```

# Passing Dynamic Arrays to Methods

Passing a dynamic array to a method is no different than passing a static array, but the dynamic array must have been created by MAKEARRAY, REDIM, COPYARRAY, or an assignment statement. If the dynamic array is not created before the method call, then an error condition will occur.

Dynamic arrays can be resized via a method if the method's parameter is a reference array and an output parameter. See "ARRAY" on page 254 for more information on reference arrays.

Suppose you have defined the resizeDynamicArray method as follows:

```
resizeDynamicArray:method parm1[*]:O:num;
declare num rc = redim(parm1, 5);
endmethod;
```

The parameter PARM1 is output parameter and a reference array. When you call this method, it will resize the dynamic array passed to it into an array with a low bound 1 and a high bound of 5. In the following code, resizeDynamicArray resizes an array with 3 elements into an array with 5 elements:

```
declare num a[*] = MAKEARRAY(3);
object.resizeDynamicArray(a);
put a;
```

The output for this code would be:

```
a[1] = .
a[2] = .
a[3] = .
a[4] = .
a[5] = .
```

Because PARM1 is a reference array, it is using the same memory as the dynamic array A.

You can now resize the array using MAKEARRAY, REDIM, COPYARRAY, DELARRAY, or an assignment statement.

# Returning Arrays From Methods

Arrays can also be assigned values from a method that returns an array. The array to which values are being assigned must have the same type, dimensions, and size as the array returned from the method. Otherwise, an error condition will occur.

Suppose you define the getArrayValues method as follows:

```
getArrayValues:method return=num(*);
declare num a[3] = (1 3 5);
return a;
endmethod;
```

To assign the values that are returned by getArrayValues to an array, you could use the following code:

```
declare num b[3];
b = object.getArrayValues();
put b;
```

The output for this example is

```
b[1] = 1
b[2] = 3
b[3] = 5
```

Dynamic arrays (that have not yet been created by other means) can be created when an array is returned from a method call. If your program returns values into a dynamic array that has been declared but not yet created, SCL will first create the new dynamic array, then copy the returned values into the new array. For example, the following code creates dynamic array B with the same size as the returned array and copies the values of the returned array into B.

```
declare num b[*];
b = getArrayValues();
put b;
```

The output of these statements is

```
b[1] = 1
b[2] = 3
b[3] = 5
```

# Deleting Dynamic Arrays

The DELARRAY function is used to delete a dynamic array that has been created using the MAKEARRAY or REDIM. The array's contents cannot be accessed after the array is deleted. If you do not delete the created dynamic array using DELARRAY, the array will be automatically deleted when exiting the routine.

# Using Temporary Arrays to Conserve Memory

If you want to use an array in an SCL program but do not need to refer to array elements by name, then you can add the _TEMPORARY_ argument to your ARRAY statement:

```
array total[4] _temporary_;
```

When you use the _TEMPORARY_ argument, you must use subscripting to refer to the array elements. For example, you must use TOTAL[2] to refer to the second element in the array TOTAL, defined above. You cannot use the variable name TOTAL2 as an alternative reference for the array element TOTAL[2]. Using the _TEMPORARY_ argument conserves memory. By default, SCL allocates memory for both the name of the array and the names of the individual array elements. However, when you use the _TEMPORARY_ argument, SCL allocates memory only for the array name. For large arrays, this can result in significant memory savings.

*Note:* Do not use the _TEMPORARY_ option if you plan to use the SET routine to read values from a SAS table directly into array elements. You must use the GETVARN or GETVARC function to read values from a SAS table into the elements of a temporary array. △

# 5

# SCL Lists

# Introduction

SCL supports data structures and functions for manipulating data in SCL lists. SCL lists, like arrays, are ordered collections of data. However, lists are more flexible than arrays in many ways. For example, SCL lists are dynamic. Therefore, a program can create a list only when and if it is needed. Lists grow and shrink to accommodate the number of items or the size of items that you assign to them. Also, an SCL list can contain items of differing data types.

Chapter 15, "SCL Elements by Category," on page 235 lists the SCL list functions. Each function and the tasks it can perform are described in Chapter 16, "SAS Component Language Dictionary," on page 249.

# Creating Data Dynamically

SCL lists are dynamic rather than static. That is, SCL programs create these lists at run time. This means that list sizes are computed at run time rather than before the list is created. Further, unlike arrays, which have a fixed size, a list's length can grow or shrink to accommodate the amount of data you want to maintain.

SCL lists can contain items of mixed types, whereas SCL arrays are fixed in type. (Depending on its declaration, an array contains either numeric data or character data, but not both). One item in an SCL list can be a number and the next item can be a character string, while a third might be another list. Further, you have the freedom to replace a numeric value with a character value in a list, and vice versa. Although you can make lists that are of fixed type, you have the freedom to allow multiple types in the same list.

*Note:*   Character values that are stored in SCL lists can be up to 32,766 characters per item. △

# Identifying SCL Lists

You access lists with a list identifier, a unique value assigned to each list that you create. You must store the list identifier in an SCL variable and then reference that variable in each operation that you perform on the list. All the SCL functions that manipulate lists use the list identifier as an argument.

*Note:*    Assigning a list identifier to another variable does not copy the list. The two variables simply refer to the same list. To copy the contents of a list to an existing or new list, use the COPYLIST function. △

# Creating New Lists

SCL lists can be declared using the LIST data type, which is a reference type that stores the identifier assigned when you create the list. You assign the LIST type with the DECLARE statement. For example:

```
declare list carlist;
```

After you declare a list, you actually create it with the MAKELIST or MAKENLIST function. You can then insert numbers, characters, other lists, or objects into the list with the INSERTN, INSERTC, INSERTL, or INSERTO function, respectively. You can also specify the default number of items in the initial list by supplying an argument to the MAKELIST function. For example, the following statement makes a list that contains *n* items:

```
carlist=makelist(n);
```

Each of the *n* items is initialized to a numeric missing value. Note that *n* can be any nonnegative SCL numeric expression that is computed at run time, or it can be a simple nonnegative numeric constant such as 12, if you want to create a list with a known initial number of items. No matter how you create the list, you are free to expand or shrink it to contain as many items as you need, from 0 to as many items as your computer has memory to hold. To determine the length of a list, use the LISTLEN function.

*Note:* It is recommended that you declare lists with the LIST keyword to avoid problems in calling overloaded methods. See "Overloading and List, Object, and Numeric Types" on page 111 △

## Example: Creating an SCL List

This section shows an SCL program that creates an SCL list, along with the output that the program produces. The program reads the columns in DICTIONARY.TABLES, a special read-only SQL view that stores information about all the SAS tables and SAS views that are allocated in the current SAS session. The columns in this view are the attributes (items of information) that are available for SAS tables. The example program stores the column values in an SCL list that is sorted in table order (the order of the columns in the ATTRIBUTES view), name order, and length order.

To create the view that lists the SAS tables, submit the following SQL procedure from the PROGRAM EDITOR window:

```
/* Create the PROC SQL view ATTRIBUTES   */
/* which contains information about all   */
/* the members of type DATA in the SAS   */
/* data libraries that are associated     */
/* with the SAS session.                  */
proc sql noprint;
create view attributes as
    select *
        from dictionary.tables
        where memtype="DATA";
quit;
```

The SCL program creates and displays an SCL list whose values come from the view ATTRIBUTES.

```
/* Declare COLUMNS as a list */
declare list columns;
INIT:
        /* Open the view ATTRIBUTES for reading */
    attrs=open('attributes', 'I');
    if (attrs > 0) then do;
        /* Make a list containing the same    */
        /* number of items as the number of   */
        /* columns in the view ATTRS.         */
        numcols=attrn(attrs, 'NVARS');
        columns=makelist(numcols);
        do i=1 to numcols;
            /* Set item I in list COLUMNS to   */
            /* the length of the column. The   */
            /* SETITEMN call is similar to     */
            /* the array assignment:           */
            /*    array{i} = colLen;           */
```

```
            colLen=varlen(attrs, i);
            rc=setitemn(columns, colLen, i);
                /* NAMEITEM gives item I the name */
                /* of the Ith column              */
            colName=varname(attrs, i);
            itemName=nameitem(columns, i, colName);
        end;
        sysrc=close(attrs);
            /* Print the column names in their   */
            /* order in the SAS table.  Sort by  */
            /* name and print. Then sort by      */
            /* length and print.                 */
        rc=putlist(columns,'SAS Table Order:',0);
        columns=sortlist(columns, 'NAME ASCENDING');
        rc=putlist(columns, 'Name Order:', 0);
        vars=sortlist(columns,'value');
        rc=putlist(columns, 'Length Order:', 0);
            /* Cleanup: delete the list  */
        rc=dellist(columns);
    end;
    else
        _msg_=sysmsg();
return;
```

This program produces the following output:

```
SAS Table Order:(LIBNAME=8
                MEMNAME=32
                MEMTYPE=8
                MEMLABEL=256
                TYPEMEM=8
                CRDATE=8
                MODATE=8
                NOBS=8
                OBSLEN=8
                NVAR=8
                PROTECT=3
                COMPRESS=8
                REUSE=3
                BUFSIZE=8
                DELOBS=8
                INDXTYPE=9
                )[5]
Name Order:(BUFSIZE=8
            COMPRESS=8
            CRDATE=8
            DELOBS=8
            INDXTYPE=9
            LIBNAME=8
            MEMLABEL=256
            MEMNAME=32
            MEMTYPE=8
            MODATE=8
            NOBS=8
            NVAR=8
```

```
            OBSLEN=8
            PROTECT=3
            REUSE=3
            TYPEMEM=8
            )[5]
Length Order:(PROTECT=3
             REUSE=3
             BUFSIZE=8
             COMPRESS=8
             CRDATE=8
             DELOBS=8
             LIBNAME=8
             MEMTYPE=8
             MODATE=8
             NOBS=8
             NVAR=8
             OBSLEN=8
             TYPEMEM=8
             INDXTYPE=9
             MEMNAME=32
             MEMLABEL=256
             )[5]
```

*Note:* [5] is the list identifier that was assigned when this example was run and may be different each time the example is run. △

# Initializing the Values in a List

You can initialize an SCL list

□ in a DCL statement. For example, to create a list with the constants 1, 2, 'a', 3, 'b', and 'c', you can declare the list as follows:

```
DCL list mylist={1,2,'a',3,'b','c'};
```

Your list may also contain sublists. For example:

```
DCL list mylist={1,2,'a',mysub={'A','B','C',
                3,'b','c'}};
```

□ in an assignment statement after you have declared the list. For example, the following assignment statement initializes the employee list with an employee ID, name, and office location. The location is a sublist.

```
DCL list employee;

emp = {id=9999, name='Thomas',
       locate={bldg='R', room='4321'}};
```

□ by specifying the InitialValue attribute when you create a class. In the following example, the class InitVal initializes three list attributes, which also contain sublists.

```
class work.a.InitVal.class;
public list list1 / (InitialValue=
  {COPY={
```

```
            POPMENUTEXT='Copy here',
            ENABLED='Yes',
            METHOD='_drop'
            },
         MOVE={
            POPMENUTEXT='Move here',
            ENABLED='Yes',
            METHOD='_drop'
            }
      }
   );
   public list list2 / (initialValue=
      {1,2,3,{'abc','def',{1,2,'abc'},3},'def'});
   public list list3 / (initialValue=
      {id=888,name=Rob,
       answers={mchoice={'a','c','b','e'},
       math={1,4,8,9,}}
      }
   );
```

For more information about creating classes, see "CLASS" on page 277.

*Note:*   Even if you initialize a list with a DCL or assignment statement or with the **initialValue** attribute (rather than using one of the INSERT functions), you must still explicitly delete the list as described in "Deleting Lists and List Items" on page 54. △

---

# Manipulating SCL Lists

You can create new lists and then insert numbers, character strings, objects, and even other lists into them. You can replace or delete list items, and you can move them around by reversing, rotating, or sorting a list. You can also assign names to the items in a list, and you can refer to items by their names rather than by their index (position) in the list. Thus, you can use a list to implement data structures and to access and assign values to list items by their names. Using this feature, you can add new fields to the list data structure or change the order of the list's items without modifying your SCL program.

SCL lists are maintained entirely in memory. Keep this in mind as you develop your applications. If your data is more appropriately maintained in a SAS table, you will probably want to design your application in that manner instead of trying to read the entire SAS table into a list. However, if you know your SAS table will not contain a large number of rows and many columns, and if you do not need to maintain data sharing, then you may find it convenient to read the SAS table into a list. That is, you can use SCL lists for data that you would have liked to put into an array but could not because of the restrictions imposed by arrays.

---

# Determining the Type of a List Item

In general, SCL list functions that process data values are suffixed with either N, C, L, or O to denote the item types of numeric, character, list, or object, respectively. You can use the ITEMTYPE function to determine the type of a list element and then use a condition statement to determine which functions are used.

# Passing Lists as Arguments for Methods

Lists that are not declared as LIST type are treated by the compiler as numeric types in order to maintain compatibility with Version 6. However, the more accurate specification of LIST should be used in Version 7 programs, particularly those that use lists in conjunction with method overloading. For example, suppose you use the list MYLIST as an argument for a method that has one version that takes a numeric argument and another that takes a list argument. If MYLIST is not declared as LIST type, then it is treated as a numeric type and the wrong method is called: the one that takes the numeric argument, instead of the one that takes the list argument.

When a list with type LIST is passed as an argument to a method, SCL seeks a method that accepts a LIST argument. If no exact type match is found, the list is passed to a method that accepts an numeric argument. For example, if MYLIST is declared as LIST type and is passed as an argument to method MYMETHOD, SCL will first search for a MYMETHOD that accepts lists as arguments. If none is found, SCL will pass MYLIST to a MYMETHOD that accepts numeric arguments.

# Inserting and Replacing Items in Lists

To insert and replace items in a list, use the SETITEMN, SETNITEMN, SETITEMC, SETNITEMC, SETITEML, SETNITEML, SETITEMO, or SETNITEMO function. These functions can assign values to existing items or they can add new items.

With arrays, you use

```
A{i}=x;
```

but with SCL lists, you use

```
rc=setitemn(listid,x,i);
```

To add a new item to a list without replacing the existing items, use the INSERTC, INSERTL, INSERTN, or INSERTO function.

See also "Assigning Names to List Items" on page 59.

# Retrieving Values from Lists

To retrieve the value of an item in a list, use the GETITEMN, GETNITEMN, GETITEMC, GETNITEMC, GETITEML, GETNITEML, GETITEMO, or GETNITEMO function.

With arrays, you use

```
x=A{i};
```

but with SCL lists, you use

```
x=getitemn(listid,i);
```

See also "Assigning Names to List Items" on page 59.

# Deleting Lists and List Items

You can delete items from SCL lists by specifying the position, or index, of the item to delete; by clearing all of the values from a list; or by deleting the entire list. You can also pop items from lists, which enables you to create queues or stacks. See "Using Lists as Stacks and Queues" on page 61.

- □ To delete a single list item, use the DELITEM or DELNITEM function, specifying either the index or the name of the item to delete.
- □ To clear all the values from a list, use the CLEARLIST function, which leaves the list with a length of 0.
- □ To delete an entire list, use the DELLIST function. This function returns to the system the memory that was required for maintaining the list and its items.

*Note:* When you delete a list that has sublists, you should delete the list recursively if you do not need to use the information in the sublists. When you do not delete a list, the memory occupied by the list is not available for other tasks. To delete a list recursively, specify **Y** as the value of the *recursively* argument in the DELLIST function. For example:

```
rc=dellist(mylist,'Y');
```

△

For more information, see "Assigning Names to List Items" on page 59 and "DELLIST" on page 336.

# Referencing List Items by Index Number

List indexing is similar to array indexing. An index I specifies the position of an item in the list. The first item is at index I=1, and the last item is at index I=LISTLEN(mylistid), which is the length of the list. Thus, you can use DO loops to process all items in a list, as shown in the following example:

```
do i=1 to listlen(mylistid);
    t=itemtype(mylistid,i);
    put 'Item ' i ' is type ' t;
end;
```

# Accessing Items Relative to the End of a List

It is also useful for you to be able to access items at or relative to the end of an SCL list. You can use negative indices to index an item from the end of the list. Counting from the end of a list, the last item is at index −1 and the first item is at position −*n*, where *n* is the length of the list. Thus, you do not need to subtract indices from *n* to access items relative to the end of the list. All of the SCL list functions recognize negative indices.

# Indexing Errors

Indexing errors occur when you supply an invalid index to an SCL list function, just as it is an error to use an invalid array index. Valid values for list indexes depend on the function. Some functions do not accept 0 as the index, whereas other functions do. Refer to the *index* or *start-index* arguments in the dictionary entries for the SCL list functions.

# Implementing Sublists and Nested Structures

SCL allows you to put one list of items inside another SCL list, thereby making a sublist. For example, you can read the columns of a SAS table row into a list. You could then insert each row into another list, and repeat this process for a range of rows in the SAS table. You then have a list of lists, where the "outer" list contains an element for each row in the SAS table, and the "inner" sublists contain each row. These lists are called nested lists.

To illustrate, consider the SAS table WORK.EMPLOYEES, created with the following DATA step program:

```
data employees;
   input fname $ 1-9 lname $ 10-18
         position $ 19-28 salary 29-34;
datalines;
Walter    Bluerock Developer 36000
Jennifer Godfrey  Manager   42000
Kevin     Blake    Janitor   19000
Ronald    Tweety   Publicist 29000
;
```

The following example reads the WORK.EMPLOYEES table into an SCL list. The outer list is the list in the variable OUTERLIST. Each time through the loop, a new inner list is created. Its identifier is stored in the variable INNERLIST, and INNERLIST is inserted at the end of OUTERLIST.

```
INIT:
     /* Open the EMPLOYEES table and   */
     /* create the SCL list OUTERLIST  */
  dsid=open('employees');
  outerList=makelist();
     /* Read the first table row and   */
     /* find the number of its columns */
  rc=fetch(dsid);
  numcols=attrn(dsid,'NVARS');
       /* For each row, make a new INNERLIST   */
       /* and create and insert the sublists   */
  do while (rc=0);
     innerList=makelist();
          /* For each column, return the name   */
          /* and type.  Insert a list item of   */
          /* that name and type into the        */
          /* row's INNERLIST.                    */
     do i=1 to numcols;
        name=varname(dsid,i);
        type=vartype(dsid,i);
        if type='N' then
           rc=insertn(innerList,(getvarn
                     (dsid,i)),-1,name);
        else
```

```
        rc=insertc(innerList,(getvarc
                   (dsid,i)),-1,name);
    end;
        /* Insert each INNERLIST as an item   */
        /* into OUTERLIST and read the next    */
        /* row of the EMPLOYEES table          */
    outerList=insertl(outerList,innerList,-1);
    rc=fetch(dsid);
  end;
        /* Close the EMPLOYEES table.  Print and  */
        /* then delete OUTERLIST and its sublists. */
  sysrc=close(dsid);
  call putlist(outerList,'Nested Lists',2);
  rc=dellist(outerList,'y');
  return;
```

This program produces the following output:

```
Nested Lists( ( FNAME='Walter'
                LNAME='Bluerock'
                POSITION='Developer'
                SALARY=36000
              )[7]   ❶
              ( FNAME='Jennifer'
                LNAME='Godfrey'
                POSITION='Manager'
                SALARY=42000
              )[9]   ❶
              ( FNAME='Kevin'
                LNAME='Blake'
                POSITION='Janitor'
                SALARY=19000
              )[11]  ❶
              ( FNAME='Ronald'
                LNAME='Tweety'
                POSITION='Publicist'
                SALARY=29000
              )[13]  ❶
              )[5] ❶     ❷
```

1  [5], [7], [9], [11], and [13] are the list identifiers that were assigned when this example was run. These values may be different each time the example runs.

2  List identifier 5 identifies the "outer" list. Each row is an inner or nested list (list identifiers 7, 9, 11, and 13).

## Limitless Levels of Nesting

Nested lists are highly useful for creating collections of records or data structures. There is no limit to the amount of nesting or to the number of sublists that can be placed in a list, other than the amount of memory available to your SAS application. Further, you can create *recursive* list structures, where the list A can contain other lists that contain A either directly or indirectly. The list A can even contain itself as a list item.

## Simulating Multidimensional Arrays with Nested Lists

You can declare multidimensional arrays in SCL, but all lists are one-dimensional. That is, to access an item in a list, you specify only one index. However, you can use nested lists to simulate multidimensional arrays. For example, to create a list structure that mimics a 2 by 3 array, you can use the following example:

```
array a[2,3] 8 _temporary_;
init:
   listid = makelist(2);
   lista = setiteml(listid, makelist(3), 1);
   listb = setiteml(listid, makelist(3), 2);
   call putlist(listid);
   do i = 1 to dim(a,1);
      list=getiteml(listid,i);
      do j = 1 to dim(a,2);
         a[i, j] = 10*i + j;
         put a[i,j]=;
         rc = setitemn(list,a[i,j], j);
      end;
   end;
   call putlist(listid);
return;
```

This example produces the following output:

```
((.  .  . )[7] (.  .  . )[9] )[5]
a[ 1 , 1 ]=11
a[ 1 , 2 ]=12
a[ 1 , 3 ]=13
a[ 2 , 1 ]=21
a[ 2 , 2 ]=22
a[ 2 , 3 ]=23
((11 12 13 )[7] (21 22 23 )[9] )[5]
```

*Note:*   Not all of the program is shown here. You would need to delete these lists before ending the program. [7], [9], and [5] are the list identifiers that were assigned when this example was run and may be different each time the example is run. △

## Saving Nested Lists to SCL Entries

When you save a list that contains sublists, both the list and its sublists are saved in the same SLIST entry. Thus, if you create list data structures that are highly recursive and have many cycles, you should be careful about saving your lists.

For example, suppose list A contains list B. When you save list A, you also save list B; you do not need to save list B separately, because list B is already stored in list A. In fact, if you store the lists in two separate SLIST entries and then try to read them back, you do not get the same list structure that you stored originally.

The following example creates two lists, A and B, (with text values in them to identify their contents) and inserts list B into list A. It then saves each list in separate SLIST entries, A.SLIST and B.SLIST. Then, the program creates two more lists, APRIME and BPRIME, reads the two saved SLIST entries into those two lists, and then prints all the list identifiers and list values.

```
INIT:
      /* Make lists A and B and insert an item */
      /* of text into each list.  Then, insert */
      /* list B into list A.                    */
   a = makelist();
   a = insertc(a, 'This is list A');
   b = makelist();
   b = insertc(b, 'This is list B');
   a = insertl(a, b);
      /* Save lists A and B into separate  */
      /* SLIST entries.                     */
   rc=savelist
      ('CATALOG','SASUSER.LISTS.A.SLIST', A);
   rc=savelist
      ('CATALOG','SASUSER.LISTS.B.SLIST', B);

      /* Make lists APRIME and BPRIME.  Fill  */
      /* APRIME with the contents of A.SLIST  */
      /* and BPRIME with B.SLIST              */
   aPrime=makelist();
   bPrime=makelist();
   rc=fillist
      ('CATALOG','SASUSER.LISTS.A.SLIST', aPrime);
   rc=fillist
      ('CATALOG','SASUSER.LISTS.B.SLIST', bPrime);
      /* Store list APRIME into list BINA */
   bInA = getiteml(aPrime);
   put a= b= aPrime= bPrime= bInA= ;
   call putlist(a, 'List A:',0);
   call putlist(b, 'List B:',0);
   call putlist(aPrime, "List aPrime:",0);
   call putlist(bPrime, "List bPrime:",0);
      /* Delete list A and its sublist B  */
      /* Delete lists APRIME, BPRIME, and BINA */
   rc=dellist(a,'y');
   rc=dellist(aPrime);
   rc=dellist(bPrime);
return;
```

Here is the output:

```
a=5 b=7 aPrime=9 bPrime=11 bIna=13
List A:(('This is list B
        )[7]
        'This is list A
        )[5]
List B:('This is list B
        )[7]
List aPrime:(('This is list B
          )[13]
          'This is list A
          )[9]
List bPrime:('This is list B
          )[11]
```

Note that the sublist B (13) that was read from A.SLIST is not the same as the sublist BPRIME (11) that was read from B.SLIST. That is, A contains B, but B does not contain BPRIME. Therefore, changes made to B are inherently reflected in A, whereas changes to BPRIME are not reflected in APRIME.

Also note that the structures of list A and list APRIME are the same, but the list identifiers are different and do not match any of the list identifiers that were read from B.SLIST.

*Note:* [5], [7], [9], [11], and [13] are the list identifiers that were assigned when this example was run and may be different each time the example runs. △

### Advantages of SAVELIST Recursiveness

There is an advantage to the recursive nature of the SAVELIST function. For example, if list A contains sublists B and C, SAVELIST saves all three lists when you save A to an SLIST entry. Your application can take advantage of this if you have several unrelated lists that you want to save. By creating a new list and inserting the lists that you want saved into the new list, you can save them all in one SLIST entry with one SAVELIST call, instead of saving each sublist in a separate SLIST entry with separate SAVELIST calls.

# Assigning Names to List Items

SCL supports a feature called named lists, which enable you to assign a name to each item in a list, or only to some list items. The name can be any SCL character string, not just character strings that are valid SAS column names, unless the list has the SASNAMES attribute. As with SAS names, list item names can contain mixed-case characters—for example, EmployeeLocation.

If you search a list for which the HONORCASE attribute has not been set, then SCL will uppercase the item names for the search operation only. The item names are not permanently changed to uppercase.

You can use the GETNITEMC, GETNITEMN, GETNITEML, and GETNITEMO functions to access named list items by their name rather than by their position. This feature enables you to vary the contents of the list according to your application needs without having to keep track of where a particular item is located in a list. To assign or replace values that are associated with a name, use the SETNITEMC, SETNITEMN, SETNITEML, or SETNITEMO function. To delete an item by its name, use the DELNITEM function.

Item names in a list do not have to be unique unless the NODUPNAMES attribute has been assigned to the list. Item names are stored as they are entered. If the list has the HONORCASE attribute (the default), then 'abc' and 'Abc' are two different item names. Otherwise, if the list has the IGNORECASE attribute, these names are duplicate names.

To search for an item by its name, you use the NAMEDITEM function. If the list has the HONORCASE attribute, this function searches for item names that match the case specified for the search unless you use the FORCE-UP attribute for NAMEDITEM. This attribute overrides the HONORCASE attribute and converts the item name to upper case for the search. However, the case of the item name is converted only for the search; the name continues to be stored as you entered it. The function ignores trailing blanks when searching for a matching name. If a list contains duplicate names, the search function finds the first occurrence of the name unless you have specified a different occurrence of the item for the search. By inserting a new item at the beginning of the list, you can "hide" a previous value because a named search will find your new item first by default. To restore the previous value, simply delete the new item from the list.

You can freely mix named items with unnamed items in a list. You can also use both kinds of indexing (by name or by index) in any list, regardless of how the list was created or whether all, some, or no items have names.

## Indexing a Named Item by its Position

To find the index of a named item in a list, use the NAMEDITEM function. This enables you to access an item later by its index in the list, which is a faster search. However, searching by index is not safe if the index of the item might change between the time you find the index and the time you use the index.

The following statement replaces the value associated with the first occurrence of the item named **ACME** in the list NUMBERS with the value **(201) 555-2263**. These statements do not modify the list if the name **ACME** is not found:

```
i=nameditem(numbers,'Acme');
if i>0 then
   rc=setitemc(numbers,'(201) 555-2263',i);
```

## Determining or Replacing an Item's Name

To replace the name of an item, use the NAMEITEM function. You can also use NAMEITEM when you want to find out the name of an item but you do not want to change the item's name.

## Finding an Occurrence of a Name

In general, the functions that enable you to access a list item by its name operate on the first occurrence of the name by default. However, you can combine the optional arguments *occurrence*, *start-index*, and *ignore-case* to refer to items other than the first occurrence. *Occurrence* enables you to specify the number of the occurrence of a named item that you want to find. For example, a value of three references the third occurrence, and a value of ten references the tenth occurrence. The following example demonstrates how to find the indexes of the first and third item named **SCL**:

```
   /* default occurrence is 1    */
first=nameditem(listid,'SCL');
   /* Find the third occurrence */
third=nameditem(listid,'SCL',3);
```

## Specifying Where the Search for an Item Starts

The *start-index* argument specifies the position in the list in which to begin the search for a named item. The default is 1, which starts the search at the first item in the list. If the value for *start-index* is negative, then the search starts at position ABS(*start-index*) from the end of the list and searches toward the front of the list. For example, a *start-index* of −1 references the list's last item, whereas a *start-index* of −2 references the list's second-to-last item. Thus, to change the value of the last occurrence of a list item named **x** to the value *y*, you can use a statement like the following:

```
listid=setnitemn(listid,y,'X',1,-1);
```

# Using Shared Data Environments

SCL lists support shared data environments. (Without a shared data environment, if you wanted an entry to pass data to many other entries, you had to pass the data explicitly in each CALL DISPLAY statement, or else you had to put the values in macro variables. However, macro variables are limited in the amount of data they can contain (only scalar values), and their names must be valid SAS names.) By placing data in a shared data environment, other programs and even other SAS applications can retrieve the data via a name. These names can be any valid SCL string, and the value associated with a name can be a numeric value, a character value, or an entire list.

The two kinds of shared data environments are implemented with local SCL lists and global SCL lists.

## Local Data Environment

Each SAS software application (such as an FSEDIT application, or a SAS/AF application started with the AF command) maintains its own application environment in a local environment list. You can store information that is local to the application, but which you want to be shared among all of an application's entries, in this local environment list. The function ENVLIST('L') returns the list identifier of the environment list for the current application. Other applications' lists are maintained in the memory of each application, and even though two lists in different applications may have the same list identifier, the lists are actually different. This is analogous to the same SAS table identifier being used by different SAS applications: the identifier actually refers to different SAS tables that are opened at different times.

## Global Data Environment

There is also a global environment list that stores data that can be shared across all SAS applications started in the same SAS session or process. For example, one SAS application may place some data in the global environment list and then close. Another application may then open and read the data that was created by the first application. To access the global environment list, use the list identifier returned by ENVLIST('G').

# Using Lists as Stacks and Queues

You can create lists that function as stacks (first in, last out lists) or queues (first in, first out lists).

## Using a List as a Stack

To use a list as a stack, use the INSERTC, INSERTN, INSERTL, or INSERTO function to insert items into a list. The default insertion position for these functions is the beginning of the list, so you need only specify the list identifier and the data to be inserted.

To pop (or delete) an item from a stack, use the POPN, POPC, POPL, or POPO function. You can use the ITEMTYPE function to determine the type of the item at the top of the stack if your application does not know the type. If your application always puts the same data type onto your stack (for example, if the stack is a stack of character strings and you use only INSERTC to put items into the list), then you do not need to use ITEMTYPE to check the type of the item at the top of the stack before popping.

If you do not want to keep the top value, use the DELITEM or DELNITEM function to delete the top item in the stack.

To replace the top item, use the SETITEMN, SETITEMC, SETITEML, or SETITEMO function.

You should not attempt to pop or delete an item unless you are sure the list contains at least one item. You can use the LISTLEN function to return the length of the list before you use a function to pop or delete an item.

## Using a List as a Queue

When you use a list as a queue, you also use the INSERTN, INSERTC, INSERTL, or INSERTO function to put items in the list. However, you use an item index of −1 to insert an item at the end of the list.

To remove an item from a queue, use the POPN, POPC, POPL, or POPO function. As with stacks, you should use the ITEMTYPE and LISTLEN functions to verify the item's type and the list's length before popping an item from the list. Here is an example:

```
INIT:
   listid=makelist();
   rc=insertc(listid,'1st',-1);
   rc=insertc(listid,'2nd',-1);
   rc=insertc(listid,'3rd',-1);
   rc=insertc(listid,'4th',-1);
   rc=insertc(listid,'5th',-1);
   put 'Test of first in, first out queue:';
   do i=1 to listlen(listid);
      cval=popc(listid);
      put 'Popping item' i cval=;
   end;
   rc=dellist(listid);
return;
```

This program produces the following output:

```
Test of first in, first out queue:
Popping item 1 cval=1st
Popping item 2 cval=2nd
Popping item 3 cval=3rd
Popping item 4 cval=4th
Popping item 5 cval=5th
```

# Assigning List and Item Attributes

You can assign attributes to lists or to items in a list. Attributes are useful for controlling the use and modification of lists. For example, you can specify that a list is not available for update, which means that other programs called by your program (for example, via CALL DISPLAY) cannot change the data in the list or cannot add or delete items from the list. You can also assign attributes such as NOUPDATE or NODELETE to individual items in a list.

Because it is easy to change the type of any item in a list simply by replacing the value with a new value, it would be quite easy for one application to accidentally change a list in a way that you did not intend. To prevent this possibility, you may want to specify that a list or items in a list have a fixed type. When you assign the proper attributes to the lists and items that you create, you do not need to worry about other parts of the application corrupting your data, and you can avoid adding data validation statements to your programs.

Assigning list and item attributes is not required. However, doing so can facilitate application development, because an attempt to violate an attribute, which indicates a bug in the application, causes the application to stop with a fatal error.

To set the attributes of a list or item, use the SETLATTR function. The GETLATTR function returns a string that describes the current attributes. The HASATTR function returns 1 if the list or item has the specified attribute and 0 if it does not.

# Using File Interfaces

Two SCL list functions enable you to store lists in SAS catalog entries or in external files and to read lists from these files. The SAVELIST function stores a list, and the FILLIST function reads data from a catalog entry or external file and fills a list with the text from the file.

# Debugging List Problems

SCL provides a List Diagnostic Utility (or list analyzer), which reports any SCL lists that are not freed at the appropriate time in a program. SCL lists that are not deleted when they are no longer needed can waste significant amounts of memory. The list analyzer highlights every statement in an SCL program that creates an SCL list that is not deleted directly or indirectly by the program.

To use the list analyzer, issue the command **SCLPROF LIST ON** from any SAS window to start the data collection phase. Then invoke the window associated with the program that you want to test. When you return to the window from which you issued the SCLPROF LIST ON command, issue the command **SCLPROF LIST OFF** to end the data collection phase. The data collected during this phase is stored in the SAS table WORK.SCLTRAC1. If you end the task from which you started the data collection phase, the data collection phase ends.

*Note:* To avoid collecting lists that are not deleted until the end of the task or application, begin the data collection phase on the second invocation of the window that you are testing. △

As soon as the data collection phase ends, the interactive data presentation phase begins. From the data presentation phase, you can save the data by selecting **Save As** from the File menu. To view the stored data, issue the command **SCLPROF LIST DATA=*analysis-data-set*.** The interactive presentation phase opens two windows:

   □ The SUMMARY window displays summary statistics of the list analysis.

   □ The List Diagnostic Utility window lists the catalog entries containing SCL programs that created lists that were not deleted during the analysis.

If warnings were generated during the analysis, a third window opens to display the warning messages.

CHAPTER

*6*

# Controlling Program Flow

# Introduction

You can control the flow of execution of your SCL application by

- using any of several programming constructs such as DO loops and IF/THEN-ELSE statements
- branching to labeled sections with the LINK statement
- branching to PROGRAM, FRAME, MENU, CBT, or HELP entries with the GOTO statement
- branching to another SCL entry with CALL DISPLAY
- executing a method that is stored in a separate SCL entry with CALL METHOD
- executing an object method by using dot notation
- sending a method to an object with CALL SEND
- sending a method to a FRAME entry control with CALL NOTIFY
- specifying how labeled sections are executed, when and where submit blocks are executed, and whether execution halts when errors are encountered in dot notation with the CONTROL statement
- creating a program halt handler to control how run-time errors are processed.

For more information about controlling the flow of execution in applications that use frames, refer to *SAS Guide to Applications Development.*

# Using DO Loops

There are four forms of the DO statement:

☐ The DO statement designates a group of statements that are to be executed as a unit, usually as a part of IF-THEN/ELSE statements.

☐ The iterative DO statement executes a group of statements repetitively based on the value of an index variable. If you specify an UNTIL clause or a WHILE clause, then the execution of the statements is also based on the condition that you specify in the clause.

☐ The DO UNTIL statement executes a group of statements repetitively until the condition that you specify is true. The condition is checked *after* each iteration of the loop.

☐ The DO WHILE statement executes a group of statements repetitively as long as the condition that you specify remains true. The condition is checked *before* each iteration of the loop.

For more information about DO statements, in addition to the information in this documentation, refer to *SAS Language Reference: Dictionary*.

## DO Statement

The DO statement designates a group of statements that are to be executed as a unit. The simplest form of the DO loop is

DO;

. . .*SAS statements*. . .

END;

This simple DO statement is often used within IF-THEN/ELSE statements to designate a group of statements to be executed if the IF condition is true. For example, in the following code, the statements between DO and END are performed only when YEARS is greater than 5.

```
if years>5 then
  do;
    months=years*12;
    put years= months=;
  end;
```

## Iterative DO Loops

The iterative DO loop executes the statements between DO and END repetitively based on the value of an index variable.

DO *index-variable* = *start* TO *stop* <BY *increment*>;

*Note:*  In SCL applications, both *start* and *stop* are required, and *start*, *stop*, and *increment* must be numbers or expressions that yield a number. The TO and BY clauses cannot be reversed, and *start* cannot be a series of items separated by commas. You can use only one *start* TO *stop* specification (with or without the BY clause) in a DO loop. △

If *increment* is not specified, then *index-variable* is increased by 1. If *increment* is positive, then *start* must be the lower bound and *stop* must the be upper bound for the loop. If *increment* is negative, then *start* must be the upper bound and *stop* must be the lower bound for the loop.

The values of *start*, *stop*, and *increment* are evaluated before the first execution of the loop. Any changes made to *stop* or *increment* within the DO group do not affect the number of times that the loop executes.

**CAUTION:**

**Changing the value of *index-variable* within the DO group may produce an infinite loop.** If you change the value of *index-variable* inside of the DO group, then *index-variable* may never become equal to the value of *stop*, and the loop will not stop executing. △

For example, the following code prints the numbers 20, 18, 16, 14, 12, and 10.

```
dcl num k=18 n=11;
do i=k+2 to n-1 by -2;
   put i;
end;
```

The following code uses the DOPEN and DNUM functions to execute SAS statements once for each file in the current directory:

```
rc=filename('mydir','.');
dirid=dopen('mydir');
do i=1 to dnum(dirid);
   ...SAS statements...
end;
rc=dclose(dirid);
```

## Using UNTIL and WHILE Clauses

You can add either an UNTIL clause or a WHILE clause to your DO statements.

DO *index-variable* = *start* TO *stop* <BY *increment*>

<WHILE (*expression*)> | <UNTIL (*expression*)>;

The UNTIL expression is evaluated *after* the statements in the DO loop have executed, and the WHILE expression is evaluated *before* the statements in the DO loop have executed. The statements in a DO UNTIL loop are always executed at least once, but the statements in a DO WHILE loop will not execute even once if the DO WHILE expression is false.

If *index-variable* is still in the range between *start* and *stop*, then if you specify an UNTIL clause, the DO group will execute until the UNTIL expression is true. If you specify a WHILE clause, the loop will execute as long as the WHILE expression is true.

The following example uses an UNTIL clause to set a flag, and then it checks the flag during each iteration of the loop:

```
flag=0;
do i=1 to 10 until(flag);
  ...SAS statements...
  if expression then flag=1;
end;
```

The following loop executes as long as I is within the range of 10 to 0 and MONTH is equal to **JAN**.

```
do i=10 to 0 by -1 while(month='JAN');
   ...SAS statements...
end;
```

## DO WHILE Statement

The DO WHILE statement works like the iterative DO statement with a WHILE clause, except that you do not specify an *index-variable* or *start, stop*, or *increment*.

DO WHILE (*expression*);

. . .*SAS statements*. . .

END;

Whether the loop executes is based solely on whether the expression that you specify evaluates to true or false. The expression is evaluated before the loop executes, and if the expression is false, then the loop is not executed. If the expression is false the first time it is evaluated, then the loop will not execute at all.

For example, the following DO loop is executed once for each value of N: 0, 1, 2, 3, and 4.

```
n=0;
do while(n<5);
  put n=;
  n+1;
end;
```

## DO UNTIL Statement

The DO UNTIL statement works like the iterative DO statement with an UNTIL clause, except that you do not specify an index variable nor *start, stop*, or *increment*.

DO UNTIL (*expression*);

. . .*SAS statements*. . .

END;

Whether the loop executes is based solely on whether the expression that you specify evaluates to true or false. The loop is always executed at least once, and the expression is evaluated after the loop executes.

For example, the following DO loop is executed once for each value of N: 0, 1, 2, 3, and 4.

```
n=0;
do until(n>=5);
  put n=;
  n+1;
end;
```

## Controlling DO Loops (CONTINUE and LEAVE)

You can use the CONTINUE and LEAVE statements to control the flow of execution through DO loops.

The CONTINUE statement stops the processing of the current DO loop iteration and resumes with the next iteration of the loop. For example, the following code reads each row in the DEPT table, and if the status is not **PT**, it displays a frame that enables the user to update the full-time employee's salary.

```
deptid=open('dept');
call set(deptid);
```

```
do while (fetch(deptid) ne -1);
  if (status='PT') then continue;
  newsal=display('fulltime.frame');
end;
```

The LEAVE statement stops processing the current DO loop and resumes with the next statement after the DO loop. With the LEAVE statement, you have the option of specifying a label for the DO statement:

LEAVE < *label*>;

If you have nested DO loops and you want to skip out of more than one loop, you can specify the label of the loop that you want to leave. For example, the following LEAVE statement causes execution to skip to the last PUT statement:

```
myloop:
do i=1 to 10;
  do j=1 to 10;
    if j=5 then leave myloop;
    put i= j=;
  end;
end;
put 'this statement executes next';
return;
```

In SCL applications, the LEAVE statement can be used only within DO loops, not in SELECT statements (unless it is enclosed in a DO statement).

For more information, refer to "CONTINUE" on page 300, "LEAVE" on page 504, and *SAS Language Reference: Dictionary*.

# Using SELECT-WHEN/OTHERWISE Conditions

The SELECT statement executes one of several statements or groups of statements based on the value of the expression that you specify.

SELECT< (*select-expression*)>;

WHEN-1 (*when-expression-1*) *statement(s)*;

<WHEN-*n* (*when-expression-n*) *statement(s)*;>

<OTHERWISE *statement*;>

END;

SAS evaluates *select-expression*, if present, as well as *when–expression-1*. If the values of both expressions are equal, then SAS executes the statements associated with *when-expression-1*. If the values are *not* equal, then SAS evaluates *when-expression-n*, and if the values of *select–expression-1* and *when-expression-1 are* equal, SAS executes the statements associated with *when-expression-n*. SAS evaluates each when expression until it finds a match or until it has evaluated all of the when expressions without finding a match. If you do not specify a select expression, then SAS evaluates each when expression and executes only the statements associated with the first when expression that evaluates to true.

If the value of none of the when expressions matches the value of the select expression, or if you do not specify a select expression and all of the when expressions are false, then SAS executes the statements associated with the OTHERWISE statement. If you do not specify an OTHERWISE statement, the program halts.

In SCL applications, you cannot specify a series of when expressions separated by commas in the same WHEN statement. However, separating multiple WHEN statements with a comma is equivalent to separating them with the logical operator OR, which is acceptable in SCL applications.

The statements associated with a when expression can be any executable SAS statement, including SELECT and null statements. A null statement in a WHEN statement causes SAS to recognize a condition as true and to take no additional action. A null statement in an OTHERWISE statement prevents SAS from issuing an error message when all of the when expressions are false.

Each WHEN statement implies a DO group of all statements until the next WHEN or OTHERWISE statement. Therefore the following program is valid:

```
select (paycat);
   when ('monthly')
     amt=salary;
   when ('hourly')
     amt=hrlywage*min(hrs,40);
     if hrs>40 then put 'Check timecard.';
   otherwise put 'problem observation';
end;
```

However, if you need to include a LEAVE statement as part of your WHEN statement, then you must explicitly specify the DO statement in your WHEN statement.

You can specify expressions and their possible values in either of the following ways:

**1**

SELECT;

WHEN (*variable operator value*) *statement(s)*;

END;

**2**

SELECT (*variable*);

WHEN (*value*) *statement(s)*;

END;

For example, both of the following SELECT statements are correct:

```
select;
  when (x<=5) put '1 to 5';
  when (x>=6) put '6 to 10';
end;

select (x);
  when (1) put 'one';
  when (2) put 'two';
end;
```

The following code is incorrect because it compares the value of the expression X with the value of the expression X=1. As described in "Boolean Numeric Expressions" on page 31, in Boolean expressions, a value of 0 is false and a value of 1 is true. Therefore, the expression X is false and the expression X=1 is false, so the program prints **x is 1**.

```
x=0;
select (x);
  when (x=0) put 'x is 0';
```

```
      when (x=1) put 'x is 1';
      otherwise put x=;
   end;
```

For more information about the SELECT statement, refer to "SELECT" on page 640 and to *SAS Language Reference: Dictionary*.

# Using IF-THEN/ELSE Conditions

The IF-THEN/ELSE statement executes a statement or group of statements based on a condition that you specify.

IF *expression* THEN *statement*;

<ELSE *statement*;>

If *expression* is true, then SAS executes the statement in the THEN clause. If the *expression* is false and if an ELSE statement is present, then SAS executes the ELSE statement. The statement following THEN and ELSE can be either a single SAS statement (including an IF-THEN/ELSE statement) or a DO group.
For example:

```
if (exist(table)) then
   _msg_='SAS table already exists.';
else do;
   call new(table,'',1,'y');
   _msg_='Table has been created.';
end;
```

Suppose your application is designed to run in batch mode and you do not want to generate any messages. You could use a null statement after THEN:

```
if (exist(table)) then;
   else call new(table,'',1,'y');
```

For more information, refer to *SAS Language Reference: Dictionary*.

# Using the RETURN Statement

The RETURN statement stops the execution of the program section that is currently executing.

RETURN <*value*>;

The RETURN statement at the end of a reserved program section (FSEINIT ,INIT, MAIN, TERM, and FSETERM) sends control to the next program section in the sequence.

The first RETURN statement after a LINK statement returns control to the statement that immediately follows the LINK statement.

When the RETURN statement is encountered at the end of a window variable section, control returns to the next section in the program execution cycle. That next section may be another window variable section or it may be the MAIN section. When the current program execution cycle finishes, control returns to the application window.

The RETURN statement at the end of a method returns control to the calling program.

The RETURN statement for an ENTRY or METHOD block can return *value* if the ENTRY or METHOD statement contains RETURN=*data-type*. The returned value has no effect if control does not immediately return to the calling program.

For an example of the RETURN statement, see the example in "Branching to Another Entry (GOTO)" on page 72. For more explanation and an additional example, see "RETURN" on page 615.

# Branching to a Labeled Section (LINK)

The LINK statement tells SCL to jump immediately to the specified statement label.

LINK *label*;

SCL then executes the statements from the statement *label* up to the next RETURN statement. The RETURN statement sends program control to the statement that immediately follows the LINK statement. The LINK statement and the *label* must be in the same entry.

The LINK statement can branch to a group of statements that contains another LINK statement; that is, you can nest LINK statements. You can have up to ten LINK statements with no intervening RETURN statements.

See "Branching to Another Entry (GOTO)" on page 72 for an example that includes LINK statements.

For more information, refer to *SAS Language Reference: Dictionary*.

# Branching to Another Entry (GOTO)

You can use the GOTO statement to transfer control to another SAS/AF entry.

CALL GOTO (*entry*<, *action*<, *frame*>>);

*Entry* specifies a FRAME, PROGRAM, MENU, CBT, or HELP entry. By default, when the entry ends, control returns to the parent entry that was specified in *entry*. If a parent entry is not specified, then the window exits.

For example, suppose WORK.A.A.SCL contains the following code:

```
INIT:
  link SECTONE;
  put 'in INIT after link to SECTONE';
return;

SECTONE:
  put 'in SECTONE before link to TWO';
  link TWO;
  put 'in SECTONE before goto';
  call goto('work.a.b.frame');
  put 'in SECTONE after goto to frame';
return;

TWO:
  put 'in TWO';
return;
```

WORK.A.B.SCL contains the following code:

```
INIT:
   put 'in WORK.A.B.FRAME';
return;
```

If you compile WORK.A.B.FRAME and WORK.A.A.SCL, and then test WORK.A.A.SCL, you will see the following output:

```
in SECTONE before link to TWO
in TWO
in SECTONE before goto
in WORK.A.B.FRAME
```

The PUT statement in the INIT section of A.SCL and the last PUT statement in SECTONE are never executed. After WORK.A.B.FRAME is displayed and the user exits from the window, the program ends.

For more information, see "GOTO" on page 455.

# Calling SCL Entries

SAS/AF software provides SCL entries for storing program modules. SCL programs can access a module that is stored in another SCL entry. They can pass parameters to the module and can receive values from the module. An SCL module can be used by any other SCL program.

You call an SCL module with a CALL DISPLAY routine that passes parameters to it and receives values that are returned by the SCL entry. The module's ENTRY statement receives parameters and returns values to the calling program.

For example, if you were creating an SCL module to validate amounts and rates that are entered by users, you could store the labeled sections in separate SCL entries named AMOUNT.SCL and RATE.SCL. Then, you could call either of them with a CALL DISPLAY statement like the following:

```
call display('methdlib.validate.amount.scl',amount,error);
```

For more information, see "DISPLAY" on page 350.

# Stopping Execution of the Current Section

The STOP statement stops the execution of the current section. If a MAIN or TERM section is present, control passes to MAIN or TERM. For example, in the following program, control passes from INIT to SECTONE. Since X=1 is true, the STOP statement is executed, so control never passes to TWO. Control passes directly from the STOP statement in SECTONE to MAIN. The STOP statement at the end of MAIN has no effect, and control passes to TERM.

```
INIT:
   put 'beginning INIT';
   x=1;
   link SECTONE;
   put 'in INIT after link';
stop;

MAIN:
   put 'in MAIN';
stop;
```

```
SECTONE:
  put 'in SECTONE';
  if x=1 then stop;
  link TWO;
return;

TWO:
  put 'in TWO';
return;

TERM:
  put 'in TERM';
return;
```

This program produces the following output:

```
beginning INIT
in SECTONE
in MAIN
in TERM
```

For more information, see "STOP" on page 674.

# Executing Methods

In object-oriented applications, methods are implemented in CLASS blocks or USECLASS blocks. These methods are usually invoked with dot notation. See "Accessing Object Attributes and Methods With Dot Notation" on page 119 for information about dot notation.

You can also send methods to an object by using CALL SEND, and you can send a method to a control in a FRAME entry by using CALL NOTIFY. See "SEND" on page 644 and "NOTIFY" on page 572 for more information.

Methods may also be stored in SCL, PROGRAM, or SCREEN entries. If the method is stored in an SCL entry, then call the method with the CALL METHOD routine. If the method is stored in a PROGRAM or SCREEN entry, you can use the LINK or GOTO statements to call it. See "Calling a Method That Is Stored in an SCL Entry" on page 13, "Branching to a Labeled Section (LINK)" on page 72, and "Branching to Another Entry (GOTO)" on page 72 for more information.

# Using the CONTROL Statement

The CONTROL statement enables you to specify options that control the execution of labeled sections, the formatting of submit blocks, and whether an error in dot notation causes a program halt.

CONTROL *options*;

You can specify the following options with the CONTROL statement:

ALLCMDS | NOALLCMDS
   determines whether SCL can intercept procedure-specific or custom commands that are issued in the application. This option also determines if and when the MAIN section executes.

ALWAYS | NOALWAYS
>  determines whether the MAIN section executes if the user enters a command that SCL does not recognize.

ASIS NOASIS
>  determines whether SCL eliminates unnecessary spaces and line breaks before submit blocks are submitted.

BREAK *label* | NOBREAK
>  enables you to specify a labeled program section that will be executed if an interrupt or break occurs while your program is executing.

HALTONDOATTRIBUTE | NOHALTONDOTATTRIBUTE
>  determines whether execution halts if SCL finds an error in the dot notation that is used in your program.

ENDSAS | NOENDSAS
>  determines whether the TERM section executes when the user enters the ENDSAS or BYE commands.

ENDAWS | NOENDAWS
>  determines whether the TERM section executes when a user ends a SAS session by selecting the system closure menu in a FRAME entry that is running within the SAS application workspace.

ENTER | NOENTER
>  determines whether the MAIN section executes when the user presses the ENTER key or a function key without modifying a window variable.

ERROR | NOERROR
>  determines whether the MAIN section executes if a control or field contains a value that causes an attribute error.

LABEL | NOLABEL
>  determines whether the MAIN section executes before or after the window variable sections.

TERM | NOTERM
>  determines whether the TERM section executes even if a user does not modify any columns in the current row of the SAS table.

For more information, see "CONTROL" on page 302.

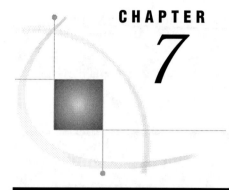

CHAPTER

*7*

# Using Other SAS Software Products

## Introduction

SCL provides many of the same features as the base SAS language. However, some SCL features differ slightly in functionality from base SAS language features. Also, although SCL provides a rich set of features, it does not provide functions and statements to accomplish directly all of the data access, management, presentation, and analysis tasks that SAS software can perform, nor can it provide the equivalent for every command that is available under your host operating system. However, SCL does provide the following features:

☐ the SUBMIT statement, which provides access to other features of SAS software by generating SAS statements and then submitting them to SAS software for processing.

☐ the SYSTEM function, which provides access to host operating systems by issuing host operating system commands.

# Using SAS DATA Step Features in SCL

SCL supports the syntax of the SAS DATA step with the exceptions and additions noted. Refer to *SAS Language Reference: Dictionary* for details about the SAS language elements that are available in the DATA step.

SCL does not support the DATA step statements that relate specifically to creating SAS data tables, such as the DATA, SET, INFILE, and DATALINES statements. However, SCL does provide special functions that can perform equivalent SAS table manipulations. See Chapter 11, "Using SAS Tables," on page 165 for details.

## Statements

"SCL Language Elements by Category" on page 235 lists the statements that are supported by SCL and tells you where they are documented. The ARRAY, DO, LENGTH, PUT, and SELECT statements are different in SCL. The differences are documented in their entries in Chapter 16, "SAS Component Language Dictionary," on page 249. The following list shows the DATA step statements that are valid in SCL programs and notes differences between a statement's support in SCL and in the DATA step.

ARRAY (Explicit)
defines the elements of an explicit array. _NUMERIC_, _CHARACTER_, and _ALL_ are not supported.

assignment
assigns values to variables.

comment
documents the purpose of a program.

CONTINUE
stops the processing of the current DO loop and resumes with the next iteration of that DO loop. See the dictionary entries for DO as well as CONTINUE for information about the differences in the behavior of this statement in SCL.

DO, iterative DO, DO-UNTIL, DO-WHILE
repetitively execute one or more statements. SCL does not support the DO-list form of the DO statement, but it does support LEAVE and CONTINUE statements that extend the capabilities of DO-group processing.

END
designates the end of a DO group or SELECT group.

GOTO
jumps to a specified program label.

IF-THEN-ELSE
enables conditional execution of one or more statements.

%INCLUDE
> accesses statements (usually from an external file) and adds them to the program when the SCL program compiles.

LEAVE
> stops executing the current DO group and resumes with the next sequential statement. See the dictionary entries for DO as well as LEAVE for information about the differences in the behavior of this statement in SCL.

LENGTH
> allocates storage space for character and numeric variables. In SCL, the LENGTH statement can set only the lengths of nonwindow variables.

LINK
> jumps to a specified program label but allows a return to the following statement. SCL allows nesting of up to 25 LINK statements.

NULL
> is an executable statement that contains a semicolon (;) and acts as a place holder.

PUT
> writes text to the LOG window.

RETURN
> returns control or a value to the calling routine or application. In SCL, RETURN can also return a value from the execution of a method.

RUN
> is an alias for the RETURN statement.

SELECT-WHEN
> enables conditional execution of one or several statements or groups of statements.

STOP
> is an alias for the RETURN statement.

SUM
> adds the result of an expression to an accumulator variable.

## Functions

SCL supports all DATA step functions except LAG and DIF. See Table 15.1 on page 235 for a list of the DATA step functions that are supported by SCL. See *SAS Language Reference: Dictionary* for details about other DATA step functions that are supported by SCL.

## Variables

Variables in SCL programs share most of the characteristics of variables in the DATA step such as default length and type. However, you should be aware of the differences described in the following sections. In addition, SCL variables can be declared to be local in scope to a DO or SELECT block.

### Numeric Variables

A variable is assigned the numeric data type if its data type is not explicitly declared.

### Character Variables

In SCL, the length of a character variable is determined as follows:

□ For window variables, the maximum length of a variable is equal to the length of the corresponding control or field in the window.

□ For character-type nonwindow variables, the length is 200 characters unless a different length is explicitly declared. However, you can use the DECLARE or LENGTH statement to change the length from a minimum of 1 character to a maximum of 32K characters. The maximum length of a nonwindow variable is not affected by the length of a string that is assigned to the variable in the SCL program. For example, suppose your SCL program contains the following statement and that the window for the application does not include a field named LongWord:

```
LongWord='Thisisaverylongword';
```

As a result of this assignment statement, SCL creates a nonwindow variable named LongWord with a maximum length of 200 characters. The length of the string in the assignment statement has no effect on the maximum length of the variable. By contrast, this same assignment in a DATA step would create a variable with a maximum length of 19 characters.

As in the DATA step, the LENGTH function in SCL returns the current trimmed length of a string (the position of the nonblank character at the right end of the variable value). However, SCL also provides the MLENGTH function, which returns the maximum length of a character variable, as well as the LENGTH function with the NOTRIM option, which returns the untrimmed length of a string.

## Expressions

SCL supports the standard DATA step expressions in an identical manner. The only exception is the IN operator, which has the following syntax:

*i*=*variable* IN (*list-of-values*) | *array-name*;

In SCL, the IN operator returns the index of the element if a match is found, or it returns 0 if no match is found. However, in the DATA step, the IN operator returns 1 if a match is found and 0 if no match is found. The IN operator is valid for both numeric and character lists as well as for arrays. If a list that is used with the IN operator contains values with mixed data types, then those values are converted to the data type of the first value in the list when the program is compiled.

In the following example, the statements using the IN operator are equivalent:

```
array list{3}$ ('cat','bird','dog');
i='dog' in ('cat','bird','dog');
i='dog' in list;
```

In SCL, this example produces I=3, whereas in the DATA step the example produces I=1. Also, the DATA step does not support the form **i='dog' in list**.

## Submitting SAS Statements and SQL Statements

SCL programs can submit statements to execute both DATA steps and all the procedures in any product in SAS software. SCL programs can also submit Structured Query Language (SQL) statements directly to SAS software's SQL processor without submitting a PROC SQL statement. SQL statements enable you to query the contents of SAS files and to create and manipulate SAS tables and SAS views. SCL programs also enable you to submit command line commands to the Program Editor window for processing. Finally, SCL programs can submit statements for processing on your local host or on a remote host, if SAS/CONNECT software is installed at your site.

## Submitting Statements Compared to Using SCL Features

You should submit statements when the task you want to perform is difficult or impossible using SCL features alone. Whenever equivalent SCL features are available, it is more efficient to use them than to submit SAS statements. For example, the following two sets of statements produce the same result, opening an FSEDIT window to display the SAS data table WORK.DATA1 for editing:

```
    /* This uses the SCL Feature. */
call fsedit('work.data1');
```

```
    /* This uses submitted statements. */
submit continue;
    proc fsedit data=work.data1;
    run;
endsubmit;
```

From within an application, fewer computer resources are required to execute the CALL routine in SCL than to submit statements to SAS software. Thus, the CALL routine is a better choice unless you need features of the procedure that the CALL routine does not provide (for example, the VAR statement in PROC FSEDIT to select which variables to display to the user).

## Designating Submit Blocks

In SCL programs, you designate statements to be submitted to SAS software for processing by placing them in submit blocks. A *submit block* begins with a SUBMIT statement, ends with an ENDSUBMIT statement, and consists of all the statements in between. The following statements illustrate these characteristics:

```
SUBMIT;   ❶
    proc print data=work.data1;   ❷
        var a b c;       ❷
    run;
endsubmit;   ❸
```

**1** The SUBMIT statement starts the submit block.
**2** These statements are submitted to SAS software when the program executes.
**3** The ENDSUBMIT statement ends the submit block.

For details, see "SUBMIT" on page 676.

## How Submit Blocks Are Processed

Figure 7.1 on page 82 illustrates how submit blocks are processed when they are executed (not when they are compiled). Submit blocks are not processed when you test a SAS/AF application with the TESTAF command.

**Figure 7.1**  Default Processing of Submit Blocks

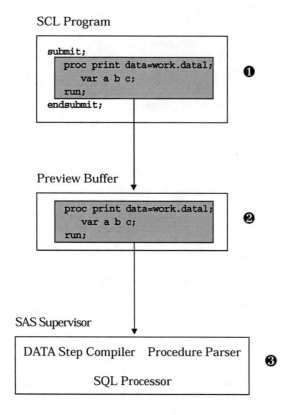

1  All of the code between a SUBMIT statement and the next ENDSUBMIT statement is copied into a special storage area called the *preview buffer*. The submitted code is not checked for errors when it is copied to the preview buffer. Errors in the submitted code are not detected until the statements or commands are executed.

2  The text in the preview buffer is scanned, and any requested substitutions are made. Substitution is discussed in "Substituting Text in Submit Blocks" on page 85.

3  The contents of the preview buffer are submitted to SAS software for execution. You can specify options to change where and when the contents of the preview buffer are submitted and to specify the actions that the SCL program takes after the statements are submitted. See "Modifying the Behavior of Submit Blocks" on page 83 for details.

*Note:*  By default, code is not submitted immediately when the submit block is encountered in an executing program. Also, when a nested entry (that is, an entry that is called by another entry in the application) contains a submit block, the submitted code is not executed until the calling task ends, or until another submit block with a CONTINUE or IMMEDIATE option is encountered. Simply ending the entry that contains the submit block does not process submitted code. △

# How Submitted Statements Are Formatted

By default, SCL reformats the submitted code when it copies it to the preview buffer. To conserve space, all leading and trailing spaces in the submitted text are removed. Semicolons in the submitted statements cause line breaks in the submitted text.

In some situations (for example, when the submitted code includes lines of raw data), you may want to prevent this formatting by SCL. You can do this by using a CONTROL statement with the ASIS option. When an SCL program contains a CONTROL ASIS statement, SCL honors the indention and spacing that appears in the submit block. Programs that use CONTROL ASIS are more efficient because the time spent on formatting is reduced. A CONTROL NOASIS statement restores the default behavior.

# Modifying the Behavior of Submit Blocks

You can modify the default processing of submit blocks by specifying options in the SUBMIT statement. SUBMIT statement options control the following behaviors:

- □ when the code in the preview buffer is submitted for execution
- □ when the submitted code is processed and what happens after the submitted code is executed
- □ whether the submitted code is executed in the local SAS session or in a remote SAS session.

## Controlling Where Submitted Code Is Executed

By default, code that is collected in the preview buffer using SUBMIT blocks is sent to SAS software for execution. SCL provides options for the SUBMIT statement that alter the default behavior. If you specify the CONTINUE option in the SUBMIT statement, you can control where code is submitted with the following options:

COMMAND
  submits the code in the preview buffer to the command line of the next window that is displayed. The code should contain valid commands for that window; otherwise, either errors are reported or the submitted commands are ignored.

EDIT
  sends the code in the preview buffer to the Program Editor window. You can modify your code in the Program Editor window and then submit it for execution.

SQL
  submits the code in the preview buffer to SAS software's SQL processor, from both TESTAF and AF modes. The SUBMIT SQL option enables you to submit the SQL statements without having to specify a PROC SQL statement. Submitting SQL statements directly to the SQL processor is more efficient than submitting PROC SQL statements.

## Controlling What Happens After a Submit Block Executes

SCL also provides SUBMIT statement options that you can use to control what action, if any, the application takes after a submit block executes. These options are CONTINUE, IMMEDIATE, PRIMARY, and TERMINATE. Without one of these options, the code in a submit block is simply passed to the preview buffer, the application continues executing, and the code in the submit block is not processed by SAS software until the application ends.

CONTINUE

> suspends program execution while the submit block executes and then continues program execution at the statement that immediately follows the ENDSUBMIT statement. (CONTINUE is the only SUBMIT option that is valid in FSEDIT and FSBROWSE applications.)

IMMEDIATE

> stops program execution after the generated statements are submitted. Use this option with caution. Using this option in a labeled section that is executed individually when a CONTROL LABEL statement is in effect can prevent the execution of other labeled sections. A program in a FRAME entry does not compile if it contains a SUBMIT IMMEDIATE statement.

PRIMARY

> returns the program to the application's initial window after the generated statements are submitted. This option is useful when you want all the intermediate windows to close and you want control to return to a primary window in the current execution stream. This option causes looping if the current program is the primary window.

TERMINATE

> stops the SAS/AF task after the statements in the submit block are processed. This option is useful when an application does not need to interact with users after the submitted statements are processed. However, use TERMINATE with caution because re-invoking the application can be time-consuming.

## Using SUBMIT CONTINUE in FSEDIT Applications

The behavior of a SUBMIT CONTINUE block in an FSEDIT application depends on how the application was invoked.

☐ If you invoked the application with a PROC FSEDIT statement, then the statements in the submit block cannot be processed until the FSEDIT session ends, even when you specify SUBMIT CONTINUE. The statements cannot be executed as long as the FSEDIT procedure is executing.

☐ If you invoked the application with an FSEDIT command or with a CALL FSEDIT routine from another SCL program, then the statements in the submit block can execute immediately as long as no other procedure is currently executing.

## Submitting Statements to a Remote Host

By default, statements in a submit block are executed for processing on the local host. If SAS/CONNECT software is available at your site, you can also submit statements for processing on a remote host. To send submitted statements to a remote host, use the following form of the SUBMIT statement:

```
submit remote;
...SAS or SQL statements to execute
on a remote host...
endsubmit;
```

In situations where an application user can switch between a remote host and the local host, the user can issue the REMOTE command to force all submits to be sent to a remote host. The syntax of the REMOTE command is REMOTE <ON|OFF>. If neither ON nor OFF is specified, the command acts like a toggle.

The REMOTE option in the SUBMIT block takes precedence over a REMOTE command that is issued by an application user. A SAS/AF application must have a display window in order to issue and recognize the REMOTE command. Before SCL submits the generated code for execution, it checks to see whether the user has issued the REMOTE ON command. If a user has issued the command, SCL checks to see whether the remote link is still active. If the remote link is active, SCL submits the code for execution. If the remote link is not active, SCL generates an error message and returns. The preview buffer is not cleared if the submit fails.

# Substituting Text in Submit Blocks

In interactive applications, values for statements in a submit block may need to be determined by user input or program input in the application. An SCL feature that supports this requirement is the substitution of text in submit blocks, based on the values of fields or SCL variables.

## How Values Are Substituted in Submit Blocks

SCL performs substitution in submit blocks according to the following rules:

- □ When SCL encounters a name that is prefixed with an ampersand (&) in a submit block, it checks to see whether that name is the name of an SCL variable. If it is, then SCL substitutes the value of that variable for the variable reference in the submit block. For example, suppose a submit block contains the following statement:

  ```
  proc print data=&table;
  ```

  If the application includes a variable named TABLE whose value is **work.sample**, then this statement is passed to the preview buffer:

  ```
  proc print data=work.sample;
  ```

- □ If the name that follows the ampersand does not match an SCL variable, then no substitution occurs. The name is passed unchanged (including the ampersand) with the submitted statements. When SAS software processes the statements, it attempts to resolve the name as a macro variable reference. SCL does not resolve macro variable references within submit blocks. For example, suppose a submit block contains the following statement:

  ```
  proc print data=&table;
  ```

  If there is no SCL variable named TABLE in the application, then the statement is passed unchanged to the preview buffer. SAS software attempts to resolve &TABLE as a macro reference when the statements are processed.

*CAUTION:*
  **Avoid using the same name for both an SCL variable and a macro variable that you want to use in submitted statements.** SCL substitutes the value of the corresponding SCL variable for any name that begins with an ampersand. To guarantee that a name is passed as a macro variable reference in submitted statements, precede the name with two ampersands (for example, &&TABLE). △

## Specifying Text for Substitutions

If an SCL variable that is used in a substitution contains a null value, then a blank is substituted for the reference in the submitted statements. This can cause problems if the substitution occurs in a statement that requires a value, so SCL allows you to define a replacement string for the variable. If the variable's value is not blank, the complete replacement string is substituted for the variable reference. To define a replacement string, you can use either the Replace attribute (for a control or field) or the REPLACE statement.

## Using the REPLACE Statement

The REPLACE statement acts as an implicit IF-THEN statement that determines when to substitute a specified string in the submit block. Consider the following example:

```
replace table 'data=&table';
   ...more SCL statements...
submit;
   proc print &table;
   run;
endsubmit;
```

If the SCL variable TABLE contains '' (or **_BLANK_**), then these statements are submitted:

```
proc print;
run;
```

If the SCL variable TABLE contains **work.sample**, then these statements are submitted:

```
proc print data=work.sample;
run;
```

## Using the Replace Attribute

In SAS/AF applications, you can also can define replacement strings for a window variable using the Replace attribute in the properties window (for a control) or the attribute window (for a field). The text that you specify for the Replace attribute is substituted for the variable name when the variable name is preceded with an ampersand in submitted statements.

# Issuing Commands to Host Operating Systems

SCL programs can use the SYSTEM function to issue commands to host operating systems. For example, an SCL program may need to issue commands to the operating system in order to perform system-specific data management or control tasks or to invoke non-SAS applications.

An SCL program can issue any command that is valid for the operating system under which an application runs. SCL places no restrictions on commands that are issued to an operating system, nor does SCL check command strings for validity before passing them to the operating system.

# Using Macro Variables

Macro variables, which are part of the macro facility in base SAS software, can be used in SCL programs. Macro variables are independent of any particular SAS table, application, or window. The values of macro variables are available to all SAS software products for the duration of a SAS session. For details, refer to macro variables in *SAS Macro Language: Reference*. In SCL programs, you can

- □ store values in macro variables (for example, to pass information from the current SCL program to subsequent programs in the application, to subsequent applications, or to other parts of SAS software).
- □ retrieve values from macro variables (for example, to pass information to the current SCL program from programs that executed previously or from other parts of SAS software, or to pass values from one observation to another in FSEDIT applications).

Examples of types of information that you frequently need to pass between entries in an application include

- □ names of SAS tables to be opened
- □ names of external files to be opened
- □ identifiers of open SAS tables
- □ file identifiers of open external files
- □ the current date (instead of using date functions repeatedly)
- □ values to be repeated across rows in an FSEDIT session.

# Storing and Retrieving Macro Variable Values

To assign a literal value to a macro variable in an SCL program, you can use the standard macro variable assignment statement, %LET. For example, the following statement assigns the literal value **sales** (not the value of an SCL variable named SALES) to a macro variable named DSNAME:

```
%let dsname=sales;
```

Macro variable assignments are evaluated when SCL programs are compiled, not when they are executed. Thus, the %LET statement is useful for assigning literal values at compile time. For example, you can use macro variables defined in this manner to store a value or block of text that is used repeatedly in a program. However, you must use a different approach if you want to store the value of an SCL variable in a macro variable while the SCL program executes (for example, to pass values between SCL programs).

Macro variables store only strings of text characters, so numeric values are stored as strings of text digits that represent numeric values. To store values so that they can be retrieved correctly, you must use the appropriate CALL routine. The following routines store the value of a macro when an SCL program runs:

CALL SYMPUT
    stores a character value in a macro variable.

CALL SYMPUTN
    stores a numeric value in a macro variable.

For example, the following CALL routine stores the value of the SCL variable SALES in the macro variable TABLE:

```
call symput('table',sales);
```

To retrieve the value of a macro variable in an SCL program, you can use a standard macro variable reference. In the following example, the value of the macro variable TABLE is substituted for the macro variable reference when the program is *compiled*:

```
dsn="&table";
```

The function that you use to retrieve the value of a macro variable determines how the macro variable value is interpreted. The following functions return the value of a macro variable when a program runs:

SYMGET
> interprets the value of a macro variable as a character value.

SYMGETN
> interprets the value of a macro variable as a numeric value.

## Using the Same Name for Macro Variables and SCL Variables

Using the same name for a macro variable and an SCL variable in an SCL program does not cause a conflict. Macro variables are stored in SAS software's global symbol table, whereas SCL variables are stored in the SCL data vector (SDV). However, if your program uses submit blocks and you have both a macro variable and an SCL variable with the same name, then a reference with a single ampersand substitutes the SCL variable. To force the macro variable to be substituted, reference it with two ampersands (&&). The following example demonstrates using a reference that contains two ampersands:

```
dsname='sasuser.class';
call symput('dsname','sasuser.houses');
submit continue;
   proc print data=&dsname;
   run;
   proc print data=&&dsname;
   run;
endsubmit;
```

The program produces the following:

```
proc print data=sasuser.class;
run;
proc print data=sasuser.houses;
run;
```

## Using Automatic Macro Variables

In addition to macro variables that you define in your programs, SAS software provides a number of predefined macro variables for every SAS session or process. These automatic macro variables supply information about the current SAS session or process and about the host operating system on which the SAS session is running. For example, you can use the automatic macro variable SYSSCP to obtain the name of the current operating system. Automatic macro variables are documented in *SAS Macro Language: Reference*.

When you use automatic macro variables, remember to use the appropriate routines and functions to set and retrieve variable values. For example, consider the following program statements. The first uses a macro variable reference:

```
jobid="&sysjobid";
```

The second uses an SCL function:

```
jobid=symget('sysjobid');
```

The macro variable reference, designated by the & (ampersand), is evaluated when the program is compiled. Thus, the identifier value for the job or process that compiles the program is assigned to the variable JOBID. Assuming that the preceding two statements were compiled by an earlier SAS process, if you want the JOBID variable to contain the identifier for the current process, then you must use the second form (without the &). The SYMGET function extracts the macro variable value from the global symbol table at execution.

*Note:* The values that are returned by SYSJOBID and other automatic macro variables depend on your host operating system. △

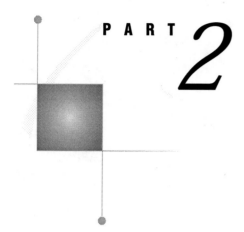

**P A R T** *2*

# Developing Object-Oriented Applications

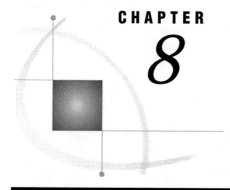

# SAS Object-Oriented Programming Concepts

# Introduction

*Object-oriented programming* (OOP) is a technique for writing computer software. The term *object oriented* refers to the methodology of developing software in which the emphasis is on the data, while the procedure or program flow is de-emphasized. That is, when designing an OOP program, you do not concentrate on the order of the steps that the program performs. Instead, you concentrate on the data in the program and on the operations that you perform on that data.

Advocates of object-oriented programming claim that applications that are developed using an object-oriented approach

- are easier to understand because the underlying code maps directly to real-world concepts that they seek to model
- are easier to modify and maintain because changes tend to involve individual objects and not the entire system
- promote software reuse because of modular design and low interdependence among modules
- offer improved quality because they are constructed from stable intermediate classes
- provide better scalability for creating large, complex systems.

*Object-oriented application design* determines which operations are performed on which data, and then groups the related data and operations into categories. When the design is implemented, these categories are called *classes*. A class defines the data and the operations that you can perform on the data. In SCL, the data for a class is defined through the class's *attributes*, *events*, *event handlers*, and *interfaces*. (Legacy classes store data in *instance variables*.) The operations that you perform on the data are called *methods*.

*Objects* are data elements in your application that perform some function for you. Objects can be *visual* objects that you place on the frame—for example, icons, push buttons, or radio boxes. Visual objects are called *controls*; they display information or accept user input.

Objects can also be *nonvisual* objects that manage the application behind the scenes; for example, an object that enables you to interact with SAS data sets may not have a visual representation but still provides you with the functionality to perform actions on a SAS data set such as accessing variables, adding data, or deleting data. An *object* or *component* is derived from, or is an *instance* of, a class. The terms object, component, and instance are interchangeable.

Software objects are self-contained entities that possess three basic characteristics:

behavior
: a collection of operations that an object can perform on itself or on other objects. *Methods* define the operations that an object can perform. For example, you can use the _onGeneric method in **sashelp.classes.programHalt.class** to trap all generic errors.

state
: a collection of attributes and their current values. Two of the programHalt component's attributes are **stopExecution** (which determines whether the program continues to execute after the program halt occurs) and **dump** (which contains the program-halt information). You can set these values through SCL.

identity
: a unique value that distinguishes one object from another. This identifier is referred to as its *object identifier*. The object identifier is created by SCL when you instantiate an object with the _NEW_ operator. This identifier is also used as the first-level qualifier in SCL dot notation.

This chapter describes how object-oriented techniques and related concepts are implemented in SCL.

# Object-Oriented Development and the SAS Component Object Model

The SAS Component Object Model (SCOM) provides a flexible framework for SCL component developers. With SCOM, you can develop model components that communicate with viewer components that are built with other SAS software (such as SAS/AF and WebAF) or with software from other vendors.

A component in SCOM is a self-contained, reusable object that has specific properties, including

- □ a set of attributes and methods
- □ a set of events that the object sends
- □ a set of event handlers that execute in response to various types of events
- □ a set of supported or required interfaces.

With SCL, you can design components that communicate with each other, using any of the following processes:*

---

*  Drag and drop operations can be defined only through SAS/AF software, not through SCL.

Attribute linking
> enabling a component to change one of its attributes when the value of another attribute is changed.

Model/view communication
> enabling a view (typically a visual control) to communicate with a model, based on a set of common methods that are defined in an interface.

Event handling
> enabling a component to send an event that another component can respond to by using an associated event handler.

Classes form the foundation of the SCOM architecture by defining these attributes, methods, events, event handlers and interfaces. There are two ways to construct a class that uses the SAS Component Object Model:

☐ You can build a class with the Class Editor that is available in SAS/AF software.

☐ You can use SCL class syntax to construct a class.

This chapter provides detailed information about using SCL to create and modify classes.

# Classes

A *class* defines a set of data and the operations you can perform on that data. *Subclasses* are similar to the classes from which they are derived, but they may have different properties or additional behavior. In general, any operation that is valid for a class is also valid for each subclass of that class.

## Relationships among Classes

Classes that you define with SCL can support two types of relationships:

☐ inheritance

☐ instantiation.

## Inheritance

Generally, the attributes, methods, events, event handlers, and interfaces that belong to a parent class are automatically inherited by any class that is created from it. One metaphor that is used to describe this relationship is that of the *family*. Classes that provide the foundation for other classes are called *parent* classes, and classes that are derived from parent classes are *child* classes. When more than one class is derived from the same parent class, these classes are related to each other as *sibling* classes. A *descendent* of a class has that class as a parent, either directly or indirectly through a series of parent-child relationships. In object-oriented theory, any subclass that is created from a parent class *inherits* all of the characteristics of the parent class that it is not specifically prohibited from inheriting. The chain of parent classes is called an *ancestry*.

**Figure 8.1** Class Ancestry

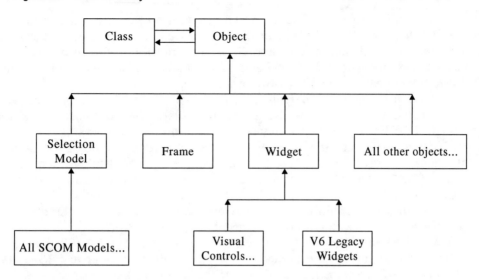

Whenever you create a new class, that class inherits all of the properties (attributes, methods, events, event handlers, and interfaces) that belong to its parent class. For example, the Object class is the parent of all classes in SAS/AF software. The Frame and Widget classes are subclasses of the Object class, and they inherit all properties of the Object class. Similarly, every class you use in a frame-based application is a descendent of the Frame, Object, or Widget class, and thus inherits all the properties that belong to those classes.

## Instantiation

In addition to the inheritance relationship, classes have an *instantiation* or an "is a" relationship. For example, a frame is an instance of the Frame class; a radio box control is an instance of the Radio Box Control class; and a color list object is an instance of the Color List Model class.

All classes are instances of the Class class. The Class class is a metaclass. A *metaclass* collects information about other classes and enables you to operate on other classes. For more information about metaclasses, see "Metaclasses" on page 98.

## Types of Classes

Some SAS/AF software classes are specific types of classes.

□ Abstract classes

□ Models and views

□ Metaclasses.

## Abstract Classes

*Abstract classes* group attributes and methods that are common to several subclasses. These classes themselves cannot be instantiated; they simply provide functionality for their subclasses.

The Widget class in SAS/AF software is an example of an abstract class. Its purpose is to collect properties that all widget subclasses can inherit. The Widget class cannot be instantiated.

## Models and Views

In SAS/AF software, components that are built on the SAS Component Object Model (SCOM) framework can be classified either as *views* that display data or as *models* that provide data. Although models and views are typically used together, they are nevertheless independent components. Their independence allows for customization, flexibility of design, and efficient programming.

*Models* are non-visual components that provide data. For example, a Data Set List model contains the properties for generating a list of SAS data sets (or tables), given a specific SAS library. A model may be attached to multiple views.

*Views* are components that provide a visual representation of the data, but they have no knowledge of the actual data they are displaying. The displayed data depends on the state of the model that is connected to the view. A view can be attached to only one model at a time.

It may be helpful to think of model/view components as client/server components. The view acts as the client and the model acts as the server.

For more information on interfaces, see "Interfaces" on page 128. For more information on implementing model/view communication, refer to *SAS Guide to Applications Development* and to the SAS/AF online Help.

## Metaclasses

As previously mentioned, the Class class (`sashelp.fsp.Class.class`) and any subclasses you create from it are metaclasses. *Metaclasses* enable you to collect information about other classes and to operate on those classes.

Metaclasses enable you to make changes to the application at run time rather than only at build time. Examples of such changes include where a class's methods reside, the default values of class properties, and even the set of classes and their hierarchy.

Metaclasses also enable you to access information about parent classes, subclasses, and the methods and properties that are defined for a class. Specifically, through methods of the Class class, you can

- retrieve information about an application, such as information about the application's structure, which classes are being used, and which legacy classes use particular instance variables. Each class has a super class that is accessed by the _getSuper method. Every class also maintains a list of subclasses that is accessed with the _getSubclassList and _getSubclasses methods.

- list the instances of a class and process all of those instances in some way. Each class maintains a list of its instances. You can use _getInstanceList and _getInstances to process all the instances.

- create objects and classes at run time with the _new method. Instances of the metaclass are other classes.

For more information about metaclasses, see the Class class in the SAS/AF online Help.

---

## Defining Classes

You can create classes in SCL with the CLASS block. The CLASS block begins with the CLASS statement and ends with the ENDCLASS statement:

<**ABSTRACT**> **CLASS** *class-name*<EXTENDS *parent-class-name*>
    <SUPPORTS *supports-interface-clause*>
    <REQUIRES *requires-interface-clause*>
    < / (*class-optional-clause*)>
    <(*attribute-statements*)>

```
        < (method-declaration-statements) >
         < (method-implementation-blocks) >
        < (event-declaration-statements) >
        < (eventhandler-declaration-statements) >
```

**ENDCLASS**;

The CLASS statement enables you to define attributes, methods, events, and event handlers for a class and to specify whether the class supports or requires an interface. The remaining sections in this chapter describe these elements in more detail.

The EXTENDS clause specifies the parent class. If you do not specify an EXTENDS clause, SCL assumes that `sashelp.fsp.object.class` is the parent class.

Using the CLASS block instead of the Class Editor to create a class enables the compiler to detect errors at compile time, which results in improved performance during run time.

For a complete description of the CLASS statement, see "CLASS" on page 277. For a description of using the Class Editor to define classes, refer to *SAS Guide to Applications Development.*

## Generating CLASS Entries from CLASS Blocks

Suppose you are editing an SCL entry in the Build window and that the entry contains a CLASS block. For example:

```
class Simple extends myParent;
  public num num1;
  M1: method n:num return=num / (scl='work.a.uSimple.scl');
  M2: method return=num;
    num1 = 3;
    dcl num n = M1(num1);
    return (n);
  endmethod;
endclass;
```

To generate a CLASS entry from the CLASS block, issue the SAVECLASS command or select

| File | ► | Save as class... |

Generating the CLASS entry from the CLASS block is equivalent to using the Class Editor to create a CLASS entry interactively.

## Generating CLASS Blocks from CLASS Entries

The CLASS block is especially useful when you need to make many changes to an existing class. To make changes to an existing class, use the CREATESCL function to write the class definition to an SCL entry. You can then edit the SCL entry in the Build window. After you finish entering changes, you can generate the CLASS entry by issuing the SAVECLASS command or selecting

| File | ► | Save as class... |

For more information, see "CREATESCL" on page 316.

## Referencing Class Methods or Attributes

Any METHOD block in a class can refer to methods or attributes in its own class without specifying the _SELF_ system variable (which contains the object identifier for the class). For example, if method M1 is defined in class X (and it returns a value), then any method in class X can refer to method M1 as follows:

```
n=M1();
```

You do not need to use the _SELF_ system variable:

```
n=_SELF_.M1();
```

Omitting references to the _SELF_ variable (which is referred to as *shortcut syntax*) makes programs easier to read and maintain. However, if you are referencing a method or attribute that is not in the class you are creating, you must specify the object reference.

## Instantiating Classes

To instantiate a class, declare a variable of the specific class type, then use the _NEW_ operator. For example:

```
dcl mylib.classes.collection.class C1;
C1 = _new_ Collection();
```

You can combine these two operations as follows:

```
dcl mylib.classes.collection.class C1 = _new_ Collection();
```

The _NEW_ operator combines the actions of the LOADCLASS function, which loads a class, with the _new method, which initializes the object by invoking the object's _init method.

You can combine the _NEW_ operator with the IMPORT statement, which defines a search path for references to CLASS entries, so that you can refer to these entries with one or two-level names instead of having to use a four-level name in each reference.

For example, you can use the following statements to create a new collection object called C1 as an instance of the collection class that is stored in **mylib.classes.collection.class**:

```
    /* Collection class is defined in    */
    /* the catalog MYLIB.MYCAT         */
import mylib.mycat.collection.class;
    /* Create object C1 from a collection class  */
    /* defined in MYLIB.MYCAT.COLLECTION.CLASS */
declare Collection C1=_new_ Collection();
```

For more information, see "_NEW_" on page 563 and "LOADCLASS" on page 525.

## Methods

*Methods* define the operations that can be executed by any component that you create from that class. In other words, methods are how classes (and instances of those classes) do their work.

Methods can be *declared* in CLASS blocks. To declare a method, include the following METHOD statement in your CLASS block:

*label* : < *scope* > METHOD < *parameter-list* ></ (*method-options*) >;

The statements that implement the method can either follow the declaration, or they can reside in a separate SCL entry.

Methods are *implemented* in METHOD blocks. A METHOD block begins with the METHOD statement, includes the SCL code that implements the method, and then ends with the ENDMETHOD statement.

*label* : *<scope>* METHOD *<parameter-list>*
  *<*OPTIONAL=*parameter-list>*
  *<*ARGLIST=*parm-list-id* | REST=*rest-list-id>*
  RETURN=*limited-data-type*
  *</* (*method-options*)*>*;

. . .*SCL statements that implement the method.* . .

ENDMETHOD;

If your program is an object-oriented program, the METHOD blocks are contained either in the CLASS block or in a USECLASS block that is stored in a separate SCL entry from the CLASS block. To store the method implementation in a separate SCL entry, when you declare the method in the CLASS block, you specify (with the SCL=*entry-name* option) the name of another SCL entry that contains the method implementation.

For example, the Add method can be implemented in the CLASS block as follows:

```
class Arithmetic;
   add: method n1 n2:num;
      return(n1 + n2);
   endmethod;
endclass;
```

If you want to implement the Add method in a separate SCL entry, then the CLASS block would contain only the method declaration:

```
class Arithmetic;
   add: method n1 n2:num / (scl='work.a.b.scl');
endclass;
```

The **work.a.b.scl** entry would contain a USECLASS block that implements the Add method:

```
useclass Arithmetic;
   add: method n1 n2: num;
      return (n1 + n2);
   endmethod;
enduseclass;
```

See "METHOD" on page 540 for a complete description of implementing methods with the METHOD statement. See Chapter 2, "The Structure of SCL Programs," on page 9; "Implementing Methods Outside of Classes" on page 115; and "USECLASS" on page 698 for more information about implementing methods in USECLASS blocks.

*Note:*  The method options that you specify in the CLASS block can also be specified in the USECLASS block. Any option that is included in the CLASS block and is used to specify a nondefault value must be repeated in the USECLASS block. For example, if you specify **State='O'** or **Signature='N'** in the CLASS block, then you must repeat those options in the USECLASS block. However, the SCL option will be ignored in the USECLASS block. △

For compatibility with Version 6, you can also define METHOD blocks in a separate SCL entry outside of CLASS and USECLASS blocks. However, such an application is not a strictly object-oriented application. For these methods, SCL will not validate method names and parameter types during compile time. See "Defining and Using

Methods" on page 13 for more information about methods that are not declared or implemented within a class.

## Defining Method Scope

SCL supports variable method scope, which gives you considerable design flexibility. Method scope can be defined as Public, Protected, or Private. The default scope is Public. In order of narrowing scope,

- □ Public methods can be accessed by any other class and are inherited by subclasses.
- □ Protected methods can be accessed only by the same class and its subclasses; they are inherited by subclasses.
- □ Private methods can be accessed only by the same class and are not inherited by subclasses.

For example, the Scope class defines two public methods (m1 and m4), one private method (m2), and one protected method (m3):

```
class Scope;
   m1: public method n:num return=num
       /(scl='work.a.uScope.scl');
   m2: private method :char;
       /(scl='work.b.uScope.scl');
   m3: protected method return=num;
       num = 3;
       dcl num n = m1(num);
       return(n);
   endmethod;
   m4: method
       /(scl='work.c.uScope.scl');
endclass;
```

By default, method m4 is a public method.

## Defining Method Names and Labels

Method names can be up to 256 characters long. Method labels can be up to 32 characters long. The name of a method should match its label whenever possible.

*Note:* A method that has the same name as the class that contains it is called a *constructor*. See "Defining Constructors" on page 112 for more information. △

### Specifying a Name That Is Different from the Label

If you need the method name to be different from the method label, you must specify either the METHOD or LABEL option in the METHOD statement. These options are mutually exclusive.

*Note:* In dot notation, always use the method name. When implementing the method, always use the method label. △

For example, a label of MyMethod may be sufficient, but if you want the method name to be MySortSalaryDataMethod, you can declare the method as follows:

```
class a;
MyMethod: public method sal:num
    /(Method='MySortSalaryDataMethod', SCL='work.a.a.scl');
```

```
endclass;
```

When you implement the method in **work.a.a.scl**, you identify the method by using the method label as follows:

```
useclass a;
   MyMethod: public method sal:num;
      ...SCL statements...
   endmethod;
enduseclass;
```

You would reference this method in dot notation by using the method name as follows:

```
obj.MySortSalaryDataMethod(n);
```

Alternatively, you can specify the LABEL option. For example, to specify a method name of Increase and a method label of CalculatePercentIncrease, you could declare the method as follows:

```
class a;
   Increase: public method
      /(Label='CalculatePercentIncrease', SCL='work.a.b.scl');
endclass;
```

As in the previous example, you use the method label when you implement the method, and you use the method name when you refer to the method in dot notation. In **work.a.b.scl**, you would implement the method as follows:

```
useclass a;
   CalculatePercentIncrease: public method;
      ...SCL statements...
   endmethod;
enduseclass;
```

You would reference the method in dot notation as follows:

```
obj.Increase();
```

## Using Underscores in Method Names

In Version 6, SAS/AF software used underscores to separate words in method names (for example, _set_background_color_). The current convention is to use a lowercase letter for the first letter and to subsequently uppercase the first letter of any joined word (for example, _setBackgroundColor).

The embedded underscores have been removed to promote readability. However, for compatibility, the compiler recognizes _set_background_color_ as equivalent to _setBackgroundColor. All Version 6 code that uses the old naming convention in CALL SEND or CALL NOTIFY method invocations will still function with no modification.

Although it is possible for you to name a new method using a leading underscore, you should use caution when doing so. Your method names may conflict with future releases of SAS/AF software if SAS Institute adds new methods to the parent classes.

## Specifying Parameter Types and Storage Types

When you define a method parameter, you must specify its data type. Optionally, you can also specify its storage type: input, output, or update. The storage type determines how methods can modify each other's parameters:

input    The values of the caller's parameters are *copied into* the corresponding parameters in the called method. When the called method's ENDMETHOD statement is executed, any updated values are *not copied out* to the caller's parameters.

output    The values of the caller's parameters are *not copied into* the corresponding parameters in the called method. When the called method's ENDMETHOD statement is executed, any updated values are *copied out* to the caller's parameters.

update    The values of the caller's parameters are *copied into* the corresponding parameters in the called method. When the called method's ENDMETHOD statement is executed, any updated values are *copied out* to the caller's parameters.

The default parameter storage type is update.

You use the colon (:) delimiter to specify both the storage type and the data type for each method parameter:

*variables<:storage>:type*

In the following example, the TypeStore class defines four methods:

```
import sashelp.fsp.collection.class;
class TypeStore;
  m1: method n:num a b:update:char return=num
      /(scl = 'work.a.uType.scl');
  m2: method n:output:num c:i:char
      /(scl = 'work.b.uType.scl');
  m3: method s:i:Collection
      /(scl = 'work.c.uType.scl');
  m4: method l:o:list
      /(scl = 'work.d.uType.scl');
endclass;
```

The parameter storage type and data type for each method are as follows:

| Method | Parameter | Data Type | Storage |
| --- | --- | --- | --- |
| m1 | n | numeric | update |
|  | a | character | update |
|  | b | character | update |
| m2 | n | numeric | output |
|  | c | character | input |
| m3 | s | Collection class | input |
| m4 | l | list | output |

*Note:*   If you specify the storage type for a parameter in the CLASS block, then you must also specify the storage type in the USECLASS block. △

## Passing Objects as Arguments for Methods

An object can be declared as an INTERFACE object, a CLASS object, or a generic OBJECT. If you declare an object as a generic OBJECT, then the compiler cannot validate attributes or methods for that object. Validation is deferred until run time.

Any error that results from using incorrect methods or attributes for the generic object will cause the program to halt. For example, if you pass a listbox class to a method that is expecting a collection object, the program will halt.

Object types are treated internally as numeric values. This can affect how you overload methods. See "Overloading and List, Object, and Numeric Types" on page 111 for more information.

## Returning Values From Methods

When you declare or implement a method, you can specify the data type of the return value with the RETURN option. If the method has a RETURN option, then the method implementation must contain a RETURN statement. The method's RETURN statement must specify a variable, expression, or value of the same type. In the following example, method m1 returns a numeric value:

```
class mylib.mycat.myclass.class;
  /* method declaration */
  m1: method n:num c:char return=num;
    /* method implementation */
    return(n+length(c));
  endmethod;
endclass;
```

## Method Signatures

A method's *signature* is a set of parameters that uniquely identifies the method to the SCL compiler. Method signatures enable the compiler to check method parameters at compile time and can enable your program to run more efficiently. All references to a method must conform to its signature definition. Overloaded methods must have signatures. (See "Overloading Methods" on page 108.)

A signature is automatically generated for each Version 8 method unless you specify **Signature='N'** in the method's option list. By default, **Signature='Y'** for all Version 8 methods. When you edit a class in the Build window, a signature is generated for each method that is declared in that class when you issue the SAVECLASS command or select

| File | ▶ | Save as class... |

For all Version 6 methods, the default is **Signature='N'**. See "Converting Version 6 Non-Visual Classes to Version 8 Classes" on page 131 for information about adding signatures to Version 6 methods.

For example, the following method declarations show methods that have different signatures:

```
Method1: method name:char  number:num;
Method2: method number:num name:char;
Method3: method name:char;
Method4: method return=num;
```

Each method signature is a unique combination, varying by argument number and type:

  □ The first signature contains a character argument and a numeric argument.

  □ The second signature contains a numeric argument and a character argument.

  □ The third signature contains a single character argument.

  □ The fourth signature contains no arguments.

These four method signatures have the following sigstrings (see "Signature Strings (SIGSTRINGs)" on page 106):

```
Method1 sigstring: (CN)V
Method2 sigstring: (NC)V
Method3 sigstring: (C)V
Method4 sigstring: ()N
```

The order of arguments also determines the method signature. For example, the getColNum methods below have different signatures — (CN)V and (NC)V — because the arguments are reversed. As a result, they are invoked differently, but they return the same result.

```
/* method1 */
getColNum: method colname:char number:update:num;
  number = getnitemn(listid, colname, 1, 1, 0);
endmethod;

/* method2 */
getColNum: method number:update:num colname:char;
  number = getnitemn(listid, colname, 1, 1, 0);
endmethod;
```

You can also use the Class Editor to define method signatures. See *SAS Guide to Applications Development* for more information.

## Signature Strings (SIGSTRINGs)

Signatures are usually represented by a shorthand notation, called a *sigstring*. This sigstring is stored in the method metadata as SIGSTRING.

A sigstring has the following compressed form:

(<*argument-type-1 argument-type-2...argument-type-n*>)*return-type*

Each argument type can be one of the following:

| | |
|---|---|
| N | Numeric |
| C | Character string |
| L | SCL list |
| O | Generic object |
| O:<*class-name*>; | Specific class. The class name should be preceded by **O:** and followed by a semi-colon. |

*Return-type* can be any of the above types, or **V** for void, which specifies that the method does not return a value. The return type cannot be an array.

Arrays are shown by preceding any of the above types with a bracket ( [ ). For example, a method that receives a numeric value and an array of characters and returns a numeric value would have the signature **(N[C)N**.

Here are some examples of method signatures:

□ A method that does not receive any parameters and does not return a value: **()V**. This sigstring is the default signature.

□ A method that returns a numeric value and that requires three parameters, numeric, character, and list: **(NCL)N**.

□ A method that does not have a return value and that requires an object of type ProgramHalt and a numeric value:

```
(O:sashelp.classes.programHalt.class;N)V
```

□ A method that returns a character value and receives a generic object and a character value: **(OC)C**.

*Note:* Although the return type is listed as part of the *sigstring*, it is not used by SCL to identify the method. Therefore, it is recommended that you do not define methods that differ only in return type. See "Overloading Methods" on page 108 for more information. △

## How Signatures Are Used

Signatures are most useful when SCL has to distinguish among the different forms of an overloaded method. The SCL compiler uses signatures to validate method parameters. When you execute your program, SCL uses signatures to determine which method to call.

For example, suppose your program contains the following class:

```
class Sig;
        /* Signature is (N)C */
  M1: method n:num return=char /(scl='work.a.uSig.scl');
        /* Signature is ([C)V */
  M1: private method n(*):char /(scl='work.a.uSig.scl');
        /* Signature is ()V */
  M1: protected method /(scl='work.a.uSig.scl');
        /* Signature is (NC)V
  M1: method n:num c:char /(scl='work.a.uSig.scl');
endclass;
```

Suppose also that your program calls M1 as follows:

```
dcl char ch;
ch = M1(3);
```

SCL will call the method with the signature (N)C. If your program calls M1 like this:

```
M1();
```

SCL will call the method with the signature ()V.

## Altering Existing Signatures

After defining a signature for a method and deploying the class that contains it for public use, you should not alter the signature of the method in future versions of the class. Doing so could result in program halts for users who have already compiled their applications. Instead of altering an existing signature, you should overload the method to use the desired signature, leaving the previous signature intact.

## Forward-Referencing Methods

Within a CLASS block, if a method invokes a another method within that same class, then either the second method must be implemented before the first, or the second method must be declared with the **Forward='Y'** option.

*Note:* Any methods that are forward-referenced must be implemented in the class in which they are declared. △

In the following example, m1 calls m2, so the compiler needs to know the existence of m2 before it can compile m1.

```
class mylib.mycat.forward.class;
  m2: method n:num c:char return=num / (forward='y');
```

```
m1: method n1 n2:num mylist:list return=num;
    dcl num listLen = listlen(mylist);
    dcl num retVal;
    if (listLen = 1) then
        retVal=m2(n1,'abc');
    else if (listLen = 2) then
        retVal=m2(n2,'abc');
endmethod;
m2:method n:num c:char return=num;
    return(n+length(c));
endmethod;
endclass;
```

## Overloading Methods

You can overload methods only for Version 8 classes. Method overloading is the process of defining multiple methods that have the same name, but which differ in parameter number, type, or both. Overloading methods enables you to

☐ use the same name for methods that are related conceptually.

☐ create methods that have optional parameters.

All overloaded methods must have method signatures because SCL uses the signatures to differentiate between overloaded methods. If you call an overloaded method, SCL checks the method arguments, scans the signatures for a match, and executes the appropriate code. A method that has no signature cannot be overloaded.

If you overload a method, and the signatures differ only in the return type, the results are unpredictable. The compiler will use the first version of the method that it finds to validate the method. If the compiler finds the incorrect version, it generates an error. If your program compiles without errors, then when you run the program, SCL will execute the first version of the method that it finds. If it finds the incorrect version, SCL generates an error. If it finds the correct version, your program might run normally.

Each method in a set of overloaded methods can have a different scope, as well. However, the scope is not considered part of the signature, so you may not define two methods that differ only by scope. (See "Defining Method Scope" on page 102.)

### Example: Different Parameter Types

Suppose you have the following two methods, where each method performs a different operation on its arguments:

```
CombineNumerics: public method a :num b :num
                 return=num;
                 endmethod;
CombineStrings:  public method c :char d :char
                 return=char;
                 endmethod;
```

Assume that CombineNumerics adds the values of A and B, whereas CombineStrings concatenates the values of C and D. In general terms, these two methods combine two pieces of data in different ways based on their data types.

Using method overloading, these methods could become

```
Combine: public method a :num  b :num
         return=num;
         endmethod;
Combine: public method c :char d :char
```

```
        return=char;
    endmethod;
```

In this case, the Combine method is overloaded with two different parameter lists: one that takes two numeric values and returns a numeric value, and another that takes two character parameters and returns a character value.

As a result, you have defined two methods that have the same name but different parameter types. With this simple change, you do not have to worry about which method to call. The Combine method can be called with either set of arguments, and SCL will determine which method is the correct one to use, based on the arguments that are supplied in the method call. If the arguments are numeric, SCL calls the first version shown above. If the arguments are character, SCL calls the second version. The caller can essentially view the two separate methods as one method that can operate on different types of data.

Here is a more complete example that shows how method overloading fits in with the class syntax. Suppose you create X.SCL and issue the SAVECLASS command, which generates the X class. (Although it is true here, it is not necessary that the class name match the entry name.)

```
class X;

Combine: public method a:num b:num  return=num;
    dcl num value;
    value = a + b;
    return value;
endmethod;

Combine: public method a:char b:char return=char;
    dcl char value;
    value = a || b;
    return value;
endmethod;

endclass;
```

You can then create another entry, Y.SCL. When you compile and execute Y.SCL, it instantiates the X class and calls each of the Combine methods.

```
import X.class;
init:
    dcl num n;
    dcl char c;
    dcl X xobject = _new_ X();
    n = xobject.Combine(1,2);
    c = xobject.Combine("abc","def");
    put n= c=;
```

The PUT statement produces

```
n=3 c=abcdef
```

## Example: Different Numbers of Parameters

Another typical use of method overloading is to create methods that have optional parameters.

*Note:* This example shows two implementations of an overloaded method that each accept different numbers of parameters. "Defining One Implementation That Accepts Optional Parameters" on page 111 describes how to use the OPTIONAL option to create a method with one implementation that accepts different numbers of parameters. △

For example, suppose we have a method that takes a character string and a numeric value, where the numeric value is used as a flag to indicate a particular action. The method signature would be (CN)V.

```
M: public method c :char f :num;
   if (f = 1) then
     /* something */
   else if (f = 2)
     /* something else */
   else
     /* another thing */
endmethod;
```

If method M is usually called with the flag equal to one, you can overload M as (C)V, where that method would simply include a call to the original M. The flag becomes an optional parameter.

```
M:  public method c: char;
  M(c, 1);
endmethod;
```

When you want the flag to be equal to one, call M with only a character string parameter. Notice that this is not an error. Method M can be called with either a single character string, or with a character string and a numeric — this is the essence of method overloading. Also, the call **M(c,1);** is not a recursive call with an incorrect parameter list. It is a call to the original method M.

This example can also be turned around for cases with existing code. Assume that we originally had the method M with signature (C)V and that it did all the work.

```
M: public method c: char;
   /* A lot of code for processing C. */
endmethod;
```

Suppose you wanted to add an optional flag parameter, but did not want to change the (possibly many) existing calls to M. All you need to do is overload M with (CN)V and write the methods as follows:

```
M:  public method c: char f: num;
   Common(c, f);
endmethod;

M:  public method c: char;
   Common(c, 0);
endmethod;

Common:  public method c: char f: num;
   if (f) then
      /* Do something extra. */
/* Fall through to same old code for */
/* processing S.                     */
endmethod;
```

Notice that when you call M with a single character string, you get the old behavior. When you call M with a string and a (non-zero) flag parameter, you get the optional behavior.

## Defining One Implementation That Accepts Optional Parameters

You can use the OPTIONAL option to create an overloaded method with only one implementation that will accept different numbers of parameters, depending on which arguments are passed to it.

In the following example, the method M1 will accept from two to four parameters:

```
class a;
M1: public method p1:input:num p2:output:char
    optional=p3:num p4:char
    / (scl='mylib.classes.old.scl');
endclass;
```

SCL will generate three signatures for this method:

(NC)V

(NCN)V

(NCNC)V

## Overloading and List, Object, and Numeric Types

Lists and objects (variables declared with either the OBJECT keyword or a specific class name) are treated internally as Numeric values. As a result, in certain situations, variables of type List, Numeric, generic Object, and specific class names are interchangeable. For example, you can assign a generic Object or List to a variable that has been declared as Numeric, or you can assign a generic Object to a List. This flexibility enables Version 6 programs in which list identifiers are stored as Numeric variables to remain compatible with Version 8.

The equivalence between objects, lists, and numeric variables requires that you exercise caution when overloading methods with these types of parameters. When attempting to match a method signature, the compiler first attempts to find the best possible match by matching the most parameter types exactly. If no exact match can be found, the compiler resorts to using the equivalence between List, generic Object, and Numeric types.

For example, suppose you have a method M with a single signature (L)V. If you pass a numeric value, a list, or an object, it will be matched, and method M will be called. If you overload M with signature (N)V, then Numeric values will match the signature (N)V, and List values will match the signature (L)V. However, List values that are undeclared or declared as Numeric will now match the wrong method. Therefore, you must explicitly declare them with the LIST keyword to make this example work correctly. Also, if you pass an object, it will match both (L)V and (N)V, so the compiler cannot determine which method to call and will generate an error message.

## Overriding Existing Methods

When you instantiate a class, the new class (or subclass) inherits the methods of the parent class. If you want to use the signature of one of the parent's methods, but you want to replace the implementation with your own implementation, you can *override* the parent's method. To override the implementation of a method, specify **State='O'** in the method declaration and in the method implementation. Here is an example for a class named State:

```
class State;
  _init: method / (state='o');
    _super();
  endmethod;
endclass;
```

## Defining Constructors

*Constructors* are methods that are used to initialize an instance of a class. The Object class provides a default constructor that is inherited for all classes. Unless your class requires special initialization, you do not need to create a constructor.

Each constructor has the following characteristics:

☐ It has the same name as the class in which it is declared.

☐ It is run automatically when the class is instantiated with the _NEW_ operator. If you do not create your own constructor, the default constructor is executed.

*Note:* Using the _NEW_ operator to instantiate a class is the only way to run constructors. Unlike other user-defined methods, you cannot execute constructors using dot notation. If you instantiate a class in any way other than by using the _NEW_ operator (for example, with the _NEO_ operator), constructors are not executed. △

☐ It is intended to run as an initializer for the instance. Therefore, only constructors can call other constructors. A constructor cannot be called from a method that is not a constructor.

☐ It cannot return a value; it must be void a method. The _NEW_ operator returns the value for the new instance of the class; it cannot return a value from an implicitly called constructor.

For example, you could define a constructor X for class X as follows:

```
class X;
  X: method n: num;
    put 'In constructor, n=';
  endmethod;
endclass;
```

You can instantiate the class as follows:

```
init:
  dcl X x = _new_ X(99);
return;
```

The constructor is run automatically when the class is instantiated. The argument to _NEW_, 99, is passed to the constructor. The output is

```
In constructor, n=99
```

## Overloading Constructors

Like other methods, constructors can be overloaded. Any void method that has the same name as the class is treated as a constructor. The _NEW_ operator determines which constructor to call based on the arguments that are passed to it. For example, the Complex class defines two constructors. The first constructor initializes a complex number with an ordered pair of real numbers. The second constructor initializes a complex number with another complex number.

```
class Complex;
  private num a b;

  Complex: method r1: num r2: num;
    a = r1;
    b = r2;
  endmethod;

  Complex: method c: complex;
    a = c.a;
    b = c.b;
  endmethod;
endclass;
```

This class can be instantiated with either of the following statements:

```
dcl Complex c  = _new_(1,2);
dcl Complex c2 = _new_(c);
```

These statements both create complex numbers. Both numbers are equal to **1 + 2i**.

## Overriding the Default Constructor

The default constructor does not take any arguments. If you want to create your own constructor that does not take any arguments, you must explicitly override the default constructor. To override the default constructor, specify **State='o'** in the method options list.

```
class X;
  X: method /(state='o');
      ...SCL statements to initialize class X...
  endmethod;
endclass;
```

## Calling Constructors Explicitly

Constructors can be called explicitly only from other constructors. The _NEW_ operator calls the first constructor. The first constructor can call the second constructor, and so on.

When a constructor calls another constructor within the same class, it must use the _SELF_ system variable. For example, you could overload X as follows:

```
class X;
  private num m;

  X: method n: num;
    _self_(n, 1);
  endmethod;

  X: method n1: num n2: num;
    m = n1 + n2;
  endmethod;

endclass;
```

The first constructor, which takes one argument, calls the second constructor, which takes two arguments, and passes in the constant **1** for the second argument.

The following labeled section creates two instances of X. In the first instance, the **m** attribute is set to **3**. In the second instance, the **m** attribute is set to **100**.

```
init:
  dcl X x  = _new_ X(1,2);
  dcl X x2 = _new_ X(99);
return;
```

Constructors can call parent constructors by using the _SUPER operator. For example, suppose you define class X as follows:

```
class X;
  protected num m;

  X: method n: num;
     m = n * 2;
  endmethod;

endclass;
```

Then, you create a subclass Y whose parent class is X. The constructor for Y overrides the default constructor for Y and calls the constructor for its parent class, X.

```
class Y extends X;
  public num p;

  Y: method n: num /(state='o');
     _super(n);
     p = m - 1;
  endmethod;

endclass;
```

You can instantiate Y as shown in the following labeled section. In this example, the constructor in Y is called with argument **10**. This value is passed to the constructor in X, which uses it to initialize the **m** attribute to **20**. Y then initializes the **p** attribute to **19**.

```
init:
  dcl Y y = _new_ Y(10);
  put y.p=;
return;
```

The output would be:

```
y.p=19
```

*Note:*  As with other overridden methods that have identical signatures, you must explicitly override the constructor in Y because there is a constructor in X that has the same signature. △

## Specifying That a Method Is Not a Constructor

The compiler automatically treats as a constructor any void method that has the same name as the class. If you do not want such a method to be treated as a constructor, you can specify **constructor='n'** in the method declaration.

```
class X;
  X: method /(constructor='n');
     put 'Is not constructor';
```

```
    endmethod;
endclass;

init:
  dcl X x = _new_ X();
  put 'After constructor';
  x.x();
return;
```

This will result in the following output:

```
After constructor
Is not constructor
```

## Implementing Methods Outside of Classes

You can define the implementation of methods outside the SCL entry that contains the CLASS block that defines the class. This feature enables multiple people to work on class methods simultaneously.

To define class methods in a different SCL entry, use the USECLASS statement block. The USECLASS block binds methods that it contains to the class that is specified in the USECLASS statement. The USECLASS statement also enables you to define implementations for overloading methods. (See "Overloading Methods" on page 108. )

Method implementations inside a USECLASS block can include any SCL functions and routines. However, the only SCL statements that are allowed in USECLASS blocks are METHOD statements.

The USECLASS block binds the methods that it contains to a class that is defined in a CLASS statement block or in the Class Editor. Therefore, all references to the methods and the attributes of the class can bypass references to the _SELF_ variable completely as long as no ambiguity problem is created. Because the binding occurs at compile time, the SCL compiler can detect whether an undefined variable is a local variable or a class attribute. See also "Referencing Class Methods or Attributes" on page 99.

## Method Metadata

SCL stores metadata for maintaining and executing methods. You can query a class (or a method within a class) to view the method metadata. For example, to list the metadata for a specific method, execute code similar to the following:

```
init:
  DCL num rc metadata;
  DCL object obj;

  obj=loadclass('class-name');

  /* metadata is a numeric list identifier */
  rc=obj._getMethod('getMaxNum',metadata);
  call putlist(metadata,'',2);
return;
```

# Attributes

*Attributes* are the properties that specify the information associated with a component, such as its name, description, and color. Attributes determine how a component will look and behave. For example, the Push Button Control has an attribute named **label** that specifies the text displayed on the button. You can create two instances of the Push Button Control on your frame and have one display "OK" and the other display "Cancel," simply by specifying a different value for the **label** attribute of each instance.

You can define attributes with attribute statements in CLASS blocks:

*scope data-type attribute-name/(attribute-options)*;

Attribute names can be up to 256 characters long.

Like methods, attributes can have public, private, or protected scope. The scope works the same for attributes as it does for methods. See "Defining Method Scope" on page 102 for more information.

Examples of attribute options include the attribute description, whether the attribute is editable or linkable, custom access methods that are to be executed when the attribute is queried or set, and whether the attribute sends events.

If an attribute is editable, you can use the Editor option to specify the name of the FRAME, SCL, or PROGRAM entry that will be used to edit the attribute's value. This entry is displayed and executed by the Properties window when the ellipsis button (...) is selected.

To specify an attribute's category, use the Category attribute option. The category is used for grouping similar types of options in the Class Editor or for displaying related attributes in the Properties window. You can create your own category names. Components that are supplied by SAS may belong to predefined categories.

## Creating Attributes Automatically

With the Autocreate option, you can control whether storage for list attributes and class attributes is automatically created when you instantiate a class. By default, **Autocreate='Y'**, which means that SCL automatically uses the _NEW_ operator to instantiate class attributes and calls the MAKELIST function to create the list attributes.

*Note:*  Even when **Autocreate='Y'**, storage is not created for generic objects because the specific class is unknown. △

If you specify **Autocreate='N'**, then storage is not automatically created, and it is your responsibility to create (and later destroy) any list attributes or class attributes after the class is instantiated.

```
import sashelp.fsp.collection.class;
class myAttr;
  public list myList / (autocreate='N');
  public list listTwo;   /* created automatically */
  public collection c1;  /* created automatically */
  public collection c2 / (autocreate='N');
endclass;
```

## Specifying Where an Attribute Value Can Be Changed

An attribute's scope and the value of its Editable option determines which methods can change an attribute's value.

- ☐ If the scope is public and **Editable='Y'**, then the attribute can be accessed (both queried and set) from any class method as well as from a frame SCL program.
- ☐ If the scope is public and **Editable='N'**, then the attribute can only be queried from any class method or frame SCL program. However, only the class or subclasses of the class can modify the attribute value.
- ☐ If the scope is protected and **Editable='N'**, then the class and its subclasses can query the attribute value, but only the class itself can set or change the value. A frame SCL program cannot set or query the value.
- ☐ If the scope is private and **Editable='N'**, then the attribute value can be queried only from methods in the class on which it is defined, but it cannot be set by the class. Subclasses cannot access these attributes, nor can a frame SCL program. This combination of settings creates a private, pre-initialized, read-only constant.

## Setting Initial Values and the List of Valid Values

Unless you specify otherwise, all numeric attributes are initialized to missing values, and all character attributes are initialized to blank strings. You can use the initialValue attribute option to explicitly initialize an attribute. For example:

```
class myAttr;
   public num n1 / (initialvalue = 3);
   public list list2 / (initialvalue = {1, 2, 'abc', 'def'};
endclass;
```

Explicitly initializing attribute values improves the performance of your program.

You can use the ValidValues attribute option to specify a list of values that the attribute can have. This list is used as part of the validation process that occurs when the value is set programmatically by using either dot notation or the _setAttributeValue method.

If you specify the ValidValues option and the InitialValue option, the value that you specify with the InitialValue option must be included in the values that you specify with the ValidValues option.

In the list of valid values, you can use blanks to separate values, or, if the values themselves contain blanks, use a comma or a slash (/) as the separator. For example:

```
class business_graph_c;
  public char statistic
          / (ValidValues='Frequency/Mean/Cumulative Percent',
             InitialValue='Mean');
  public char highlightEnabled
          / (ValidValues='Yes No',
             InitialValue='Yes');
  endclass;
```

You can also specify an SCL or SLIST entry to validate values. For more information on how to use an SCL entry to perform validation, refer to *SAS Guide to Applications Development*.

# Associating Custom Access Methods with Attributes

A custom access method (CAM) is a method that is executed automatically when an attribute's value is queried or set using dot notation. When you query the value of an attribute, SCL calls the _getAttributeValue method. When you set the value of an attribute, SCL calls the _setAttributeValue method. These methods are inherited from the Object class.

You can use the getCAM and setCAM attribute options to specify additional methods that you want _getAttributeValue or _setAttributeValue to execute. For example:

```
class CAM;
  public char A / (getCAM='M1');
  public num B / (setCAM='M2');
  protected M1: method c:char;
    put 'In M1';
  endmethod;
  protected M2: method b:num;
    put 'In M2';
  endmethod;
endclass;
```

When the value of A is queried, _getAttributeValue is called, then M1 is executed. When the value of B is set, _setAttributeValue is called, then M2 is executed.

CAMs always have a single signature and cannot be overloaded. The CAM signature contains a single argument that is the same type as its associated attribute. A CAM always returns a numeric value.

You should never call a CAM directly; instead, use the _getAttributeValue or _setAttributeValue methods to call it automatically. To prevent CAMs from being called directly, it is recommended that you define them as protected methods.

# Linking Attributes

Attribute linking enables one component to automatically upate the value of one of its attributes when the value of another component attribute is changed. You can link attributes between components or within the same component. Only public attributes are linkable.

To implement attribute linking, you need to identify attributes as either source attributes or target attributes. You can identify source and target attributes either in the Properties window or with SCL. To identify an attribute as a source attribute with SCL, specify **SendEvent='Y'** in the attribute's option list. To identity an attribute as a target attribute, specify **Linkable='Y'** in the attribute's option list.

You can then link the attributes (specify the **LinkTo** option) in the Properties window.

When **SendEvent='Y'**, SAS/AF software registers an event on the component. For example, the **textColor** attribute has an associated event named "textColor Changed". You can then register an event handler to trap the event and to conditionally execute code when the value of the attribute changes.

If you change the **SendEvent** value from **'Y'** to **'N'**, and if **Linkable='Y'**, then you must send the "*attributeName* Changed" event programmatically with the attribute's setCAM in order for attributes that are linked to this attribute to receive notification that the value has changed. If the linked attributes do not receive this event, attribute linking will not work correctly. In the previous example, the setCAM for the **textColor** attribute would use the _sendEvent method to send the "textColor Changed" event.

Refer to *SAS Guide to Applications Development* for more information on attribute linking.

## Attribute Metadata

SCL uses a set of attribute metadata to maintain and manipulate attributes. This metadata exists as a list that is stored with the class. You can query a class (or an attribute within a class) with specific methods to view attribute metadata. To list the metadata for a specific attribute, execute code similar to the following:

```
init:
    DCL num rc;
    DCL list metadata;
    DCL object obj;

    obj=loadclass('class-name');

    rc=obj._getAttribute('attribute-name',metadata);
    call putlist(metadata,'',3);
return;
```

# Accessing Object Attributes and Methods With Dot Notation

SCL provides dot notation for directly accessing object attributes and for invoking methods instead of using the SEND and NOTIFY routines. Thus, dot notation provides a shortcut for invoking methods and for setting or querying attribute values. Using dot notation reduces typing and makes SCL programs easier to read.

Using dot notation enhances run-time performance if you declare the object used in the dot notation as an instance of a predefined class instead of declaring it as a generic object. The object's class definition is then known at compile time, enabling the SCL compiler to verify the method and to access attributes at that time. Moreover, since dot notation checks the method signature, it is the only way to access an overloaded method. SEND does not check method signatures. It executes the first name-matched method, and the program might halt if the method signature does not match.

## Syntax

The syntax for dot notation is as follows:

```
object.attribute
```

or

```
object.method(<arguments>)
```

Where

*object*
> specifies an object or an automatic system variable (for example, _SELF_). An object must be a component in a FRAME entry or a variable that is declared as an Object type in the SCL program. Automatic system variables like _SELF_ are declared internally as Object type, so they do not have to be declared explicitly as such in a program.

*attribute*
> specifies an object attribute to assign or query. It can be of any data type, including Array. If the attribute is an array, use the following syntax to reference its elements:

```
object.attributeArray[i]
```

You can also use parentheses instead of brackets or braces when referencing the array elements. However, if you have declared the object as a generic object, the compiler interprets it as a method name rather than an attribute array. If you have declared a type for the object, and an attribute and method have the same name, the compiler still interprets the object as a method. To avoid this ambiguity, use brackets when referencing attribute array elements.

*method*
specifies the name of the method to invoke. If an object is declared with a specific class definition, the compiler can perform error checking on the object's method invocations.

If the object was declared as a generic object (with the OBJECT keyword), then the method lookup is deferred until run time. If there is no such method for the object, the program halts. If you declare the object with a specific definition, errors such as this are discovered at compile time instead of at run time.

*arguments*
are the arguments passed to the method. Enclose the arguments in parentheses. The parentheses are required whether or not the method needs any arguments.

You can use dot notation to specify parameters to methods. For example:

```
return-value = object.method (object.id);
```

However, if you use dot notation to specify an update or output parameter, then SCL executes the _setAttributeValue method, which may produce side effects. See "What Happens When Attribute Values Are Set or Queried" on page 122 for more information.

Some methods may be defined to return a value of any SCL type. You can access this returned value by specifying a variable in the left side of the dot notation. For example:

```
return-value = object.method (<arguments>);
```
or

```
if ( object.method (<arguments>) ) then ...
```

The return value's type defaults to Numeric if it is not explicitly declared. If the declared type does not match the returned type, and the method signature is known at compile time, the compiler returns an error. Otherwise, a data conversion might take place, or the program will halt at run time.

If you override an object's INIT method, you must call _SUPER._INIT before you can use dot notation to set attribute values or to make other method calls.

Dot notation is not available in the INPUT and PUT functions.

By default, your application halts execution if an error is detected in the dot notation that is used in the application. You can control this behavior with the HALTONDOTATTRIBUTE or NOHALTONDOTATTRIBUTE option in the CONTROL statement. See "CONTROL" on page 302 for more information.

## Using Nested Dot Notation

You can also use dot notation in nested form. For example,

```
value = object.attribute1.method1().attribute2;
```

is equivalent to the following:

```
dcl object object1 object2;
object1 = object.attribute1;  /* attribute1 in object
```

```
                                     is of OBJECT type */
object2 = object1.method1();   /* method1 in object1
                                     returns an object */
value   = object2.attribute2; /* assign the value of
                                     attribute2 in object2
                                     to the variable
                                     'value'. */
```

You can also specify the nested dot notation as an l-value. For example,

```
object.attribute1.method1().attribute2 = value;
```

is equivalent to the following:

```
dcl object object1 object2;

object1 = object.attribute1;
object2 = object1.method1();
object2.attribute2 = value; /* assume 'value' has
                                   been initialized.
                                   This would set
                                   attribute2 in object2
                                   to the value */
```

## Examples

An application window contains a text entry control named clientName. The following examples show how to use dot notation to invoke methods and to query and assign attribute values. For example, the following statement uses dot notation to invoke the _gray method of the control:

```
clientName._gray();
```

This is equivalent to

```
call send('clientName','_gray');
```

You can change the text color to blue, using dot notation to set the value of its **textColor** attribute:

```
name.textColor='blue';
```

You can also use dot notation to query the value of an attribute. For example:

```
color=clientName.textColor;
```

You can use dot notation in expressions. You can use a method in an expression only if the method can return a value via a RETURN statement in its definition. For example, suppose you create a setTable method, which is a public method and accepts an input character argument (the name of a SAS table). The method determines whether a SAS table exists and uses the RETURN statement to pass the return code from the EXIST function.

```
setTable: public method dsname:i:char(41) return=num;
  rc = exist(dsname, 'DATA');
  return rc;
endmethod;
```

Then you could use a statement like the following to perform actions that depend on the value that the setTable method returned.

```
if (obj.setTable('sasuser.houses')) then
   /*  the table exists, perform an action */
else
   /*  the table doesn't exist,    */
   /*  perform another action      */
```

The next example shows how to use dot notation with an object that you create in an SCL program. Suppose class X is saved in the entry X.SCL, and the INIT section is saved in the entry Y.SCL.

```
class x;
  public num n;
  m: public method n1: num n2: num return=num;
    dcl num r;
    r = n1 + n2;
    /* return sum of n1 and n2 */
    return r;
  endmethod;
  m: public method c1: char c2:char return=char;
    dcl num s;
    /* concatenate c1 and c2 */
    s = c1 || c2;
    return s;
  endmethod;
endclass;

init:
  dcl x xobj = _new_ x();
  dcl num n;
  dcl string s;
  n = xobj.m(99,1);
  s = xobj.m("abc","def");
  put n= s=;
  return;
```

If you compile and run Y.SCL, it produces

```
n=100  s=abcdef
```

# What Happens When Attribute Values Are Set or Queried

When you use dot notation to change or query an attribute value, SCL translates the statement to a _setAttributeValue method call (to change the value) or to a _getAttributeValue method call (to query the value). As a result, defining the attribute with a getCAM or setCAM method could produce side effects.

When you use dot notation to specify a parameter to a method, SCL executes the _setAttributeValue method if the parameter is an update or output parameter. SCL executes the _getAttributeValue method if the parameter is an input parameter. However, if the object is declared as a generic object or if the method does not have a signature, then all of the method's parameters are treated as update parameters. Therefore, SCL will execute the _setAttributeValue method even if the parameter is an input parameter, which could execute a setCAM method and send an event.

*Note:*  If you use dot notation to access a class attribute, program execution halts if any error is detected while the _getAttributeValue or _setAttributeValue method is running. Explicitly invoking the _getAttributeValue or _setAttributeValue method allows the program to control the halt behavior. The _getAttributeValue or _setAttributeValue method also enables you to check the return code from the method. For example:

```
rc = obj._setAttributeValue ('abc');
if ( rc ) then do;
    /* error detected in the _setAttributeValue method */
    ...more SCL statements...
    end;
```

△

## Setting Attribute Values

When you use dot notation to set the value of an attribute, SCL follows these steps:

1 Verify that the attribute exists.

2 Verify that the type of the attribute matches the type of the value that is being set.

3 Check whether the attribute value is in the ValidValues list. If the ValidValues metadata is an SCL entry, it is executed first to get the list of values to check the attribute value against.

4 Run the setCAM method, if it is defined, which gives users a chance to perform additional validation and to process their own side effects.

   *Note:*  If the Editable metadata is set to **No**, the custom set method is not called (even if it was defined for the attribute). △

5 Store the object's value in the attribute.

6 Send the "*attributeName* Changed" event if the SendEvent metadata is set to **Yes**.

7 sends the "contents Updated" event if the attribute is specified in the object's **contentsUpdatedAttributes** attribute. This event notifies components in a model/view relationship that a key attribute has been changed.

**Figure 8.2**   Flow of Control for _setAttributeValue

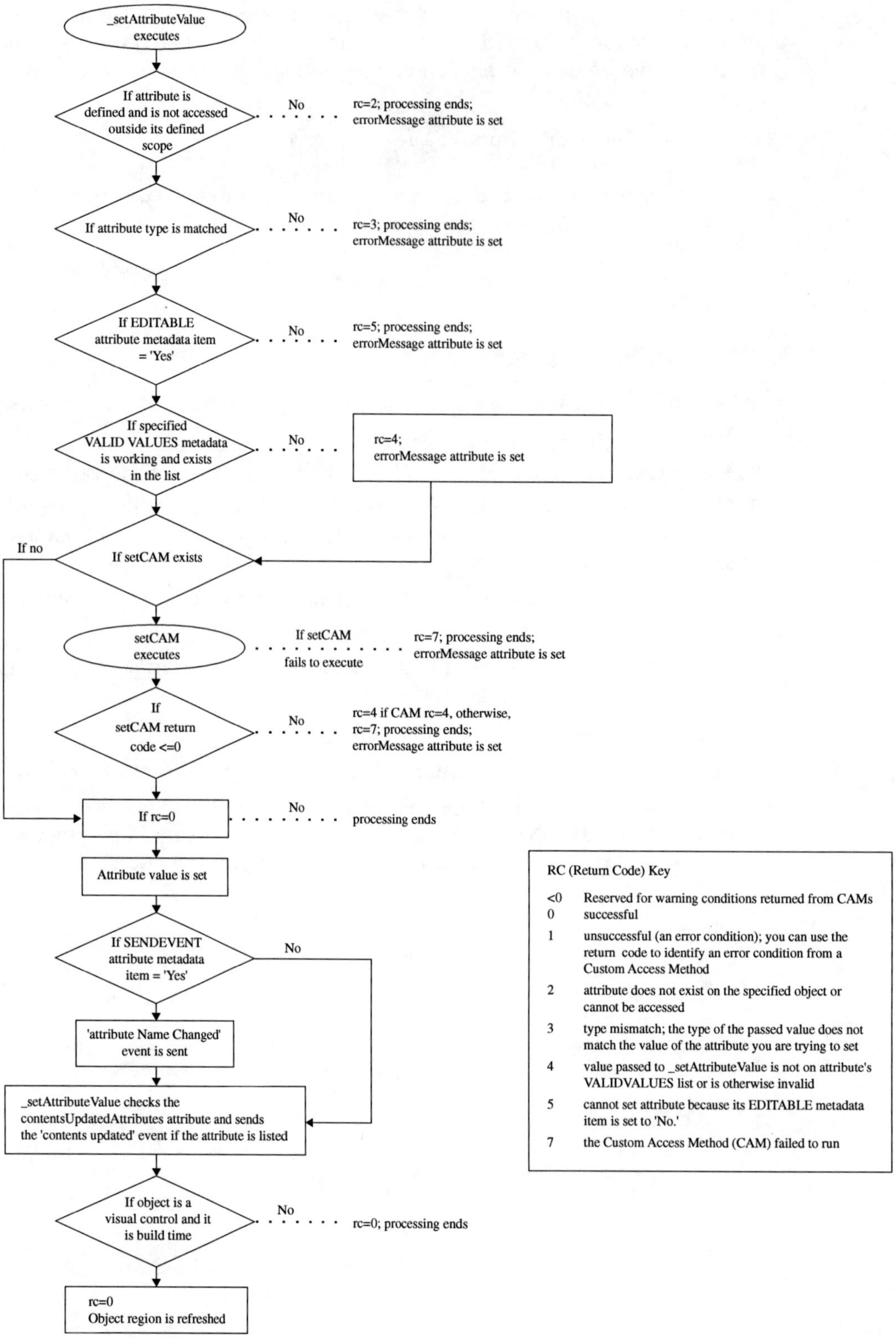

## Querying Attribute Values

When you use dot notation to query the value of an attribute, SCL follows these steps:

1 Execute the getCAM method to determine the attribute value, if a getCAM method has been defined.

2 Return the attribute value, if a value has been set.

3 Return the initial class value, if no attribute value has been set.

The following figure shows this process in detail.

**Figure 8.3** Flow of Control for _getAttributeValue

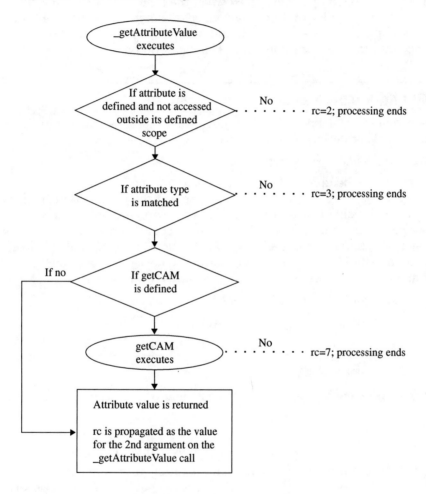

# Events and Event Handlers

Events alert applications when there is a change of state. Events occur when a user action takes place (such as a mouse click), when an attribute value is changed, or when a user-defined condition occurs. Events are essentially generic messages that are sent to objects from the system or from SCL applications. These messages usually direct an object to perform some action such as running a method.

Event handlers are methods that listen for these messages and respond to the them. Essentially, an event handler is a method that determines which method to execute after the event occurs.

SCL supports both system events and user-defined events.

## System Events

System events include user interface events (such as mouse clicks) as well as "attribute changed" events that occur when an attribute value is updated. SCL automatically defines system events for component attributes when those attributes are declared.

SCL can also automatically send system events for you when a component's attribute is changed. If you want "attribute changed" events to be sent automatically, specify **SendEvent='Y'** in the options list for the attribute.

If you want an action to be performed when the system event occurs, then you need to define the event handler that you want to be executed when the event occurs. You define event handlers for system events in the same way that you define them for user-defined events. See "Defining Event Handlers" on page 126 for more information.

## Defining and Sending Events

You can create user-defined events through the Properties window in the Class Editor or with event declaration statements in CLASS blocks.

EVENT event-name</(event-options)>;

Event names can be up to 256 characters long.

For the event options, you can specify the name of the method that handles the event and when an object should send the event. Events can be sent automatically either before (specify **Send='Before'**) or after (**Send='After'**) a method executes or they can be programmed manually (**'Manual'**) with SCL. New events default to **'After'**. You must specify a method name for events that are to be sent automatically.

After an event is defined, you can use the _sendEvent method to send the event:

object._sendEvent("event-name"<, event-handler-parameters>);

For a complete description of _sendEvent, refer to the SAS/AF online Help.

## Defining Event Handlers

You can define event handlers with event handler declaration statements in CLASS blocks.

EVENTHANDLER event-handler-name</(event-handler-options)>;

As part of the event handler options, you can specify the name of the event, the name of the method that handles the event, and the name of the object that generates the event (the sender). As the sender, you can specify **'_SELF_'** or **'_ALL_'**. When **Sender='_SELF_'**, the event handler listens only to events from the class itself. When **Sender='_ALL_'**, the event handler listens to events from any other class.

Using the _addEventHandler method, you can dynamically add a sender to trigger the event. For a complete description of _addEventHandler, refer to the SAS/AF online Help.

For more information about defining event handlers, see "CLASS" on page 277.

## Example

The following class defines one user-defined event, myEvent, and the event handler for this event, M2. When this class is created, SCL also assigns the system event name "n Changed" for the attribute **n** and registers the event name with the component.

```
class EHclass;
  public num n;     /* system event */
  event 'myEvent' / (method='M2');
  eventhandler M1 / (sender = '_SELF_',
                     event = 'n Changed');
  eventhandler M2 / (sender = '_SELF_',
                     event = 'myEvent');

M1: method a:list;
  put "Event is triggered by attribute n";
endmethod;

M2: method a:string n1:num n2:num;
  put "Event is triggered by _sendEvent";
  put a= n1= n2=;
endmethod;
endclass;
```

When the value of the attribute **n** is changed, the system automatically sends the "n Changed" event, and method M1 is executed. Method M2 is not executed until myEvent is sent with the _sendEvent method.

The next class, EHclass1, defines a second event handler, M3, that is also executed when myEvent is sent.

```
class EHclass1;
  /* Sender='*' means that the sender */
  /* is determined at run time.       */
  eventhandler M3 / (sender = '*', event='myEvent');
  M3: method a:string n1:num n2:num;
    put "Event myEvent is defined in another class";
    put "that is triggered by _sendEvent.";
    put a= n1= n2=;
  endmethod;
endclass;
```

In the following program, the system event "n Changed" is triggered when the value of the **n** attribute is modified. The user-defined event myEvent is triggered with the _sendEvent method.

```
import work.a.EHclass.class;
import work.a.EHclass1.class;
init:
  dcl EHclass obj = _new_ EHclass();
  dcl EHclass1 obj1 = _new_ EHclass1();

  /* Trigger the system event. */
  obj.n = 3;

  /* Trigger the user-defined event. */
  obj._sendEvent("myEvent", 'abc', 3, 4);
return;
```

The order in which the two classes are instantiated determines the order in which the event handlers for myEvent are executed. EHclass is instantiated first, so when myEvent is sent, event handler M2 is executed first, followed by the event handler defined in EHclass1, M3.

The output from this test program is

```
Event is triggered by attribute n
Event is triggered by _sendEvent
a=abc n1=3 n2=4
Event myEvent is defined in another class
that is triggered by _sendEvent.
a=abc n1=3 n2=4
```

## Event and Event Handler Metadata

Events and event handlers are implemented and maintained with metadata. This metadata exists as a list that is stored with the class. You can query a class (or an event within a class) to view the event and event handler metadata. To list the metadata for the an event, execute code similar to the following:

```
init:
    DCL num rc;
    DCL list metadata;
    DCL object obj;

    obj=loadclass('class-name');

    rc=obj._getEvent('event-name',metadata);
    call putlist(metadata,'',3);
    rc=obj._getEventHandler('_self_','event-handler-name',
                                '_refresh',metadata);
    call putlist(metadata,'',3);
return;
```

# Interfaces

Interfaces are groups of method declarations that enable classes to possess a common set of methods even if the classes are not related hierarchically. An interface is similar to a class that contains only method declarations.

A class can either *support* or *require* an interface. A class that supports an interface must implement all of the methods in the interface. A class that requires an interface can invoke any of the methods in the interface.

Suppose you have the following interface:

```
interface I1;
  M1: method;
endinterface;
```

If class A supports the interface, then it must implement the method M1:

```
class A supports I1;
  M1: method;
     put 'Implementation of M1';
  endmethod;
endclass;
```

Class B requires the interface, which means that it can invoke the methods declared in the interface.

```
class B requires I1;
  M2: method;
```

```
      dcl I1 myObj = _new_ I1;
      myObj.M1();
   endmethod;
endclass;
```

Interfaces are especially useful when you have several unrelated classes that perform a similar set of actions. These actions can be declared as methods in an interface, and each class that supports the interface provides its own implementation for each of the methods. In this way, interfaces provide a form of multiple inheritance.

A class can be defined to support or require one or more interfaces. If two components share an interface, they can indirectly call each others' methods via that interface. For example, model/view component communication is implemented with the use of interfaces. The model typically *supports* the interface, whereas the view *requires* the same interface. The interfaces for the components must match before a model/view relationship can be established. A class stores interface information as a property to identify whether it supports or requires an interface. Refer to *SAS Guide to Applications Development* for more information about model/view communication.

Although classes that support or require an interface are often used together, they are still independent components and can be used without taking advantage of an interface.

## Defining Interfaces

You define interfaces with the INTERFACE statement block:

INTERFACE *interface-name*
    &lt;EXTENDS *interface-name*&gt;
    &lt;/ (*interface-optional-clause*)&gt;;

&lt; *limited-method-declaration-statements*&gt;

ENDINTERFACE;

For more information about defining interfaces, see Chapter 9, "Example: Creating An Object-Oriented Application," on page 137 and "INTERFACE" on page 486.

## Example

The following INTERFACE block declares two methods for reading and writing data.

```
interface Reader;
   Read: method return=string;
   Write: method data:string;
endinterface;
```

Only the method declarations are given in the INTERFACE block. The method implementations are given in any class that supports the interface.

For example, the Lst and Ddata classes both implement the Read and Write methods. These classes *support* the Reader interface. In the Lst class, these methods read and write items from and to an SCL list.

```
class Lst supports Reader;
   dcl list L;
   dcl num cur n;

   /* Override the class constructor. */
   /* Create a new list.               */
   Lst: method/(state='o');
```

```
      L = makelist();
      cur = 0;
      n = 0;
   endmethod;

   Read method: return=string;
      if (cur >= n) then do;
        put 'End of file';
        return "";
        end;
      else do;
        cur + 1;

        /* Get the current item from the list. */
        return getitemc(l,cur);
      end;
   endmethod;

   Write method: c:string;
      n + 1;

      /* Insert a new item into the list. */
      insertc(l,c,-1);
   endmethod;

endclass;
```

The method implementations in the Ddata class read and write data from and to a SAS table.

```
class Ddata supports Reader;
   protected num fid;
   protected num obs n;

   /* Override the class constructor. */
   /* Use the open function to open a SAS table. */
   Ddata: method name: string mode: string;
      fid = open(name, mode);
      obs = 0;
      n = 0;
   endmethod;

   Read method: return=string;
      if (obs >= n) then do;
        put 'End of file';
        return "";
      end;
      else do;
        dcl string c;

        /* Fetch an observation from the table. */
        obs + 1;
        fetchobs(fid, obs);

        /* Get the contents of table column 1. */
```

```
        c = getvarc(fid, 1);
        return c;
    end;
 endmethod;

 Write method: c:string;
   dcl num rc;

   /* Add a new row to the table and      */
   /* write the contents of C into column 1. */
   append(fid);
   call putvarc(fid, 1, c);
   rc = update(fid);
   n + 1;
 endmethod;

endclass;
```

Using the interface, you can read and write data without knowing the data source. In the following example, the Read class implements method M, which calls the method that was declared in the Reader interface. The interface determines which method implementation is executed.

```
class Read;
  M: method r:Reader;

    /* Write a string to the data source, */
    /* then read it back.                  */
    r.write("abc");
    put r.read();
  endmethod;
endclass;
```

The following labeled program section reads and writes data to both a list and a SAS table. This code passes a Lst class and a Ddata class to the Read class, which treats the list and the table in the same way. The data is read and written transparently. The Read class does not need to know what the actual implementation of the Reader is — it only needs to know the interface.

```
init:
  dcl Lst L = _new_ Lst();
  dcl Ddata D = _new_Ddata("test","un");
  dcl read R = _new_ read();

  R.M(L);
  R.M(D);
return;
```

# Converting Version 6 Non-Visual Classes to Version 8 Classes

You do not need to convert Version 6 classes to Version 8 classes in order to run programs from the previous versions. Version 6 classes are automatically loaded into Version 8 formats when they are instantiated. Existing Version 6 SCL programs should run normally in Version 8 environments.

However, you can use Version 8 SAS Component Object Model (SCOM) features to make your programs more object-oriented, easier to maintain, and more efficient. Using SCOM features also enables you to reuse model classes in the future development of client/server applications.

To convert Version 6 model classes to Version 8 classes, you must modify the method implementation files and regenerate the class files. To modify the method implementation files, follow these steps:

1 Remove global variables. Declare them as private attributes or, if they are referenced in only one method, declare them as local variables within that method. See "Removing Global Variables" on page 132 for more information.

2 Declare all variables. See "Declaring Variables" on page 133 for more information.

3 Convert labels to method names and convert LINK statements to method calls. Declare the labeled sections as private methods. If necessary, specify the **Forward='Y'** option for the method. See "Converting Labels and LINK Statements" on page 133 for more information.

4 Convert CALL SEND statements to dot notation. See "Converting CALL SEND to Dot Notation" on page 134 for more information.

To regenerate the class files, follow these steps:

1 Use CREATESCL to convert Version 6 class files to Version 8 class files. See "Converting Class Definitions with CREATESCL" on page 134 for more information.

2 Convert instance variables to attributes, if appropriate. See "Using Instance Variables" on page 135 for more information.

3 Make sure signatures are generated for all methods. The best way to ensure that signatures are generated is to delete the method declarations from the class files and to replace them with the METHOD blocks from the method implementation files.

4 Change the class names specified in the CLASS statements if you do not want to overwrite the existing Version 6 classes.

5 Issue the SAVECLASS command to generate the new Version 8 class.

## Removing Global Variables

Remove all global variables from the Version 6 method implementation entries. Convert them either to local variables through DECLARE or to private attributes in the class definition file. For example, suppose that a Version 6 method implementation file contains the variables N1, N2, C1 and C2 as shown:

```
length n1 n2 8;
length c1 c2 $200;
```

In this example, four attributes need to be added to **mylib.classes.newclass.scl**, as follows:

```
Private num n1;
Private num n2;
Private char c1;
Private char c2;
```

After the attributes are added, issue the SAVECLASS command to generate the new class.

## Declaring Variables

Declare all of the variables in your program. Lists should be declared with the LIST keyword rather than allowing them to default to a Numeric type. Objects should be declared either as generic objects (with the OBJECT keyword) or as specific class objects. You can use dot notation with an object only if it is declared as an object. Using specific LIST and object declarations can avoid problems with overloading methods. For more information, see "Overloading and List, Object, and Numeric Types" on page 111.

Whenever possible, classes should be declared with a specific class declaration such as

```
dcl work.a.listbox.class lboxobj;
```

Try to avoid using generic object declarations such as

```
dcl object lboxobj;
```

Also, the compiler cannot check method signatures or validate methods and attributes if it does not know the specific class type. If the compiler is not able to do this checking and validation at compile time, then SCL must do it at run time, which makes your program less efficient.

For example, assume that you declare a generic object named SomeC that has a method Get, which returns a numeric value. You also declare a class named XObj that has a method M, which is overloaded as (N)V and (C)V. Suppose you need to pass the return value of Get to the M method:

```
dcl object SomeC = _new_ someclass.class();
dcl work.a.xclass.class XObj = _new_ xclass.class();
XObj.M(SomeC.Get());
```

SomeC is declared as a generic object, so the compiler cannot determine what object it contains at compile time. Even though there is a specific object assignment to SomeC, the compiler cannot guarantee what type it will contain at any given point, because the value could be changed elsewhere when the program runs.

Therefore, the compiler cannot look up the Get method to find that it returns a Numeric value, and it cannot determine which method M in Xclass to call. This method validation must be deferred until run time, when the return type of the Get method will be known (because the actual call will have taken place and the value will have been returned).

The problem can be remedied by declaring SomeC as a specific object:

```
dcl someclass SomeC = _new_ someclass.class();
```

If this is not possible, then you could declare a Numeric variable to hold the result of the Get method, as shown in this example:

```
dcl object SomeC = _new_ someclass.class();
dcl xclass XObj = _new_ xclass.class();
dcl num n;
n = SomeC.Get();
XObj.M(n);
```

Even though the compiler cannot validate the Get method for the SomeC class, it can validate the method name and parameter type for XObj.

## Converting Labels and LINK Statements

The next step is to remove all link labels from the Version 6 method implementation catalog entries. Convert them to private methods in the class definition file, and convert the link to a method call. For example, suppose that **myclass.classes.old.scl** contains the following:

```
m1: method;
    link a1;
endmethod;

a1:
   ...SCL statements...
return;
```

To change the labeled section to a private method in **mylib.classes.newclass.scl**, add the following:

```
a1: Private method;
    ...SCL statements...
endmethod;
```

If needed, you can also add parameters to the method. To change the link to a method call, change the following:

```
m1: method;
    a1();
endmethod;
```

In the old entry, the A1 labeled section is after the M1 method. In the new entry, the labeled section has been converted to a method. However, you cannot call a method before it is declared. To fix this problem, you must either move the A1 method before the M1 method, or you can declare A1 with the **Forward='Y'** option:

```
a1: Private method / (Forward='y');
    ...SCL statements...
endmethod;
```

## Converting CALL SEND to Dot Notation

The final step in modifying your method implementation files is converting CALL SEND statements to METHOD calls that use dot notation.

*Note:* To use dot notation, the method that you specify must have a signature. Therefore, you cannot convert CALL SEND statements to dot notation unless your class files have been converted to Version 8 class files. Also, the object that you specify should be declared as a specific class type to enable the compiler to validate method parameters. △

For example, suppose that a Version 6 program contains the following line:

```
call send(obj1,'m1',p1);
```

Converting this line to dot notation results in

```
obj1.m1(p1);
```

## Converting Class Definitions with CREATESCL

Assume that the Version 6 class is **mylib.classes.oldclass.class** and that the method implementation file is **mylib.classes.old.scl**.

**1** Use CREATESCL to create an SCL entry that contains the following SCL statements:

```
Init:
    rc=createscl('mylib.classes.oldclass.class',
                 'mylib.classes.newclass.scl');
return;
```

**2** Issue the SAVECLASS command to generate the Version 6 class file **mylib.classes.newclass.class**.

**3** Open this entry in the Build window and modify the class definition as needed. Reissue the SAVECLASS command to generate the new class file in Version 8 format.

## Using Instance Variables

The object model in Version 6 uses instance variables. In Version 8, instance variables have been replaced with attributes.

When a class is loaded, the class loader automatically converts Version 6 formats to the Version 8 format. This process includes converting instance variables to public or private attributes with the option IV, which specifies the name of the Version 6 instance variable.

In the following example, the Version 6 instance variable ABC is converted to the Version 8 attribute **abc**.

```
class IVclass;
  public char abc / (iv='ABC');
endclass;
```

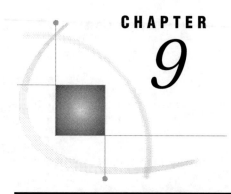

# CHAPTER 9

# Example: Creating An Object-Oriented Application

## Introduction

Version 8 SCL provides many object-oriented programming features such as class and useclass syntax, method overloading, and interfaces. This tutorial demonstrates how to use many of these new features by creating a class-based version of a simple data input facility that is based on traditional SCL library functions.

The tutorial is organized in sections by level of difficulty, with Level Zero being the most elementary and Level Five the most challenging. A beginner should work through sections Zero, One, and Two. The remaining sections can then be reviewed as the user progresses. For example, a beginner may want to return to the tutorial after gaining additional experience with the basics. A user who is more experienced in object-oriented programming may want to work through them at once. Level Five should be reviewed by all users because it contains an example that shows how the SCL class syntax can be used with SAS/AF software.

## Simple Class Syntax — Level Zero

Before beginning the tutorial, you must have a clear understanding of a simple SCL class. A CLASS statement enables you to use SCL to create a SAS/AF class and to define all the properties for the class, including attributes, methods, events, and interfaces. An SCL class is created with SCL class syntax. The simplest class is an empty class, which is defined using the following code:

```
class x;
endclass;
```

Enter the above code in an SCL entry such as X.SCL and then create the class by using the SAVECLASS command. You should now see a CLASS entry for X in the current catalog.

*Note:*  The name of the entry does not have to match the name of the class, but for beginners this is the easiest way to name an entry. △

To add functionality to this class, you can create a simple method by using the following code:

```
class x;

  m: method;
      put 'Hello';
  endmethod;

  endclass;
```

The PUT statement will write **Hello** to the SAS procedure output file or to a file that is specified in the most recent FILE statement. To run this method, you need to create an example of the class and call the method. In an SCL entry called Y.SCL, enter the following code:

```
init:
   dcl x x = _new_ x();
   x.m();
   return;
```

The _NEW_ operator is used to create an example of the class X and to assign it to the variable *x*. The _NEW_ operator provides a faster and more direct way to create an object by combining the actions of loading a class with LOADCLASS and initializing the object with the _new method, which invokes the object's _init method. You then call method M using the object variable *x* in the dot notation expression x.m().

*Note:*  dot notation provides a shortcut for invoking methods and for setting or querying attribute values. Using dot notation reduces typing and makes SCL programs easier to read. It also enhances run-time performance if you declare the object used in the dot notation as an example of a predefined class instead of a generic object. The object's class definition is then known at compile time. Because dot notation checks the method signature, it is the only way to access an overloaded method as illustrated in "Overloaded Methods — Level Two" on page 145. △

Compile Y.SCL, and then use the TESTAF command to run it. You should see the following output:

```
Hello
```

# Creating a Data Set Class — Level One

In this exercise you will read a simple SAS data set that contains two character variables. You will learn how to open the data set, fetch an observation, copy a data set character variable, and close the data set. The SCL functions that will be used are

- □ OPEN
- □ FETCH
- □ GETVARC
- □ CLOSE

You will build a class that encapsulates these operations so that they can be called as methods on any given data set. Because of this, the class itself should represent a data set.

Before you can begin converting these functions to class methods, you must create the class data, as shown in the next section, "Class Data — Level One" on page 139.

## Class Data — Level One

Class data is declared with the DCL statement by using the following code:

```
class x;
  dcl num n;
endclass;
```

Here class X contains a numeric variable called *n*.

The DCL statement can be omitted when you provide a variable scope modifier such as public, private or protected. *Scope modifiers* indicate how the variable is to be accessed from locations outside the class. By default, the scope modifier is public, which indicates that anyone can access the variable. Both private and protected scope modifiers restrict access to the variable.

## The Data Set Class — Level One

For the data set class, begin with the following class data:

```
DDATA class;
public-string-dname;
public-string-mode;
protected-num-fid;
protected-num-nvars; endclass;
```

where

| | |
|---|---|
| *dname* | is the name of the data set |
| *mode* | is the access mode |
| *fid* | is the file identifier that will be returned from the OPEN call |
| *nvars* | is the number of variables in the data set. |

In this case, public access is given to *dname* and *mode*, but access is restricted for *fid* and *nvars*.

You will create one method for each of the SCL functions OPEN, FETCH, GETVARC, and CLOSE. The following example shows how to use the FETCH function to take an action that is based on the value of its return code:

```
read: method return=num;
      dcl num rc;
      rc = fetch(fid);
      return rc;
endmethod;
```

You can use a function such as GETVARC directly in the IF statement. In this case, the VARTYPE function is executed, and then the IF expression evaluates the return code to determine whether to perform the conditional action. The following method takes a parameter *n*, which represents the variable number, and returns the character variable *c* from GETVARC.

```
cpy: method n: num return=string;
     dcl string c = "";
     if (vartype(fid, n) = 'C') then
         c = getvarc(fid, n);
     return c;
endmethod;
```

CLOSE is used to close a data set as soon as it is no longer needed by the application. The method in this example for CLOSE is

```
_term: method /(state='O');
       if (fid) then close(fid);
       _super();
endmethod;
```

This method closes the data set represented by *fid*. It also contains two items that refer to the parent class of DDATA (State='O' and _super()). A *parent class* is the class from which a particular class was extended or derived. In this case, DDATA was implicitly extended from OBJECT.CLASS. Since OBJECT.CLASS contains a _term method, you must indicate that you are overriding it in DDATA by specifying State='O'. Because OBJECT.CLASS is being overridden, to ensure that the _term method in OBJECT.CLASS is still executed, use the function call _super().

## Constructors — Level One

The method that will be used for opening the data set is called a constructor. A *constructor* is a method that is used to instantiate a class and provides a way for initializing class data. In order for a method to be a constructor, it must be a void method (one that does not have a return value), and it must have the same name as the class. Here is the constructor for DDATA:

```
ddata: method n: string m:string nv:num;
       fid = open(n, m);
       dname = n;
       mode = m;
       nvars = nv;
endmethod;
```

where *n* is a parameter containing the name of the data set, *m* is the input mode, and *nv* is the number of variables.

This constructor method will be called when an example of the DDATA class is created using the _NEW_ operator. For example, the following code creates an example of the DDATA class representing the data set **sasuser.x**. The data set will be opened in input mode and has two variables.

```
init:
  dcl ddata d = _new_ ddata("sasuser.x", "i", 2);
  return;
```

## Using the Data Set Class — Level One

The entire data set class is

```
class ddata;

  /* Data */
  public string dname;
  public string mode;
  protected num fid;
  protected num nvars;

  /* Constructor method */
  ddata: method n: string m:string nv:num;
        fid = open(n, m);
        dname = n;
        mode = m;
        nvars = nv;
  endmethod;

  /* FETCH method */
  read: method return=num;
      dcl num rc;
      rc = fetch(fid);
      return rc;
  endmethod;

  /* GETVARC method */
  cpy: method n: num return=string;
      dcl string c = "";
      if (vartype(fid, n) = 'C') then
          c = getvarc(fid, n);
      return c;
  endmethod;

  /* CLOSE method */
  _term: method /(state='O');
        if (fid) then close(fid);
        _super();
  endmethod;
endclass;
```

You can use this class as follows:

```
init:
  dcl ddata d = _new_ ddata("sasuser.x", "i", 2);
  dcl num more = ^d.read();
  do while(more);
     dcl string s s2;
     s = d.cpy(1);
     s2 = d.cpy(2);
     put s s2;
     more = ^d.read();
  end;
  d._term();
```

```
      return;
```

In this example, the data set **sasuser.x** has two character variables, which you read and print until the end of the file is reached.

Now suppose that you create the following data set:

```
data sasuser.x;
 input city $1-14;
 length airport $10;
 if city='San Francisco' then airport='SFO';
 else if city='Honolulu' then airport='HNL';
 else if city='New York' then airport='JFK';
 else if city='Miami' then airport='MIA';
 cards;
 San Francisco
 Honolulu
 New York
 Miami
 ;
```

The output from the program will be

```
San Francisco SFO
Honolulu HNL
New York JFK
Miami MIA
```

# Extending Classes — Level Two

While designing the class structure, you might find that some classes share functionality with other classes. In that case, you can extend classes by creating subclasses to prevent duplication of functionality.

In "Constructors — Level One" on page 140, the DDATA class implicitly extended OBJECT.CLASS. In fact, any class without an explicit EXTENDS clause in the CLASS statement extends OBJECT.CLASS. To explicitly extend a class, add the EXTENDS clause shown below:

```
class y extends x;
endclass;
```

In this case, class Y extends the class X. Alternatively, Y is a subclass of X, and X is the parent class of Y.

This enables Y to share X's functionality. For example, if the class X were

```
class x;
 m: method;
     put 'Hello';
 endmethod;
endclass;
```

and the class y were

```
class y extends x;
endclass;
```

then you could call the method M using an example of the class Y:

```
init:
 dcl y y = _new_ y();
 y.m();
 return;
```

## Access Modifiers — Level Two

The access modifiers that we mentioned above – public, private and protected – can now be explained. A variable (or method) that is declared as public can be accessed anywhere. A variable (or method) that is declared as protected can be accessed only by non-proper subclasses of the class in which its declared. Protected variables can be accessed only from the class in which they are declared. This is also true for protected variables that are accessed from the subclasses of those classes.

These modifiers restrict access to certain variables (or methods) that should not be seen outside the class or class hierarchy in which they are declared. For example, there is no need for any class outside the DATA class hierarchy to access the *fid* variable, so it is declared as protected but could also be declared as private.

## The DDATA Class as a Subclass — Level Two

To illustrate how subclassing works with the DDATA class, this exercise creates a similar class for external data files. The following SCL functions will be used:

- □ FOPEN
- □ FREAD
- □ FGET
- □ FCLOSE

These SCL functions will be used to create a class called FDATA to represent an external file. It is important to note similarities to the DDATA class. In particular, each class will have a name, input mode, and file identifier, so a class will be created to store this information. Then the subclasses DDATA and FDATA will be created from the DATA class. The parent data class will be

```
class data;
    public num type;
    public string dname;
    public string mode;
    protected num fid;

data: method f: num n: string m:string;
        fid = f;
        dname = n;
        mode = m;
endmethod;

endclass;
```

In addition to the *name*, *mode* and *file id*, a type variable is stored to indicate whether FDATA is an external file or a SAS data set.

The constructor DATA will be called whenever an example of the DATA class is created. It will also be called automatically whenever any subclasses of data are created if the constructor in the subclass has not be overridden. If the constructor has been overridden, you must use _super to call the parent constructor. You must also use _super if the argument list that is used in the _NEW_ operator does not match the argument list of the parent constructor. This will be the case for DDATA and FDATA.

To extend the DATA class, modify the DDATA CLASS statement, data declarations, and constructor as follows:

```
class ddata extends data;

    /* Class data */
    protected num nvars;

    /* Constructor method */
    ddata: method n: string m:string nv:num;
        fid = open(n, m);
        _super(fid, n, m);
        nvars = nv;
        type = 1;
    endmethod;
```

In this example, the DDATA constructor will call the data constructor via the _super call. This sets the name, mode and file identifier that are stored in the parent class data. The DDATA constructor still sets *nvars* and also sets the type field to indicate that the file is a data set. The rest of the class will remain the same.

## The FDATA Class — Level Two

The declaration and constructor of the FDATA class will be similar to those of the DDATA class, as shown in the following:

```
class fdata extends data;

    /* Constructor method */
    fdata: method n: string m: string;
        dcl string ref = "";
        dcl num rc = filename(ref, n);
        fid =  fopen(ref, m);
        _super(fid, n, m);
        type = 2;
    endmethod;

    /* FREAD method */
    read: method return=num;
        dcl num rc = fread(fid);
        return rc;
    endmethod;

    /* FGET method */
    cpy: method n: num return=string;
        dcl string c = "";
        dcl num rc = fget(fid, c);
        return c;
    endmethod;

    /* FCLOSE method */
    _term: method /(state='O');
```

```
        if (fid) then fclose(fid);
        _super();
    endmethod;
endclass;
```

Use FDATA to read an external class by instantiating it and looping through the data:

```
init:
dcl fdata f = _new_ fdata("some_file", "i");
dcl num more = ^f.read();
do while(more);
    dcl string s s2;
    s = f.cpy(1);
    s2 = f.cpy(2);
    put s s2;
    more = ^f.read();
end;
f._term();
return;
```

This code assumes that the external file is formatted with each line containing two character variables separated by a blank. For example:

```
Geoffrey Chaucer
Samuel Johnson
Henry Thoreau
George Eliot
Leo Tolstoy
```

# Overloaded Methods — Level Two

*Method overloading* is the process of defining multiple methods that have the same name, but which differ in parameter number, type, or both. Method overloading lets you use the same name for methods that are related conceptually but take different types or numbers of parameters.

For example, you may have noticed that the CPY method in FDATA has a numeric parameter that apparently serves no useful purpose. You do not need to specify a variable number for an external file. This parameter is used so that in the future when you use interfaces, the CPY method in FDATA matches the one in DDATA. For now, the parameter is not needed. One way of resolving this is to overload the CPY method by creating another CPY method with a different parameter list, as shown in the following code:

```
cpy: method return=string;
    dcl string c="";
    dcl num rc = fget(fid, c);
    return c;
endmethod;

cpy: method n: num return=string;
    return cpy();
endmethod;
```

In this example, the original CPY method ignores the parameter and calls a CPY method that returns the character value. By doing this, you have defined two methods that have the same name but different parameter types. With this simple change, you do not have to worry about which method to call.

The CPY method can be used as follows:

```
s = f.cpy();
```

Overloaded methods can be used any time you need to have multiple methods with the same name but different parameter lists. For example, you may have several methods that are conceptually related but which operate on different types of data, or you may want to create a method with an optional parameter, as in the CPY example.

To differentiate between overloaded methods, the compiler refers to the *method signature*, which is a list of the method's parameter types. A method signature provides a means of extending a method name, so that the same name can be combined with multiple different signatures to produce multiple different actions. Method signatures are created automatically when a method is added to a class and when the compiler is parsing a method call. Method signatures appear as part of the information that the Class Editor displays about a method.

# Interfaces and Higher Levels of Abstraction — Level Three

The routines that use DDATA and FDATA are very similar. In fact, the set of methods for each class is similar by design. The actual implementations of the methods differ. For example, the CPY method in DDATA is different from the CPY method in FDATA, but the basic concept of reading character data is the same. In effect, the interface for both classes is essentially the same.

You can exploit this similarity to make it easier to use the two classes. In fact, you can have one data loop that handles both types of classes by defining an SCL interface for both classes. To define the interface, you generalize the functionality and create the following SCL entry:

```
interface reader;
   read: method return=num;
   cpy: method n: num return=string;
endinterface;
```

Use SAVECLASS to create an interface entry with two abstract methods, READ and CPY. The abstract methods are by definition the interface itself. Any class that supports this interface will need to supply the implementations for these methods.

When you use the SAVECLASS command in an SCL entry that contains a CLASS block, the class is generated and its CLASS entry is created. This is the equivalent of using the Class Editor to interactively create a CLASS entry.

Once you have created the interface, you must modify the DDATA and FDATA classes to support it. To do that, change the CLASS statements in each class as follows:

```
class ddata extends data supports reader;
```

and

```
class fdata extends data supports reader;
```

Since DDATA and FDATA contain READ and CPY methods, no other changes are needed in the classes.

To use the new interface, you will create two helper classes. One is an iterator class that will be used to abstract the looping process over both DDATA and FDATA. Use the following code to create the two helper classes:

```
class iter;

    private num varn nvars;
    public reader r /(autocreate='n');

    /* Constructor */
    iter: method rdr: reader n: num;
          varn = 1;
          nvars = n;
          r = rdr;
    endmethod;

    /* Check if there are more elements to iterate over */
    more: method return=num;
          dcl num more = ^r.read();
          varn = 1;
          return more;
    endmethod;

    /* Return the next element */
    next: method return=string;
          dcl string c = "";
          c =  r.cpy(varn);
          varn + 1;
          return c;
    endmethod;

  endclass;
```

Several things require explanation for this class. First, note that it has two private variables, *varn* and *nvars*, to keep track of where it is in the iteration process.

It also has a variable *r* which is an interface type. Since we cannot create the interface automatically when an example of ITER is created, we specify the AUTOCREATE='N' option.

The iterator has three methods. In the first method, the constructor stores the reader variable and the number of variables in the reader. A *reader variable* is any class that supports the READER interface. The MORE method reads from the reader to check whether there are any more elements. The NEXT method returns the next element.

The other helper class uses the iterator to loop over the data in a reader.

```
class read;

  private iter i;

  read: method r: reader;
        i = _new_ iter(r, 2);
  endmethod;

  loop:method;
      do while(i.more());
      dcl string s s2;
      s = i.next();
      s2 = i.next();
      put s s2;
    end;
```

```
endmethod;

_term: method /(state='O');
  i._term();
  _super();
endmethod;

endclass;
```

The constructor will create a new iterator, and the LOOP method will use it to loop over the data.

The SCL to use these classes is

```
init:
dcl string filename;
dcl fdata f;
dcl ddata d;
dcl read r;

/* Read an external file */
filename = "some_file";
f = _new_ fdata(filename, "i");
r = _new_ read(f);
r.loop();
r._term();

/* Read a dataset */
filename = "sasuser.x";
d = _new_ ddata(filename, "i", 2);
r = _new_ read(d);
r.loop();
r._term();
return;
```

This code will successfully read an external file and a data set.

# Other Classes and Further Abstraction — Level Four

Given the reader interface, you can now use other classes – even ones outside the data class hierarchy – as readers, as long as they support the reader interface. Using the abstract reader interface enables you to read from many different types of objects as well.

For example, consider the following class, which uses SCL lists to maintain data:

```
class lst supports reader;
  private list l;
  private num nvars;
  private num nelmts;
  private num cur;

  /* Constructor */
  lst: method n:num;
      l = makelist();
      nvars = n;
      nelmts = 0;
```

```
          cur = 1;
    endmethod;

    /* Copy method */
    cpy: method n: num return=string;
         dcl string c = "";
         if (cur <= nelmts) then do;
           c = getitemc(l, cur);
           cur + 1;
         end;
         return c;
    endmethod;

  /* Read method */
  read: method return=num;
     if (cur > nelmts) then
         return 1;
     else
         return 0;
  endmethod;

  /* Add an element to the list */
  add: method c:string;
       nelmts + 1;
       setitemc(l, c, nelmts, 'Y');
  endmethod;

  /* Add two elements to the list */
  add: method c1:string c2:string;
       add(c1);
       add(c2);
  endmethod;

  /* Terminate the list */
  _term: method /(state='O');
       if (l) then dellist(l);
       _super();
  endmethod;
 endclass;
```

This class represents a list, and because it supports the READER interface, it can be read in the same way as the DDATA and FDATA classes.

The SCL for reading from the list is

```
init:
 dcl lst l;
 dcl read r;
 l = _new_ lst(2);

 /* Notice the overloaded add method */
 l.add("123", "456");
 l.add("789", "012");
 l.add("345", "678");

 /* Create a read class and loop over the data */
```

```
r = _new_ read(l);
r.loop();

r._term();
return;
```

The output for this program will be

```
123 456
789 012
345 678
```

# USECLASS — Level One

This section presents the USECLASS statement and is intended for those users who are unfamiliar with USECLASS. It is not required for the remainder of the tutorial.

A USECLASS statement binds methods that are implemented within it to the specified class definition. USECLASS allows a class's method implementations to reside in different entries other than the class declaration's entry. This is helpful if a class is complex enough to require several developers to write its methods.

The DDATA class will be modified to use USECLASS. Although this class is certainly not complex enough to require USECLASS, it illustrates its use.

First, rewrite the class specification, using the following code:

```
class ddata;

   /* Data */
   public string dname;
   public string mode;
   protected num fid;
   protected num nvars;

   /* Constructor method */
   ddata: method n: string m:string nv:num /
   (scl='sasuser.a.constr.scl');

   /* FETCH method */
   read: method return=num                    /
   (scl='sasuser.a.read.scl');

   /* GETVARC method */
   cpy: method n: num return=string           /
   (scl='sasuser.a.cpy.scl');

   /* CLOSE method */
   _term: method                              /
   (state='O', scl='sasuser.a.trm.scl');
 endclass;
```

The method implementations are removed, and the method declaration statements are modified to indicate which SCL entry contains each method implementation. This new class specification should be compiled with the SAVECLASS command.

Next, create the method implementations in each entry. These should be compiled with the COMPILE command, not with SAVECLASS. SASUSER.A.CONSTR.SCL should contain

```
useclass ddata;

  /* Constructor method */
  ddata: method n: string m:string nv:num;
         fid = open(n, m);
         dname = n;
         mode = m;
         nvars = nv;
  endmethod;

enduseclass;
```

SASUSER.A.READ.SCL should contain

```
useclass ddata;

  /* FETCH method */
  read: method return=num;
      dcl num rc;
      rc = fetch(fid);
      return rc;
  endmethod;

enduseclass;
```

SASUSER.A.CPY.SCL should contain

```
useclass ddata;

  /* GETVARC method */
  cpy: method n: num return=string;
      dcl string c = "";
      if (vartype(fid, n) = 'C') then
         c = getvarc(fid, n);
      return c;
  endmethod;

enduseclass;
```

SASUSER.A.TRM.SCL should contain

```
useclass ddata;

 /* CLOSE method */
  _term: method /(state='O');
         if (fid) then close(fid);
         _super();
  endmethod;
enduseclass;
```

# Using SCL Class Syntax with SAS/AF — Level Five

So far you have created stand-alone SCL classes. SCL class syntax can be used to create SAS/AF visual objects.

This exercise will extend the SAS/AF List Box class. The readers that were previously developed in this tutorial will be used to read data that will be used to initialize the items in the List Box.

To extend the List Box class, you must write a class to extend List Box and modify the READ class that was created in "Other Classes and Further Abstraction — Level Four" on page 148. The READ class will then be able to pass the new class to the list box to use for initializing the item list instead of having it simply print the character data after reading it.

You must create a new interface and make a minor modification to the LOOP method in READ.

The interface has a single method, CALLBACK:

```
interface call;
 callback: method s:string;
endinterface;
```

The modified LOOP method in READ is

```
loop: method caller:call;
        do while(i.more());
          caller.callback(i.next());
        end;
    endmethod;
```

The method now takes a CALL interface parameter and calls its CALLBACK method.

*Note:* You do not specify the implementation of a method in an interface; you simply supply the name and parameter list. △

It is not necessary to know what the implementation for CALLBACK is at this point, only that you call it in the read loop and pass a character value to it. Whatever class supports the interface will supply the implementation for CALLBACK.

Now, create the extended List Box class (depending on which version of SAS you have, you may need to create an empty MLIST class first in order for the following to work).

```
import sashelp.classes;
class mlist extends listbox_c supports call;

    /* Local item list */
    private list l;

    /* Set method */
    set: method r: read;
        l = makelist();
        r.loop(_self_);
    endmethod;

    /* Store the character value in the local list */
    callback: method s:string;
            insertc(l, s, -1);
    endmethod;

    /* Set the items attribute */
    setattr: method;
            _self_.items = l;
    endmethod;

endclass;
```

Note how the IMPORT statement and the LOOP, SET, SETATTR, and CALLBACK methods will be used:

☐ The IMPORT statement defines a search path for CLASS entry references in an SCL program so that you can refer to a class by its two-level name instead of having to specify the four-level name each time. It is used to specify a catalog to search for abbreviated class names. For example, the MLIST class extends LISTBOX_C, but if LISTBOX_C is not in the current catalog, the compiler will not know where to find it. The IMPORT statement tells the compiler to search the SASHELP.CLASSES catalog for any classes it cannot find in the current catalog.

☐ The SET method is used to set up a local list that will hold the new set of items for the list box. It will also call the LOOP method in READ, with MLIST's object as a parameter. Recall that MLIST supports the CALL interface, so this will work with the new LOOP method that was created above.

☐ As the LOOP method executes, it will call the CALLBACK method for each character variable that it reads. The CALLBACK method will store the variable in the local list that was created in the SET method.

☐ Finally, the SETATTR method will assign the local list to MLIST's item list, thus changing the list of items seen when the List Box, which is actually MLIST, is displayed.

To see how this works, create the CALL interface, as well as the classes READ and MLIST, by using the SAVECLASS command. Then edit a frame. In the Components window, add the MLIST class to the class list (via **AddClasses** on the pop-up menu). After it appears on the list, drag and drop MLIST to the frame. In the frame's source, enter

```
init:
 dcl ddata d;
 dcl read r;
 dcl string filename = "sasuser.x";
 d = _new_ ddata(filename, "i", 2);
 r = _new_ read(d);
 mlist1.set(r);
 mlist1.setattr();
 return;
```

This will create a DDATA reader with an associated READ class. Now call the SET and SETATTR methods on the new List Box class (MLIST).

Compile and use the TESTAF command on the frame. The initial list of items will be

```
San Francisco
Honolulu
New York
Miami
```

## Flexibility — Level Five

Using the CALL interface in the above exercise allows a great deal of flexibility in modifying the MLIST and READ classes.

For example, to process numeric data instead of character data, you could simply overload the CALLBACK method in the interface

```
interface call;
 callback: method s:string;
```

```
callback: method n:num;
endinterface;
```

and support it in the MLIST class

```
callback: method n:num;
                /* process numeric value */
endmethod;
```

Now, the READ class – or any class that supports CALL – can call the CALLBACK method with a numeric parameter. Clearly, this process can be generalized to make use of any possible parameter lists that are needed for CALLBACK.

Another feature is that any class that supports the READER interface can be used to read the data into the list box. For example, to use an external file, change the frame's SCL to

```
init:
 dcl fdata f;
 dcl read r;
 dcl string filename = "some_file";
 f = _new_ fdata(filename, "i");
 r = _new_ read(f);
 mlist1.set(r);
 mlist1.setattr();
 return;
```

We can consolidate the code further by creating another class to set up the reader:

```
init:
 dcl SetReader g = _new_ SetReader();
 dcl read r = g.get();
 mlist1.set(r);
 mlist1.setattr();
 return;
```

SetReader sets up whatever reader is necessary even if your program is using external data. Then, at the frame level, you can read from any type of data source, such as a data set, an external file, an SCL list, or any other user-defined data source. The only requirement is that SetReader support the reader interface.

P A R T *3*

# Application Considerations

CHAPTER

*10*

# Handling Exceptions

## Introduction

SCL provides two mechanisms for handling error conditions:

The program halt handler
　Program halt handlers typically allow your application to print a message, save
　some information, and then either try to continue execution or halt the
　application. The SCL generic program halt handler is sort of an all-purpose
　routine for handling program halts that occur for a variety of different reasons at
　any point in the program.

The CATCH and THROW statements
　The SCLException class and the CATCH and THROW statements enable you to
　define specific exceptions and recovery routines that are specific to each exception.
　You can define the exceptions and recovery routines in the locations in your code
　where the exceptions may be encountered, thus making error recovery code a
　natural part of the program.

## Using the Program Halt Handler

The program halt handler is designed to handle unexpected run-time errors. The
programHalt class contains methods that are called when certain run-time exceptions
occur. By overriding these methods, you can specify whether an application should halt
immediately or continue executing. You can control how exceptions are handled.

In the following example, the _onGeneric method creates a list named MSGS, inserts
information about the location where the application failed into the list, and displays
the list with the MESSAGEBOX function. You can use this code to create your own
program halt handler.

```
class myHalt extends
    sashelp.classes.programHalt.class;
```

```
_onGeneric:method / (STATE='O');
    dcl list msgs=makelist();
    rc = insertc(msgs, "SCL program failed at ", 1);
    rc = insertc(msgs, "Entry=" || entry, 2);
    rc = insertc(msgs, "Line=" || putn(lineNumber, "3.0"), 3);
    if (keywordType = 'function') then
        rc = insertc(msgs, "Function=" || keyword, 4);
    else
        rc = insertc(msgs, "Method=" || keyword, 4);

    rc = messageBox(msgs);

    /* continue execution */
    stopExecution = 'No';
    endmethod;
endclass;
```

*Note:* **Entry**, **lineNumber**, **keyword**, and **keywordType** are all object attributes that are defined in the class sashelp.classes.programHalt.class. △

The _onGeneric method traps any error messages that are generated by SCL and saves them in the MSGS list. Developers can use this list to identify and fix potential problems in their code.

The programHalt handler must be declared at the beginning of your application. For example:

```
dcl myHalt obj = _new_ myHalt();
```

Your program can instantiate multiple programHalt handlers, or your program may instantiate only one handler, but then call a second program that instantiates its own handler. The last programHalt handler that is instantiated is the *current* programHalt handler. Only the current programHalt handler is active at any one time.

SCL uses a stack to keep track of programHalt handlers. Each time a programHalt handler is instantiated, the new instance is pushed onto the stack. The handler on the top of the stack is always the active handler. Before a program terminates it must terminate (using the _term method) its programHalt handler. For example:

```
obj._term();
```

Terminating a programHalt handler pops it from the stack, and makes the next programHalt handler on the stack the active handler.

For example, if your program instantiates the programHalt handler, and then calls another SCL program, the second program may also instantiate a programHalt handler. The second programHalt handler becomes the current programHalt handler. Before the second program ends, it must terminate the second programHalt handler. The first programHalt handler then becomes the current programHalt handler. If the second programHalt handler is not terminated, it will remain active even after the program that instantiated it has terminated.

# Handling Exceptions with CATCH and THROW

All exceptions are subclasses of the SCLException class, which is a subclass of the SCLThrowable class. You can use the CLASS statement to define your own exception classes, and then use the THROW and CATCH statements to handle the exception.

Because an exception is a class, you can design the class to contain any information that is relevant to recovering from the specific exception. A simple exception class may contain only an error message. For example, the following class defines a subclass of SCLException called NewException, which defines an error message string named SecondaryMessage:

**Example Code 10.1**  NewException Class

```
Class NewException extends SCLException
   dcl string SecondaryMessage;
endclass;
```

You can then create a new instance of NewException and raise this exception with the THROW statement, as shown in the ThrowIt class:

**Example Code 10.2**  ThrowIt Class

```
Class ThrowIt;
  m: method;
  dcl NewException NE = _new_ NewException('Exception in method m');
  NE.SecondaryMessage = "There's no code in m!";
  throw NE;
  endmethod;
endclass;
```

*Note:*  You must always declare a variable to hold the thrown exception. △

The code that processes the exception is enclosed in CATCH blocks. CATCH blocks can contain any code needed to process the exception, including more CATCH and THROW statements.

When an exception is thrown, normal execution of the entry stops, and SCL begins looking for a CATCH block to process the thrown class. The CATCH block can contain any statements needed to process the exception. For example, the following code prints the stack traceback at the point of the throw.

```
do;
dcl NewException NE = new NewException('Exception in method m');
NE.SecondaryMessage = "There's no code in m!";
throw NE;

catch NE;
   put NE.getMessage();          /* Print exception information. */
   call putlist(NE.traceback);
   put NE.SecondaryMessage=;     /* Print secondary message. */
endcatch;
end;
```

*Note:*  CATCH blocks must always be enclosed in DO statements. △

The traceback information that is printed by this example is stored automatically by SCL when an exception is thrown. See "The SCLThrowable and SCLException Classes" on page 163 for more information.

*Note:*  When a CATCH block has finished executing, control transfers to the end of the current DO statement, and the program resumes normal execution. If no exception has been thrown and SCL encounters a CATCH block, control transfers to the end of the current DO statement and execution resumes at that location. Therefore, any SCL statements the occur between CATCH blocks or following the last CATCH block within the same DO group will never be executed. Any SCL statements within the DO group that are not part of a CATCH block but must execute must be entered at the beginning of the DO group. △

After an exception is processed, program execution continues normally.

## Example

Suppose you have the following class Y. This class defines a method called update that throws an exception that is an instance of the SCLException class.

```
import sashelp.classes;
class Y;
update: method;
   if (_self_.readOnly) then
      /* Throw an exception.  Set message via constructor. */
      throw _new_ SCLException('Cannot update when in ready-only mode');
endmethod;
endclass;
```

Class X defines method M, which declares a local variable to hold the exception, and then calls the update method, which throws the exception. The exception is then processed by the CATCH block for SCLE.

```
import sashelp.classes;
class X;
M: method;
   do;
   /* Declare the local exception variable. */
   dcl SCLException scle;
   dcl Y y = _new_ y();

   /* Call update method, which throws SCLEception. */
   y.update();

   /* Process the SCLException. */
   catch scle;
      /* Print exception information. */
      put scle.getMessage();
      call putlist(scle.traceback);
   endcatch;
   end;
endmethod;
endclass;
```

## How SCL Determines Which CATCH Block To Execute

SCL uses the scope of the DO group that contains the CATCH block and the class of the exception to determine which CATCH block to execute.

☐ SCL first looks in the scope of the DO group where the exception was initially thrown. If SCL does not find a corresponding CATCH block, it expands its search outward to the next enclosing DO group.

*Note:* If you are rethrowing an exception that has been thrown and caught at least once already, then SCL automatically passes the exception outside of the DO group where the exception was rethrown. △

SCL continues expanding the scope of its search until it finds a corresponding CATCH block or it has searched the current SCL entry. If the current SCL entry does not contain a CATCH block for the thrown class, then the exception is passed up the stack to the calling entry where the process is repeated. If the calling entry contains a CATCH statement for the thrown class, then execution resumes at the location of the CATCH statement. If the calling entry does not contain a CATCH statement for the thrown class, then the exception is passed up the stack until SCL finds a corresponding CATCH statement or until the stack is completely unwound. If SCL does not find a corresponding CATCH statement, then the exception is treated the same as a program halt.

☐ SCL uses the class hierarchy to determine which CATCH block to execute. Within the scope that it is currently searching, SCL chooses the CATCH block for the class that is most closely related to the class of the thrown exception. For example, if the current scope contains a CATCH block for the thrown class, then SCL will execute that CATCH block. If the current scope does not contain a CATCH block for the thrown class, but does contains a CATCH block for the parent class of the thrown exception, then SCL will execute the CATCH block for the parent class. If none of the CATCH blocks in the current scope are related to the thrown class, then SCL continues its search for an appropriate CATCH block.

Suppose that in addition to the NewException class (see Example Code 10.1 on page 159) you define a subclass of NewException called SubException:

**Example Code 10.3**   SubException Class

```
Class SubException extends NewException
   ...code to process SubExceptions...
endclass;
```

As with all exceptions, SCL first searches the current DO group for a CATCH block that is related to the thrown class. In this example, because NEsub is an instance of SubException and SubException is a subclass of NewException, SCL will execute the CATCH block for NE because it is in the scope of the current DO group. The CATCH block for NEsub is in a different scope (the outer DO group), so it will not be executed unless the CATCH block for NE is modified to rethrow (see "Catching and Rethrowing Exceptions" on page 162) the exception. If the CATCH block for NE rethrows the exception, then both CATCH blocks will be executed.

**Example Code 10.4**   Nested DO Statements

```
dcl NewException NE;
dcl SubException NEsub;

do;
   do;
   NEsub = _new_ SubException('Exception in method m');
   NEsub.SecondaryMessage = "There's no code in m!";
   throw NEsub;

   catch NE;
      put NE.getMessage();          /* Print exception information. */
      call putlist(NE.traceback);
      put NE.SecondaryMessage=;   /* Print secondary message. */
      /* Could rethrow the NEsub exception if needed. */
   endcatch;
   end;

/* The following CATCH block will not be executed */
/* unless the CATCH block for NE rethrows the exception. */
```

```
catch NEsub;
    ...code to process NEsub exceptions...
endcatch;
end;
```

## Catching and Rethrowing Exceptions

Each entry in the stack can process an exception and then pass it back up the stack by rethrowing it, which allows the calling entry to perform additional processing. Each entry can perform whatever processing is relevant to that entry.

```
do;
catch e1;
    ...process the exception...
    throw e1;  /* Rethrow the exception. */
endcatch;
end;
```

*Note:* If an exception is rethrown within a CATCH block, no CATCH block within the same scope can recatch the exception. The exception is passed out of the scope where it was thrown. △

If SCL finds a second CATCH block for E1 within the same SCL entry but outside of the scope of the DO group where the exception was thrown, then execution continues with that second CATCH block. If SCL does not find another CATCH block for E1 in that same SCL entry, then the exception is passed up the stack to the calling entry.

Suppose you have defined the NewException class (see Example Code 10.1 on page 159) and the ThrowIt class (see Example Code 10.2 on page 159). The following program section calls method M, which throws the exception NE. The two CATCH blocks catch, rethrow, and recatch the exception.

```
init:
dcl ThrowIt TI = _new_ThrowIt( );
dcl NewException NE;
do;
    do;
    TI.m( );

    catch NE;
        put 'caught it';
        throw NE;
    endcatch;
    end;

catch NE;
    put 'caught it again';
endcatch;
end;
return;
```

*Note:* You cannot define multiple CATCH blocks for the same exception within the same scope. △

## Nested CATCH Blocks

You can nest CATCH blocks. For example, suppose you define the class W as follows:

```
class w;
m: method n:num;
do;
dcl e1 e1;
dcl e2 e2;
    do;
    if (n < 0) then throw _new_ e2();
        else throw _new_ e1();
    catch e2;
        put 'caught inner e2';
        do;
        dcl e1 e1;
        if (n<0) then throw _new_ e2();
            else throw _new_ e1();
        catch e1;
            put 'caught inner e1';
        endcatch;
        end;
    endcatch;
    end;
    catch e1;
        put 'caught outer e1';
    endcatch;

    catch e2;
        put 'caught outer e2';
    endcatch;
end;
endmethod;
endclass;
```

If you invoke method M with a negative argument as in the following program section:

```
init:
dcl w w = _new_ w();
w.m(-2);
return;
```

then the output would be

```
caught inner e2
caught outer e2
```

## The SCLThrowable and SCLException Classes

All exceptions are subclasses of the SCLException class, which is a subclass of the SCLThrowable class. When an exception is thrown, SCL automatically stores the name of the entry that throws the exception, the line number where the throw occurs, and the stack traceback at the point of the throw. You can set the message attribute via the constructor when an instance of the exception is created. You can use the getMessage method to return the message.

**Example Code 10.5**  SCLThrowable Class

```
class SCLThrowable;
    public string(32767) message;
    public list traceback;  /* stack traceback */
    public string entry;    /* SCL entry name */
    public num line;        /* line number */

    SCLThrowable: public method s:string;
        message = s;
    endmethod;

    getMessage: public method return=string;
        return message;
    endmethod;
endclass;
```

**Example Code 10.6**  SCLException Class

```
class SCLException extends SCLThrowable;
    SCLException: public method /(state='o');
        _super("SCLException");
    endmethod;

    SCLException: public method s:string /(state='o');
        _super(s);
    endmethod;
endclass;
```

# CHAPTER
## *11*

# Using SAS Tables

# Introduction

SCL provides a group of features that can read or manipulate data stored in SAS tables. For example, you may want an SCL program to update one or more SAS tables, based on user transactions from a single user interface. For a data entry and retrieval system, you may want to use a secondary table to supplement the primary table. You might use the secondary table as a lookup table for sophisticated error checking and field validation. In addition, you may want to manipulate SAS tables to perform tasks like the following:

□ displaying table values in a window

□ creating a new table

□ copying, renaming, sorting, or deleting a table

□ indexing a SAS table.

Many functions that perform SAS table operations return a SAS software return code, called sysrc. Chapter 14, "SAS System Return Codes," on page 227 contains a list of return codes with a section for operations that are most commonly performed on SAS tables. You can check for these codes to write sophisticated error checking for your SCL programs.

The following sections describe the tasks that SCL programs can perform on SAS tables, along with summary information about the SCL function or routine to use to perform that task. These functions and routines are described in Chapter 16, "SAS Component Language Dictionary," on page 249.

# Accessing SAS Tables

Before an SCL program can access the values in a SAS table, a communication link must be established between SAS software, the SAS tables, and the SCL program. You link SAS software to the tables by assigning librefs to the data libraries in which the SAS tables are stored. You complete the communication by linking the SAS tables and the SCL program, using the OPEN function to open the SAS tables. (Some SCL routines, such as CALL FSEDIT and CALL FSVIEW automatically open the SAS table that they are displaying. Therefore, the OPEN function is not needed to open the specified table.)

# Assigning Librefs

SCL provides the LIBNAME function for assigning a libref in an SCL program. You can also assign librefs outside an SCL program that works with SAS tables by putting the appropriate LIBNAME statement in the application's start-up file, the autoexec file. For more information about assigning librefs outside an SCL program, see the SAS software documentation for your host operating system.

If you have SAS/SHARE software or SAS/CONNECT software installed at your location, you can also use Remote Library Services (RLS) to assign librefs. RLS gives your SCL applications "read" or "write" access to SAS tables, views and catalogs across hardware platforms and SAS releases. Once an RLS libref is established, the RLS functionality is transparent to SAS tables and views in SCL programs. Catalog compatibility across platforms is architecture dependent. For further information, see *SAS/SHARE User's Guide.*

# Opening SAS Tables

To open a SAS table, use the OPEN function. Opening a SAS table provides the gateway through which an SCL program and a SAS table can interact. This process does not actually access the information in a SAS table, but it makes the table available for the program's use. To access the data in the SAS table, the program must perform "read" operations on the table. When you open a SAS table, the following actions take place:

□ The SAS table data vector (TDV) for the table is created to store copies of the table's column values.

□ A unique numeric identifier is assigned to the SAS table. This identifier is used by other functions that manipulate data.

□ An access control level is assigned to the SAS table. This control level determines the level of access to the SAS table that is permitted to other users or applications that try to use the SAS table at the same time.

The identifier number identifies the table to the application, and you pass it to other SCL functions that manipulate the SAS table. Because this number is unique for each table that is currently open, it is useful for tracking multiple SAS tables that are open at the same time.

*Note:* If for some reason a SAS table cannot be opened, the OPEN function returns a value of 0 for the table identifier. Therefore, to determine whether a SAS table has been opened successfully, you should test the value of the return code for the OPEN function in your SCL program. Doing this ensures that you don't cause a program to halt by passing a 0 to another function that uses that SAS table identifier. To determine why the table could not be opened, use the SYSMSG function to retrieve the message that is associated with the return code. △

## Number of Open SAS Tables Allowed

An application can have a maximum of 999 SAS tables open simultaneously. However, your operating system may impose other limits. For details, see the documentation provided by the vendor for your operating system.

Although SCL permits you to have a large number of tables open simultaneously, be aware that memory is allocated for each SAS table from the time the SAS table is opened until it is closed. Therefore, try to minimize the number of tables that are open at the same time, and close them as soon as a program finishes with them for that session.

## SAS Table and SCL Data Vectors

When an application opens a SAS table, its TDV is empty. However, to enable the program to work with the SAS table columns, SCL provides functions for copying table rows one at a time from the SAS table to the TDV. Once column values for a row are in the TDV, you can copy these values into the SCL data vector (SDV), and the application can manipulate the column values.

Before you can display or manipulate the values of SAS table columns, those columns must be linked to SCL variables through the TDV and the SDV. Special SCL functions and storage locations facilitate the transfer of values between SAS table columns and SCL variables. Figure 11.1 on page 168 illustrates the SDV and TDV that are created for an application that opens a SAS table. This figure shows the paths that rows take when they are read from the table, displayed in the window, processed, and then returned to the table.

**Figure 11.1**   Path of Data in SAS Table "Read" and "Write" Operations

Two steps are required in order to transfer data from an open SAS table to an SCL program:

1   The values of the columns in a row in the open SAS table are copied into the TDV.

2   The values of the columns in the TDV are copied to the SDV, which contains all of the SCL variables (window variables, nonwindow variables, system variables, and so on). The transfer of data from the TDV to the SDV can be either automatic (when the SET routine is used) or under program control (when the GETVARC or GETVARN functions are used).

Once the values are in the SDV, you can manipulate them by using SCL statements. Two steps are also required in order to transfer data from an SCL program to an open SAS table:

1   The column values in the SDV are transferred to the TDV. The transfer of data from the SDV to the TDV can be either automatic (when the SET routine is used) or under program control (when PUTVARC or PUTVARN is used).

2   The values in the TDV are written to the columns in a row in the open table.

## Access Control Levels

When a SAS table is opened, SAS software determines the control level for the table. The control level determines the extent to which access to the table is restricted. For example, an application may be able to gain exclusive update access to the entire SAS table, or it may be able to gain exclusive update access to only the row that is currently in use. In either case, there are ramifications for any users or applications that need to access the SAS table at the same time. You can open a SAS table with one of the following control levels:

RECORD

provides exclusive update access only to the SAS table row that is currently in the TDV (as with the FETCH and FETCHOBS functions). With this control level, the same user can open the same SAS table multiple times (multiple concurrent access). In addition, if SAS/SHARE software is used, then multiple users can open the same SAS table simultaneously for browsing or for editing. For more information, see *SAS/SHARE User's Guide*.

MEMBER

provides exclusive update access to an entire SAS table. While this control level is in effect, no other user can open the table, and the same user cannot open the table multiple times.

## Specifying a Control Level

When you use the OPEN function to open a SAS data set in UPDATE mode, by default the table is opened with RECORD-level control. However, in SCL you can use the OPEN function with the SAS data set option CNTLLEV= to set the control level when a SAS table opens. See "OPEN" on page 576 for more information.

# Reading SAS Tables

You may want to use an SCL program to manipulate column values from SAS tables. For example, you may want to do one or more of the following:

□ display data values in a window

□ use the values in arithmetic calculations

□ determine data values before taking certain actions.

Before a program can manipulate the data, it must read the data from the table. After column values are changed, the program can update the values of columns in the table. In addition to updating existing column values, programs also can add new rows or delete obsolete rows.

After a SAS table is open, you can access any column value for any row in the SAS table. The first step in accessing the data involves reading (or copying) a row from the SAS table to the TDV—for example, by using the FETCH function. By default, the FETCH function starts with the first row in the SAS table and reads the next row from the SAS table each time it executes.

## Linking SAS Table Columns And SCL Variables

The next step in accessing the data is to link the SAS table columns in the TDV with the SCL window variables and nonwindow variables in the SDV. The function that you use depends on whether the SCL variables and SAS table columns have the same name and type. If an application has some SCL variables that match SAS table columns and others that do not, then you can use a combination of these techniques.

### Matched Column and Variable Names

If columns of a SAS table and SCL variables have the same names and types, then you can use the SET routine to link all of them automatically with a single program statement. The SET routine is typically invoked immediately following the OPEN function.

*Note:* If you use the SET routine and then also use the PUTVARC or PUTVARN routine for an SCL variable that has a matching SAS table column, the SET routine overrides the PUTVARC or PUTVARN routine. Doing this is inefficient because duplicate actions are performed. △

## Unmatched Column and Variable Names

When the SCL variables do not have the same names or types as SAS table columns, you must use a GETVARC or GETVARN statement (for character and numeric values, respectively) for each unmatched column to link them from the TDV to the SDV. Once the columns have been manipulated, use an individual PUTVARC or PUTVARN routine to link each one from the SDV back to the TDV.

*Note:* The GETVARC and GETVARN functions establish only a temporary link between a SAS table column and an SCL variable. When the statement executes, the columns are linked. After the statement executes, the link is terminated. Therefore, you must use the GETVARC or GETVARN function one time for each SAS table column that you want to link. This is different from the SET routine, which establishes a permanent link between any matching SAS table and SCL variables until the open SAS table is closed. △

## Determining a Column's Position in a SAS Table

Some functions, such as GETVARC, GETVARN, PUTVARC and PUTVARN, require the position of a column in the SAS table row. Use the VARNUM function to determine the position, and then use the position repeatedly throughout your program. The following example uses the VARNUM function to determine the position of several columns. After the column positions have been determined, the program links to a labeled section called GETVALUE to determine the column values.

```
INIT:
    control enter;
    houses=open('sasuser.houses','u');
    if (houses=0) then _msg_=sysmsg();
    else
        do;
            vtype=varnum(houses,'style');
            vsize=varnum(houses,'sqfeet');
            vbedrms=varnum(houses,'bedrooms');
            vbathrms=varnum(houses,'baths');
            vaddress=varnum(houses,'street');
            vcost=varnum(houses,'price');
            link getvalue;
        end;
return;

MAIN:
    ...more SCL statements...
return;

TERM:
    if (houses>0) then rc=close(houses);
return;

GETVALUE:
    rc=fetch(houses);
    type=getvarc(houses,vtype);
```

```
      size=getvarn(houses,vsize);
      bedrms=getvarn(houses,vbedrms);
      bathrms=getvarn(houses,vbathrms);
      address=getvarc(houses,vaddress);
      cost=getvarn(houses,vcost);
   return;
```

## Using Table-Lookup Techniques

Table lookup, the process of looking up data in a data structure, has several useful applications for data entry applications. For example, you may want to display certain information in a window based on a value that a user has entered. If this information is stored in another SAS table, then you can use table-lookup techniques to read and display this information. In addition, you can use table lookup to perform field validation by ensuring that a value entered by a user is a value that is contained in a specified SAS table.

To validate a field value, you can use the LOCATEC, LOCATEN, or WHERE function to search a secondary SAS table for a specific character or numeric value that has been entered by a user. For example, you might want to make sure that users enter names that exist in another SAS table. You also can use these techniques to display text from a secondary SAS table, based on values that users enter in the fields. For example, when a user enters a valid name in the **Employee Name** field, you can look up the associated sales region and sales to date in the secondary SAS table and then display this information in the window.

# Controlling Access to SAS Table Rows

For many applications, you may want an SCL program to read from a SAS table only the rows that meet a set of search conditions. For example, if you have a SAS table that contains sales records, you may want to read just the subset of records for which the sales are greater than $300,000 but less than $600,000. To do this, you can use WHERE clause processing, which is a set of conditions that rows must meet in order to be processed. In WHERE clause processing, you can use either permanent or temporary WHERE clauses.

## Permanently Subsetting Data

A permanent WHERE clause applies a set of search conditions that remain in effect until the SAS table is closed. You might use a permanent WHERE clause to improve the efficiency of a program by reading only a subset of the rows in a SAS table. You might also want to use a permanent WHERE clause in applications when you want to limit the SAS table rows that are accessible, or visible, to users. For example, if you are working with a large SAS table, users may not need access to all the rows to use your application. Or, for security reasons, you may want to restrict access to a set of rows that meet certain conditions.

SCL provides several features that enable you to subset a SAS table based on specified search conditions. To apply a permanent WHERE clause to a SAS table, you can use the SAS data set option WHERE= with the OPEN function. For example, the following WHERE clause selects only the records for which the sales are greater than $300,000 but less than $600,000:

```
/* Open the SAS table and display a  */
/* subset of the SAS table rows      */
salesid=open
  ("sample.testdata(where=((sales > 300000)"||
                "and (sales < 600000)))",'i');
```

You can also use the WHERE= option in SCL with the FSEDIT and FSVIEW routines.

## Temporarily Subsetting Data

In addition to restricting access to SAS table rows, you may want to enable users to subset the accessible records even further. In this case, you can use the WHERE function to apply a temporary WHERE clause. A temporary WHERE clause applies a set of search conditions that can be modified or canceled by subsequent SCL statements. For example, you could apply a temporary WHERE clause like the following:

```
rc=where(dsid,'SSN='||ssn);
```

When a SAS table is indexed, you can use the SETKEY function for subsetting. For example, if a SAS table is indexed on the column SSN, you could use:

```
rc=setkey(dsid,'SSN','eq');
```

## Searching with WHERE versus LOCATEC or LOCATEN

You can search efficiently with the WHERE function if you are working with a large SAS table that is indexed by the column or columns for which you are searching. It is also appropriate to use the WHERE function when you are using an expression that involves several columns to locate rows.

However, you can use LOCATEC or LOCATEN to find a row when one or more of the following conditions are met:

□ The SAS table is small.

□ You are searching for one row that meets a single search condition (for example, the row that contains a particular name).

□ You are looking for one row that meets a single search condition in a large SAS table, if the SAS table is sorted by the column for which you are searching, and if you are using the more efficient binary search. See the following section for more information.

## Searching Efficiently

By default, LOCATEC and LOCATEN search a SAS table sequentially. However, a sequential search is not always the most efficient way to locate a particular row, especially if your SAS table has been sorted. If a SAS table has already been sorted by the column for which you want to search, you can specify a faster, more efficient binary search. For a binary search, use an additional optional argument with LOCATEC or LOCATEN to specify the order in which the SAS table has been sorted (A for ascending order or D for descending order). For example, assuming that the SAS table MYSCHOOL.CLASS has been sorted in ascending order by NAME, you can use the following statements to perform a binary search:

```
dsid=open('myschool.class');
vnum=varnum(dsid,'name');
```

```
sname='Gail';
val=locatec(dsid,vnum,sname,'a');
```

## Undoing WHERE Clauses

WHERE clauses impose certain restrictions on other SCL functions that manipulate data. Therefore, in some cases, you may need to undo a WHERE clause in an SCL program before using other functions. When you specify a WHERE clause, the WHERE conditions replace the conditions that were specified in the previous WHERE clause. However, you can augment a WHERE condition with the ALSO keyword. For example, the following WHERE clause adds the condition of "age greater than 15" to an existing WHERE clause:

```
rc=where(dsid,'also age > 15');
```

To undo the condition that was added by the ALSO keyword, you could use the following statement:

```
rc=where(dsid,'undo');
```

To undo (or delete) a *temporary* WHERE clause, use the WHERE function and specify only the SAS table identifier argument. This process undoes all temporary WHERE clauses that are currently in effect.

# Changing the Sequence of Reading Rows

When an application displays a subset of a SAS table, you may want to let users display and scroll through all rows that meet the search conditions. To do this, you can use a set of SCL functions that reread table rows. For example, when a program displays the first row that meets the conditions, SCL provides functions that you can use to mark the row. Then a user can continue to search the rest of the SAS table for any other rows that meet the search conditions, counting them along the way. After finding the last row that meets the search conditions, the user can redisplay the first row in the subset (the row that was marked earlier). The following sequence of steps implements this technique:

1 Use the NOTE function to mark a row in the subset for later reading.

2 Use the POINT function to return to the marked row after you have located all rows that meet the search conditions.

3 Use the DROPNOTE function to delete the NOTE marker and free the memory used to store the note after the program finishes using the noted row.

# Updating SAS Tables

When a table row is read, its data follow a path from the SAS table through the TDV to the SDV, where finally they can be manipulated. After the data is manipulated, it must follow the reverse path from the SDV through the TDV back to the SAS table. If you use the SET routine to link the values from the TDV to the SDV, then any changed values are automatically linked from the SDV back to the TDV. If you do not use SET, then you must explicitly copy the value of each variable to the TDV. In either case, you use the UPDATE function to copy the values from the TDV to the SAS table.

## Appending Rows

To add new rows to a SAS table rather than updating the existing rows, use the APPEND function. If the SCL variables have the same name and type as the SAS table columns and you use the SET routine to link them, then using the APPEND function is straightforward, and the values are automatically written from the TDV to the SAS table.

*Note:*   If the program does not use the SET routine, or if the APPEND function is used with the NOSET option, a blank row is appended to the SAS table. This is a useful technique for appending rows when the SCL program or the window variables do not match the SAS table columns. For example, when the SET routine is not used, you would use a sequence of statements like those below to append a blank row and then update it with values. △

```
rc=append(dsid);
...PUTVARC or PUTVARN program statement(s)...
rc=update(dsid);
```

## Deleting Rows

To delete rows from a SAS table, use the DELOBS function. In order to use this function, the SAS table must be open in UPDATE mode. The DELOBS function performs the following tasks:

□ marks the row for deletion from the SAS table. However, the row is still physically in the SAS table.

□ prevents any additional editing of the row. Once a row has been marked for deletion, it cannot be read.

## Remaining Rows Not Renumbered

Although deleted rows are no longer accessible, all other rows in the SAS table retain their original physical row numbers. Therefore, it is important to remember that a row's physical number may not always coincide with its relative position in the SAS table. For example, the FETCHOBS function treats a row value as a relative row number. If row 2 is marked for deletion and you use FETCHOBS to read the third row, FETCHOBS reads the third *non-deleted* row—in this case, row 4. However, you can use FETCHOBS with the ABS option to count deleted rows.

Non-deleted rows are intentionally not renumbered so that you can continue to use row numbers as pointers. This is important when you are using the FSEDIT procedure or subsequent SAS statements that directly access table rows by number, such as the POINT= option in a SAS language SET statement.

You can control row renumbering if necessary. See the next section for details.

## Renumbering Rows

To renumber accessible SAS table rows, an SCL program must use one of the following techniques to process the SAS table:

□ Sort the table, using either the SORT function in SCL or the SORT procedure. If the SAS table is already in sorted order, then you must use the FORCE option.

*Note:* The SORT function and PROC SORT do not sort and replace an indexed SAS table unless you specify the FORCE option, because sorting destroys indexes for a SAS table. △

☐ Copy the table, using either the COPY function in SCL or the COPY procedure. In this case, the input and output tables must be different. The output table is the only one that is renumbered.

☐ Read the remaining data table rows, using the SAS language SET statement in a DATA step (not the SCL SET statement), and write these rows to a data table. To avoid exiting from SCL, you can use a submit block. For example:

```
houseid=open('sasuser.houses','u');
   ...SCL statements that read rows and delete rows...
submit continue;
   data sasuser.houses;
      set sasuser.houses;
   run;
endsubmit;
```

# Closing SAS Tables

After an SCL program has finished using a SAS table, the program should close the table with the CLOSE function at the appropriate point in your program. If a SAS table is still open when an application ends, SAS software closes it automatically and displays a warning message. In general, the position of the CLOSE function should correspond to the position of the OPEN function, as follows:

☐ If the OPEN function is in the initialization section, then put the CLOSE function in the termination section.

☐ If the OPEN function is in MAIN, then put the CLOSE function in MAIN.

*Note:* If you're designing an application system in which more than one program uses a particular SAS table, and if the identifier for this table can be passed to subsequent programs, then close the SAS table in the termination section of the program that uses the table last. △

# Determining Attributes of SAS Tables and Columns

SCL provides features for determining characteristics (or attributes) of the SAS table or columns with which a program is working. For example, one approach is to open a table, determine how many columns are in the table, and then set up a program loop that executes once for each column. The loop can query the attributes of each column. To do this, the program needs to determine how many columns are in the SAS table, as well as the name, type, length, format, informat, label, and position of each column.

## Querying Attributes of SAS Tables

SAS tables have a variety of numeric and character attributes associated with them. These attributes can provide some basic information to your SCL program. For example, to determine the number of columns in an existing SAS table, use the NVARS argument with the ATTRN function. For a list of other table attributes and how to retrieve them, see "ATTRC and ATTRN" on page 258.

## Querying Attributes of SAS Table Columns

Columns in a SAS table also have several attributes that your program may need to query. Here is a list of column attributes and the SCL functions that you can use to retrieve those attributes:

| | |
|---|---|
| name | VARNAME function |
| number | VARNUM function |
| data type | VARTYPE function |
| length | VARLEN function |
| label | VARLABLE function |
| format | VARFMT function |
| informat | VARINFMT function. |

## Defining New Columns

After determining the name, type, length, label, format, and informat of each column, you can add a new column that has these attributes to the column list for a new SAS table. To do this, first use the OPEN function with the **N** argument (for NEW mode), and then use the NEWVAR function.

*CAUTION:*

**Your program should check to see whether the SAS table exists before opening it in NEW mode.** When used with the **N** argument (for NEW mode), the OPEN function replaces an existing SAS table that has the same name. If you do not want to delete an existing SAS table by opening it in NEW mode, then use the EXIST function to confirm that the table does not exist before using OPEN to create a new SAS table.  △

# Performing Other SAS Table Operations

There are other SCL functions that you can use to perform operations on SAS tables. The tasks that you can perform, along with the function to use, are as follows:

- □ To copy a table, use the COPY function. By default, if the target file already exists, the COPY function replaces that file without warning. To avoid unintentionally overwriting existing files, your program should use the EXIST function to determine whether the target file exists before executing the COPY function. (You can use COPY with a WHERE clause to create a new table that contains a subset of the rows in the original table.)

- □ To create a new table, use the OPEN function with the **N** option. (The table must be closed and then reopened in UPDATE mode if the program will update it). Then, use NEWVAR to create columns.

- □ To enable users to create a new table interactively, use the NEW function.

- □ To enable users to create a new table interactively from an external file, use the IMPORT function or the IMPORT wizard.

□ To delete a table, use the DELETE function. (The table must be closed).

□ To rename a table, use the RENAME function. (The table must be closed.)

□ To sort a table, use the SORT function. (The table must be open in UPDATE mode.)

# Preserving the Integrity of Data

SCL provides a group of functions that specify and enforce integrity constraints for SAS tables. Integrity constraints preserve the consistency and correctness of stored data, and they are automatically enforced for each addition, update, and deletion activity for a SAS table to which the constraints have been assigned. For such a table, value changes must satisfy the conditions that have been specified with constraints.

There are two basic types of integrity constraints: general constraints and referential constraints. The following list shows the specific types of integrity restraints that you can apply through SCL. The first four items are general constraints, which control values in a single SAS table. The last item is a referential constraint, which establishes a parent-child relationship between columns in two or more SAS tables.

□ A column can contain only non-null values.

□ A column can contain only values that fall within a specific set, range, or list of values, or that duplicate a value in another column in the same row.

□ A column can contain only values that are unique.

□ A column that is a primary key can contain only values that are unique and that are not missing values.

□ A column that is a foreign key (the child) can contain only values that are present in the associated primary key (the parent) or null values. A column that is a primary key can contain only values that cannot be deleted or changed unless the same deletions or changes have been made in values of the associated foreign key. Values of a foreign key can be set to null, but values cannot be added unless they also exist in the associated primary key.

SCL provides the following functions for creating and enforcing integrity constraints:

ICCREATE
  creates and specifies integrity constraints for a SAS table.

ICDELETE
  drops an integrity constraint.

ICTYPE
  returns the type of constraint that is assigned to a SAS table.

ICVALUE
  returns the varlist or WHERE clause that is associated with an integrity constraint.

For more information about integrity constrains, see *SAS/SHARE User's Guide*.

# Manipulating SAS Table Indexes

When you develop an application that creates a SAS table, you may want to give users the option of creating an index for the table. An index, which provides fast access to rows, is an auxiliary data structure that specifies the location of rows, based on the values of one or more columns, known as key columns. Both compressed and uncompressed SAS tables can be indexed by one or more columns to aid in the subsetting, grouping, or joining of rows. SAS table indexes are particularly useful for optimizing WHERE clause processing.

SCL provides a set of functions for creating and manipulating SAS table indexes. However, SCL functions are just one way of building and querying SAS table indexes. Other ways include:

- the DATASETS procedure in base SAS software
- the INDEX= option (when you are creating a SAS table)
- the SQL procedure in base SAS software.

There are two types of indexes: simple indexes and composite indexes. A simple index is an index on a single column, and a composite index is an index on more than one column. A SAS table can have multiple simple indexes, multiple composite indexes, or a combination of simple and composite indexes.

SCL provides the following functions for manipulating indexes:

ICREATE
: creates an index for SAS tables that are open in UTILITY mode.

IVARLIST
: returns a list of one or more columns that have been indexed for the specified key in the table.

ISINDEX
: returns the type of index for a column in a SAS table, as follows:

| | |
|---|---|
| BOTH | The column is a member of both simple and composite indexes. |
| COMP | The column is a member of a composite index. |
| REG | The column is a member of a regular (simple) index. |
| (blank) | No index has been created for the specified column. |

IOPTION
: returns a character string that consists of the options for the specified key and index columns. The options are separated by blanks.

IDELETE
: deletes an index for a SAS table that is open in UTILITY mode. You can delete an index when a program finishes with it, or if you find that the index is not operating efficiently. Keep in mind that indexes are not always advantageous. Sometimes the costs outweigh the savings. For a detailed discussion of when to use indexes, see the information about SAS files in *SAS Language Reference: Concepts*.

CHAPTER

*12*

# Using External Files

## Introduction

In addition to using SCL to manipulate SAS tables, you can use it to manipulate external files. External files are files that are created and maintained on a host operating system (for example, files that you have created with your system editor or files in which you have stored the output of SAS procedures). They have different internal formats than SAS files.

When you use external files to store data or other information, you can use SCL functions to read, update, and write information to new files, and to perform utility operations on existing files. These functions enable you to create SCL programs that do the following:

☐ read values from external files for field validation

☐ manipulate data values that your site maintains in external files

☐ write information in a form that can be read by applications that were created with the software of other vendors.

*Note:* Your operating system maintains groups of external files in an aggregate storage location, which this book calls a directory. However, your operating system may identify these locations with different names (for example, folder, subdirectory, partitioned data set, or MACLIB). If you need more information, see the SAS documentation for your operating environment. △

Ordinarily, you must use a logical name called a fileref to identify the location of an external file to SAS software. SCL allows you to assign a fileref to a directory and then to open and perform operations on as many of its files as the program requires.

Many functions that perform external file operations return a SAS system return code, called *sysrc*. Chapter 14, "SAS System Return Codes," on page 227 contains a list of return codes with a section for operations that are commonly performed on external files. You can check for these codes to write more sophisticated error checking for your SCL programs.

# Accessing External Files

Before SCL programs can work with external files, you must establish a communication link between SAS software, the file, and your SCL program. You start the communication link by assigning a fileref to the file, which links the file to SAS software. You complete the communication link by using an SCL function to open the file, which links the file to the SCL program. SCL also enables you to establish this communication link between SAS software, a directory, and your SCL program. Your program can then use any file in that directory without assigning a fileref to it. This can make it easier for you to process multiple files in the same directory.

# Assigning Filerefs

To establish the communication between SAS software and an external file, you must assign a fileref to the file with the FILENAME function. If an application requires that users specify the name of the physical file, then create a block of SCL code labeled with a window variable name to run only when a user enters a filename in that field. You can also put the FILENAME function in the MAIN section so that it executes after a user specifies the filename. In this case, add a statement to check that the field containing the filename has been modified so that the FILENAME function does not run every time the MAIN section runs. When a program can specify the name of the physical file without user input, put the function in the initialization section so that the function executes only once, before the window opens.

You can also assign filerefs outside of an application when files are used by all or large parts of your application. You assign filerefs to these files by using the FILENAME statement in base SAS in the application's start-up file (the autoexec file). For more information about assigning filerefs, see the SAS documentation for your operating environment.

There are other SCL functions that you can use to manipulate filerefs. Use these functions to prevent programs from terminating prematurely because of possible errors (for example, a fileref is already assigned or a physical file does not exist).

□ Use the FILEREF function to verify that a fileref has been assigned to a physical file for the current SAS session or process.

□ Use the FEXIST function to verify that the file associated with a specified fileref exists.

□ Use the FILEEXIST function to verify that the file associated with a physical name exists.

# Opening Files

To complete the communication link between an application and an external file, use the FOPEN function to open the file. Opening a file does not access the information in the file. It simply makes the file available to the program.

When you open an external file, a unique identifier is assigned to the external file. This identifier is used by any other SCL functions that manipulate the file. In addition, a temporary storage buffer is automatically created for the external file. This storage area is used to store copies of file records.

The FOPEN function returns the program's identification number for that file. This unique number is called the file identifier. You use this identifier by storing it in an SCL variable and passing the variable name as an argument to all the SCL functions that manipulate that file or directory. This technique enables you to open and manipulate multiple files at the same time and to clearly identify which file to manipulate.

When you open a file, you specify an open mode. The open mode determines the actions that can be performed on the file. With the FOPEN function, you can also specify the file's record length. If you specify a record length of 0, the existing record length is used. For details about the modes and record lengths and how to specify them, see "FOPEN" on page 420.

## Making an Open File Available to Other Programs

After you open an external file, its contents are available to all programs in your application. However, you must link the file to the programs by using one of the following techniques to pass them the variable that contains the file identifier.

□ You can pass the file identifier as a parameter to other programs by using the parameter-passing mechanism of the DISPLAY or METHOD routine with the ENTRY or METHOD statement. This is the preferred method.

□ You can store the file identifier value by using the SETPARMID routine, and you can retrieve it by using the GETPARMID function. This method limits you to passing only one file identifier at a time.

□ You can pass the file identifier value as a macro variable by using the SYMPUTN routine, and you can retrieve it by using the SYMGETN function.

□ You can pass the file identifier as an item in the local environment list. For details about this list, see Chapter 5, "SCL Lists," on page 47.

## Number of Open Files Allowed

SCL allows a maximum of 999 external files to be open simultaneously in an application. However, your operating system may impose other limits. For further details, refer to the documentation provided by the vendor for your operating system.

Although SCL allows you to have a large number of files open simultaneously, you should be aware that memory is allocated for each file from the time the file is opened until it is closed. Therefore, you should try close files as soon as your program is finished with them.

# File Data Buffers and SCL Data Vectors

When an SCL program starts executing, an SCL Data Vector (SDV) is created for the program. The SDV contains temporary storage areas for the program's SCL variables. Values of program variables are manipulated and stored in the SDV before they are written to or deleted from an external file. When an external file is opened, a temporary storage buffer called the file data buffer (FDB) is created for it. The FDB is the length of the file's records, and it is empty until a record is read from the file. A "read" function copies a record from the file into the FDB. A "write" function moves the contents of the FDB to a record in the physical file and clears the file's FDB. Once a record is in the FDB, it remains there until the record is written back to the file, until another record is read in, or until the file is closed.

Figure 12.1 on page 182 illustrates the SDV and the FDB for an application that uses an external file. This figure shows the paths that file records take when they are read from the file, displayed in the window, processed, and then returned to the file.

**Figure 12.1**   Path of Data in File "Read" and "Write" Operations

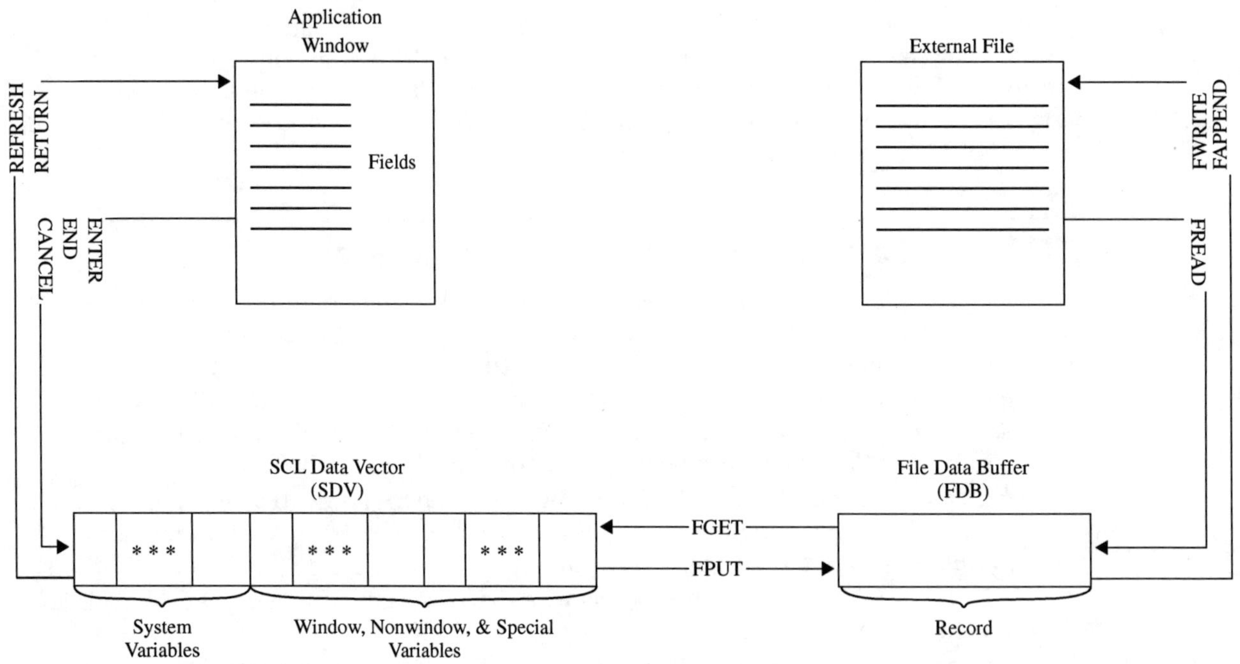

Application Window

External File

REFRESH
RETURN

Fields

FWRITE
FAPPEND

ENTER
END
CANCEL

FREAD

SCL Data Vector (SDV)

File Data Buffer (FDB)

***   ***   ***

FGET

FPUT

System Variables

Window, Nonwindow, & Special Variables

Record

# Reading Values from External Files

Before an SCL program can use the information in an external file, the program must read the file's records. For example, an application may need to use external file records to do the following:

□ display the values for users to browse or edit

□ modify existing values

□ add new values or records

□ delete values or records.

In order to read record values from the external file, your SCL program must first copy a record from the file into the FDB. Then it must copy the contents of the FDB into the SDV to make the values available to your SCL program. A value can be either part of a record or an entire record. Unless you must read values separately for some reason, reading an entire record as a single value is the easier technique to use. To complete the process of reading values from an open file, follow these steps:

1  A record must be copied from the file to the FDB. Use the FREAD function to copy the values to the FDB, starting at the file's first record and reading each record sequentially.

2  Each value in the record must be copied from the FDB to the SDV, where the value can be used by the application. Use the FGET function to copy the contents of the FDB (interpreted as values) to the SDV.

## Order of Reading Records

Many types of external files can be read only sequentially, from the first record to the last. However, when a file supports random access, you can use SCL functions to change that sequence and either reread a particular record or start at the first record and reread the entire file. For more information, see "Changing the Sequence of Reading Records" on page 185.

## Reading Record Values into the SDV

When the FGET function reads values from the FDB into the SDV, it makes the contents of the FDB available to the SCL program. You can control how this step processes the contents of the FDB by reading the FDB contents either as one single value or as a series of separate values. Reading the contents of the FDB as a single value can simplify your program. To do this, you can design a single control or field in the window to display the entire contents of the record. If you need to read record values into separate window variables, you can read the FDB contents as a single value into a program variable in the SDV. Then, you can use SAS character functions (like SCAN or SUBSTR) to assign parts of that program variable to window variables. The following example finds the length of a record and then reads the entire record as a single value into the window variable ROW.

```
length=finfo(fileid,'lrecl');
reclen=inputn(length,'best.');
rc=fget(fileid,row,reclen);
```

If ROW is a nonwindow variable instead of a window variable, then values that are read from the FDB are in the SDV, but they are not displayed in the window until they are assigned to a window variable.

*Note:*  The code in the preceding example is host specific. See the SAS documentation for your operating environment for more information. △

You determine whether the contents are treated as one value or as a series of values. There is a column pointer in the FDB that is set to 1 when the contents are read. By default, the FGET function copies the value from the current position of the column pointer to the next separator character. The default separator character is one blank. Therefore, the default action of the FGET function is to copy the value from the current position of the column pointer to the next blank. (To designate a different character as the separator character, use the FSEP function).

After each FGET function, the column pointer is positioned one column past the last character that was read. When the FDB contains no more values, the FGET function returns −1 to signal that it has reached the end of the FDB.

## Reading Records as Separate Values

Reading the contents of the FDB as a series of separate values brings up a different set of considerations. Your applications must process a specified number of file values and display them in window variables of a particular size. Also, in order to read separate values, you need to know more about the external files that your application will process. You need to know how many values a record contains, and it is helpful if you know the starting columns for the values or the characters that separate the values. Finally, you need to define separate controls or fields to display the values.

When you read the FDB contents as separate values, you can locate these values by positioning the FDB column pointer at the column where the value begins or by specifying the character that separates these values. By default, the separator character for file records is a blank.

## Identifying a Value's Starting Column

When you know the numbers of the columns where the values start, you can use the FPOS function to move the "read" pointer to the column where the next value begins. When the FPOS and FGET functions are used together, the FPOS function sets the starting column for the FGET function, which reads the FDB contents up to the next separator character unless a length is specified.

The following example shows how to read separate values when you know the numbers of the columns where the values start. This example reads record values into the variables NAME, HEIGHT, and WEIGHT by using the FPOS function to specify the position of the "read" pointer.

```
rc=fget(fileid,name,20);
rc=fpos(fileid,21);
rc=fget(fileid,height);
rc=fpos(fileid,28);
rc=fget(fileid,weight);
```

# Modifying External Files

An application can enable users to modify the values in external files interactively. External files can be modified by updating existing records, by adding new records, or by deleting records. To store record values in external files, you can use functions to update the FDB with values that are stored in window variables or program variables. When you write the contents of the FDB to a file, you can update an existing record, or you can append the record at the end of the file.

## Writing Modified Records or New Records to a File

In order to return values to a file that is open for writing, an application must do the following:

1 Write each value from a window or program variable. Use the FPUT function to copy values from the SDV to the FDB.

2 Write record values from the FDB to the external file. Use the FWRITE or FAPPEND function to write the current values to the external file and to clear the FDB.

Some operating systems do not allow new records to be appended to external files. For example, you cannot append records to members of partitioned data sets under the OS/390 operating system. If you use this type of operating system, you can append records to files by maintaining blank records in the file, usually at the end of the file. Then, when you want to add a record, you can update an existing blank record.

After a value is written to the FDB with the FPUT function, the column pointer moves to the first column following that value.

To return modified records as updates to the file's records, use the FWRITE function to overwrite each record in the physical file with the contents of the FDB. After the FDB contents are written to the file, the FDB's column pointer is positioned in column 1, and the FDB is filled with blanks.

# Closing Files

You should close an external file or directory when your application is finished with it. To close a file, use the FCLOSE function. To close a directory, use the DCLOSE function. Ordinarily, when you open a file or directory in the initialization section for the window, you close it in the window's termination section. When you open a file or directory in MAIN, you also close it in MAIN.

# Changing the Sequence of Reading Records

To start reading a file from its beginning, you can move the "read" pointer to the first record in a file. Then, the next FGET or FPUT function manipulates the first record. To return the "read" pointer to the file's first record, use the FREWIND function.

In addition to reading records sequentially, you can generally designate records for later reading, or you can re-read a file's first record. However, some file types do not support this feature.

When a record is in the FDB, you can mark it so that the "read" pointer can read it later. For example, because there are no search functions for files, you may want to mark a found record so you can use it again. To designate a record for later reading, perform these steps:

1 Use FNOTE to mark the record that is in the FDB for later reading.

2 Use FPOINT to return the "read" pointer to the marked record when you are ready to read it.

3 Use FREAD to read the record marked by the "read" pointer.

4 After you are finished using the marked record, use DROPNOTE to delete the note marker and to free the memory that was allocated to store the note.

# Other Manipulations for External Files

There are other SCL functions that enable you to determine the names and values of attributes that your operating system maintains for external files. These functions are listed in the following sections and are described completely in the appropriate entry in Chapter 16, "SAS Component Language Dictionary," on page 249.

## Determining Attributes and Attribute Values

Files and directories have several operating system attributes that are assigned and maintained by the file management system (for example, the date modified and name attributes). These attributes can vary among operating systems and are described in the SAS documentation for your operating environment. You can use the following SCL functions to determine the attributes and attribute values for external files:

FOPTNUM               reports the number of attributes maintained for files in your operating system.

FOPTNAME              returns the name of a file attribute.

FINFO                 returns the value of a file attribute.

## Determining Information about an FDB

You can also use SCL functions to find a file's record length and the position of the column pointer in the FDB.

FRLEN         returns the length of a record in the FDB.

FCOL          returns the position of the column pointer in the FDB.

## Renaming and Deleting an External File

You can use SCL functions to rename or delete an external file.

DELETE        delete an external file.
FDELETE

RENAME        renames an external file.

# Reading and Modifying Files in the Same Directory

To assign a fileref to a directory, use the FILENAME function, just as you would to assign a fileref to a file. Before you can perform operations on multiple files in a directory, you must open the directory, just as you open an external file. To open a directory, use the DOPEN function.

## Determining the Number of Files in a Directory

To find out the name of a file in a directory, you must know the number of files in the directory. You can determine that number by using the DNUM function.

In a program that displays the filenames in an extended table or in an SCL list, you use the value returned by the DNUM function to determine how many rows to display in the extended table or list.

## Finding the Names of Files

After you find the number of files in the directory, you can use the DREAD function to read their names.

If you are using DREAD in a program that is not for an extended table, put the function in a DO loop so that it processes from 1 to the value returned by the DNUM function, as follows:

```
dirid=dopen(fileref);
numfiles=dnum(dirid);
do i=1 to numfiles;
   name=dread(dirid,i);
...more SCL statements...
end;
```

## Manipulating Files in an Open Directory

When you open and close files in a directory that you opened with the DOPEN function, you can manipulate any of the files without assigning a fileref to each file. To use this technique, you must

- □ open the file
- □ manipulate the file's records
- □ close the file.

## Opening Files in an Open Directory

To open a file in a directory that you opened with the DOPEN function, use the MOPEN function. This function returns a file identifier. You can use this identifier with any function that uses a file identifier value returned by the FOPEN function. That is, you can use any SCL file function on any file that you have opened with the MOPEN function. For example, when you open files with the MOPEN function, you use the FCLOSE function to close the files.

## Closing Files in an Open Directory

When your program is finished with a file in an open directory, you must close that file. To close a file, use the FCLOSE function.

## Changing All the Files in a Directory

When you use the directory and file functions, you can create applications that enable users to make a change in each file in a directory. For example, you might want to change a date or multiply all the salaries by the same percentage when everyone represented in the file receives the same percentage raise in pay.

To make the same change to all the files in a directory, first pass the directory name to the FILENAME function, and then use the DOPEN function to open the directory. Then, follow these steps:

1  Use the DNUM function to return the number of files in the directory. Use the number as the end of a DO loop that processes each file.

2  Use the DREAD function to read the name of a file for each repetition of the loop.

3  Use the MOPEN function to open the file.

4  Use the FREAD function to read a record from the file.

5  Use the FPOS function to move the FDB column pointer to the value's start column.

6  Use the FGET function to copy data from the File Data Buffer (FDB) and to assign it to the specified character variable.

7  Use the FPOS function to return the FDB column pointer to the value's start column.

8  Use the FPUT function to write the modified value back to the FDB.

9  Use the FWRITE function to write the modified record back to the external file.

10 Use the FCLOSE function to close the file at the end of the processing loop.

## Creating a Subdirectory

You can use the DCREATE function to create a subdirectory.

## Closing a Directory

When your application is finished with the files in a directory, you should close the directory. To close a directory, use the DCLOSE function.

*CAUTION:*

**Be careful to complete operations on all files before closing the directory.** When you use the MOPEN function to open files, be sure your program completes its operations on all the directory's files before you use the DCLOSE function. When you use the DCLOSE function, SCL closes all the directory's files that were opened previously with the MOPEN function. △

## Other Manipulations for Directories

The following SCL functions provide additional information about directory attributes:

| | |
|---|---|
| DOPTNUM | reports the number of directory attributes available for a file. |
| DOPTNAME | returns the name of a directory attribute for a file. |
| DINFO | returns the value of a directory attribute for a file. |

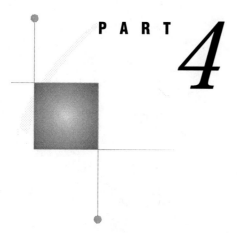

PART *4*

# Reference

CHAPTER

*13*

# The SCL Debugger

## Overview of SCL Debugger Features and Capabilities

The SAS Component Language Debugger (SCL Debugger) is a powerful window-oriented utility that can interactively monitor the execution of SCL programs, enabling you to locate run-time errors. The SCL debugger also enables you to suspend the execution of one program that is part of a series of programs and to execute the other programs in the series. The SCL debugger interface consists of two windows, the debugger SOURCE window and the debugger MESSAGE window. The debugger displays the source program, specifying which line is executing, in the SOURCE window. The MESSAGE window contains the debugger command line, as well as the results of any debugger commands.

The debugger can

- suspend execution at selected statements and programs. The point at which execution is suspended is called a breakpoint. Breakpoints can be set based on the evaluation of an expression.

- monitor the values of selected variables. This is called a watch variable. When a watch variable is set to some specified value, the debugger stops executing the program at the statement where this occurred.

- set or query the value of SCL variables.

- display the attributes of variables.

- bypass a group of statements.

- continue execution of a halted program.

- step over statements and function calls.

- display the execution stacks of active programs.

□ display the values of the arguments passed into a program.

□ display an expansion of the program's macros and macro variable references.

□ display each statement as it executes.

□ execute commands conditionally.

□ retrieve previous commands.

□ evaluate expressions, which can include functions, in the debugger command line.

□ process statements that use dot notation.

□ create and use SAS macros that contain debugger commands.

□ display help for individual commands.

# Establishing the Debugging Environment

Before you can use the SCL debugger, you must compile your SCL programs with the DEBUG option. This directs the SCL compiler to collect information from the programs that will be used in the debugging session.

You can activate the debug option in the following ways:

□ Issue the DEBUG ON command from the SOURCE or DISPLAY window of an open application. After you issue this command, it remains active in all currently running tasks, and all subsequent compiles will collect debugging information.

□ Specify the DEBUG option in the COMPILE statement of the BUILD procedure:

```
proc build c=libref.catalog.entry.type;
     compile debug;
run;
```

□ Specify the DEBUG option in the FSEDIT procedure:

```
proc fsedit data=data-set
               screen=screen-entry debug;
     run;
```

□ Select

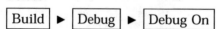

Build ▶ Debug ▶ Debug On

□ In the Explorer window, select from the pull-down menu

Tools ▶ Options ▶ Build ▶ Debugger

Change **Debugger status** to On or Off.

*Note:*  If you specify the DEBUG option from a procedure statement, the option is active only for that procedure or task. △

In the BUILD procedure, using the DEBUG option in the COMPILE statement compiles all the specified programs with the DEBUG option. For example, the following statements compile all the FRAME entries in the catalog with the DEBUG option turned on:

```
proc build c=mylib.mycat;
     compile debug entrytype=frame;
run;
```

By compiling specific SCL entries with the DEBUG option, you can debug pieces of a larger application.

The debugger session terminates and exits the current stream when you issue the QUIT command in the MESSAGE window, or when you end the procedure session. If the current stream is nested, then the last window in the previous stream will be activated. Otherwise, control returns to the point at which the application was started. A stream contains information about the entries and windows that are used in the application.

Because compiling with the DEBUG ON option results in a larger code size, you should subsequently recompile your programs with the DEBUG OFF option before installing your application in production mode.

# Invoking the Debugger

After you have successfully compiled a program with the DEBUG ON option, you can choose to invoke the debugger for that entry. For an entry that can be executed with the TESTAF, AF, or AFA command, you can invoke the debugger in the following ways:

☐ Enter the TESTAF command in the application window.

☐ If the debugging environment has not been established through the DEBUG ON command, specify DEBUG=YES in the AF or AFA command:

```
afa c=libref.catalog.entry.type debug=yes
```

Otherwise, submit the AF or AFA command.

☐ Specify the DEBUG option in conjunction with the TESTAF option in a PROC BUILD statement:

```
proc build c=libref.catalog.entry.type testaf debug;
```

☐ Select

Build ► Test

For an FSEDIT or FSVIEW application, you can invoke the debugger in the following ways:

☐ Close the SOURCE window, which compiles the program, when you build the application.

☐ Specify the DEBUG option in the procedure statement:

```
proc fsedit data=SAS-table
            screen=libref.catalog.entry.SCREEN
            debug;
run;

proc fsview data=SAS-table
            formula=libref.catalog.entry.FORMULA
            debug;
run;
```

# Using the Debugger Windows

When a debugging session starts, the debugger SOURCE window opens above the debugger MESSAGE window. The debugger SOURCE window displays the text of the current SCL program. The debugger MESSAGE window echoes the commands that you enter from the debugger command prompt, **DEBUG>**.

You can enter debugger commands from the following locations:

☐ the debugger command prompt **DEBUG>**

☐ the main SAS command line, if the command menus are active

☐ the command line at the top of the debugger MESSAGE window, if active. However, each debugger command that you enter from the command line must be preceded with the word SCL, as in this example, which sets a breakpoint at line 10:

```
scl b 10
```

When you enter a debugger command, the SCL debugger

**1** echoes the command in the debugger MESSAGE window

**2** checks the syntax of the command and the parameters that you entered. The debugger returns error messages for any syntax errors and reports the positions of the errors.

**3** prints the results of the command in the debugger MESSAGE window if there are no errors.

## Retrieving Previously Entered Commands

If the debugger detects an error in your command, you can recall the previous command, fix the error, and press the ENTER key to re-execute the command.

There are two ways to retrieve commands that you previously entered:

☐ Use the ? command, which enables you to retrieve up to the last five commands. This feature recalls a command once after you press ENTER and does not cycle through the commands again.

☐ Define a function key (using the KEYS command) to issue the AGAIN command. Once the key is defined, position the cursor on a line in the debugger MESSAGE window and press the key that is defined as the AGAIN command. The text on that line is displayed on the debugger command line. You can re-edit the line and then re-execute the command or commands.

## Using the SAS Macro Interface

The SCL debugger has a complete interface with the SAS macro facility. You can display macros with the MACEXPAND command. In addition, you can define a macro in the debugger session to replace a debugger command list that you use frequently, as in this example:

```
DEBUG> %macro ckvars; e var1 var2 %mend ckvars;
```

After the macro CKVARS is defined, you can invoke the macro as follows:

```
DEBUG> %ckvars
```

The macro CKVARS expands to

```
e var1 var2
```

*Note:*  To display the definition of a macro with the CALC command, you must enclose the macro name in quotes:

```
calc "%ckvars"
```

△

---

# Debugger Commands by Functional Category

The following sections briefly describe the commands that are available in the SCL debugger. For detailed information about a command, see its corresponding dictionary entry later in this chapter.

---

## Controlling Program Execution

While you are in a debugger session, you can use the following commands to monitor the flow of the program and even to change the way the program executes:

GO

continues program execution until a specified statement or until the next breakpoint (if any) or program is finished.

JUMP

restarts program execution at a specified executable statement. This command causes the interpreter to bypass execution of any intermediate statement.

STEP

steps through the program statement by statement. By default, the ENTER key is set to STEP.

---

## Manipulating Debugging Requests

The following debugger commands enable you to set breakpoints, tracepoints, and watched variables, which you can then use to suspend or trace the execution so that you can further manipulate the program variables. Whenever a debugging request is set, it remains in effect until you use the DELETE command to delete it.

BREAK

sets a breakpoint at a particular executable program statement. When a breakpoint is encountered, execution of the program is suspended and the cursor is placed on the DEBUG prompt line in the debugger MESSAGE window.

DELETE

removes breakpoints, tracepoints, or watched variables that were previously set by the BREAK, TRACE, and WATCH commands.

LIST

displays all the breakpoints, tracepoints, and watched variables that have been set by the BREAK, TRACE, and WATCH commands.

TRACE

sets a tracepoint. When a tracepoint is encountered, the debugger prints the information in the debugger MESSAGE window and continues processing.

WATCH

sets a watched variable. If the value of the watched variable is modified by the program, the debugger suspends execution at the statement where the change occurred, and it prints the old and the new values of the variable in the debugger

MESSAGE window. This command is especially useful in large programs to detect when the value of a particular variable is being modified.

## Manipulating Variables

When program execution is suspended, the debugger allows you to examine the values and attributes of variables. If the value of a variable would result in a logic error, you can then modify it so that you can continue the debugging session. Use these commands to manipulate SCL variables from the debugger:

ARGS
> displays the values of arguments that are passed into the current program through the ENTRY statement.

CALCULATE
> acts as an online calculator by evaluating expressions and displaying the result. This is useful when you try to set the value of a variable to the result of an expression. You can use SCL functions and dot notation in CALCULATE expressions.

DESCRIBE
> displays the name, type, length, and class attributes of a variable.

EXAMINE
> displays the values of one or more variables. You can use SCL functions with EXAMINE. You can also use dot notation to display values of object attributes and values that are returned by methods.

PARM
> displays the values of parameters that you are passing if the next executable statement contains a function call.

PUTLIST
> displays the contents of an SCL list.

SET
> changes the value of a variable in the SCL program. This enables you to continue the debugging session instead of having to stop, modify the source, and recompile the program. You can also assign new values to variables in other active entries.

## Expanding Macros and Macro Variable References

When program execution is suspended, the debugger can expand macros and macro variable references.

MACEXPAND
> displays expanded macro invocations and macro variable references. The text of the macro or the value of the macro variable is displayed in the debugger window.

## Controlling the Windows

The following commands manipulate the debugger windows:

ENVIRONMENT
> enables you to set a developer environment by redisplaying the source of any program in the execution stack. When a developer environment is set, the debugger generates messages that show you what the current program

environment and the developer environment are. You can then scroll through the source program, set debugging requests, and operate on the variables.

HELP
  displays information about debugger commands.

QUIT
  terminates a debugger session.

SWAP
  switches control between the debugger SOURCE and MESSAGE windows.

TRACEBACK
  displays the execution stack, which contains information about which entries are running.

## Customizing the Debugger Session

The following commands enable you to customize your debugging sessions:

ENTER
  enables you to assign one or more frequently used commands to the ENTER key. The default for ENTER is STEP, which steps through the program statement by statement.

IF
  enables you to conditionally execute other commands.

# ARGS

**Displays the values of arguments declared in the current program's ENTRY statement**

## Syntax

**ARGS**

## Details

The ARGS command displays the values of the arguments received from a calling program and declared in the current program's ENTRY statement. This command is valid only when the current program contains an ENTRY statement. If you use this command when you are debugging an entry that does not contain an ENTRY statement, an error message is displayed. For more information about the ENTRY statement, see "ENTRY" on page 369.

## Example

Suppose that the program being examined begins with the following statement:

```
entry d e f 8;
```

In a particular program, the ARGS command might produce the following output for the above ENTRY statement:

```
args
Arguments passed to ENTRY:
1 D = 10
2 E = 4
3 F = 6
```

## See Also

"DESCRIBE" on page 203

"EXAMINE" on page 207

"PARM" on page 215

"PUTLIST" on page 216

# BREAK

**Suspends program execution at an executable statement**

**Abbreviation:**    B

## Syntax

**BREAK** < *location* <AFTER *count*> <WHEN *clause* | DO *list*>>

### *location*

specifies where to set a breakpoint (the current line, by default):

_ALL_

sets a breakpoint at every executable statement.

ENTRY

sets a breakpoint at the first executable statement in all entries in the application catalog that contain a program.

*entry-name*\

specifies a catalog entry. A breakpoint is set at the first executable statement in the program in the specified entry. If the entry resides in the current catalog, then *entry-name* can be a one-level name. If the entry resides in a different catalog, then *entry-name* must be a four-level name, and the entry must already be loaded into the application's execution stack. A backslash must follow the entry name.

*label*

specifies a program label. A breakpoint is set at the first executable statement in the program label.

*line-num*

specifies a line number in an SCL program where a breakpoint is set. The specified line must contain at least one executable SCL statement.

### AFTER *count*

specifies the number of times for the debugger to execute a statement before executing the BREAK command.

*Note:* When multiple statements appear on a single line, the debugger treats them as separate statements. That is, the debugger will break on the same line as each statement on that line is executed. In the following example, the line will break three times in line number 10 because the condition is met three times

```
10 x=1 y=2 z=3
b10 after 3;
```

△

**WHEN** *clause*

specifies an expression that must be true in order for the command to be executed.

**DO** *list*

specifies one or more debugger commands to execute. Use semicolons to separate multiple commands.

## Details

The BREAK command sets a breakpoint at a specified statement. A breakpoint is an executable SCL program statement at which the debugger suspends program execution. An exclamation mark replaces the line number in the debugger SOURCE window to designate the line at which the breakpoint is established.

When an SCL program detects a breakpoint, it

□ suspends program execution

□ checks the count that you specified with the AFTER command and resumes program execution if the statement has not yet executed the specified number of times

□ evaluates the condition specified with the WHEN clause and resumes execution if the condition evaluates to FALSE

□ displays the entry name and line number at which execution is suspended

□ executes any command that is specified in a DO *list*

□ returns control to you.

If a breakpoint is set at a program line that contains more than one statement, then the breakpoint applies to each statement on the source line. If a breakpoint is set at a line that contains a SAS macro expansion, then the debugger breaks at each statement that is generated by the macro expansion.

## Examples

□ Set a breakpoint at line 5 in the current program:

```
DEBUG> b 5
```

The output to the debugger MESSAGE window is

```
stop at line 5 in MYLIB.MYCAT.TEST.SCL
b 5
Stop at line 5 in MYLIB.MYCAT.TEST.SCL
Set breakpoint at line 5 in program
    MYLIB.MYCAT.TEST.SCL
```

□ Set a breakpoint in each executable statement:

```
DEBUG> b _all_
```

□ Set a breakpoint in each executable line and print all the values:

```
DEBUG> b _all_ do; E _all_; end;
```

☐ Set a breakpoint at the first executable statement in each entry that contains a program in the catalog:

```
DEBUG> b entry
```

☐ Set a breakpoint at the first executable statement in the MAIN section:

```
DEBUG> b main
```

☐ Set a breakpoint at the first executable statement in the entry TEST1.SCL:

```
DEBUG> b test1\
```

☐ Set a breakpoint at line 45 in the entry TEST1.SCL:

```
DEBUG> b test1\45
```

☐ Set a breakpoint at the MAIN label in the entry TEST1.SCL:

```
DEBUG> b test1\main
```

☐ Set a breakpoint at line 45 before the fourth execution of line 45:

```
DEBUG> b 45 after 3
```

☐ Set a breakpoint at line 45 in the entry TEST1.SCL only when both the divisor and the dividend are 0:

```
DEBUG> b test1\45 when (divisor=0 AND dividend=0)
```

☐ Set a breakpoint at line 45 only when both the divisor and dividend are 0 before the fourth execution of line 45:

```
DEBUG> b 45 after 3 when (divisor=0 AND dividend=0)
```

☐ Set a breakpoint at line 12 when the value of the maxLength attribute on object1 is greater than 12:

```
DEBUG> b 12 when (object1.maxLength > 12)
```

☐ Set a breakpoint at line 45 of the program and examine the values of variables NAME and AGE:

```
DEBUG> b 45 do; e name age; end;
```

## See Also

"DELETE" on page 201

"EXAMINE" on page 207

"LIST" on page 213

"TRACE" on page 221

"WATCH" on page 224

# CALCULATE

**Evaluates a debugger expression and displays the result**

**Abbreviation:**   CALC

## Syntax

**CALCULATE** *expression*

*expression*
> is any standard debugger expression, which can include SCL functions and dot notation.

## Details

The CALCULATE command is an online calculator that evaluates expressions for the debugger. Expressions can include standard debugger expressions, SCL functions, and many of the SAS arithmetic functions. You can also use dot notation to perform operations on values that are returned by object attributes and methods.

## Examples

- □ Add 1.1, 1.2, 3.4 and multiply the result by 0.5:

  ```
  DEBUG> calc (1.1+1.2+3.4)*0.5
  ```

  The output to the debugger MESSAGE window is

  ```
  calc (1.1+1.2+3.4)*0.5
  2.85
  ```

- □ Calculate the values of the variable SALE minus the variable DOWNPAY and then multiply the result by the value of the variable RATE. Divide that value by 12 and add 50:

  ```
  DEBUG> calc (((sale-downpay)*rate)/12)+50
  ```

- □ Calculate the sum of the values of array variables A(1), A(2), and A(3):

  ```
  DEBUG> calc sum(a(1), a(2), a(3))
  ```

- □ Concatenate the string, the value of variable X, and the value returned from getMaxValue method on object1:

  ```
  DEBUG> calc ''Values=''||x||object1.getMaxValue()
  ```

- □ Display the defintion of the macro CKVARS:

  ```
  DEBUG> calc "%ckvars"
  ```

# DELETE

**Deletes breakpoints, tracepoints, or watched variables**

**Abbreviation:**   D

## Syntax

**DELETE** *debug-request* < *location*>

***debug-request***
　　is an SCL debugger command to be deleted:

　　BREAK　　　　deletes breakpoints.

　　TRACE　　　　deletes tracepoints.

　　WATCH　　　　deletes watched variables.

***location***
　　specifies where a debugging request should be deleted. For *debug-request* BREAK or
　　TRACE, *location* can be

　　_ALL_
　　　　deletes debugging requests from all programs that are in the application's
　　　　execution stack.

　　ENTRY
　　　　deletes debugging requests from the first executable statement in each entry that
　　　　contains an SCL program. If the entry resides in the current catalog, then
　　　　*entry-name* can be a one-level name.

　　*entry-name*\
　　　　specifies a catalog entry. The debugging requests on the first executable statement
　　　　of the specified catalog entry are deleted. If the entry resides in a different catalog,
　　　　then *entry-name* must be a four-level name, and it must already be loaded into the
　　　　application's execution stack. A backslash must follow the entry name.

　　*label*
　　　　specifies a program label. The debugging requests on the first executable statement
　　　　of the specified program label are deleted. *Label* can be any program label.

　　*line-num*
　　　　specifies a line number in an SCL program. The debugging requests on the
　　　　specified line are deleted.
　　　　For *debug-request* WATCH, *location* can be

　　_ALL_
　　　　deletes the watch status for all watched variables.

　　<*entry-name* \> *variable*
　　　　deletes the watch status from the first executable statement of the specified
　　　　catalog entry. If the entry resides in a different catalog, then *entry-name* must be a
　　　　four-level name, and it must already be loaded into the application's execution
　　　　stack. A backslash must follow the entry name. *Variable* specifies the name of a
　　　　particular watched variable for which the watch status is deleted.

## Details

The DELETE command deletes any breakpoint, tracepoint, or watched variable
debugger requests in one or more programs that you specify.

## Examples

□ Delete all breakpoints from the entry TEST1.SCL:

```
DEBUG> d b test1\
```

The output to the debugger MESSAGE window is

```
d b test1
Stop at line  5 in MYLIB.MYCAT.TEST1.SCL
Delete all the breakpoints in MYLIB.MYCAT.TEST1.SCL
```

□ Delete all breakpoints from the first executable statement of all entries:

```
DEBUG> d b entry
```

□ Delete the tracepoint at line 35 in the program currently executing:

```
DEBUG> d t 35
```

□ Delete the tracepoint at the first executable statement of the MAIN section of the program that is currently executing:

```
DEBUG> d t main
```

□ Delete the watch status from all variables in all programs that are in the application's execution stack:

```
DEBUG> d w _all_
```

□ Delete the watch status from the variable ABC in the program that is currently executing:

```
DEBUG> d w abc
```

□ Delete the watch status from the variable XYZ in the entry TEST3.SCL:

```
DEBUG> d w test3\xyz
```

## See Also

"BREAK" on page 198

"LIST" on page 213

"TRACE" on page 221

"WATCH" on page 224

# DESCRIBE

**Displays the attributes of a variable**

**Abbreviation:**   DES

## Syntax

**DESCRIBE** *arg-list* | _ALL_

*arg-list*
   contains one or more arguments specified in the form *<entry-name\ >variable.*

*entry-name\*

is the name of a catalog entry that contains an SCL program. If the entry resides in the current catalog, then *entry-name* can be a one-level name. If the entry resides in a different catalog, then *entry-name* must be a four-level name, and the entry must already be loaded into the application's execution stack. A backslash must follow the entry name.

*variable*

identifies an SCL variable to describe. The program that uses the specified variable must already be loaded in the application's execution stack.

**_ALL_**

describes all variables in all programs that are in the application's execution stack.

**Details** The DESCRIBE command displays the attributes of the specified variables. You can also use dot notation to specify object attributes. The attributes reported are

Name

contains the name of the variable whose attributes are displayed.

Length

contains the variable's length. All numeric variables have a length of 8 bytes. Variables of type list return the number of items in the list.

Category

contains the variable's class or category:

SYSTEM

designates a system variable.

WINDOW

designates a window variable.

NONWINDOW

designates a nonwindow variable.

Type

contains the data type of the variable:

ARRAY ELMT

array element

CHAR

character

CHAR ARRAY

character array

LIST

list

LIST ARRAY

list array

NUM

numeric

NUM ARRAY

numeric array

OBJECT

object

OBJECT ARRAY

object array

## Examples

☐ Display the name, data type, length and class of variable A:

```
DEBUG> des a
```

A is described as

```
des age
AGE          NUM    8   NONWINDOW
```

☐ Display the name, data type, length, and class of all elements in the array ARR:

```
DEBUG> des arr
```

☐ Display the attributes of array element ARR[i+j]:

```
DEBUG> des arr[i+j]
```

☐ Display the attributes of variable A in the entry TEST1.SCL:

```
DEBUG> des test1\a
```

☐ Display the attributes of all elements of array BRR in the entry TEST2.SCL:

```
DEBUG> des test2.scl\brr
```

☐ Display the attributes of object1:

```
DEBUG> des object1
```

☐ Display the attributes of the visible attribute on object1:

```
DEBUG> des object1.visible
```

☐ Display the attributes of the attribute name on object1 in the entry TEST2.SCL:

```
DEBUG> des test2\object1.name
```

## See Also

"ARGS" on page 197

"EXAMINE" on page 207

"PARM" on page 215

"PUTLIST" on page 216

# ENTER

**Assigns one or more debugger commands to the ENTER key**

## Syntax

**ENTER** < *command-list*>

***command-list***
contains one or more debugger commands, separated by semicolons.

**Details**     The ENTER command assigns one or more debugger commands to the
ENTER key. Each debugger command assignment replaces an existing debugger

command assignment. To clear the key setting, enter the command without any options. By default, the ENTER key is set to the STEP command.

## Example

Assign the commands EXAMINE and DESCRIBE, both for the variable ABC, to the ENTER key:

```
DEBUG> enter e abc; des abc
```

## See Also

"STEP" on page 219

---

# ENVIRONMENT

### Displays the developer debugging environment

**Abbreviation:**   ENV

---

## Syntax

**ENVIRONMENT** <<*entry-name\*><*line-num*> | RUN>

*entry-name\*
: sets the developer environment at the first executable statement in the program in the specified entry. If the entry resides in the current catalog, then *entry-name* can be a one-level name. If the entry resides in a different catalog, then *entry-name* must be a four-level name, and the entry must already be loaded into the application's execution stack. A backslash must follow the entry name.

*line-num*
: is the line to display in reverse-video.

**RUN**
: returns the debugger to executing the program.

**Details**    The ENVIRONMENT command enables you to display and modify the source program (that is, it sets a developer debugging environment) for any program in the application's execution stack while another program is active. When a developer environment is set, the debugger generates messages showing both the current program environment and the developer environment. In the developer environment, you can scroll through the source program, set debugging requests, and operate on the variables. For example, while TEST2.SCL is active, the ENVIRONMENT command enables you to display the source code for TEST1.SCL, reset the values of several variables in TEST1.SCL, and then return to TEST2.SCL.

By default, when you issue the ENVIRONMENT command from the current executing program without options, it sets the current program environment as the developer environment. If you issue the ENVIRONMENT command without an argument from a program other than the current program, the developer environment is reset to the program line containing the CALL DISPLAY statement.

Setting a developer environment does not change the way a program executes.

To return control to the active program, use the ENV RUN command to reset the environment to the active program, or use the GO, STEP or JUMP command to leave the developer environment and resume execution.

## Example

Assume that an execution stack looks like this:

```
TEST3.SCL    line 37
TEST2.SCL    line 24
TEST1.SCL    line 10
```

The following examples illustrate valid ENVIRONMENT commands and describe their effect on the preceding execution stack:

□ Display the source of TEST1.SCL with line 10 in reverse video:

```
DEBUG> env test1.scl\10
```

The output to the debugger MESSAGE window is

```
env test1.scl\10
Stop at line 37 in MYLIB.MYCAT.TEST3.SCL
Developer environment at line 10 in
MYLIB.MYCAT.TEST1.SCL
```

□ Display the source of TEST2.SCL with line 45 in reverse video:

```
DEBUG> env test2\45
```

□ Return to the current program environment (TEST3.SCL at line 37):

```
DEBUG> env run
```

□ Attempt to return to the program TEST4.SCL:

```
DEBUG> env test4\
```

Because TEST4.SCL is not in the SCL execution stack, the SOURCE window still displays TEST3.SCL. The output to the debugger MESSAGE window is

```
Program TEST4 is not active
```

## See Also

"SWAP" on page 220

---

# EXAMINE

**Displays the value of one or more variables**

**Abbreviations:** EX, E

---

## Syntax

**EXAMINE** *arg-list* | _ALL_

*arg-list*

contains one or more arguments specified in the form *<entry-name\>variable*.

> *entry-name\*
>> names a catalog entry that contains an SCL program.
>
> *variable*
>> identifies a standard SCL variable. The program that uses *variable* must already be loaded in the application's execution stack.

> **_ALL_**
>> examines all variables defined in all programs in the application's execution stack.

**Details**    The EXAMINE command displays the value of one or more specified variables or object attributes.

*Note:*   You can examine only one object attribute at a time. △

## Examples

- Display the values of variables N and STR:

  ```
  DEBUG> e n str
  ```

  The output to the debugger MESSAGE window is

  ```
  e n str
  N = 10
  STR = 'abcdef'
  ```

- Display variable A in the entry TEST1.SCL, variable B in the current program, and variable C in the entry TEST2.SCL:

  ```
  DEBUG> e test1\a b test2\c
  ```

- Display the elements i, j, and k of the array CRR:

  ```
  DEBUG> e crr[i, j, k]
  ```

- Display the elements i+1, j*2, k-3 of the array CRR:

  ```
  DEBUG> e crr[i+1, j*2, k-3]
  ```

- Display the value of the text in the Text Entry control NAME:

  ```
  DEBUG> e name.text
  ```

- Display the value of the enabled attribute on object1:

  ```
  DEBUG> e object1.enabled
  ```

- Display the reference ID of an object or a list:

  ```
  DEBUG> e object1
  ```

  or

  ```
  DEBUG> e object1.attributeList
  ```

  Once the reference ID is known, use PUTLIST to display the list data.

## See Also

"ARGS" on page 197

"DESCRIBE" on page 203

"PARM" on page 215

"PUTLIST" on page 216

# GO

**Starts or resumes execution of the active program from the current location**

**Abbreviation:** G

## Syntax

**GO** <*entry-name\ | line-num | label-name |* RETURN>

***entry-name\***
is the name of a catalog entry that contains the SCL program to resume executing.

***line-num***
is the number of the program line to start executing or resume executing.

***label***
is the program label where execution is to start or resume.

**RETURN**
starts or resumes execution at the next RETURN statement.

**Details**    The GO command starts or resumes execution of the active program. By default, program statements execute continuously. However, you can specify one of the optional arguments to establish a temporary breakpoint that stops the program at the corresponding statement.

A temporary breakpoint established through the GO command is ignored when the debugger encounters a breakpoint that was previously set before it encounters the temporary breakpoint. That is, program execution suspends at the breakpoint that was previously set by the BREAK command rather than at the temporary breakpoint.

## Examples

□ Resume executing the program and execute its statements continuously:

```
DEBUG> g
```

□ Resume program execution and then suspend execution at the next RETURN statement:

```
DEBUG> g return
```

□ Resume program execution and then suspend execution at the statement in line 104:

```
DEBUG> g 104
```

□ Resume program execution and then suspend execution at the first statement of the MAIN section:

```
DEBUG> go main
```

□ Resume program execution and then suspend execution at the statement in line 15 in program TEST2:

```
DEBUG> go test2\15
```

## See Also

"JUMP" on page 212

"STEP" on page 219

# HELP

**Displays information about debugger commands**

## Syntax

**HELP** < *command*>

*command*
is the debugger command for which to display help. You must use full command names rather than abbreviations.

**Details**    The HELP command displays information describing the syntax and usage of debugger commands. If *command* is not supplied, HELP displays a list of the debugger commands. You can then select any command to receive information about that command.

You can also issue the HELP command from the command line of the debugger MESSAGE window.

## Examples

□ Display a list of the debugger commands:

```
DEBUG> help
```

□ Display the syntax and usage information for the BREAK command:

```
DEBUG> help break
```

# IF

**Evaluates an expression and conditionally executes one or more debugger commands**

## Syntax

**IF** *expression* THEN *clause* <; ELSE *clause*>

*expression*
   contains a condition to be evaluated before one or more commands are executed.

*clause*
   contains either a single debugger command or a debugger DO list.

**Details**   The IF command immediately evaluates an expression and conditionally executes one or more debugger commands. The expression will contain dot notation because it resolves to a numeric variable. Character variables are converted.

   The IF command must contain a THEN clause with one or more commands to execute if the expression is true. It can also contain an ELSE clause with one or more commands to execute if the expression is false. The ELSE clause must be separated from the THEN clause with a semicolon, and the ELSE clause cannot be entered separately.

## Examples

- □ Examine the variable X if X contains a value that is greater than 0:

   ```
   DEBUG> if x > 0 then e x
   ```

- □ Examine the variable X if X is greater than 0, or examine the value of the variable Y if X is less than or equal to 0:

   ```
   DEBUG> if (x>0) then e x; else e y
   ```

- □ Execute the following actions if the value of variable X is less than variable Y and if Y is less than variable Z:

   - □ Delete all breakpoints in all program entries.
   - □ Set a breakpoint in the entry TEST2.SCL at the first executable statement.
   - □ Resume program execution.

   ```
   DEBUG> if ((x<y) & (y<z)) then
          do; d b _all_; b test2.scl\;g;end;
   ```

- □ Execute the following actions if the value of the variable X is 1:
   - □ Examine the value of variable A.
   - □ Set a breakpoint at line 5 of the program that is currently executing.

   If the value of X is not 1, then execute these actions:
   - □ Examine the value of variable B.
   - □ Set a breakpoint at line 15 of the program that is currently executing.

   ```
   DEBUG> if x=1 then do; e a; b 5; end;
          else do; e b; b 15; end;
   ```

□ Set a breakpoint at line 15 of the program. Whenever the execution suspends at line 15, if the value of the variable DIVISOR is greater than 3, execute the STEP command; otherwise, examine the value of the variable DIVIDEND.

```
DEBUG> b 15 do; if divisor>3 then st;
       else e dividend; end;
```

□ Examine the variable X if the attribute attrValue on object1 is greater than 10:

```
if object1.attrValue > 10 then e x
```

# JUMP

**Restarts execution of a suspended program**

**Abbreviation:**   J

## Syntax

**JUMP** *line-num*

*line-num*
is the number of a program line at which to restart the suspended program. The specified line must contain at least one executable SCL statement.

**Details**    The JUMP command restarts program execution at the executable statement in the specified line. It is different from the GO command because none of the statements between the suspended statement and the specified line are executed. With this capability, the JUMP command enables you to skip execution of some code that causes incorrect results or program failure.

The JUMP command can restart only the current source entry. The values of all variables are the same as the values at the original suspending point.

Although the JUMP command can jump to any statement in the current source, if the target statement resides in a different section of code, then the first RETURN statement encountered in the section that contains the target statement is treated as the RETURN statement from the section where the JUMP command was executed.

For example, suppose you were in the TERM section and you issued a JUMP command to jump to a statement in the MAIN section. When the program resumes execution, the first RETURN statement that it encounters in the MAIN section terminates the program (as the RETURN statement does in the TERM section) instead of redisplaying the screen.

*Note:*   Using the JUMP command to jump to a statement that is inside a DO loop may produce an illogical result. △

## Example

The following example illustrates the use of the JUMP command:

```
DEBUG> j 5
```

The output to the debugger MESSAGE window is

```
Stop at line 5 in MYLIB.MYCAT.TEST2.SCL
```

## See Also

"GO" on page 209

"STEP" on page 219

# LIST

**Displays a list of all program breakpoints, tracepoints, or watched variables**

**Abbreviation:**   L

## Syntax

**LIST** <<BREAK | TRACE | WATCH | _ALL_> *entry-name*\ | _ALL_>

**_ALL_**
  lists all breakpoints, tracepoints and watched variables. LIST _ALL_ performs the same function as LIST.

**BREAK**
  lists all breakpoints.

**TRACE**
  lists all tracepoints.

**WATCH**
  lists all watched variables.

***entry-name***\
  is the name of a catalog entry that contains an SCL program. If the entry resides in the current catalog, then *entry-name* can be a one-level name. If the entry resides in a different catalog, then *entry-name* must be a four-level name, and the entry must already be loaded into the application's execution stack. A backslash must follow the entry name.

**_ALL_**
  displays the debugging requests that are currently set for all entries.

**Details**     The LIST command displays a list of all debugging requests that have been set for an application. These requests include breakpoints, tracepoints, and watched variables. By default, the list contains all of the debugging requests for the current entry.

## Examples

□ List all the breakpoints, tracepoints, and watched variables for the current program:

```
DEBUG> l _all_
```

The output to the debugger MESSAGE window is

```
1 _all_
Stop at line  5 in MYLIB.MYCAT.TEST2.SCL
List all the breakpoints in program
MYLIB.MYCAT.TEST2.SCL
Breakpoint has been set at line 4
Breakpoint has been set at line 8
Breakpoint has been set at line 10
List all tracepoints in program
MYLIB.MYCAT.TEST2.SCL
No tracepoint has been set in program
MYLIB.MYCAT.TEST2.SCL
No variables have been watched in program
MYLIB.MYCAT.TEST2.SCL
```

□ List all the breakpoints, tracepoints, and watched variables for all active programs in the execution stack:

```
DEBUG> l _all_ _all_
```

□ List all the breakpoints in the current entry:

```
DEBUG> l b
```

□ List all the breakpoints in all active programs in the execution stack:

```
DEBUG> l b _all_
```

□ List all the breakpoints, tracepoints, and watched variables in the entry TEST1.SCL:

```
DEBUG> l _all_ test1\
```

□ List all the watched variables in the entry TEST3.SCL:

```
DEBUG> l w test3\
```

## See Also

"BREAK" on page 198

"DELETE" on page 201

"TRACE" on page 221

"WATCH" on page 224

---

# MACEXPAND

**Expands macro calls**

**Abbreviation:**   MACX

---

## Syntax

**MACEXPAND** *line-num*

### *line-num*

is the number of the program line that contains either a macro invocation or a macro variable reference to expand.

**Details** The MACEXPAND command expands macro invocations and macro variables. The expansion is displayed in the debugger window. If the line does not contain a macro invocation or a macro variable reference, then the MACEXPAND command is ignored.

## Example

In this example, the program contains the macro VALAMNT:

```
%macro valamnt(amount);
  if amount <0 or amount >500 then
     do;
        erroron amount;
        _msg_='Amount must be between $0 and $500.';
        stop;
     end;
  else erroroff amount;
%mend valamnt;
```

Line 33 of the SCL program calls the macro:

```
%valamnt(amt)
```

After entering 250 into the **Amount** control, enter in the debugger window:

```
DEBUG> macx 33
```

The debugger window displays the following output:

```
AMOUNT
$T0 = AMOUNT < 0
$T1 = AMOUNT > 500
$T2 = $T0 OR $T1
IF $T2 ==  0 THEN #24 ERRORON(AMOUNT)
_MSG_ = 'Amount must be between $0 and $500.'
STOP
JUMP #26
ERROROFF(AMOUNT)
```

# PARM

**Displays the values of variables that are passed as parameters to any SCL function or routine**

## Syntax

**PARM**

**Details** The PARM command displays the values of variables that are passed as parameters to an SCL function or routine. This command is valid only when the next executable statement contains a function call. Otherwise, the debugger issues a warning.

If a nested function call is encountered — that is, if the parameters passed to a function or routine are themselves function calls — then the PARM command displays the parameter list only for the nested function. You have to keep using the PARM command in order to display the parameter list for other function calls. For example, assume that the next executable statement is

```
str1=substr(upcase(string), min(x,y), max(x,y));
```

A PARM command first displays the parameter STRING, which is passed to the function UPCASE. A second PARM command displays the parameter list X, Y, which is passed to the function MIN. Subsequent PARM commands would display the parameter lists passed to the function MAX and then to SUBSTR.

*Note:*   Once the values of arguments for a function or routine have been displayed, you cannot repeat the PARM command for the same function unless you are re-executing it. △

## Example

A PARM command issued at the following statement

```
call display ('test2', x, y);
```

generates the following output:

```
parm
Arguments passed to DISPLAY:
  1 (Character Literal)='test2'
Parameters passed to DISPLAY ENTRY:
  1 X=0
  2 Y=4
```

## See Also

"ARGS" on page 197

"DESCRIBE" on page 203

"EXAMINE" on page 207

"PUTLIST" on page 216

# PUTLIST

### Displays the contents of an SCL list

## Syntax

**PUTLIST** < *arg-list* | *n*>

*arg-list*
contains one or more SCL list identifiers that are returned by the MAKELIST or COPYLIST function. Use the form < *entry-name* \ > *variable*.

*entry-name\*
　　is a catalog entry that contains the program that uses *variable*.

*variable*
　　is the variable that contains a list identifier.

***n***
　　is one or more numeric literals that represent the list to be printed.

**Details**　　The PUTLIST command displays the contents of an SCL list in the debugger MESSAGE window. The list starts with a left parenthesis, **(**, to mark its beginning, followed by the list of items separated by blanks. Each named item is preceded by its name and an equal sign, **=**, but nothing is printed before items that do not have names. The PUTLIST function ends the list with a right parenthesis, **)**, followed by the list's identifier number within square brackets.

If a list appears more than once in the list being printed, the PUTLIST command displays **(...)** *listid* for the second and subsequent occurrences of the list. You should scan the output of the PUTLIST command for another occurrence of *listid* to view the full contents of the list. This prevents infinite loops if a list contains itself as a sublist.

## Examples

□ Print the contents of List A, which contains the numbers 17 and 328 and the character string 'Any string':

```
DEBUG > putlist a
```

This produces the following output:

```
( 17
  328
  'Any string'
  )[5]
```

□ Print the list identified by number 5 (the same list shown in the previous example):

```
DEBUG> putlist 5
```

This produces the following output:

```
( 17
  328
  'Any string'
  )[5]
```

□ Print the list identified by the dot notation **object.dropoperations**, assuming that **dropoperations** is a valid list attribute on the object identified by **object**:

```
putlist object.dropoperations
( COPY=( POPMENUTEXT='Copy here'
         ENABLED='Yes'
         METHOD='_drop'
        )[11601]
   MOVE=( POPMENUTEXT='Move here'
          ENABLED='No'
          METHOD='_drop'
         )[11599]
   LINK=( POPMENUTEXT='Link here'
          ENABLED='No'
```

```
                    METHOD='_drop'
                )[11597]
            )[11593]
```

## See Also

"ARGS" on page 197

"DESCRIBE" on page 203

"EXAMINE" on page 207

"PARM" on page 215

# QUIT

**Terminates a debugger session**

**Abbreviation:**    Q

## Syntax

**QUIT**

**Details**    The QUIT command terminates a debugger session and returns control to the point at which the debugger was invoked. You can use this command on the debugger command line at any time during program execution.

# SET

**Assigns new values to a specified variable**

**Abbreviation:**    S

## Syntax

**SET** < *entry-name* \> *variable expression*

***entry-name* \**
    is the name of a catalog entry containing an SCL program entry that uses *variable*. If the entry resides in the current catalog, then *entry-name* can be a one-level name. If the entry resides in a different catalog, then *entry-name* must be a four-level name, and the entry must already be loaded into the application's execution stack. A backslash must follow the entry name.

***variable***
    is an SCL variable.

*expression*
contains a standard debugger expression.

**Details**   The SET command assigns either a value or the result of a debugger expression to the specified variable. When you detect an error during program execution, you can use this command to assign new values to variables. This enables you to continue the debugging session instead of having to stop, modify a variable value, and recompile the program. You can also assign new values to variables in other active entries.

## Examples

- Set variable A to the value of 3:

  ```
  DEBUG> s a=3
  ```

  The output to the debugger MESSAGE window is

  ```
  Stop at line 5 in SASUSER.SCL.TEST2.SCL
  A = 3
  ```

- Set X to the value of item 1 in LIST:

  ```
  DEBUG> s x=getitemc(list,1)
  ```

- Set variable A in program PROG1 to the value of the result of the expression a+c*3:

  ```
  DEBUG> s prog1\a=a+c*3
  ```

- Assign to variable B the value **12345** concatenated with the value of B:

  ```
  DEBUG> s b= 12345 || b
  ```

- Set array element ARR[1] to the value of the result of the expression a+3:

  ```
  DEBUG> s arr[1]=a+3
  ```

- Set array element CRR[1,2,3] to the value of the result of the expression crr[1,1,2]+crr[1,1,3]:

  ```
  DEBUG> s crr[1,2,3]=crr[1,1,2]+crr[1,1,3]
  ```

- Set the values of a whole array:

  ```
  DEBUG> s crr=['a', 'b', 'c', 'd']
  ```

# STEP

**Executes statements one at a time in the active program**

**Abbreviation:**   ST

## Syntax

**STEP** <OVER|O>

**OVER**

specifies that if the next executable statement is a CALL DISPLAY, FSEDIT, or FSVIEW statement, the whole reference counts as a statement. By default, the STEP command suspends program execution at the first executable statement of the called program if that program was compiled with DEBUG ON.

**Details**    The STEP command executes one statement in the active program, starting with the suspended statement. When you issue a STEP command, the command

□ executes the next statement

□ displays the entry name and line number

□ returns control to the developer and displays the **DEBUG>** prompt.

By default, the STEP command suspends the execution at the first executable statement in the called program if the current statement is a CALL DISPLAY or CALL FSEDIT statement. The OVER option forces the debugger to count the call of the DISPLAY, FSEDIT, or FSVIEW routine as a statement, and program execution stops at the statement after the CALL statement. However, if the called program contains a display, execution is not suspended until you leave the display window.

When the STEP command is used to execute a SELECT statement, it jumps directly to the appropriate WHEN or OTHERWISE clause without stepping through any intervening WHEN statements.

## Example

Suppose you are using the STEP command to execute the following program, which is stopped at line 15. If VAL contains 99, the STEP command goes to line 116 immediately.

```
line #
15    select (val);
16        when (1)
17            call display('a1');
18        when (2)
19            call display('a2');
...more SCL statements...
113        when (98)
114            call display('a98');
115        when (99)
116            call display('a99');
117        when (100)
118            call display('a100');
119        otherwise
120            call display('other');
121    end;
```

## See Also

"ENTER" on page 205

"GO" on page 209

"JUMP" on page 212

# SWAP

**Switches control between the debugger SOURCE window and MESSAGE window**

## Syntax

SWAP

## Details

The SWAP command enables you to switch control between the MESSAGE window and the SOURCE window when the debugger is running. When a debugging session is initiated, the control defaults to the MESSAGE window until you issue a command. While the program is still being executed, the SWAP command enables you to switch control between the SOURCE and MESSAGE window so that you can scroll and view the text of the program and also continue monitoring program execution.

## See Also

"ENVIRONMENT" on page 206

# TRACE

**Sets a tracepoint for tracing the execution of the corresponding statement**

**Abbreviation:** T

## Syntax

**TRACE** < *location* <AFTER *count* <<WHEN *clause* | DO *list*>>

*location*
  specifies where to set a tracepoint (at the current line, by default).

  _ALL_
    sets a tracepoint at every SCL executable program statement.

  ENTRY
    sets a tracepoint at the first executable statement in every entry in the current catalog that contains an SCL program.

  *entry-name*\
    sets a tracepoint in an SCL program.

  *label*
    sets a tracepoint at the first executable statement in an SCL reserved label or in a user-defined label.

  *line-num*
    sets a tracepoint at the specified line.

**AFTER** *count*
  is the number of times for the debugger to execute a statement before executing the TRACE command.

**WHEN** *clause*

specifies an expression that must be true in order for the command to be executed.

**DO** *list*

contains one or more debugger commands to execute. Use semicolons to separate multiple commands.

**Details**    The TRACE command sets a tracepoint at a specified statement and traces the execution of that statement.

A tracepoint differs from a breakpoint because a tracepoint resumes program execution after temporary suspension. Also, a tracepoint has a higher priority than a breakpoint. If a statement has been specified both as a tracepoint and as a breakpoint, the debugger first prints the trace message and then suspends program execution. Each time the tracepoint statement is encountered, the debugger does the following:

- □ suspends program execution

- □ checks the count that is specified with the AFTER command and resumes program execution if the specified number of tracepoint activations has not been reached

- □ evaluates any conditions specified in a WHEN clause and resumes execution if the condition evaluates as false

- □ displays the entry name and line number at which execution is suspended

- □ executes any command that is specified in a DO list

- □ resumes program execution.

## Examples

- □ Trace the statement at line 45:

    ```
    DEBUG> t 45
    ```

- □ Trace each executable statement:

    ```
    DEBUG> t _all_
    ```

- □ Trace each executable statement and print all the values:

    ```
    DEBUG> t _all_ do; e _all_; end
    ```

- □ Trace the first executable statement in each program:

    ```
    DEBUG> t entry
    ```

- □ Trace the first executable statement in the program's MAIN section:

    ```
    DEBUG> t MAIN
    ```

- □ Trace the statement at line 45 after each third execution:

    ```
    DEBUG> t 45 after 3
    ```

- □ Trace the statement at line 45 when the values of the variables DIVISOR and DIVIDEND are both 0:

    ```
    DEBUG> t 45 when (divisor=0 and dividend=0)
    ```

- □ Trace the statement at line 5 in the entry TEST1:

    ```
    DEBUG> t test1\5
    ```

### See Also

"BREAK" on page 198

"DELETE" on page 201

"LIST" on page 213

"WATCH" on page 224

# TRACEBACK

**Displays the traceback of the entire SCL execution stack**

**Abbreviation:**   TB

## Syntax

**TRACEBACK** <_ALL_>

**_ALL_**
   displays the link stack information in addition to the SCL execution stack.

**Details**    The TRACEBACK command displays the entire execution stack, which consists of the program that is currently being executed and all programs that were called to display the current program. In addition, the _ALL_ argument displays the *link stack*, which consists of the labeled sections that are called within the program.
   The display of the link stack does not include labeled sections that are called with a GOTO statement.

## Example

START.SCL contains a link at line 5 and calls ANALYZE.SCL at line 9. ANALYZE.SCL contains links at lines 5, 11, and 16.

Running the debugger and issuing TRACEBACK at line 21 of ANALYZE.SCL produces the following output:

```
---- Print The Traceback ----
In routine: TEST.TRACEBAK.ANALYZE.SCL line 21
Called from TEST.TRACEBAK.START.SCL line 9
```

Running the debugger and issuing TRACEBACK _ALL_ at line 21 of ANALYZE.SCL produces the following output:

```
---- Print The Traceback ----
In routine: TEST.TRACEBAK.ANALYZE.SCL line 21
      Linked from TEST.TRACEBAK.ANALYZE.SCL line 16
      Linked from TEST.TRACEBAK.ANALYZE.SCL line 11
      Linked from TEST.TRACEBAK.ANALYZE.SCL line 5
Called from TEST.TRACEBAK.START.SCL line 9
      Linked from TEST.TRACEBAK.START.SCL line 5
```

# WATCH

**Suspends program execution when the value of a specified variable has been modified**

**Abbreviation:**    W

## Syntax

WATCH < *entry-name* \> *variable* <AFTER *count*> <WHEN *clause* | DO *list* >

**entry-name\\**
is the name of the entry that contains the variable to be watched. The debugger starts watching the variable at the first executable statement in the program in the specified entry. If the entry resides in the current catalog, then *entry-name* can be a one-level name. If the entry resides in a different catalog, then *entry-name* must be a four-level name, and the entry must already be loaded into the application's execution stack. A backslash must follow the entry name.

**variable**
is the name of the variable to watch.

**AFTER *count***
specifies the number of times for the value of the variable to be changed before the debugger suspends program execution. Therefore, for an AFTER specification of 3, the program halts when the value of the watched variable is changed for the third time.

**WHEN *clause***
specifies an expression that must be true in order for the command to be executed. *Clause* can contain SCL functions.

**DO *list***
contains one or more debugger commands to execute. Use semicolons to separate multiple commands.

**Details**    The WATCH command monitors a variable and suspends program execution when the value of the variable is modified. A variable is called a watched entry parameter if it is defined as both a watched variable and as an ENTRY statement parameter. A program is not suspended when the value of a watched entry parameter is changed by a called program. However, a program is suspended when a changed value for a watched entry parameter is copied back to the calling program.

Each time the variable is modified, the debugger

- □  suspends program execution
- □  checks for any AFTER count and resumes program execution if the specified number of changes has not been reached
- □  evaluates the WHEN condition and resumes execution if the WHEN condition is false
- □  displays the entry name and line number at which execution has been suspended
- □  displays the variable's old value
- □  displays the variable's new value
- □  executes any commands that are provided in a DO list
- □  returns control to the developer and displays the **DEBUG>** prompt.

You can watch only variables that are in the current program.

## Examples

☐ Monitor the variable DIVISOR in TEST2 for value changes:

```
DEBUG> w divisor
```

The output to the MESSAGE window is

```
Stop at line 6 in MYLIB.MYCAT.TEST2.SCL
Watch variable DIVISOR has been modified
Old value=1
New value=99
```

☐ Monitor all the elements in the array NUM for value changes:

```
DEBUG> w num
```

☐ Monitor the variable DIVISOR in TEST1.SCL for value changes:

```
DEBUG> w test1\divisor
```

☐ Monitor an object attribute for its value changes:

```
DEBUG> w object.attribute
```

☐ Monitor the variable A[1] for value changes and suspend program execution after its value has been altered three times:

```
DEBUG> w a[1] after 3
```

☐ Monitor A[1] for value changes and suspend program execution when neither X nor Y is 0:

```
DEBUG> w a[1] when (x^=0 and y^=0)
```

☐ Monitor FIELD1 for value changes and suspend program execution after the third change in the value of FIELD1 when the variables DIVIDEND and DIVISOR both equal 0:

```
DEBUG> w field1 after 3 when (dividend=0
        and divisor=0)
```

☐ Monitor X when it has the same value as item 1 in LIST.

```
DEBUG> w x when x=getitemc(list,1)
```

## See Also

"BREAK" on page 198

"DELETE" on page 201

"LIST" on page 213

"TRACE" on page 221

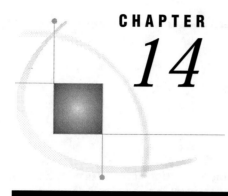

CHAPTER

*14*

# SAS System Return Codes

## Introduction

Many of the SCL functions that interface to external databases and file systems return special values called *SAS system return codes*. These return codes report the success or failure of a function, and they report error and warning conditions. You can use these system return codes to include sophisticated error checking in your applications.

## Using SAS System Return Codes

The value of a SAS system return code can be interpreted as:

| | |
|---|---|
| 0 | The operation was completed successfully. |
| >0 | An error condition was detected during the operation. |
| <0 | The operation was completed, but a warning or a note was generated. |

Not all SCL functions that return completion code values return SAS system return codes. Some functions return a completion code value that reports the success or failure of the requested operation (usually 1 for success or 0 for failure). These values are referred to in this book simply as return codes because they do not have the special property of SAS system return codes described above.

### Obtaining a SAS System Return Code

Some functions — notably OPEN, DOPEN, FOPEN, and MOPEN — return values other than SAS system return codes. For these functions, use the SYSRC function to obtain the SAS system return code for the operation. SAS software retains the value of the return code for the most recent warning or error condition, and the SYSRC function reads the stored value.

The following example assigns the SAS system return code to the variable ERRNUM if the OPEN operation fails:

```
tableid=open('prices','I');
if tableid=0 then do;
   errnum=sysrc();
   put "Open failed" errnum;
end;
```

*Note:*  If you call the SYSRC function after executing a function that returns a SAS system return code, the value that the SYSRC function returns is the same as the value that the original function returned. △

## Obtaining the Message for a SAS System Return Code

In many cases, knowing the value of a SAS system return code enables you to determine whether an operation succeeded or failed. However, in some cases warning messages can be useful for informing users of special situations that may need to be corrected.

You can use the SYSMSG function to return the text of the error message that was produced by the most recent SCL warning or error.

For example, the following statements display the SAS system message for the error condition that is produced when the FETCH function returns a nonzero return code:

```
rc=fetch(dsid);
if rc then _msg_=sysmsg();
```

The message string that SYSMSG() returns is reset to blank after each call to SYSMSG() until the next error or warning condition occurs.

## Testing for a Particular Error or Warning Condition

When an SCL function returns a nonzero SAS system return code, you can use the %SYSRC macro to determine whether the code indicates one of a defined set of error and warning conditions. The %SYSRC macro is provided in the autocall library that is supplied by SAS Institute.

*Note:*  In order for you to use autocall macros, the MAUTOSOURCE system option must be in effect, and the SASAUTOS= system option must point to the Institute-supplied autocall macro library. For more information about the autocall facility, see *SAS Macro Language: Reference* and the online Help for the SAS Macro Language. △

To test whether a specific return code is one of the documented conditions, pass a mnemonic name for the condition to the %SYSRC macro. The syntax is

```
rc=%SYSRC(mnemonic);
```

Mnemonics consist of up to eight characters, as follows:

□ an underscore (_) for the first character

□ S for the second character

□ E (for error conditions) or W (for warning conditions) for the third character

□ a shortened version of the name of the error for the remaining characters.

For example, _SWEOF is the mnemonic for the end-of-file warning condition.

*Note:*   The return code for an end-of-file condition is a warning (_SWEOF). The value of the return code is –1. This is a special return code that is explicitly documented in this book. △

Mnemonics are assigned only to error or warning conditions that are considered relevant to an application developer. In some cases, SCL returns values that do not have a corresponding mnemonic. In these cases, a negative value indicates a warning condition, and a positive value indicates an error condition. For example, the following statements can be used to test whether the row requested by the FETCH function was successfully locked:

```
rc=fetch(dsid);
if (rc) then
    do;
       if (rc=%sysrc(_swnoupd)) then _msg_=
       'Another user has locked the requested row.';
       else
               /* fetch failed for another reason*/
           _msg_=sysmsg();
    end;
```

# Mnemonics for SAS System Return Codes

Table 14.1 on page 229 lists the mnemonics for SAS system return codes along with the value and a description of the error or warning condition. This table is sorted by the mnemonic name, and the codes are grouped into general categories of operations that can produce the conditions. Table 14.2 on page 232 presents the codes sorted by the return code value.

**Table 14.1**   Warning and Error Conditions Sorted Alphabetically by Mnemonic

| Mnemonic | Value | Description |
|---|---|---|
| **Library Assign/Deassign Messages** | | |
| _SEDUPLB | 70004 | The libref refers to the same physical library as another libref. |
| _SEIBASN | 70006 | The specified libref is not assigned. |
| _SEINUSE | 70025 | The library or member is not available for use. |
| _SEINVLB | 70002 | The library is not in a valid format for the access method. |
| _SEINVLN | 20014 | The libref is not valid. |
| _SELBACC | 70029 | The action requested cannot be performed because you do not have the required access level on the library. |
| _SELBUSE | 70025 | The library is still in use. |
| _SELGASN | 70006 | The specified libref is not assigned. |
| _SENOASN | 20004 | The libref is not assigned. |
| _SENOLNM | 20031 | The libref is not available for use. |
| _SESEQLB | 630032 | The library is in sequential (tape) format. |

| Mnemonic | Value | Description |
|---|---|---|
| _SWDUPLB | –70004 | The libref refers to the same physical file as another libref. |
| _SWNOLIB | –70008 | The library does not exist. |
| **Fileref Messages** | | |
| _SELOGNM | 20002 | The fileref is assigned to an invalid file. |
| _SWLNASN | –20004 | The fileref is not assigned. |
| **SAS Table Messages** | | |
| _SEBAUTH | 70045 | The data set has passwords. |
| _SEBDIND | 630009 | The index name is not a valid SAS name. |
| _SEDSMOD | 70018 | The data set is not open in the correct mode for the specified operation. |
| _SEDTLEN | 20012 | The data length is invalid. |
| _SEINDCF | 630008 | The new name conflicts with an index name. |
| _SEINVMD | 20015 | The open mode is invalid. |
| _SEINVPN | 20017 | The physical name is invalid. |
| _SEMBACC | 70030 | You do not have the level of access required to open the data set in the requested mode. |
| _SENOLCK | 630053 | A record-level lock is not available. |
| _SENOMAC | 660025 | Member-level access to the data set is denied. |
| _SENOSAS | 70037 | The file is not a SAS data set. |
| _SEVARCF | 630019 | The new name conflicts with an existing variable name. |
| _SWBOF | –570001 | You tried to read the previous observation when you are on the first observation. |
| _SWNOWHR | –630004 | The record no longer satisfies the WHERE clause. |
| _SWSEQ | –630032 | The task requires reading observations in a random order, but the engine you are using allows only sequential access. |
| _SWWAUG | –580016 | The WHERE clause has been augmented. |
| _SWWCLR | –580017 | The WHERE clause has been cleared. |
| _SWWREP | –580015 | The WHERE clause has been replaced. |
| **SAS File Open and Update Messages** | | |
| _SEBDSNM | 630087 | The filename is not a valid SAS name. |
| _SEDLREC | 630049 | The record has been deleted from the file. |
| _SEFOPEN | 20036 | The file is currently open. |
| _SEINVON | 70022 | The option name is invalid. |
| _SEINVOV | 70023 | The option value is invalid. |
| _SEINVPS | 20018 | The value of the File Data Buffer pointer is invalid. |
| _SELOCK | 70031 | The file is locked by another user. |
| _SENOACC | 20029 | You do not have the level of access required to open the file in the requested mode. |

| Mnemonic | Value | Description |
|---|---|---|
| _SENOALL | 630100 | _ALL_ is not allowed as part of a filename in this release. |
| _SENOCHN | 630058 | The record was not changed because it would cause a duplicate value for an index that does not allow duplicates. |
| _SENODEL | 10011 | Records cannot be deleted from this file. |
| _SENODLT | 20030 | The file could not be deleted. |
| _SENOERT | 20035 | The file is not open for writing. |
| _SENOOAC | 70030 | You are not authorized for the requested open mode. |
| _SENOOPN | 20037 | The file or directory is not open. |
| _SENOPF | 20006 | The physical file does not exist. |
| _SENORD | 20032 | The file is not opened for reading. |
| _SENORDX | 630066 | The file is not radix addressable. |
| _SENOTRD | 570002 | No record has been read from the file yet. |
| _SENOUPD | 630006 | The file cannot be opened for update because the engine is read-only. |
| _SENOWRT | 70040 | You do not have write access to the member. |
| _SEOBJLK | 20025 | The file or directory is in exclusive use by another user. |
| _SERECRD | 630052 | No records have been read from the input file. |
| _SWACMEM | −630032 | Access to the directory will be provided one member at a time. |
| _SWEOF | −1 | End of file. |
| _SWNOFLE | −20006 | The file does not exist. |
| _SWNOPF | −70008 | The file or directory does not exist. |
| _SWNOREP | −630002 | The file was not replaced because of the NOREPLACE option. |
| _SWNOTFL | −20002 | The item pointed to exists but is not a file. |
| _SWNOUPD | −630054 | This record cannot be updated at this time. |

**Library/Member/Entry Messages**

| Mnemonic | Value | Description |
|---|---|---|
| _SEBDMT | 70015 | The member type specification is invalid. |
| _SEDLT | 70033 | The member was not deleted. |
| _SELKUSR | 630097 | The library or library member locked by another user. |
| _SEMLEN | 70028 | The member name is too long for this system. |
| _SENOLKH | 630099 | The library or library member is not currently locked. |
| _SENOMEM | 70009 | The member does not exist. |
| _SWKNXL | −670212 | You have locked a library, member, or entry that does not exist yet. |
| _SWLKUSR | −630097 | The library or library member is locked by another user. |
| _SWLKYOU | −630098 | You have already locked the library or library member. |
| _SWNOLKH | −630099 | The library or library member is not currently locked. |

**Miscellaneous Operations**

| Mnemonic | Value | Description |
|---|---|---|
| _SEDEVOF | 10008 | The device is offline or unavailable. |

| Mnemonic | Value | Description |
|----------|-------|-------------|
| _SEDSKFL | 70039 | The disk or tape is full. |
| _SEINVDV | 20011 | The device type is invalid. |
| _SENORNG | 20034 | There is no write ring in the tape opened for write access. |
| _SOK | 0 | The function was successful. |
| _SWINVCC | −20001 | The carriage-control character is invalid. |
| _SWNODSK | −20005 | The device is not a disk. |
| _SWPAUAC | −630104 | Pause in I/O, process accumulated data up to this point. |
| _SWPAUSL | −630105 | Pause in I/O, slide data window forward and process accumulated data up to this point. |
| _SWPAUU1 | −630106 | Pause in I/O, extra user control point 1. |
| _SWPAUU2 | −630107 | Pause in I/O, extra user control point 2. |

**Table 14.2** Warning and Error Conditions Sorted by Value

| Value | Mnemonic | Description |
|-------|----------|-------------|
| −1 | _SWEOF | End of file. |
| −20001 | _SWINVCC | The carriage control character is invalid. |
| −20002 | _SWNOTFL | The item pointed to exists but is not a file. |
| −20004 | _SWLNASN | The fileref is not assigned. |
| −20005 | _SWNODSK | The device is not a disk. |
| −20006 | _SWNOFLE | The file does not exist. |
| −70004 | _SWDUPLB | The libref refers to the same physical file as another libref. |
| −70008 | _SWNOPF | The file or directory does not exist. |
| −70008 | _SWNOLIB | The library does not exist. |
| −570001 | _SWBOF | You tried to read the previous observation when you are on the first observation. |
| −580015 | _SWWREP | The WHERE clause has been replaced. |
| −580016 | _SWWAUG | The WHERE clause has been augmented. |
| −580017 | _SWWCLR | The WHERE clause has been cleared. |
| −630002 | _SWNOREP | The file was not replaced because of the NOREPLACE option. |
| −630004 | _SWNOWHR | The record no longer satisfies the WHERE clause. |
| −630032 | _SWSEQ | The task requires reading observations in a random order, but the engine you are using allows only sequential access. |
| −630032 | _SWACMEM | Access to the directory will be provided one member at a time. |
| −630054 | _SWNOUPD | This record cannot be updated at this time. |
| −630097 | _SWLKUSR | The library or library member is locked by another user. |
| −630098 | _SWLKYOU | You have already locked the library or library member. |

| Value | Mnemonic | Description |
|---|---|---|
| –630099 | _SWNOLKH | The library or library member is not currently locked. |
| –630104 | _SWPAUAC | Pause in I/O, process accumulated data up to this point. |
| –630105 | _SWPAUSL | Pause in I/O, slide data window forward and process accumulated data up to this point. |
| –630106 | _SWPAUU1 | Pause in I/O, extra user control point 1. |
| –630107 | _SWPAUU2 | Pause in I/O, extra user control point 2. |
| –670212 | _SWKNXL | You have locked a library, member, or entry that does not exist yet. |
| 0 | _SOK | The function was successful. |
| 10008 | _SEDEVOF | The device is offline or unavailable. |
| 10011 | _SENODEL | Records cannot be deleted from this file. |
| 20002 | _SELOGNM | The fileref is assigned to an invalid file. |
| 20004 | _SENOASN | The libref is not assigned. |
| 20006 | _SENOPF | The physical file does not exist. |
| 20011 | _SEINVDV | The device type is invalid. |
| 20012 | _SEDTLEN | The data length is invalid. |
| 20014 | _SEINVLN | The libref is not valid. |
| 20015 | _SEINVMD | The open mode is invalid. |
| 20017 | _SEINVPN | The physical name is invalid. |
| 20018 | _SEINVPS | The value of the File Data Buffer pointer is invalid. |
| 20025 | _SEOBJLK | The file or directory is in exclusive use by another user. |
| 20029 | _SENOACC | You do not have the level of access required to open the file in the requested mode. |
| 20030 | _SENODLT | The file could not be deleted. |
| 20031 | _SENOLNM | The libref is not available for use. |
| 20032 | _SENORD | The file is not opened for reading. |
| 20034 | _SENORNG | There is no write ring in the tape opened for write access. |
| 20035 | _SENOERT | The file is not open for writing. |
| 20036 | _SEFOPEN | The file is currently open. |
| 20037 | _SENOOPN | The file or directory is not open. |
| 70002 | _SEINVLB | The library is not in a valid format for the access method. |
| 70004 | _SEDUPLB | The libref refers to the same physical library as another libref. |
| 70006 | _SEIBASN | The specified libref is not assigned. |
| 70006 | _SELGASN | The specified libref is not assigned. |
| 70009 | _SENOMEM | The member does not exist. |
| 70015 | _SEBDMT | The member type specification is invalid. |
| 70018 | _SEDSMOD | The data set is not open in the correct mode for the specified operation. |
| 70022 | _SEINVON | The option name is invalid. |

| Value | Mnemonic | Description |
|---|---|---|
| 70023 | _SEINVOV | The option value is invalid. |
| 70025 | _SEINUSE | The library or member is not available for use. |
| 70025 | _SELBUSE | The library is still in use. |
| 70028 | _SEMLEN | The member name is too long for this system. |
| 70029 | _SELBACC | The action requested cannot be performed because you do not have the required access level on the library. |
| 70030 | _SEMBACC | You do not have the level of access required to open the data set in the requested mode. |
| 70030 | _SENOOAC | You are not authorized for the requested open mode. |
| 70031 | _SELOCK | The file is locked by another user. |
| 70033 | _SEDLT | The member was not deleted. |
| 70037 | _SENOSAS | The file is not a SAS data set. |
| 70039 | _SEDSKFL | The disk or tape is full. |
| 70040 | _SENOWRT | You do not have write access to the member. |
| 70045 | _SEBAUTH | The data set has passwords. |
| 570002 | _SENOTRD | No record has been read from the file yet. |
| 630006 | _SENOUPD | The file cannot be opened for update because the engine is read-only. |
| 630008 | _SEINDCF | The new name conflicts with an index name. |
| 630009 | _SEBDIND | The index name is not a valid SAS name. |
| 630019 | _SEVARCF | The new name conflicts with an existing variable name. |
| 630032 | _SESEQLB | The library is in sequential (tape) format. |
| 630049 | _SEDLREC | The record has been deleted from the file. |
| 630052 | _SERECRD | No records have been read from the input file. |
| 630053 | _SENOLCK | A record-level lock is not available. |
| 630058 | _SENOCHN | The record was not changed because it would cause a duplicate value for an index that does not allow duplicates. |
| 630066 | _SENORDX | The file is not radix addressable. |
| 630087 | _SEBDSNM | The filename is not a valid SAS name. |
| 630097 | _SELKUSR | The library or library member locked by another user. |
| 630099 | _SENOLKH | The library or library member is not currently locked. |
| 630100 | _SENOALL | _ALL_ is not allowed as part of a filename in this release. |
| 660025 | _SENOMAC | Member-level access to the data set is denied. |

CHAPTER

*15*

# SCL Elements by Category

*SCL Language Elements by Category* **235**

## SCL Language Elements by Category

**Table 15.1** SCL Elements by Category

| Category | Element Name | Description |
| --- | --- | --- |
| Array | "ASORT" on page 256 | Sorts an array |
| | "COMPAREARRAY" on page 297 | Allows you to compare two arrays for size and data equality |
| | "COPYARRAY" on page 309 | Allows you to copy data from one array into another array |
| | "DELARRAY" on page 332 | Deletes a dynamic array |
| | "MAKEARRAY" on page 533 | Creates an array of the given size with all elements in the array initialized to missing for numerics or blank for characters |
| | "REDIM" on page 610 | Resizes a dynamic array |
| Catalog | "CATLIST" on page 269 | Displays a host selector window that lists entries in a SAS catalog, and returns user selections |
| | "CATNAME" on page 272 | Defines a concatenated catalog, which contains a logical combination of the entries in two or more catalogs |
| | "CEXIST" on page 276 | Verifies the existence of a SAS catalog or SAS catalog entry |
| | "CONTENTS" on page 299 | Displays the attributes of a SAS Table |
| | "IMPORT" on page 478 | Defines a search path for references to CLASS entries |
| | "SEARCH" on page 635 | Creates or manipulates the current catalog search path |
| | "SEARCHPATH" on page 638 | Reports the complete pathname of a SAS catalog entry |
| Character | "CENTER" on page 275 | Returns a centered character string |
| | "LEFT" on page 506 | Returns a left-aligned character string |

| | "LENGTH" on page 509 | Returns the length of a trimmed character string |
|---|---|---|
| | "MLENGTH" on page 549 | Returns the maximum length of a variable |
| | "RIGHT" on page 620 | Returns a right-aligned character value |
| Command | "EXECCMD" on page 380 | Executes one or more commands when control returns to the application |
| | "EXECCMDI" on page 381 | Executes one or more global commands immediately before processing the next statement, or executes one non-global command when control returns to the application |
| | "LASTCMD" on page 502 | Returns the text of the last command that was issued from the application window |
| | "LOOKUPC" on page 530 | Searches for a string among a list of valid tokens |
| | "NEXTCMD" on page 567 | Discards the current command on the command line |
| | "NEXTWORD" on page 568 | Deletes the current word and advances to the next word in the current command |
| | "SYSTEM" on page 687 | Issues a host system command |
| | "WORD" on page 725 | Returns a word from a command that was issued with the command line, function keys, command processing, or a control |
| | "WORDTYPE" on page 726 | Identifies the word type of a word on the command line |
| Control Flow | "CATCH" on page 268 | Processes an exception that has been thrown with the THROW statement |
| | "CONTINUE" on page 300 | Stops processing the current DO loop and resumes with the next iteration of that DO loop |
| | "CONTROL" on page 302 | Controls the execution of labeled program sections and the formatting of submit blocks |
| | "DO" on page 356 | Designates a group of statements to be executed as a unit |
| | "ENDCATCH" on page 365 | Ends a CATCH statement block |
| | "GOTO" on page 455 | Branches immediately to another entry |
| | "LEAVE" on page 504 | Stops processing the current DO group and resumes with the next statement in sequence |
| | "RETURN" on page 615 | Stops executing statements in the program section that is currently executing and may return a value to the caller |
| | "RUN" on page 625 | Stops executing statements in the program section that is currently executing |
| | "SELECT" on page 640 | Executes one of several statements or groups of statements |
| | "STOP" on page 674 | Stops executing statements in the program section that is currently executing |
| | "THROW" on page 688 | Raises an exception |
| | "WAIT" on page 717 | Suspends execution of the next program statement |
| Control or Field | "ACTIVATE" on page 249 | Activates or grays either a Version 6 check box or radio box widget, or a station in a choice group |

| | "CLRFLD" on page 293 | Clears the value from variables whose values match a specified value |
|---|---|---|
| | "DISPLAYED" on page 353 | Reports whether a control or field is currently visible |
| | "ERROR" on page 375 | Reports whether a FRAME entry control or field contains an invalid value |
| | "ERROROFF" on page 376 | Clears the error flag on one or more FRAME entry controls or fields |
| | "ERRORON" on page 377 | Sets the error flag for one or more FRAME entry controls or fields |
| | "GRAY" on page 457 | Grays FRAME entry controls and stations of a choice group |
| | "HOME" on page 459 | Positions the cursor on a window's command area |
| | "ISACTIVE" on page 492 | Returns the number of the active button in a radio box or check box or the active station in a choice group |
| | "ISGRAY" on page 493 | Reports whether a FRAME entry control or choice group is grayed |
| | "MODIFIED" on page 550 | Reports whether a field or FRAME entry control has been modified |
| | "PROTECT" on page 602 | Assigns protection to a FRAME entry control or field |
| | "SETCR" on page 647 | Controls the cursor's response to the carriage-return key |
| | "SETFLD" on page 650 | Assigns a value to up to ten blank variables |
| | "UNGRAY" on page 693 | Ungrays a window element |
| | "UNPROTECT" on page 695 | Removes protection from a FRAME entry control or a field |
| Cursor | "CURFLD" on page 319 | Returns the name of the FRAME or PROGRAM entry control or field on which the cursor is currently positioned |
| Declarative Statement | "ARRAY" on page 254 | Defines elements of an explicit array |
| | "DECLARE" on page 330 | Declares variables and specifies their data types |
| | "LENGTH" on page 510 | Declares variables and specifies their length and whether their data type is numeric or character |
| Directory | "DCLOSE" on page 328 | Closes a directory |
| | "DINFO" on page 346 | Returns information about a directory |
| | "DNUM" on page 355 | Returns the number of members in a directory |
| | "DOPEN" on page 357 | Opens a directory |
| | "DOPTNAME" on page 358 | Returns the name of a directory attribute |
| | "DOPTNUM" on page 359 | Returns the number of information items that are available for a directory |
| | "DREAD" on page 360 | Returns the name of a directory member |
| | "MOPEN" on page 552 | Opens a member file in a directory |
| Extended Table | "CURTOP" on page 324 | Returns the number of the row that is currently displayed at the top of an extended table |

| | | |
|---|---|---|
| "ENDTABLE" on page 368 | Stops the processing of the getrow section of a dynamic extended table |
| "ISSEL" on page 495 | Returns the selection number for a specified row of a selection list |
| "NSELECT" on page 573 | Returns the number of rows that have been selected in a selection list |
| "SELECT" on page 639 | Selects a specified row of a selection list |
| "SELECTED" on page 642 | Returns the number of the row that corresponds to a user's choice in a selection list |
| "SETROW" on page 664 | Determines the characteristics of extended tables |
| "TOPROW" on page 689 | Scrolls a row to the top of an extended table |
| "UNSELECT" on page 696 | Deselects a specified row of a selection list |

| | | |
|---|---|---|
| External File | "DCREATE" on page 329 | Creates an external directory |
| | "FAPPEND" on page 384 | Appends the current record to the end of an external file |
| | "FCLOSE" on page 386 | Closes an external file, a directory, or a directory member |
| | "FCOL" on page 387 | Returns the current column position from the File Data Buffer (FDB) |
| | "FDELETE" on page 388 | Deletes an external file |
| | "FEXIST" on page 392 | Verifies the existence of the external file that is associated with the specified fileref |
| | "FGET" on page 393 | Copies data from the File Data Buffer (FDB) |
| | "FILEDIALOG" on page 398 | Displays a selection window that lists external files |
| | "FILEEXIST" on page 400 | Verifies the existence of an external file, a directory, or a SAS data library by its physical name |
| | "FILENAME" on page 403 | Assigns or deassigns a fileref for an external file, a directory, an output device, or a catalog entry |
| | "FILEREF" on page 406 | Verifies that a fileref has been assigned for the current SAS session or process |
| | "FINFO" on page 412 | Returns a file information item |
| | "FNOTE" on page 417 | Identifies the last record that was read |
| | "FOPEN" on page 420 | Opens an external file |
| | "FOPTNAME" on page 421 | Returns the name of an item of information for a file |
| | "FOPTNUM" on page 423 | Returns the number of information items that are available for an external file |
| | "FPOINT" on page 425 | Positions the "read" pointer on the next record to be read |
| | "FPOS" on page 426 | Sets the position of the column pointer in the File Data Buffer |
| | "FPUT" on page 427 | Moves data to the File Data Buffer (FDB) for an external file, starting at the FDB's current column position |
| | "FREAD" on page 430 | Reads a record from an external file into the File Data Buffer (FDB) |

| | | |
|---|---|---|
| | "FREWIND" on page 431 | Positions the file pointer at the beginning of the file |
| | "FRLEN" on page 432 | Returns the size of the last record read, or, if the file is opened for output, returns the current record size |
| | "FSEP" on page 435 | Sets the token delimiters for the FGET function |
| | "FSLIST" on page 436 | Displays an external file for browsing |
| | "FWRITE" on page 439 | Writes a record to an external file |
| | "PATHNAME" on page 586 | Returns the physical name of a SAS data library or an external file |
| Formatting | "FORMAT" on page 424 | Verifies that the specified format is valid |
| | "INFORMAT" on page 479 | Verifies that the specified informat is valid |
| | "INPUTC and INPUTN" on page 481 | Read a character value using an informat |
| | "PUTC and PUTN" on page 605 | Return a formatted value, using the specified format |
| Image | "IMGCTRL" on page 469 | Performs control operations on the Image window |
| | "IMGINIT" on page 471 | Starts an image task |
| | "IMGOP" on page 472 | Performs image operations |
| | "IMGTERM" on page 475 | Terminates an image task |
| | "LNAMECHK" on page 522 | Validates a path string |
| | "LNAMEGET" on page 523 | Decodes a path string |
| | "LNAMEMK" on page 524 | Makes a path string for an image file |
| | "PICCLOSE" on page 587 | Closes the graphics environment |
| | "PICDELETE" on page 588 | Deletes a region |
| | "PICFILL" on page 589 | Defines a region and fills it with an image |
| | "PICOPEN" on page 591 | Initializes the graphics environment |
| Interface to SAS Software | "RLINK" on page 621 | Reports whether a link exists between the current SAS session and a remote SAS session |
| | "RSESSION" on page 623 | Returns the name, description, and SAS software version of a remote session |
| | "RSTITLE" on page 624 | Defines a description for an existing connection to a remote session |
| | "SASTASK" on page 626 | Determines whether a SAS procedure is running |
| Keys | "EVENT" on page 378 | Reports whether a user has pressed a function key, ENTER key, or mouse button |
| | "FKEYNAME" on page 413 | Returns the name of the specified function key |
| | "GETFKEY" on page 440 | Returns the command that is assigned to a function key |
| | "LASTKEY" on page 503 | Returns the number of the last function key that was pressed from the application window |
| | "NUMFKEYS" on page 574 | Returns the number of function keys that are available for the device |

| | "SETFKEY" on page 649 | Assigns a command to a function key |
|---|---|---|
| Legend | "ENDLEGEND" on page 366 | Closes the LEGEND window |
| | "LEGEND" on page 507 | Displays a legend window or refreshes the current LEGEND window |
| | "POPLEGEND" on page 596 | Restores to the LEGEND window the last contents saved with the PUSHLEGEND routine |
| | "PUSHLEGEND" on page 603 | Saves the contents of the LEGEND window |
| | "PUTLEGEND" on page 606 | Specifies the contents of one line in the LEGEND window |
| List | "CLEARLIST" on page 290 | Clears the items from an SCL list without deleting the list and optionally clears all sublist items |
| | "COMPARELIST" on page 298 | Compares two SCL lists |
| | "COPYLIST" on page 311 | Copies or merges the contents of an SCL list into an existing list or a new list |
| | "CURLIST" on page 320 | Designates or reports the current result SCL list |
| | "DELITEM" on page 335 | Deletes an item from an SCL list |
| | "DELLIST" on page 336 | Deletes a list and optionally deletes all of its sublists |
| | "DELNITEM" on page 337 | Deletes a named item from an SCL list |
| | "DESCRIBE" on page 341 | Fills an SCL list with items of system information about a SAS table, view, or catalog entry |
| | "ENVLIST" on page 373 | Returns the list identifier of an SCL environment list |
| | "FILLIST" on page 407 | Fills an SCL list with text and data |
| | "GETITEMC, GETITEML, GETITEMN, and GETITEMO" on page 442 | Returns a value that is identified by its position in an SCL list |
| | "GETLATTR" on page 443 | Returns the attributes of either an SCL list or an item in the list |
| | "GETNITEMC, GETNITEML, GETNITEMN, and GETNITEMO" on page 445 | Return a value identified by its item name in an SCL list |
| | "HASATTR" on page 458 | Reports whether an SCL list or a list item has a specified attribute |
| | "INSERTC, INSERTL, INSERTN, and INSERTO" on page 482 | Insert a value into an SCL list |
| | "ITEMTYPE" on page 497 | Reports the type of an item in an SCL list |
| | "LISTLEN" on page 521 | Reports the length of an SCL list |
| | "LVARLEVEL" on page 531 | Fills an SCL list with the unique values of a column from a SAS table |
| | "MAKELIST" on page 535 | Creates an SCL list |

| | "MAKENLIST" on page 536 | Creates an SCL list that contains named items |
|---|---|---|
| | "NAMEDITEM" on page 555 | Returns the index of a named item in a list |
| | "NAMEITEM" on page 558 | Returns and optionally replaces the name of an item in an SCL list |
| | "POPC, POPL, POPN, and POPO" on page 593 | Removes an item from an SCL list and returns the value of the item |
| | "POPMENU" on page 597 | Displays a pop-up menu that contains character items from an SCL list |
| | "PUTLIST" on page 607 | Displays the contents of an SCL list in the LOG window |
| | "REVLIST" on page 617 | Reverses the order of the items in an SCL list |
| | "ROTLIST" on page 622 | Rotates the items in an SCL list |
| | "SAVELIST" on page 629 | Stores SCL list items in a SAS catalog entry or in an external file |
| | "SEARCHC, SEARCHL, SEARCHN, and SEARCHO" on page 636 | Search for a value in an SCL list and return its position number |
| | "SETITEMC, SETITEML, SETITEMN, and SETITEMO" on page 651 | Store a value at an indexed position in an SCL list |
| | "SETLATTR" on page 656 | Sets the attributes of an SCL list or an item in a list |
| | "SETNITEMC, SETNITEML, SETNITEMN, and SETNITEMO" on page 661 | Assign a value to a named item in an SCL list |
| | "SORTLIST" on page 669 | Sorts the items in an SCL list by value or by name |
| Macro | "SYMGET and SYMGETN" on page 684 | Return the value stored in a macro variable |
| | "SYMPUT and SYMPUTN" on page 685 | Store a value in a SAS macro variable |
| Message | "STDMSG" on page 673 | Displays the text of the SAS software message that is generated by an unknown command |
| | "SYSMSG" on page 686 | Returns the text of SCL error messages or warning messages |
| | "SYSRC" on page 686 | Returns a system error number or the exit status of the most recently called entry |
| Modular Programming | "CBT" on page 274 | Runs a CBT entry |
| | "DISPLAY" on page 350 | Runs a catalog entry that was created with SAS/AF software |
| | "ENDMETHOD" on page 366 | Ends a METHOD statement block |
| | "ENTRY" on page 369 | Receives parameters from the DISPLAY function or routine |

| | | |
|---|---|---|
| | "GETPARMID" on page 448 | Returns the numeric value stored by the SETPARMID routine |
| | "METHOD" on page 539 | Executes a method block that is defined in an SCL entry |
| | "METHOD" on page 540 | Defines a method that can be called by the METHOD routine |
| | "NOCHANGE" on page 569 | Causes the called program to return the original values for the variables that it received as parameters in an ENTRY statement |
| | "SETPARMID" on page 664 | Makes the value of an SCL numeric variable available between SCL programs |
| Object Oriented | "APPLY" on page 252 | Invokes a method whose arguments are passed from an SCL list |
| | "CBT" on page 274 | Runs a CBT entry |
| | "CLASS" on page 277 | Creates a class using SCL code |
| | "CREATESCL" on page 316 | Writes class or interface information to an SCL entry |
| | "DIALOG" on page 345 | Runs a FRAME entry that was created with SAS/AF software and disables all other windows |
| | "DISPLAY" on page 350 | Runs a catalog entry that was created with SAS/AF software |
| | "ENDCLASS" on page 366 | Ends a CLASS statement block |
| | "ENDMETHOD" on page 366 | Ends a METHOD statement block |
| | "ENDPACKAGE" on page 367 | Ends a PACKAGE statement block |
| | "ENDUSECLASS" on page 369 | Ends a USECLASS statement block |
| | "ENTRY" on page 369 | Receives parameters from the DISPLAY function or routine |
| | "GETPARMID" on page 448 | Returns the numeric value stored by the SETPARMID routine |
| | "IMPORT" on page 478 | Defines a search path for references to CLASS entries |
| | "INSTANCE" on page 485 | Creates an object and returns its identifier |
| | "INTERFACE" on page 486 | Defines a group of abstract methods shared by the related classes |
| | "ITEM" on page 496 | Specifies the classes on the server that can be accessed by applications on the client |
| | "LOADCLASS" on page 525 | Loads a class and returns its identifier number |
| | "LOADRES" on page 526 | Loads a RESOURCE entry |
| | "METHOD" on page 540 | Defines a method that can be called by the METHOD routine |
| | "METHOD" on page 539 | Executes a method block that is defined in an SCL entry |

| | | |
|---|---|---|
| | "_NEO_" on page 559 | Creates an object |
| | "_NEW_" on page 563 | Creates an object and runs an associated class constructor |
| | "NOCHANGE" on page 569 | Causes the called program to return the original values for the variables that it received as parameters in an ENTRY statement |
| | "NOTIFY" on page 572 | Sends a method to a control that is identified by its name |
| | "PACKAGE" on page 585 | Defines a group of classes whose metadata must be recognized by objects defined on the client |
| | "SEND" on page 644 | Sends a method to an object using its identifier and can return a value from a called method |
| | "SETPARMID" on page 664 | Makes the value of an SCL numeric variable available between SCL programs |
| | "SUPAPPLY" on page 679 | Invokes the inherited definition of a method and passes the method's arguments in an SCL list |
| | "SUPER" on page 681 | Invokes the inherited definition of a method |
| | "USECLASS" on page 698 | Implements methods for a class and binds them to the class definition |
| SAS System Option | "COMAMID" on page 295 | Returns the list of communications access methods for an operating system |
| | "GETFOOT" on page 441 | Returns the text of a footnote definition |
| | "GETTITLE" on page 449 | Returns the text of a title definition |
| | "GGLOBAL" on page 452 | Returns the text of a SYMBOL, PATTERN, LEGEND, or AXIS statement |
| | "GGLOBALE" on page 454 | Deletes an internal table of SYMBOL, PATTERN, LEGEND, or AXIS definitions |
| | "GGLOBALN" on page 454 | Returns the number of SYMBOL, PATTERN, LEGEND, or AXIS statements that are currently defined |
| | "OPTGETC and OPTGETN" on page 583 | Return the current setting of a SAS system option |
| | "OPTSETC and OPTSETN" on page 584 | Assign a value to a SAS system option |
| | "SETFOOT" on page 650 | Sets the text of a footnote definition |
| | "SETTITLE" on page 666 | Sets the text of a title definition |
| SAS Table | "APPEND" on page 251 | Appends a new row to a SAS table |
| | "ATTRC and ATTRN" on page 258 | Return the value of an attribute for a SAS table |
| | "CLOSE" on page 292 | Closes a SAS table |
| | "CONTENTS" on page 299 | Displays the attributes of a SAS table |
| | "CUROBS" on page 321 | Returns the number of the current row in a SAS table |
| | "DATALISTC and DATALISTN" on page 326 | Displays a selection list window that contains the values of particular columns from rows in a SAS table and returns user selections |

|                 | "SELECTICON" on page 643 | Displays a dialog window that contains a list of icons, and returns the value of the selected icon |
|                 | "SHOWLIST" on page 667 | Displays a selection list window that contains up to 13 items, and returns the user's selections |
| Submit Block | "ENDSUBMIT" on page 367 | Ends statements to be submitted to SAS software for execution |
|                 | "PREVIEW" on page 599 | Manipulates an application's preview buffer |
|                 | "REPLACE" on page 614 | Substitutes a replacement string for a reference to an SCL variable in the SUBMIT block |
|                 | "SUBMIT" on page 676 | Submits statements or commands to SAS for execution |
|                 | "SUBMITCLEAR" on page 678 | Aborts a pending submit transaction |
| System Variable | "_BLANK_" on page 262 | Special missing value |
|                 | "_CFRAME_" on page 277 | Contains the identifier of the FRAME entry that is currently executing |
|                 | "_CURCOL_" on page 318 | Contains the value of the leftmost column in an extended table control in a FRAME entry |
|                 | "_CURROW_" on page 322 | Contains the number of the current row in an extended table |
|                 | "_EVENT_" on page 379 | Contains the type of event that occurred on a FRAME entry control |
|                 | "_FRAME_" on page 429 | Contains the identifier of either the FRAME entry that contains the control or the FRAME entry that is being used as a method |
|                 | "_METHOD_" on page 548 | Contains the name of the method that is currently executing |
|                 | "_MSG_" on page 554 | Contains the text to display on the window's message line the next time the window is refreshed |
|                 | "_SELF_" on page 643 | Contains the identifier of the control for the currently executing method, or the identifier of the FRAME entry if the FRAME entry is not running as a method |
|                 | "_STATUS_" on page 671 | Contains the status of program execution or overrides the normal flow of control |
|                 | "_VALUE_" on page 704 | Contains the value of a FRAME entry component |
| Utility | "ALARM" on page 250 | Sounds an alarm on a device when the current window is refreshed or redisplayed. |
|                 | "BUILD" on page 266 | Invokes the BUILD window in SAS/AF software |
|                 | "COPY" on page 307 | Copies a SAS table, view, catalog, or catalog entry |
|                 | "DELETE" on page 334 | Deletes a member of a SAS data library or an external file or directory |
|                 | "LETTER" on page 512 | Displays the FSLETTER window or sends a letter that was created with the FSLETTER procedure |
|                 | "LIBREF" on page 517 | Verifies that a libref has been assigned |

| | | |
|---|---|---|
| | "MESSAGEBOX" on page 537 | Displays a host message window with a specified text and icon |
| | "NAMEDIVIDE" on page 557 | Returns the number of parts of a compound name as well as the values of each part |
| | "NAMEMERGE" on page 559 | Returns a compound name by merging name parts |
| | "PUT" on page 604 | Writes text to the LOG window |
| | "RENAME" on page 612 | Renames a member of a SAS data library, an external file, or a directory |
| | "RGBDM" on page 619 | Returns the name supported by the SAS windowing environment for a color |
| | "SASNAME" on page 625 | Verifies that a name is a valid SAS name |
| | "TRACEBACK" on page 690 | Displays traceback information for an SCL execution stack |
| | "UNIQUENUM" on page 694 | Returns a unique number |
| | "WAIT" on page 717 | Suspends execution of the next program statement |
| Variable | "MODVAR" on page 551 | Changes the name, label, format, or informat of a column in a SAS table |
| | "VARFMT" on page 705 | Returns the format that is assigned to a SAS table column |
| | "VARINFMT" on page 706 | Returns the informat that is assigned to a SAS table column |
| | "VARLABEL" on page 706 | Returns the label that is assigned to a SAS table column |
| | "VARLEN" on page 707 | Returns the length of a SAS table column |
| | "VARLEVEL" on page 708 | Reports the unique values of a SAS table column |
| | "VARNAME" on page 712 | Returns the name of a SAS table column |
| | "VARNUM" on page 713 | Returns the number of a SAS table column |
| | "VARSTAT" on page 714 | Calculates simple statistics for SAS table columns |
| | "VARTYPE" on page 716 | Returns the data type of a SAS table column |
| Widget or Field | "CURSOR" on page 323 | Positions the cursor in a specified widget or field of a FRAME entry |
| | "CURWORD" on page 324 | Returns the word that is at the cursor position |
| | "FIELD" on page 394 | Performs an action on or reports the state of FRAME entry widgets or fields |
| | "FLDATTR" on page 414 | Changes the color and display attributes of a field, text entry widget, or text label widget to those stored in an attribute string |
| | "FLDCOLOR" on page 416 | Changes the color and display attributes of a field, text entry widget, or text label widget to those stored in an attribute string |
| | "STRATTR" on page 675 | Defines a string for color and display attributes |

| Window | "BLOCK" on page 263 | Displays a menu containing up to 12 choice blocks and returns the number of the user's choice |
|--------|---------------------|-----------------------------------------------------------------------------------------------|
|  | "DMWINDOW" on page 354 | Sets the color and highlighting for lines in the OUTPUT and LOG windows |
|  | "ENDBLOCK" on page 364 | Closes the window that is created by the BLOCK function |
|  | "ICON" on page 464 | Associates an icon with a window |
|  | "PMENU" on page 591 | Changes the PMENU for an application |
|  | "REFRESH" on page 612 | Redisplays a window using current field or control values |
|  | "SAVESCREEN" on page 634 | Saves the values of data entry fields without exiting from the window |
|  | "SCREENNAME" on page 634 | Returns the name of the current window |
|  | "WDEF" on page 718 | Resizes the active window |
|  | "WINFO" on page 721 | Returns information about the current window |
|  | "WNAME" on page 724 | Specifies a name for the active window |
|  | "WOUTPUT" on page 728 | Manipulates the OUTPUT window |
|  | "WREGION" on page 730 | Defines the boundaries for the next window that is displayed |

CHAPTER

*16*

# SAS Component Language Dictionary

---

## ACTIVATE

Activates or grays either a Version 6 check box or radio box widget, or a station in a choice group

**Category:** Control or Field

---

### Syntax

*rc*=**ACTIVATE**(*var-name,station< ,row>*);

**rc**
contains the return code for the operation:

| | |
|---|---|
| 0 | successful |
| ≠0 | not successful |

   Type: Numeric

**var-name**
is the FRAME entry control or choice group to activate.
   Type: Character

**station**
is the number of the station or item to be activated or grayed:

| | |
|---|---|
| >0 | is the number of the station to be activated. |
| <0 | is the number of the station designated by the absolute value of the argument to be grayed instead of activated. Users cannot select a station that has been grayed. |
| 0 | indicates that no station is to be activated. |

   Type: Numeric

**row**
is the row number for a choice group that is in the scrollable section of an extended table. *Row* is valid for PROGRAM entries but not for FRAME entries. Specify *row* only when you want to activate a station from outside an extended table's getrow or putrow section. Do not specify *row* if you want to activate a station with the _getrow or _putrow method or from the getrow or putrow sections.
   Type: Numeric

**Details** ACTIVATE works only for Version 6 widgets in FRAME entries and for choice groups in PROGRAM entries. Version 8 controls use attribute settings to implement this functionality. ACTIVATE is not valid in FSEDIT or FSVIEW programs.

The *station* value is the number of the check box or the item or button in a check box or choice group. For example, if your application has three fields named A, B, and C, and they all belong to the same radio box, then you can make the B field active by passing 2 for the *station* value (B is the second field).

ACTIVATE makes a check box or an item in a radio box or choice group active by assigning the station or item number to the associated window variable. ACTIVATE grays a check box or an item in a radio box or choice group when you assign the negative number of the station or item. When a window element is grayed, users cannot select it.

FRAME entry controls can also use the _activate method.

For linked action fields in choice groups, the action-type pair is considered one station. Linked action fields have the following form:

```
&  &A_____      &  &B_____      &  &C_____
```

To make the linked action pair for B active, pass 2 for the value of *station*, not 4.

## Examples

### Example 1: Activating a Radio Box Station
Activate the second station in the radio box HOBBY:

```
rc=activate('hobby',2);
```

### Example 2: Activating a Station in an Extended Table
Make the third station in the fourth row of an extended table the active station in the choice group LIST:

```
if (activate('list',3,4)) then
   do;
   ...SCL statements to handle the error condition...
   end;
```

## See Also

"GRAY" on page 457

"ISACTIVE" on page 492

"ISGRAY" on page 493

"UNGRAY" on page 693

# ALARM

**Sounds an alarm on a device when the current window is refreshed or redisplayed.**

**Category:** Utility

## Syntax

**ALARM**;

**Details** The ALARM statement sounds the bell when the current window is refreshed or redisplayed. This statement works for devices that support sounds.

## See Also

"CURSOR" on page 323

"FIELD" on page 394

# APPEND

**Appends a new row to a SAS table**

**Category:** SAS Table

## Syntax

*sysrc=*__APPEND__*(table-id< ,option>);*

*sysrc*
contains the return code for the operation:

0                              successful

≠0                            an error or warning condition occurred

*table-id*
contains the identifier for the SAS table, which is returned by the OPEN function.
Type: Numeric

**option**
is one of the following options:

**'NOSET'**
appends a row with all column values set to missing, even if the SET routine has been called.

**'NOINIT'**
appends a row with the values currently in the Table Data Vector (TDV), even if the SET routine has not been called.
Type: Character

**Details** APPEND adds a row to the end of a SAS table. By default, the added row contains missing values. However, you can add a row with the current values in the TDV if SET has been called or if the NOINIT option is specified as the second argument. If SET has been called, the NOSET argument can still force APPEND to fill the row with missing values.

If the SET routine has not been called, you can PUTVARC and PUTVARN to specify values for each column in the TDV before calling APPEND with the NOINIT option. You can use INITROW to initialize the TDV to missing to prevent APPEND from writing bad data to a row values are not explicitly assigned to some columns through PUTVARC or PUTVARN.

## Example

Add a row to the SAS table WORK.DATAONE, which has two columns, FNAME and SSN. Because SET is called, the values **ROBERT** and **999-99-9999** are written to the new row.

```
tableid=open('work.dataone','u');
call set(tableid);
fname='Fname';
ssn='999-99-9999';
if (append(tableid)) then do;
    _msg_=sysmsg();
```

If SET had not been called, then using the NOINIT option would produce the same results:

```
tableid=open('work.dataone','u');
fname='ROBERT';
ssn='999-99-9999';
call putvarc(tableid,varnum(tableid,'fname'),fname);
call putvarc(tableid,varnum(tableid,'ssn'),ssn);
if (append(tableid,'noinit')) then
        _msg_=sysmsg();
```

## See Also

"OPEN" on page 576

"PUTVARC and PUTVARN" on page 609

"SET" on page 646

"UPDATE" on page 697

"INITROW" on page 480

---

# APPLY

**Invokes a method whose arguments are passed from an SCL list**

**Category:**   Object Oriented

## Syntax

**CALL APPLY**(*control-id,method-name,arg-list-id*);

*return-value=***APPLY**(*control-id,method-name,*
     *arg-list-id*);

***control-id***
     is the control whose method is being invoked.
          Type: Numeric

***method-name***
     is the method to invoke.
          Type: Character

***arg-list-id***
> contains the identifier of a list of arguments that the method requires. An invalid *arg-list-id* produces an error condition.
> Type: Numeric

***return-value***
> contains the value returned by *method-name*. The data type for *return-value* should match the data type for the called method.
> Type: Character, List, Numeric, Object, Class, Interface.

**Details**   APPLY provides the functionality of CALL SEND except that you can build a dynamic parameter list at run time instead of coding a fixed parameter list. You can also use APPLY as a function if the called method returns a value with a RETURN statement in the program that defines the method.

**Example**   Instead of using the following statement to invoke a method that you have defined and named METHOD,

```
control.method(10,'abc','xyz',x);
```

you can use

```
args = makelist(4);
args = setitemn(args,10,1);
args = setitemc(args,'abc',2);
args = setitemc(args,'xyz',3);
args = setitemn(args,x,4);
call apply(control,'method',args);
```

More useful is the ability to combine APPLY with the ARGLIST= and REST= keywords in order to write methods that accept variable argument lists:

```
length _method_ $40;
m: method arglist=args;

call apply(otherControl,_method_, args);
```

This calls the method with the same arguments to the otherControl.

For example, a control receiving a method could rebroadcast the method to all controls on its _RECEIVERS_ list:

```
m: method arglist=args;
   _receivers_=getniteml(_self_,'_receivers_',
                         1, 1, 0);
   if _receivers_ then do
      r=listlen(_receivers_) to 1 by -1;
      call apply(getiteml(_receivers_, r),
                 _method_, args);
   end;
endmethod;
```

## See Also

"NOTIFY" on page 572

"RETURN" on page 615

"SEND" on page 644

"SUPAPPLY" on page 679

"SUPER" on page 681

# ARRAY

### Defines elements of an explicit array

**Category:**   Declarative Statement

**Comparisons:**   SAS Statement with limitations in SCL

## Syntax

**ARRAY** *array-name*<*{n}*><*$*><*length*><*elements*>
   <(*initial-values*)>;

### *array-name*

is the name of the array. It cannot be the same as the name of a window variable. However, window variables can be elements of an array.
   Type: Character

### *{n}*

is either the dimension of the array, or an asterisk (*) to indicate that the dimension is determined from the number of array elements or initial values. Multidimensional arrays are allowed. If an asterisk is specified without any array elements or initial values, then the array is a reference array. The dimension of this array will be determined at execution time, based on the corresponding array in the calling program.
   Type: Numeric

### *$*

indicates that the array type is character.

### *length*

is the maximum length of elements in the array. For character arrays, the maximum length cannot exceed 200. The default length is 8 characters. *Length* is ignored for numeric arrays.
   Type: Numeric

### *elements*

are the variables (either window or nonwindow variables) that make up the array, or you can specify '**_TEMPORARY_**' to create a list of temporary data elements.
   Type: Character

### *initial-values*

are the values to use to initialize some or all of the array elements. Separate these values with commas or blanks. By default, all the elements in an array are initialized to missing.
   Type: Character

**Details** If you have elements that you reference only with subscripting, then you can save memory by using the _TEMPORARY_ keyword. The SCL compiler has to allocate memory for the array name and the names of the array elements. However, if this keyword is used, the compiler allocates memory only for the array name. For large arrays, this could result in significant memory savings.

*Note:* Do not use '**_TEMPORARY_**' for *elements* if you plan to use the SET routine to fetch values from a SAS table directly into an array. Use GETVARN and GETVARC when '**_TEMPORARY_**' is specified. △

*Note:* You can also declare temporary arrays using the DECLARE statement. △

**Reference Array** A reference array is a pointer to another defined array. Previously, when an array needed to be passed as a parameter to a METHOD or ENTRY statement, an array of equal size needed to be defined in both the calling program and the called program. This technique used twice as much memory as was actually required. With reference arrays, only one array needs to be defined with the actual size. The array in the called program uses the actual memory of the array in the calling program.

By using reference arrays, you can create general array functions, because the array dimension is determined by the calling program. That is, you do not need to hardcode the array dimension in the SCL program that contains the ENTRY or METHOD statement. See the example later in this section for an illustration of this concept.

Using multidimensional reference arrays is allowed when the dimensions match. For example, if a two-dimensional array is passed in, the reference array must also be two-dimensional.

Reference arrays can currently be used as parameters only in a METHOD or ENTRY statement. Once a reference array has been created by a call to another program, it can be used in any way that a regular array can be used.

**Differences from DATA Step in ARRAY Statement Execution** The ARRAY statement in SCL is very similar to the ARRAY statement in the DATA step and is used to define single or multidimensional arrays. The ARRAY statement in SCL differs from the DATA step ARRAY statement in the following ways:

- □ SCL does not support implicitly subscripted arrays.
- □ SCL does not support the _NUMERIC_, _CHAR_, or _ALL_ keywords.
- □ SCL allows a repetition factor for initialization of arrays.
- □ SCL allows arrays to be used with the IN operator.
- □ SCL supports reference arrays.

For details about the ARRAY statement in the base SAS language, see *SAS Language Reference: Dictionary*.

## Examples

**Example 1: Using Repetition Factors for Array Initialization** In the following statement, note that 1 is repeated three times and the pattern 2,3,4 is repeated four times:

```
array a{16}(0,3*1 ,4*(2,3,4));
```

This statement initializes the values of the elements of array A as follows:

```
0, 1, 1, 1, 2, 3, 4, 2, 3, 4, 2, 3, 4, 2, 3, 4
```

**Example 2: Using an Array with the IN Operator** Consider the following code segment:

```
array a 8 (2 4 6 8 10);

INIT:
   b=6;
   if b in a then put 'B is in array A';
      /* returns location of B in array A */
   c=b in a;
   put c=;
return;
```

This code produces the following output:

```
B is in array A
C=3
```

**Example 3: Using a Reference Array with a METHOD Statement**     Assume that an entry SORT.SCL contains the method definition shown below. The method illustrates the use of a reference array to define a generic sort routine. The routine is termed generic because NSORT does not need to know the size of the array that is being passed: the reference array NARRAY takes on the definition of the array that is specified in the CALL METHOD routine.

```
nsort: method narray [*]:num;
   size = dim( narray );
   do i = 1 to size - 1;
      do j = i + 1 to size;
         if narray( i ) > narray( j ) then
            do;
               ntemp = narray( i );
               narray( i ) = narray( j );
               narray( j ) = ntemp;
            end;
      end;
   end;
endmethod;
```

Here is a sample calling program that executes the NSORT method:

```
array numarray(100);

MAIN:
   do i=1 to dim(numarray);
      numarray(i)=dim(numarray)-i+1;
   end;
   call method('sort.scl', 'nsort', numarray);
return;
```

## See Also

"DECLARE" on page 330

# ASORT

**Sorts an array**

**Category:** Array

## Syntax

*rc*=**ASORT**(*array*< ,*order*>< ,*elements*>);

**rc**
> contains the return code for the operation:

> 0                    successful

> ≠0                   not successful
>> Type: Numeric

**array**
> is an SCL array that was declared in an ARRAY statement.
>> Type: Character

**order**
> specifies the order for the sort:

> **'A'**                   ascending order (the default)

> **'D'**                   descending order
>> Type: Character

**elements**
> is the number of elements to sort.
>> Type: Numeric

**Details**     By default, the array is sorted in ascending order. You can use the optional *order* argument to specify either ascending or descending order.

By default, the entire array is sorted. You can use the optional *elements* argument to restrict sorting to the specified number of elements (starting from the beginning of the array).

If the value of the *elements* argument is greater than the total number of array elements, the program halts execution and sends an error message to the log.

## Example

Sort the first five items of array VALUES in ascending order:

```
array values[8] val1-val8 (3,5,2,1,6,8,7,4);

if (asort(values,'d',5)) then _msg_=sysmsg();
else do;
   _msg_='Sort was successful';
   do i=1 to dim(values);
      put values{i}=;
   end;
end;
```

This produces the following output:

```
values[ 1 ]=6
values[ 2 ]=5
values[ 3 ]=3
values[ 4 ]=2
values[ 5 ]=1
```

```
values[ 6 ]=8
values[ 7 ]=7
values[ 8 ]=4
```

---

# ATTRC and ATTRN

**Return the value of an attribute for a SAS table**

**Category:**   SAS Table

---

## Syntax

*attr-value*=**ATTRC**(*table-id,attr-name*);

*attr-value*=**ATTRN**(*table-id,attr-name*);

**attr-value**
> contains the value of the SAS table attribute. For ATTRC, the value is for a character attribute. For ATTRN, the value is for a numeric attribute.
> Type: Character, Numeric

**table-id**
> contains the identifier for the SAS table. This is the identifier that was returned by the OPEN function when the table was opened. If *table-id* is invalid, the program halts.
> Type: Numeric

**attr-name**
> is the name of the SAS table attribute. If *attr-name* is invalid, then a missing or null value is returned for *attr-value*. Values that can be used with ATTRC are listed in "Attributes for the ATTRC Function" on page 258. Values that can be used with ATTRN are listed in "Attributes for the ATTRN Function" on page 260.
> Type: Character

## Attributes for the ATTRC Function

To check for a character attribute of a SAS table, use ATTRC with one of the following values for *attr-name*:

**'CHARSET'**
> returns a string indicating the character set of the machine that created the SAS table. It returns either one of the following values, or an empty string if the SAS table is not sorted:

> ASCII
>> ASCII character set

> EBCDIC
>> EBCDIC character set

> HASCII
>> extended ASCII character set

> ANSI
>> OS/2 ANSI standard ASCII character set

OEM
  OS/2 OEM code format

**'ENCRYPT'**
  returns **'YES'** or **'NO'** depending on whether the SAS table is encrypted.

**'ENGINE'**
  returns the name of the engine used to access the SAS table.

**'LABEL'**
  returns the label assigned to the SAS table.

**'LIB'**
  returns the libref of the SAS data library in which the SAS table resides.

**'MEM'**
  returns the name of the SAS data library member.

**'MODE'**
  returns the mode in which the SAS table was opened, such as:

| | |
|---|---|
| I | INPUT mode, allows random access if the engine supports it; otherwise, defaults to IN mode |
| IN | INPUT mode, reads sequentially and allows revisiting rows |
| IS | INPUT mode, reads sequentially but does not allow revisiting rows |
| N | NEW mode (to create a new SAS table) |
| U | UPDATE mode, allows random access if the engine supports it; otherwise, defaults to UN mode |
| UN | UPDATE mode, reads sequentially and allows revisiting rows |
| US | UPDATE mode, reads sequentially but does not allow revisiting rows |
| V | UTILITY mode, allows modification of column attributes and indexes that are associated with the SAS table. |

For more information about open modes, see "OPEN" on page 576.

**'MTYPE'**
  returns the type of the SAS data library member.

**'SORTEDBY'**
  returns an empty string if the SAS table is not sorted. Otherwise, returns the names of the BY columns in the standard BY statement format.

**'SORTLVL'**
  returns an empty string if the SAS table is not sorted. Otherwise, returns one of the following:

  WEAK
    The sort order of the SAS table is not validated. That is, the sort order was established by a user (for example, through a SORTEDBY SAS data set option). The system cannot validate its correctness, so the order of the rows cannot be depended upon.

  STRONG
    The sort order of the SAS table is validated. That is, the order of its rows can be depended upon. The sort order was established by the software (for example, through PROC SORT or through the OUT= option on the CONTENTS procedure).

**'SORTSEQ'**
    returns an empty string if the SAS table is sorted on the native machine or if the
    sort collating sequence is the default for the operating system. Otherwise, returns
    the name of the alternate collating sequence that is used to sort the file.

**'TYPE'**
    is the SAS table type.

## Attributes for the ATTRN Function

To check for a numeric attribute, use ATTRN with one of the following values for
*attr-name*:

**'ANY'**
    specifies whether the table has rows or columns:

| | |
|---|---|
| -1 | The table has no rows or columns. |
| 0 | The table has no rows. |
| 1 | The table has both rows and columns. |

**'ALTERPW'**
    indicates whether a password is required in order to alter the SAS table:

| | |
|---|---|
| 1 | The SAS table is alter protected. |
| 0 | The SAS table is not alter protected. |

**'ANOBS'**
    indicates whether the engine knows the number of rows:

| | |
|---|---|
| 1 | The engine knows the correct number of rows. |
| 0 | The engine does not know the correct number of rows. |

**'ARAND'**
    indicates whether the engine supports random access:

| | |
|---|---|
| 1 | The engine supports random access. |
| 0 | The engine does not support random access. |

**'ARWU'**
    indicates whether the engine can manipulate files:

| | |
|---|---|
| 1 | The engine is not read-only. It can create or update SAS files. |
| 0 | The engine is read-only. |

**'CRDTE'**
    returns the SAS table creation date. The value returned is the internal SAS
    DATETIME value for the creation date. Use the DATETIME format to display this
    value.

**'GENMAX'**
    returns the maximum number of generations.

**'GENNEXT'**
    returns the next generation number to generate.

**'ICONST'**
    returns information on the existence of integrity constraints for a SAS table:

| | |
|---|---|
| 0 | No integrity constraints. |
| 1 | One or more general integrity constraints. |

| | |
|---|---|
| 2 | One or more referential integrity constraints. |
| 3 | Both one or more general integrity constraints and one or more referential integrity constraints. |

**'INDEX'**
indicates whether the SAS table supports indexing:

| | |
|---|---|
| 1 | Indexing is supported. |
| 0 | Indexing is not supported. |

**'ISINDEX'**
indicates whether the SAS table is indexed:

| | |
|---|---|
| 1 | At least one index exists for the SAS table. |
| 0 | The SAS table is not indexed. |

**'ISSUBSET'**
indicates whether the SAS table is a subset:

| | |
|---|---|
| 1 | At least one WHERE clause is active. |
| 0 | No WHERE clause is active. |

**'LRECL'**
returns the logical record length.

**'LRID'**
returns the length of the record ID.

**'MODTE'**
returns the last date and time the SAS table was modified. Use the DATETIME format to display this value.

**'NDEL'**
returns the number of deleted rows in the SAS table.

**'NLOBS'**
returns the number of logical rows (those not marked for deletion). An active WHERE clause does not affect this number.

**'NLOBSF'**
returns the number of logical rows (those not marked for deletion) that match the active WHERE clause.

*Note:* NLOBSF should be used with caution. Passing NLOBSF to ATTRN requires the engine to read every row from the table that matches the WHERE clause. Based on the file type and size, this can be a time-consuming process. △

**'NOBS'**
returns the number of physical rows (including those marked for deletion). An active WHERE clause does not affect this number.

**'NVARS'**
returns the number of columns in the SAS table.

**'PW'**
indicates whether a password is required in order to access the SAS table:

| | |
|---|---|
| 1 | The SAS table is protected. |
| 0 | The SAS table is not protected. |

**'RADIX'**
indicates whether access by row number is allowed:

| | |
|---|---|
| 1 | Access by row number is allowed. |

0                      Access by row number is not allowed.

*Note:* A SAS table on a tape engine is index addressable even though it cannot be accessed by row number.

**'READPW'**
indicates whether a password is required in order to read the SAS table:

1                      The SAS table is read protected.

0                      The SAS table is not read protected.

**'TAPE'**
indicates whether the SAS table is a sequential tape file:

1                      The SAS table is a sequential tape file.

0                      The SAS table is not a sequential tape file.

**'WHSTMT'**
returns information about active WHERE clauses:

0                      No WHERE clause is active.

1                      A permanent WHERE clause is active.

2                      A temporary WHERE clause is active.

3                      Both permanent and temporary WHERE clauses are active.

**'WRITEPW'**
indicates whether a password is required in order to write to the SAS table:

1                      The SAS table is write protected.

0                      The SAS table is not write protected.

## Examples

**Example 1: Using the ATTRC Function**    Ensure that the SAS table has been opened in UPDATE mode and display an error message if it is not open:

```
mode=attrc(tableid,'MODE');
if (mode ne 'U') then _msg_=
   'Table not open in UPDATE mode.';
else rc=sort(tableid,'name');
```

**Example 2: Using the ATTRN Function**    Determine whether a WHERE clause is currently active for a SAS table:

```
iswhere=attrn(tableid,'whstmt');
if (iswhere) then _msg_=
   'A WHERE clause is currently active.';
```

## See Also

"DESCRIBE" on page 341

"OPEN" on page 576

# _BLANK_

**Special missing value**

**Category:** System Variable

---

**Details**    _BLANK_ is a system variable that is created for every SCL program that you compile. The compiler creates a space for _BLANK_ in the SCL data vector. In SAS/AF applications, you can compare the value of window variables against the value _BLANK_ to test whether a value has been entered in a field in the window. The test is valid for both numeric and character variables. You can also use _BLANK_ in assignment statements to reset a window variable to a blank, as if the user had not entered a value in the field. You cannot reset the value of the _BLANK_ variable itself.

In comparison operations, _BLANK_ is considered the smallest missing value.

## Example

The following code fragment prints a message if X is modified and is blank:

```
if modified(x) and x eq _blank_ then
    _msg_ = 'Please enter a value';
```

## See Also

"CLRFLD" on page 293

"SETFLD" on page 650

---

# BLOCK

**Displays a menu containing up to 12 choice blocks and returns the number of the user's choice**

**Category:** Window

---

## Syntax

*choice*=**BLOCK**(*window-name,title,color,text-1,* . . . ,
    *text-12*<*,icon-1,* . . . *, icon-12*>);

*choice*
    returns either the number (1-12) of the selected block, or one of the following:
    –99
        if a user requested help for SAS software
    –1 to –12
        if a user requested help for the block
    0
        if a user issued the END, CANCEL, or BYE command
    99
        if an unknown command is issued (see "WORD" on page 725).
    Type: Numeric

*window-name*
    is the title (up to 80 characters) for the window.
        Type: Character

*title*
>   is the title (up to 60 characters) for the menu's title box.
>       Type: Character

*color*
>   is a number from 0 to 33 that represents the combination of colors to be used for the
>   blocks. The colors and numbers are listed in Table 16.1 on page 265. Some devices do
>   not support changing the background color. If you have specified that icons be used
>   with BLOCK, then the specified color combination may not take effect. The display of
>   icons is host specific, and therefore the color may be controlled by the host operating
>   system. (Under Windows or OS/2, use the Color Palette to alter icon colors. Under X
>   windows, set X resources to control icon colors.)
>       Type: Numeric

*text-1, . . . , text-12*
>   is the text for each block or icon to display (up to 14 characters). The blocks or icons
>   are displayed in groups of four. Blocks for the first four *text* values are displayed on
>   the first row, blocks for the second four *text* values are displayed on the middle row,
>   and blocks for the last four *text* values are displayed on the last row. Twelve values
>   are required, but you can use null values for block positions that you do not want
>   displayed.
>       Type: Character

*icon-1, . . . , icon-12*
>   are numbers for icons to display in place of the blocks. If no values are provided for
>   icons, or if the host system does not support icons, then standard rectangular blocks
>   are displayed. If you specify a number for which no icon is defined, then the default
>   SAS icon is displayed. If at least one icon number is specified, and the total number
>   of icons is less than the total number of text labels, then the default SAS icon is
>   displayed for text labels that lack an associated icon number.
>       Type: Numeric

**Details**     The number of text values that you specify determines how many blocks of
icons are displayed in the menu. In order to display an icon menu, you must specify at
least one icon position, although you can display the default SAS icon by specifying 0
for positions for which a value for *text* is supplied.

Because BLOCK does not generate a physical display window, window options such
as KEYS are not recognized. The BLOCK function windows recognize only DMKEYS
settings. To alter DMKEYS settings for a BLOCK menu, you can use GETFKEY and
SETFKEY in a program that runs before the BLOCK menu opens. This program must
have a display screen associated with it.

This function attempts to display the blocks in the best manner depending upon the
characteristics of the user's display device. The function displays up to three rows of
four blocks. Blocks are displayed in the order in which the *text* arguments appear in the
function. Only the nonblank choices are displayed, and the blocks in each row are
centered in the row.

When the function is called, it queries the current value of *choice*. If the value of
*choice* corresponds to a valid selection number, the cursor is positioned on the correct
block. Otherwise, the cursor is positioned in the upper-left corner of the window.

To make a selection from the block menu, a user must move the cursor to the
appropriate block and then press ENTER or click the mouse. BLOCK returns the index
of the selection.

If a user presses the HELP key on one of the selections, then the negative of the
selection is returned. If a user presses the HELP key while the cursor is not on one of
the blocks, then the value –99 is returned.

If a user issues the END or CANCEL command via a function key, then the value 0
is returned.

Use ENDBLOCK to close the menu window that is opened by BLOCK.
Table 16.1 on page 265 lists values that can be used for *color*.

## Values For The Color Argument

**Table 16.1** Values for the *Color* Argument

| Color | Background | Border | Text | Icon | Shadow |
|---|---|---|---|---|---|
| 0 | black | white | white | white | white |
| 1 | black | gray | cyan | gray | blue |
| 2 | black | gray | cyan | gray | blue |
| 3 | black | cyan | cyan | gray | cyan |
| 4 | black | gray | white | cyan | gray |
| 5 | black | cyan | yellow | cyan | blue |
| 6 | black | gray | white | blue | gray |
| 7 | black | gray | yellow | blue | gray |
| 8 | black | gray | white | red | gray |
| 9 | black | gray | white | pink | gray |
| 10 | black | gray | white | yellow | gray |
| 11 | black | gray | white | red | blue |
| 12 | blue | gray | cyan | gray | black |
| 13 | blue | gray | yellow | gray | black |
| 14 | blue | gray | white | gray | black |
| 15 | blue | gray | white | magenta | black |
| 16 | blue | gray | white | red | black |
| 17 | blue | gray | white | cyan | black |
| 18 | blue | yellow | white | yellow | black |
| 19 | blue | gray | white | magenta | gray |
| 20 | blue | gray | white | red | gray |
| 21 | gray | blue | black | blue | black |
| 22 | gray | red | black | red | black |
| 23 | gray | magenta | black | magenta | black |
| 24 | gray | blue | black | cyan | blue |
| 25 | gray | cyan | black | cyan | black |
| 26 | red | gray | white | gray | black |
| 27 | red | gray | black | gray | black |
| 28 | pink | gray | white | gray | black |
| 29 | pink | gray | black | gray | black |
| 30 | yellow | gray | black | gray | black |
| 31 | brown | gray | gray | gray | black |

| Color | Background | Border | Text | Icon | Shadow |
|---|---|---|---|---|---|
| 32 | background* | border* | foreground* | secondary background* | black |
| 33 | secondary background* | secondary border* | foreground* | background* | black |

\* SASCOLOR window element names.

## Example

Create a menu with five choices represented by icons. The first row contains two icons, **Outline** and **Index**. The second row contains two icons, **Compare Files** and **Calendar**. The third row contains a single icon, **End**.

Because the CHOICE variable is assigned the value 5 before BLOCK is called, the cursor is positioned on the Compare Files icon when the window opens. When a user makes a selection, the SELECT statement either exits the DO loop or calls another PROGRAM entry. When control returns from the called program, the menu is displayed again.

```
INIT:
choice=5;
LOOP:
   do while(choice ne 0);
      choice=block('Writers Toolbox',
        'Main Menu',6,'Outline','Index',
        '','','Compare Files',
        'Calendar','','',
        'End','','','',
        1,2,0,0,3,4,0,0,111,0,0,0);
      select(choice);
         when(1) call display('outl.scl');
         when(2) call display('index.scl');
         when(5) call display('compare.scl');
         when(6) call display('calend.scl');
         when(9) leave LOOP;
         otherwise do;
            if (choice<0) then
            call display('help.scl',choice);
         end;
      end;
   end;
   call endblock();
return;
```

## See Also

"ENDBLOCK" on page 364

# BUILD

**Invokes the BUILD window in SAS/AF software**

**Category:** Utility

## Syntax

**CALL BUILD**(*entry*< ,*open-mode*< ,*resource*>< ,*pmenu*>>);

*entry*
> is the name of an entry in a SAS catalog. A one-level name is assumed to be WORK.*catalog*. A two-level name is assumed to be *libref.catalog*. A three-level name is assumed to be *libref.catalog.entry*.PROGRAM. A four-level name is assumed to be *libref.catalog.entry.type*.
>
> If a catalog is specified instead of a catalog entry, the Explorer window is brought up and the three optional parameters are ignored.
> Type: Character

*open-mode*
> is the mode in which to open the catalog:

> **'EDIT' | 'E'**
>> opens the catalog entry for editing. (This is the default.)

> **'BROWSE' | 'B'**
>> opens the catalog entry for browsing.

> **'COMPILE <NOMSG>' | 'C <NOMSG>'**
>> compiles the FRAME, PROGRAM, or SCL entry specified in *entry*. The **NOMSG** option prevents NOTE messages from being sent to the SAS log when batch files are being run (or to the LOG window for all other files) when the program is compiled, but it does not suppress compiler error or warning messages.
>> Type: Character

*resource*
> is the RESOURCE entry if *entry* is a FRAME entry. A one- or three-level name can be specified. A one-level name assumes that the RESOURCE entry is in the current catalog, the SASUSER.PROFILE catalog, or the SASHELP.FSP catalog.
> Type: Character

*pmenu*
> is the PMENU entry for the DISPLAY window. If *pmenu* is not supplied, a default PMENU entry is displayed. A one-level name assumes that the PMENU entry is in either the current catalog, the SASUSER.PROFILE catalog, or the SASHELP.FSP catalog. For FRAME and PROGRAM entries, you can specify a secondary PMENU entry for the SOURCE window. Use a space to separate a secondary PMENU name from a main PMENU name.
> Type: Character

**Details**    You can use the BUILD routine to

- □ open catalog entries from within an application
- □ compile PROGRAM, FRAME, or SCL entries without displaying the contents of the entries
- □ view SAS/GRAPH or SAS/AF entries.

If a catalog entry is specified in the first parameter instead of an entry, none of the optional parameters are honored.

*Note:* When a program uses the BUILD routine, SAS/AF software must be licensed at sites where the application is executed. △

## Examples

**Example 1: Opening an Entry**     Open a PROGRAM entry named NAME in edit mode in the catalog MYLIB.MYCAT:

```
call build('mylib.mycat.name');
```

**Example 2: Compiling a FRAME Entry**     Compile the source code for the entry A.FRAME in the WORK.TEST catalog without opening a DISPLAY window for the entry and without displaying any NOTES:

```
call build('work.test.a.frame','compile nomsg');
```

**Example 3: Specifying RESOURCE and PMENU Entries**     Edit a FRAME using a particular RESOURCE and PMENU:

```
call build('lib.cat.name.frame','e',
    'lib.cat.build.resource','lib.cat.build.pmenu');
```

**Example 4: Specifying a Secondary PMENU Entry**     Edit a FRAME entry using a custom PMENU for both the DISPLAY and SOURCE windows. The DISPLAY window uses MYPMENU1.PMENU, and the SOURCE window uses MYPMENU2.PMENU.

```
call build('lib.cat.a.frame','e','',
    'mypmenu1 mypmenu2');
```

## See Also

"CBT" on page 274

"DISPLAY" on page 350

# CATCH

**Processes an exception that has been thrown with the THROW statement**

**Category:**   Control Flow

## Syntax

**CATCH** *exception*;
        /* *SCL statements to process the exception* */

**ENDCATCH**;

   *Note:*   CATCH blocks must always be enclosed in DO statements. △

*exception*
   is the local variable for the exception (which is an instance of the SCLException class) that you want to process.

## Details

When an exception is raised via the THROW statement, normal execution of the program stops, and SCL begins looking for a CATCH block to process the exception.

The CATCH block can contain any statements needed to process the exception, including additional CATCH and THROW statements.

SCL uses the scope of the DO group that contains the CATCH block and the class of the exception to determine which CATCH block to execute. For details, see "How SCL Determines Which CATCH Block To Execute" on page 160.

Each entry in the stack can process an exception and then pass it back up the stack by rethrowing it, which allows the calling entry to perform additional processing. Each entry can perform whatever processing is relevant to that entry.

If an exception is rethrown within a CATCH block, no other CATCH block within the same scope can recatch the exception. The exception is passed out of the scope where it was thrown. Also, you cannot define multiple CATCH blocks for the same exception within the same scope.

## Example

The following DO group declares a local exception variable called NE, creates a new instance of NE, and throws the new exception. The CATCH block prints the traceback information that is automatically stored by SCL when an exception is thrown.

```
do;
dcl SCLException NE = _new_ NewException('Exception in method m');
throw NE;

catch NE;
    put NE.getMessage();              /* Print exception information. */
    call putlist(NE.traceback);
endcatch;
end;
```

## See Also

"THROW" on page 688

Chapter 10, "Handling Exceptions," on page 157

# CATLIST

**Displays a host selector window that lists entries in a SAS catalog, and returns user selections**

**Category:** Catalog, Selection List

## Syntax

*selections*=**CATLIST**(*catalog-name,type,num-sel,prefix< ,message>*);

### *selections*

contains one or more user selections from the list. Separate multiple selections with one or more blanks. By default, *selections* is 200 bytes long. To accommodate values longer than 200 bytes, explicitly declare *selections* with a longer length.
Type: Character

**catalog-name**

is either a SAS catalog name, in the form *libref.catalog*, or * to allow a user to interactively select a libref, catalog, and entry.

Type: Character

**type**

is the entry type to list for selection (for example, SCL or FRAME). To display the names of all entries in the catalog, use '**ALL**' or ' '.

**num-sel**

is the maximum number of items a user can select. To display the list for information only (no selections allowed), specify **0**. To specify an unlimited number of selections, use a value that is equal to or larger than the number of available selections. A user cannot make a number of selections that exceeds the number of items in the list.

Type: Numeric

**prefix**

specifies whether selected entries are prefixed by the catalog name:

'**Y**'  returns selected names in the form *libref.catalog.entry.type*. This is the default value if *catalog-name* is *.

'**N**' | ' '  returns selected names in the form *entry.type*.

Type: Character

**message**

is the text for the message that is displayed at the top of the selection list window. The default message tells users to make up to *num-sel* selections.

Type: Character

**autoclose**

is an obsolete argument but is retained for compatibility with earlier releases. If you want to specify a value for *num-sel*, then specify ' ' as a placeholder for this argument.

Type: Character

**Details**    You can provide default values that will be initially selected when the catalog selection list is displayed. To do this, assign the values to the *selections* variable before calling CATLIST. If *selections* contains valid values when the function is invoked, then those names are automatically designated as selected when the selection list is displayed.

If a user closes the Catalog Entry Selector window without making a selection, then CATLIST returns a blank value unless there was an initial value for the *selections* variable before CATLIST was called.

Selections from the window can be returned in the current result list, if one is available. The current result list is a special SCL list that is automatically filled with the values that have been selected from a selection list. To create a current result list, use the MAKELIST function to create it, and use the CURLIST function to designate it as the current result list. The current result list must exist before you call the CATLIST function.

When CATLIST is invoked, the current result list is cleared. After CATLIST is invoked, the result list contains the following named items:

TAG

identifies the list as one that was created by CATLIST.

Type: Character

COUNT

contains either the number of selected elements, or 0 if a user makes no selections or issues a CANCEL command in the list window.

Type: Numeric

NAME
> contains the uppercase name of each selected catalog entry. If the value of *prefix* is
> **Y**, then the prefix is appended to the beginning of each name. There is one NAME
> element for each selection.
> > Type: Character

DESC
> contains the description of each selected catalog entry. There is one DESC element
> for each selection. The value of DESC is in the same case that was entered
> originally.
> > Type: Character

DATE
> contains the date of last modification for each selected catalog entry. There is one
> DATE element for each selected catalog entry.
> > Type: Character

Because some engines support mixed-case filenames, CATLIST now retains the cases of
the returned selected items. This may cause your application to fail if your application
contains code that assumes the returned selection is uppercased. For example,

```
if (catlist(dsid, 'TESTNDX')='NDXVAR')
```

must be changed to

```
if (upcase(catlist(dsid, 'TESTNDX'))='NDXVAR'
```

If the application cannot be modified, you may need to specify the
VALIDVARNAME=V6 system option when you run the application to ensure that the
selections returned from the CATLIST function will be uppercased.

## Example

Display a selection list that contains the entries in the catalog MYLIB.TEST, and
allow users to make up to five selections. Use GETNITEMC to retrieve the selected
values from the current result list.

```
listid=makelist();
rc=curlist(listid);
selections=catlist('mylib.test','all',5);
n=getnitemn(listid,'COUNT');
do i=1 to n;
   name=getnitemc(listid,'NAME',i);
   desc=getnitemc(listid,'DESC',i);
   date=getnitemc(listid,'DATE',i);
   put name= desc= date=;
end;
```

## See Also

"CURLIST" on page 320

"DIRLIST" on page 347

"FILELIST" on page 401

"LIBLIST" on page 513

---

# CATNAME

**Defines a concatenated catalog, which contains a logical combination of the entries in two or more catalogs**

**Category:**   Catalog

---

## Syntax

*rc*=**CATNAME**(*cat-name,action<,catalog-list><,list-id>*);

**rc**
   contains the return code for the operation:

   | | |
   |---|---|
   | 0 | successful |
   | 1 | not successful |

   Type: Numeric

**cat-name**
   is a two-level name (*libref.catalog*) for the concatenated catalog. The libref must already be defined.
   Type: Character

**action**
   specifies the action to take on *cat-name*:

   | | |
   |---|---|
   | **'SET'** | sets the definition. |
   | **'CLEAR'** | clears the definition. |
   | **'LIST'** | lists the members and saves them in the SCL list referenced by *list-id*. |

   Type: Character

**catalog-list**
   lists the two-level names (*libref.catalog*) of two or more SAS catalogs whose entries are logically combined in *cat-name*. Use at least one blank space to separate catalog names. This list can contain concatenated catalogs that were previously defined with the CATNAME function.
   Type: Character

**list-id**
   contains the identifier for the list of catalogs to be logically combined in *cat-name*, if *action* is **SET** and *catalog-list* is not specified. If *action* is **LIST**, then the list contains the following information about all of the entries:

**CATNAME**
> The catalog name, which is a two-level name (libref.catalog) for the concatenated catalog.
> > Type: Character

**LEVELS**
> The total number of levels of the defined catalog name.
> > Type: Numeric

**(sublist1...sublist*n*)**
> Sublist number 1 to *n*, where *n* is the total number of levels.
> > Type: List
> > The sublist elements are as follows:
>
> > ☐ **LEVEL**, which is the level number. Type: Numeric
>
> > ☐ **CATALOG**, which is the catalog name. Type: Character
>
> > ☐ **ENGINE**, which is the engine name. Type: Character
>
> > ☐ **PHYSICAL NAME OF LIBRARY**, which is the physical name of the library.
> > > Type: Character

> Type: Numeric or List

**Details**    CATNAME defines a concatenated catalog that is a logical combination of the entries in two or more SAS catalogs. When the program uses *cat-name* as the catalog in a catalog entry name, SAS searches for the specified entry in the catalogs specified in *catalog-list* or *list-id*. A concatenated catalog name that is defined with CATNAME can be part of *catalog-list* or *list-id* for another CATNAME function.

This feature is most useful for debugging and testing during application development. It eliminates the need to copy a whole catalog when you need to test and change a single catalog entry that contains a particular method.

## Examples

**Example 1: Defining a CATNAME**    Create concatenated catalog S.T, which logically combines the entries in catalogs A.B and C.D. Then, create concatenated catalog E.F, which contains the logical combination of the entries in the concatenated catalog S.T as well as the entries in Q.T and X.Y. A subsequent reference in a program to S.T.TEST.SCL causes SAS to search for A.B.TEST.SCL and then for C.D.TEST.SCL. A reference to E.F.TEST.SCL causes SCL to search for A.B.TEST.SCL, then for C.D.TEST.SCL, then for Q.T.TEST.SCL, and finally for X.Y.TEST.SCL.

```
rc=catname ('s.t','set','a.b c.d');
rc=catname ('e.f','set','s.t q.t x.y');
```

**Example 2: Defining a CATNAME for a *list-id***    Use the 'LIST' action to query the definition of E.F from Example 1.

```
list=makelist();
rc=catname('e.f','list','',list);
call putlist(list);
```

## See Also

"SEARCH" on page 635

# CBT

**Runs a CBT entry**

**Category:** Modular Programming and Object Oriented

## Syntax

**CALL CBT**(*entry<,frame><,frame-name>*);

*entry*
> is the name of a CBT entry. Specify a CBT entry in the current catalog with *entry*. Specify an entry in the current catalog with *entry.type*. Specify a CBT entry in a different catalog with *libref.catalog.entry*. Specify a different type of entry in a different catalog with *libref.cat-name.entry.type*.

*frame*
> is the number of the frame in the CBT entry to be displayed initially.
> Type: Numeric

*frame-name*
> is the name assigned to the frame in the CBT to be displayed initially. If this argument is specified, the value of *frame* is ignored.
> Type: Character

**Details**    The CBT routine opens a CBT entry window. You can optionally specify the name or number of the CBT frame to display initially. For information about CBT entries, see the SAS documentation for SAS/AF software. You can use CBT entries to link detailed instructional information with an application so that the information is readily available.

The following restrictions apply for users of a CBT entry that is called from an SCL program:

- □ The SAVE command is not recognized.
- □ =X returns the user to the calling program.
- □ QCANCEL returns the user to the calling program.
- □ QEND returns the user to the calling program.

## Examples

**Example 1: Displaying a Particular CBT Frame**    Display the second frame of the entry EXAMPLE.CBT:

```
call cbt('example',2);
```

Display the frame named ABC of the entry EXAMPLE.CBT:

```
call cbt('example',1,'abc');
```

**Example 2: Calling a CBT Entry**    Suppose an application requires users to be familiar with a particular set of terminology. You use the following program to call a CBT course (in this example, TERMINAL.CBT) that teaches the appropriate information. The following example runs the CBT entry if a user issues the command TEACH. Then, when the user exits the CBT course, it returns control to the SCL statement that follows the call to TERMINAL.CBT.

```
control always;
if (upcase(word(1))='TEACH') then
    do;
        call nextcmd();
        call cbt('terminal');
    end;
```

## See Also

"DISPLAY" on page 350

"GOTO" on page 455

# CENTER

**Returns a centered character string**

**Category:**  Character

## Syntax

*centered-string*=**CENTER**(*string*<,*length*>);

**centered-string**
   contains the centered character string. If *centered-string* already exists, then specifying *length* changes the length of *centered-string* to the number of characters specified in *length*.
      Type: Character

**string**
   contains the character string to be centered.
      Type: Character

**length**
   contains the length in which the character string is to be centered. The default is the maximum length of *centered-string*.
      Type: Numeric

**Details**   The default length is the maximum length of *centered-string*. The string is centered by padding with spaces. To enable CENTER to work properly when *centered-string* is a window variable, set the justification attribute (**JUST**) for the control or field to **NONE**.

To left- or right-justify a string, use LEFT or RIGHT, respectively.

## See Also

"LEFT" on page 506

"RIGHT" on page 620

---

# CEXIST

Verifies the existence of a SAS catalog or SAS catalog entry

**Category:** Catalog

---

## Syntax

*rc*=**CEXIST**(*entry*< ,'U'>);

*rc*
   contains the return code for the operation:

1                    The SAS catalog or catalog entry exists.

0                    The SAS catalog or catalog entry does not exist.
   Type: Numeric

*entry*
   is SAS catalog, or the name of an entry in a catalog. A one- or two-level name is assumed to be the name of a catalog. To test for the existence of an entry within a catalog, use a three- or four-level name.
   Type: Character

**'U'**
   tests whether the catalog specified in *entry* can be opened for updating.
   Type: Character

## Examples

**Example 1: Testing Whether a Catalog Can Be Updated**    Test whether the catalog LIB.CAT1 exists and can be opened for update. If the catalog does not exist, a message is displayed on the message line.

```
if (cexist('lib.cat1','u')) then
   _msg_='The catalog LIB.CAT1 exists and can be
                        opened for update.';
else _msg_=sysmsg();
```

**Example 2: Verifying the Existence of a Catalog**    Verify the existence of the entry X.PROGRAM in LIB.CAT1:

```
if (cexist('lib.cat1.x.program')) then
   _msg_='Entry X.PROGRAM exists';
else _msg_=sysmsg();
```

## See Also

"EXIST" on page 383

# _CFRAME_

**Contains the identifier of the FRAME entry that is currently executing**

**Category:** System Variable

**Details** _CFRAME_ is a system variable that is provided automatically for FRAME entries. _CFRAME_ has a valid value only when a FRAME entry's SCL code is running or when a FRAME entry or component method is running.

## Example

Suppose the entry FIRST.FRAME contains an icon. The icon's _select method is defined to run SECOND.FRAME, which contains the following program:

```
INIT:
        /* Send a method to the current FRAME */
    _CFRAME_._setMsg('Running the Select method');
return;
TERM:
        /* Send a method to the FRAME that  */
        /* contains the icon                */
    _FRAME_._setMsg('The Select method has finished.');
return;
```

When FIRST.FRAME displays and a user selects the icon, SECOND.FRAME displays with the message "Running the Select method." After the user ends from SECOND.FRAME, FIRST.FRAME displays the message "The Select method has finished." This is accomplished by sending the _setMsg method to _CFRAME_ (the FRAME entry that is currently running) in the INIT section and by sending _setMsg to _FRAME_ (the FRAME entry that contains the icon) in the TERM section.

## See Also

"_FRAME_" on page 429

# CLASS

**Creates a class using SCL code**

**Category:** Object Oriented

## Syntax

<ABSTRACT> CLASS *class-name*<EXTENDS *parent-class-name*>
    <SUPPORTS *supports-interface-clause*>

```
        <REQUIRES requires-interface-clause>
        < / (class-optional-clause)>
         <(attribute-statements)>
        <(method-declaration-statements)>
         <(method-implementation-blocks)>
        <(event-declaration-statements)>
         <(eventhandler-declaration-statements)>
      ENDCLASS;
```

**ABSTRACT**

is an optional keyword used to define a class as an abstract class. Methods defined inside an abstract class are not required to have method implementations. Abstract classes are used to specify a common interface for several classes. An abstract class can not be instantiated through the _NEW_ operator.

*class-name*

is the name of a class that you are creating, which can be specified as a one- to four-level name.

*parent-class-name*

specifies the parent class of *class-name* and is specified as EXTENDS *parent-class-name*. *Parent-class-name* can be specified as a one- to four-level name.

If no EXTENDS clause is supplied, *parent-class-name* defaults to SASHELP.FSP.OBJECT.CLASS, which is the parent class of all SAS/AF classes.

*supports-interface-clause*

lists the interfaces that this class supports. Interfaces can be specified as follows:
      SUPPORTS*interface-1<,interface-2...>*

The *interface* names can be specified as one- to four-level names. All of the methods listed in SUPPORTS must be implemented in the CLASS block.

*requires-interface-clause*

lists the interfaces required for this class. Interfaces are specified as follows:
      REQUIRES *interface-1<,interface-2...>*

The *interface* names can be specified as one- to four-level names. The REQUIRES interfaces are used for the client-server model. For more information, see "INTERFACE" on page 486.

*class-optional-clause*

specifies options for the class. Options should be placed inside parentheses following a / (slash). Separate multiple options with commas. Class options can be any of the following:

`Description`=*description*

is a description of the CLASS entry

`MetaClass`=*class-name*

is the four-level name of the CLASS entry that contains the model of a class. The default MetaClass is SASHELP.FSP.CLASS.CLASS.

*attribute-statements*

defines the class attributes, which determine how an object will look and behave. Attributes can either be scalars or arrays. The syntax of a class attribute statement is: *access-scope type var-name< / (attribute options)>*;

*access-scope*

can be one of the following:

**'PUBLIC'**
> specifies that the attribute can be accessed by any SCL program. DECLARE may be used in place of public scope.

**'PRIVATE'**
> specifies that the attribute can be accessed only from methods in the class where the attribute is defined.

**'PROTECTED'**
> specifies that the attribute can be accessed only from methods in subclasses of the class where the attribute is defined. Since a class can be considered a subclass of itself, a protected attribute can also be accessed from the class where it is defined.

*type*
> is the data type of the attribute. NUM, CHAR, LIST, OBJECT or a four-level *class-name* are possible values of *type*.

*var-name*
> is the name of the attribute. You can specify a multi-dimensional array by providing an array dimension after *var-name*. For example:

```
PRIVATE num narray{3, 2, 3};
```

> If an array variable has the same name as a method, the method name has higher precedence when referencing that array. To avoid ambiguity, use **[ ]** or **{ }** instead of **( )** to specify the array reference.

*attribute-options*
> specifies options for a class attribute. List options inside parentheses following a / (slash). Separate multiple options with commas. *Attribute-options* can be any of the following:

**AutoCreate='N' | 'Y'**
> determines whether an SCL list is created automatically when an instance of the class is created. If **AutoCreate='Y'** (default), a four-level object name or SCL list is created depending on the attribute type. If **'N'**, then a four-level object name or SCL list is not created, and the user is responsible for creating and deleting this list.

**Category**=*category-name*
> specifies the category for an attribute. Categories organize attributes so that you can display only attributes for the category. You can create your own category names. Components that are supplied with SAS software belong to the following categories:
>
> > Appearance
> >
> > Data
> >
> > Drag and drop
> >
> > Help
> >
> > Misc (Miscellaneous)
> >
> > Region
> >
> > Size/location
>
> Misc is the default.

**Description**=*attribute-description*
> specifies the description of the attribute. When you click on an attribute in the Class Editor, this text is displayed below the list of attributes.

**Editable=**'**N**' | '**Y**'

determines whether attributes can be altered. '**Y**' is the default.

If **EDITABLE='Y'**, then the attribute can be set anywhere that it is in scope:

□ If the attribute is defined in class C and it is a public attribute, then it can be set anywhere.

□ If the attribute is defined in class C and it is a private attribute, then it can only be set from methods in the class C.

□ If the attribute is defined in class C and it is a protected attribute, then it can only be set from methods in C and subclasses of C.

If **EDITABLE='N'**, then the ability to set the attribute is restricted based on its scope:

□ If the attribute is defined in a class C and it is a public attribute, then it can only be set from methods in C and subclasses of C.

□ If the attribute is defined in class C and it is a protected attribute, then it can only be set from methods in C.

□ If the attribute is defined in class C and it is a private attribute, it cannot be set anywhere. (It is effectively a constant.)

**Editor=**editor-entry-name

specifies a FRAME, SCL, or PROGRAM entry that returns a value. The **Editor=** option is available for attributes of all types except OBJECT. If supplied, the specified entry is displayed and executed by the Properties window when the ellipsis button (...) in the cell is clicked. The value that is returned from the entry is displayed in the cell in the Properties window.

Editors are typically FRAME entries that are designed to aid an application developer in specifying a value for an attribute. For example, for an attribute called 'textColor' that can be assigned to any hexcolor string, you could design a FRAME entry window to help the user visually see what the hexcolor string represents. The window could contain an RGB slider control with a sample box that shows the color that is being created as a user manipulates the red/green/ blue sliders. In this example, you assign the name of the FRAME entry as the value of **EDITOR=**, and this window opens when a user selects the **...** button for the TEXTCOLOR attribute in the Properties window.

**GetCAM=**method-name

specifies the custom access method to be executed when the value of the attribute is queried. Using dot notation to query an attribute for which a getCAM method has been defined may result in side effects. See "What Happens When Attribute Values Are Set or Queried" on page 122.

**InitialValue=**initial-values

specifies an initial value for the attribute. This option is valid only for attributes with types CHAR , NUM, and SCL LIST.For an example of using an SCL list as an initial value, see "Initializing the Values in a List" on page 51.

**Linkable=**'**N**' | '**Y**'

determines whether an attribute is linkable from the Properties window. Only public attributes are linkable. Private and protected attributes are not displayed in the Properties window. **Y** is the default.

**SendEvent=**'**N**' | '**Y**'

determines whether an attribute sends an event when modified. When **SENDEVENT='Y'**, SAS assigns the Event Name, which has the format ''attributeName **Changed**'', and registers it with the component. **Y** is the default. When **SENDEVENT='N'**, no Event name will be registered

**SetCAM**=*method-name*
> specifies the custom access method to be executed when the attribute value is assigned.Using dot notation to set an attribute for which a setCAM method has been defined may result in side effects. See "What Happens When Attribute Values Are Set or Queried" on page 122.

**State='N'|'O'**
> determines whether the attribute is new or is overridden. **N** is the default.

**ValidValues**=*valid-values*
> specifies the values that are valid for the CHARACTER attribute. Use a space or '/' or ',' to separate the values.
> The following options are used for compatibility with Version 6 classes:

**Automatic='Y' | 'N'**
> specifies whether *var-name* is an automatic instance variable.

**IV**=*V6-instance-variable-name*
> specifies the name of a Version 6 instance variable.

**PureIV='Y' | 'N'**
> When **PureIV='Y'**, it specifies that *var-name* is a pure Version 6 instance variable and that no associated Version 8 attribute will be created. **N** is the default.

***method-declaration-statements***
> list the class methods.
> For *method-declaration-statements*, use the following syntax:

```
method-label-name : <access-scope> METHOD<parameter-list>
              < / (method-options)>;
```

*method-label-name*
> can be up to 32 characters and has the same restrictions as an SCL label. By default, you should treat *method-label-name* the same as the method name. To define a more descriptive method name which is over 32 characters, use the **method=** option.

*access-scope*
> can be one of the following:

> **PUBLIC**
>> designates a method that can be inherited by subclasses and accessed anywhere the corresponding object exists. This is the default.

> **PRIVATE**
>> designates a method that can be accessed only by methods in the class in which the method is defined. Private methods will not be inherited by subclasses of the class.

> **PROTECTED**
>> designates a method that can be accessed only by subclasses in which the method is defined. Since a class can be considered a subclass of itself, a protected method can also be accessed from the class in which it is defined.

*parameter-list*
> For parameter options such as using Input/Output/Update to store the parameter storage, using ":" operator to specify the parameter type, using **Optional=** to specify the varying arguments in the method, and using **Return=** to specify the

method return type, as well as **Arglist=** and **Rest=**, can all be applied in the parameter list. For more information, see "METHOD" on page 540.

*method-options*

specify options for a class method. You must put the list inside parentheses that follow a / (slash). Separate multiple options with commas. The available options are

**Abstract='N' | 'Y'**

specifies that the method is an abstract method and does not have an implementation associated with it. Abstract methods can be declared only in abstract classes. The default is **'N'**.

**Description=**ment*method-description-string*

specifies the description of the method.

**Enabled='N' | 'Y'**

determines whether a method can be temporarily disabled. **Y** is the default.

**Label=**'*method-label*'

identifies a method whose label is different from the method-label-name. If the **Label=** option exists, the **Method=** option cannot be used.

**Method=**'*method-name*'

identifies the *method-label-name* as the label name and the 'method-name' will be used for the method reference in the dot notation or CALL SEND routine. Since the '*method-name*' is a string, you can extend the method name up to 256 characters. If the **Method=** option exists, the **Label=** option cannot be used.

**Native=**'/*executable-name:n*

specifies the name of a system-implemented method.

> *Note:* This option is generated by the CREATESCL function. △

**SCL | Entry=**four-level-entry-name-string

identifies the entry that contains the USECLASS block that implements the method. This option is required when the method is not implemented in the SCL entry that contains the CLASS statement block.

**Signature='N' | 'Y'**

determines whether the method has a signature. Y is the default. All methods in Version 6 classes have **Signature='N'**. Adding *parameter-list* and removing **Signature='N'** for each method will cause the SCL compiler to generate signatures for that method. **Signature='Y'** is required for method overloading.

**State='O' | 'N'**

determines whether the method has been overridden or is new.

**Forward='N' | 'Y'**

determines whether the method can be forward referenced when **Forward='Y'**. The SCL compiler is a one-pass compiler and will report errors when referencing a method that has not been defined in the current class. Using **Forward='Y'** will allow the SCL compiler to suppress the error messages and delay validation of the forward methods which are required to be defined later in the current class. If the forward method is not defined before the ENDCLASS statement, the SCL compiler will report the error. **N** is the default. This option can be used for methods calling each other.

**ArgDesc1 | ArgDesc2 |...| ArgDescN** =*each-argument-description-string*

specifies each argument description. This option is used for documenting the parameters.

**ReturnDesc**=*return-argument-description-string*
> specifies the return argument description. This option is used for documenting the return parameter.

***method-implementation-blocks***
> contain any SCL statements for the defined methods. These statements perform the operations of the method.

***event-declaration-statements***
> define the class events. Declare the events as follows:
> > EVENT *event-string-name* < / (*event-options*)>;

*event-string-name*
> is the name of the event you are declaring.

*event-options*
> specifies options for the event. You must put the list inside parentheses that follow a / (slash). Separate multiple options with commas. Event options can be

**Description**=*event-description*
> specifies the description of the event.

**Enabled**='**N**' | '**Y**'
> determines whether an event can be temporarily disabled. **Y** is the default.

**Method**=*string*
> identifies the method that handles the event.

**Send**='**Manual**' | '**After**' | '**Before**'
> determines when the object sends the event.
> > After is the default.

***eventhandler-declaration-statements***
> define the event handler to be executed after the events are triggered. The event handler is an SCL method that handles the event. Declare the event handler as follows:

> > EVENTHANDLER *eventhandler-name*< / (*eventhandler-options*)>;

*eventhandler-name*
> is the name of the event handler of an SCL class method that you are declaring.

*eventhandler-options*
> specifies options for the event handler. You must put the list inside parentheses that follow a / (slash). Separate multiple options with commas. Event handler options can be

**Description**=*eventhandler-description*
> specifies the description of the event handler.

**Enabled**='**N**' | '**Y**'
> determines whether an event handler can be temporarily disabled. **Y** is the default.

**Event**=*event-name*
> specifies the name of the event.

**Method**=*string*
> identifies the method that handles the event.

**Sender=' _SELF_ '** │ **' _ALL_ '**

identifies the location of the sender to trigger the event handler. When **Sender=' _SELF_ '**, the event handler will only listen to events from the class itself. When **Sender=' _ALL_ '**, the event handler will listen to events from any other class. Using the method _addEventHandler, you can dynamically add a sender to trigger the event.

**Details**   The CLASS statement enables you to use SCL to create a class and to define attributes, methods, events and event handlers for the class. The CLASS block is especially useful when you need to make many changes to an existing class such as adding signatures to an existing class, or when you want to create a class in batch mode. Using the CLASS block provides the advantages of error detection at compile time and improved performance during run time. It also enables you to use short-cut notation. Instead of using _SELF_.*attribute* or _self.*method*(...) to reference the name of a class attribute or a class method, you simply specify the attribute or method name. This makes programs easier to read and maintain. In addition, you can overload method definitions, which means that multiple methods can have the same name, but have different numbers and types of parameters.

The program block that defines a class starts with a CLASS statement and ends with an ENDCLASS statement. A CLASS block can contain statements that define attributes, methods, events, event handlers and even METHOD statement blocks implementing the operations for methods. You can also put the METHOD statements that implement class methods in another SCL entry when you use the SCL= method option to specify the name of that entry. Then, in the SCL entry that is specified with SCL=, define the methods for the class within a USECLASS statement block. Defining methods in a separate entry is useful for enabling class methods to be created, tested, or maintained by multiple application developers. For more information, see "METHOD" on page 539.

To create a class from an SCL entry that contains a CLASS block, you must compile and save the SCL entry as a CLASS entry. To do this, either issue the SAVECLASS command or select

| File | ► | Save Class |

from the SCL Source Editor. This is equivalent to using the Class Editor to interactively create a CLASS entry. However, the Class Editor provides a graphical view of the class, whereas the CLASS statement in SCL provides a language view of the class.

Do not declare the _SELF_, _FRAME_, _CFRAME_, _METHOD_, or _EVENT_ system variables inside a CLASS or USECLASS block. SCL automatically sets these values when it is running methods that are defined in CLASS or USECLASS blocks. Redefining any of these system variables can introduce unexpected behavior.

In methods that are defined in a CLASS statement block, all references to the methods and the attributes of the class can bypass two-level references to _SELF_.*attribute* and _SELF_.*method*(...). Because these methods are defined within the class, the SCL compiler can detect whether an undefined variable is a local variable or a class attribute.

You can also use the _super method in method code inside a CLASS statement block without having to specify either an object identifier or the method whose super method you are calling. You can use the _super method to call any method. For example, to invoke the super ADD method, you would use

```
_super.add();
```

To override the _init method, you must first call the super _init method before overriding the _init method. For example:

```
_super._init();
    ...statements that define the
    overridden _init method ...
```

Any SCL function or routine can be called inside a METHOD statement block that is inside a CLASS block. Outside the METHOD statement block, only class attribute statements, event statements and event handlers are allowed in a CLASS block. Other than the IMPORT statement, no SCL statements can be written outside the CLASS block.

METHOD blocks can include labeled sections. However, labeled sections that are outside a method block must be re-coded as PRIVATE methods, and the LINK statements that call them must be changed to method calls. This programming style will make your applications more consistent with the object-oriented paradigm.

If a local variable that is defined in a METHOD block has the same name as a class attribute, SCL gives precedence to the local variable. If a class method has the same name as any SCL-supported function, SCL gives precedence to the function. If an attribute array has the same name as a class method, SCL gives precedence to the method. It is probably best to avoid using the same name for multiple local variables, class attributes, method names or arrays to avoid problems.

The CLASS statement also enables you to define method definitions for overloading methods, which means that multiple methods have the same name. Methods that have the same names are allowed in a CLASS block only if the signatures, or parameter numbers or types, are different. For example, a class can have one COMBINE method that has numeric parameters and adds parameter values, and another COMBINE method that has character parameters and concatenates parameter values.

Inheritance from multiple classes is not supported in class syntax, but is allowed with interface syntax. For more information, see "INTERFACE" on page 486.

## Examples

**Example 1: A CLASS Block with Method Implementation**    This example defines the Arith class, a subclass of Sashelp.Fsp.Object.class, and implements the methods in the CLASS entry. The example shows the METHOD statements using the RETURN= option and then RETURN statements returning values to the caller.

```
class work.classes.arith.class;
    public  num  total;
    public  char catstr;
        /* A method that adds numeric values */
    add:  public method n1:num n2:num return=num;
        total = n1 + n2;
        return (total);
    endmethod;
        /* A method that concatenates */
        /* character values           */
    concat: public method c1:char  c2:char return=char;
        catstr = c1 || c2;
        return (catstr);
    endmethod;
endclass;
```

**Example 2: A CLASS Block without Method Implementation**    This example defines the Combine class and specifies the SCL entry in which the methods are implemented. The class uses overloaded COMBINE methods, one to process numeric values and another to process character values. The code that implements the methods is defined in a USECLASS block.

```
class work.classes.combine.class;
    public   num   total;
    public   char catstr;

    combine: public method n1:num  n2:num   return=num
        / (scl='work.classes.combine.scl');

    combine:  public method c1:char c2:char
        return=char
        / (scl='work.classes.combine.scl');
endclass;
```

Here is the USECLASS block that contains the method implementations for WORK.CLASSES.COMBINE.CLASS:

```
useclass work.classes.combine.class;
    combine:  public method
          n1:num  n2:num   return=num;
      total = n1 + n2;
      return (total);
    endmethod;

    combine: public method
          c1:char  c2:char return=char;
      catstr = c1 || c2;
      return (catstr);
    endmethod;
enduseclass;
```

**Example 3: Definition of a Class**   This example imports the Collection class, which is provided with SAS/AF software, and shows several forms of attribute declarations, method declarations, and overloading methods. Attributes list1 and list2, which define SCL list initialization, can also be found in this example.

```
import sashelp.fsp.collection.class;
class work.classes.myclass.class
    extends sashelp.fsp.object.class
    / (description = 'my first class file');
      /* simple attribute with no options */
    public num num1;
      /* Attribute with options */
    public num num2
      / (description = 'second numeric attribute',
         initialvalue= 3,
         validvalues = '1 2 3');
      /* Another attribute with options */
    public char string1
      / (editable = 'n', linkable = 'n',
         initialvalue = 'abc');

  /* SCL List initializations:items without name*/
    public list list1
  / (InitialValue={1, 2, 3, 'abc', 'def', 4, 5, 6}
    );
```

```
/* SCL List initializations:Items with name.*/
/* Address is a sublist of list2          */
   public list list2
/ (InitialValue={name='John Doe', Number=100,
   Address={State='NC', CITY='CARY'},
   Office='Bldg Z'} )
   /* Private array attribute  */
   private num arr(3) ;
       /* Private list attribute   */
   private list list;
       /* Protected collection attribute */
   protected collection coll;

       /* public method m0 */
   m0:  Public method
           /* External method implementations */
       / (scl='mylib.classes.b.scl',
         label = 'M0',
         description='test method m0');

       /* Public method m1          */
       /* with no method options   */
   m1:  public method ;
       ...more SAS statements...
   endmethod;

       /* Private overloading method m1 */
       /* with numeric parameter         */
   m1:  private method n: num;
       ...more SAS statements...
   endmethod;

       /* Protected overloaded method m1.
        * Method implementations should be placed in
        * work.classes.c.scl */
   m1:  protected method s: char
     /* external method implementation */
     / (scl = 'work.classes.c.scl');

       /* Other public method */
   m2: method return=num;
       ...more SAS statements...
       return (1);
   endmethod;

       /* Private method */
   m3: private method;
       ...more SAS statements...
   endmethod;
endclass;
```

**Example 4: Illustrating Short-Cut References**  This example shows how to use the _super method as well as short-cut references to _SELF_:

```
CLASS work.classes.another.class;
    Public Num n1;
    Public Num n2;
    Public Char c1;
    Public Char c2;
    Public Num m(3);

    _Init:  method / (State='O');
        DCL Num  n2;
        DCL Char c2;
            /* Equivalent to call super(_init); */
        _SUPER();
            /* Equivalent to _SELF_.N1 = 1    */
        n1 = 1;
            /* Local variable N2 dominates class */
            /* attribute N2                      */
        n2 = 1;
        m{1} = abs(n2);
            /* Uses { to avoid ambiguity     */
            /* Equivalent to _SELF_.C1 = 'a' */
        c1 = 'a';
            /* Local variable C2 dominates */
            /* class attribute C2          */
        c2 = 'a';
    endmethod;
        /* commonly used method can be PRIVATE */
    Common: Private Method a:Num;
        ...more SCL statements...
        a = a + 1;
    endmethod;

    M: method;
        /* Equivalent to                */
        /*    if _SELF_.N1 > 0 then     */
      if n1 > 0 then
            /* Equivalent to        */
            /*    _SELF_.N1 + 1; */
        n1 + 1;
      common(n1);
    endmethod;
          /* Method M1 with numeric parameter */
    M: method n: Num;
          /* Equivalent to _SELF_.M(); */
      M();
      common(n1);
    endmethod;

  endclass;
```

### Example 5: Illustrating Set Custom Access(setCAM) Method

This example shows a setCAM method, M1, which will be invoked when the attribute N is modified in the _init method.

```
Class work.mycat.camDemo.class;
    Public num n / (initialValue = 5,
```

```
                     setCam='m1');
    _init: Method / (State='O');
           _super();
           n = 3;
           EndMethod;
    m1:    Method nParm:Num;
    /* - nParm is input value of attribute n */
           nParm = nParm + 100;
    /*  nParm is output value of attribute n */
           EndMethod;
EndClass;
```

To reference the camDemo class, you can code the following program:

```
Init:
    DCL  camDemo  obj = _new_ camDemo();
    obj.n = 7;
    /*  Using the SCL debugger to trace the sequence
     *  of this program, you will find the value
     *  of obj.n = 107 */
    put obj.n=;
    Return;
```

**Example 6: Illustrating User-defined Events and Event Handlers**    This example shows a system-defined event, 'n Changed', which will be automatically generated to associate with the attribute N. An event handler, M1, which is associated with the 'n Changed' event is also written and will be executed when the attribute N is modified. Another user-defined event, 'myEvent', is created by the EVENT statement. The associated event handler, M2, will be executed when an explicit _sendEvent method is executed.

```
Class work.mycat.eDemo.class;
    Public num n; /* sendEvent='Y' is default*/
    Public char c / (sendEvent='N');
    Event 'myEvent'
       / (method='m2');
    EventHandler m1
       / (Sender='_SELF_',
          Event='n Changed');
    EventHandler m2
       / (Sender='_ALL_',
          Event='myEvent');
    m1: method a:list;
      Put 'Event is triggered by attribute N';
        endMethod;
    m2: method a:string b:num ;
      Put 'Event is triggered by _sendEvent';
        return (100);
        endMethod;
EndClass;
```

You could use the following program to trace the control sequence of the event handler by using the SCL debugger.

```
init:
    DCL eDemo obj = _new_ eDemo();
    obj.n = 3;  /* will trigger the m1 */
```

```
obj._sendEvent('myEvent','abc',3);
Return;
```

**Example 7: Illustrating Forward Method, Optional= and ArgList=**    This example shows how to use the method option Forward='Y' to write a method, M1, which can invoke another method, M2, defined after the current method, M1. Without the Forward='Y' option, the SCL compiler will issue an error. The M1 method contains Optional=, which actually includes two overloading methods.

```
Class mylib.mycat.forward.class;
   m2: Method n:num c:char Return=Num / (Forward='Y');
   m1: Method n1:num Optional=n2:num Arglist=argList
Return=Num;
         DCL Num listLen = listlen(argList);
         DCL Num retVal;
         if (listLen = 1) then
            retVal = m2(n1, 'abc');
         else if (listLen = 2) then
            retVal = m2(n2, 'abc');
         Return(retVal);
      EndMEthod;
   m2: Method n:num c:char  Return=Num;
         Return(n+length(c));
      EndMethod;
EndClass;
```

## See Also

"ARRAY" on page 254

"CREATESCL" on page 316

"ENDCLASS" on page 366

"METHOD" on page 540

"USECLASS" on page 698

---

# CLEARLIST

**Clears the items from an SCL list without deleting the list and optionally clears all sublist items**

**Category:**  List

---

## Syntax

*rc*=**CLEARLIST**(*list-id<,recursively>*);

***rc***

indicates whether the operation is successful:

0                          successful

≠0                          not successful
    Type: Numeric

*list-id*

is the identifier of the list that contains the items to clear. An invalid *list-id* produces
an error condition.
    Type: Numeric or List

*recursively*

indicates whether to recursively clear all the list's sublists as well as all sublists of
its sublists.

'**N**'                          Sublists are not cleared. (This is the default.)

'**Y**'                          All sublists are cleared.
    Type: Character

**Details**    CLEARLIST clears all the items from the SCL list identified by *list-id*. The
list is not deleted, but its length is reduced to 0. If *recursively* is '**Y**', then all the list's
sublists, including sublists of sublists, are also cleared.

*CAUTION:*

**Before you clear a list recursively, make sure it is not needed by other parts of the SCL
program.** The *recursively* option clears all of a list's sublists, even if they are
referenced in other SCL lists or by other SCL variables. △

An error condition results if

☐ the list has the NOUPDATE or FIXEDLENGTH attribute.

☐ any item in the list (or in its sublists, if *recursively* is '**Y**') has the NODELETE
attribute.

☐ *recursively* is '**Y**', and any sublist has the NOUPDATE or FIXEDLENGTH
attribute.

☐ *list-id* is a component or class identifier.

If an error condition results, no further items or sublists are cleared.

## Example

Clear all sublists from an existing list identified by MYLIST without deleting items
that are not sublists:

```
    /* Copy the list.  */
cp=copylist(mylist);
  /* Clear the entire list, including sublists  */
  /* that also appear in CP.                    */
rc=clearlist(mylist,'Y');

   /* Copy the old list data.  */
   /* Sublists have been cleared.  */
mylist=copylist(cp,'N',mylist);

   /* Delete the copied list. */
rc=dellist(cp);
```

## See Also

"COPYLIST" on page 311

"DELITEM" on page 335

"DELLIST" on page 336

"DELNITEM" on page 337

"SETLATTR" on page 656

# CLOSE

**Closes a SAS table**

**Category:** SAS Table

## Syntax

*sysrc*=**CLOSE**(*table-id*);

**sysrc**
contains the return code for the operation:

| | |
|---|---|
| 0 | successful |
| ≠0 | not successful |

  Type: Numeric

**table-id**
is the identifier that was assigned when the table was opened. A *table-id* value of **–999** closes all tables that were opened with OPEN. If *table-id* is invalid, the program halts.

  Type: Numeric

**Details**   Close all SAS tables as soon as they are no longer needed by an application. You do not need to open and close a SAS table in each program of an application. If an application contains several programs that use the same table, the first program can open the table and can use the parameter passing mechanism with the DISPLAY routine or method calls to make the table identifier value available to other programs.

## Example

Use OPEN to open a SAS table. If the table opens successfully, as indicated by a positive value for the PAYID variable, then use CLOSE to close the PAYROLL table.

```
payid=open('payroll','u');
   ...SCL statements...
if (payid>0) then payid=close(payid);
```

## See Also

"OPEN" on page 576

---

# CLRFLD

**Clears the value from variables whose values match a specified value**

**Category:** Control or Field

---

## Syntax

**CALL CLRFLD**(*pattern,variable-1*<, . . . ,*variable-10*>);

*pattern*
> is the character string to match.
> Type: Character

*variable-1, . . . , variable-10*
> names up to ten character variables. If the value of a variable in this list matches *pattern*, then that value is cleared.
> Type: Character

**Details**   Variables in the variable list whose values do not match *pattern* exactly are not changed. No error occurs if there are no matches.

## Example

Clear the value of any variable in the group SYM1 through SYM5 whose value is **BLUE**:

```
call clrfld('blue',sym1,sym2,sym3,sym4,sym5);
```

## See Also

"SETFLD" on page 650

---

# COLORLIST

**Displays a selection list of the names of a device's valid colors and returns user selections**

**Category:** Selection List

---

## Syntax

*selections*=**COLORLIST**(*color-set,num-sel*< ,*message* <,*autoclose*>>);

**selections**

contains one or more user selections from the list. Multiple selections are separated by blanks. By default, *selections* is 200 bytes long. To accomodate values longer than 200 bytes, you should explicitly declare *selections* with a longer length.

Type: Character

**color-set**

specifies the set of colors to display in the selection list:

| | |
|---|---|
| *device* | specifies the name of a SAS/GRAPH device. If *device* is supplied, the selection list includes only the colors that are valid for the specified device, and an **All...** choice to display all possible colors. *Device* can be the name of a monitor, plotter, printer, or camera. This name can be up to eight characters long and must be specified within quotes. If the device entry is not found, the list contains all possible colors without regard to whether the device supports them. |
| **'?'** | opens the Color Selector window in which a user can design a color. Only one color can be defined, so *num-sel* is ignored. For additional information, use the window's online help. |

Type: Character

**num-sel**

is the maximum number of items that a user can select from the list. To display the list for information purposes only (no selections allowed), specify **0**. To specify an unlimited number of selections, use a value such as 9999 that is larger than the number of available selections. A user cannot make a number of selections that exceeds the number of items in the list.

Type: Numeric

**message**

is the message text to display above the selection list. The default message tells users to make up to the number of selections specified in *num-sel*.

Type: Character

**autoclose**

specifies whether the selection list window closes automatically after a user makes a selection when only one choice is allowed:

| | |
|---|---|
| **'Y'** | closes the window automatically. (This is the default.) |
| **'N'** | leaves the window open until the user explicitly closes it. |

This option is ignored when *num-sel* is not 1.

Type: Character

**Details**   By default, the message above the selection list asks the user to make *num-sel* selections. Also by default, the selection list window closes when the user makes a choice and presses ENTER if the selection list allows only one choice.

The FIND item in the selection list window enables you to specify characters that a value in the list contains. If the value is found, it is displayed as selected. If the value is not found, a message is displayed in the selection list window.

You can provide default values that will be initially selected when the color selection list is displayed. To do this, assign the values to the *selections* variable before calling COLORLIST.

If a user closes the selection list window without making a selection, COLORLIST returns a blank value unless there was an initial value for the *selections* variable before COLORLIST was called.

Selections from the window can be placed in the current result list, if one is available. The current result list is a special SCL list that is automatically filled with the values that are selected from a selection list. To use a current result list, use the MAKELIST function to create it, and use the CURLIST function to designate it as the current result list. The current result list must exist before you call the COLORLIST function.

You can use COLORLIST to enable a user to interactively design the RGB components for a color. If a user designs a color that is not supported on that device, SCL uses the closest color that is supported.

When COLORLIST is invoked, the current result list is cleared. After COLORLIST is invoked, the result list contains one element for each selected color name. The selections can be retrieved by using GETITEMC.

## Example

Display a list of devices of type MONITOR that are available in the catalog SASHELP.DEVICES and allow users to select a device. Users can choose up to four colors from the selection list. If no device is chosen, display a list of all possible colors.

```
usrdev=devlist('sashelp.devices','monitor',
                    'Select a device. ');
device=substr(usrdev,41,8);
devcolor=colorlist(device,4);
```

Use a current result list to process multiple selections:

```
listid=makelist();
rc=curlist(listid);
selection=devlist('sashelp.devices','monitor',
                      'Select a device.');
device=substr(selection,41,8);
devcolor=colorlist(device,4);
n=listlen(listid);
do i=1 to n;
   color=getitemc(listid,i);
   put color=;
end;
```

Display a color selection dialog window:

```
color=colorlist('?',1,'Design a color for the
                                        bars');
```

## See Also

"CURLIST" on page 320

"DEVLIST" on page 342

# COMAMID

**Returns the list of communications access methods for an operating system**

**Category:** SAS System Option

## Syntax

*comamids=***COMAMID**(*options*);

**comamids**
> are the communications access methods (comamids) for the operating system or for SAS/SHARE software or SAS/CONNECT software, if they are requested. Multiple values are separated by blanks.
>    Type: Character

**options**
> requests comamid values that are supported by SAS/SHARE software or SAS/CONNECT software for your operating system:

> **'S'**          requests comamid values that are supported by SAS/SHARE software.

> **'C'**          requests comamid values that are supported by SAS/CONNECT software.

**Details**    COMAMID provides a list of communication access method values for a user's operating system. If no value is provided for *options*, then all comamid values for the operating system are returned.

You can display the list to application users by using other SCL features. For example, you can display the values in a list box by specifying that the source of list box values is the variable that you used as the return value for COMAMID.

*Note:*   COMAMID verifies communication access method values so that if the module to support a value has not been installed, that value is not returned in the string of comamid values. △

## Examples

**Example 1: Finding the Comamids for an Operating System**    Find out which comamids are valid for the operating system:

```
INIT:
    comamids=COMAMID();
    put comamids=;
return;
```

This example produces the following output on an HP-UX system:

```
COMAMIDS= TCP
```

**Example 2: Finding Comamids for SAS/SHARE Software**    Find out which comamids are supported by SAS/SHARE software:

```
INIT:
    comamids=COMAMID('S');
    put 'Comamids for SAS/SHARE are 'comamids=;
return;
```

This example produces the following output on an HP-UX system:

```
Comamids for SAS/SHARE are COMAMIDS=TCP
```

# COMPAREARRAY

**Allows you to compare two arrays for size and data equality**

**Category:** Array

---

## Syntax

*rc*=**COMPAREARRAY**(*array1,array2*);

*rc*
   indicates whether the two arrays match.

| | |
|---|---|
| 0 | arrays match |
| 1 | arrays do not match |

    Type: Numeric

*array1*
   is one of the two arrays to be compared.
    Type: Array

*array2*
   is one of the two arrays to be compared.
    Type: Array

**Details**    The COMPAREARRAY function allows you to compare two arrays for size and data equality. To be considered equal, the arrays must:

☐ have the same number of dimensions

☐ be of the same type

☐ have the same bounds

☐ have the same values in each element.

## Examples

**Example 1: Compare Arrays**    The example compare several different arrays.

```
DCL num n1(5) n2(5,5) n3(*) n4(5) n5(*,*);
DCL char c1(5);
DCL num rc;

rc = comparearray(n1,n2); put rc=;
rc = comparearray(n1,c1); put rc=;
rc = comparearray(n1,n3); put rc=;
rc = makearray(n3,3);
rc = comparearray(n1,n3); put rc=;
rc = redim(n3,5);
rc = comparearray(n1,n3); put rc=;
do i=1 to 5;
   n1[i] = i;
   n4[i] = i;
end;
```

```
rc = comparearray(n1,n4); put rc=;
rc = copyarray(n2,n5);
rc = comparearray(n2,n5); put rc=;
rc = delarray (n3); rc delarray (n5);
```

The output for this code would be:

```
rc=1
rc=1
rc=1
rc=1
rc=0
rc=0
rc=0
```

## See Also

"COPYARRAY" on page 309

"DELARRAY" on page 332

"MAKEARRAY" on page 533

Chapter 4, "SCL Arrays," on page 37

---

# COMPARELIST

### Compares two SCL lists

**Category:**   List

---

### Syntax

*rc*=**COMPARELIST**(*list1-id,list2-id< ,options>*);

*rc*
    contains the return code for the operation:

    0              The lists match.

    1              The lists do not match.

*list1–id, list2–id*
    contain the identifiers for the two SCL lists to be compared.

*options*
    specify one or more comparison options. Use a space to separate multiple options.
    The available options are:

    NAME (Default)|NONAME
        determine whether the comparison is performed on the names of list items that
        are in the same position in both lists. NONAME does not compare item names.

    NOHONORCASE (Default)|MIXEDCASE
        determine whether the comparison is performed on the uppercase or mixed case
        values of all item values and names. NOHONORCASE compares the uppercase

values of item names and values. MIXEDCASE compares mixed case names and values.

ITEM (Default) | NOITEM

determine whether the comparison is performed on the values of list items that are in the same position in both lists. NOITEM does not compare list values.

NODUMP (Default) | LONGDUMP | SHORTDUMP

determine the extent to which differences are reported. NODUMP produces no messages. LONGDUMP displays all differences in the LOG window. SHORTDUMP displays the first five differences.

### Details

COMPARELIST enables you to compare the information in two SCL lists. This comparison can include item names, values, or both. Names and items can be compared in mixed case.

### Example

Compare the item names and values in OLDLIST and NEWLIST. If the lists are not the same, write all the error messages to the SAS log. If the lists are the same, delete OLDLIST.

```
rc=comparelist(oldlist,newlist,'name item nohonorcase
    longdump');
if rc=0 then
    rc=dellist(oldlist);
else do;
   ...SCL statements to run
   when the lists do not match...
end;
```

# CONTENTS

**Displays the attributes of a SAS table**

**Category:** Catalog and SAS Table

### Syntax

*rc*=**CONTENTS**(*SAS-table*<,*mode*>);

***rc***

contains the return code for the operation:

| | |
|---|---|
| 0 | The attributes of the specified table were displayed. |
| ≠0 | An error or warning condition occurred during the operation. |

Type: Numeric

***SAS-table***

is the name of the SAS table. (SAS data set options are ignored in this argument.) The name of the data set would have to include the #nnn number of the generation set. For example to view the third generation data set of WORK.ONE:

```
rc=contents('work.one#003');
```

Type: Character

*mode*

specifies whether the information can be modified:

'**B**'                           displays the Properties window for browsing only.

'**E**'                           allows information in the Properties window to be modified. (This is the default.) If member-level locking is not available, then the Properties window is displayed in BROWSE mode instead.

> *Note:*  Any value that begins with a character other than **B** or **b** also selects EDIT mode. △

Type: Character

**Details**    The CONTENTS function opens the Properties window, which enables an application user to browse or modify column names, formats, informats, and labels of a SAS table. By default, the Properties window is opened in edit mode. However, if the specified table is currently open, then you must specify **B** for *mode*.

Initially, General Properties (that is, attributes, but not column names) are listed in the Properties window. To change the value of an attribute, do the following:

1  Click the mouse menu button on the attribute that you want to change and then click on Modify .

2  In the dialog window that appears, make the desired changes to the text.

To change a column name, do the following:

1  Click on the down arrow at the upper right corner of the window. The menu that appears contains information about the table, including column names. Select the column name that you want to change.

2  Click the mouse menu button on the column name that you want to change, and then select Modify .

3  In the dialog window that appears, make the desired change to the column name.

## Example

Display the attributes for the table MYLIB.HOUSES:

```
if (contents('mylib.houses')) then
   do;
       _msg_=sysmsg();
       ...SCL statements to handle case where
       contents cannot be displayed...
   end;
```

# CONTINUE

**Stops processing the current DO loop and resumes with the next iteration of that DO loop**

**Category:**   Control Flow

**Comparisons:**   SAS Statement with limitations in SCL

## Syntax

**CONTINUE**;

**Details** The CONTINUE statement is provided in SCL to control the execution of DO loops. When you need to force the statements in a DO loop to stop executing, you can use the CONTINUE statement to stop executing successive statements in a DO loop, and to move back up and re-execute the DO loop, starting with the header statement.

*Note:* In DATA step code, the CONTINUE statement stops processing only the current DO loop. In SCL code, the CONTINUE statement stops processing the current DO loop *or DO group*, whichever is closest. For example, suppose your code contains a DO loop that contains DO groups:

```
do n=1 to 5;      /* DO loop */
  if n=2 then do; continue; end;    /* DO group */
  put n=;
end;
```

When this code is compiled and run as part of an SCL program, the output is:

```
n=1
n=2
n=3
n=4
n=5
```

When this code is submitted as part of a DATA step, the output is:

```
n=1
n=3
n=4
n=5
```

See "DO" on page 356 for more information on DO groups and DO loops. △

When you use DO WHILE and DO UNTIL statements, use caution to prevent the CONTINUE statement from forcing the program into an infinite loop. For example, the following statements produce an infinite loop because the value of the variable I never exceeds 2. When I has the value of 2, the IF statement always causes a branch around the next two SCL statements.

```
    /* This example causes an infinite loop */
INIT:
i=1;
do while (i<1000);
   if mod(i,2)=0 then
      continue;
   sum+i;
   i+1;
end;
return;
```

See the documentation for the CONTINUE statement in *SAS Language Reference: Dictionary* for more information.

## Example

Count the number of females in the SAS table WORK.PERSONEL and display their average age. WORK.PERSONEL contains the column GENDER, which contains the values **F** for female and **M** for male, as well as the column AGE, which contains numeric values for age. The display window contains two numeric controls: AVGAGE and FEMALES. If the value of GENDER is not **F** (female), then the CONTINUE statement skips the other statements and returns to the DO WHILE statement to read the next row. The results are displayed in the application window, although the individual records are not displayed.

```
INIT:
   females=0;
   total=0;
   persnlid=open('personel');
   call set(persnlid);
 /* Process rows until all the */
 /* rows are read. */
   do while (fetch(persnlid) ne -1);
        /* Skip males when processing. */
      if gender ne 'F' then
         continue;
      females+1;
      total+age;
   end;
 /* Display the results in the fields */
 /* FEMALES and AVGAGE. */
      avgage=total/females;
return;
MAIN:
   ...other SCL statements...
return;

TERM:
   rc=close(persnlid);
return;
```

## See Also

"DO" on page 356

"LEAVE" on page 504

# CONTROL

**Controls the execution of labeled program sections and the formatting of submit blocks**

**Category:**   Control Flow

**Comparisons:**   SAS Statement with limitations in SCL

## Syntax

**CONTROL** *options*;

## *options*

specify the type of control for program statements. The available options are described below. You can use one or more options.

Type: Character

### ALLCMDS | NOALLCMDS

NOALLCMDS is in effect by default. Global or procedure-specific commands execute immediately without executing the SCL program. The program cannot intercept any procedure-specific commands that are issued in the application. Use CONTROL ALLCMDS to enable SCL to intercept procedure-specific or custom commands that are issued in the application. You can use the NEXTCMD routine to ignore invalid commands. Use CONTROL NOALLCMDS to restore the default behavior.

ALLCMDS provides the same functionality as the ALWAYS option and enables a program to intercept custom commands. In addition, ALLCMDS allows an SCL program to intercept procedure-specific commands. In FRAME entries only, ALLCMDS allows an SCL program to intercept full-screen global commands. For a listing of full-screen global commands, see "EXECCMDI" on page 381 .

In PROGRAM entries, ALLCMDS combines the effects of ENTER and ERROR and forces statements in the MAIN section to execute even if a user issues commands that are not recognized by the procedure.

In FSEDIT applications, ALLCMDS and ALWAYS have the same functionality, and both enable an SCL program to intercept any procedure-specific or custom commands.

When ALLCMDS is specified, statements execute in the MAIN section before a command that is issued with the EXECCMD routine. This behavior could introduce an infinite loop. Either execute the EXECCMD routine conditionally or specify the command using EXECCMDI with the NOEXEC parameter.

FSVIEW applications ignore these options.

### ALWAYS | NOALWAYS

NOALWAYS is in effect by default. The MAIN section executes only when a user modifies a window variable with a valid value and then presses either ENTER or a function key. Use CONTROL ALWAYS to force statements in the MAIN section to execute even if a user issues commands that are not recognized by the procedure. ALWAYS combines the effects of ENTER and ERROR.

ALWAYS can be used if your application supports custom commands. When ALWAYS is specified, FSEDIT applications execute statements in the MAIN section before handling a command that is issued with the EXECCMD routine. This behavior could introduce an infinite loop. Either execute the EXECCMD routine conditionally or specify the command using EXECCMDI with the NOEXEC parameter.

FSVIEW applications ignore this option.

### ASIS | NOASIS

NOASIS is in effect by default. SCL formats submit-block code and eliminates unnecessary spaces and line breaks. Use CONTROL ASIS so that submit blocks are submitted without formatting. You must use this option when the position of elements in the SAS code is important (for example, if you are submitting a DATALINES statement with a DATA step). ASIS is more efficient than NOASIS because it reduces the time spent on formatting.

### BREAK *label* | NOBREAK

NOBREAK is in effect by default. If a program interrupt occurs while the SCL statements are executing, a requestor window opens and asks the user whether program execution should resume (that is, ignore the interrupt) or the program should quit. If a user chooses to quit execution, no more statements are executed for the current program, and control returns to the calling program. Use CONTROL BREAK so that you can specify a labeled section to which control passes if an interrupt or break condition occurs while the SCL statements are executing. *Label* is the program label of the section to execute after the current statement finishes execution. This labeled section can include SCL statements that report status and handle the interrupt. Use the _STATUS_ system variable to control execution such as **H** to halt and **R** to resume.

A program can contain any number of CONTROL BREAK statements. For example, there can be one in each of the INIT, MAIN, and TERM sections or in any other labeled section. When a CONTROL BREAK statement executes, any previous CONTROL BREAK statement is overwritten so that only one is in effect at a time.

Use NOBREAK to restore the default behavior. NOBREAK clears the current CONTROL BREAK specification.

FSVIEW applications ignore this option.

HALTONDOTATTRIBUTE/NOHALTONDOTATTRIBUTE
HALTONDOTATTRIBUTE is in effect by default. If SCL detects an error in the dot notation used in your application, the application halts execution. If you specify NOHALTONDOTATTRIBUTE, the application will continue to execute when errors are detected in the dot notation, but the results will be unpredictable. See "Accessing Object Attributes and Methods With Dot Notation" on page 119 for more information.

ENDSAS/NOENDSAS
NOENDSAS is in effect by default. When a user issues the ENDSAS or BYE command, the TERM sections of SCL programs in the current execution stack do not execute. This is called an ENDSAS event. Use CONTROL ENDSAS to force execution of the TERM section in an SCL program when an ENDSAS event occurs. ENDSAS has no effect on the _term method.

ENDAWS/NOENDAWS
NOENDAWS is in effect by default. When a user ends a SAS session by selecting the system closure menu in a FRAME entry that is running with the Application Work Space (AWS), the TERM sections of SCL programs in the current execution stack do not execute. This is called an ENDAWS event. Use CONTROL ENDAWS to force execution of the TERM section in an SCL program when an ENDAWS event occurs. ENDAWS has no effect on the _term method.

ENTER | NOENTER
NOENTER is in effect by default. The MAIN section executes only when a user modifies the value of a window variable and then presses either ENTER or a function key that is recognized by the procedure. Use CONTROL ENTER to force MAIN to execute when a user presses the ENTER key or a function key without modifying a window variable.

In FSVIEW applications, this option has an effect only if the cursor is on a valid row when ENTER or a function key is pressed.

ERROR | NOERROR
NOERROR is in effect by default. Statements in MAIN do not execute if a control or field contains a value that causes an attribute error. Thus, some statements in MAIN do not execute if multiple fields are in error and a user has not modified all of these fields. Use CONTROL ERROR to force statements in MAIN to execute even if the window contains fields that are in error.

If you use ERROROFF to remove the error status from a continued portion of a field in an FSEDIT application, then you must also use a CONTROL ERROR statement in the program. If a user does not type in the continued portion of the field and the program does not have a CONTROL ERROR statement, the error flag is not removed from the continued portion of the field. As a result, the default error message may be displayed, saying that a data value is not valid.

LABEL | NOLABEL

NOLABEL is in effect by default for PROGRAM and SCREEN entries. MAIN executes after any window variable is modified. Use CONTROL LABEL to force sections that are labeled with a window variable name (called window variable sections) to execute before MAIN executes. For FRAME entries, CONTROL LABEL is the default.

Statements in a window variable block execute after the associated window variable is modified, but only if the value does not introduce an error. That is, the value must satisfy any attributes that have been defined for the window variable.

Statements in MAIN do not execute until statements in all the window variable sections for modified fields execute successfully. The sequence for executing window variable sections is determined by the physical position of the field in the window from left to right and from top to bottom.

If a field modification introduces an attribute error, the associated window variable section does not execute. However, other window variable sections for modified window variables do execute. To correct an attribute error, you can allow users to correct the error in the window, or you can include SCL statements that make a correction in the labeled section for other fields.

If ERROR, ALWAYS, or ALLCMDS is also specified, then MAIN executes after the window variable sections even if an error was introduced.

If the window contains an extended table, the window variable section for each modified window variable executes for a row before the putrow section executes. MAIN executes after the putrow section executes.

*Note:* If CONTROL LABEL is specified, a window variable section must not contain a SUBMIT IMMEDIATE block. △

TERM | NOTERM

This option is valid only for FSEDIT applications. NOTERM is in effect by default. Statements in the TERM section of FSEDIT applications do not execute when a user scrolls off the current row in a SAS table unless the user changed the values of one or more columns so that the current row needs to be updated in the table, or unless the row is new. Use the TERM option to force execution of the statements in the TERM section even if a user does not modify any columns in the current row.

**Details**    The CONTROL statement controls the execution of labeled program sections and also controls the formatting of code in a submit block. A CONTROL statement option remains in effect until another CONTROL statement option overrides it. Multiple CONTROL statement options can be in effect at the same time.

## Examples

### Example 1: Using the ASIS Option    Use the ASIS option:

```
control asis;
submit;
   data a;
      input x y z;
      datalines;
      10 20 30
      40 50 60
```

```
    run;
  endsubmit;
  rc=preview('display');
```

With the CONTROL ASIS statement in effect, the submit block executes without errors. If you remove the CONTROL ASIS statement, SCL formats the code within the block as follows when the code is submitted for processing:

```
data a;
input x y z;
datalines;
0 20 30 40 50 60 run;
```

When formatted in this manner, the final statement contains a syntax error and the code cannot execute properly.

**Example 2: Controlling a Program Interrupt**    Define a break handler section labeled STOPINIT. When a user interrupts processing while SCL statements in INIT are executing, the STOPINIT label executes. If the loop index I is less than 350, execution of the program halts and control returns to the calling program. Otherwise, execution resumes. After the first loop is finished, execute CONTROL NOBREAK so that there is no break handler. If a user interrupts processing during the second loop, the SCL Break requestor window is displayed, and the statements in STOPINIT do not execute. The user can either abort or resume processing. Follow the same steps to define a new break handler section labeled STOPTERM in the TERM section.

```
INIT:
     /* define break label STOPINIT       */
  control break stopinit;
     /* loop 500 times to allow interrupt */
     /* checking with control break       */
     /* if user interrupts, statements in */
     /* label STOPINIT execute */
  do i=1 to 500;
     put i=;
  end;

     /* reset so there is no break handler */
  control nobreak;

     /* loop 500 times to allow interrupt */
     /* checking without control break    */
  do i = 1 to 500;
     if (int(i/25) eq (i/25)) then put i=;
  end;
return;
MAIN: return;
TERM:
     /* Define the new break label STOPTERM. */
  control break stopterm;

     /* Loop 500 times to allow */
     /* interrupt checking with control */
     /* break.  If user interrupts,      */
     /* statements in label STOPTERM     */
     /* execute.                         */
  do j=1 to 500;
```

```
        put j=;
    end;

        /* Reset so there is no break handler.  */
    control nobreak;

        /* Loop 500 times to allow */
        /* interrupt checking without control  */
        /* break.                              */
    do j = 1 to 500;
        if (int(j/25) eq (j/25)) then put j=;
    end;
return;

STOPINIT:
        /* HALT if loop counter is less than 350, */
        /* otherwise RESUME.                      */
        /* Report the current status.             */
    put i=;
    if (i < 350) then
        _status_ = 'H';
    else
        _status_ = 'R';
return;

STOPTERM:
        /* HALT if loop counter is less than 350, */
        /* otherwise RESUME.                      */
        /* Report the current status.             */
    put j=;
    if (j < 350) then
        _status_ = 'H';
    else
        _status_ = 'R';
return;
```

## See Also

"WORD" on page 725

# COPY

**Copies a SAS table, view, catalog, or catalog entry**

**Category:**  Utility

## Syntax

*sysrc=***COPY**(*old-name,new-name<,type>*);

*sysrc*
> contains the return code for the operation:
>
> | | |
> |---|---|
> | 0 | successful |
> | ≠0 | not successful |
>
> Type: Numeric

*old-name*
> is the name of the SAS file or catalog entry to copy. This can be a one-, two-, or four-level name and can include SAS data set options.
> Type: Character

*new-name*
> is the new name for the SAS file or catalog entry. This must be a three- or four-level name if *type* is `'CATALOG'`. If a catalog entry is being copied, the function sets the entry type of the new entry to that of the old entry. You can also specify SAS data set options.
> Type: Character

*type*
> is the type of SAS file or catalog entry to be copied:
>
> `'ACCESS'`
> > The member is an access descriptor that was created using SAS/ACCESS software.
>
> `'CATALOG'`
> > The member is a SAS catalog or a catalog entry.
>
> `'DATA'`
> > The member is a SAS data file. (This is the default.)
>
> `'VIEW'`
> > The member is a SAS data view.
> > Type: Character

**Details**   To copy a catalog entry, specify the complete four-level name of the entry for *old-name*, a three-level name for *new-name*, and `'CATALOG'` for *type*.

You can use the WHERE= data set option to copy only those rows that meet a WHERE subset to the new table.

The COPY function does not copy existing integrity constraints to the new SAS table. Use the ICCREATE function to define new integrity constraints.

If the SAS table that is being copied is indexed, then all indexes are rebuilt for the new SAS table. *New-name* is ignored when you use COPY to copy GRSEG catalog entries that were created using SAS/GRAPH software. A copied GRSEG entry will have either the same name as the original entry or, if an entry with that name already exists in the target catalog, a unique name generated by SAS software.

*CAUTION:*
> **This function can overwrite existing files.** If a table or catalog with the specified new name already exists, COPY overwrites the existing table or catalog without warning. △

## Example

Copy the SAS table DATA1 to DATA2 and copy WORK.TEMP.A.SCL to SASUSER.PROFILE.B.SCL:

```
if (copy('data1','data2')) then
   do;
```

```
      _msg_=sysmsg();
      ...SCL statements to handle the
               error condition...
   end;
rc=copy('work.temp.a.scl',
      'sasuser.profile.b.scl', 'catalog');
if (rc) then
   do;
      _msg_=sysmsg();
      ...SCL statements to handle the
               error condition...
   end;
```

Copy from the SAS table SASUSER.CLASS to WORK.CLASS only those rows in which the variable GENDER=**M**:

```
if (copy('sasuser.class(where=(GENDER=''M''))',
      'work.class')) then
   do;
      _msg_=sysmsg();
      ...SCl statements to handle the
         error condition...
   end;
```

## See Also

"DELETE" on page 334

"ICCREATE" on page 460

"RENAME" on page 612

---

# COPYARRAY

**Copies data from one array into another array**

**Category:** Array

---

## Syntax

*rc*=**COPYARRAY**(*source_array,target_array*<*,ignoresize*>);

***rc***
indicates whether the operation was successful.

| | |
|---|---|
| 0 | successful |
| ≠0 | not successful |

Type: Numeric

***source_array***
is the array to copy the values from.
Type: Array

***target_array***
    is the array to copy the values into.
        Type: Array

***ignoresize***
    indicates whether to check for array sizes to be the same.

'Y'                         tells SCL to check whether the source and target arrays are the
                            same size.

'N'                         tells SCL to ignore array sizes. (This value is the default.)

    Type: Character

**Details**    The COPYARRAY function allows you to copy data from one array
(*source_array*) into another array (*target_array*). The arrays must have the same
dimensions and size and be of the same type. The source array being copied from can
be a static or dynamic array, but if it is a dynamic array then its size must already have
been set using MAKEARRAY or REDIM. The target array being copied into can also be
a static or dynamic array. If it is dynamic and has not yet been created, then
COPYARRAY will create the array to the same size of the source array. However, the
low bound of a dynamic array is always 1, so the resultant target array may end up
with different low or high bounds in each of its dimensions.
    If you set *ignoresize* to '**Y**', then the sizes of the arrays do not have to match. Only
the types and dimensions of the arrays have to match. In this case, if the source array
is bigger than the target array, then the elements in the source array will be truncated,
and you will lose the data in the elements that do not coincide. If the source array is
smaller than the target array, then the elements in target array that are not set will be
automatically set to missing values.
    If the COPYARRAY is used to create a dynamic array, the DELARRAY function
should be used to delete the dynamic array.

# Examples

### Example 1: Copy Elements of a One–Dimensional Array    The example copies the
elements of the one–dimensional array A into the one–dimensional array B and prints
out the contents of the arrays.

```
DCL num a(5) b(5);
do i=1 to 5;
   a[i] = i;
end;
rc = copyarray(a,b);
put a=; put b=;
```

The result of this code would be:

```
a=
a[1] = 1
a[2] = 2
a[3] = 3
a[4] = 4
a[5] = 5
b=
b[1] = 1
b[2] = 2
b[3] = 3
b[4] = 4
```

```
b[5] = 5
```

**Example 2: Copy Elements of a Two–Dimensional Array**    The example copies the elements of the two–dimensional array A into the two–dimensional array B and prints out the contents of the arrays.

```
DCL num a(2,2) b(3,4);
count=0;
do i=1 to 2;
  do j=1 to 2;
    a[i,j] = count;
  end;
end;
rc = copyarray(a,b,'y');
put a=; put b=;
```

The result of this code would be:

```
a=
a[1,1] = 1
a[1,2] = 2
a[2,1] = 3
a[2,2] = 4
b=
b[1,1] = 1
b[1,2] = 2
b[1,3] = .
b[1,4] = .
b[2,1] = 3
b[2,2] = 4
b[2,3] = .
b[2,4] = .
b[3,1] = .
b[3,2] = .
b[3,3] = .
b[3,4] = .
```

## See Also

"DELARRAY" on page 332

"MAKEARRAY" on page 533

"REDIM" on page 610

Chapter 4, "SCL Arrays," on page 37

# COPYLIST

**Copies or merges the contents of an SCL list into an existing list or a new list**

**Category:**  List

## Syntax

*new-list-id*=**COPYLIST**(*list-id*<,*options*>
    <,*target-list-id*>);

***new-list-id***

> is either the identifier of the new list to contain a copy of the contents of *list-id*, if *target-list-id* is not supplied, or *target-list-id*, if a target list is supplied.
> Type: Numeric

***list-id***

> is the identifier of the list to copy or merge into the target list. An invalid *list-id* produces an error condition.
> Type: Numeric or List

***options***

> specify whether list values are merged and control how sublists are copied or merged. You can use one or more of the following values, separated by spaces. Later keywords override previous keywords.

> `'NONRECURSIVELY'` | `'NO'` | `'N'`

> > copies or merges only sublist identifiers as values for sublist items. (This is the default.)

> `'MERGE'` | `'M'`

> > merges the contents of the source *list-id* into the *target-list-id*, replacing like-named existing items in the target list. You may combine this option with the recursive option. An error occurs if *target-list-id* is not supplied or is not a valid list identifier.

> `'RECURSIVELY'` | `'YES'` | `'Y'`

> > copies or merges all items of sublists and of sublists of sublists, and so on.
> > Type: Numeric

***target-list-id***

> is the identifier of the list into which the source list is copied or merged. If supplied, *target-list-id* is also returned. Otherwise, a new list is created and returned. New sublists are created with the same environment (local or global) as the target list.
> An error condition results if the target list has attributes such as NOUPDATE and FIXEDLENGTH that prevent copying data into it.
> Type: Numeric

**Details**   The copy operation appends items from the source list to the end of the target list, whereas the merge operation copies them into the target list, replacing existing named items.

If an SCL object is passed to COPYLIST as *list-id*, the resulting copy is not an SCL object. Although the new list contains all items from the original object, methods can not be called on this copy. The copied list is also treated as a regular list for comparisons (e.g., COMPARELIST).

If *target-list-id* is omitted, the function creates a new list in the same environment (L or G) as the list being copied and makes the new list the *target-list-id*. (For a description of list environments, see "ENVLIST" on page 373.) If *target-list-id* is supplied, its identifier is returned in *new-list-id*.

When a list is copied recursively, the items in all sublists are also copied, not just the sublist identifiers. However, even this duplication is avoided if it would result in an infinite recursion. When copying a list recursively, SCL does not perform an infinite recursive copy. For example, if a list contains itself, COPYLIST detects the circular structure and recreates the structure in the copy.

Merging occurs by item names. All items in the source list (and in its sublists, if merging is recursive) must have names. For each item, the name is used to find a matching name in the target list, as with NAMEDITEM(*list-id name*). If the same name appears multiple times in the source list, each item is merged independently. That is, the last occurrence of the name overwrites previous merged values and does *not* match with subsequent items in the target list. Thus, you should strive to keep item names unique in the source list in order to avoid wasted processing. If the corresponding item is not found in the target list, a new item is created.

In the merge operation, a list or sublist is merged only once, even if it appears multiple times. Also, a warning is printed for items that do not have names.

If an item in the source list has the NOWRITE attribute, then the corresponding item in the target list is *deleted*, unless it has the NODELETE attribute, in which case it is not merged. If a scalar item replaces a sublist item in a merge, the replaced list is not deleted because it may be used elsewhere. The SCL program must explicitly delete the old list.

All attributes of the list and its contents are preserved when a list is copied. The password is not copied so that you can modify the copy without knowing the password of the original list. The copy has no password. (See "SETLATTR" on page 656 for a discussion of passwords for lists.)

COPYLIST ignores any invalid options and uses its defaults instead.

## Examples

### Example 1: Copying a Single List

```
    /* make B a local named list */
    /* with 2 items named x, y    */
b=makenlist('L','x','y');
b=setnitemc(b,'ABC','x');
b=setnitemc(b,'XYZ','y');
    /* make A a local named list       */
    /* with 3 items named A, B, and C */
a=makenlist('L','A','B','C');
a=setnitemn(a,3.5,'A');
a=setniteml(a,b,'B');
a=setnitemn(a,9.75,'C');

call putlist(a,'A=',2);
NREC=copylist(a,'N');
    /* nonrecursive copy */
call putlist(NREC,'NREC=',2);
REC=copylist(a,'Y');
    /* recursive copy */
call putlist(REC,'REC=',2);
```

This program produces the following output:

```
A=(   A=3.5
      B=(   x='ABC'
            y='XYZ'
          )[3]
      C=9.75
    )[5]
NREC=(   A=3.5
         B=(   x='ABC'
               y='XYZ'
             )[3]
         C=9.75
       )[7]
```

```
REC=(  A=3.5
       B=(  x='ABC'
            y='XYZ'
          )[11]
       C=9.75
     )[9]
```

The sublist named B in the outer list NREC is the same list as the sublist named B in the outer list named A, from which NREC was copied non-recursively. Both lists named B have the same list identifier (3), which means they are in fact the same list. However, the sublist named B in the outer list REC, which was copied recursively from list A, is a different list, although it has the same contents as the list named B from A. The sublist in the outer list REC has a list identifier of 11, not 3, which shows it is a different list.

*Note:*   [5], [7], and [9] are the list identifiers that were assigned when this example was run and may be different each time the example is run. △

**Example 2: Appending a List to Itself**    Append the list MYLIST to itself. Both NEWLIST and MYLIST contain the list identifier for the copy of MYLIST.

```
mylist=makelist();
mylist=insertn(mylist,1,-1);
mylist=insertn(mylist,2,-1);
mylist=insertn(mylist,3,-1);
newlist = copylist(mylist,'N',mylist);
```

NEWLIST contains the values 1, 2, 3, 1, 2, 3.

**Example 3: Merging One List into Another List**

```
INIT:
    a = makenlist('L','A','B','C','D','E','F');
    do i = 1 to listlen(a);
       a = setitemc(a, nameitem(a,i),i);
    end;
    c = insertc(makelist(),'?',-1,'NOT');
    a = insertl(a, c,-1,'WHY');
    b = makenlist('L','A','E','I','O','U');
    do i = 1 to listlen(b);
       b = setitemn(b, rank(nameitem(b,i)),i);
    end;
    b =
    insertl(b, insertn(makelist(),0,-1,'NOT'),-1,
                                        'WHY');
    call putlist(a,'A before merge:');
    call putlist(b,'B before merge:');
    b = copylist(a,'yes merge',b);
    call putlist(b,'B after merge :');
return;
```

The result is

```
A before merge:(A='A' B='B' C='C' D='D' E='E'
                                        F='F'
WHY=(NOT='?' )[7] )[5]
B before merge:(A=65 E=69 I=73 O=79 U=85
WHY=(NOT=0 )[11] )[9]
B after  merge :(A='A' E='E' I=73 O=79 U=85
```

```
WHY=(NOT='?'  )[11] B='B' C='C'
D='D' F='F'  )[9]
```

The result list B contains items from A where the names intersect as well as original items from B for items that were not found in A. Because the sublist WHY was found in both, a recursive merge replaced 0 from the sublist of B with '?' from the sublist of A.

*Note:* 7, 5, 11, and 9 are the list identifiers that were assigned when this example was run and may be different each time the example is run. △

**Example 4: Copying Multiple Instances of a List**   Copy a list, which contains a copy of itself, non-recursively and recursively. The outer list R1 contains two items, named SELF and R1, which are actually the same list as R1. When a non-recursive copy, R2, is made, the copy has items named SELF and R1 which are still the list R1. Only when R1 is copied recursively as R3 does the copy contain itself instead of R1.

```
/*  Create the list L, fill it, and print R1.  */
   r1=makenlist('l','a','SELF','r1', 'x');
   r1=setniteml(r1,r1,'SELF'));
   r1=setniteml(r1,r1,'r1'));
   r1=setnitemn(r1,1,'a'));
   r1=setnitemn(r1,99,'x'));
   call putlist(r1,'R1=',2));
/*  Copy R1 nonrecursively into R2 and print R2 */
   r2=copylist(r1,'n');
   call putlist(r2,'R2=',2);
/*  Copy R1 recursively into R3 and print R3 */
   r3=copylist(r1,'y');
   call putlist(r3,'R3=',2);
```

The list R2, which was created with a nonrecursive copy operation, contains the list R1. Note that the structure of the list R3 is identical to that of R1: it contains two copies of itself, at items named SELF and R1, because these items are lists whose list identifier is the same as the list R3.

This program produces the following output:

```
R1=(   a=1
       SELF=(...)[13]
       R1=(...)[13]
       x=99
     )[13]
R2=(   a=1
       SELF=(   a=1
                SELF=(...)[13]
                R1=(...)[13]
                x=99
              )[13]
       R1=(...)[13]
       x=99
     )[15]
R3=(   a=1
       SELF=(...)[17]
       R1=(...)[17]
       x=99
     )[17]
```

*Note:*   13, 15, and 17 are the list identifiers that were assigned when this example was run and may be different each time the example is run. △

**Example 5: Merging Nonrecursively and Recursively**   Merge the contents of the list identified in SOURCEID into the list identified in TARGETID. The second call does a recursive merge.

```
targetid=copylist(sourceid,"MERGE",targetid);
targetid=copylist(sourceid,"MERGE YES",targetid);
```

## See Also

"DELLIST" on page 336

"GETLATTR" on page 443

"HASATTR" on page 458

"MAKELIST" on page 535

"MAKENLIST" on page 536

"PUTLIST" on page 607

"SETLATTR" on page 656

# CREATESCL

**Writes class or interface information to an SCL entry**

**Category:**   Object Oriented

## Syntax

*entry-id*=**CREATESCL**(*entry-name, scl-entry<,description><,proxy>*);

**entry-id**
   contains the identifier that is assigned to the class, interface, or class package. If the class does not exist, *entry-id* contains 0.
      Type: Numeric

**entry-name**
   is the one- to four-level name of the CLASS, INTERFACE, or CLASSPKG catalog entry to load. If *entry-name* is a one- or two-level name, then the current search path is used to find the CLASS, INTERFACE, or CLASSPKG entry. If the entry was previously loaded, then the same identifier is returned. Otherwise, the entry is loaded from the catalog into the application class list, and the entry identifier is returned in *entry-id*.
      Type: Character

**scl-entry**
   is the one- to four-level name of the SCL entry to be created. If *proxy* is **1** and *entry-name* is a CLASSPKG entry, then you can specify a two-level name for *scl-entry*, and CREATESCL will generate a series of proxy entries for the classes in the class package.
      Type: Character

*description*
> is the description of the SCL entry.
>> Type: Character

*proxy*
> specifies whether CREATSCL should generate proxy entries. The default value of **0** means that CREATESCL will not generate proxy entries.
>
> Specify **1** if you want CREATESCL to generate proxies. If *entry-name* is a CLASS or an INTERFACE entry, then CREATESCL will generate a proxy entry for the class or interface. If *entry-name* is a CLASSPKG entry, and *scl-entry* is a two-level name, then CREATESCL will generate a proxy entry for each of the classes in the package (each class specified in an ITEM statement).
>> Type: Numeric

**Details**   CREATESCL writes the class or interface definition that is in *entry-name* to an SCL entry. The class definition is written to a CLASS or INTERFACE statement block in the SCL entry that is specified in *scl-entry*.

You can revise the code in *scl-entry* and use the SAVECLASS command to create a new or revised class/interface. For example, you can use the CREATESCL function to generate a Version 8 class that contains Version 6 class information. You can add the method signatures, scope, and so on, and then generate a new class using the SAVECLASS command. This process is described in "Converting Version 6 Non-Visual Classes to Version 8 Classes" on page 131.

For more information on the SAVECLASS command, see the online Help for SAS/AF software.

For a description of the CLASS and INTERFACE statement syntax that is written to the SCL entry, see "CLASS" on page 277 and "INTERFACE" on page 486.

## Examples

**Example 1: Generate CLASS SCL Entry**   Generate the SCL code for SASHELP.CLASSES.CHECKBOX_C.CLASS. Store the SCL code in WORK.A.CHECKBOX_C.SCL:

```
myClass=CREATESCL('sashelp.classes.checkbox_c.class',
   'work.a.checkbox_c.scl',
   'CheckBox class to convert');
```

**Example 2: Generate CLASSPKG SCL Entry**   Generate the SCL code for SASHELP.IOMSAMP.TSTPKG.CLASSPKG. Store the SCL code in WORK.A.B.SCL:

```
rc = createscl('sashelp.iomsamp.tstpkg.classpkg','work.a.b.scl');
```

**Example 3: Generate A Proxy Entry**   Generate a proxy entry for SASHELP.CLASSES.SCLLIST.CLASS.

```
rc = createscl('sashelp.classes.scllist.class','work.a.c.scl','',1);
```

The CLASS statement needed to generate the proxy class is stored in WORK.A.C.SCL. If you issue the SAVECLASS command for WORK.A.C.SCL, then SCL will generate the associated proxy class SCLLISTPROXY.CLASS.

*Note:* CREATESCL will generate **native='/sasprxy:0'** for each of the methods defined in the class. Do not modify this method option. △

**Example 4: Generate A Series of Proxy Entries**   Generate an SCL proxy file for each of the classes specified in SASHELP.IOMSAMP.TSTPKG.CLASSPKG. This class package contains a ITEM statement for these classes:

      □ SASHELP.IOMSAMP.AFTESTTYPES.CLASS
      □ SASHELP.CLASSES.SCLLIST.CLASS

```
rc = createscl('sashelp.iomsamp.tstpkg.classpkg','work.a','',1);
```

This statement creates two SCL entries in the WORK.A catalog:
AFTESTTYPESPESPROXY.SCL and SCLLISTPROXY.SCL. These SCL entries contain
the CLASS statements needed to generate the proxy classes. If you issue the
SAVECLASS command for these SCL entries, SCL will generate the proxy CLASS files.

   *Note:*   CREATESCL will generate **native='/sasprxy:0'** for each of the methods
defined in the class. Do not modify this method option. △

## See Also

"APPLY" on page 252

"INSTANCE" on page 485

"LOADRES" on page 526

"NOTIFY" on page 572

"SEND" on page 644

"SUPAPPLY" on page 679

"SUPER" on page 681

# _CURCOL_

**Contains the value of the leftmost column in an extended table control in a FRAME entry**

**Category:**   System Variable

**Details**     _CURCOL_ is a system variable. It is provided automatically by the FRAME
entry in SAS/AF, and the SCL compiler automatically creates a space for it in the SCL
data vector.

   The value of _CURCOL_ is updated when the getrow or putrow section or the
_getrow or _putrow method of an extended table is executing. Therefore, _CURCOL_
must be referenced only within these sections.

   _CURCOL_ is available only in SAS/AF FRAME entries.

## Example

   Suppose you have a text entry control, TEXT, in an extended table control. TEXT is
assigned a value in the getrow section, based on a substring of a longer string. When
the extended table is scrolled left and right, the value of _CURCOL_ is updated and is
used as the *position* argument to the SUBSTR function.

```
GET1:
   text = substr( longstring, _curcol_ );
return;
```

For more information about extended table controls for horizontal scrolling, see the
documentation for SAS/AF classes.

### See Also

"_CURROW_" on page 322

# CURFLD

**Returns the name of the FRAME or PROGRAM entry control or field on which the cursor is currently positioned**

**Category:** Cursor

## Syntax

*wvar-name*=**CURFLD**();

**wvar-name**
  contains the name of the FRAME or PROGRAM entry control or field on which the cursor is currently positioned.
  Type: Character

**Details**   The CURFLD function returns the name of the field FRAME or PROGRAM entry control on which the cursor is located. If the cursor is not positioned on a window variable, a null string is returned. CURFLD is usually used in conjunction with a CONTROL statement that includes the ENTER, ALWAYS, or ALLCMDS option. You can use CONTROL LABEL to achieve the same result more efficiently. FRAME or PROGRAM entries can also use the _getCurrentName method.

## Example

Use CURFLD to control the behavior of an SCL entry application:

```
INIT:
   control enter;
return;

MAIN:
   select( curfld() );
      when('PHONE') call display('phone.help');
      when('EMPLOYEE') call display
                            ('employee.scl');
      otherwise;
   end;
return;
```

This example can be implemented without CURFLD if the program contains a program block that is labeled with the name of the window variable. If the program is in a SCL entry, then the window variables must be of type PUSHBTNC or PUSHBTNN, and the INIT section must contain CONTROL LABEL.

```
INIT:
   controllable;
   return;
```

```
PHONE:
   call display('phone.help');
return;
EMPLOYEE:
   call display('employee.scl');
return;
```

## See Also

"CONTROL" on page 302

"CURSOR" on page 323

"CURWORD" on page 324

---

# CURLIST

**Designates or reports the current result SCL list**

**Category:** List

---

## Syntax

*list-id*=**CURLIST**(<*new-list-id*>);

*list-id*
  is the identifier of the list to receive the values returned by the next SCL selection list function that is invoked.

  >0              is the list identifier of the SCL list that was previously defined as current with the CURLIST function.

  0               indicates that no list is defined as the current list.

  Type: Numeric or List

*new-list-id*
  is the identifier of the list to be designated as the current list. An invalid *new-list-id* produces an error condition.
    Type: Numeric

**Details**    When a value is provided for *new-list-id*, CURLIST designates the SCL list that is identified by *new-list-id* as the current result list. *New-list-id* must be the list identifier that was returned by the MAKELIST, MAKENLIST, or COPYLIST function that created this list. If you omit *new-list-id*, then CURLIST returns the identifier of the SCL list that was already designated as the current result list by CURLIST. If no argument is passed to CURLIST and no current result list has been specified, CURLIST returns 0.

The current result list is filled automatically with the values that are selected when the next SCL selection list function executes.

The functions that can fill the current result list are the SCL selection list functions CATLIST, COLORLIST, DATALISTC, DATALISTN, DEVLIST, DIRLIST, FILELIST, LIBLIST, LISTC, LISTN, LVARLEVEL, and VARLIST. For example, CATLIST opens a selection list window that displays the names of catalog entries. The value returned by CATLIST is a character string containing each catalog name that users select, separated by blanks. Selection list functions like CATLIST can also automatically fill the current result list, as specified by CURLIST, with a character item for each selection that users make. The length of that list is unbounded.

When one of the selection list functions is invoked, the values that users select replace the entire contents of the current result list. To preserve the contents of the current result list, use COPYLIST to copy the list before calling another selection list function.

## Example

Set up a selection list, invoke a selection list function, and access the selections:

```
clist=makelist();
oldcurlist=curlist(clist);
   /* Allow user to choose up to 16 graphs.  */
graphs=catlist('SASUSER.DEMO','GRSEG',16,'Y');
n=getnitemn(clist,'COUNT');
do g=1 to n;
     graphName=getnitemc(clist,'name',g);
   put 'Selection #' g ' is ' graphName;
end;
/* Delete temporary curlist and restore +/
/* previous curlist. */
rc=dellist(clist);
oldcurlist=curlist(oldcurlist);
```

## See Also

"CATLIST" on page 269

"COLORLIST" on page 293

"COPYLIST" on page 311

"DATALISTC and DATALISTN" on page 326

"DELLIST" on page 336

"DEVLIST" on page 342

"DIRLIST" on page 347

"FILELIST" on page 401

"LIBLIST" on page 513

"LISTC and LISTN" on page 518

"LVARLEVEL" on page 531

"MAKELIST" on page 535

"MAKENLIST" on page 536

"PUTLIST" on page 607

"VARLIST" on page 709

# CUROBS

**Returns the number of the current row in a SAS table**

Category:   SAS Table

## Syntax

*row-number*=**CUROBS**(*table-id*);

**row-number**
> is the current row number.
> Type: Numeric

**table-id**
> is the table identifier that was assigned when the table was opened. If *table-id* is
> invalid, the program halts.
> Type: Numeric

## Details

*CAUTION:*
> **This function should be used only with an uncompressed SAS table that is accessed using
> a native library engine.** △

If the engine that is being used does not support row numbers, the function returns a
missing value.

In FSEDIT and FSVIEW applications, specifying a value for *table-id* is optional. If
the argument is not specified, CUROBS returns the value for the SAS table displayed
by FSEDIT or FSVIEW. For a SAS table view, the function returns the relative row
number. Also, on engines that do not support absolute row numbers, such as ORACLE,
CUROBS returns the relative row number.

## Examples

**Example 1: Getting the Row Number of a Control**   Use FETCHOBS to fetch the tenth
row in the SAS table MYDATA. CUROBS returns a value of 10 for *row-number*.

```
tableid=open('mydata','i');
rc=fetchobs(tableid,10);
rownum=curobs(tableid);
```

**Example 2: Getting the Current Row Number**   In an FSEDIT SCL program, retrieve
the number of the row that is currently displayed:

```
rownum=curobs();
```

# _CURROW_

**Contains the number of the current row in an extended table**

Category:   System Variable

**Details**     _CURROW_ is a system variable that is created for every SCL program that
you compile. The compiler creates a space for _CURROW_ in the SCL data vector.

_CURROW_ is updated when the getrow or putrow section of an extended table is executing or when the _getrow or _putrow method of an extended table control is executing. Therefore, _CURROW_ must be referenced only within these sections of an SCL program.

_CURROW_ is available in PROGRAM and FRAME entries.

## Example

The following getrow section of a FRAME entry fetches a row from a previously opened SAS table, using _CURROW_ as the row number.

```
GET1:
   if fetchobs( tableid, _currow_ ) ne 0 then
      call notify('table','endtable');
return;
```

## See Also

"_CURCOL_" on page 318

"SETROW" on page 664

# CURSOR

**Positions the cursor in a specified widget or field of a FRAME entry**

**Category:** Widget or Field

## Syntax

**CURSOR** *wvar-name*;

***wvar-name***
specifies which FRAME entry widget or field to position the cursor on.
Type: Character

**Details** The CURSOR statement does not move the cursor immediately while the SCL program is executing. Rather, it specifies where the cursor will be positioned when SCL returns control to the procedure after the frame is updated. If multiple cursor statements execute, the cursor is positioned on the FRAME entry widget or field that was specified in the last CURSOR statement. In SAS/AF applications, a REFRESH statement also positions the cursor, based on the last cursor statement.

The FRAME entry widget or field cannot be an element of an array. For an array element, use the FIELD function instead.

FRAME entry widgets can also use the _cursor method.

## Example

Move the cursor to ADDRESS if NAME is filled in:

```
if modified (name) and name ne '' then
   cursor address;
```

## See Also

# CURTOP

**Returns the number of the row that is currently displayed at the top of an extended table**

**Category:**   Extended Table

## Syntax

*row=***CURTOP**();

***row***

is the number of the row that is currently displayed at the top of an extended table.
Type: Numeric

**Details**     CURTOP can be used only on extended tables in PROGRAM entries. Because extended tables can be defined only in SAS/AF software, this function cannot be used in FSEDIT or FSVIEW programs.

## Example

Store the number of the table's top row in the column TOPROW:

```
toprow=curtop();
```

## See Also

# CURWORD

**Returns the word that is at the cursor position**

**Category:** Widget or Field

## Syntax

*word*=**CURWORD**();

**word**
    is the text of the word.
        Type: Character

**Details**    CURWORD returns the word on which the text cursor was located when the user last pressed ENTER. The retrieved character string begins with the first character of the word on which the cursor was positioned and extends to the first space after the word. CURWORD is usually used in conjunction with a CONTROL statement that includes the ENTER, ALWAYS, or ALLCMDS option.

    If CURWORD is used on a window variable that has been modified, the field value is justified before CURWORD executes.

## Example

Suppose a PROGRAM entry window contains text entry widgets that contain the words **PROJECT1** and **PROJECT2**. The entry's program determines which action to perform by determining which word the cursor is positioned on when the user presses ENTER.

```
INIT:
   widget enter;
return;
MAIN:
   word=curword();
   if (word='PROJECT1') then
      submit continue;
         proc print data=project1;
         run;
      endsubmit;
   else if (word='PROJECT2') then
      submit continue;
         proc print data=project2;
         run;
      endsubmit;
   else _msg_=
      'Please position the cursor on a valid selection.';
return;

TERM:
return;
```

## See Also

"CONTROL" on page 302

"CURFLD" on page 319

"CURSOR" on page 323

"LOOKUPC" on page 530

---

# DATALISTC and DATALISTN

**Displays a selection list window that contains the values of particular columns from rows in a SAS table and returns user selections**

**Category:**   SAS Table

---

## Syntax

*selection*=**DATALISTC**(*table-id*,
      *col-list*<,*message*<,*autoclose*<,*num-sel*>>>);

*selection*=**DATALISTN**(*table-id*,
      *col-list*<,*message*<,*autoclose*<,*num-sel*>>>);

**selection**
is the value of the first column from the selected row. For DATALISTC, the value is the first character column. For DATALISTN, the value is the first numeric column. *Selection* is a missing value (period) if the user closes the selection list window without making a selection.

For DATALISTC, *selection* is blank if the selection list window is closed and no selections are made. By default, *selection* is 200 bytes long. To accommodate a value longer than 200 bytes, explicitly declare *selection* with a longer length.
     Type: Character, Numeric.

**table-id**
is the identifier that was assigned when the table was opened. If *table-id* is invalid, the program halts.
     Type: Numeric

**col-list**
is a list of column names, separated by blanks, from the SAS table to be displayed. For DATALISTC, the first column in this list must be character or else the program halts. For DATALISTN, the first column must be numeric or else the program halts. However, the remaining columns in the list can be of any type.
     Type: Character

**message**
is the text for a message to be displayed above the selection list. The default message tells users to make up to the number of selections specified in *num-sel*.
     Type: Character

**autoclose**
specifies whether the selection list window closes automatically after a user makes a selection when only one choice is allowed:

'**Y**'                              closes the window automatically. (This is the default.)

'**N**'
    leaves the window open until the user explicitly closes it.
    This option is ignored when *num-sel* is not 1. However, use ' ' as a placeholder if you are also specifying a value for *num-sel*.
    Type: Character

***num-sel***
    specifies the maximum number of items a user can select from the list. To display the list for information purposes only (no selections allowed), specify **0**. To specify unlimited selections, use a value that is larger than the number of available selections, such as 9999.
    Type: Numeric

**Details**    If a user ends the selection list window without making a selection, DATALISTC and DATALISTN return a blank value. If the user exits by using OK without making a selection, then the selection variable is set to blank. However, if the user exits using CANCEL without making a selection, the selection variable retains any previous value it may have had.

Although a user can position the cursor or mouse pointer anywhere in a row to make a selection from the list, only the value of the first column is returned. (The other column values are displayed for information only.)

When multiple selections are allowed, *selection* contains only the value of the first column in the last selected row. However, values for displayed columns for all rows that are selected can be returned in the current result list if one is available. The current result list is a special SCL list that is automatically filled with the values selected from a selection list. To create a current result list, use the MAKELIST function to create it, and use the CURLIST function to designate it as the current result list. The current result list must exist before you call the DATALISTC or DATALISTN function.

By default, a message is displayed asking the user to make one selection, and the selection list window closes automatically when the user makes a selection.

When DATALISTC or DATALISTN is invoked, the current result list is cleared. After DATALISTC or DATALISTN is invoked, the result list contains the following named items:

TAG
    identifies the list as one that was created by the DATALISTC function.
    Type: Character

COUNT
    contains either the number of selected elements, or 0 if a user makes no selections or issues a CANCEL command in the list window.
    Type: Numeric

*var-name*
    contains the value of column *var-name* in *var-list* for each selection.
    Type: Numeric or Character

## Examples

**Example 1: Using DATALISTC to Return a Single Selection**    Create a selection list whose rows contain the values of the columns NAME, STREET, CITY, STATE, and ZIP from the SAS table identified by the SCL variable CLASSID, which was returned by the OPEN function. NAME contains the value for the selected row. The other columns are displayed for information purposes only.

```
name=datalistc(classid,'name street city state zip');
```

**Example 2: Using DATALISTN to Return Multiple Selections**   Create a selection list whose rows contain the values of the columns ITEMNUM, ITEMAMT, CUSTNAM, and CUSTADR from the SAS table identified by the SCL variable SALESID. Allow users to make up to three selections from this selection list. Then retrieve the values for each column for each of the selected rows from the current result list.

```
salesid=open('sales');
listid=makelist();
rc=curlist(listid);
itemnum=datalistn(salesid,
   'itemnum itemamt custnam custadr','','',3);
n=getnitemn(listid,'COUNT');
do i=1 to n;
   itemnum=getnitemn(listid,'ITEMNUM',i);
   itemamt=getnitemn(listid,'ITEMAMT',i);
   custnam=getnitemc(listid,'CUSTNAM',i);
   custadr=getnitemc(listid,'CUSTADR',i);
   put itemnum= itemamt= custnam= custadr=;
end;
rc=close(salesid);
```

## See Also

"LISTC and LISTN" on page 518

"LOCATEC and LOCATEN" on page 527

"SHOWLIST" on page 667

"VARLIST" on page 709

# DCLOSE

**Closes a directory**

**Category:**   Directory

## Syntax

*sysrc=***DCLOSE**(*directory-id*);

*sysrc*
contains the return code for the operation:

0                   successful

≠0                  not successful
   Type: Numeric

*directory-id*
is the identifier that was assigned when the directory was opened. If *directory-id* is invalid, the program halts.
   Type: Numeric

**Details**    The DCLOSE function closes a directory that was previously opened by the DOPEN function. DCLOSE also closes any open members of the directory before closing the directory.

## Example

Open the directory to which the fileref MYDIR has previously been assigned, return the number of members, and then close the directory:

```
rc=filename('mydir','fname')
did=dopen('mydir');
memcount=dnum(did);
if (dclose(did)) then
   do;
      _msg_=sysmsg();
      ...SCL statements to handle the error condition...
   end;
```

## See Also

"DOPEN" on page 357

"FCLOSE" on page 386

"FOPEN" on page 420

"MOPEN" on page 552

# DCREATE

**Creates an external directory**

**Category:**  External File

## Syntax

*new-directory*=**DCREATE**(*dir-name*<,*parent-dir*>);

**new-directory**
>    contains the complete pathname of the new directory, or an empty string if the directory cannot be created.
>       Type: Character

**dir-name**
>    is the name of the directory to create. This must be only the directory name and cannot include a pathname.
>       Type: Character

**parent-dir**
>    is the complete pathname of the directory in which to create the new directory. If *parent-dir* is not supplied, then the current directory is the parent directory.
>       Type: Character

**Details**    DCREATE enables you to create a directory in your operating environment.

*Operating Environment Information:* On CMS, DCREATE works only for shared file system (SFS) directories. △

## Example

☐ Create a new directory on UNIX, using the name stored in the variable DIRNAME:

```
newdir=dcreate(dirname,'/local/u/abcdef/');
```

☐ Create a directory on Windows, using the name stored in the variable DIRNAME:

```
newdir=dcreate(dirname,'d:\testdir\');
```

☐ Create a new directory on CMS, using the name stored in the variable DIRNAME:

```
newdir=dcreate(dirname,'auser.');
```

# DECLARE

**Declares variables and specifies their data types**

**Alias:** DCL

**Category:** Declarative Statement

## Syntax

**DECLARE | DCL** *data-type-1 argument-1 < . . . ,data-type-nargument-n >*;

*data-type*

specifies the data types to assign. Multiple data types may be declared with one DECLARE statement. Use a comma to separate multiple data types. If you omit a comma between data types, then subsequent data type names are interpreted as variable names until the next comma is encountered.

The following are valid data types:

**'CHAR <(*n*)>'**

is for variables that can contain character values. Optionally, *n* is the length. Default: 200. Declaring a length for CHAR variables that will store values shorter than 200 characters can reduce the amount of memory required to store a program's variables.

**'LIST'**

is for variables that can reference an SCL list.

**'NUM'**

is for variables that can contain numeric values.

**'OBJECT'**

is for variables that can contain the identifier of a component.

*Note:* The compiler cannot validate attributes or methods for objects declared with the OBJECT keyword (generic objects). Consequently, using generic objects is less efficient (possibly up to 25 percent less efficient) than declaring objects with the CLASS or INTERFACE keyword. See "Objects" on page 19 for more information. △

*class-name*
> is for variables that can contain the identifier of an instance of a particular class. It can be a one– to four–level name.
> Type: Character

***argument-1< . . . argument-n>***
> can be either one or more constants and/or one or more variable names. The constants and/or variable names should be separated by spaces. Variable names can be any of the following:
> *variable*
> *variable = initial-value*
> *variable = expression*
> *variable-1 – variable-n = (value-1,...,value-n)*
> *listname={value-1,...,value-n }*
> Constants have the following form:
>
> *constant-n<=value-n>*
>
>> Type: Character or Numeric (for variables).
>>
>> Type: Character (for constants).

**Details**   The DECLARE statement declares a variable of any SCL data type. DECLARE can be used within a DO, SELECT, or USECLASS block to define variables that are available only within that block. This enables you to enforce variable scoping, because variables that you declare within a DO, SELECT, or USECLASS block are local to that block.

You can use the DECLARE statement to declare any type of array. However, arrays that are declared with the DECLARE statement are all temporary arrays. See "Using Temporary Arrays to Conserve Memory" on page 46.

Although you can use the LENGTH statement to declare numeric and character variables, you might want to use the DECLARE statement in order to enforce variable scoping.

Place DECLARE statements either before the first labeled section of an SCL program or inside a DO or SELECT block.

## Comparisons

- □ You can use the DECLARE statement to declare any SCL data type, whereas the LENGTH statement can declare only numeric and character variables.

- □ You can use the DECLARE statement inside a DO block, whereas the LENGTH statement cannot be used inside a DO block.

- □ You can use the DECLARE statement to declare temporary arrays, but you must use the ARRAY statement to declare indirect or non-temporary arrays.

For details about the LENGTH statement in the base SAS language, see *SAS Language Reference: Dictionary*.

## Examples

```
dcl char  s;
dcl num x y;
dcl char s, num x y;
dcl char(10) ar[3] x y z;
dcl list mylist;
dcl sashelp.fsp.collection.class obj3;
dcl object obj4;
dcl num m n, char(300) string, list newlist;
```

Each variable or array can be followed by an initial value or expression. The following example declares and initializes various variables and arrays.

```
dcl num      x=1 y=20+x;
dcl num      i1-i4=(1, 2, 3, 4);
dcl num      arr(3)=(1, 2, 3);
dcl char(10) s='abc';
dcl char     sarr(3)=('abc', 'def', 'ghi');
dcl list     mylist = {1, 'abc', 2, 'def'};  /* Initialize a list */
dcl list l = (100, 'abc', 200);
```

## Defining a Constant List with a Sublist

A constant list can be defined with a sublist.

```
init:               /*To edit a frame. As the frame runs,*/
                    /*it will display */
  dcl list l ;      /* a pop-up menu when you hit the ENTER key.*/;
  control enter
/* Initialize a list with three pop-menu items: Select 1, Numeric*/
/*and  Character. This will also define a separator between item*/
/*'Select 1'and 'Numeric'.   */
  list = { {text='Select 1',
           helpText='This is a selection.',
           mnemonic='S',
           classifier = 107},
        ''_'',
        ''Numeric'',
        ''Character''};

    return;
main:
 rc = popmenu (list);
 put rc=;
 return;

term:
 /* Delete the list recursively to avoid a memory leak */
 rc = dellist ( list, 'y');
 return;
```

*Note:*  The form of the physical filename depends on the host operating system. △

## See Also

"ARRAY" on page 254

"LENGTH" on page 510

"USECLASS" on page 698

---

# DELARRAY

### Deletes a dynamic array

**Category:**  Array

## Syntax

*rc*=**DELARRAY**(*array*);

**rc**

indicates whether the operation was successful.

| | |
|---|---|
| 0 | successful |
| ≠0 | not successful |

Type: Numeric

**array**

is the dynamic array to delete. A non-dynamic array causes an error condition.

Type: Array

**Details**    The DELARRAY function deletes dynamic arrays. An array's contents cannot be accessed after the array is deleted. Dynamic arrays are only accessible within the scope that they are declared. In the following example, array B is not accessible outside of the scope of the DO group:

```
m1:method;
     DCL num a(*,*) rc;
     rc = makearray(a,5,5);
     do;
         DCL num b(*);
         rc = makearray(b,10);
     end;
endmethod;
```

## Examples

**Example 1: Create an Array and Delete It**    The example creates a 1-dimensional array of 5 elements, resizes it to 10 elements (preserving the data), and deletes the array.

```
DCL num a(*);
rc = makearray(a,3);
do i=1 to dim(a);
    a[i]=i;
end;
rc = redim(a,5);
put a=;
rc = delarray(a);
```

The output would be:

```
a[1]=1
a[2]=2
a[3]=3
a[4]=.
a[5]=.
```

## See Also

"COPYARRAY" on page 309

"MAKEARRAY" on page 533

"REDIM" on page 610

# DELETE

**Deletes a member of a SAS data library or an external file or directory**

**Category:**   Utility

## Syntax

*sysrc*=**DELETE**(*name*<,*type*,<,*password*<,*generation*>>>);

### *sysrc*
contains the return code for the operation:

| | |
|---|---|
| 0 | successful |
| ≠0 | not successful |

   Type: Numeric

### *name*
is the name of the member of the SAS data library or the physical pathname of an external file or directory. If a one-level name is specified for a SAS data library member, the library is assumed to be USER.
   Type: Character

### *type*
specifies the type of element to delete:

**'ACCESS'**
   an access descriptor that was created using SAS/ACCESS software.

**'CATALOG'**
   a SAS catalog or catalog entry. If a one- or two-level name is specified, the catalog is deleted. If a four-level name is specified, the entry is deleted.

**'DATA'**
   a SAS table. (This is the default.)

**'VIEW'**
   a SAS table view.

**'FILE'**
   an external file or directory.
   Type: Character

### *password*
is the password that is assigned to the SAS table when *type* is **DATA**.
   Type: Character

### *generation*
is the generation number of the SAS table that is being deleted.
   Type: Numeric

**Details**    DELETE attempts to delete the specified member and returns a value indicating whether the operation was successful. You can use DELETE to delete files or empty directories that are external to a SAS session, as well as members of a SAS data library.

## Examples

**Example 1: Deleting Tables and Catalog Entries**    Delete the SAS table LIB1.MYDATA and the SAS catalog entry LIB2.CAT1.MYPROG.PROGRAM:

```
rc=delete('lib1.mydata');
rc=delete('lib2.cat1.myprog.program','catalog');
```

When deleting generation tables, if you delete the current (base) table without specifying the *generation* parameter, all tables in the generation group are deleted. For example:

```
rc=delete('one');
/* Deletes all tables in the generation group named 'one'*/
```

If you specify the current (base) table using the *generation* parameter, only that table is deleted. The youngest historical table becomes the new base. For example:

```
rc=delete('one','data','',0);
/* Deletes only the table work.one (relative generation number=0) */
```

**Example 2: Deleting Files**    Delete an external file:
In UNIX:

```
/* delete a file in a different directory */
rc=delete('/local/u/abcdef/testfile','file');
```

In Windows:

```
/* delete a file in a different directory */
rc=delete('D:\testfile','file');
```

**Example 3: Deleting Data Set Generations**    Delete the third generation of a data set:

```
    /* delete the third generation of the data set 'work.one' */
rc=delete('work.one','data','',3);
```

## See Also

"NEW" on page 561

---

# DELITEM

**Deletes an item from an SCL list**

**Category:**  List

---

## Syntax

*list-id*=**DELITEM**(*list-id*< ,*index*>);

*list-id*
> is the identifier of the list from which the item is to be deleted. The function returns the list identifier that is passed in. An invalid *list-id* produces an error condition.
>    Type: Numeric or List

*index*
> is the position of the item in the list. The position can be specified as either a positive or negative number. By default, *index* is 1 (the first item). If *index* is a positive number, then the item is at position *index* from the beginning of the list. If *index* is a negative number, then the item is at position ABS(*index*) from the end of the list. An error condition results if the absolute value for *index* is zero or if it is greater than the number of items in the list.
>    Type: Numeric

**Details**    The item to be deleted is specified by its position in the list that is passed in. DELITEM does not make a copy of the list before deleting the specified item. The delete operation is performed in place on the list, and the list identifier is returned.

When the item to be deleted is a sublist, DELITEM deletes the item but not the sublist, because the sublist may be referenced by other SCL variables or lists.

An error condition results if

☐ the item has the NODELETE attribute

☐ the list has the NOUPDATE or FIXEDLENGTH attribute.

To check the attributes of a list or list item, use HASATTR. To change attributes, use SETLATTR.

## See Also

"DELLIST" on page 336

"DELNITEM" on page 337

"POPC, POPL, POPN, and POPO" on page 593

# DELLIST

**Deletes a list and optionally deletes all of its sublists**

**Category:**  List

## Syntax

*rc*=**DELLIST**(*list-id*<,*recursively*>);

*rc*
> contains the return code for the operation:

| | |
|---|---|
| 0 | successful |
| ≠0 | not successful |

>    Type: Numeric

*list-id*
> is the identifier of the list to be deleted. An invalid *list-id* produces an error condition.
>    Type: Numeric or List

*recursively*
  specifies whether to recursively delete all the list's sublists and all sublists of its sublists.

  `'N'`              Sublists are not deleted. (This is the default.)

  `'Y'`              Sublists are deleted.
        Type: Character

**Details**    A list's contents cannot be retrieved after the list is deleted.

If *recursively* is `'Y'`, DELLIST recursively deletes all sublists that do not have the NODELETE attribute. For sublists that have the NODELETE attribute, the sublist identifiers are removed from the deleted list, but the sublist is not deleted. Thus, you should store list identifiers for sublists either in another list or in an SCL variable so that you can access the lists later. All local lists that are not explicitly deleted are deleted when the application ends, at the same time that SCL closes open tables and files.

*CAUTION:*
**Be careful when deleting lists recursively because you may inadvertently delete lists that are needed by other parts of the SCL program.** Recursively deleting a list deletes all of its sublists even if they are referenced in other SCL lists or by other SCL variables. If you do not want a list to be deleted when it is a sublist item in a deleted list, use SETLATTR to assign the NODELETE attribute to the sublist. See "SETLATTR" on page 656 for a discussion of the NODELETE attribute. △

To conserve memory, delete lists when they are no longer needed. Typically, a DELLIST statement is placed in the termination section (TERM or FSETERM) of the program. Although the program that creates a list is most often responsible for deleting the lists that it creates, it does not have to delete them unless that is the appropriate action for the application; it may return the list that it created to its caller.

The list is not deleted, and a non-zero value is returned to *rc*, if

  □ the list has the NODELETE attribute
  □ the list is the local or global environment list (the lists returned by the ENVLIST function)
  □ *list-id* is a component identifier or a class list identifier.

To check attributes, use HASATTR. To change attributes, use SETLATTR.

If DELLIST fails because of a condition listed above, the list and/or sublists may be partially cleared, and no further items or sublists are cleared.

## See Also

"CLEARLIST" on page 290

"DELITEM" on page 335

"DELNITEM" on page 337

"SETLATTR" on page 656

# DELNITEM

**Deletes a named item from an SCL list**

**Category:**  List

## Syntax

*list-id*=**DELNITEM**(*list-id,name,< occurrence*
  *<,start-index<,index<,forceup>>>>*);

**list-id**
: is the identifier of the list from which the item is to be deleted. The function returns the list identifier that is passed in. An invalid *list-id* produces an error condition.
  Type: Numeric or List

**name**
: is the name of the item to delete. Item names are converted to uppercase and trailing blanks are ignored when searching the list for a matching name. Thus, the names 'abc' and 'Abc' are converted to 'ABC'.
  Type: Character

**occurrence**
: is the number of the occurrence of the named item to delete. The default, 1, specifies the first occurrence of the item.
  Type: Numeric

**start-index**
: specifies where in the list to begin searching for the item. By default, *start-index* is 1 (the first item). If *start-index* is positive, then the search begins at position *start-index* items from the beginning of the list. If *start-index* is negative, then the search begins at the item specified by ABS(*start-index*) items from the end of the list. An error condition results if the absolute value of *start-index* is zero or if it is greater than the number of items in the list.
  Type: Numeric

**index**
: specifies the variable to contain the position number of the deleted item. *Index* must be initialized to a nonmissing value; otherwise, errors result.

  *Note:* This parameter is an update parameter. See "Input, Output, and Update Parameters" on page 34 for more information. △
  Type: Numeric

**forceup**
: can have one of the following values:

  'Y'
  : specifies a case-insensitive search, which overrides the HONORCASE or NOHONORCASE list attribute.

  'N'
  : specifies a search that uses the HONORCASE or NOHONORCASE list attribute and is the default action for lists when FORCEUP is not specified.

  IGNORECASE
  : IGNORECASE is the alias for NOHONORCASE and is the default for a list. But you can use the SETLATTR function to set a list's attribute to HONORCASE.

**Details**    DELNITEM searches for a named item and deletes it from the list. Case is ignored only if *forceup* is 'Y'; otherwise, it searches according to the list attribute HONORCASE and NOHONORCASE.

If a list has the NOHONORCASE attribute, the case is also ignored.

If *occurrence* and *start-index* are both positive or both negative, then the search proceeds forward from the *start-index* item. For forward searches, the search continues only to the end of the list and does not wrap back to the front of the list. If *occurrence* or *start-index* is negative, then the search is backwards. For backward searches, the search continues only to the beginning of the list and does not wrap back to the end of the list.

DELNITEM does not make a copy of the list. The delete operation is performed in place on the list. For example, the following statement deletes the first item named **app** in the list identified by LISTID:

```
listid=delnitem(listid,'app');
```

When the item to be deleted is a sublist, DELNITEM deletes the item but not the sublist, because the sublist may be referenced by other SCL variables or lists.

An error condition results if

☐ the item has the NODELETE attribute

☐ the list has the NOUPDATE or FIXEDLENGTH attribute

☐ the named item is not found in the list.

To check the attributes of a list or list item, use HASATTR. To change these attributes, use SETLATTR.

## Example

The following code creates a list named A, adds four items to the list, and prints the list. Then it deletes the third item in the list and prints the list again.

```
a=makelist();
rc=insertc(a,'a',-1,'var1');
rc=insertc(a,'b',-1,'var2');
rc=insertc(a,'c',-1,'var1');
rc=insertc(a,'d',-1,'var2');
call putlist(a,'Before deleting',0);
pos=0;
rc=delnitem(a,'var1',2,1,pos);
put pos=;
call putlist(a,'After deleting',0);
```

The results of this program are:

```
Before deleting(VAR1='a'
                VAR2='b'
                VAR1='c'
                VAR2='d'
                )[5]
POS=3
After deleting(VAR1='a'
               VAR2='b'
               VAR2='d'
               )[5]
```

*Note:* [5] is the list identifier that was assigned when this example was tested and may be different each time the example is run. △

### See Also

"DELITEM" on page 335

"DELLIST" on page 336

"LISTLEN" on page 521

"SETLATTR" on page 656

# DELOBS

**Deletes a row from a SAS table**

**Category:** SAS Table

## Syntax

*sysrc*=**DELOBS**(*table-id*);

**sysrc**
contains the return code for the operation:

| | |
|---|---|
| 0 | successful |
| ≠0 | not successful |

Type: Numeric

**table-id**
is the identifier that was assigned when the SAS table was opened. If *table-id* is invalid, the program halts.
Type: Numeric

**Details**    You must fetch a row before it can be deleted. Some functions that fetch a row include FETCH, FETCHOBS, LOCATEC, LOCATEN, APPEND, DATALISTC, and DATALISTN.

## Example

Delete the current row from an open SAS table. (The example assumes that the table identifier returned by the OPEN function was stored in the SCL variable MYDATAID.) If the function is unable to delete the row, a message is displayed on the message line.

```
if (delobs(mydataid)) then _msg_=sysmsg();
```

### See Also

"APPEND" on page 251

"DATALISTC and DATALISTN" on page 326

"FETCH" on page 389

"FETCHOBS" on page 390

"LOCATEC and LOCATEN" on page 527

---

# DESCRIBE

**Fills an SCL list with items of system information about a SAS table, view, or catalog entry**

**Category:** List

---

## Syntax

*sysrc*=**DESCRIBE**(*source-name,list-id<,type>*);

*sysrc*
   contains the return code for the operation:

   0               successful

   ≠0            not successful
      Type: Numeric

*source-name*
   is the name of the table, view, or catalog entry.
      Type: Character

*list-id*
   contains the identifier of an existing list to contain the control's description. An invalid *list-id* produces an error condition.
      Type: Numeric or List

*type*
   specifies the type of control to be described:

   **'CATALOG'**
   SAS catalog entry (This is the default.) For three- or four-level names, the default entry type is PROGRAM.

   **'DATA'**
   SAS table (This is the default for one- or two-level names.)

   **'VIEW'**
   SAS data view.
      Type: Character

**Details**   Because DESCRIBE replaces the previous values in the list, the same list can be used repeatedly.

The items of descriptive information are placed into the list as named items, and the names of the list items are the names of the attributes described. Only the named attributes that appear in the list are filled in.

The attributes that DESCRIBE can place in an SCL list are determined by the value of *type*. If *type* is DATA or VIEW, then the items named in the list are attributes that are returned by the ATTRN and ATTRC functions. If *type* is CATALOG, then the items named in the list are DESC (the description of the catalog), EDESC (the extended description of the catalog entry), CRDATE (the date that the entry was created), and DATE (the date that the entry was last modified). CRDATE and DATE are SAS date values.

For catalog entries, if a numeric list item named DATE exists in the list, then DESCRIBE sets that item's values to a SAS date value. Otherwise, if DATE is a character list item, then DESCRIBE assigns a formatted date string using the MMDDYY10. format. Use ITEMTYPE to determine the type of a list item.

## Example

Create an SCL list containing items named DESC and DATE. DESCRIBE fills the DESC and DATE items in the list with information about the catalog entry MYLIB.MYCAT.A.SCL.

```
init:
  desc_list=makenlist('L','DESC','DATE');
 /* set DATE to character list item */
  rc=setnitemc(desc_list,' ','DATE');
  rc=describe('MYLIB.MYCAT.A.SCL',desc_list,'CATALOG');
  call putlist(desc_list);
return;
```

The output would be similar to:

```
(DESC='A.SCL' DATE='03/25/1999' )[5]
```

## See Also

"ATTRC and ATTRN" on page 258

# DEVLIST

**Displays a selection list of graphic hardware devices and returns user selections**

**Category:**   Selection List

## Syntax

*selections*=**DEVLIST**(*catalog-name,device< ,message*
   *< ,autoclose< ,num-sel>>>*);

*selections*
   are one or more user selections from the list, or blank if the selection list window is closed and no selections are made.
      Type: Character

*catalog-name*
   is the catalog that lists the devices. Usually the catalog SASHELP.DEVICES is used as *catalog-name*.
      Type: Character

***device***
> is the type of device to be listed:
>
> **'CAMERA'**
> > lists device catalog entries for film recorders.
>
> **'DEFAULT'**
> > returns the current device name, description, and type instead of displaying a list.
>
> **'EXPORT'**
> > lists device catalog entries for device drivers that produce a graphics stream file.
>
> **'MONITOR'**
> > lists device catalog entries for video displays.
>
> **'PLOTTER'**
> > lists device catalog entries for plotters.
>
> **'PRINTER'**
> > lists device catalog entries for printers.
> > Type: Character

***message***
> is the text for a message to be displayed above the selection list. The default message tells users to make up to the number of selections specified in *num-sel*.
> Type: Character

***autoclose***
> specifies whether the selection list window closes automatically after a user makes a selection when only one choice is allowed:
>
> **'Y'**          closes the window automatically. (This is the default.)
>
> **'N'**          leaves the window open until the user explicitly closes it.
> > This option is ignored when *num-sel* is not 1. However, use ' ' as a placeholder if you are also specifying a value for *num-sel*.
> > Type: Character

***num-sel***
> specifies the maximum number of items a user can select from the list. To display the list for information purposes only (no selections allowed), specify 0. To specify an unlimited number of selections, use a value that is larger than the number of available selections about graphic device drivers such as 9999.
> Type: Numeric

**Details**    The value in *selections* consists of a 40-character description, an 8-character device name, and an 8-character device type. For additional details about graphic device drivers, see *SAS/GRAPH Software: Reference* and the SAS online Help for SAS/ GRAPH software.

You can provide a default value or an initial selected value in the list by providing a value for the *selections* variable before calling DEVLIST. If *selections* contains valid entry names when the function is invoked, those names are automatically designated as selected when the selection list is displayed.

If a user closes the selection list window without making a selection, then DEVLIST returns a blank value unless there was an initial value for the *selections* variable before DEVLIST was called.

When multiple selections are allowed, *selections* contains the first value selected from the list. However, the values for all selections can be returned in the current result list, if one is available. The current result list is a special SCL list that is automatically filled with the values selected from a selection list. To use a current result list, use the

MAKELIST function to create the list, and use the CURLIST function to designate it as the current result list. The current result list must exist before you call DEVLIST.

When DEVLIST is invoked, the current result list is cleared. After DEVLIST is invoked, the result list contains the following named items:

TAG
> identifies the list as one that was created by the DEVLIST function.
>> Type: Character

COUNT
> contains either the number of selected elements, or 0 if a user makes no selections or issues a CANCEL command in the list window.
>> Type: Numeric

DESC
> contains the description of the selected device. There is one DESC element for each selection. The value of DESC is in the case that was entered originally.
>> Type: Character

DEVICE
> contains the name for each selected device. There is one DEVICE element for each selection.
>> Type: Character

TYPE
> contains the type of each selected device. There is one TYPE element for each selection.
>> Type: Character

## Examples

**Example 1: Displaying the Printer Devices of a Catalog**   Display a list of devices of type PRINTER that are available in the catalog SASHELP.DEVICES. After the user selects one device from the list, the program uses the SUBSTRING function to extract the individual items of information returned by DEVLIST.

```
select=devlist('sashelp.devices','printer',
   'Select a device.');
descript=substr(select,1,40);
device=substr(select,41,8);
devtype=substr(select,49,8);
```

**Example 2: Using the Results of a DEVLIST**   Use the current result list to process multiple selections:

```
listid=makelist();
rc=curlist(listid);
selection=devlist('sashelp.devices','printer',
   'Select a device',' ',3);
n=getnitemn(listid,'COUNT');
do i=1 to n;
   descript=getnitemc(listid,'DESC',i);
   device=getnitemc(listid,'DEVICE',i);
   devtype=getnitemc(listid,'TYPE',i);
   put descript= device= devtype=;
end;
```

## See Also

"COLORLIST" on page 293

# DIALOG

**Runs a FRAME entry that was created with SAS/AF software and disables all other windows**

**Category:** Modular Programming

## Syntax

**CALL DIALOG**(*entry<,parameters>*)

*entry*
 is a FRAME entry to be displayed. It is specified as

*entry.type*
 for a FRAME entry in the current catalog.

*libref.catalog.entry.type*
 for a FRAME entry in a specified catalog.
 Type: Character

*parameters*
 lists one or more parameters to pass to the called entry. In order for the called entry
 to accept these parameters, it must contain a corresponding ENTRY statement.

 *Note:* These parameters are update parameters. See "Input, Output, and Update
 Parameters" on page 34 for more information. △
 Type: Numeric, Character

## Details

 DIALOG runs a FRAME entry, makes it the active entry, and disables all other
windows. When the called entry is exited, control returns to the calling program. With
the exception of disabling all other windows, DIALOG is similar to DISPLAY.

 *Note:* From the window created with the CALL DIALOG routine, you cannot
execute a SUBMIT statement with the CONTINUE option. See "Controlling What
Happens After a Submit Block Executes" on page 83. △

 DIALOG can pass parameters through the ENTRY statement to the called Frame entry.
Parameters can be numeric constants, character constants, variables, expressions, and
array variables.

 Using DIALOG without any options in the associated ENTRY statement requires a
strict correspondence between DIALOG parameters and ENTRY statement arguments.
The arguments and parameters must agree in number, data type, and relative position.
If you pass an incorrect number of parameters or a parameter of the incorrect type,
SCL halts the execution of the program. The argument-parameter correspondence is
less restrictive when you use the options REST=, ARGLIST=, and OPTIONAL= in the
ENTRY statement.

 Names listed in *parameter* do not have to match the argument names in the ENTRY
statement.

 Parameters are passed in the following ways:

call-by-reference
>    passes window variables and local variables and allows values to be returned to the calling program. This method allows the called program to modify values and then return them. If you do not want to return the new values, use the NOCHANGE routine. Or, if you do not want to return the new values for particular parameters, use the INPUT option for that parameter in the ENTRY statement. Here is an example of call-by-reference:

```
array employee{50};
call dialog('b.frame',var1,name,num,employee{1});
```

call-by-value
>    is used for all numeric constants, character constants, and expressions. It does not allow values to be returned to the calling program. Here is an example of call-by-value:

```
call dialog('b.frame',100,'hello',x+y);
```

## See Also

"DISPLAY" on page 350

"ENTRY" on page 369

"NOCHANGE" on page 569

"RETURN" on page 615

# DINFO

### Returns information about a directory

**Category:**   Directory

## Syntax

*attribute*=**DINFO**(*directory-id,info-item*);

**attribute**
>    contains the value of the information item, or a blank if *info-item* is invalid.
>    Type: Character

**directory-id**
>    is the identifier that was assigned when the directory was opened. If *directory-id* is invalid, the program halts.
>    Type: Numeric

**info-item**
>    is the information item to be retrieved.
>    Type: Character

**Details**   DINFO returns the value of a system-dependent directory parameter. The available information varies according to the operating system. See the SAS documentation for your host operating system for information about system-dependent directory parameters.

Use DOPTNAME to determine the names of the available system-dependent directory information items. Use DOPTNUM to determine the number of directory information items available.

## Example

Open the directory MYDIR, determine the number of directory information items available, and retrieve the value of the last item:

```
   /* Assign the fileref MYDIR to the */
   /* pathname stored in the variable */
   /* or entered in the DIRNAME field and open it.*/
   rc=filename('mydir',dirname);
did=dopen('mydir');
numopts=doptnum(did);
foption=doptname(did,numopts);
charval=dinfo(did,foption);
rc=dclose(did);
```

## See Also

"DOPTNAME" on page 358

"DOPTNUM" on page 359

"FINFO" on page 412

"FOPTNAME" on page 421

"FOPTNUM" on page 423

# DIRLIST

**Opens a host selection list window that lists members of one or more SAS data libraries, and returns a user's selections**

**Category:**   Selection List

## Syntax

*selections*=**DIRLIST**(*lib-spec,member-type,num-sel,prefix<,table-type<,sel-excl<,message>>>*);

***selections***
contains one or more user selections. Multiple selections are separated by blanks. By default, *selections* is 200 bytes long. To accommodate values longer than 200 bytes, explicitly declare *selections* with a longer length.
   Type: Character

***lib-spec***
lists one or more librefs that are associated with particular SAS data libraries. To include or exclude SAS data libraries, use a name specification style from "Name Specifications for Arguments" on page 348. By default, SASHELP is not included in the selection window.
   Type: Character

*member-type*

lists one or more types of SAS data library members. For example, a few common *member-types* are DATA, VIEW, and CATALOG. To include or exclude particular *member-types*, use a name specification style from "Name Specifications for Arguments" on page 348.

Type: Character

*num-sel*

is the maximum number of items that a user can select from the list. To display the list for information purposes only (no selections allowed), specify 0. To specify an unlimited number of selections, use a value such as 9999 that is larger than the number of available selections.

Type: Numeric

*prefix*

specifies whether names that are selected are prefixed with the libref:

**'Y'**

Selected names are returned as *libref.name*.

**'N'** or **' '**

Selected names are returned as *name*.

*table-type*

lists one or more SAS table types. By default, the selection list displays members of all SAS table types. To include or exclude specific table types, use a name specification style from "Name Specifications for Arguments" on page 348. This argument is ignored unless **DATA** is one of the values of *member-type*. For information about table types, see the description of the TYPE= data set option in *SAS Language Reference: Dictionary*.

Type: Character

*sel-excl*

lists one or more SAS data library members to include or exclude from the list. Use a name specification style from "Name Specifications for Arguments" on page 348. If *prefix* is **N**, then specify the name here as *member*. If *prefix* is **Y**, then specify the name here as *libref.member*.

Type: Character

*message*

is the text for a message to be displayed above the selection list. The default message tells users to make up to the number of selections specified in *num-sel*.

Type: Character

*autoclose*

is an obsolete arument bur is retained for compatibility with earlier releases. If you want to specify a value for *num-sel*, then specify **' '** as a placeholder for this argument.

## Name Specifications for Arguments

For *lib-spec*, *member-type*, and *table-type*, use these guidelines for specifying names:

- □ To specify one or more specific names, separate the names with a space.
- □ To specify all names, use an asterisk (*) or a null string (' ').
- □ To specify all names *except* those listed, use a NOT sign (^ or ¬) followed by one or more names.

**Details**   If a user closes the selection list window without making a selection, *selections* contains a blank value unless that variable contained a valid value before DIRLIST was called.

The values for all selections can be returned in the current result list, if one is available. The current result list is a special SCL list that is automatically filled with the values selected from a selection list. To use a current result list, use the MAKELIST function to create the list, and use the CURLIST function to designate it as the current result list. The current result list must exist before you call the DIRLIST function.

When the function is invoked, the current result list is cleared. After DIRLIST is invoked, the current result list contains the following named elements:

TAG
> identifies the list as one that was created by DIRLIST.
>> Type: Character

COUNT
> contains the number of selected items or contains 0 if a user makes no selections or issues a CANCEL command in the list window.
>> Type: Numeric

NAME
> contains the uppercase name of each selected catalog entry. If *prefix* is **Y**, then the name is in the form *libref.member*. Otherwise, it is in the form *member*. There is one NAME element for each selection made.
>> Type: Character

DESC
> contains the description of each selected catalog entry. There is one DESC element for each selection made. The value of DESC is in the case entered originally. If the SAS system option DETAILS is in effect, then DESC contains the table label.
>> Type: Character

TYPE
> contains the type of each selected library member. There is one TYPE element for each selection.
>> Type: Character

Because some engines support mixed-case filenames, DIRLIST now retains the cases of the returned selected items. This may cause your application to fail if your application contains code that assumes the returned selection is uppercased. For example,

```
if (dirlist(dsid, 'TESTNDX')='NDXVAR')
```

must be changed to

```
if (upcase(dirlist(dsid, 'TESTNDX'))='NDXVAR'
```

If the application cannot be modified, you may need to specify the VALIDVARNAME=V6 system option when you run the application to ensure that the selections returned from the DIRLIST function will be uppercased.

## Example

Display a selection list of SAS tables in the SAS libraries MYLIB1 and MYLIB2 except MYLIB1.ANSWERS, and enable users to select up to three table names. The selections are retrieved from the current environment list by using GETNITEMC.

```
listid=makelist();
rc=curlist(listid);
selections=dirlist('mylib1 mylib2','data',3,'Y',
                   ' ','^ mylib1.answers');
n=getnitemn(listid,'COUNT');
do i=1 to n;
```

```
      member=getnitemc(listid,'NAME',i);
      descript=getnitemc(listid,'DESC',i);
      memtype=getnitemc(listid,'TYPE',i);
      put member= descript= memtype=;
   end;
```

## See Also

"CATLIST" on page 269

"FILELIST" on page 401

"LIBLIST" on page 513

---

# DISPLAY

**Runs a catalog entry that was created with SAS/AF software**

**Category:** Modular Programming and Object Oriented

---

## Syntax

**CALL DISPLAY**(*entry<,parameters>*);

*return-value*=**DISPLAY**(*entry<,parameters>*);

*entry*
> is a display entry (FRAME, PROGRAM, SCL, MENU, HELP, or CBT) that was created using SAS/AF software. It is specified as

*entry-name*
> for a PROGRAM entry in the current catalog.

*entry.type*
> for an entry of the specified type in the current catalog.

*libref.catalog.entry*
> for a PROGRAM entry in the specified catalog.

*libref.catalog.entry.type*
> for an entry of a specified type in a specified catalog.
> Type: Character

*parameters*
> lists one or more parameters to pass to the called entry. You can pass parameters to FRAME, PROGRAM, and SCL entries. In order for the called entry to accept these parameters, it must contain a corresponding ENTRY statement.
>
> *Note:* These parameters are update parameters. See "Input, Output, and Update Parameters" on page 34 for more information. △
> Type: Numeric, Character

*return-value*
> contains the value that is returned by the called entry. The data type for *return-value* should match the data type for the called entry.
> Type: Numeric, Character, List, Object, Class, or Interface

**Details**     DISPLAY can run a FRAME, PROGRAM, SCL, MENU, HELP, or CBT entry and make it the active entry. When the called entry is exited, control returns to the calling program.

DISPLAY can pass parameters to a FRAME, PROGRAM, or SCL entry and receive a return value. Parameters can be numeric constants, character constants, variables, expressions, and array variables. Parameters are passed to the ENTRY statement in the called entry.

Using DISPLAY without any options in the associated ENTRY statement requires a strict correspondence between DISPLAY parameters and ENTRY statement arguments. The arguments and parameters must agree in number, data type, and relative position. If you pass an incorrect number of parameters or a parameter of the incorrect type, SCL halts the execution of the program. The argument-parameter correspondence is less restrictive when you use the options REST=, ARGLIST=, and OPTIONAL= in the ENTRY statement. See "ENTRY" on page 369 for examples of these options.

Names listed in *parameter* do not have to match the argument names in the ENTRY statement.

Parameters are passed in the following ways:

call-by-reference
>    enables the specified entry to change the values of the parameters. If you do not want the values of the parameters to be modified, use the NOCHANGE routine. Or, if you do not want to return the new values for specific parameters, use the INPUT option for that parameter in the ENTRY statement. Here is an example of call-by-reference:

```
array employee{50};
call display('b.frame',var1,name,num,employee{1});
```

call-by-value
>    prevents the specified entry from changing the values of the parameters. Call-by-value is used for all numeric constants, character constants, and expressions. Here is an example of call-by-value:

```
call display('b.frame',100,'hello',x+y);
```

*Note:*   Use CALL CBT to run CBT applications, because it provides more options used by CBT entries. In general, you may want to use CALL GOTO instead of CALL DISPLAY if you do not need control to return to the calling program. This may be helpful for applications that have memory constraints. △

## Examples

**Example 1: Passing Parameters**     Use DISPLAY in program X to pass parameters to program Y. Program Y then declares these arguments with an ENTRY statement. Variables I and S are call-by-reference parameters, and the constant 1 is a call-by-value parameter.

X.SCL contains the following program:

```
INIT:
   s = 'abcd';
   i = 2;
   call display('y.frame', i, 1, s);
      /* At this point, after the return from Y, */
      /* i=7 and s='abcde'                       */
   put i= s=;
```

```
return;
MAIN:
TERM:
return;
```

Y.SCL contains the following program:

```
entry j c:num str:char;
init:
    j = length(str) + c;
    j = j + 2;
    str = str || 'e';
    c = 2;
return;
```

The following correspondence occurs:

☐ The value of variable I passes to variable J.

☐ The literal value 1 passes to variable C.

☐ The value of variable S passes to variable STR.

After program Y runs, the values of variables J and STR are returned to the variables I and S, respectively. The variable C cannot return a value, however, because the corresponding parameter in DISPLAY is a constant.

**Example 2: Passing Array Parameters by Reference**　Use DISPLAY to pass array parameters by reference. In this example, the variables S and A are call-by-reference parameters, and the constant 4 is a call-by-value parameter.

X.SCL contains the following program:

```
array a{4} 8;
INIT:
    a{1} = 1; a{2} = 2; a{3} = 3; a{4} = 4;
    s = 0;
    call display('y.frame', s, a, 4);
      /*  At this point, after the return
                                    from Y, */
      /*  s=10, a{1}=2, a{2}=4, a{3}=6,
                             a{4}=8.   */
    put s= a=;
return;

MAIN:
TERM:
return;
```

Y.SCL contains the following program:

```
array arr{*} 8;
entry sum arr[*] len:num;
INIT:
    do i = 1 to len;
        sum = sum + arr{i};
        arr{i} = 2 * arr{i};
    end;
return;
```

The following correspondence occurs:

- □ The value of variable S passes to variable SUM.
- □ The array variable A is passed to the array variable ARR.
- □ The literal value 4 passes to variable LEN.

After program Y runs, the value of the variable SUM is returned to the variable S, and the values in the array ARR are returned to the corresponding values in the array A. The variable LEN cannot return a value, however, because the corresponding parameter in DISPLAY is a constant.

## See Also

"DIALOG" on page 345

"ENTRY" on page 369

"GOTO" on page 455

"INPUTC and INPUTN" on page 481

"NOCHANGE" on page 569

"RETURN" on page 615

# DISPLAYED

**Reports whether a control or field is currently visible**

**Category:**  Control or Field

## Syntax

*rc*=**DISPLAYED**(*wvar-name*);

**rc**

indicates whether the FRAME entry control or field is visible:

1                     visible

0                     not visible
   Type: Numeric

**wvar-name**

is the name of a control or field. This name cannot be an element of an array or an expression. An invalid *wvar-name* halts the program.
   Type: Character

**Details**    In SAS/AF applications, DISPLAYED reports whether a control is currently visible or whether it has the NONDISPLAY attribute. In FSEDIT, DISPLAYED tells you whether a field is visible on the current screen of a multiscreen application, regardless of whether the control has the NONDISPLAY attribute. This function is useful in multiscreen applications in which the application developer wants to be on a specific screen for a field.

If a control is not currently displayed, then your application can use the EXECCMD routine to issue scrolling commands to change the screen position or to issue scrolling commands that are specific to the procedure (for example, the =*n* command in the FSEDIT procedure).

The control or field cannot be an element of an array. To report this information for an array element, use FIELD instead.

FRAME entry controls can also use the _isDisplayed or _isHidden method.

## Example

Test whether the SALARY field is displayed on the current screen of an FSEDIT application. If not, issue an FSEDIT scrolling command to display the screen that contains the field:

```
if (displayed(salary)=0) then
   call execcmd('=salary');
```

## See Also

"ERROR" on page 375

"ERROROFF" on page 376

"ERRORON" on page 377

"FIELD" on page 394

"MODIFIED" on page 550

# DMWINDOW

**Sets the color and highlighting for lines in the OUTPUT and LOG windows**

**Category:**   Window

## Syntax

*rc*=**DMWINDOW**(*window-name,line-type,color,attribute*);

**rc**
contains the return code for the operation:

| | |
|---|---|
| 0 | successful |
| ≠0 | not successful |

Type: Numeric

**window-name**
is the window for which you want to assign colors and display attributes:

**'OUTPUT'**
the OUTPUT window

**'LOG'**
the LOG window
Type: Character

**line-type**
is the output area to which the colors and highlighting attributes are to be assigned:

'DATA'
> Data line

'ERROR'
> Error line

'NOTES'
> Notes line (LOG window only)

'SOURCE'
> Source line (LOG window only)

'WARNING'
> Warning line (LOG window only)

'BYLINE'
> Byline line (OUTPUT window only)

'HEADER'
> Header line (OUTPUT window only)

'TITLE'
> Title line (OUTPUT window only)
> Type: Character

*color*
> is a color name: BLACK, BLUE, BROWN, CYAN, GRAY, GREEN, MAGENTA, ORANGE, PINK, RED, WHITE, or YELLOW. SASCOLOR window elements can also be used for *color*.
> Type: Character

*attribute*
> is a display attribute: NONE, BLINKING, HIGHLIGHT, HIREV, REVERSE, or UNDERLINE. If you specify a SASCOLOR window element for *color*, then *attribute* is ignored, because the SASCOLOR window element contains a display attribute.
> Type: Character

**Details**   The device must support the specified color or highlighting attribute in order for SAS to enable the attribute.

## Example

Set the highlighting attribute of the title line in the OUTPUT window to blinking and set its color to yellow:

```
rc=dmwindow('output','title','yellow','blinking');
```

# DNUM

### Returns the number of members in a directory

**Category:** Directory

## Syntax

*nval*=**DNUM**(*directory-id*);

***nval***
> contains the number of members in the directory.
> Type: Numeric

***directory-id***
> is the identifier that was assigned when the directory was opened. If *directory-id* is invalid, the program halts.
> Type: Numeric

**Details** You can use DNUM to determine the largest member number that can be passed to DREAD.

## Example

Open the directory MYDIR, determine the number of members, and close the directory:

```
      /* Assign the fileref MYDIR to the        */
      /* filename stored in the variable DIRNAME */
      /* and open it.                            */
rc=filename('mydir',dirname);
dirid=dopen('mydir');
memcount=dnum(dirid);
rc=dclose(dirid);
```

## See Also

"DREAD" on page 360

# DO

**Designates a group of statements to be executed as a unit**

**Category:** Control Flow

**Comparisons:** SAS Statement with limitations in SCL

## Syntax

**DO** *do-clause*;

**END;**

**Details** The following forms of the *do-clause* are supported:

iterative DO
> executes a group of statements repetitively, based on the value of an index variable. However, the form DO *i=item-1, . . . , item-n* is not supported.

DO UNTIL
> executes a group of statements repetitively until a condition is true.

DO WHILE

executes a group of statements repetitively as long as a condition is true.

The form DO OVER is not supported.

To force the statements in a DO group to stop executing, you can use the SCL statements CONTINUE or LEAVE.

For details about the DO statement in the base SAS language, see *SAS Language Reference: Dictionary*.

## See Also

"CONTINUE" on page 300

"LEAVE" on page 504

# DOPEN

**Opens a directory**

**Category:** Directory

## Syntax

*directory-id=***DOPEN**(*fileref*);

### directory-id

contains the return code for the operation:

0                     indicates that the directory could not be opened.

>0                   is the identifier that was assigned to the opened directory.

Type: Numeric

### fileref

is the fileref that is assigned to the directory.

Type: Character

**Details**     DOPEN opens a directory and returns a directory identifier value (a number greater than 0), which can then be used to identify the open directory to other SCL functions. The directory to be opened must be identified by a fileref. You must associate a fileref with the directory before calling DOPEN.

You can assign filerefs by using either the FILENAME statement or the FILENAME function in SCL. Under some operating systems, you can also use system commands to assign filerefs.

*Operating Environment Information:*    The term *directory* used in the description of this function and related SCL functions refers to an aggregate grouping of files that are managed by the host operating system. Different host operating systems identify such groupings with different names, such as directory, subdirectory, MACLIB, or partitioned data set. See the SAS documentation for your operating environment for details. △

## Example

Assign the fileref MYDIR to a directory. Then open the directory, determine how many system-dependent directory information items are available, and close the directory. DIRNAME is an SCL variable with a value that represents the actual name of the directory in the form required by the host operating system.

```
rc=filename('mydir',dirname);
did=dopen('mydir');
infocnt=doptnum(did);
rc=dclose(did);
```

## See Also

"DCLOSE" on page 328

"FOPEN" on page 420

"MOPEN" on page 552

---

# DOPTNAME

**Returns the name of a directory attribute**

**Category:** Directory

---

## Syntax

*attribute*=**DOPTNAME**(*directory-id,attribute-number*);

**attribute**
> contains the directory option. If *nval* is out-of-range, the program halts and *attribute* contains the value that it held before the program halt.
> Type: Character

**directory-id**
> contains the identifier that was assigned when the directory was opened. If *directory-id* is invalid, the program halts.
> Type: Numeric

**attribute-number**
> is the sequence number of the option.
> Type: Numeric

**Details** DOPTNAME works only if the directory was previously opened by the DOPEN function. The names and nature of directory information items vary depending on the operating system. The number of attributes that are available for a directory also varies depending on the operating system.

## Example

Open the directory identified by the fileref MYDIR, retrieve all system-dependent directory information items, write them to the SAS log, and then close the directory:

```
/* Assign the fileref MYDIR to the  */
/* filename stored in the variable DIRNAME  */
```

```
      /* and open it.                     */
rc=filename('mydir',dirname);
dirid=dopen('mydir');
numitems=doptnum(dirid);
do j=1 to numitems;
   opt=doptname(dirid,j);
   put 'Directory information=' opt;
end;
rc=dclose(dirid);
```

## See Also

"DINFO" on page 346

"DOPTNUM" on page 359

# DOPTNUM

**Returns the number of information items that are available for a directory**

**Category:** Directory

## Syntax

*num-attributes*=**DOPTNUM**(*directory-id*);

**num-attributes**
 contains the number of available directory information items. If an error condition occurs, the program halts and *num-attributes* contains the value that it held before the program halt.
 Type: Numeric

**directory-id**
 contains the identifier that was assigned when the directory was opened. If *directory-id* is invalid, the program halts.
 Type: Numeric

**Details**   DOPTNUM works only if the directory was previously opened by the DOPEN function.

## Example

Retrieve the number of system-dependent directory information items that are available for the directory MYDIR and then close the directory:

```
   /* Assign the fileref MYDIR to the       */
   /* filename stored in the variable DIRNAME */
   /* and open it.                           */
rc=filename('mydir',dirname);
dirid=dopen('mydir');
infocnt=doptnum(dirid);
rc=dclose(dirid);
```

### See Also

"DINFO" on page 346

"DOPTNAME" on page 358

---

# DREAD

**Returns the name of a directory member**

**Category:**  Directory

---

## Syntax

*name*=**DREAD**(*directory-id,member-num*);

**name**
> contains either the name of the member, or a blank if an error occurs (for example, if
> *nval* is out-of-range).
>> Type: Character

**directory-id**
> contains the identifier that was assigned when the directory was opened. If
> *directory-id* is invalid, the program halts.
>> Type: Numeric

**member-num**
> is the sequence number of the member within the directory.
>> Type: Numeric

**Details**    Use DNUM to determine the highest possible member number that can be
passed to DREAD. DREAD works only if the directory was previously opened by the
DOPEN function.

## Example

Open the directory identified by the fileref MYDIR, retrieve the number of members
and place the number in the variable MEMCOUNT, retrieve the name of the last
member and place the name in the variable LSTNAME, and then close the directory:

```
    /* Assign the fileref MYDIR to the      */
    /* filename stored in the variable DIRNAME */
    /* and open it.                          */
rc=filename('mydir',dirname);
dirid=dopen('mydir')
lstname='';
memcount=dnum(dirid);
if (memcount>0) then
    lstname=dread(dirid,memcount);
rc=dclose(dirid);
```

## See Also

"DNUM" on page 355

"DOPEN" on page 357

# DROPNOTE

**Deletes a note marker from either a SAS table or an external file**

**Category:** SAS Table

## Syntax

*rc*=**DROPNOTE**(*table-id* | *file-id*,*note-id*);

**rc**
> contains the return code for the operation:

| | |
|---|---|
| 0 | successful |
| ≠0 | not successful |

> Type: Numeric

**table-id** or **file-id**
> contains the identifier that was assigned when the table or external file was opened. If this variable contains an invalid value, the program halts.
> Type: Numeric

**note-id**
> contains the identifier that was assigned by the NOTE or FNOTE function. If *note-id* contains an invalid value, the program halts.
> Type: Numeric

**Details**    DROPNOTE deletes a marker that was set by NOTE or FNOTE.

## Example

Open the SAS table MYDATA, fetch the first row, and set a note ID at the beginning of the table. Return to the first row by calling POINT, and then delete the note ID by calling DROPNOTE.

```
dsid=open('mydata','i');
rc=fetch(dsid);
noteid=note(dsid);
   /* more SCL statements */
rc=point(dsid,noteid);
rc=fetch(dsid);
rc=dropnote(dsid,noteid);
```

## See Also

"FNOTE" on page 417

"FPOINT" on page 425

"NOTE" on page 570

"POINT" on page 592

---

# DSID

**Searches for a SAS table name and returns the table identifier**

**Category:** SAS Table

## Syntax

*dsid*=**DSID**(< *table-name*< ,*mode*< ,*nth*< ,*gen-num*>>>>);

### *dsid*
contains either the identifier for the table, or

| | |
|---|---|
| 0 | if the table is not currently open, if the table is not open in the requested mode, or if no *nth* open occurrence exists. |
| <0 | if an error occurs. SYSMSG contains the error text. |

Type: Numeric

### *table-name*
names the SAS table to search for. The default is _LAST_, which is the last table that was created in the current SAS session. A one-level name is assumed to be a SAS table name in the default SAS data library, WORK. A two-level name is assumed to be *libref.table*.

Type: Character

### *mode*
specifies whether to limit the search to tables that are open in one of the modes listed below. If *mode* is not specified, DSID returns the *dsid* for the first occurrence of *table-name* that is open in any mode. Values for *mode* are

| | |
|---|---|
| 'I' | INPUT mode, allows random access if the engine supports it; otherwise, defaults to IN mode. |
| 'IN' | INPUT mode, reads sequentially and allows revisiting rows. |
| 'IS' | INPUT mode, reads sequentially but does not allow revisiting rows. |
| 'N' | NEW mode, creates a new SAS table. |
| 'U' | UPDATE mode, allows random access if the engine supports it; otherwise, defaults to UN mode. |
| 'UN' | UPDATE mode, reads sequentially and allows revisiting rows. |
| 'US' | UPDATE mode, reads sequentially but does not allow revisiting rows. |

'V'                    UTILITY mode, allows modification of column attributes and indexes that are associated with the SAS table.

For more information about open modes, see "OPEN" on page 576.
   Type: Character

***nth***
   specifies which occurrence of *table-name* opened in the specified *mode* to search for. By default, the search returns the first occurrence.
   Type: Numeric

***gen-num***
   is the generation number of the SAS table for which the DSID is returned.
   Type: Numeric

**Details**    DSID searches all SAS tables that are currently open. This function is useful for accessing table identifiers across entries.

## Examples

**Example 1: Working with Several Tables**    Open several SAS tables and find the first occurrence in various modes:

```
/* Open several SAS tables, varying the open mode */
dsid1 = open('sasuser.class', 'I');
dsid2 = open('sasuser.class', 'U');
dsid3 = open('sasuser.class', 'U');
dsid4 = open('sasuser.houses', 'U');
dsid5 = open('sasuser.class', 'I');
dsid6 = open('sasuser.houses', 'U');
dsid7 = open('sasuser.houses', 'I');
dsid8 = open('sasuser.class', 'U');

 /* Find the first occurrence open in any mode.*/
first = DSID( 'sasuser.houses' );
put first=;

 /* Find the first occurrence open in 'I' */
firstI = DSID( 'sasuser.houses', 'I' );
put firstI=;

 /* Find the second occurrence open in 'I' */
secondI = DSID( 'sasuser.class', 'I', 2 );
put second=;

 /* Return the fourth occurrence open in 'U' */
secondU = DSID( 'sasuser.class', 'U', 4 );
put secondU=;
```

This example produces the following output:

```
first=4
firstI=7
secondI=5
secondU=0
```

**Example 2: Returning the DSID of a Generation Data Set**    The following code returns the DSID of the SAS table WORK.ONE#003.

```
dsid=DSID('work.one','IN',1,3);
```

## See Also

"OPEN" on page 576

---

# DSNAME

### Returns the SAS table name that is associated with a table identifier

**Category:**   SAS Table

---

## Syntax

*table-name=***DSNAME**(< *table-id*>);

***table-name***
contains either the table name that is associated with the specified *table-id* value, or a blank if an invalid value is specified.
  Type: Character

***table-id***
contains the identifier that was assigned when the table was opened. If DSNAME is called from FSEDIT, FSBROWSE, or FSVIEW, this value is optional. If *table-id* is not specified in an FSEDIT or FSVIEW application, then DSNAME returns the name of the current table. If *table-id* is not specified in a SAS/AF application, then DSNAME returns a blank.
  Type: Character

## Examples

☐ Determine the name of the SAS table that is associated with the table identifier TABLEID and display this name on the message line:

```
_msg_='The open table is '||dsname(tableid)||'.';
```

☐ In an FSEDIT or FSVIEW SCL program, display on the command line the name of the table that is currently being edited:

```
_msg_='The table being edited is '||dsname()||'.';
```

## See Also

"OPEN" on page 576

---

# ENDBLOCK

### Closes the window that is created by the BLOCK function

**Category:**   Window

## Syntax

**CALL ENDBLOCK();**

## Example

Create a menu that contains four choices. The first row of blocks contains two blocks with the labels Outline and Index. The second row contains two blocks with the labels Compare Files and Calendar. No third row of blocks is displayed. The memory that was used in displaying the menu is freed when the ENDBLOCK routine is executed and the window is closed.

```
INIT:
   choice=block('Writers Toolbox','Main Menu',6,
         'Outline','Index','','',
         'Compare Files','Calendar','','',
         '','','','');
   ...more SCL statements...
return;
MAIN:
   ...more SCL statements...
return;

TERM:
   call endblock();
return;
```

## See Also

"BLOCK" on page 263

# ENDCATCH

**Ends a CATCH statement block**

**Category:** Control Flow

## Syntax

**ENDCATCH;**

## Details

The ENDCATCH statement marks the end of a CATCH block.

### See Also

"CATCH" on page 268

# ENDCLASS

**Ends a CLASS statement block**

**Category:**   Object Oriented

### Syntax

**ENDCLASS;**

**Details**     The ENDCLASS statement marks the end of a CLASS block in an SCL program. Use ENDCLASS to designate the end of a block of SAS statements that define a class.

### See Also

"CLASS" on page 277

# ENDLEGEND

**Closes the LEGEND window**

**Category:**   Legend

### Syntax

**CALL ENDLEGEND();**

**Details**     If the LEGEND window is not currently displayed, the routine has no effect.
For an example of using ENDLEGEND as well as other functions that manipulate the LEGEND window, see "LEGEND" on page 507.

### See Also

"POPLEGEND" on page 596

"PUSHLEGEND" on page 603

"PUTLEGEND" on page 606

# ENDMETHOD

**Ends a METHOD statement block**

**Category:**  Modular Programming and Object Oriented

## Syntax

**ENDMETHOD**;

**Details**    The ENDMETHOD statement marks the end of a method block in an SCL program. Use ENDMETHOD with a METHOD statement to indicate a block of statements that can be called by the METHOD routine. When the method block is executed, control returns to the calling program when ENDMETHOD is encountered.

## Example

End a METHOD block:

```
METHOD;
    ...SCL statements...
endmethod;
```

## See Also

"METHOD" on page 540

# ENDPACKAGE

**Ends a PACKAGE statement block**

**Category:**  Object Oriented

## Syntax

**ENDPACKAGE**;

## Details

The ENDPACKAGE statement marks the end of a PACKAGE block. Use ENDPACKAGE to designate the end of a block of ITEM statements that define a package.

## See Also

"PACKAGE" on page 585

# ENDSUBMIT

**Ends statements to be submitted to SAS software for execution**

**Category:**  Submit Block

## Syntax

**ENDSUBMIT**;

**Details**    The ENDSUBMIT statement marks the end of a SUBMIT block in an SCL program. Use ENDSUBMIT with SUBMIT to indicate a block of SAS statements to submit to SAS software for execution.

The ENDSUBMIT statement instructs SCL to stop collecting statements in the PREVIEW buffer and to submit the collected statements, based on the options that were specified for the SUBMIT statement.

## Example

Use SUBMIT to invoke the PRINT procedure and use ENDSUBMIT to mark the end of the SUBMIT block:

```
submit immediate;
data one;
   do x=1 to 10;
   output;
   end;
run;
proc print;
run;

endsubmit;
```

## See Also

"SUBMIT" on page 676

# ENDTABLE

**Stops the processing of the getrow section of a dynamic extended table**

**Category:**    Extended Table

## Syntax

**CALL ENDTABLE()**;

**Details**    The ENDTABLE routine stops the processing of the getrow section of a dynamic extended table. A *dynamic extended table* is a table whose maximum number of rows is determined when the program executes. Call the ENDTABLE routine from the getrow section of the SCL program when the end of the extended table has been reached.

Because you can define extended tables only in SAS/AF software, you cannot use ENDTABLE in FSEDIT or FSVIEW programs.

The ENDTABLE routine marks only the end of the table for this invocation of the GETROW label. If the user issues a scroll command, the GETROW label is driven again until ENDTABLE is called. This allows the size of the table to change dynamically.

## Example

In this example, data for the extended table comes from the open SAS table that is identified by the value in the variable DSID. The _CURROW_ variable, which identifies the current row of the extended table, specifies which row to fetch. When the value of _CURROW_ exceeds the number of rows in the table, FETCHOBS returns a nonzero value, which indicates that the end of the extended table has been reached. ENDTABLE is then called to stop the processing of the GETROW label.

```
GETROW:
   ...SCL statements...
   if (fetchobs(dsid,_currow_) =-1) then
      call endtable();
   else do;
      ...more SCL statements...
   end;
return;
```

## See Also

"CURTOP" on page 324

"SETROW" on page 664

"TOPROW" on page 689

---

# ENDUSECLASS

**Ends a USECLASS statement block**

**Category:** Object Oriented

---

## Syntax

**ENDUSECLASS;**

**Details** The ENDUSECLASS statement marks the end of a USECLASS block in an SCL program. Use ENDUSECLASS with USECLASS to designate a block of SAS statements that define methods for a class that was previously defined in the Class Editor.

## See Also

"USECLASS" on page 698

---

# ENTRY

**Receives parameters from the DISPLAY function or routine**

**Category:** Modular Programming and Object Oriented

## Syntax

ENTRY <*argument-list*> <RETURN=*data-type*> <OPTIONAL=*argument-list* |
  <ARGLIST=*arg-list-id* | REST=*rest-list-id*>>;

***argument-list***
> lists one or more sets of arguments, with each set specified as follows:
>> *var-list* <: INPUT | UPDATE | OUTPUT> :*data-type*
>
> *var-list*
>> lists one or more variables to which the parameter in the corresponding position in the DISPLAY routine or function is passed. For details, see "DISPLAY" on page 350.
>
> **INPUT | I**
>> specifies that, at run time, the variable contains the value that is copied from the corresponding parameter of the calling program. However, when the program finishes, the value is not copied back to the calling program. This is equivalent to using CALL NOCHANGE() in the calling program.
>
> **UPDATE | U**
>> specifies that, at run time, the variable contains the value that is copied from the corresponding parameter of the calling program. When the program finishes, the value is copied back to that parameter (unless CALL NOCHANGE is specified).
>
> **OUTPUT | O**
>> specifies that, when the program finishes, the value is copied back to the corresponding parameter in the calling program. An error condition results if the corresponding parameter in the calling program is a constant, because a constant cannot receive a value.
>
> *data-type*
>> specifies the data type of the variable. Any valid SCL data type may be specifid. A named data type (for example, CHAR or LIST) must be preceded by the **:** delimiter. The delimiter is optional for unnamed data types (for example, $).
>
> *arg-list-id*
>> contains the identifier for the SCL list that will contain all the arguments passed to the ENTRY statement. This includes all optional arguments.
>> Type: List
>
> *rest-list-id*
>> contains the identifier for the SCL list that will contain all arguments that are passed to the ENTRY statement but are not explicitly specified in *argument-list* for either ENTRY or OPTIONAL=.
>> Type: List

**Details**   The ENTRY statement receives parameters from the DISPLAY routine or function. It can also return a value if the ENTRY statement contains both the RETURN= option to declare the data type of the returned value and a RETURN statement that specifies either the variable containing the value or the literal value to be returned.

   To be compatible with the applications built in earlier releases of SAS software, the **:** delimiter is optional for variables that are assigned unnamed data types (for example,

\$), but it is required for variables that are assigned named data types. The following example shows a variety of data type declarations:

```
ENTRY:   char1   :$20
         char2   $20
         char3   :input :char(20)
         char4 char5:char
         num1    :8
         num2    8
         num3    :  num
         mylist :list
         myobj  :object
         mybutton :mylib.mycat.button.class return=char;
```

RETURN=*data-type* enables you to return a value to the calling program. An error condition is produced if *data-type* is not the same as the type of data to be returned to the calling program. Use a RETURN statement in the program to specify the value to return.

When there are no options in the ENTRY statement, there is a strict correspondence between DISPLAY parameters and ENTRY statement arguments. The arguments and parameters must agree in number, data type, and relative position. If you pass an incorrect number of parameters or a parameter of the incorrect type, SCL stops executing the program. The correspondence of arguments to parameters is less restrictive when you use the options REST=, ARGLIST=, and OPTIONAL= in the ENTRY statement.

OPTIONAL= enables you to specify a list of optional arguments that are used only if the calling program supplies the corresponding parameters in the DISPLAY parameter list. If the corresponding parameters in the DISPLAY routine are not supplied, then the optional arguments are initialized to missing values.

ARGLIST= and REST= enable you to pass a variable number of parameters to the ENTRY statement. You determine the types and order of the variable arguments. The lists identified by *arg-list-id* and *rest-list-id* are created automatically when the entry is called, and they are deleted automatically when the entry ends. When arrays are passed as parameters, the array is expanded into individual items, and these items are inserted into the *arg-list-id* and *rest-list-id* lists. ARGLIST= and REST= are mutually exclusive, so you can use only one or the other.

The called program can modify all call-by-reference arguments that it receives. However, it cannot modify any call-by-value arguments. For a description of call-by-reference and call-by-value, see "DISPLAY" on page 350 .

By default, values for call-by-reference arguments are returned to the calling program. If you want a called program to receive values but not to return values to its calling program, use the NOCHANGE routine. Or, you can use the INPUT, OUTPUT, or UPDATE option for each variable to specify how its value is passed and returned.

An SCL program with ENTRY statement arguments cannot be executed by itself due to the uninitialized arguments. To test a program that receives parameters via the ENTRY statement, run it with the SCL debugger. The debugger enables you to initialize all the ENTRY arguments before program execution starts.

## Examples

### Example 1: Returning a Value from the ENTRY Statement
B.SCL contains the following ENTRY statement, which uses several numeric arguments:

```
entry x  y z u v :i :num return=num;
INIT:
   total=x+y+z+u+v;
```

```
        return(total);
```

A.SCL contains

```
total=display('b.scl',1,2,3,4,5);
put total=;
```

The output of A.SCL is

```
total=15
```

### Example 2: Using ENTRY with OPTIONAL=    B.SCL contains the following ENTRY
statement, which defines multiple character variables:

```
entry x   :char(10)
      y z :num
      optional=u v w :num ;
INIT:
   put x= y= z= u= v= w=;
return;
```

Suppose A.SCL contains

```
call display('b.program','one',2,3,4,5);
```

The output would be

```
X='one' Y=2 Z=3 U=4 V=5 W=.
```

### Example 3: Using ENTRY with ARGLIST=    B.SCL contains the following ENTRY
statement, declaring both numeric, character, and list variables:

```
entry x   :char(10)
      y z :num
      optional=u v    :num
      arglist=mylist;

 INIT:
   put x= y = z= u= v=;
   call putlist(mylist);
return;
```

Suppose A.SCL contains

```
call display('b.scl','one',2,3,4,5);
```

The output would be

```
x='one'
y=2
z=3
u=4
v=5('one' 2 3 4 5) [list-id]
```

### Example 4: Using ENTRY with ARGLIST=    Suppose B.SCL contains

```
entry arglist=mylist;
 INIT:
    call putlist(mylist);
 return;
```

Suppose A.SCL contains

```
call display('b.scl','one',2,3,4,5);
```

The output would be

```
('one' 2 3 4 5) [list-id]
```

### Example 5: Using ENTRY with REST=    B.SCL contains the following ENTRY statement, which declares numeric variables:

```
entry x y :num
      rest=mylist;
INIT:
   put x= y=;
   call putlist(mylist);
 return;
```

Suppose A.SCL contains

```
call display('b.scl',1,2,3,4,5);
```

The output would be

```
x=1
y=2
(3 4 5) [list-id]
```

### Example 6: Using ENTRY with OPTIONAL= and REST=    B.SCL contains the following ENTRY statement, which declares both numeric and character variables along with parameter Z, which is optional:

```
entry x y :num optional=z :num rest=mylist;
INIT:
   put x= y= z=;
   call putlist(mylist);
 return;
```

Suppose A.SCL contains

```
call display('b.scl',1,2,3,4,5);
```

The output would be

```
x=1
y=2
z=3
(4 5) [list-id]
```

## See Also

"DISPLAY" on page 350

"NOCHANGE" on page 569

"METHOD" on page 540

"RETURN" on page 615

# ENVLIST

**Returns the list identifier of an SCL environment list**

**Category:** List

---

## Syntax

*list-id*=**ENVLIST**(<*envlist-type*>);

*list-id*
> contains the identifier of the SCL environment list.
>> Type: Numeric or List

*envlist-type*
> specifies which environment list to return:

> 'G'                   returns the identifier for the global environment list.

> 'L'                   returns the identifier for the local environment list. (This is the default.)
>> Type: Character

**Details**    When the SAS session starts, a global environment list that persists for the entire session is created. When a SAS/AF or FSEDIT application starts executing, a local environment list is created for that application. This local environment list persists for the duration of that application and is available to each program that runs in that application (for example, a program that is invoked by the DISPLAY routine).

Environment lists are special lists that can contain numeric items, character items, and sublist items. You use the item names to fetch the items. You can use the item names to fetch the items. Environment lists provide a means of creating global variables that can be shared among different SCL programs, much like macro variables. However, unlike macro variables, the names in an environment list do not have to be valid SAS names, and the values in an environment list can be other lists, if you want to associate a lot of data with a single name. For example, you can read the contents of a small SAS table into a list and place the contents in the global environment list so that other SCL programs do not have to read the table to fetch data.

You can also insert items that do not have names.

**The Local Environment List**    The local environment list, which is returned by ENVLIST('L'), contains data that is available only to the current application. Each executing application has its own unique local environment list. Both the contents of an application's environment list and the list itself are deleted when the application ends.

**The Global Environment List**    The global environment list, which is returned by ENVLIST('G'), contains data that all SAS applications can share during the same SAS session. The data remains in the global environment list until an SCL program explicitly removes it. Thus, after one application puts data into the global environment list, the application can exit, and another application can fetch the data.

You can insert only global lists into the global environment list. Global lists are created with MAKELIST or MAKENLIST (using the 'G' visibility value), or they can be new lists that have been copied from other global lists. A fatal error results if you try to insert a local list into the global list.

**Recommendations for Modifying Environment Lists**    It is strongly recommended that you insert only named items into environment lists and that you choose names that are unambiguous. If you add items that have simple names, other applications are more likely to unknowingly use the same name and to accidentally overwrite your data.

## See Also

"CURLIST" on page 320

"DELLIST" on page 336

"MAKELIST" on page 535

"MAKENLIST" on page 536

# ERROR

**Reports whether a FRAME entry control or field contains an invalid value**

**Category:** Control or Field

## Syntax

*rc*=**ERROR**(*wvar-name*);

**rc**

indicates whether the FRAME entry control or field in the window is in error:

1                              in error

0                              not in error
   Type: Numeric

**wvar-name**

is the name of a FRAME entry control or field in the window. This argument cannot be an expression.
   Type: Character

**Details**     Use ERRORON and ERROROFF to set and reset error conditions for the FRAME entry control or field.

The FRAME entry control or field cannot be an element of an array. To report this information for an array element, use FIELD instead.

FRAME entry controls can also use the _inError method.

## Examples

**Example 1: Using ERROR to Report Invalid Values**     Specify the CONTROL statement with the ERROR option in the INIT section of the program. The statements in the MAIN section are submitted only if the FRAME entry control OBJ1 is not in error.

```
INIT:
   control error;
return;
MAIN:
   if (error(obj1)=0) and obj1 NE _blank_ then
      submit continue;
         proc print data=&obj1;
         run;
      endsubmit;
   else
```

```
_msg_='Nothing submitted.  Please correct error.';
return;
```

**Example 2: Generating a Compile Error with ERROR**    The following sequence generates a compile error because the variable DS is not a window variable but contains the name of a window variable. ERROR expects to be passed the window variable itself.

```
ds='tablename';
if (error(ds)) then
    do;
    ...SCL statements to handle the error condition...
    end;
```

## See Also

"DISPLAYED" on page 353

"ERROROFF" on page 376

"ERRORON" on page 377

"FIELD" on page 394

"MODIFIED" on page 550

# ERROROFF

**Clears the error flag on one or more FRAME entry controls or fields**

**Category:**   Control or Field

## Syntax

**ERROROFF** *wvar-names* | _ALL_;

*wvar-names*
:   specifies one or more window variables for which to turn off the error flag, or **_ALL_** to turn off the error flag for all window variables.
    Type: Character

**Details**    An error flag can be set either by attributes that are assigned to fields or FRAME entry controls, or by the ERRORON statement.

Use the following statement to clear the error flag for all FRAME entry controls or all fields in the window:

```
erroroff _all_;
```

Statements in MAIN do not execute by default if a field is placed in error. Therefore, use a CONTROL statement that specifies the ERROR option to enable ERROROFF to remove the error flag.

The FRAME entry control or field cannot be an element of an array. To remove the error flag for an array element, use FIELD instead.

FRAME entry controls can also use the _erroroff method.

## Example

If a user enters an invalid value in the field TABLENAME, this SAS/AF program resets the value of TABLENAME to the default and turns off the error flag. The field TABLENAME is assigned type INPUT, so the procedure checks to see whether the SAS table exists when a user enters a value for TABLENAME.

```
INIT:
   control error;
return;
MAIN:
   if (error(tablename)= 1) then
      do;
         tablename='my.default';
         erroroff tablename;
      end;
return;
```

## See Also

"CONTROL" on page 302

"DISPLAYED" on page 353

"ERROR" on page 375

"ERRORON" on page 377

"FIELD" on page 394

# ERRORON

Sets the error flag for one or more FRAME entry controls or fields

**Category:** Control or Field

## Syntax

**ERRORON** *wcol-names* | _ALL_;

### *wcol-names*

specifies one or more window variables for which to turn on the error flag, or **_ALL_** to turn the error flag on for all window variables.
Type: Character

**Details**   To set an error flag for multiple fields, specify the field names following ERRORON, separated by blanks. To set an error flag for all fields in the window, use the following statement:

```
erroron _all_;
```

To clear the error flag for one or more fields, use ERROROFF (see the preceding entry).

In SAS program entries, ERRORON causes the SCL program to execute when a user presses any key the next time the window is displayed. Any fields for which the error flag is set are marked as modified regardless of whether or not the user has changed the value in the field.

In FSEDIT applications where a field is placed in error with ERRORON, a user can enter a new value and the error status is removed from the field and reset if the error condition is still met. In SAS/AF applications where a field is placed in error with ERRORON, entering a valid value is not enough to remove the error flag. You must use ERROROFF.

The FRAME entry control or field cannot be an element of an array. To set the error flag for an array element, use FIELD instead.

FRAME entry controls can also use the _erroron method.

## Example

Suppose your application manipulates a SAS table that contains information about employees and the number of hours they work each week. Because only weekly personnel are paid for overtime, the application should verify that all employees who have reported overtime hours are weekly employees.

```
if (weekly='N' and overtime>0) then
   do;
      erroron overtime;
      _msg_ =
      'Only weekly personnel can have overtime.';
      return;
   end;
```

## See Also

"CONTROL" on page 302

"DISPLAYED" on page 353

"ERROR" on page 375

"ERROROFF" on page 376

"FIELD" on page 394

# EVENT

**Reports whether a user has pressed a function key, ENTER key, or mouse button**

**Category:** Keys

## Syntax

*rc*=**EVENT**();

**rc**

contains the return code for the operation:

1                  A function key, ENTER key, or mouse button was pressed since the last event call.

SAS Component Language Dictionary △ _EVENT_ 379

| | |
|---|---|
| 0 | A function key, ENTER key, or mouse button was not pressed since the last event call. |

Type: Numeric

**Details**    A mouse click registers as an event only when it occurs in a FRAME entry control that responds to mouse events (for example, pushbuttons, check boxes, radio boxes, icons, and blocks).

EVENT is useful when you want your program to continue a task while it waits for user input. For example, your application can read data from an external source and display the results. When a user presses an appropriate key, you can stop processing and handle the request.

*Operating Environment Information:   OS/390 and CMS*

EVENT does not work under OS/390 or CMS, nor on ASCII DRIVER machines. On these systems you should use the attention handler exit that is provided in SCL. Refer to the discussion of the BREAK option for "CONTROL" on page 302. △

## Example

Display the date and time until a user presses either ENTER or one of the function keys. The variable DATETIME is a numeric window variable with the format DATETIME17.2. When a user presses ENTER or a function key, the program exits the loop and returns control to the application. In this example, when a user issues a RUN command, the loop resumes.

```
INIT:
   control allcmds;
return;
MAIN:
   if _status_ in ('C','E') then return;
   if (word(1,'U')='RUN') then
      do while(event()=0);
         datetime=datetime();
         refresh;
      end;
return;

TERM:
return;
```

## See Also

"CONTROL" on page 302

---

# _EVENT_

**Contains the type of event that occurred on a FRAME entry control**

**Category:** System Variable

## Details

_EVENT_ is a character system variable. It is provided automatically by the FRAME entry in SAS/AF, and the SCL compiler automatically creates a space for it in the SCL data vector.

In order to use _EVENT_, you must use the DECLARE or LENGTH statement to declare it as a character variable. If _EVENT_ is not declared, the following error is produced when the _select or _objectLabel method executes:

```
ERROR: Expecting string (P), received SCL number
       (symbol '_EVENT_').
```

_EVENT_ has a valid value only when a window control's _select or _objectLabel method is executing. _EVENT_ can have one of the following values:

| | |
|---|---|
| ' ' (blank) | Modification or selection |
| 'D' | Double click (An 'S' select event always precedes a 'D' double click event.) |
| 'C' | Command |
| 'P' | Pop-up menu request |
| 'S' | Selection or single click |

## Example

The following _select method prints the value of _EVENT_ when a window control is modified.

```
length _event_ $1;

SELECT: method;
   call super(_self_,_select);
   put _event_=;
endmethod;
```

## See Also

"_METHOD_" on page 548

"_SELF_" on page 643

"_STATUS_" on page 671

"_VALUE_" on page 704

# EXECCMD

**Executes one or more commands when control returns to the application**

**Category:**   Command

## Syntax

**CALL EXECCMD**(*cval*);

*cval*

specifies one or more commands to execute. To specify multiple commands, place a semicolon between each command.

Type: Character

**Details**   The commands are collected until another window is displayed or until SCL has finished executing and control is returned to the procedure. The commands are then submitted to the command-line processor before the next window is displayed or before the current window is redisplayed.

The commands collected with EXECCMD will not be executed if the next window displayed is a host window (such as CATLIST, DIRLIST, LIBLIST, FILELIST or MESSAGEBOX). The commands will be held in a buffer until a non-host selector window is displayed or the current window is redisplayed.

With CONTROL ALWAYS in FSEDIT applications or CONTROL ALLCMDS in other SAS/AF applications, statements in MAIN execute before a command that is issued with CALL EXECCMD. This behavior could introduce an infinite loop. Either execute the EXECCMD routine conditionally or specify the command using EXECCMDI with the NOEXEC parameter.

## Example

If the table is empty, add a new row:

```
call execcmd('end');
```

## See Also

"EXECCMDI" on page 381

# EXECCMDI

**Executes one or more global commands immediately before processing the next statement, or executes one non-global command when control returns to the application**

**Category:**   Command

## Syntax

**CALL EXECCMDI**(*command<,when>*);

*command*

specifies one or more commands to execute. To specify multiple commands, place a semicolon between each command.

Type: Character

*when*

specifies when the commands will be executed:

**'EXEC'**

executes commands in the command buffer immediately. (This is the default.)

**'NOEXEC'**

executes the specified non-global command when control returns to the application. Global commands are still executed immediately.

Type: Character

**Details**   By default, the EXECCMDI routine immediately executes the specified global command or list of global commands. After executing the command, the program statement that immediately follows the call to EXECCMDI is executed. EXECCMDI is valid only in SCL applications that display a window.

If you specify **EXEC**, which is the default for the *when* argument, then you should issue only windowing environment global commands and full-screen global commands through this routine. Any procedure-specific commands that are executed with EXECCMDI are ignored.

An error is displayed on the message line if the string that is passed to EXECCMDI is not a valid command, but the SCL program is not halted. Any statements that follow the call to the routine are still executed. If multiple commands are specified and one is invalid, none of the remaining commands are executed.

With the NOEXEC option, EXECCMDI allows only one procedure-specific or custom command to be executed. EXECCMDI saves the command in the command buffer and does not execute the command immediately. The program statement that immediately follows the CALL EXECCMDI routine is executed. The command in the command buffer is executed when control returns to the application.

If multiple EXECCMDI routines each have the NOEXEC option specified, then only the command that was issued by the last EXECCMDI routine is executed. The previous commands are cleared.

The NOEXEC option does not alter the way global commands are handled. Global commands are still executed immediately.

With CONTROL ALWAYS in FSEDIT applications or CONTROL ALLCMDS in SAS/AF applications, issuing EXECCMDI with the NOEXEC option from MAIN tells SAS not to execute statements in MAIN again before executing the specified procedure-specific or custom command. This is different from issuing an EXECCMD routine from MAIN, which would execute statements in MAIN again before executing the specified command.

*Note:*   We do not recommend combining EXECCMD and EXECCMDI routines, because the order of execution may be unexpected. △

## Examples

### Example 1: Using EXECCMDI to Ensure Correct Window Size
Ensure that the window is the correct size when the application runs:

```
INIT:
   call execcmdi('zoom off');
return;
```

### Example 2: Using EXECCMDI to Confirm a Delete Request
From an FSEDIT SCREEN entry, open CONFIRM.FRAME to confirm the delete request before the row is actually deleted:

```
FSEINIT:
   control always;
   length confirm $ 3;
return;

INIT:
return;

MAIN:
   if word(1, 'U') =: 'DEL' then
      do;
```

```
call display('confirm.frame', confirm);
if confirm =
  'YES' then call execcmdi('delete', 'noexec');
      end;
return;

TERM:
return;
```

CONFIRM.FRAME contains two pushbutton controls, YES and NO, and is controlled by the following program:

```
entry confirm $ 3;
YES:
   confirm = 'YES';
   _status_='H';
return;

NO:
   confirm = 'NO';
   _status_='H';
 return;
```

## See Also

"EXECCMD" on page 380

# EXIST

**Verifies the existence of a member of a SAS data library**

**Category:** SAS Table

## Syntax

*rc*=**EXIST**(*member-name*<,*member-type*<,*generation*>> );

**rc**
    contains the return code for the operation:

    1                The library member exists.

    0                Either *member-name* does not exist or *member-type* is invalid.
    Type: Numeric

**member-name**
    is the name of the SAS data library member.
    Type: Character

**member-type**
    is the type of SAS data library member:

    **'ACCESS'**
        indicates an access descriptor that was created using SAS/ACCESS software.

**'CATALOG'**
indicates a SAS catalog or catalog entry.

**'DATA'**
indicates a SAS data file. (This is the default.)

**'VIEW'**
indicates a SAS data view.
Type: Character

*generation*
is the generation number of the SAS table whose existence you are checking. If *member-type* is not DATA, *generation* is ignored.
Type: Numeric

**Details**    If *member-name* is not specified, EXIST verifies the existence of the member specified by the system variable _LAST_. If *member-type* contains an invalid value, EXIST returns the value 0.

## Examples

**Example 1: Verifying the Existence of a SAS Table**    Call the FSEDIT function only if the SAS table specified in the variable TABLENAME exists. If the table does not exist, display a message on the message line.

```
if (exist(tablename)) then call fsedit(tablename);
else _msg_='Table '||tablename||' does not exist.';
```

**Example 2: Verifying the Existence of a SAS Data View**    Verify the existence of the SAS table view TEST.MYVIEW:

```
rc=exist('test.myview','view');
```

**Example 3: Determining if a Data Set Generation Exists**    Determine if the third generation of the data set **work.one** exists:

```
rc=exist('work.one','data',3);
```

## See Also

"CEXIST" on page 276

"FEXIST" on page 392

"FILEEXIST" on page 400

# FAPPEND

Appends the current record to the end of an external file

Category:   External File

## Syntax

*sysrc*=**FAPPEND**(*file-id*< ,*cc*>);

*sysrc*
contains the return code for the operation:

0                      successful

≠0                     not successful
Type: Numeric

*file-id*
contains the identifier that was assigned when the file was opened. If *file-id* is invalid, the program halts.
Type: Numeric

*cc*
specifies a carriage-control character:

*blank*
indicates that the record starts a new line.

`'0'`
skips one blank line before this new line.

`'-'`
skips two blank lines before this new line.

`'1'`
specifies that the line starts a new page.

`'+'`
specifies that the line overstrikes a previous line.

`'P'`
specifies that the line is a terminal prompt.

`'='`
specifies that the line contains carriage-control information.

*all else*
specifies that the record starts a new line.
Type: Character

**Details**   FAPPEND adds the record currently contained in the File Date Buffer (FDB) to the end of an external file.

*Operating Environment Information:   OS/390*
Records cannot be appended to partitioned data sets. △

## Example

Use FAPPEND to append a record to a file:

```
/* Assign the fileref THEFILE to the physical */
/* filename that the user entered in the      */
/* field FNAME and open it in append mode.     */
rc=filename( 'thefile',fname);
fid=fopen('thefile','a');
if (fid>0) then
   do;
        /* Append a new record to the file. */
      rc=fput(fid,'Data for the new record');
```

```
            rc=fappend(fid);
            rc=fclose(fid);
        end;
    else
        do;
            ...other SCL statements...
        end;
rc=filename('thefile'','');
```

## See Also

"DOPEN" on page 357

"FGET" on page 393

"FOPEN" on page 420

"FPUT" on page 427

"FWRITE" on page 439

"MOPEN" on page 552

# FCLOSE

**Closes an external file, a directory, or a directory member**

**Category:**   External File

## Syntax

*sysrc=***FCLOSE***(file-id)*;

**sysrc**
   contains the return code for the operation:

   0                      successful

   ≠0                     not successful
      Type: Numeric

**file-id**
   contains the identifier that was assigned when the file was opened. A *file-id* value of
   **-999** closes all files opened with FOPEN. If *file-id* contains an invalid value, the
   program halts.
      Type: Numeric

## Example

Close a file after manipulating it:

```
/* Assign the fileref THEFILE to the physical */
/* filename that is stored in the variable FNAME    */
/* and open it in append mode.    */
rc=filename( 'thefile',fname);
```

```
fileid=fopen('thefile');
if (fileid>0) then
   do;
      rc=fread(fileid);
      rc=fclose(fileid);
   end;
else
   do;
      _msg_=sysmsg();
      return;
   end;
rc=filename('thefile','');
```

## See Also

"DCLOSE" on page 328

"DOPEN" on page 357

"FOPEN" on page 420

"MOPEN" on page 552

# FCOL

**Returns the current column position from the File Data Buffer (FDB)**

**Category:**   External File

## Syntax

*col-num*=**FCOL**(*file-id*);

**col-num**
   contains the current column position.
      Type: Numeric

**file-id**
   contains the identifier that was assigned when the file was opened. If *file-id* contains
   an invalid value, the program halts.
      Type: Numeric

**Details**    Use FCOL in conjunction with FPOS to move the pointer in the FDB and
manipulate the data.

## Example

Use FCOL and FPOS to set the pointer in the FDB:

```
/* Assign the fileref THEFILE to the physical  */
/* filename that the user entered in the field */
/* FNAME.                                       */
rc=filename( 'thefile',fname);
```

```
      fileid=fopen('thefile','o');
      if (fileid>0) then do;
            /* Put data into the FDB, get the     */
            /* current column, move the pointer    */
            /* by 1 and add more data to the FDB.  */
         record='This is data for the record';
         rc=fread(fileid);
         rc=fput(fileid,record);
         pos=fcol(fileid);
         rc=fpos(fileid,pos+1);
         rc=fput(fileid,'and more data');
         rc=fwrite(fileid);
         rc=fclose(fileid);
      end;
      rc=filename('thefile','');
```

The record written to the external file is

```
This is data for the record and more data
```

## See Also

"FPOS" on page 426

"FPUT" on page 427

"FWRITE" on page 439

# FDELETE

**Deletes an external file**

**Category:**   External File

## Syntax

*sysrc*=**FDELETE**(*fileref*);

**sysrc**
   contains the return code for the operation:

   0                         successful

   ≠0                        not successful
      Type: Numeric

**fileref**
   is the fileref that was assigned to the external file to be deleted. The fileref cannot be associated with a list of concatenated filenames or directories. If the fileref is associated with a directory, a PDS or a PDSE, then the directory, PDS, or PDSE must be empty. You must have permission to be able to delete the file or directory.
      Type: Character

**Details**    You can use either the FILENAME statement or the FILENAME function in SCL to assign a fileref. Under some operating environments, you can also use system commands to assign filerefs.

## Example

Generate a fileref for an external file and assign it to the variable FREF. Then call FDELETE to delete the file and call the FILENAME function again to deassign the fileref.

```
length fref $ 8;
fref = _blank_;
   /* Assign a fileref generated by the system */
   /* to the physical filename that is stored  */
   /* in the variable FNAME.                    */
 rc=filename(fref,fname);
if (rc=0) and (fexist(fref)) then
   rc=fdelete(fref);
rc=filename(fref,'');
```

## See Also

"FEXIST" on page 392

"FILENAME" on page 403

# FETCH

**Reads the next nondeleted row from a SAS table into the Table Data Vector (TDV)**

**Category:** SAS Table

## Syntax

*sysrc*=**FETCH**(*table-id*<,'NOSET'>);

**sysrc**
  contains the return code for the operation:

| | |
|---|---|
| 0 | successful |
| >0 | not successful |
| <0 | the operation was completed, but a warning or a note was generated. If the row is locked, it is still fetched (read in) but a *sysrc* of **_SWNOUPD** is returned. |
| −1 | the end of the table was reached |

  Type: Numeric

**table-id**
  is the identifier that was assigned when the table was opened. If *table-id* is invalid, the program halts.
  Type: Numeric

**'NOSET'**
  prevents the automatic passing of SAS table column values to SCL variables even if the SET routine has been called.
  Type: Numeric

**Details**   FETCH skips rows that have been marked for deletion. When a WHERE clause is active, the function reads the next row that meets the WHERE condition.

If the SET routine has previously been called, the values for any table columns that are also window variables or SCL variables for the application are automatically passed from the TDV to the SCL Data Vector (SDV). To temporarily override this behavior so that fetched values are not automatically copied to the SDV, use the NOSET option.

## Example

Fetch the next row from the SAS table MYDATA. If the end of the table is reached or if an error occurs, SYSMSG retrieves the appropriate message and displays it on the message line.

```
INIT:
   tableid=open('mydata','i');
return;

MAIN:
   rc=fetch(tableid);
   if rc then _msg_=sysmsg();
   else
      do;
         ...more SCL statements...
      end;
return;

TERM:
   rc=close(tableid);
return;
```

## See Also

"APPEND" on page 251

"FETCHOBS" on page 390

"GETVARC and GETVARN" on page 450

"LOCATEC and LOCATEN" on page 527

"PUTVARC and PUTVARN" on page 609

"SET" on page 646

"UPDATE" on page 697

# FETCHOBS

**Reads a specified row from a SAS table into the Table Data Vector (TDV)**

**Category:**   SAS Table

## Syntax

*sysrc=***FETCHOBS**(*table-id,row-number*<*,options*>);

*sysrc*
> contains the return code for the operation:

| | |
|---|---|
| 0 | successful |
| >0 | not successful |
| <0 | the operation was completed, but a warning or a note was generated. If the row is locked, it is still fetched (read in) but a *sysrc* of **_SWNOUPD** is returned. |
| −1 | the end of the table was reached |

> Type: Numeric

*table-id*
> is the identifier that was assigned when the table was opened. If *table-id* is invalid, the program halts.
> Type: Numeric

*row-number*
> is the number of the row to read.
> Type: Numeric

*options*
> is one or both of the following options, separated by blanks:

> **'ABS'**
>> specifies that the value of *row-number* is absolute; that is, deleted rows are counted.

> **'NOSET'**
>> prevents the automatic passing of SAS table column values to SCL variables even if the SET routine has been called.
>> Type: Character

**Details**    If SET has previously been called, the values for any table columns that are also window variables or SCL variables for the application are automatically passed from the TDV to the SCL Data Vector (SDV) with FETCHOBS. You can use NOSET in the FETCHOBS function to temporarily override this behavior so that fetched values are not automatically copied to the SDV. FETCHOBS treats the row value as a relative row number unless the ABS option is specified.

The row value may or may not coincide with the physical row number on disk. For example, the function skips rows that have been marked for deletion. When a WHERE clause is active, the function counts only rows that meet the WHERE condition. If *row-number* is less than 0, the function returns an error condition. If *row-number* is greater than the number of rows in the SAS table, an 'End of file' warning is returned.

## Example

Fetch the tenth row from the SAS table MYDATA. If the end of the table is reached, a message to that effect is displayed on the message line. If an error occurs, the SYSMSG function retrieves the error message and displays it on the message line.

```
rc=fetchobs(mydata,10);
if (rc=-1) then
  _msg_='End of table has been reached.';
if (rc ne 0) then _msg_=sysmsg();
```

## See Also

"APPEND" on page 251

"FETCH" on page 389

"GETVARC and GETVARN" on page 450

"LOCATEC and LOCATEN" on page 527

"PUTVARC and PUTVARN" on page 609

"SET" on page 646

"UPDATE" on page 697

---

# FEXIST

**Verifies the existence of the external file that is associated with the specified fileref**

**Category:**  External File

---

## Syntax

*rc*=**FEXIST**(*fileref*);

**rc**

contains the return code for the operation:

| | |
|---|---|
| 1 | successful |
| 0 | not successful, or there was no logical assignment for the fileref |

Type: Numeric

**fileref**

is the fileref that was assigned to the external file.

Type: Character

**Details**    You can use either the FILENAME statement or the FILENAME function in SCL to assign filerefs. Under some operating systems, you can also use system commands to assign filerefs. Use FILEEXIST to verify the existence of a file based on its physical name.

## Example

Verify the existence of an external file for a fileref that the user enters in the field for the window variable FREF. A message informs the user whether the file exists.

```
 if (fexist(fref)) then
_msg_=
   'The file does exist.';
else
   _msg_=sysmsg();
```

## See Also

"EXIST" on page 383

"FILEEXIST" on page 400

"FILENAME" on page 403

"FILEREF" on page 406

"PATHNAME" on page 586

# FGET

### Copies data from the File Data Buffer (FDB)

**Category:** External File

## Syntax

*sysrc=***FGET**(*file-id,cval< ,length>*);

**rc**
> contains the return code for the operation:
>
> 0                 successful
>
> −1             the end of the FDB was reached, or no more tokens were available.
>     Type: Numeric

**file-id**
> is the identifier that was assigned when the file was opened. If *file-id* is invalid, the program halts.
>     Type: Numeric

**cval**
> is a character variable to hold the data.
>
>     *Note:* This parameter is an update parameter. See "Input, Output, and Update Parameters" on page 34 for more information. △
>     Type: Character

**length**
> specifies how many characters to retrieve from the FDB.
>     Type: Numeric

**Details**     FGET copies data from the FDB into a character variable. If *length* is specified, then only the specified number of characters is retrieved (or the number of characters remaining in the buffer, if that number is less). If *length* is omitted, then all characters in the FDB from the current column position to the next delimiter are returned. The default delimiter is a blank. The delimiter is not retrieved. (See "FSEP" on page 435 for more information about delimiters.)

After FGET is executed, the column pointer is automatically moved to the next "read" position in the FDB.

## Example

Read the first record in the file specified by the user and copy the first token into the variable THESTRING.

```
     /* Assign the fileref THEFILE to the physical */
     /* filename that is stored in the       */
     /* variable FNAME and open it in append mode.  */
rc=filename( 'thefile',fname);
fileid=fopen('thefile');
if (fileid>0) then
    do;
            /* Read the first record, retrieve the  */
            /* first token of the record and store  */
            /* it in the variable THESTRING.        */
        rc=fread(fileid);
        rc=fget(fileid,thestring);
        put thestring;
        rc=fclose(fileid);
    end;
rc=filename('thefile','');
```

## See Also

"FPOS" on page 426

"FREAD" on page 430

"FSEP" on page 435

---

# FIELD

**Performs an action on or reports the state of FRAME entry widgets or fields**

**Category:**  Widget or Field

## Syntax

*rc*=**FIELD**(*action*<,*wvar-name-1*<,*wvar-name-2*
   <,*wvar-name-3*>>>);

**rc**
   contains the return code for the operation. The return value is dependent on the
   action.
      Type: Numeric

**action**
   is an action from the list of actions described in "Values for the *action* Argument" on
   page 395.
      Type: Character

**wvar-name-1, wvar-name-2, wvar-name-3**
   are character columns or expressions whose values are the names of one or more
   FRAME entry widgets or fields in a window, separated by spaces. At least one name
   is required for all actions except ALARM, BLOCKCUROFF, BLOCKCURON,
   CURSCREEN, HOME, NSCREEN, and SMOOTHSCRL.
      Type: Character

# Values for the *action* Argument

The following list contains the values that you can specify for *action*. The list also includes the corresponding methods that can be used in FRAME entries, which are documented with FRAME entry classes in the online Help for SAS/AF software.

**'ALARM'**

sounds a bell. This action has a corresponding SCL statement.

**'BLOCKCUROFF'**

turns the block cursor off so that fields or text entry widgets are not highlighted when a user tabs or moves the cursor to them.

**'BLOCKCURON'**

turns the block cursor on, which causes input fields to be highlighted when the cursor is on the text entry widget or field.

**'COLOR *color* <*attribute*>'**

changes the color and display attribute of a field, text entry widget, or text label widget in the window. Colors are: BLACK, BLUE, BROWN, CYAN, GRAY, GREEN, MAGENTA, ORANGE, PINK, RED, WHITE, and YELLOW. Attributes are: NONE, BLINKING, HIGHLIGHT, HIREV, REVERSE, and UNDERLINE. SASCOLOR window elements can be used for *color*. If you specify a SASCOLOR window element for *color*, then *attribute* is not allowed, because the SASCOLOR window element already contains a display attribute.

**'COLUMN'**

returns the column where a FRAME entry widget or field is located. This option is valid only in SAS/AF software. FRAME entry widgets can also use the _column method.

**'CUROBS'**

returns the current row number for FSEDIT and FSVIEW for the specified field.

**'CURSOR'**

positions the cursor in the FRAME entry widget or field. If more than one field or widget is specified, the cursor is positioned in the last one specified. This action has a corresponding SCL statement. FRAME entry widgets can also use the _cursor method.

**'CURSCREEN'**

returns the current screen number. For SAS/AF software, this is valid only for multipage PROGRAM entries. For FSEDIT, it reports which screen of a multiscreen application is displayed.

**'DISPLAYED'**

returns the total number of FRAME entry widgets or fields that are visible, or 0 if none of them are currently displayed. For example, if you pass three field names and two are visible, then *rc* is 2. This action has a corresponding SCL function. FRAME entry widgets can also use the _isDisplayed and _isHidden methods.

**'ERROR'**

returns the total number of FRAME entry widgets or fields that are in error, or 0 if none of the specified fields are in error. For example, if you pass two field names and one is in error, then *rc* is 1. This action has a corresponding SCL function. FRAME entry widgets can also use the _inError method.

**'ERROROFF'**

removes the error status from one or more FRAME entry widgets or fields. This action has a corresponding SCL statement. FRAME entry widgets can also use the _erroroff method.

**'ERRORON'**

turns on the error status for one or more FRAME entry widgets or fields. Turning on the error status prevents users from ending the SAS/AF application or from leaving the current row in FSEDIT. The error status also highlights the field or widget, using the error color and display attributes that were assigned in the Attribute (or ATTR) window. This action has a corresponding SCL statement. FRAME entry widgets can also use the _erroron method.

**'GETOBS'**

reports whether a formula is being executed in an FSVIEW application because a column is being read. If *rc* is 1, then the formula is being executed because a column is being read. If *rc* is 0, then the formula is being executed because a column has been modified. If you are on a new row, *rc* is always 1. This is the opposite of PUTOBS.

**'HOME'**

moves the cursor to the command line. This entry has a corresponding SCL statement.

**'ICON *icon-number*'**

assigns a number for an icon that represents the field if it is a pushbutton in PROGRAM entries. This option is valid only in SAS/AF software. FRAME entry widgets can use the _setIcon method.

**'MODIFIED'**

returns the total number of FRAME entry widgets or fields that were modified, or 0 if none of them were modified. For example, if you pass two field names and both were modified, then *rc* is 2. This action has a corresponding SCL function. FRAME entry widgets can also use the _isModified method.

**'NSCREEN'**

returns the number of screens (for FSEDIT applications) or the number of panes (for SAS/AF applications).

**'PROTECT'**

protects one or more FRAME entry widgets or fields. This prevents a user from modifying the FRAME entry widget or field. This action has a corresponding SCL statement. FRAME entry widgets can also use the _protect method.

**'PROTECTED'**

reports whether a FRAME entry widget or field is protected. FRAME entry widgets can also use the _isProtected method.

**'PUTOBS'**

reports whether a formula is being executed in an FSVIEW application because a column has been modified. If *rc* is 1, then the formula is being executed because a column has been modified. If *rc* is 0, then the formula is being executed to read a column. If you are on a new row, *rc* is always 0. This is the opposite of GETOBS.

**'ROW'**

returns the row where a FRAME entry widget or field is positioned. This option is valid only in SAS/AF software. FRAME entry widgets can also use the _row method.

**'SMOOTHSCRL'**

sets smooth scrolling to **ON**, **OFF**, or **TOGGLE**. Allows smooth scrolling when users drag the thumb in the scroll bar. When smooth scrolling is on, the getrow sections of AF extended tables are called while the thumb is dragged. In the FSVIEW procedure, the display is refreshed while the thumb is dragged. When smooth scrolling is turned off, the redisplay is deferred until the thumb is released. By default, smooth scrolling is off for SAS/AF and on for FSVIEW.

If you do not specify ON or OFF, SMOOTHSCRL is toggled from OFF to ON or from ON to OFF.

**'UNPROTECT'**

unprotects one or more fields or FRAME entry widgets. This enables a user to modify the field or FRAME entry widget. This action has a corresponding SCL statement. FRAME entry widgets can also use the _unprotect method.

**Details** The FIELD function combines the functionality of the field statements (CURSOR, DISPLAYED, ERROROFF, ERRORON, PROTECT, and so on). It also provides additional widget over the fields.

At least one window column name is required for all actions except ALARM, BLOCKCUROFF, BLOCKCURON, CURSCREEN, HOME, NSCREEN, and SMOOTHSCRL.

The smooth scrolling action enables you to turn on, turn off, or toggle the scrolling mode.

## Examples

### Example 1: Using FIELD to Allow Smooth Scrolling     Allow smooth scrolling:

```
rc=field ('smoothscrl', 'on');
```

### Example 2: Using FIELD to Check for Error Status of Fields     Create the array
FLDNAMES and pass its elements to the FIELD function to check the error status of the fields. If necessary, move the cursor to the field that contains invalid data.

```
array fldnames{*} $ 8 ('tablename','colname','list',
                       'x','y');
do i=1 to dim(fldnames);
   if (field('error',fldnames{i})) then
      do;
          _msg_='Field name '||
          fldnames{i}||' is bad.';
          rc=field('cursor',fldnames{i});
          return;
      end;
end;
```

### Example 3: Using FIELD to Turn on an Error Flag     Turn on the error flag for FIELD1
and FIELD2:

```
rc=field('erroron','field1','field2');
```

### Example 4: Using FIELD to Change a Field's Color     Change the color of FIELD1:

```
rc=field('color blue','FIELD1');
```

### Example 5: Using FIELD to Change Color and Display Attributes for a Field     Change
FIELD1's color and display attributes:

```
rc=field('color red reverse','field1');
```

### Example 6: Using FIELD to Specify a SASCOLOR Window Element     Specify FIELD1's
color, using the name of a SASCOLOR window element:

```
rc=field('color foreground','field1');
```

## See Also

"ALARM" on page 250

"CURSOR" on page 323

"DISPLAYED" on page 353

"ERROR" on page 375

"ERROROFF" on page 376

"ERRORON" on page 377

"HOME" on page 459

"MODIFIED" on page 550

"PROTECT" on page 602

"UNPROTECT" on page 695

# FILEDIALOG

**Displays a selection window that lists external files**

**Category:**   External File

## Syntax

*rc*=**FILEDIALOG**(*dialog-type,filename<,default-file <,default-dir<,filter-1<. . .
,filter-11<,description-1 . . .<description-11>>>>>>*);

**rc**
  contains the return code for the operation:

  | | |
  |---|---|
  | −1 | A user cancelled without selecting a file. |
  | 0 | Either *dialog-type* is **OPEN** and the file exists, or *dialog-type* is **SAVEAS** and the file does not exist. |
  | 1 | *Dialog-type* is **SAVEAS**, the file exists, and the user wants to replace the file. |
  | 2 | *Dialog-type* is **SAVEAS**, the file exists, and a user wants to append to the file. |

  Type: Numeric

**dialog-type**
  specifies the type of dialog window to open. An invalid type specification produces an error and halts the program. Types are

  **'AGGREGATE'**
    lists aggregate storage areas — for example, directories, partitioned data sets, or MACLIBs.

  **'LIBRARY'**
    lists SAS data libraries.

**'OPEN'**

lists files that a user can open.

**'SAVEAS'**

lists files that a user can write to.
Type: Character

*filename*

is the fully qualified name of the selected file, including the directory.

*Note:*  This parameter is an update parameter. See "Input, Output, and Update Parameters" on page 34 for more information. △
Type: Character

*default-file*

is the name of the file (without directory information) to display as selected when the dialog window opens. If you specify a null string (' '), the file that was selected last is the default file.
Type: Character

*default-dir*

is the directory whose files are listed when the dialog window opens. If you specify a null string (' '), the directory that was selected last is the default directory.
Type: Character

*filter1 ... filter11*

are up to 11 name specifications to narrow the list of files to display — for example, *.html. The number of filter arguments is host specific. If you do not supply a filter, the list contains all files in *default-dir*.
Type: Character

*description1 ... description11*

are up to 11 descriptions, one for each *filter*, to make the dialog window more informative for application users. If no descriptions are supplied, a default description is displayed for each specified filter. If you provide a description for any filter, then you must supply a description for each filter that you specify.
Type: Character

**Details**     Depending on the values of *default-dir* and *filter*, *default-file* may not be in the list of files displayed. Therefore, *default-file* will not be selected.

An error condition is produced if you supply a description for at least one filter but fail to supply a description for each specified filter.

*Operating Environment Information:*  The formats of the files and filter parameters are all host specific. The UNIX and MicroSoft Windows platforms use all of the passed filters. The Macintosh platform ignores the filter argument. All other platforms use only the first filter that is passed. △

## Examples

□ Enable a user to select a file to open, and see whether the user cancelled the window:

```
rc=filedialog('saveas',selfile,'autoexec.sas',
              '/sas','*.sas');
   /* Process the selected file  */
select(rc);
   when(0) put 'New file selected';
   when(1) put 'REPLACE an existing file';
```

```
              when(2) put 'APPEND to an existing file';
              when(-1) put 'User pressed cancel';
              otherwise put 'ERROR occurred';
          end;
```

☐ Display a list of filenames that have .SAS, .HTML, and .GIF extensions, and
provide descriptions for these filters:

```
    rc=filedialog('open',selfile,'','',
       '*.sas','*.html','*.gif','','','','','','','','',
       'SAS Files','Web Pages','Images');
```

### See Also

"FILELIST" on page 401

---

# FILEEXIST

**Verifies the existence of an external file, a directory, or a SAS data library by its physical name**

**Category:** External File

---

### Syntax

*sysrc=***FILEEXIST**(*filename*);

**rc**
  contains the return code for the operation:

  1            The external file exists.

  0            The external file does not exist.
       Type: Numeric

**filename**
  is the name that identifies the external file to the host operating system. The
  *filename* specification varies according to the operating system.
       Type: Character

**Details**    FILEEXIST verifies the existence of an external file, a directory, or a SAS
data library.
  Although your system utilities may recognize partial physical filenames, you must
always use fully qualified physical filenames with FILEEXIST.

### Example

Verify the existence of an external file whose filename the user enters in the field for
the window variable FNAME. Display a message on the message line to tell the user
whether the file exists.

```
    if (fileexist(fname)) then
       _msg_='The external file '||fname||' exists.';
    else
       _msg_=sysmsg();
```

### See Also

"EXIST" on page 383

"FEXIST" on page 392

"FILENAME" on page 403

"FILEREF" on page 406

"PATHNAME" on page 586

# FILELIST

**Displays a host selection window that lists the currently assigned filerefs, and returns user selections**

**Category:**  Selection List

## Syntax

*selections=***FILELIST**(< *sel-excl*< *,message*< *,autoclose* <*,num-sel*>>>>);

### selections

contains the user's selections, or a blank if no fileref was selected. Multiple selections are separated by blanks. By default, *selections* is 200 bytes long. To accomodate values longer than 200 bytes, explicitly declare *selections* with a longer length.
Type: Character

### sel-excl

specifies which filerefs to include in the selection window. Specify as

- □ one or more filerefs that have been assigned for the current SAS session. Use spaces to separate multiple filerefs.

- □ an asterisk (' * ') or a null string (' ') to display all the filerefs that are defined for the current SAS session.

- □ a NOT sign (¬ or ^) followed by one or more filerefs, to display all filerefs except those listed after the NOT sign. For example, '^ MYFILE1 MYFILE2' displays all defined filerefs except MYFILE1 and MYFILE2.
Type: Character

### message

is the text for a message to display above the selection list. The default message tells users to make up to the number of selections specified in *num-sel*.
Type: Character

### autoclose

is an obsolete argument but is retained for compatibility with earlier releases. If you want to specify a value for *num-sel*, then specify ' ' as a placeholder for this argument.
Type: Character

### num-sel

is the maximum number of items a user can select from the list. To display the list for information purposes only (no selections allowed), specify 0. To specify an unlimited number of selections, use a value such as 9999 that is larger than the number of available selections. A user cannot make a number of selections that exceeds the number of items in the list.

   Type: Numeric

**Details**    The selection list displays both filerefs and the corresponding physical names of the external files to which the filerefs are assigned, but only the selected fileref is returned.

   If you omit all the arguments for FILELIST (for example, `selections=filelist();`), the selection list window contains all filerefs that have been assigned in the current SAS session.

   You can provide default values that will be initially selected when the fileref selection list is displayed. To do this, assign the values to the *selections* variable before calling FILELIST.

   If a user closes the selection list window without making a selection, FILELIST returns a blank value unless there was an initial value for the *selections* variable before FILELIST was called.

   Selections from the window can be returned in the current result list, if one is available. The current result list is a special SCL list that is automatically filled with the values that are selected from a selection list. To use a current result list, use the MAKELIST function to create the list, and use the CURLIST function to designate it as the current result list. The current result list must exist before you call the FILELIST function.

   When FILELIST is invoked, the current result list is cleared. After FILELIST is invoked, the current result list contains the following named items:

TAG
   identifies the list as one that was created by FILELIST.
      Type: Character

COUNT
   contains the number of selected filerefs, or 0 if a user makes no selections or issues a CANCEL command in the list window.
      Type: Numeric

FILEREF
   contains the name of each selected fileref. There is a FILEREF element for each selected fileref.
      Type: Character

FILENAME
   contains the physical name of the external file for each selected fileref. There is a FILENAME element for each selection made.
      Type: Character

   Because some engines support mixed-case filenames, FILELIST now retains the cases of the returned selected items. This may cause your application to fail if your application contains code that assumes the returned selection is uppercased. For example,

```
if (filelist(dsid, 'TESTNDX')='NDXVAR')
```

must be changed to

```
if (upcase(filelist(dsid, 'TESTNDX'))='NDXVAR'
```

If the application cannot be modified, you may need to specify the VALIDVARNAME=V6 system option when you run the application to ensure that the selections returned from the FILELIST function will be uppercased.

## Examples

**Example 1: Displaying Specified Filerefs**    Open a window that displays a list of all defined filerefs except for LISTNUM.

```
select=filelist('^listnum');
```

**Example 2: Using a Current Result List for Multiple User Selections**    Open a window that displays a list of all defined filerefs except LISTNUM. Users can make up to five selections. The selections are retrieved from the current result list.

```
listid=makelist();
rc=curlist(listid);
select=filelist('^listnum',' ',' ',5);
n=getnitemn(listid,'COUNT');
do i=1 to n;
   fileref=getnitemc(listid,'FILEREF',i);
   physname=getnitemc(listid,'FILENAME',i);
   put fileref= physname=;
end;
```

## See Also

"CATLIST" on page 269

"DIRLIST" on page 347

"LIBLIST" on page 513

---

# FILENAME

**Assigns or deassigns a fileref for an external file, a directory, an output device, or a catalog entry**

**Category:**   External File

---

## Syntax

*sysrc*=**FILENAME**(*fileref,filename<,device <,host-options<,dir-ref>>>*);

**sysrc**
contains the return code for the operation:

| | |
|---|---|
| 0 | successful |
| ≠0 | not successful |

Type: Numeric

**fileref**
is the fileref to assign. A blank *fileref* (' ') causes an error condition. If the fileref is an SCL character variable that has a blank value, a fileref will be generated for you.
Type: Character

**filename**
is the physical name of an external file. Specifying a blank *filename* deassigns one that was previously assigned.
Type: Character

**device**
is the type of device if the fileref points to something other than a physical file:

CATALOG
a catalog entry

DUMMY
output to the file is discarded

FTP
the file transfer protocol (FTP) access method

GTERM
graphics on the user's terminal

NAMEPIPE
a named pipe

PIPE
an unnamed pipe

> *Note:*　Some host operating systems do not support pipes. △

PLOTTER
an unbuffered graphics output device

PRINTER
a printer or printer spool file

SOCKET
the Transmission Control Protocol/Internet Protocol (TCP/IP) socket access method

TERMINAL
the user's terminal

TAPE
a tape drive

URL
the URL access method
Type: Character

**host-options**
are host-specific details such as file attributes and processing attributes. *Host-options* can also be used to specify device options. For example, they could include output destinations, and CATALOG, FTP, URL, TCPIP, and SOCKET options. For details about host and device options for the FILENAME statement, see *SAS Language Reference: Dictionary* and the SAS documentation for your operating environment.
Type: Character

**dir-ref**
is the fileref assigned to the directory or partitioned data set in which the external file resides.
Type: Character

**Details**　The name associated with the file or device is called a *fileref* (file reference name). Other SCL functions that manipulate external files and directories require that the files be identified by a fileref rather than by a physical filename. A system-generated fileref is not displayed in the FILENAME window.

The association between a fileref and a physical file lasts only for the duration of the current SAS session or until you use FILENAME to change or discontinue the association. You can de-assign filerefs by specifying a null string for the *filename* argument in FILENAME.

For more information about the arguments that you can use with FILENAME, see *SAS Language Reference: Dictionary* and the SAS documentation for your operating environment.

*Operating Environment Information:* The term *directory* in this description refers to an aggregate grouping of files that are managed by the host operating system. Different host operating systems identify such groupings with different names, such as directory, subdirectory, MACLIB, or partitioned data set. See the SAS documentation for your operating environment for details.

Under some operating systems, you can also use system commands to assign filerefs. Depending on the operating system, FILENAME may be unable to change or de-assign filerefs that are assigned outside of a SAS session.

See the SAS documentation for your host operating system for information about the system-dependent options that you can specify for *options.* △

## Examples

**Example 1: Assigning a Fileref**   Assign the fileref MYFILE to an external file:

```
    /* Assign fileref MYFILE to the physical */
    /* filename stored in the variable FNAME   */
rc=filename('myfile',fname);
if (rc ne 0) then
    _msg_=sysmsg();
```

**Example 2: Using a System-Generated Fileref**   Assign a system-generated fileref, stored in the variable FNAME, to the file whose physical name is in the control FNAME:

```
fname=' ';
    /* Assign a system-generated fileref to the */
    /* filename stored in the variable FNAME     */
rc=filename(fname,fname);
if (rc) then
    _msg_=sysmsg();
else
    do;
        ...more SCL statements...
    end;
    /* De-assign the fileref */
rc=filename('myfile','');
```

**Example 3: Making an External File Accessible to a Client**   Assign a fileref to an external file:

```
rc=filename('sharedfl','\ABC\XYZ\AUTOEXEC.SAS');
```

**Example 4: Assigning a Fileref for a Pipe File**   Assign a fileref for a pipe file with the output from the UNIX command LS, which lists the files in the directory /u/myid:

```
rc=filename('myfile','ls /u/myid','pipe');
```

## See Also

"FEXIST" on page 392

"FILEEXIST" on page 400

"FILEREF" on page 406

"PATHNAME" on page 586

---

# FILEREF

**Verifies that a fileref has been assigned for the current SAS session or process**

**Category:**   External File

---

## Syntax

*sysrc*=**FILEREF**(*fileref*);

**sysrc**
   contains the return code for the operation:

| | |
|---|---|
| 0 | Both the fileref and the external file exist. |
| < 0 | The fileref has been assigned, but the file that it points to does not exist. |
| > 0 | The fileref has not been assigned. |

      Type: Numeric

**fileref**
   is the fileref to be validated (up to eight characters).
      Type: Character

**Details**   A negative return code indicates that the fileref exists but that the physical file associated with the fileref does not exist. A positive, nonzero value indicates that the fileref has not been assigned.

   A fileref can be assigned to an external file by using the FILENAME statement or the FILENAME function in SCL. Under some operating systems, you can also use system commands to assign filerefs. See the SAS documentation for your operating environment.

## Examples

**Example 1: Determining Whether a Fileref Has Been Assigned to an External File**   Test whether the fileref MYFILE is currently assigned to an external file. A system error message is issued if the fileref is not currently assigned.

```
if (fileref('myfile') > 0) then _msg_=sysmsg();
```

**Example 2: Determining Whether a Fileref and Its File Exist**   Test the fileref MYFILE to determine whether the fileref is assigned and whether the file that it refers to exists:

```
if (fileref('myfile') ne 0) then _msg_=sysmsg();
```

### See Also

"FEXIST" on page 392

"FILEEXIST" on page 400

"FILENAME" on page 403

"PATHNAME" on page 586

# FILLIST

**Fills an SCL list with text and data**

**Category:**  List

## Syntax

*sysrc*=**FILLIST**(*type,source,list-id< ,attr-list-id< ,description>>*);

*sysrc*

contains the return code for the operation:

0                              successful

≠0                            not successful
Type:  Numeric

*type*

specifies the type of file or data source named in *source* and one or more options to use:

**'CATALOG**<(*options*)>**'**

specifies that *source* names a catalog entry.

**'FILE**<(*options*)>**'**

specifies that *source* names an external file.

**'FILEREF**<(*options*)>**'**

specifies that *source* names a fileref that has been assigned to an external file.

**'SASICONS**<(*numbers*)>**'**

specifies the numbers for icons that are provided with SAS software. (When you specify SASICONS, *source* is ignored. Specify a null argument '' for *source*.)

**'SEARCH'**

specifies catalog names in the current search path (*source* is ignored). Use the SEARCH function to define the search path, or specify '' for *source*.

The available options are described in "*Type* Options" on page 408. Separate multiple options with blanks. For example, to fill a list from an external print file and to strip carriage-control characters, specify **FILE(PRINT STRIPCC)** for *type*.
Type:  Character

*source*

is a catalog entry (specified as *libref.catalog.entry.type*), an external file, or a fileref.
Type:  Character

*list-id*
> contains the identifier of the list to fill. An invalid *list-id* produces an error condition.
> Type: Numeric or List

*attr-list-id*
> contains the identifier of the list to fill with text attribute *source* information when *type* is **CATALOG** and the entry type is LOG, OUTPUT, or SOURCE. An invalid *attr-list-id* produces an error condition.
> Type: Numeric

*description*
> is the name of the variable in which you want to store the text of the catalog entry description. This argument is ignored if *type* is **FILE** or **FILEREF**.
>
> *Note:*   This parameter is an update parameter. See "Input, Output, and Update Parameters" on page 34 for more information. △
> Type: Character

## *Type* Options

**ADDCC**
> adds default host carriage-control characters. Used with *type* **FILE**, **FILEREF**, and **CATALOG** and with catalog entry types **LOG**, **OUTPUT**, and **SOURCE**.

**PRINT**
> designates an external file as a PRINT file (uses the host carriage-control characters). Used with *type* **FILE** and **FILEREF**.

**STRIPCC**
> removes carriage-control characters. Used with *type* **FILE**, **FILEREF**, and **CATALOG** and with catalog entry types **LOG**, **OUTPUT**, and **SOURCE**.

**TRIM**
> trims trailing blanks. Used with *type* **FILE**, **FILEREF** and **CATALOG** and with catalog entry types **LOG**, **OUTPUT**, and **SOURCE**. **TRIM** is used if you want to use FILLIST to fill a list with items that contain trailing blanks and then remove the blanks so that they will not be displayed in a pop-up menu that is produced by POPMENU.

**Details**    Each line of text in the source file is placed in a separate character item of the list identified by *list-id*. The number of items in the filled list is determined by the number of lines of text. All SCL lists must be created with MAKELIST before you call FILLIST. FILLIST automatically clears the lists before it fills the lists.

Data from the external file or catalog entry cannot exceed the maximum length of a character value in an SCL list item, which is 32,766 characters.

**External Files**    If *type* is **FILE**, then *source* is the name of an external file. If *type* is **FILEREF**, then *source* is a SAS fileref. FILLIST reads each record of the file into a separate character item.

**SLIST Catalog Entries**    If *type* is **CATALOG** and the catalog entry type in *source* is **SLIST**, then the types of the items in the filled list are determined by the saved list, and they may be character strings, numbers, or other lists. All item attributes and names are duplicated, as are the list attributes. However, the list identifier numbers are different.

**LIST Catalog Entries**    If *type* is **CATALOG** and the catalog entry type in *source* is **LIST**, FILLIST reads the contents of a SAS/AF LIST entry into *list-id*. The list contains either all numeric or all character items, depending on the contents of the LIST entry. The attribute list contains the following named values, which are all character type:

INFORMAT
> is the SAS informat that was specified in the LIST entry.

FORMAT
> is the SAS format that was specified in the LIST entry.

MESSAGE
> is the error message that was specified in the LIST entry.

CAPS
> reports whether the LIST entry has the CAPS attribute. **Y** or **N**.

SORTED
> reports whether the LIST entry has the SORT attribute. **Y** or **N**.

NOHONORCASE
> reports whether the LIST entry has the CASE-INSENSITIVE attribute. **Y** or **N**.

TYPE
> is the TYPE attribute that was specified in the LIST entry. **N** for numeric, **C** for character.

JUST
> is the JUST attribute that was specified in the LIST entry. **L**, **R**, **C**, or **N** for left, right, center, or none.

**SOURCE, OUTPUT, and LOG Catalog Entries**    If *type* is **CATALOG** and the entry type is **OUTPUT, LOG**, or **SOURCE**, the first character in each list item contains a FORTRAN carriage-control character: 1 means that a new page starts with this line. See **STRIPCC** above. **ADDCC** converts all carriage-control characters to ' '(blank).

If *type* is **CATALOG** and the entry type is **OUTPUT, LOG**, or **SOURCE**, then any text attributes (such as color and display attributes), are read one element per line into *attr-list-id*, if it is specified. These attributes consist of a character item for each line of text. Each character item contains one character for each character in the line, plus a prefix descriptor character. The prefix character is **T** for a title line, **H** for a header line, or **D** for a data line. The other characters represent the text display attributes and color, as described in the tables below.

Do not confuse text attributes (color, display, and so on) with list attributes that are specified with SETLATTR.

The attribute list that is filled by FILLIST contains one item for each line of text from the SAS catalog entry. The attribute string for each line has one character for each character of text. Each attribute character represents the SAS windowing environment color and display attribute. Not all display devices support all colors.

Color attributes are represented as follows:

| Color | Value | Color | Value |
|-------|-------|-------|-------|
| BLUE  | '10'x | WHITE   | '70'x |
| RED   | '20'x | ORANGE  | '80'x |
| PINK  | '30'x | BLACK   | '90'x |
| GREEN | '40'x | MAGENTA | 'A0'x |

| Color | Value | Color | Value |
|-------|-------|-------|-------|
| CYAN | '50'x | GRAY | 'B0'x |
| YELLOW | '60'x | BROWN | 'C0'x |

Display attributes are represented as follows:

| Attribute | Value |
|-----------|-------|
| NONE | '00'x |
| HIGHLIGHT | '01'x |
| UNDERLINE | '02'x |
| BLINK | '04'x |
| REVERSE | '08'x |

You combine the color and display attributes by adding them together. For example, you can specify GREEN UNDERLINE by adding '40'x to '02'x to yield '42'x. To assign GREEN UNDERLINE to the first 4 characters of a string, you could use a statement like:

```
str = '42424242'x;
```

See also "STRATTR" on page 675, which creates attribute strings.
You can use GETITEMC or POPC to retrieve an item from this list.
An error condition is produced if

□ either list has the NOUPDATE, NUMONLY, or FIXEDLENGTH attribute

□ any item in either list cannot be removed because it has the NODELETE attribute.

## Examples

**Example 1: Reading Text and Attributes Into a List** Suppose you have an OUTPUT entry named FINANCE.REPORTS.MONTHLY.OUTPUT that contains the text "Net:($45,034)" on line 45. The text **Net:** is white with no highlight attributes, whereas the text **($45,034)** is red reverse. The following statements read the text and attributes and print line 45.

```
INIT:
   text_list=makelist();
   attr_list=makelist();
   rc=fillist('CATALOG',
      'FINANCE.REPORTS.MONTHLY.OUTPUT',
      text_list,attr_list);
   text=substr(getitemc(text_list,45),2);
   attr=substr(getitemc(attr_list,45),2);
   len=compress(put(2*length(text), 4.));
   attrhex=putc(attr,'$HEX'||len||'.');
   put attr;
   put text;
   put attrhex;
return;
```

*Note:* SUBSTR removes the carriage-control characters. △

This example produces the following output:

```
PPPPP((((((((((
Net: ($45,034)
707070707028282828282828282828
```

The line of text consists of five white characters with no attributes, represented by the attribute value '70'x, followed by nine red reverse characters, represented by '28'x.

**Example 2: Performing a Recursive List Copy**    The following statements perform an operation similar to a recursive list copy:

```
rc=savelist('CATALOG','WORK.TEMP.MYLIST.SLIST',
   mylist);
new_list=makelist();
rc=fillist('CATALOG','WORK.TEMP.MYLIST.SLIST',
   new_list);
rc=delete('WORK.TEMP.TEMP.SLIST','CATALOG');
```

Lists that are saved in a permanent catalog with SAVELIST can persist across SAS sessions.

**Example 3: Reading and Printing Out Data and Attributes from LIST Entries**    Consider two LIST entries: SASUSER.DATA.A.LIST, which contains some character data, and SASUSER.DATA.DATES.LIST, which contains formatted numeric data. The following program reads the data and attributes from these entries and uses PUTLIST to print the results.

```
INIT:
items=makelist();
attrs=makelist();
rc=fillist('catalog','sasuser.data.a.list',
   items,attrs);
call putlist(items,'A.LIST contents:',0);
call putlist(attrs,'A.LIST attributes:',0);
rc=fillist('catalog','sasuser.data.dates.list',
   items,attrs);
call putlist(items,'DATES.LIST contents:',0);
call putlist(attrs,'DATES.LIST attributes:',0);
rc=dellist(items);
rc=dellist(attrs);
return;
```

The output for these entries may look like this:

```
A.LIST contents:('THIS      '
                'IS        '
                'A         '
                'LIST      '
                'ENTRY     '
                'WITH      '
                'EIGHT     '
                'ITEMS     '
                )[5]
A.LIST attributes:(INFORMAT=''
                   FORMAT=''
                   MESSAGE=''
                   CAPS='Y'
```

```
                      SORTED='N'
                      NOHONORCASE='Y'
                      TYPE='C'
                      JUST='L'
                      )[7]
        DATES.LIST contents:(1765
                      11162
                      11813
                      12072
                      )[5]
        DATES.LIST attributes:(INFORMAT='DATE.'
                      FORMAT='DATE.'
                      MESSAGE=''
                      CAPS='Y'
                      SORTED='Y'
                      NOHONORCASE='N'
                      TYPE='N'
                      JUST='L'
                      )[7]
```

*Note:*  [5] and [7] are the list identifiers that were assigned when this example was run and may be different each time the example is run. △

## See Also

"SAVELIST" on page 629

---

# FINFO

**Returns a file information item**

**Category:** External File

---

## Syntax

*item-value=***FINFO**(*file-id,info-item*);

**item-value**
   contains the value of the file parameter, or a blank if *info-item* is invalid.
   Type: Character

**file-id**
   is the identifier that was assigned when the file was opened. If *file-id* is invalid, the program halts.
   Type: Numeric

**info-item**
   specifies which file information item to retrieve.
   Type: Character

**Details**   FINFO returns the value of a system-dependent information item for an external file. The information that is available for files depends on the operating system.

FOPTNUM determines how many system-dependent information items are available. FOPTNAME determines the names of the available items.

## Example

Assign the fileref MYFILE to an external file. Then open the file and determine whether LRECL is one of the available information items. If the value of the variable CHARVAL is nonblank, then a value for LRECL (logical record length, an attribute used on some host systems), is displayed to the user.

```
rc=filename('myfile',fname);
fid=fopen('myfile');
charval=finfo(fid,'lrecl');
if (charval=' ') then
_msg_= 'The LRECL attribute is not available.';
else
    _msg_='The LRECL for the file is||charval||'.';
rc=fclose(fid);
rc=filename('myfile','');
```

## See Also

"DINFO" on page 346

"FOPEN" on page 420

"FOPTNAME" on page 421

"FOPTNUM" on page 423

# FKEYNAME

**Returns the name of the specified function key**

**Category:** Keys

## Syntax

*key-name*=**FKEYNAME**(*key-number*);

**key-name**
contains a function key name as listed in the KEYS window. Function key names vary according to the device.
Type: Character

**key-number**
is the number that corresponds to the order in which the keys are displayed in the KEYS window.
Type: Numeric

**Details** The *key-number* argument identifies a key by its ordinal position in the KEYS window, not by its label. For example, if the first key in the KEYS window is named PF1, use a 1 rather than PF1 for the *key-number* argument to identify that key. To retrieve the corresponding key definitions, use GETFKEY.

You can use this function only in entries that have a DISPLAY window.

## Example

Return the name of function key 12:

```
keyname=fkeyname(12);
```

## See Also

"GETFKEY" on page 440

"NUMFKEYS" on page 574

"SETFKEY" on page 649

---

# FLDATTR

**Changes the color and display attributes of a field, text entry widget, or text label widget to those stored in an attribute string**

**Category:**   Widget or Field

---

## Syntax

*rc*=**FLDATTR**(*wcol-name*,*string*);

**rc**
   contains the return code for the operation:

   0                         successful

   ≠0                        not successful
      Type: Numeric

**wcol-name**
   specifies the field, text entry widget, or text label widget to be changed.
      Type: Character

**string**
   specifies the color and display attributes to apply and the starting and ending
   character positions within the field.
      Type: Character

**Details**    You can use STRATTR or FILLIST to generate the attribute string. You can
also generate the attribute string by assigning hexadecimal values directly to the string.
   Color attributes are represented as

| Color | Value | Color | Value |
|-------|-------|-------|-------|
| BLUE | '10'x | WHITE | '70'x |
| RED | '20'x | ORANGE | '80'x |
| PINK | '30'x | BLACK | '90'x |

| Color | Value | | Color | Value |
|---|---|---|---|---|
| GREEN | '40'x | | MAGENTA | 'A0'x |
| CYAN | '50'x | | GRAY | 'B0'x |
| YELLOW | '60'x | | BROWN | 'C0'x |

Display attributes are represented as

| Attribute | Value |
|---|---|
| NONE | '00'x |
| HIGHLIGHT | '01'x |
| UNDERLINE | '02'x |
| BLINK | '04'x |
| REVERSE | '08'x |

To preserve a color, use the special hexadecimal value 'F0'x. To preserve a display attribute, use '0F'x. To preserve both the color and display attribute, add the two special characters together ('FF'x).

For programs with extended tables you must call this function in the getrow section of your SCL program.

FRAME entry widgets can also use the _setColorStr method.

## Example

Change the first half of the field, ABC, to red reverse.

```
str=strattr('red','reverse',1,mlength(abc)/2);
rc=fldattr('abc',str);
```

Suppose the FRAME text entry widget, OBJ1, is BLUE REVERSE. To change the third through the seventh character positions of OBJ1 to yellow, you must initialize the first two characters of the attribute string to 'FF'x, then assign YELLOW in the third through seventh characters. You can assign YELLOW to the attribute string either by using STRATTR or by assigning the hexadecimal values directly to the string.

```
st ='FFFF6060606060'x;
rc=fldattr('obj1',str);
```

The previous example could have been written as follows:

```
str='FFFF'x;
str=strattr('yellow','',3,5);
rc=fldattr('obj1',str);
```

You can also use the REPEAT function to initialize a string.

```
str=repeat('FF'x,2 );
str=strattr('yellow','',3,5);
rc=fldattr('obj1',str);
```

### See Also

"FLDCOLOR" on page 416

"STRATTR" on page 675

---

# FLDCOLOR

**Changes the color and display attributes of a field, text entry widget, or text label widget to those stored in an attribute string**

**Category:** Widget or Field

---

## Syntax

*rc*=**FLDCOLOR**(*wcol-name,color,attribute,start,length*);

**rc**

contains the return code for the operation:

| | |
|---|---|
| 0 | successful |
| ≠0 | not successful |

Type: Numeric

**wcol-name**

specifies the field, text entry widget, or text label widget to be changed.
Type: Character

**color**

specifies either a color name, or ''to retain the current color. Colors are BLACK, BLUE, BROWN, CYAN, GRAY, GREEN, MAGENTA, ORANGE, PINK, RED, WHITE, and YELLOW. SASCOLOR window elements can also be used for *color*.
Type: Character

**attribute**

specifies either a display attribute, or ''to retain the current attribute. Attributes are NONE, BLINKING, HIGHLIGHT, HIREV, REVERSE, and UNDERLINE. If you specify a SASCOLOR window element for *color*, then *attribute* is ignored because the SASCOLOR window element contains a display attribute. However, you must specify a placeholder ('') for *attribute* when you specify arguments after it.
Type: Character

**start**

specifies the position in the field at which to begin applying the specified color and display attributes.
Type: Numeric

**length**

specifies the number of positions to which the specified color and display attributes are to be applied.
Type: Numeric

**Details**   FRAME entry widgets can also use the _setColor method.

To change the color for the entire field or FRAME entry widget, you can use the FIELD function.

## Examples

**Example 1: Changing the Color and Attributes of Character Positions**  Change the color of the third through seventh character positions in field ABC to red, and change the display attribute of those positions to high intensity:

```
rc=fldcolor('abc','red','highlight',3,5);
```

**Example 2: Changing the Color of a Field**  Change the color of a field, but leave the attributes the same:

```
rc=fldcolor('abc','red','',3,7);
```

**Example 3: Using a SASCOLOR Window Element to Change the Color of a Field**  Change the color of a field, using a SASCOLOR window element:

```
rc=fldcolor('abc','foreground','',3,7);
```

## See Also

"FIELD" on page 394

"FLDATTR" on page 414

"STRATTR" on page 675

# FNOTE

**Identifies the last record that was read**

**Category:**  External File

## Syntax

*note-id*=**FNOTE**(*file-id*);

**note-id**
contains the identifier assigned to the last record that was read. The *note-id* value is used by the FPOINT function to reposition the file pointer on a particular record. SCL programs should not modify the value of the *note-id* variable.
Type: Numeric

**file-id**
is the identifier that was assigned when the file was opened. If *file-id* is invalid, the program halts.
Type: Numeric

**Details**  You can use FNOTE like a bookmark, marking the position in the file so that your application can later use FPOINT to return to that position.

FNOTE is limited to noting 1,000 records. When that limit is reached, the program halts. To free the memory that is associated with each note identifier, use DROPNOTE.

## Example

Assign the fileref THEFILE to an external file. Then attempt to open the file. If the file is successfully opened, indicated by a positive value in the variable FID, then read the records, use the variable NOTE3 to save the position of the third record that is read, and then later use FPOINT to point to NOTE3 to update the file. After the record is updated, close the file.

```
      /* Assign the fileref THEFILE to the      */
      /* filename stored in the variable FNAME  */
      /* and open it in UPDATE mode.            */
rc=filename('thefile',fname);
fileid=fopen('thefile','u');
if (fileid>0) then do;
      /* Read the first record. */
   rc=fread(fileid);
      /* Read the second record. */
   rc=fread(fileid);
      /* Read the third record. */
   rc=fread(fileid);
      /* Note the position of third record. */
   note3=fnote(fileid);
      /* Read the fourth record. */
   rc=fread(fileid);
      /* Read the fifth record. */
   rc=fread(fileid);
      /* Point to the third record. */
   rc=fpoint(fileid,note3);
      /* Read the third record. */
   rc=fread(fileid);
      /* Copy the new text to the FDB. */
   rc=fput(fileid,'New text');
      /* Update the third record with data in the FDB. */
   rc=fwrite(fileid);
      /* Close the file. */
   rc=fclose(fileid);
end;
      /* Deassign the fileref.  */
rc=filename('thefile','');
```

## See Also

"DROPNOTE" on page 361

"FPOINT" on page 425

"FREAD" on page 430

"FREWIND" on page 431

# FONTSEL

**Opens the selector window for host fonts or for portable fonts**

**Category:**   Selection List

## Syntax

*newfontlist-id=***FONTSEL**(*oldfontlist-id,font-selector*);

*newfontlist-id*
> contains the identifier of the list that contains the selected font family, size, weight, and style.
> Type: Numeric

*oldfontlist-id*
> contains the identifier of the list that contains the font information for the selection list. An invalid *oldfontlist-id* produces an error condition. This list can be empty.
> Type: Numeric

*font-selector*
> specifies which font selector window to open:
>
> **'Y'**
> > the host font selector window
>
> **'N'**
> > the portable font selector window
>
> **'H'**
> > the portable font selector window, displaying only the hardware fonts
>
> **' '** (blank)
> > the default font selector window
> > Type: Character

**Details**     If *oldfontlist-id* is not empty, then the selector window opens with the font family, size, weight, and style selections that are specified in the list. If *oldfontlist-id* is an empty list, then the selector window opens with the default selections for font family, size, weight, and style. The *newfontlist-id* identifier contains information about the font family, size, weight, and style that the user selected.

The host font selector window enables a user to select fonts that are available on the host in an environment-specific way. The portable font selector window enables a user to select a portable font specification, which is used to find the closest match among fonts that are available on a host. The host font selector window can also be opened from the portable font selector window by using the System button.

For more information about how to use the font information that is returned, see the documentation for the extended text entry class in SAS/AF software and its _setFont method.

To change the default font selector window, use the SAS system option MULTENVAPPL, which is described in *SAS Language Reference: Dictionary*.

## Example

Make a FRAME entry with a pushbutton control named PUSHBTN and a Version 8 text entry control named TEXTENTRY1. Clicking on the pushbutton executes the code to display the portable font selector window. Change the font selector value from **N** to **Y** to use the host font selector window.

```
INIT:
    fontid=makelist();
return;
PUSHBTN:
    fontid=fontsel(fontid,'n');
    rc=putlist(fontid,'FONT',1);
    textentry1.font=fontid;
return;
```

```
TERM:
    rc=dellist(fontid);
return;
```

## See Also

"MAKELIST" on page 535

# FOPEN

### Opens an external file

**Category:**   External File

## Syntax

*file-id*=**FOPEN**(*fileref*< ,*open-mode*< ,*record-length*
    < ,*record-format*>>>);

**file-id**
> contains the identifier for the file, or 0 if the file could not be opened.
>> Type: Numeric

**fileref**
> is the fileref that is assigned to the external file.
>> Type: Character

**open-mode**
> specifies the type of access to the file:

| | |
|---|---|
| **'A'** | APPEND mode, which allows writing new records after the current end of the file. |
| **'I'** | INPUT mode, which allows reading only. (This is the default.) |
| **'O'** | OUTPUT mode, which defaults to the OPEN mode specified in the host option in the FILENAME statement or function. If no host option is specified, it allows writing new records at the beginning of the file. If the file exists, its contents are overwritten, destroying any previous contents. If the file does not exist, it is created. |
| **'S'** | Sequential input mode, which is used for pipes and other sequential devices such as hardware ports. |
| **'U'** | UPDATE mode, which allows both reading and writing records. |
| **'W'** | Sequential output mode, which is used for pipes and other sequential devices such as hardware ports. |

> Type: Character

**record-length**
> is the logical record length of the file. To use the existing record length for the file, either specify a length of 0 or do not provide a value here.
>> Type: Numeric

***record-format***
>is the record format of the file. To use the existing record format, do not specify a value here.
>
>| | |
>|---|---|
>| `'B'` | The data is to be interpreted as binary data. |
>| `'D'` | Use the default record format. |
>| `'E'` | Use an editable record format. |
>| `'F'` | The file contains fixed-length records. |
>| `'P'` | The file contains printer carriage-control characters in a host-dependent record format. |
>| `'V'` | The file contains variable-length records. |
>
>Type: Character

### Details

***CAUTION:***
>**Use OUTPUT mode with care.** Opening an existing file in OUTPUT mode overwrites the current contents of the file without warning. △

The FOPEN function opens an external file for reading or updating and returns a file identifier value that can then be used to identify the open file to other functions. You must associate a fileref with the external file before calling the FOPEN function.

In SCL you can assign filerefs by using either the FILENAME statement or the FILENAME function. Under some operating systems, you can also use operating system commands to assign filerefs.

*Operating Environment Information: OS/390*
>For OS/390 data sets that have the VBA record format, specify 'P' for the *record-format* argument. △

### Examples

□ Assign the fileref MYFILE to an external file. Then attempt to open the file for input, using all defaults:

```
rc=filename('myfile',fname);
fid=fopen('myfile');
```

□ Attempt to open the file for input, this time not using defaults:

```
fid=fopen('file2','o',132,'e');
```

### See Also

"DOPEN" on page 357

"FCLOSE" on page 386

"FILENAME" on page 403

"FILEREF" on page 406

"MOPEN" on page 552

---

# FOPTNAME

**Returns the name of an item of information for a file**

**Category:**  External File

---

## Syntax

*item-name*=**FOPTNAME**(*file-id*,*item-num*);

**item-name**
> contains the name of the information item, or a blank if an error occurred.
> Type: Character

**file-id**
> contains the identifier that was assigned when the file was opened. If *file-id* is invalid, the program halts.
> Type: Numeric

**item-num**
> is the number of the information item.
> Type: Numeric

**Details**  The number, value, and type of available information items depend on the operating system.

## Example

Retrieve the system-dependent file information items and write them to the log:

```
length name $ 8;
rc=filename('myfile',fname);
fid=fopen('myfile');
infonum=foptnum(fid);
do j=1 to infonum;
  name=foptname(fid,j);
  value=finfo(fid,name);
  put 'File attribute' name 'has a value of' value;
end;
rc=fclose(fid);
rc=filename('myfile','');
```

The example produces the following output:

```
File attribute LRECL has a value of 256.
```

### See Also

"DINFO" on page 346

"DOPTNAME" on page 358

"DOPTNUM" on page 359

"FINFO" on page 412

"FOPEN" on page 420

"FOPTNUM" on page 423

"MOPEN" on page 552

# FOPTNUM

**Returns the number of information items that are available for an external file**

**Category:** External File

## Syntax

*num-items*=**FOPTNUM**(*file-id*);

**num-items**
    contains the number of information items that are available.
      Type: Numeric

**file-id**
    contains the identifier that was assigned when the file was opened. If *file-id* is
    invalid, the program halts.
      Type: Numeric

**Details**    The number, value, and type of available information items depend on the
operating system.

    Use FOPTNAME to determine the names of the items that are available for a
particular operating system. Use FINFO to retrieve the value of a particular
information item.

## Example

    Open the external file that has the fileref MYFILE and determine how many
system-dependent file information items are available:

```
fileid=fopen('myfile');
infonum=foptnum(myfile);
```

## See Also

"DINFO" on page 346

"DOPTNAME" on page 358

"DOPTNUM" on page 359

"FINFO" on page 412

"FOPTNAME" on page 421

---

# FORMAT

**Verifies that the specified format is valid**

**Category:**   Formatting

---

## Syntax

*rc*=**FORMAT**(*format,type*);

**rc**
    contains the return code for the operation:

    1                successful

    0                not successful
        Type: Numeric

**format**
    contains a format that is either supplied by SAS or created using the FORMAT
    procedure. The format name must contain a period (for example, dollar6. or
    dollar8.2).
        Type: Character

**type**
    specifies the type of the format:

    '**C**'             character

    '**N**'             numeric.
        Type: Character

**Details**    If the specified format is not known to the SAS session, then the operation is
unsuccessful. The function verifies that valid widths are specified for formats.
    See *SAS Language Reference: Dictionary* for details about formats.

## Examples

**Example 1: Verifying the Validity of a Character Format**    Assume that you want to use
the $CHAR12. format and to verify that $CHAR12. is a valid character format. (If the
format name is valid, then the value returned to the variable RC is 1.)

```
rc=format('$char12.','c');
```

**Example 2: Verifying the Validity of a Numeric Format**    Verify that **5.6** is not a valid format for numeric values. (If it is not valid, then the value returned to the variable RC is 0.)

```
rc=format('5.6','n');
```

## See Also

"INFORMAT" on page 479

---

# FPOINT

**Positions the "read" pointer on the next record to be read**

**Category:**   External File

---

## Syntax

*sysrc*=**FPOINT**(*file-id,note-id*);

**sysrc**
   contains the return code for the operation:

   0                          successful

   ≠0                         not successful
      Type: Numeric

**file-id**
   contains the identifier that was assigned when the file was opened. If *file-id* is invalid, the program halts.
      Type: Numeric

**note-id**
   contains the identifier that was assigned by the FNOTE function.
      Type: Numeric

**Details**    Use FNOTE to provide the *note-id* value that identifies the record. FPOINT determines only the record to read next. It has no impact on which record is written next. When you open the file for update, FWRITE writes to the most recently read record.

## Example

Assign the fileref MYFILE to an external file. Then attempt to open the file. If the file is opened successfully, then read the records and use NOTE3 to store the position of the third record read. Later, point back to NOTE3 to update the file, closing the file afterward.

```
      /* Assign the fileref MYFILE to the physical */
      /* filename stored in the variable FNAME     */
      /* and open it in UPDATE mode.               */
   rc=filename('myfile',fname);
   fileid=fopen('myfile','u');
```

```
if (fileid>0) then do;
      /* Read the first record. */
   rc=fread(fileid);
      /* Read the second record. */
   rc=fread(fileid);
      /* Read the third record. */
   rc=fread(fileid);
      /* Note the position of the third record. */
   note3=fnote(fileid);
      /* Read the fourth record. */
   rc=fread(fileid);
      /* Read the fifth record. */
   rc=fread(fileid);
      /* Point to the third record. */
   rc=fpoint(fileid,note3);
      /* Read the third record. */
   rc=fread(fileid);
      /* Copy the new text to the FDB. */
   rc=fput(fileid,'new text');
      /* Write data in the FDB to the third record. */
   rc=fwrite(fileid);
      /* Close the file. */
   rc=fclose(fileid);
end;
   /* Clear the fileref. */
rc=filename('myfile','');
```

## See Also

"DROPNOTE" on page 361

"FNOTE" on page 417

"FREAD" on page 430

"FREWIND" on page 431

# FPOS

**Sets the position of the column pointer in the File Data Buffer**

**Category:**  External File

## Syntax

*sysrc*=**FPOS**(*file-id,nval*);

*sysrc*
    contains the return code for the operation:

    0                          successful

    ≠0                        not successful
        Type: Numeric

*file-id*
> contains the identifier that was assigned when the file was opened. If *file-id* is invalid, the program halts.
> Type: Numeric

*nval*
> is the number of the column at which to set the pointer.
> Type: Numeric

**Details**   If the specified position is past the end of the current record, then the size of the record is increased appropriately. However, in a fixed block file or a VBA file, if you specify a column position beyond the end of the record, the record size does not change, and the text string is not written to the file.

## Example

Assign the fileref THEFILE to an external file and then attempt to open the file. If the file is opened successfully, as indicated by a positive value in the variable FID, then place data into the file's buffer at column 12, write the record, and close the file.

```
    /* Assign the fileref THEFILE to the physical */
    /* filename stored in the variable FNAME      */
    /* and open it in append mode.                */
rc=filename('thefile',fname);
fileid=fopen('thefile','o');
if (fileid>0) then do;
   rc=fread(fileid);
   dataline='This is some data.';
      /* Position at column 12 in the FDB. */
   rc=fpos(fileid,12);
      /* Put the data in the FDB. */
   rc=fput(fileid,dataline);
      /* Write the record. */
   rc=fwrite(fileid);
      /* Close the file. */
   rc=fclose(fileid);
end;
   /* Clear the fileref. */
rc=filename('thefile','');
```

## See Also

"FCOL" on page 387

"FPUT" on page 427

---

# FPUT

**Moves data to the File Data Buffer (FDB) for an external file, starting at the FDB's current column position**

**Category:**   External File

## Syntax

*sysrc*=**FPUT**(*file-id,cval*<, *length*>);

**rc**
> contains the return code for the operation:

0                    successful

≠0                  not successful
> Type: Numeric

**file-id**
> contains the identifier that was assigned when the file was opened. If *file-id* is
> invalid, the program halts.
> Type: Numeric

**cval**
> is the data to be moved to the FDB.
> Type: Character

**length**
> is the length of the string to move to the FDB. If *length* is greater than *cval*, then the
> string is padded with blanks when it is moved. If *length* is less than *cval*, the string
> is truncated when it is moved. If *length* is less than 1, the program halts.
> Type: Numeric

**Details**    The unformatted value of *cval* is passed to FPUT. The number of bytes moved
to the FDB is determined by the length of the variable, or by the value of *length*, if
*length* is specified. The value of the column pointer is then incremented to one position
past the end of the new text.

## Example

Move data to the FDB and write it to the external file:

```
/* Assign the fileref THEFILE to the physical */
/* filename stored in the variable FNAME      */
/* and open it in append mode.                */
rc=filename('thefile',fname);
fileid=fopen('thefile','a');
if (fileid>0) then
    do;
        thestring='This is some data.';
        rc=fput(fileid,thestring);
        rc=fwrite(fileid);
        rc=fclose(fileid);
    end;
else
    _msg_=sysmsg();
rc=filename('thefile','');
```

## See Also

"FNOTE" on page 417

"FPOINT" on page 425

"FPOS" on page 426

"FWRITE" on page 439

---

# _FRAME_

**Contains the identifier of either the FRAME entry that contains the control or the FRAME entry that is being used as a method**

**Category:**  System Variable

---

**Details**    _FRAME_ is a system variable that is provided automatically by the FRAME entry in SAS/AF software. A space is automatically created for it in the SCL data vector (SDV). _FRAME_ contains the identifier of the FRAME entry that contains a component. Otherwise, it contains the identifier of the FRAME that is running.

You can use this variable to send methods to a FRAME entry from a control's method. For example, a control method can send a _refresh method to the FRAME entry, causing the FRAME entry to refresh its display.

## Example

Suppose the entry FIRST.FRAME contains an icon. The icon's _select method is defined to run the SAS/AF FRAME entry SECOND.FRAME, which contains the following program:

```
INIT:
     /* Send a method to the current FRAME */
  _CFRAME_._setMsg('Running the Select method');
return;
TERM:
     /* Send a method to the FRAME that */
     /* contains the icon               */
  _FRAME_._setMsg('Select method has finished.');
return;
```

When FIRST.FRAME displays and a user selects the icon, SECOND.FRAME displays with the message "Running the Select method". After the user ends from SECOND.FRAME, FIRST.FRAME displays the message "Select has finished." This is accomplished by sending the _setMsg method to _CFRAME_ (the FRAME entry that is currently running) in the INIT section and by sending _setMsg to _FRAME_ (the FRAME entry that contains the icon) in the TERM section.

## See Also

"_CFRAME_" on page 277

# FREAD

**Reads a record from an external file into the File Data Buffer (FDB)**

**Category:** External File

## Syntax

*sysrc*=**FREAD**(*file-id*);

**sysrc**
contains the return code for the operation:

0            successful

≠0          not successful
    Type: Numeric

**file-id**
contains the identifier that was assigned when the file was opened. If *file-id* is invalid, the program halts.
    Type: Numeric

**Details**    The position of the file pointer is automatically updated after the read operation so that successive FREAD functions read successive file records.
Use FNOTE, FPOINT, and FREWIND to position the file pointer explicitly.

## Example

Assign the fileref MYFILE to an external file and attempt to open the file. Read each record from the file and list it in the LOG window.

```
/* Assign the fileref MYFILE to the physical */
/* filename stored in the variable FNAME     */
/* and open it.                              */
rc=filename('myfile',fname);
fileid=fopen('myfile');
if (fileid>0) then
   do while(fread(fileid)=0);
      rc=fget(fileid,c,200);
      put c;
   end;
rc=fclose(fileid);
rc=filename('myfile','');
```

### See Also

"FGET" on page 393

"FNOTE" on page 417

"FPOINT" on page 425

"FREWIND" on page 431

# FREWIND

**Positions the file pointer at the beginning of the file**

**Category:** External File

## Syntax

*sysrc*=**FREWIND**(*file-id*);

**sysrc**
  contains the return code for the operation:

  0                          successful

  ≠0                         not successful
    Type: Numeric

**file-id**
  contains the identifier that was assigned when the file was opened. If *file-id* is invalid, the program halts.
    Type: Numeric

**Details**    FREWIND has no effect on a file that was opened with sequential access.

## Example

Assign the fileref THEFILE to an external file. Then open the file and read the records until the end of the file is reached. The FREWIND function then repositions the pointer to the beginning of the file. The first record is read again and is stored in the File Data Buffer (FDB). The first token is retrieved and is stored in the variable VAL.

```
    /* Assign the fileref THEFILE to the physical */
    /* filename stored in the variable FNAME      */
    /* and open it.                               */
rc=filename('thefile',fname);
fileid=fopen('thefile');
do while (rc ne -1);
     /* Read a record. */
   rc=fread(fileid);
end;

    /* Reposition the pointer at the beginning of */
    /* the file.                                  */
if rc= -1  then rc=frewind(fileid);
```

```
    /* Read the first record. */
rc=fread(fileid);
    /* Read the first token into VAL. */
rc=fget(fileid,val);
put val= ;
rc=fclose(fileid);
rc=filename('thefile','');
```

## See Also

"FGET" on page 393

---

# FRLEN

Returns the size of the last record read, or, if the file is opened for output, returns the current record size

**Category:** External File

---

## Syntax

*length*=**FRLEN**(*file-id*);

**length**
  contains the length of the current record if the file is opened for output. Otherwise, it is the length of the last record read.
  Type: Numeric

**file-id**
  is the identifier that was assigned when the file was opened. If *file-id* is invalid, the program halts.
  Type: Numeric

## Example

Open the file identified by the fileref THEFILE. Determine the minimum and maximum lengths of records in the external file, and write the results to the LOG window.

```
    /* Assign the fileref THEFILE to the physical */
    /* filename stored in the variable FNAME      */
    /* and open it.                               */
rc=filename('thefile',fname);
fileid=fopen('thefile');
min=0;
max=0;
if (fread(fileid)=0) then do;
    min=frlen(fileid);
    max=min;
    do while(fread(fileid)=0);
        reclen=frlen(fileid);
        if (reclen>max) then max=reclen;
```

```
         if (reclen<min) then min=reclen;
      end;
      rc=fclose(fileid);
   end;
   put min= max=;
```

## See Also

"FCLOSE" on page 386

"FOPEN" on page 420

"FREAD" on page 430

# FSEDIT

**Displays a SAS table by row**

**Category:**  SAS Table

## Syntax

**CALL FSEDIT**(*table-name*<,*screen-name*
   <,*open-mode*<,*row-number*>>>);

**table-name**
   is the SAS table to display, in the form <*libref.*>*member-name*<(*data-set-options*)>. If
   you omit the libref, the default WORK library is used.
      You can add a list of SAS data set options in parentheses following the table name.
   All data set options are valid except FIRSTOBS= and OBS=. See *SAS Language
   Reference: Dictionary* for a list of SAS data set options and their descriptions.
      Type: Character

**screen-name**
   is a SCREEN entry for the FSEDIT session. (Screen entries are SAS catalog entries
   of type SCREEN that define custom features for the FSEDIT session.) For
   *screen-name,* use the form <*libref.*>*catalog-name*<.*entry-name*<.SCREEN>>. A one-
   or two-level name is interpreted as a catalog name, and the default screen entry
   name, FSEDIT.SCREEN, is assumed. (A one-level name is interpreted as a catalog
   in the default SAS data library, WORK.) If the specified catalog does not already
   exist, it is created.
      If the screen entry does not already exist, a new screen entry is not created unless
   the user issues a MODIFY command during the FSEDIT session.
      If you want to use predefined SAS table labels, use an equal sign (=) for
   *screen-name.* (A modified SCREEN entry is not saved.) Column names are used for
   any fields that lack labels.
      Type: Character

**open-mode**
   specifies the type of access to the SAS table:

   **'ADD'**
      adds a new blank row to the table, then opens the FSEDIT window with the new
      row displayed for editing.

**'BROWSE'**
>opens the FSBROWSE window for reading rows.

**'EDIT'**
>opens the FSEDIT window for editing rows. (This is the default.)

**'NEW'**
>opens the FSEDIT NEW window for creating the specified SAS table as a new table, then opens the FSEDIT window for entering values into the new table.
>Type: Character

***row-number***
>is the first row to be displayed when the FSEDIT or FSBROWSE window is opened. This argument is ignored unless the value of *open-mode* is **'EDIT'** or **'BROWSE'**.
>Type: Numeric

**Details**    The FSEDIT routine calls the FSEDIT procedure, which opens the FSEDIT window to display the specified SAS table. You can specify BROWSE for *open-mode* to open the FSBROWSE window for browsing the table instead. You can optionally specify the name of a screen entry to provide a custom display and the number of the row to be displayed when the window is opened.

If you want to specify *open-mode* or *row-number* but do not want to specify a screen entry, use a null string (' ') for *screen-name*.

For more information about the commands that are available in the FSEDIT procedure, see *SAS/FSP Software Procedures Guide*.

## Examples

□ Open a SAS table named PERSONAL (in the default SAS data library WORK) for editing:

```
call fsedit('personal');
```

□ Open the SAS table PERSONAL in the library MASTER for editing, using a custom SCREEN entry named PER1 in the catalog MASTER.DISPLAY:

```
call fsedit ('master.personal','master.display.per1');
```

□ Open a SAS table named MASTER.PERSONAL for browsing, using the default FSBROWSE window display:

```
call fsedit('master.personal',' ','browse');
```

□ To display the predefined labels that are associated with the SAS table columns instead of the column names, specify an equal sign (=) for the *screen-name* argument, as in the following example:

```
call fsedit('master.personal','=','browse');
```

Specify SAS data set options by enclosing them within parentheses immediately following the SAS table name in the *table-name* argument, as in the following examples.

□ Open a SAS table named MASTER.PERSONAL and subset the rows based on the value that is entered for the numeric column SCRNUM:

```
call fsedit('master.personal(where=(num='||
            put(scrnum,5.)||'))');
```

□ Open a SAS table named MASTER.PERSONAL and subset the rows based on the value that is entered for the character column SCRNAME:

```
call fsedit('master.personal(where=(name='||
            quote(scrname)||'))');
```

## See Also

"NEW" on page 561

# FSEP

**Sets the token delimiters for the FGET function**

**Category:**  External File

## Syntax

*sysrc*=**FSEP**(*file-id*,*delimiter*);

***sysrc***

contains the return code for the operation:

0                              successful

≠0                            not successful
     Type: Numeric

***file-id***

specifies the identifier that was assigned when the file was opened. If *file-id* is invalid, the program halts.
     Type: Numeric

***delimiter***

specifies the token delimiter that separates items in the File Data Buffer (FDB). If multiple characters are specified, each character is considered a delimiter. The default delimiter is a blank.
     Type: Character

## Example

Suppose the external file contains data in this form:

```
John J. Doe,Male,25,Weight Lifter
```

Note that each field is separated by a comma.

Read the file identified by the fileref THEFILE, using the comma as a separator, and write the values for NAME, GENDER, AGE, and WORK to the LOG window:

```
fileid=fopen('thefile');
rc=fsep(fileid,',');
sysrc=fread(fileid);
rc=fget(fileid,cval);
do while (rc ne -1);
   put cval=;
   rc=fget (fileid,cval);
end;
rc=fclose(fileid);
```

The output of the program is

```
cval=John J. Doe
cval=Male
cval=25
cval=Weight Lifter
```

## See Also

"FGET" on page 393

"FREAD" on page 430

# FSLIST

**Displays an external file for browsing**

**Category:**   External File

## Syntax

**CALL FSLIST**(*file< ,options>*);

*file*
>    is the fileref or physical filename of the external file. A physical name must be enclosed in quotation marks.
>    Type: Character

*options*
>    specifies one or more carriage-control options for formatting the display, with multiple options separated by blanks and enclosed in one set of quotation marks:

>    **'CC'**
>>    Use the host operating system's native carriage-control characters.

>    **'FORTCC'**
>>    Use FORTRAN-style carriage-control characters.

>    **'NOCC'**
>>    Treat carriage-control characters as regular text. (This is the default.)
>>    For CC or FORTCC, you can also specify an overprinting control option:

>    **'OVP'**
>>    Print the current line over the previous line when the overprint code is encountered. The OVP option is valid only if the CC or FORTCC option is also specified. The default is NOOVP.

>    **'NOOVP'**
>>    Ignore the overprint code and print each line from the file on a separate line of the display.
>>    If you use the FORTCC option, the first column of each line in the external file is not displayed. The character in this column is interpreted as a carriage-control code. Under some operating systems, FORTRAN-style carriage control is the native carriage control. For these systems, the FORTCC and CC options produce the same behavior.
>>    Under some operating systems, the CC option is the default for print files.
>>    Type: Character

**Details** The FSLIST routine calls the FSLIST procedure, which opens the FSLIST window to display an external file for interactive browsing. This routine provides a convenient method for examining the information stored in an external file.

For more information about the commands that are available in the FSLIST procedure, see *SAS Language Reference: Dictionary*.

External files (files maintained by the host operating system rather than by SAS software) can contain various types of information:

- □ data records
- □ output from previous SAS sessions
- □ SAS source statements
- □ carriage-control information.

### Examples

- □ Browse an external file to which the fileref MYFILE has previously been assigned. The file contains FORTRAN-style carriage-control characters, and overprinting is allowed.

  ```
  call fslist('myfile','fortcc ovp');
  ```

- □ Browse the external file named FSLIST.PUB. Double quotation marks surrounding the filename string indicate that a physical filename, not a fileref, is being passed to the FSLIST routine.

  ```
  call fslist('"fslist.pub"');
  ```

*Note:* The form of the physical filename depends on the host operating system. △

### See Also

"FILENAME" on page 403

---

# FSVIEW

**Displays a SAS table in tabular format**

**Category:** SAS Table

---

### Syntax

**CALL FSVIEW**(*table-name*<,*open-mode*
   <,*formula-entry*<,*options*>>>);

*table-name*

is the SAS table to be displayed. Use the format <*libref.*>*member-name*<(*data-set options*)>. If the libref is omitted, the default SAS data library, WORK, is assumed. You can add a list of SAS data set options in parentheses following the table name. All data set options are valid except FIRSTOBS= and OBS=. Refer to *SAS Language Reference: Dictionary* for a list of SAS data set options and their descriptions.

   Type: Character

*open-mode*

specifies the type of access to the SAS table:

**'ADD'**

Add a new blank row to the table, and then open the FSVIEW window with the new row displayed for editing.

**'BROWSE'**

Open the FSVIEW window for reading rows. (This is the default.)

**'EDIT'**

Open the FSVIEW window for editing rows.

**'NEW'**

Open the FSVIEW NEW window for creating the specified SAS table as a new table, then open the FSVIEW window for entering values into the new table.
Type: Character

*formula-entry*

is the FORMULA catalog entry that defines custom features for the FSVIEW session or that controls the display and behavior of the session.

Specify this argument as *<libref.>catalog-name<.entry-name<.FORMULA>>*. A one- or two-level name is interpreted as a catalog name, and the default formula entry name is assumed. The default formula entry name is the same as the member name of the table specified in the *table-name* argument. (A one-level name is assumed to refer to a catalog in the default SAS data library, WORK.) If the specified catalog does not exist, it is created. If the specified formula entry does not already exist, a new formula entry is created.
Type: Character

*options*

specifies whether to disable certain FSVIEW window commands for the duration of the FSVIEW session. Separate multiple options with blanks.

**'BRONLY'**

disables the MODIFY command so that only browsing is allowed and **'EDIT'** and **'ADD'** modes are ignored.

**'NOADD'**

disables the ADD command so that new rows cannot be added to the table.

**'NODELETE'**

disables the DELETE command so that rows cannot be deleted.
Type: Character

**Details**    The FSVIEW routine calls the FSVIEW procedure, which opens the FSVIEW window to display the specified SAS table. By default, the SAS table is opened for browsing. You can use the *open-mode* argument to specify that the table should instead be opened for editing. You can also specify a formula entry and other options for the FSVIEW session.

If you specify NEW for the *open-mode* argument, the FSVIEW NEW window is opened for the user to define a new SAS table before the FSVIEW window is opened to enter values for that table.

You can specify SAS data set options by enclosing them within parentheses immediately following the SAS table name in the *table-name* argument, as in the second example in the "Examples" section.

If you want to specify the *options* argument but do not want to specify a formula entry, then use a null string (' ') for the *formula-name* argument.

To specify multiple values for the *options* argument, separate the values with blanks.

For more information about the commands that are available in the FSVIEW procedure, see *SAS Language Reference: Dictionary*.

## Examples

☐ Browse a SAS table named PERSONAL in the default SAS data library WORK:

```
call fsview('personal');
```

☐ Edit a SAS table named PERSONAL in the library MASTER. Only those rows in which the SITE column has the value 5 are displayed.

```
call fsview
('master.personal(where=(site=5))','edit');
```

☐ Edit a SAS table named PERSONAL in the library MASTER. Rows cannot be added or deleted during the FSVIEW session.

```
call fsview
('master.personal','edit','','noadd nodelete');
```

## See Also

"FSEDIT" on page 433

"NEW" on page 561

# FWRITE

**Writes a record to an external file**

**Category:** External File

## Syntax

*sysrc*=**FWRITE**(*file-id*< ,*cc*>);

**sysrc**

contains the return code for the operation:

| | |
|---|---|
| 0 | successful |
| ≠0 | not successful |

Type: Numeric

**file-id**

contains the identifier that was assigned when the file was opened. If *file-id* is invalid, the program halts.

Type: Numeric

**cc**

specifies a carriage-control character:

| | |
|---|---|
| '0' | skips one blank line before a new line. |
| '-' | skips two blank lines before a new line. |
| '1' | starts the line on a new page. |
| '+' | overstrikes the line on a previous line. |
| 'P' | interprets the line as a terminal prompt. |

'=' interprets the line as carriage-control information.
Any other character (including a blank) starts the record on a new line.
If *cc* is not provided, FWRITE writes to the current line.
Type: Character

**Details**   FWRITE moves text from the File Data Buffer (FDB) to the external file. In order to use the carriage-control characters, you must open the file with a RECORD format of P (PRINT format) with FOPEN.

## Example

Write the numbers 1 to 50 to an external file, skipping two blank lines. Then call FSLIST to display the newly created file.

```
    /* Assign the fileref THEFILE to the external */
    /* filename stored in the variable FNAME.     */
rc=filename('thefile',fname);
fileid=fopen('thefile','o',0,'P');
do i=1 to 50;
   rc=fput(fileid,put(i,2.));

 if (fwrite(fileid,'-') ne 0) then do;
    _msg_=sysmsg();
    put msg;
    return;
  end;
end;

rc=fclose(fileid);
call fslist('thefile','cc');
```

## See Also

"FAPPEND" on page 384

"FGET" on page 393

"FPUT" on page 427

# GETFKEY

**Returns the command that is assigned to a function key**

**Category:**   Keys

## Syntax

*key-command*=**GETFKEY**(*key-name*);

**key-command**
    returns the command that is currently assigned to the function key.
       Type: Character

### key-name

specifies the name of the function key as listed in the KEYS window. Function key names vary according to the device. Use FKEYNAME to retrieve the name of a function key.

Type: Character

**Details** GETFKEY returns the command that is assigned to a function key for the current window. This is the same as the text displayed for the key in the KEYS window. You can use this function only in entries that have a DISPLAY window.

## Examples

### Example 1: Using GETFKEY When the Function Key Name Is Unknown Return the
command assigned to the first function key if the name of the function key is not known:

```
command=getfkey(fkeyname(1));
```

### Example 2: Using GETFKEY When the Function Key Name Is Known If the value of the
first function key is F1, return the command that is assigned to the first function key:

```
command=getfkey('F1');
```

## See Also

"FKEYNAME" on page 413

"NUMFKEYS" on page 574

"SETFKEY" on page 649

# GETFOOT

**Returns the text of a footnote definition**

**Category:** SAS System Option

## Syntax

*foot-text*=**GETFOOT**(*foot-num*);

### foot-text

contains the text of the footnote definition, or a blank if the footnote is not defined.

Type: Character

### foot-num

is the number (1 to 10) of the footnote definition.

Type: Numeric

**Details** Use GETFOOT to retrieve any footnote text that was previously defined in the SAS session by either the FOOTNOTE statement or the SCL SETFOOT routine. Only the footnote text is retrieved. Graphic options such as color or font are not returned.

You can view footnotes in the FOOTNOTES window by using the FOOTNOTE command. Changing any text in the FOOTNOTES window, however, resets all graphically defined FOOTNOTE options, such as color, font, and position.

For more information about footnotes, see *SAS Language Reference: Dictionary*. For more information about graphical footnotes, see *SAS/GRAPH Software: Reference*.

## Example

Store the text of FOOTNOTE2 in the variable FNOTE2:

```
fnote2=getfoot(2);
```

## See Also

"GETTITLE" on page 449

"SETFOOT" on page 650

"SETTITLE" on page 666

# GETITEMC, GETITEML, GETITEMN, and GETITEMO

**Returns a value that is identified by its position in an SCL list**

**Category:**   List

## Syntax

*cval*=**GETITEMC**(*list-id<,index>*);

*sublist-id*=**GETITEML**(*list-id<,index>*);

*nval*=**GETITEMN**(*list-id<,index>*);

*object-id*=**GETITEMO**(*list-id<,index>*);

**cval**
> contains the character value (returned by GETITEMC) of the item that is stored at the specified position in list identified by *list-id*.
> Type: Character

**sublist-id**
> contains the list identifier (returned by GETITEML) of the sublist that is stored at the specified position in the list identified by *list-id*.
> Type: Numeric

**nval**
> contains the numeric value (returned by GETITEMN) of the item that is stored at the specified position in the list identified by *list-id*.
> Type: Numeric

**object-id**
> contains the object identifier (returned by GETITEMO) of the object that is stored at the specified position in the list identified by *list-id*.
> Type: Numeric

**list-id**
> contains the identifier of the list that you want to query. An invalid *list-id* produces an error condition.
> Type: Numeric or List

*index*
> is the position in the list of the item to return. The position can be specified as a positive or negative number. By default, *index* is 1 (the first item). If *index* is a positive number, then the item is at position *index* from the beginning of the list. If *index* is a negative number, then the item is at position ABS(*index*) from the end of the list. An error condition results if the absolute value for *index* is zero or if it is greater than the number of items in the list.
>   Type: Numeric

**Details**   An error results if you use any of these functions to return an indexed item that has a different data type. You can determine the data type of an item in a list by using ITEMTYPE before using GETITEMC, GETITEML, GETITEMN, or GETITEMO.

## Examples

**Example 1: Using the GETITEMC Function**   Return the character values stored in the first and third items of the list identified by the MYLIST variable:

```
citem=getitemc(mylist);
citem=getitemc(mylist,3);
```

**Example 2: Using the GETITEML Function**   Return the list identifier stored in the eighth item of the list identified by the MYLIST variable:

```
slist=getiteml(mylist,8);
```

**Example 3: Using the GETITEMN Function**   Return the numeric value stored in the fifth item of the list identified by the MYLIST variable:

```
nitem=getitemn(mylist,5);
```

**Example 4: Using the GETITEMO Function**   Return the object identifiers stored in the third and ninth item of the list identified by the MYLIST variable:

```
sublist=getitemo(mylist,3);
oitem=getitemo(mylist,9);
```

## See Also

"GETNITEMC, GETNITEML, GETNITEMN, and GETNITEMO" on page 445

"POPC, POPL, POPN, and POPO" on page 593

"SETITEMC, SETITEML, SETITEMN, and SETITEMO" on page 651

# GETLATTR

**Returns the attributes of either an SCL list or an item in the list**

**Category:**   List

## Syntax

*attributes*=**GETLATTR**(*list-id*<,*index*>);

***attributes***

contains a string of words separated by blanks. Each word is a separate attribute for a list or item.

Type: Character

***list-id***

contains the identifier of the list that GETLATTR processes. An invalid *list-id* produces an error condition.

Type: Numeric or List

***index***

is the position of the item in the list. The position can be specified as a positive or negative number. By default, *index* is 1 (the first item). If *index* is a positive number, then the item is at position *index* from the beginning of the list. If *index* is a negative number, then the item is at position ABS(*index*) from the end of the list. An error condition results if the absolute value for *index* is zero or if it is greater than the number of items in the list.

If *index* is 0 or is omitted, then the attributes returned by GETLATTR are list attributes. If *index* is nonzero, then GETLATTR returns the attributes associated with the indexed item instead of the attributes for the entire list.

Type: Numeric

**Details**    The items in *attributes* can be used to assign attributes to another list or item. The string returned as *attributes* contains a blank before and after each attribute, which makes it easy to determine whether an attribute is set by searching *attributes* for an attribute name. Use the INDEX function to search the string for a specified attribute.

If *index* is omitted, *attributes* contains one attribute from each row of the following table:

| Default Setting | Alternate Setting |
|---|---|
| UPDATE | NOUPDATE |
| NOFIXEDTYPE | FIXEDTYPE |
| NOFIXEDLENGTH | FIXEDLENGTH |
| ANYNAMES | SASNAMES |
| DUPNAMES | NODUPNAMES |
| NOCHARONLY | CHARONLY |
| NONUMONLY | NUMONLY |
| COPY | NOCOPY |
| HONORCASE | NOHONORCASE |

If *index* is supplied, then *attributes* is the set of item attributes consisting of one attribute from each row of the following table:

| Default Setting | Alternate Setting |
|---|---|
| ACTIVE | INACTIVE |
| DELETE | NODELETE |
| NOFIXEDTYPE | FIXEDTYPE |

| Default Setting | Alternate Setting |
| --- | --- |
| UPDATE | NOUPDATE |
| WRITE | NOWRITE |

For detailed information about these attributes, see "SETLATTR" on page 656.

## Example

Create a list LISTID with one item and print the sets of list attributes for LISTID as well as the item attributes that are associated with the first item of LISTID. Note the leading and trailing blanks in the attribute strings, which are made evident by embedding the attribute strings in double quotation marks.

```
INIT:
   listid = makelist(1);
   listattrs = '"' || getlattr(listid) || '"';
   put listattrs=;
   found = index(listattrs,'UPDATE');
   put found=;
   itemattrs = '"' || getlattr(listid,1) || '"';
   put itemattrs=;
   rc = dellist(listid);
return;
```

The output of this example is

```
LISTATTRS=" DELETE UPDATE NOFIXEDTYPE
NOFIXEDLENGTH ANYNAMES DUPNAMES
NOCHARONLY NONUMONLY COPY NOHONORCASE"
FOUND=10;
ITEMATTRS=" ACTIVE WRITE NOAUTO NOEDIT
DELETE UPDATE NOFIXEDTYPE "
```

FOUND returns the starting position of the word "UPDATE" in the string of list attributes.

## See Also

"HASATTR" on page 458

"SETLATTR" on page 656

# GETNITEMC, GETNITEML, GETNITEMN, and GETNITEMO

**Return a value identified by its item name in an SCL list**

**Category:** List

## Syntax

*cval*=**GETNITEMC**(*list-id,name*<*,occurrence*
    <*,start-index*<*,default*<*,force*>>>>);

*sublist-id*=**GETNITEML**(*list-id,name<,occurrence*
    *<,start-index<,default<,force>>>*);

*nval*=**GETNITEMN**(*list-id,name<,occurrence*
    *<,start-index<,default<,force>>>*);

*obj-val*=**GETNITEMO**(*list-id,name<,occurrence*
    *<,start-index<,default<,force>>>*);


**cval**
    contains the character value that is returned by GETNITEMC.
        Type: Character

**list-id**
    is the identifier of the list to search. An invalid *list-id* produces an error condition.
        Type: List

**name**
    is the name of the item to search in the list. Item names are converted to uppercase
    during the search if *force* is **'Y'** or if the searched list has the attribute
    NOHONORCASE set. Trailing blanks are ignored when the list is searched for a
    matching name. Thus, the names 'abc' and 'Abc' are converted to 'ABC'.
        IGNORECASE is the alias for NOHONORCASE and is the default for a list. But
    you can use the SETLATTR function to set a list's attribute to HONORCASE.
        Type: Character

**occurrence**
    is the number of the occurrence of the named item to be searched. The default, 1,
    indicates the first occurrence of the item.
        Type: Numeric or List

**start-index**
    specifies where in the list to begin searching for the item. By default, *start-index* is 1
    (the first item). If *start-index* is positive, the search begins at position *start-index*
    items from the beginning of the list. If *start-index* is negative, the search begins at
    the item specified by ABS(*start-index*) items from the end of the list. An error
    condition results if the absolute value of *start-index* is zero or if it is greater than the
    number of items in the list.
        Type: Numeric

**default**
    is a default value to return if the named item is not found in the list. This value
    must have the appropriate data type for the function that is being used:

GETNITEMC
    a character value

GETNITEML
    a sublist identifier or a list value

GETNITEMN
    a numeric value

GETNITEMO
    an object identifier.

    Type: Character, Numeric, List, or Object

**sublist-id**
    is the identifier for the sublist that is returned by GETNITEML.
        Type: List

*nval*
> is the numeric value that is returned by GETNITEMN.
> Type: Numeric

*obj-val*
> is the object identifier that is returned by GETNITEMO.
> Type: Object

*force*
> specifies whether to conduct the name search in uppercase.

> `'N'`    searches according to the list attributes HONORCASE and NOHONORCASE, which are specified with SETLATTR. (This is the default.)

> `'Y'`    conducts the name search in uppercase regardless of list attributes specified with SETLATTR.
> Type: Character

**Details**    By default, the search starts at the beginning of the list and returns the first item found that has the specified item name. However, you can start the search at a different place in the list by specifying a *start-index* other than 1. You can also specify a different occurrence of the item (for example, the second, tenth, or twentieth) by specifying an *occurrence* other than 1. If the item is not found and you have specified a value for *default* as the fifth parameter, then that value is returned instead of an error condition.

If *occurrence* and *start-index* are both positive or both negative, the search proceeds forward from the *start-index* item. For forward searches, the search continues only to the end of the list and does not wrap back to the front of the list. If *occurrence* or *start-index* is negative, then the search is backwards. For backward searches, the search continues only to the beginning of the list and does not wrap back to the end of the list.

GETNITEMC combines the actions of NAMEDITEM and GETITEMC. GETNITEML combines the actions of NAMEDITEM and GETITEML. GETNITEMN combines the actions of NAMEDITEM and GETITEMN. GETNITEMO combines the actions of NAMEDITEM and GETITEMO.

In situations where your application manipulates an SCL list and you cannot guarantee that the named item is character, you should not use GETNITEMC. Instead, when manipulating SCL lists which may contain other types, you should use NAMEDITEM with ITEMTYPE with GETITEMC, GETITEML, GETITEMN, or GETITEMO.

An error condition results if

□ the named item is not a character value and you are using GETNITEMC

□ the item is not a list identifier and you are using GETNITEML

□ the item is not a numeric value and you are using GETNITEMN

□ the item is not an object and you are using GETNITEMO.

□ the named item does not exist and *default* is not specified.

## Examples

**Example 1: Using the GETNITEMC Function**    Halt the program if there are fewer than two items named `'Software Sales'` in the list identified by DIRECTORY. Omitting the default value from GETNITEMC designates that the character item must exist in the list.

```
s=getnitemc(directory,'Software Sales',2,-1);
```

This statement is equivalent to the following statements:

```
ssi=nameditem(directory,'Software Sales',2,-1);
s=getitemc(directory,ssi);
```

Both of the preceding examples search for the second occurrence of **'Software Sales'**, starting from the end of the list.

**Example 2: Searching for an Item of Unknown Type**   This example shows how to search for a named item in an SCL list when you do not know the type of that item.

```
index = nameditem(listid, 'A', occurrence,
                               startIndex);
if index then
   select (itemtype(listid, index));
     when ('C') c = getitemc(listid, index);
     when ('L') l = getiteml(listid, index);
     when ('N') n = getitemn(listid, index);
     when ('O') o = getitemo(listid, index);
   end;
```

**Example 3: Using GETNITEML and Specifying a Default Value**   If the named item may not be in the list, supply a list identifier value for *default* for GETNITEML:

```
sslistid=getniteml
(emp_list,'Marketing',2,-10,-1);
```

The preceding program statement is equivalent to the following:

```
mpos=nameditem(emp_list,'Marketing',2,-10);
if mpos ne 0 then
   sslistid=getiteml(emp_list,mpos);
else
   sslistid=-1;
```

**Example 4: Using GETNITEMC and Specifying a Default Value**   This example shows GETNITEMC, using a default value that contains an error message.

```
defaultc='Value not found';
s=getnitemc
(directory,'Software Sales',2,-1,defaultc);
```

## See Also

"GETITEMC, GETITEML, GETITEMN, and GETITEMO" on page 442

"NAMEDITEM" on page 555

"NAMEITEM" on page 558

"SEARCHC, SEARCHL, SEARCHN, and SEARCHO" on page 636

"SETLATTR" on page 656

"SETNITEMC, SETNITEML, SETNITEMN, and SETNITEMO" on page 661

# GETPARMID

**Returns the numeric value stored by the SETPARMID routine**

**Category:** Modular Programming and Object Oriented

## Syntax

*nval*=**GETPARMID**();

*nval*
   contains the numeric value stored by a previous call to the SETPARMID routine.
   Type: Numeric

**Details**     SETPARMID stores a value, and GETPARMID retrieves the stored value.
SETPARMID and GETPARMID allow only one value to be passed. To pass multiple
values between entries, use the ENTRY statement. Additional ways of making values
available to other SCL programs include using macro variables and SCL lists.

## Example

Retrieve the table identifier value that was stored in another program by
SETPARMID:

```
dsid=getparmid();
```

## See Also

   "DISPLAY" on page 350

   "ENTRY" on page 369

   "SETPARMID" on page 664

# GETTITLE

**Returns the text of a title definition**

**Category:** SAS System Option

## Syntax

*title-text*=**GETTITLE**(*title-num*);

*title-text*
   is the text of the title definition, or a blank if the title is not defined.
   Type: Character

*title-num*
   is the number (1 to 10) of the title definition.
   Type: Numeric

**Details**     Use GETTITLE to retrieve any title text that was previously defined in the
SAS session by either the TITLE statement or the SCL SETTITLE routine. Only the
title text is retrieved. Graphic options, such as color or font, are not returned.

You can view titles in the TITLES window by using the TITLE command. Changing any text in the TITLES window, however, resets all graphically defined title options, such as color, font, and position.

For more information about titles, see *SAS Language Reference: Dictionary.* For more information about graphical titles, see *SAS/GRAPH Software: Reference.*

## Example

Put the text of TITLE2 into the variable TITLE2:

```
title2=gettitle(2);
```

## See Also

"GETFOOT" on page 441

"SETFOOT" on page 650

"SETTITLE" on page 666

# GETVARC and GETVARN

**Assign the value of a SAS table column to an SCL variable**

**Category:**  SAS Table

## Syntax

*cval*=**GETVARC**(*table-id,col-num*);

*nval*=**GETVARN**(*table-id,col-num*);

**cval**
is the value of the character column that is returned by GETVARC.
Type: Character

**table-id**
is the identifier for a table that is open. If *table-id* is invalid, the program halts.
Type: Numeric

**col-num**
is the number of the column in the Table Data Vector (TDV). This value can be obtained by using the VARNUM function. If the column specified in *col-num* is invalid, the program halts.
Type: Numeric

**nval**
is the value of the numeric column that is returned by GETVARN.
Type: Numeric

**Details**    Before you use GETVARC or GETVARN, you can use VARNUM to obtain the number of a column in a SAS table. You can nest VARNUM, or you can assign it to a column that can be passed as the second argument. GETVARC and GETVARN read the value of the specified column that is in the current row in the TDV and copy that value to the specified SCL variable in the SCL data vector (SDV).

## Examples

**Example 1: Using GETVARN to Search for a Value**    Assign VARNUM to a column that can be passed as the second argument to GETVARN. Read row number 10 into the TDV.

```
pricenum=varnum(mydataid,'price');
rc=fetchobs(mydataid,10);
price=getvarn(mydataid,pricenum);
```

**Example 2: Using GETVARC with a Nested VARNUM**    Nest VARNUM in the GETVARC function to search for the value of the character column NAME from the tenth row of the open SAS table whose identifier is stored in the column MYDATAID.

```
rc=fetchobs(mydataid,10);
user=getvarc(mydataid,varnum(mydataid,'name'));
```

## See Also

"FETCH" on page 389

"FETCHOBS" on page 390

"LOCATEC and LOCATEN" on page 527

"PUTVARC and PUTVARN" on page 609

"UPDATE" on page 697

"VARNUM" on page 713

# GETVARF

**Assigns the formatted value of a SAS table column to a character SCL variable**

**Category:**   SAS Table

## Syntax

*cval*=**GETVARF**(*table-id,col-num*);

**cval**
>   is the formatted value of the table column that is returned by GETVARF.
>       Type: Character

**table-id**
>   is the identifier for a table that is open. If *table-id* is invalid, the program halts.
>       Type: Numeric

**col-num**
>   is the number of the column in the Table Data Vector (TDV). This value can be obtained by using the VARNUM function. If the column specified in *col-num* is invalid, the program halts.
>       Type: Numeric

**Details**   GETVARF assigns the formatted value of a SAS table column to a character SCL variable. If no format has been assigned to the specified column, GETVARF returns the raw value for a character column or _BLANK_ for a numeric column.

## Examples

**Example 1: Print Formatted Table Column Values**   The example first creates a SAS table with a character column, NAME, and two numeric columns, BDAY and GENDER. It then reads each row from the table and prints the values of each column plus the formatted values of the two numeric columns.

```
control asis;
submit continue;
  proc format; value sexfmt 1='Male' 2='Female';
  data work.samplef; input name $ 1-10  bday date. gender;
  format  bday date. sex sexfmt.  ;
  cards;
Jane      16oct63   2
Bill      15may62   1
Mary      25jan64   2
;
endsubmit;

id = open ( 'work.samplef');
do while (fetch(id)=0 );
  name  = getvarc ( id, 1);
  bdayn = getvarn (id, 2);
  bday  = getvarf (id, 2);
  gender  = getvarn (id, 3);
  fgender = getvarf (id, 3);
  put name= bdayn= bday= gendern= gender=;
  end;
rc = close (id);
```

The output would be like the following:

```
name=Jane bdayn=1384 bday= 16OCT63 gendern=2 gender=Female
name=Bill bdayn=865 bday= 15MAY62 gendern=1 gender=Male
name=Mary bdayn=1485 bday= 25JAN64 gendern=2 gender=Female
```

## See Also

"GETVARC and GETVARN" on page 450

"GETVARC and GETVARN" on page 450

# GGLOBAL

**Returns the text of a SYMBOL, PATTERN, LEGEND, or AXIS statement**

**Category:**   SAS System Option

## Syntax

*stmt-text*=**GGLOBAL**(*stmt-type,stmt-num*);

***stmt-text***

contains the text of the retrieved SYMBOL, PATTERN, LEGEND, or AXIS statement. If *stmt-type* is invalid, a missing value is returned.

Type: Character

***stmt-type***

is the type of statement to retrieve:

**'SYMBOL'**

**'PATTERN'**

**'LEGEND'**

**'AXIS'**

Type: Character

***stmt-num***

is the number of the SYMBOL, PATTERN, LEGEND, or AXIS statement to retrieve. Valid values are from 1 to the number of statements that are defined for the specified type, which is returned by the GGLOBALN function.

Type: Numeric

**Details** Because a user can change SYMBOL, PATTERN, LEGEND, or AXIS statements during the execution of an application, GGLOBALN must be executed before the GGLOBAL function in order to set up an internal table that is used by GGLOBAL.

*Note:* SYMBOL and PATTERN can generate more than one definition per statement. For more information about the SYMBOL, PATTERN, LEGEND, and AXIS statements, see *SAS/GRAPH Software: Reference.* △

## Example

Assume that the following SYMBOL statements have been defined for the current SAS session:

```
symbol1 c=red;
symbol30 c=blue;
```

Check to see that at least two SYMBOL statements are available. If this condition is true, the text of the second SYMBOL statement is returned to the variable SYMBOL2.

```
numsymb=gglobaln('symbol');
if (numsymb >= 2)
then symbol2=gglobal('symbol',2);
```

The value returned to NUMSYMB is 2. The following value is returned to SYMBOL2:

```
SYMBOL30 CV=BLUE CO=BLUE CI=BLUE;
```

The value of HEIGHT is also returned:

```
SYMBOL30 CV=BLUE CO=BLUE CI=BLUE HEIGHT=1 ;
```

## See Also

"GGLOBALE" on page 454

"GGLOBALN" on page 454

# GGLOBALE

**Deletes an internal table of SYMBOL, PATTERN, LEGEND, or AXIS definitions**

**Category:**   SAS System Option

## Syntax

*sysrc=***GGLOBALE**(*stmt-type*);

*sysrc*
  contains the return code for the operation:

  0                         successful

  ≠0                        not successful

     Type: Numeric

*stmt-type*
  specifies the type of statement to delete:

        **'SYMBOL'**
        **'PATTERN'**
        **'LEGEND'**
        **'AXIS'**
  Type: Character

**Details**    When you have completed processing information concerning the SYMBOL, PATTERN, LEGEND, or AXIS statements, use GGLOBALE to free the memory used for storing the internal table that was created with GGLOBALN. For more information about the SYMBOL, PATTERN, LEGEND, and AXIS statements, see *SAS/GRAPH Software: Reference.*

## Example

Free the internal table that was created by GGLOBALN for the SYMBOL statements, and check the return code to determine whether a message needs to be issued:

```
rc=gglobale('symbol');
if rc then _msg_=sysmsg();
```

## See Also

"GGLOBAL" on page 452

"GGLOBALN" on page 454

# GGLOBALN

**Returns the number of SYMBOL, PATTERN, LEGEND, or AXIS statements that are currently defined**

**Category:** SAS System Option

## Syntax

*num-stmts*=**GGLOBALN**(*stmt-type*);

**num-stmts**
> contains the number of SYMBOL, PATTERN, LEGEND, or AXIS definitions that are currently defined.
> Type: Numeric

**stmt-type**
> specifies the type of statement to return:
>
> > `'SYMBOL'`
> >
> > `'PATTERN'`
> >
> > `'LEGEND'`
> >
> > `'AXIS'`
>
> Type: Character

**Details**  Information about SYMBOL, PATTERN, LEGEND, or AXIS statements is stored in an internal table and can be retrieved with GGLOBAL. To delete the internal table created by GGLOBALN, use GGLOBALE.

*Note:*  SYMBOL and PATTERN can generate more than one definition per statement. For more information about SYMBOL, PATTERN, LEGEND, and AXIS statements, see *SAS/GRAPH Software: Reference.*  △

## Example

Assume that the following SYMBOL statements have been defined for the current SAS session:

```
symbol1 c=red;
symbol30 c=blue;
```

In the variable NUMSYMB, return the number of SYMBOL statements that are currently available. The value returned for NUMSYMB is 2, not 30.

```
numsymb=gglobaln('symbol');
```

## See Also

"GGLOBAL" on page 452

"GGLOBALE" on page 454

# GOTO

**Branches immediately to another entry**

**Category:**  Control Flow

## Syntax

**CALL GOTO**(*entry< ,action< ,frame>>*);

*entry*
> is the name of the entry to branch to. The entry can be any of the SAS/AF display entry types (FRAME, PROGRAM, MENU, CBT, or HELP). The *entry* argument can be in the following forms:

> *entry*
>> to specify a PROGRAM entry in the current catalog.

> *entry.type*
>> to specify an entry in the current catalog.

> *libref.catalog.entry*
>> to specify a PROGRAM entry in a different catalog.

> *libref.cat-name.entry.type*
>> to specify an entry in a different catalog.
>> Type: Character

*action*
> specifies how the execution stack is to be handled and where control transfers to when the specified entry ends:

> **'A'**
>> adds *entry* to the top of the execution stack. The specified entry is displayed immediately. When the entry ends, the user returns to the window that was displayed before the program with the CALL GOTO was executed.

> **'C'**
>> clears the current execution stack. The specified entry is displayed immediately, and the stack is cleared. When the entry ends, the user returns to the parent entry, if one was specified in the entry, or exits the AF window. This option may be useful if you have memory constraints. (This is the default.)

> **'R'**
>> removes the top entry from the execution stack and places the entry specified in the GOTO routine on the top of the execution stack. The specified entry is displayed immediately. When the entry ends, the user returns to the next entry on the stack rather than to the program that contains the GOTO call.
>> Type: Character

*frame*
> is the number of the CBT frame if you are branching to a CBT entry.
> Type: Numeric

**Details**    The GOTO routine branches immediately to a CBT, HELP, MENU, FRAME, or PROGRAM entry and transfers control to it. Statements that appear after GOTO are not executed, because control is transferred to the entry that is specified in the GOTO routine.

GOTO, which always starts a new stream, cannot be used in FSEDIT or FSVIEW programs.

## Example

Pass control to MYEND.PROGRAM, and end the SAS/AF session if the user issues the END command. Assume there is no parent entry specified.

```
if _status_='E'
then call goto('myend.program','C');
```

## See Also

"DISPLAY" on page 350

# GRAY

**Grays FRAME entry controls and stations of a choice group**

**Category:** Control or Field

## Syntax

*rc*=**GRAY**(*var-name*< ,*station*< ,*row*>>);

*rc*
> contains the return code for the operation:

| 0 | successful |
| ≠0 | not successful |

> Type: Numeric

*var-name*
> is the name of a window control or choice group to be grayed.
> Type: Character

*station*
> is the number of the button in a radio box or field in a choice group. This value must be greater than 0 and no larger than the total number of stations defined for the choice group. For PROGRAM entries, use the value 0 as a placeholder if the entire choice group at a specified row is to be grayed.
> Type: Numeric

*row*
> is the number of the row when the choice group is in the scrollable section of an extended table. *Row* can be used in PROGRAM entry programs but not for FRAME entry programs. Specify *row* only when you want to gray a station from outside an extended table's getrow or putrow section. Do not specify *row* if you want to gray a station from a getrow or putrow section.
> Type: Numeric

**Details**    Users cannot select a FRAME entry control, choice group, or choice group station that is grayed.

For linked action fields in choice groups, the ACTION-type pair is considered one station. For example, the following line in a PROGRAM entry window defines three linked action fields:

```
&  &A_____       &  &B_____       &  &C_____
```

To gray the linked action pair for field B, pass in 2 for the value of *station*, not 4.
Window controls can also use the _gray method. You cannot use GRAY in FSEDIT or
FSVIEW programs.

## Example

Prevent users from selecting CONTINUE when the value of AGE is less than 21:

```
if (age<21) then
      rc=gray('CONTINUE');
   else
      rc=ungray('CONTINUE');
```

## See Also

"ACTIVATE" on page 249

"ISACTIVE" on page 492

"ISGRAY" on page 493

"UNGRAY" on page 693

# HASATTR

**Reports whether an SCL list or a list item has a specified attribute**

**Category:**   List

## Syntax

*rc*=**HASATTR**(*list-id,attribute<,index>*);

*rc*
   contains the return code for the operation:

   1                         The list or item has the specified attribute.

   0                         The list or item does not have the specified attribute.
        Type: Numeric

*list-id*
   is the identifier of the list that HASATTR searches. An invalid *list-id* produces an
   error condition.
        Type: Numeric or List

*attribute*
   is an attribute for a list or list item, as described in SETLATTR. In addition, you can
   test for the following special attributes:

   'G'                       returns 1 if the list is a global list.

   'L'                       returns 1 if the list is a local list.

   'C'                       returns 1 if the list identifier is also a class identifier.

'O'   returns 1 if the list identifier is also an object identifier.
  Type: Character

*index*

is the position of the item in the list. The position can be specified as a positive or negative number. By default, *index* is 1 (the first item). If *index* is omitted, HASATTR checks to see if the specified list has the named *attribute*. If *index* is specified, HASATTR checks to see if the specified item has the named *attribute*. If *index* is a positive number, then the item is at position *index* from the beginning of the list. If *index* is a negative number, then the item is at position ABS(*index*) from the end of the list. An error condition results if the absolute value for *index* is zero or if it is greater than the number of items in the list.
  Type: Numeric

**Details**   If no value is specified for *index*, HASATTR queries the attribute of the list. If a nonzero value is specified for *index*, HASATTR queries the attribute of an item in the list.

For a list of attributes for lists and list items, see "SETLATTR" on page 656.

## Examples

### Example 1: Clearing a List That Has a Particular Attribute   Clear the list identified by MYLIST only if it has the UPDATE attribute:

```
if hasattr(mylist,'UPDATE') then rc=clearlist
                              (mylist);
```

### Example 2: Determining Whether a List Item Has a Particular Attribute   Determine whether the third item in a list has the FIXEDTYPE attribute:

```
isfixed=hasattr(mylist,'FIXEDTYPE',3);
```

## See Also

"GETLATTR" on page 443

"SETLATTR" on page 656

# HOME

**Positions the cursor on a window's command area**

**Category:**  Control or Field

## Syntax

**HOME**;

**Details**   In SAS/AF applications, the HOME statement moves the cursor immediately. In FSEDIT and FSVIEW applications, the cursor is moved when control is returned to the application.

See "CURSOR" on page 323 for more information about how to position the cursor in a field.

If the PMENU facility is active, the command area for a dialog window is at the bottom of the window.

Some systems do not position the cursor on the pull-down menu for standard windows nor on the command area for dialog windows.

## See Also

"CURSOR" on page 323

"FIELD" on page 394

---

# ICCREATE

### Creates integrity constraints on a SAS table

**Category:**  SAS Table

---

## Syntax

*sysrc*=**ICCREATE**(*table-id,icname,ictype,icvalue*<, *argument-1*<, . . . <,*argument-3*>>>);

**sysrc**
contains the status of the operation:

| | |
|---|---|
| =0 | successful |
| >0 | not successful |
| <0 | the operation was completed with a warning |

Type: Numeric

**table-id**
contains the identifier for the SAS table, which is returned by the OPEN function. Integrity constraints can be set for a new SAS table only when it is opened in NEW mode. Integrity constraints can be set for an existing table only when it is opened in UTILITY or NEW mode. (Remember that if you open an existing table in NEW mode, the table is replaced without warning.)

Type: Numeric

**icname**
is the name of the integrity constraint.

Type: Character

**ictype**
specifies the type of integrity constraint to create:

**'CHECK'**
specifies that column values must fall within a particular set, range, or list of values, or that values must meet a condition or be the same as values in other columns in the same row.

**'FOREIGN'**
specifies that a column is linked to a column in another SAS table. A foreign key column can contain only a null value or a value that is present in the associated primary key column.

**'NOT-NULL'**
specifies that column values cannot contain missing values.

**'PRIMARY'**
specifies that column values must be unique and that they cannot be missing values. If there is an associated foreign key column, then primary key values cannot be deleted or changed unless the same deletions or changes have been made in values of that foreign key column.

**'UNIQUE'** | **'DISTINCT'**
specifies that column values must be unique. If more than one column is specified, then their concatenated values must be unique.
Type: Character

*icvalue*
specifies the names of one or more columns from the SAS table to which the constraint is applied. Separate multiple column names with blanks. If *ictype* is **CHECK**, then *icvalue* can contain a condition that values must meet.
Type: Character

*argument-1,...,argument-3*
are additional specifications that are used when *ictype* is **FOREIGN**.

*argument-1*
is the name of the SAS table in which one or more associated primary keys are defined. This links the two SAS tables and creates the primary/foreign key relationship. Use *libref.member* to specify the SAS table. This argument is required for foreign keys.

*argument-2*
is the restriction option for update operations on values in foreign key columns:

**'RESTRICT'**
allows the primary key value to be updated only if no foreign key matches the current value to be updated.

**'NULL'**
specifies that when the primary key value is modified, all matching foreign key values are set to NULL.

*argument-3*
is the restriction option for delete operations in foreign key columns:

**'RESTRICT'**
allows the primary key row to be deleted only if no foreign key values match the deleted value.

**'NULL'**
allows the primary key row to be deleted and sets the values of corresponding foreign keys to null.
Type: Character

**Details**     ICCREATE defines integrity constraints for a SAS table that has been opened in an SCL program. Integrity constraints guarantee the correctness and consistency of data that is stored in a SAS table. Integrity constraints are enforced automatically for each addition, update, or deletion of data in a table that contains a constraint.

You can define integrity constraints for SAS tables that contain zero or more rows. For tables that already contain data, an integrity constraint is compared to values in all table rows. If a single row does not comply with the constraint being defined, then the creation of the constraint fails. When rows are added to tables that have integrity constraints, the new rows are checked against the constraints. If a row violates an integrity constraint, the row is not added to the table. Also, a primary key column cannot be dropped until all foreign key columns that reference the primary key are deleted.

The basic types of integrity constraints are general constraints and referential constraints. The general constraints, which control values in a single SAS table, are CHECK, NOT-NULL, PRIMARY key, and UNIQUE. Referential constraints, which establish a parent-child relationship between columns in two SAS tables, include FOREIGN keys and PRIMARY keys that have one or more FOREIGN key references. A FOREIGN key column (the child) can contain only null values or values that are present in its associated PRIMARY key (the parent). Values for a FOREIGN key cannot be added unless the same values also exist in the associated PRIMARY key.

For more information about integrity constraints, see "Preserving the Integrity of Data" on page 177.

## Example

This example creates integrity constraints for the SAS tables MYLIB.ONE and MYLIB.TWO. Although they contain different data, they have one column with shared data, an identifier number that is stored in IDNUM in MYLIB.ONE and in EMPID in MYLIB.TWO. The following *icname*s are used in the example:

UQ
: is a UNIQUE constraint which specifies that the concatenated values of columns D and E must be unique.

WH
: is a CHECK constraint which specifies that the sum of the values of columns B and C must be less than 1000.

PK
: is a PRIMARY constraint which specifies that the IDNUM column can contain only unique and non-missing values. Because IDNUM is associated with the foreign key column EMPID in the table MYLIB.TWO, values for IDNUM cannot be deleted or changed unless the same changes have been made to the values in the foreign key EMPID.

FK
: is a foreign key in the table MYLIB.TWO. EMPID is the foreign key column whose primary key is IDNUM in MYLIB.ONE. Because EMPID is a foreign key column, it can contain only values that are present in IDNUM. The first **RESTRICT** specifies that a value in IDNUM can be changed only if EMPID does not contain a value that matches the IDNUM value to be changed. The second **RESTRICT** specifies that a row can be deleted from MYLIB.ONE only if the value of IDNUM does not match a value in EMPID in MYLIB.TWO.

NONULL
: is a NOT-NULL constraint which specifies that the EMPID column cannot contain a null value.

```
table1=open('mylib.one','V');
rc=iccreate(table1,'uq','Unique','d e');
rc=iccreate(table1,'wh','Check','(b + c)< 1000');
rc=iccreate(table1,'pk','Primary','idnum');
rc=close(table1);

table2=open('mylib.two','V');
rc=iccreate(table2,'fk','Foreign','empid',
    'mylib.one','restrict','restrict');
```

```
rc=iccreate(table2,'nonull','Not-null','empid');
    ...more SCL statements...
rc=close(table2);
```

## See Also

"ICDELETE" on page 463

"ICTYPE" on page 466

"ICVALUE" on page 467

---

# ICDELETE

### Drops an integrity constraint from a SAS table

**Category:**  SAS Table

---

## Syntax

*sysrc=***ICDELETE**(*table-id,icname*);

**sysrc**
   contains the status of the operation:

| | |
|---|---|
| =0 | successful |
| >0 | not successful |
| <0 | the operation was completed with a warning |

   Type: Numeric

**table-id**
   contains the identifier for the SAS table, which is returned by the OPEN function.
   An integrity constraint can be dropped only from a SAS table that is open in NEW or
   UTILITY mode.
   Type: Numeric

**icname**
   is the name of the integrity constraint to delete.
   Type: Character

**Details**    Referential integrity constraints (where *ictype* is **FOREIGN**) provide a link
between SAS tables. Part of the link mechanism involves the name of the table.
Therefore, renaming or deleting a table that has a FOREIGN integrity constraint is not
allowed until after the FOREIGN key is deleted.

## Example

Delete the integrity constraint UQ from the table MYLIB.ONE. The constraint was
created in "Example" on page 462.

```
table1=open('mylib.one','V');
rc=icdelete(table1,'uq');
rc=close(table1);
```

## See Also

"ICCREATE" on page 460

"ICTYPE" on page 466

"ICVALUE" on page 467

# ICON

**Associates an icon with a window**

**Category:**   Window

## Syntax

*rc*=**ICON**(*icon-number*);

**rc**
   contains the return code for the operation:

   0                        successful

   ≠0                       not successful
      Type: Numeric

***icon-number***
   is the number of the icon to use to represent the application window when it is
   minimized. If you specify a number for which no icon is defined, the SAS icon is used.
      Type: Numeric

**Details**    When a user minimizes a window into an icon, SAS uses the specified icon to
represent the window.
   Only systems that display icons support this function. Non-graphical devices ignore
the icon setting.
   The ICON function is ignored if you are running with the SAS software Application
Work Space (AWS). To run an application without the AWS, specify the AWS=NO option
in the AF command.

## Example

Assign icon number 107 as the icon for the current window:

```
rc=icon(107);
```

# ICREATE

**Creates an index for a SAS table**

**Category:**   SAS Table

## Syntax

*sysrc*=**ICREATE**(*table-id,key-name<,var-list<,options>>*);

**sysrc**
> contains the return code for the operation:

> 0                           successful

> ≠0                         not successful
>> Type: Numeric

**table-id**
> is the identifier that was assigned when the table was opened. If *table-id* is invalid or if the table is not opened in UTILITY mode, the index is not created and the function returns a nonzero value.
>> Type: Numeric

**key-name**
> is the name of the index key to be created.
>> Type: Character

**var-list**
> is one or more columns from the SAS table to be indexed. Separate multiple names with blanks.
>> Type: Character

**options**
> are index attributes, with multiple values separated by blanks within a single set of parentheses:

> `'NONUNIQUE'` | `'UNIQUE'`
>> specifies whether the values of the key columns must be unique. The default is `'NONUNIQUE'`.

> `'MISSING'` | `'NOMISS'`
>> specifies whether the index can point to missing values. The default is `'MISSING'`.
>> Type: Character

**Details**    An *index* is an auxiliary data structure used to speed up searches for records that are specified by the value of a column (for example, "all the records for which AGE is greater than 65"). To create an index for a SAS table, you must open the table in UTILITY mode (see "OPEN" on page 576 for details).

An index on a single column is called a *simple index*. If *var-list* contains only one column name, then a simple index is created.

*Note:*  For a simple index, *key-name* and *var-list* must both contain the same value. If *var-list* is omitted, then *key-name* specifies the index column. △

An index on more than one column is called a *composite index*. If *var-list* contains more than one column name, a composite index is created. In this case, *key-name* can be any valid SAS name that is not already used as a column name in the table. A composite index is based on the values of these columns, concatenated to form a single value.

UNIQUE specifies that the index contains only unique values of the key columns. The creation of such an index prohibits duplicate values for its columns from being stored in the SAS table. For columns that must be uniquely specified in a row, such as passport numbers, this option is useful for preventing duplicate values from incorrectly getting into a table. The function returns an error condition if non-unique values are present and UNIQUE is specified. By default, duplicate values are permitted in an index and thus in its table.

NOMISS prevents missing values from being pointed to by an index. Unlike UNIQUE, NOMISS does not prevent missing values from being stored in the SAS table. This feature is useful if the key columns contain many missing values that would make the index large and thus slower to access than if they were excluded. By default, missing values are stored in the index.

Indexes can also be created using

☐ the DATASETS and SQL procedures in base SAS software

☐ SAS/IML software

☐ the CONTENTS function in SCL

☐ the ACCESS procedure in SAS/ACCESS software.

## Example

Create a simple index for the SAS table WORK.INVOICE. The key column for the index is the table column ITEMTYPE.

```
tableid=open('work.invoice','v');
    /* open in UTILITY mode */
rc=icreate(tableid,'itemtype',' ','unique nomiss');
```

In this example, because the value of the *var-list* argument is blank, the key column for the index is the column named in the *key-name* argument.

## See Also

"CONTENTS" on page 299

"IDELETE" on page 468

"IOPTION" on page 490

"ISINDEX" on page 494

"IVARLIST" on page 498

"OPEN" on page 576

# ICTYPE

**Returns the type of integrity constraint that is assigned to a SAS table**

**Category:** SAS Table

## Syntax

*ictype*=**ICTYPE**(*table-id*,*icname*);

*ictype*
> contains the type of integrity constraint that is returned. The constraints are listed below and are defined in "ICCREATE" on page 460:
>> `'CHECK'`
>>
>> `'FOREIGN'`
>>
>> `'NOT-NULL'`
>>
>> `'PRIMARY'`
>>
>> `'UNIQUE'`
>
> Type: Character

*table-id*
> contains the identifier for the SAS table, which is returned by the OPEN function.
> Type: Numeric

*icname*
> is the name of the integrity constraint.
> Type: Character

**Details**    ICTYPE returns the type of integrity constraint for a SAS table when you specify the name of the constraint.

## Example

Return the type of the UQ integrity constraint that is assigned to the SAS table MYLIB.ONE. Because the constraint UQ (which was created in "ICCREATE" on page 460 )was UNIQUE, the value of TYPE will be **UNIQUE**.

```
tableid=open('mylib.one','i');
type=ictype(tableid,'uq');
   ...more SCL statements...
rc=close(tableid);
```

## See Also

"ICCREATE" on page 460

"ICDELETE" on page 463

"ICVALUE" on page 467

# ICVALUE

**Returns the column names or the condition associated with an integrity constraint**

**Category:**  SAS Table

## Syntax

*icvalue*=**ICVALUE**(*table-id,icname*);

*icvalue*
> contains the names of one or more columns from the SAS table identified by *table-id*.
> When *ictype* is **CHECK**, *icvalue* returns the condition that values must meet.
> Type: Character

***table-id***
contains the identifier for the SAS table, which is returned by the OPEN function.
Type: Numeric

***icname***
is the name of the integrity constraint.
Type: Character

**Details** ICVALUE returns the names of columns that are associated with the specified integrity constraint. If *ictype* is **CHECK** and is specified as a condition, then ICVALUE returns the condition that is assigned to the constraint.

## Example

Return the value of the UQ integrity constraint. If ICVALUE returns a blank, then display the error message. Because the constraint UQ (which was created in "ICCREATE" on page 460 )specified that columns D and E must contain unique values, COLLIST would contain **D E**.

```
tableid=open('mylib.one','i');
collist=icvalue(tableid,'uq');
if (collist=' ') then _msg_=sysmsg();
```

## See Also

"ICCREATE" on page 460

"ICDELETE" on page 463

"ICTYPE" on page 466

# IDELETE

**Deletes an index from a SAS table**

**Category:** SAS Table

## Syntax

*sysrc=***IDELETE**(*table-id,key-name*);

***sysrc***
contains the return code for the operation:

| | |
|---|---|
| 0 | successful |
| ≠0 | not successful |

Type: Numeric

***table-id***
is the identifier that was assigned when the table was opened. If *table-id* is invalid, the program halts.
Type: Numeric

*key-name*
> is the name of the index key to be deleted.
> Type: Character

**Details**    In order to delete an index for a SAS table, you must open the table in UTILITY mode (see "OPEN" on page 576 for details).
> You can also delete indexes using

- the DATASETS and SQL procedures in base SAS software
- the CONTENTS function in SCL
- the ACCESS procedure in SAS/ACCESS software.

## Example

Delete an index for the SAS table WORK.INVOICE. The name of the index key is ITEMTYPE.

```
tableid=open('work.invoice','v');
rc=idelete(tableid,'itemtype');
```

## See Also

"CONTENTS" on page 299

"ICREATE" on page 464

"IOPTION" on page 490

"ISINDEX" on page 494

"IVARLIST" on page 498

# IMGCTRL

**Performs control operations on the Image window**

**Category:**  Image

## Syntax

*rc*=**IMGCTRL**(*task-id,command,< other-arguments>*);

*rc*
> contains the return code for the operation:

| | |
|---|---|
| 0 | successful |
| >0 | not successful |

> Type: Numeric

*task-id*
> contains the identifier of the image task, which is returned by a previous IMGINIT function.
> Type: Numeric

***command***
> is the control command to be executed. Commands are described in "Commands Used with IMGCTRL" on page 470.
> Type: Character

***other-arguments***
> lists the argument(s) required with each command.
> Type: Character or Numeric

## Commands Used with IMGCTRL

**`'WAIT'`** *seconds*
> specifies the amount of time to wait before executing the next command. *Seconds* specifies the number of seconds to wait.

**`'WRAISE'`**
> attempts to force the Image window to the top while IMGOP or IMGCTRL commands are executing. This command may not be honored by some window managers. Note that the 'TOPWINDOW' option can be set at IMGINIT time to force the window to always be on top.

**`'WSIZE'`** *width, height <xpos, ypos>*
> specifies the width and height of the Image window in pixels. It optionally positions the window at *xpos* and *ypos* of the top left corner. Some window managers may not support positioning.

**`'WTITLE'`** *title*
> specifies a title for the Image window. The specified title appears in parentheses after 'SAS: IMAGE'.

**Details**  IMGCTRL enables you to control the Image window. It includes, for example, commands to assign a window title and set the window size.

## Examples

**Example 1: Using the WTITLE Command**  Extract the name of the IMAGE entry and then use the WTITLE command to assign that name to the window:

```
path=lnamemk(5,catname,'format=cat');
rc=lnameget(path,type,name,form);
gname=scan(name,3,'.');
rc=imgop(taskid,'READ',path);
rc=imgctrl(taskid,'WTITLE',gname);
rc=imgop(taskid,'PASTE',1,1);
```

**Example 2: Using the WAIT Command**  Wait 5 seconds before displaying the image after each PASTE command:

```
rc=imgop(taskid,'READ',path);
rc=imgop(taskid,'PASTE');
rc=imgctrl(taskid,'WAIT',5);
rc=imgop(taskid,'READ',path2);
rc=imgop(taskid,'PASTE');
rc=imgctrl(taskid,'WAIT',5);
```

**Example 3: Using the WRAISE Command**  Force the Image window to the top:

```
pop:
   rc=imgctrl(taskid,'WRAISE');
```

```
    return;
```

### Example 4: Using the WSIZE Command    Make the Image window match the size of the
image that is being displayed:

```
height=0;
width=0;
rc=imgop(taskid,'READ',path);
rc=imgop(taskid,'QUERYN','WIDTH',iwidth);
rc=imgop(taskid,'QUERYN','HEIGHT',iheight);
rc=imgctrl(taskid,'WSIZE',iwidth,iheight);
rc=imgop(taskid,'PASTE',1,1);
```

### Example 5: Using the WTITLE and WRAISE Commands    Change the window title and
then force the Image window to the top:

```
path=lnamemk(5,catname,'format=cat');
rc=lnameget(path,type,name,form);
gname=scan(name,3,'.');
rc=imgop(taskid,'READ',path);
rc=imgctrl(taskid,'WTITLE',gname);
rc=imgop(taskid,'PASTE',1,1);
rc=imgctrl(taskid,'WRAISE');
```

# IMGINIT

**Starts an image task**

**Category:**  Image

## Syntax

*task-id*=**IMGINIT**(< *list-id*>,< *option*>);

**task-id**
> contains the identifier for the image task. This identifier is used by other SCL image
> functions.
>     Type: Numeric

**list-id**
> contains the identifier for an SCL list that contains image operation (IMGOP) and
> image control (IMGCTRL) commands to pass to the function. The commands are
> processed as the task starts. For command descriptions, see "Commands Used with
> IMGCTRL" on page 470 and Appendix 1, "Commands Used with the IMGCTRL,
> IMGOP and PICFILL Functions," on page 735.
>     A value of zero means that no list is passed.
>     Type: Numeric or List

**option**
> specifies a window option:

> **'NODISPLAY'**
> > prevents the Image window from being created. This can be useful in SCL
> > programs that read, process, or write images without displaying them.

**'TOPWINDOW'**
causes the Image window to stay on top of the FRAME or SCL window when it is created.
Type: Character

**Details**    The IMGINIT function initializes the image environment. This usually means opening the Image window, but you must use this function even if you plan to manipulate images without displaying them.

When you initialize the Image window, the list that you pass to IMGINIT can include commands to initialize the window size.

## Example

Initialize the Image window size:

```
width=700;
height=520;
xpos=0;
ypos=0;

cmdid=makelist();
allcmdid=makelist();
rc=insertc(cmdid,'WSIZE',-1);
rc=insertn(cmdid,width,-1);
rc=insertn(cmdid,height,-1);
rc=insertn(cmdid,xpos,-1);
rc=insertn(cmdid,ypos,-1);
rc=insertl(allcmdid,cmdid,-1);

taskid=imginit(allcmdid,'TOPWINDOW');
```

Start the image task without displaying the Image window:

```
taskid=imginit(allcmdid,'nodisplay');
```

# IMGOP

**Performs image operations**

**Category:**   Image

## Syntax

*rc*=**IMGOP**(*task-id*,*command*,<*other arguments*>);

***rc***
contains the return code for the operation:

| | |
|---|---|
| 0 | successful |
| >0 | not successful |

Type: Numeric

***task-id***

contains the identifier (returned by a previous IMGINIT function) of the task to be operated upon.

Type: Numeric

***command***

is the command to execute. Valid commands are listed in "Commands Used with IMGOP" on page 473.

Type: Character

***other-arguments***

lists arguments that are used for a command. The arguments required for a command may include image file attributes. You can specify image file attributes by enclosing the attributes in quotation marks and separating multiple attributes with blanks. For example:

```
rc=imgop(tid,"WRITE",filename,
         "FORMAT=TIFF
         COMPRESS=G3FAX"):
```

Type: Character or Numeric

## Commands Used with IMGOP

For detailed information about these commands, see Appendix 1, "Commands Used with the IMGCTRL, IMGOP and PICFILL Functions," on page 735 .

CONVERT

converts an image to the specified image type and depth.

COPY

copies an image.

CREATE_IMAGE

creates a new image that is stored in memory.

CROP

crops the selected image.

DESTROY

removes an image from memory and from the display.

DESTROY_ALL

removes all images from memory and from the display.

DITHER

dithers an image to a color map.

DITHER_BW

dithers the selected image to a monochrome black and white image.

EXECLIST

executes a list of commands.

FILTER

applies a filter to an image.

GAMMA

applies a gamma value to the selected image.

GENERATE_CMAP

generates a color map for the selected image.

GET_BARCODE
   returns the value of the specified bar code.

GET_COLORS
   returns the RGB values of the index positions of a color map for the selected image.

GET_PIXEL
   returns the pixel value of a specified position in the selected image.

GRAB_CMAP
   grabs the color map from the selected image.

MAP_COLORS
   maps colors to the closest color in the selected color map.

MIRROR
   mirrors an image.

NEGATE
   changes the image to a negative.

PASTE
   displays an image at a specified location.

PASTE_AUTO
   displays an image automatically.

PRINT
   prints an image.

QUANTIZE
   reduces the number of colors used for an image.

QUERYC, QUERYL, and QUERYN
   query information about images.

READ
   reads an image from an external file, a SAS catalog, or a device.

READ_CLIPBOARD
   reads an image from the host clipboard.

READ_PASTE
   reads and displays an image.

READ_PASTE_AUTO
   reads and automatically displays an image.

ROTATE
   rotates an image clockwise by 90, 180, or 270 degrees.

SCALE
   scales an image.

SELECT
   selects the image identifier to be used in other commands.

SET_COLORS
   assigns the RGB values for the index positions of a color map for the current image.

SET_PIXEL
   assigns the pixel value in an image at the specified position.

STANDARD_CMAP
   selects a color map.

THRESHOLD
:   converts color images to black and white, using the value that is specified with the THRESHOLD command.

TILE
:   replicates the current image into a new image.

UNPASTE
:   removes an image from the display.

WRITE
:   writes an image to a file or to a SAS catalog.

WRITE_CLIPBOARD
:   writes an image to the host clipboard.

# IMGTERM

**Terminates an image task**

**Category:** Image

## Syntax

*rc*=**IMGTERM**(*task-id*);

*rc*
:   contains the return code for the operation:

    | | |
    |---|---|
    | 0 | successful |
    | >0 | not successful |

    Type: Numeric

*task-id*
:   contains the identifier of the task, which was returned by a previous IMGINIT function.
    Type: Numeric

## Example

This example shows IMGTERM used within the TERM section:

```
term:
   if (task-id ne 0) then
      rc=imgterm(task-id);
return;
```

# IMPORT

**Creates a SAS table from an external file**

**Category:**   SAS Table

---

## Syntax

*name*=**IMPORT**(*table-name,file*<,'DEFINE'>);

**name**
> contains the name of the last SAS table that was created.
>> Type: Character

**table-name**
> is the new SAS table to create. If the table already exists, a warning message is displayed when the IMPORT window opens.
>> Type: Character

**file**
> is the fileref or physical filename of the external file from which data are to be imported. A physical filename must be enclosed in quotation marks. (See the example.)
>> Type: Character

**'DEFINE'**
> specifies to open the DEFINE window before opening the IMPORT window.
>> Type: Character

## Details

*CAUTION:*
> **Blank lines in files can cause problems.** Under some host operating systems, blank lines in an external file may adversely affect the ability of the IMPORT function to extract data from the file. △

The IMPORT function returns the name of the last SAS table that it created from an external data file. This function enables users to easily import raw data from an external file into a SAS table.

Two auxiliary windows are associated with IMPORT: the IMPORT window and the DEFINE window.

**The IMPORT Window**    The IMPORT window, which defines the columns for the SAS table, is the primary window for the IMPORT function. The first two lines of the external file are displayed below a ruler in order to help the application user identify the variables for the columns.

If numbers for start and end columns are not supplied, then list input is used, and items in the file must be separated by at least one blank. Users can use the following fields in the IMPORT window to specify information about the table columns:

Name
> specifies the name for the table column. This can be any valid SAS name that is up to 32 characters long.

Start/End Column
> specify the starting and ending columns of the value in the external file. These fields are optional. You can specify a starting column without specifying an ending column but not vice versa. If you omit the ending column, it is calculated to be one less than the next starting column.

Type
> specifies the data type of the table column. Choose the type by pressing ENTER or clicking with the mouse on the appropriate type.

Format
> specifies a SAS format. Enter a '?' to display a list of some common formats. This field is optional.

Informat
> specifies a SAS informat. Enter a '?' to display a list of some common informats. This field is optional.

Label
> specifies a label for the table column. The label can be up to eight characters long. This field is optional.

**IMPORT Window Command Menu**    The File menu enables you to perform save operations, to import data with the Import Wizard, to export data using the Export Wizard, to perform print operations, to send mail, and to close the window.

The Edit menu enables you to copy marked text, to select or deselect marked text, to set the horizontal and vertical scroll amounts, to perform find operations, and to set the keyfield (the field to search with the next Find command).

The View menu enables you to scroll right and left, to specify the sort order for fields in the window, to display the first record in hexadecimal representation, and to open other SAS windows.

The Tools menu enables you to specify conditions for querying values in the file, to open a Viewtable window, and to run a session of graphics editors, the Report Editor or Text Editor. You can also set a variety of options.

The Data menu enables you to create a SAS table from contents of the external file, to test read the file, to define fields with the Define window, to specify a different external file for input, to specify a new name for the SAS table to create, to display the length of the longest record that has been read, to view the external file, and to edit or browse the data set that was created from the external file.

**The DEFINE Window**    The DEFINE window is displayed when you use the DEFINE option with the IMPORT function or when you select

| Data | ► | Define fields |

from the IMPORT window. It displays the first line from the external file, along with a ruler and delimiter lines. On the delimiter lines, you can use < and > to mark the beginning and end of a column, respectively. If the column is only one character wide, use a vertical bar (|).

In order to use the DEFINE window, you must align the data values in columns in the data records.

When you issue the END command to exit from this window, the fields are given default column names and types (numeric or character). The IMPORT window then opens so that you can change the column names and optionally add formats and informats.

## Examples

☐ Create a new SAS table named MYLIB.NEW using data in the file to which the fileref EXTERN has previously been assigned:

```
name=import('mylib.new','extern');
```

☐ Create a new SAS table named MYLIB.NEW using data in the file with the physical name SAMPLE1.DATA. The name of the file is enclosed in quotation marks to indicate that a physical filename, not a fileref, is being passed to the IMPORT function.

```
name=import('mylib.new',"'sample1.data'");
```

*Note:* The form of the physical filename depends on the host operating system. △

# IMPORT

**Defines a search path for references to CLASS entries**

**Category:** Catalog, Object Oriented

## Syntax

**IMPORT** *class-specification*;

*class-specification*
  is the two- to four-level name of a CLASS entry. If it is a four-level name, then that CLASS entry is imported. If it is a two-level name, then it is used as the *libname.catalog* prefix for any one- or two- level CLASS entry names in the program. This prefix is concatenated to the one- or two-level CLASS entry name, and that is the CLASS entry that is searched for. The first CLASS entry that is found is the one that is imported. Any subsequent entries that are found are flagged as warnings.

**Details**    The IMPORT statement defines a search path for CLASS entry references in an SCL program so that you can refer to CLASS entries with one- or two-level names instead of having to use a four-level name in each reference. The current catalog is always the first catalog to be searched for a one- or two-level class name, regardless of whether there are any imported catalogs. References to CLASS entries are resolved by the SCL compiler at compile time. The SEARCH function can be used to define a search path that will resolve at run time.

## Examples

**Example 1: Defining a Search Path**    Define a MYLIB.MYCAT as a search path for the program.

```
    /* All the program's classes  */
    /* are defined in MYLIB.MYCAT *
IMPORT mylib.mycat;
    /* collobj1 is defined in      */
    /* mylib.mycat.collection.class */
DECLARE Collection c1=_new_ Collection();
    /* collobj2 is defined in            */
    /* mylib.mycat.OrderedCollection.class */
DECLARE OrderedCollection c2=_new_ OrderedCollection();
```

**Example 2: Importing a Class from Another Catalog**    This example imports class X from another catalog. Class Y is in the current catalog.

```
X.SCL
class work.cat.x;
  public num n;
endclass;

Y.SCL
import work.cat2;
class y;
  m: method o: x;
    o.n=99;
  endmethod;
endclass;

Z.SCL
init:
  import work.cat2;
  dcl y yobj=_new_ y();
  dcl x xobj=_new_ x();
  yobj.m(xobj);
  put xobj.n=;
return;
```

This example should produce the following output:

```
xobj.n=99
```

### See Also

"DECLARE" on page 330

"SEARCH" on page 635

# INFORMAT

**Verifies that the specified informat is valid**

**Category:** Formatting

## Syntax

*rc=***INFORMAT**(*informat,type*);

***rc***
contains the return code for the operation:

| | |
|---|---|
| 1 | successful |
| 0 | not successful |

  Type: Numeric

***informat***
is an informat that is supplied by SAS or created using the FORMAT procedure. The name of an informat must include a period (for example, **date7**. or **comma10.2**).
  Type: Character

*type*
specifies the type of the informat:

'C'               character

'N'               numeric
Type: Character

**Details**   If the specified informat is not known to the SAS session, then the operation is unsuccessful. The function verifies that valid widths are specified for informats.
See *SAS Language Reference: Dictionary* for details about informats.

## Examples

**Example 1: Verifying the Validity of a Character Informat**   Verify that $MYFMT. is a valid character informat that has been defined for the current SAS session. (The value returned to the variable RC is 1.)

    rc=informat('$myfmt.','c');

**Example 2: Verifying the Validity of a Numeric Informat**   Verify that 5.6 is not a valid informat for numeric values. (The value returned to the variable RC is 0.)

    rc=informat('5.6','n');

## See Also

"FORMAT" on page 424

# INITROW

Initializes the Table Data Vector (TDV) for a SAS table to missing values

Category:   SAS Table

## Syntax

*rc=**INITROW**(table-id);*

*rc*
contains the return code for the operation:

0                 successful

≠0                not successful
Type: Numeric

*table-id*
is the identifier that was assigned when the SAS table was opened.
Type: Numeric

**Details**   INITROW initializes the TDV to missing values. This prevents bad data from being written to a table row when you do not explicitly assign values to columns with the PUTVARC or PUTVARN function and you use the APPEND function with the NOINIT option.

## Example

Open the table whose name is saved in the variable TABLE, initialize a new row to missing, and then write a value for the NAME column. When the new row is appended to the data table, the column NAME is initialized to the value JOHN while values in all other columns are set to missing.

```
tableid=open(table);
rc=initrow(tableid);
call putvarc(tableid,varnum(tableid,'name'),'JOHN');
rc=append(tableid,'noinit');
rc=close(tableid);
```

# INPUTC and INPUTN

### Read a character value using an informat

**Category:** Formatting

## Syntax

*char-value*=**INPUTC**(*char-string,char-informat*);

*num-value*=**INPUTN**(*char-string,num-informat*);

**char-value**
> contains *char-string* with the character informat applied to it.
> Type: Character

**num-value**
> contains *char-string* converted to a numeric value with the numeric informat applied to it.
> Type: Numeric

**char-string**
> is the character string to be read.
> Type: Character

**char-informat**
> is the character informat to use for reading *char-string*.
> Type: Character

**num-informat**
> is the numeric informat to use for reading *char-string*.
> Type: Numeric

**Details**    INPUTC and INPUTN both read a character value. However, INPUTC applies a character informat and returns a character value, and INPUTN applies a numeric informat and returns a numeric value. These functions are similar to the INPUT function in the DATA step.

*Note:*  Dot notation cannot be used with the INPUTC or INPUTN functions. This restriction is necessary to allow proper parsing of the *char-informat* and *num-informat* parameters. △

For more information about using an informat to read a value, see the INPUT function for the DATA step in *SAS Language Reference: Dictionary*.

## Examples

### Example 1: Using the INPUTC Function
Read the character variable NAME, using the $UPCASE3. informat:

```
name='sas';
cval=inputc(name,'$upcase3.');
put cval=;
```

This program produces the following output:

```
cval=SAS
```

### Example 2: Using the INPUTN Function
Read the character variable AMOUNT, containing the value $20,000.00, into the numeric variable SALARY, using the COMMA10.2 informat:

```
amount='$20,000.00';
informat='comma10.2';
salary=inputn(amount,informat);
put salary=;
```

This program produces the following output:

```
salary=20000
```

### Example 3: Using INPUTN with a DATE Value
Read the value in DATE and apply the JULIAN8. informat:

```
date='90091';
ndate=inputn(date,'julian8.');
put ndate=;
```

This program produces the following output:

```
ndate=11048
```

### See Also

"PUTC and PUTN" on page 605

---

# INSERTC, INSERTL, INSERTN, and INSERTO

**Insert a value into an SCL list**

**Category:** List

---

## Syntax

*rc*=**INSERTC**(*list-id,cval<,index<,name>>*);

*rc*=**INSERTL**(*list-id,sublist-id<,index< name>>*);

*rc*=**INSERTN**(*list-id,nval<,index< name>>*);

*rc*=**INSERTO**(*list-id,object-id< ,index< name>>*);

**rc**
> is the *list-id*, which is the identifier of the modified list.
> Type: Numeric

**list-id**
> is the identifier of the list into which to insert the item. An invalid *list-id* produces an error condition.
> Type: Numeric or List

**cval**
> is the character value to insert into the list with INSERTC.
> Type: Character

**sublist-id**
> is the identifier of the sublist to insert into the list with INSERTL. An invalid *sublist-id* produces an error condition.
> Type: Numeric

**nval**
> is the numeric value to insert into the list with INSERTN.
> Type: Numeric

**object-id**
> is the identifier of the object to insert into the list with INSERTO. An invalid *object-id* produces an error condition.
> Type: Numeric or Object

**index**
> is the position at which to insert the item into the list. The position can be specified as a positive or negative number. By default, *index* is 1 (the first item). If *index* is a positive number, then the item is at position *index* from the beginning of the list. If *index* is a negative number, then the item is at position ABS(*index*) from the end of the list. *Index* must be in the range [−(*n*+1),−1] or [1,*n*+1] where *n* is the length of the list. An error condition results if the absolute value for *index* is zero or if it is greater than the number of items in the list.
> Type: Numeric

**name**
> is the name to assign to the item. If *name* is omitted, a name is not assigned to the item.
> Type: Character

**Details**    The item is inserted such that after you insert an item at position *index*, you can retrieve it from position *index* with any of these functions.

These functions do not make a copy of the list. The insertion is performed in place. You can append an item to an SCL list of length *n* by inserting at *index*=n+1 or at *index*=−1.

*Note:*   The return value of these functions is not used to indicate whether an error has been detected. When an error occurs, the program simply halts. △

An error condition results if

☐ the list has any of the following attributes:

    ☐ NOUPDATE

    ☐ FIXEDLENGTH

        □ CHARONLY, and you use an insert function other than INSERTC
        □ NUMONLY, and you use an insert function other than INSERTN
        □ SASNAMES, and *name* is omitted or is not a valid SAS name
        □ NODUPNAMES, and *name* duplicates the name of a list item.
    □ the absolute value for *index* is greater than 1 plus the number of items in the list or is 0.
    □ you attempt to insert a local list into a global list with INSERTL.

You can use HASATTR to check the attributes of a list or list item. To change attributes, use SETLATTR.

## Examples

**Example 1: Using the INSERTC Function**   Insert **CANADA** as the third item in the list:

```
listid=insertc(listid,'CANADA',3);
```

After this insertion, return the value that was third in the list before the insertion of **CANADA** shifted the value from the third to the fourth position:

```
cval=getitemc(listid,4);
```

**Example 2: Using the INSERTL Function**   Insert the sublist NEWLIST as the third item from the end of the list:

```
listid=insertl(listid,newlist,-3);
```

**Example 3: Using the INSERTN Function**   Assume that the list MYLIST contains four items, named **A**, **B**, **C**, and **D**, with the values 1, 4, 9, and 16, respectively. Insert two new items: a string at the default position 1 (the beginning of the list), and a number at position –1 (the end of the list). The new number is given the name **E**.

```
call putlist(mylist,'Before: ',0);
mylist=insertc(mylist,'Squares');
mylist=insertn(mylist,25, -1,'E');
call putlist(mylist,'After: ',0);
```

This program produces the following output:

```
Before: (A=1
         B=4
         C=9
         D=16
         )[3]
After: ('Squares'
        A=1
        B=4
        C=9
        D=16
        E=25
        )[3]
```

*Note:* [3] is the list identifier that was assigned when this example was run and may be different each time the example is run. △

**Example 4: Using the INSERTO Function**   Create the list MYLIST, insert the item whose identifier is stored in the variable MYOBJECT, and assign the name **My Object** to the item:

```
declare sashelp.fsp.object myobject, =_new_ sashelp.fsp.object(),
         list mylist;
mylist=makelist();
rc=inserto(mylist,myobj,-1,'My Object');
```

## See Also

"GETITEMC, GETITEML, GETITEMN, and GETITEMO" on page 442

"GETNITEMC, GETNITEML, GETNITEMN, and GETNITEMO" on page 445

"POPC, POPL, POPN, and POPO" on page 593

"SETITEMC, SETITEML, SETITEMN, and SETITEMO" on page 651

"SETNITEMC, SETNITEML, SETNITEMN, and SETNITEMO" on page 661

# INSTANCE

**Creates an object and returns its identifier**

**Category:**   Object Oriented

## Syntax

*object-id*=**INSTANCE**(*class-id*<,*arg*>);

### object-id
contains the identifier that was assigned to the new object.
   Type: Numeric or Object

### class-id
is the identifier for the class, which is returned by the LOADCLASS function.
   Type: Numeric

### arg
is an argument to pass to the _init method.
   Type: Numeric

**Details**    When creating an object (or instance) of a class, INSTANCE sends the _init method for the specified class to the new instance and passes *arg* as an argument to the _init method. If *arg* is not specified, then no argument is passed to the _init method. To indicate that the numeric parameter is optional, the _init method of all classes should use the OPTIONAL= option in the METHOD statement or ENTRY statement.

A common practice is to use an SCL list as *arg*. You can then pass an arbitrary list of data which will be accessible in the _init method.

To delete an object that was created with INSTANCE, use its _term method. For example:

```
dcl object objectid;
objectid=instance(classid);
objectid._term();
```

You cannot use the INSTANCE function to create instances of the Frame class.

For more information about classes and methods, see the documentation for SAS/AF classes.

## Example

Load a class named Queue, a subclass of the Object class, and create two instances of the Queue class. The Inqueue class is created with a maximum number of items. The Outqueue class does not have a maximum.

```
queue=loadclass('applib.classes.queue');
inqueue=instance(queue, max_items);
outqueue=instance(queue);
```

Assume that the _init method of the Queue class is declared as

```
_init: method optional= maxItems 8;
    ...more SCL statements...
endmethod;
```

## See Also

"APPLY" on page 252

"ENTRY" on page 369

"LOADCLASS" on page 525

"LOADRES" on page 526

"METHOD" on page 540

"_NEO_" on page 559

"NOTIFY" on page 572

"SEND" on page 644

"SUPAPPLY" on page 679

"SUPER" on page 681

# INTERFACE

**Defines a group of abstract methods shared by the related classes**

**Category:**   Object Oriented

## Syntax

**INTERFACE** *interface-name*
    <EXTENDS *interface-name*>
    </ (*interface-optional-clause*)>;
    <(*limited-method-declaration-statements*)>

**ENDINTERFACE**;

*interface-name*
    is the name of the interface that you are defining, which can be specified as a one- to four-level name. The entry type is INTERFACE.

**EXTENDS**-*interface-name*
>specifies the parent interfaces as a one- to four-level name. An interface can inherit from parent interfaces. If you do not use the EXTENDS clause, the *parent-interface* defaults to SAS HELP.FSP.INTERFACE.CLASS.

*interface-optional-clause*
>specifies options for the interface. You must put the list inside the parentheses that follow a / (slash). Separate multiple options with commas. The only option currently supported is

Description = *description*
>is a description of the INTERFACE entry.

*limited-method-declaration-statements*
>defines the interface methods. Declare the methods as follows:

>```
>method-label-name: METHOD <argument-list><OPTIONAL=argument-list>
></(method-options)>;
>```

>*method-label-name*
>>can be up to 32 characters and has the same restrictions as an SCL label.

>*argument-list*
>>list one or more sets of arguments, with each set specified as follows:

>>```
>>var-list <:INPUT|UPDATE|OUTPUT>:data-type(length)
>>```

>>*var-list*
>>>lists one or more variables to contain values that are passed in from a method call using either dot notation or the METHOD, SEND, SUPER, APPLY or SUPAPPLY routine or function. Variables can also be reference arrays. Reference array dimensions are specified by '*'. Use commas to separate '*' for multiple dimensions. The actual size of the reference array will be determined at run time based on the dimensions specified in the array parameter of the calling method. For more information, see "ARRAY" on page 254 and Example 3 on page 546.

>>**INPUT** | **I**
>>>specifies that, at run time, the variable contains the value that is copied from the corresponding parameter of the calling method. However, when the program finishes, the value is not copied back to the calling method.

>>**UPDATE** | **U**
>>>specifies that, at run time, the variable contains the value that is copied from the corresponding parameter of the calling method. When the program finishes, the value is copied back to that parameter.

>>**OUTPUT** | **O**
>>>specifies that, when the program finishes, the value is copied back to the corresponding parameter in the calling program. An error condition results if the corresponding parameter in the calling program is a constant, because a constant cannot receive a value.

>>*data-type*
>>>specifies the type of data that the variable will contain. A named data type (for example, CHAR or LIST) must be preceded by the : delimiter. The delimiter is optional for unnamed data types (for example, $).

**CHAR**<(*length*)>

specifies that the variable will contain character data. *Length* can be 1 to 32,767 characters. If *length* is not provided, the default length is 200.

**LIST**

specifies that the variable will contain an SCL list identifier.

**NUM**

specifies that the variable will contain a numeric value.

**OBJECT**

specifies that the variable will contain the identifier for an object when it is defined at run time.

This type causes the SCL compiler to generate extra conversion instructions. Consequently, you should use it only when necessary so as to achieve optimal run-time performance.

*class-name*

specifies that the variable will contain the identifier for an object of the class specified in *class-name*. *Class-name* must be a three- or four-level name unless an IMPORT statement has specified the libref and catalog. In that case, the name can be a one- to four-level name. If the entry type is not specified, it is assumed to be CLASS.

*interface-name*

specifies that the variable will contain the identifier for an object of the class that supports the interface specified in *interface-name*. *Interface-name* must be a three– or four-level name unless an IMPORT statement has been used to specify the libref and catalog. In that case, the name can be a one- to four-level name.

If the entry type is not specified and a class with that name does not exist, the default entry type of INTERFACE is assumed.

To be compatible with the applications built in earlier releases of SAS software, the **:** delimiter is optional for variables that have been declared with unnamed data types (for example, $), but it is required for variables that have been assigned named data types. The following example shows a variety of data type declarations, including reference arrays that use * as the dimensions:

```
mymethod: method
  char1  : Char(20)
    char2  : Char(10)
    char3  :input :char(50)
    charArr(*):u:char /* a reference array */
    num1   : num
    num2   : num
    num3   : num
    numArr(*):num      /* a reference array */
    myList :list
    myObj  :object
    myCol :Sashelp.Fsp.Collection.class ;
```

Type: Character

*length*

is a numeric constant that specifies the length of the preceding variable or variables. The length of a character variable does not have to match the length of the corresponding passed parameter. SCL pads or truncates as necessary. When a

length is specified for a variable that is declared as CHAR, the length specification must be enclosed in parentheses.
Type: Character

**OPTIONAL=**

enables you to specify one or more optional arguments that are used only if the calling program supplies the corresponding parameters in the parameter list of the calling routine. If corresponding parameters are not supplied, then the optional arguments are initialized to missing values.

*method-options*

specify options for an interface method. You must put the list inside parentheses that follow a / (slash). The only option currently supported is Description = *description*, which may be used to provide a description of the method.

**Details**    In order to group related classes which share similar method names, a superclass can be created. One approach to create the superclass is to use the INTERFACE block. You can use the INTERFACE and ENDINTERFACE statements to create an INTERFACE block that contains method definitions. Method implementations are not allowed in the INTERFACE block, so all methods are defined as abstract methods.

Interfaces describe "contracts" in a pure, abstract form, but an interface is interesting only if a class supports it. Any class that supports an interface must implement all of the methods defined in the interface. Since the INTERFACE block does not contain any method implementations, class developers can use the INTERFACE block to reflect the high- level design of their applications. Any class can also be specified with the "required" interface using the "Required-Clause". The SCL compiler will generate information that will be used to validate whether the actual method used at run time matches the required interface.

To create an interface from an SCL entry that contains an INTERFACE block, you must issue either the SAVECLASS command or from FILE menu Save Class Pmenu. This compiles the entry and creates the INTERFACE entry that is specified by *interface-name*. This is equivalent to using the Interface Editor to interactively create an INTERFACE entry. However, the Interface Editor provides a tabular view of the interface, whereas the INTERFACE statement in SCL provides a language view of the interface. For maintenance purposes, the existing INTERFACE entry can also be converted to SCL syntax by using the CreateSCL function. For more detailed information, please refer to the CREATESCL"CREATESCL" on page 316 function.

## Examples

**Example 1: Defining a Simple Interface**    The following INTERFACE block defines a simple myWidget interface with four GUI methods.

```
interface work.a.myWidget.interface;
    refresh: method;
    needRefresh: method;
    select: method;
    tab: method n1:NUM n2:NUM;
endinterface;
```

The following INTERFACE block defines an I/O interface with two I/O methods.

```
interface work.a.myIO.
interface;
  read: method string buffer;
  write: method string buffer;
```

```
endinterface;
```

**Example 2: Defining Classes That Support Interfaces**   The INTERFACE blocks cannot contain method implementations, so any class that supports an interface must implement all of the methods defined in the interface. The following class implements methods that are defined in **work.a.myIO.interface:**

```
class work.a.model.class supports work.a.myIO.interface;
  read: method string buffer
         / (scl='work.a.model.scl');
  write: method string buffer
         / (scl='work.a.model.scl');
  /* The following method is not in the interface */
  myMethod: method n:Num
         / (scl='work.a.myscl.scl');
endclass;
```

The following class supports both the myWidget interface and the myIO interface.

```
class work.a.modelViewer.class
      supports work.a.myWidget.interface,
               work.a.myIO.interface;
  refresh: method / (scl='work.a.mv.scl');
  needRefresh: method / (scl='work.a.mv.scl');
  select: method / (scl='work.a.mv.scl');
  tab: method n1:NUM n2:NUM
         / (scl='work.a.mv.scl');
  read: method string buffer
         / (scl='work.a.model.scl');
  write: method string buffer
         / (scl='work.a.model.scl');
  myMethod: method n: num
         / (scl='work.a.myscl.scl');
endclass;
```

**Example 3: Defining Classes That Require Interfaces**   The following class requires both the myWidget interface and the myIO interface. By specifying which interfaces are required, you allow the SCL compiler to generate information that will be used to validate whether the actual methods used at run time matched the required interface.

```
class work.a.myRequired.class
      Requires work.a.myWidget.interface,
               work.a.myIO.interface;
  ...Other implementations...
endClass;
```

## See Also

"CLASS" on page 277

# IOPTION

**Returns options for index columns and key columns**

**Category:**   SAS Table

## Syntax

*options*=**IOPTION**(*table-id,key-name*);

**options**
> contains options for the specified index *key-name,* separated by a blank:

MISSING
> The index can contain missing values.

NOMISS
> The index does not contain missing values.

NONUNIQUE
> The index can contain non-unique values.

UNIQUE
> The index contains only unique values.
> Type: Character

**table-id**
> is the identifier that was assigned when the table was opened. If *table-id* is invalid, the program halts.
> Type: Numeric

**key-name**
> is the name of an index key.
> Type: Character

**Details** An *index* is an auxiliary data structure used to speed up the selection of records that are specified by the value of a column.
> You can create indexes using

☐ the ICREATE function in SCL

☐ the DATASETS and SQL procedures in base SAS software

☐ SAS/IML software

☐ the CONTENTS function in SCL

☐ the ACCESS procedure in SAS/ACCESS software.

When an error occurs, IOPTION returns a blank string.

## Example

Return the options of the defined key index ITEMTYPE for the SAS table WORK.DATAONE. If the value returned to the OPTIONS column is blank, then the message returned by the SYSMSG function is displayed on the message line.

```
tableid=open('work.invoice','i');
options=ioption(tableid,'itemtype');
if (options=' ') then _msg_=sysmsg();
```

## See Also

---

# ISACTIVE

**Returns the number of the active button in a radio box or check box or the active station in a choice group**

**Category:** Control or Field

---

## Syntax

*station*=**ISACTIVE**(*var-name*<,*row*>);

**station**
contains the status of a selection:

>0                  the number of the button or station that is active

0                    no button or station is active
     Type: Numeric

**var-name**
is the radio or choice group to be tested.
     Type: Character

**row**
is the row number when the button or choice group is in the scrollable section of an extended table in a PROGRAM entry. Do not specify *row* in programs for FRAME entries. Specify *row* only when you want to check the active station from outside the extended table's getrow or putrow section.
     Type: Numeric

**Details**    You cannot use ISACTIVE in FSEDIT or FSVIEW programs.
Window controls can also use the _isActive method.

## Example

Suppose your application has a radio box named HOBBY in which the third button displays the value **TENNIS**. Branch to an appropriate program when a user selects the **TENNIS** station (either by pressing ENTER or by clicking the mouse button).

```
if (isactive('hobby')=3)
then call display('tennis.frame');
```

### See Also

"ACTIVATE" on page 249

"GRAY" on page 457

"ISGRAY" on page 493

"UNGRAY" on page 693

# ISGRAY

**Reports whether a FRAME entry control or choice group is grayed**

**Category:** Control or Field

## Syntax

*rc*=**ISGRAY**(*var-name*< ,*station*< ,*row*>>);

***rc***

contains the return code for the operation:

| | |
|---|---|
| 1 | the specified station is grayed |
| 0 | the specified station is not grayed, or no station in the choice group is grayed |
| *m* | the number of stations that are grayed, when an entire choice group is not grayed |
| −*n* | the total number of stations, when an entire choice group is grayed. |

Type: Numeric

***var-name***

is the window control or choice group to be tested.
Type: Character

***station***

is the number of the choice group station or the button in a radio box. *Station* must be greater than 0 and must be no greater than the total number of buttons in a radio box or the number of stations in a choice group.
Type: Numeric

***row***

is the number of the row when the control or choice group is in the scrollable section of an extended table. *Row* is valid for PROGRAM entries. Specify *row* only when you want to determine whether the station is gray from outside the extended table's getrow or putrow section.
Type: Numeric

**Details**    Window controls can also use the _isGray method.

Because choice groups can be defined only in SAS/AF software, you cannot use ISGRAY in FSEDIT or FSVIEW programs.

## Examples

**Example 1: Determining Whether an Extended Table Row Is Grayed**    Test whether the
choice group WINE at the third row of an extended table is grayed:

```
if (isgray('wine',0,3)) then
      do;
         ...SCL program statements...
      end;
```

**Example 2: Finding the Number of Stations in a Choice Group**    Find out how many
stations are defined for a choice group:

```
rc=gray('wine');
    total=abs(isgray('wine'));
```

## See Also

"ACTIVATE" on page 249

"GRAY" on page 457

"ISACTIVE" on page 492

"UNGRAY" on page 693

# ISINDEX

**Returns the type of index for a SAS table column**

**Category:**   SAS Table

## Syntax

*index=***ISINDEX**(*table-id,col-name*);

***index***
contains the type of the index:

(blank)
No index has been created for the specified column.

BOTH
The column is a member of both simple and composite indexes.

COMP
The column is a member of a composite index.

REG
The column is a regular (simple) index.
Type: Character

***table-id***
is the identifier that was assigned when the table was opened. If *table-id* is invalid,
the program halts.
Type: Numeric

*col-name*
>    is the name of a column in the SAS table. If *col-name* is not a column in the table,
>    then ISINDEX returns a blank value.
>    Type: Character

**Details**    An *index* is an auxiliary data structure used to assist in the location (that is,
selection) of rows that are specified by the value of a column. An index is called a
*simple index* if it contains the value of only one column. A *composite index* merges the
values for more than one column to form a single value. A given SAS table can have
multiple simple indexes, composite indexes, or any combination of these.
>    You can create indexes using

□ the ICREATE function in SCL

□ the DATASETS and SQL procedures in base SAS software

□ SAS/IML software

□ the CONTENTS function in SCL

□ the ACCESS procedure of SAS/ACCESS software.

## Example

Return the type of index for the FNAME column in the SAS table WORK.DATAONE:

```
dsid=open('work.dataone','i');
ixtype=isindex(dsid,'fname');
```

## See Also

"CONTENTS" on page 299

"ICREATE" on page 464

"IDELETE" on page 468

"IOPTION" on page 490

"IVARLIST" on page 498

# ISSEL

**Returns the selection number for a specified row of a selection list**

**Category:**   Extended Table

## Syntax

*selection*=**ISSEL**(*row*);

*selection*
>    contains the row's selection number, or 0 if the row is not selected.
>    Type: Numeric

*row*
>    is the number of the row that is being queried.
>    Type: Numeric

**Details**   You can use the ISSEL function in two ways:

□ to determine the order in which a certain row was selected

□ to determine whether a row is being selected or deselected.

Because you can define extended tables only with SAS/AF software, you cannot use ISSEL in FSEDIT or FSVIEW programs. ISSEL is valid only for PROGRAM entries. Window controls must use the _issel method.

In order for an extended table to be considered a selection list, you must specify a number of selections in the SETROW routine.

## Example

Suppose that your application has a selection list with ten rows and that the user has just selected row 3 and then row 5. If ISSEL is called with the *row* argument equal to 5, then the value 2 is returned for *selection*, because row 5 was the second selection.

You can also use ISSEL in the putrow section of an extended table application to test whether a row is selected. Call the function for the desired row and check the *selection* value to see whether its value is positive (the row has been selected) or zero (the row has been deselected):

```
PUTROW:
   if (issel(_CURROW_)) then
      do;
         ...SCL statements to process the selected row...
      end;
   else
      do;
         ...SCL statements to process the deselected row...
      end;
return;
```

## See Also

"NSELECT" on page 573

"SELECT" on page 640

"SELECTED" on page 642

"UNSELECT" on page 696

# ITEM

**Specifies the classes on the server that can be accessed by applications on the client**

**Category:**   Object Oriented

## Syntax

**ITEM** *class-name*;

**class-name**
> is the name of a class that you want included in the class package that you are defining. The class name is a one- to four-level name of the form *library.catalog.member.*CLASS.

## Details

ITEM statements define the classes on the server whose methods and attributes can be accessed by applications on the client.

## See Also

> "PACKAGE" on page 585

# ITEMTYPE

**Reports the type of an item in an SCL list**

**Category:** List

## Syntax

*type=***ITEMTYPE**(*list-id<,index>*);

**type**
> contains the type of the specified item:

| | |
|---|---|
| C | The item is a character item. |
| N | The item is a numeric item. |
| L | The item is a sublist item. |
| O | The item is a component item. |

> Type: Character

**list-id**
> is the identifier of the list containing the item whose type is returned by ITEMTYPE. An invalid *list-id* produces an error condition.
> Type: Numeric or List

**index**
> is the position of the item in the list. The position can be specified as a positive or negative number. By default, *index* is 1 (the first item). If *index* is a positive number, then the item is at position *index* from the beginning of the list. If *index* is a negative number, then the item is at position ABS(*index*) from the end of the list. An error condition results if the absolute value for *index* is zero or if it is greater than the number of items in the list.
> Type: Numeric

**Details**    An item's type depends on which function was used to create the item:

C (character) items
> are created by SETITEMC, SETNITEMC, INSERTC.

N (numeric) items
> are created by SETITEMN, SETNITEMN, INSERTN, MAKELIST, MAKENLIST.

L (sublist) items
> are created by SETITEML, SETNITEML, INSERTL.

O (component) items
> are created by SETITEMO, SETNITEMO, INSERTO.

## See Also

"INSERTC, INSERTL, INSERTN, and INSERTO" on page 482

"MAKELIST" on page 535

"MAKENLIST" on page 536

"SETITEMC, SETITEML, SETITEMN, and SETITEMO" on page 651

"SETNITEMC, SETNITEML, SETNITEMN, and SETNITEMO" on page 661

# IVARLIST

**Returns the column names for an index key**

**Category:** SAS Table

## Syntax

*varlist*=**IVARLIST**(*table-id,key-name*);

**varlist**
> contains one or more index columns (separated by a blank) for the specified key, or a blank if *key-name* is invalid.
> > Type: Character

**table-id**
> contains the identifier that was assigned when the table was opened. If *table-id* is invalid, the program halts.
> > Type: Numeric

**key-name**
> is the name of an index key.
> > Type: Character

**Details**    An *index* is an auxiliary data structure used to speed up the selection of records that are specified by the value of a column.

An index is called a *simple index* if it contains the value of only one column. A *composite index* merges the values for more than one column to form a single value. A given SAS table can have multiple simple indexes, composite indexes, or a combination of these.

You can create indexes using

□ the ICREATE function in SCL

□ the DATASETS and SQL procedures in base SAS software

□ SAS/IML software

□ the CONTENTS function in SCL

□ the ACCESS procedure of SAS/ACCESS software.

*Note:* Because some engines now support mixed-case filenames, IVARLIST now retains the cases of the returned selected items. If your application contains code that assumes that the returned selection is in uppercase, your application may fail. You may need to modify your application. For example, you can use the UPCASE* function to convert the returned selection to uppercase:

```
if (upcase(ivarlist(dsid, 'TESTNDX'))='NDXVAR'
```

If the application cannot be modified, you may need to specify the VALIDVARNAME=V6 system option when you run the application to ensure that the selections returned from the IVARLIST function are in uppercase. △

## Example

Return the column list that is indexed for the key ITEMTYPE in the SAS table MYLIB.DATAONE. Assume that ITEMTYPE is a simple index (that is, it contains the values of only one column). The returned VARLIST contains the string ITEMTYPE.

```
tableid=open('mylib.dataone','i');
varlist=ivarlist(tableid,'itemtype');
```

## See Also

VALIDVARNAME system option in *SAS Language Reference: Dictionary*

"ICREATE" on page 464

"IDELETE" on page 468

"IOPTION" on page 490

"ISINDEX" on page 494

---

# KEYCOUNT

**Returns the number of rows that meet the criteria specified by an index key**

**Category:** SAS Table

---

## Syntax

*nrow=*__KEYCOUNT__(*table-id*);

**nrow**

contains the number of rows that meet the criteria, or <0 if an error occurred. The error message can be retrieved by using SYSMSG.
Type: Numeric

---

* For documentation for the UPCASE function, refer to *SAS Language Reference: Dictionary*.

*table-id*
> is the identifier that was assigned when the table was opened. If *table-id* is invalid, the program halts.
> Type: Numeric

**Details**    KEYCOUNT returns the number of rows that meet the criteria specified by the index key column. The index key column was specified with the last SETKEY function that was used on the table. After KEYCOUNT executes, the table points to the first row that meets the criteria defined by the last SETKEY function. Use FETCH or FETCHOBS to read the row.

*CAUTION:*

**Using KEYCOUNT with composite keys may show a larger number of rows matching the search criteria than you expect.** Using a composite key with SETKEY operates the same way as the WHERE function only when the condition is EQ. The value returned when the condition is EQ is the same as if the columns specified in the composite key are connected by WHERE conditions using AND or ALSO. (See Example 1.)

For all other conditions (GT, GE, LT, or LE) specified with SETKEY for a composite key, the composite key columns are concatenated to form the index key. The number that the KEYCOUNT function returns is the number of rows in the table that satisfy the composite key. For example, if the composite index consists of columns GENDER and AGE and the condition is GT (greater than), the values to search for are concatenated such that key values of **F** for GENDER and **13** for AGE yield an index key of **F13**. Because the search is performed on the concatenated values, some values that you did not expect may meet the search condition . For example, key values of **M** for GENDER and **11** for AGE meet the search condition, because the string **M11** is considered greater than the string **F13**. (See Example 2.) △

## Examples

Suppose you have the following examples which use rows from the WORK.CLASS table. Create a simple index for the table WORK.CLASS, using ICREATE or the DATASETS procedure, with AGE as the index column. Also, create a composite index for WORK.CLASS called COMP that consists of columns GENDER and AGE.

**Example 1: Using a Simple Index Key**    Set up a search criteria of AGE=13. SETKEY specifies that the key column is AGE and the condition is equality.

```
/*  Locate rows where 'age = 13'  */
   tableid = open( 'work.class', 'v' );

      /* Create the simple index */
   rc = icreate(tableid,'age');
   name = ''; gender = '';
   age = 13;
   call set(tableid);
   rc = setkey(tableid,'age','eq');
   nrow = keycount(tableid);

 if (nrow < 0) then _msg_ = sysmsg();
   else
      do;
         put 'Number of rows found:' nrow;
         do while (fetch(tableid) ne -1);
            put name= gender= age=;
         end;
```

```
          end;
```
This program produces the following output:

```
Number of rows found: 3
   name=Alice gender=F age=13
   name=Becka gender=F age=13
   name=Jeffery gender=M age=13
```

**Example 2: Using a Composite Index Key with Condition 'EQ'**    Set up search criteria of
GENDER=F and AGE=13. SETKEY specifies that the key is named COMP and the
condition for the search is equality.

```
/* Locate rows where 'gender="F"' */
/* and 'age=13' */
   tableid = open( 'work.class', 'v' );

      /*  Create index */
   rc = icreate(tableid,'comp','gender age');
   name = ''; gender = 'F'; age = 13;
   call set(tableid);
   rc = setkey(tableid,'comp','eq');
   nrow = keycount(tableid);

   if (nrow < 0) then _msg_ = sysmsg();
   else
   do;
      put 'Number of rows found:' nrow;
      do while (fetch(tableid) ne -1);
         put name= gender= age=;
      end;
   end;
```

This program produces the following output:

```
Number of rows found: 2
   name=Alice gender=F age=13
   name=Becka gender=F age=13
```

**Example 3: Using a Composite Index Key with Condition 'GT'**    Set up search criteria of
GENDER=F and AGE greater than 13. SETKEY specifies that the key is named COMP
and the condition for the search is greater-than. This example illustrates the
unexpected results returned by KEYCOUNT when you use composite index keys and
SETKEY using a 'GT' argument.

```
/*  Locate rows where 'genderage' > 'F13'  */
   tableid = open( 'work.class', 'v' );

      /* Create index */
   rc=icreate(tableid,'comp','gender age');
   name = ''; gender = 'F'; age = 13;
   call set(tableid);
   rc = setkey(tableid,'comp','gt');
   nrow = keycount( tableid);

   if (nrow < 0) then _msg_ = sysmsg();
   else
   do;
```

```
            put 'Number of rows found:' nrow;
            do while (fetch(tableid) ne -1);
                put name= gender= age=;
            end;
        end;
```

This program lists 14 rows from the indexed table that met the search criteria of GENDER||AGE>=F13.

```
Number of rows found: 14
    name=Gail gender=F age=14
    name=Tammy gender=F age=14
    name=Mary gender=F age=15
    name=Sharon gender=F age=15
    name=Thomas gender=M age=11
    name=James gender=M age=12
    name=John gender=M age=12
    name=Robert gender=M age=12
    name=Jeffrey gender=M age=13
    name=Alfred gender=M age=14
    name=Duke gender=M age=14
    name=Guido gender=M age=15
    name=William gender=M age=15
    name=Philip gender=M age=16
```

You can see that James at AGE=12 does not meet the SETKEY requirement of AGE > 13 and GENDER > 'F'. However, his row was selected because the values were concatenated before the comparison was made.

## See Also

"SETKEY" on page 653

---

# LASTCMD

**Returns the text of the last command that was issued from the application window**

**Category:**   Command

---

## Syntax

*cmdtext*=**LASTCMD**();

**cmdtext**
contains the text of the last command that was issued from the application window. Type: Character

**Details**   If the command contains multiple words, only the first word is returned. LASTCMD is usually used in conjunction with CONTROL ENTER, ALWAYS, or ALLCMDS.

## Example

Retrieve the last command that was issued in the window and display a message, based on that command name:

```
INIT:
    control always;
return;
MAIN:
    cmd=lastcmd();
    if cmd='GO' then
        _msg_='Last command was '||cmd;
return;
```

## See Also

"WORD" on page 725

---

# LASTKEY

**Returns the number of the last function key that was pressed from the application window**

**Category:** Keys

---

## Syntax

*keynum*=**LASTKEY**();

***keynum***
    contains the number of the function key that was pressed from the application window, or 0 if ENTER was pressed.
      Type: Numeric

**Details**    The returned value is the ordinal position of the key definition in the KEYS window. In order for this function to work, you must have a window variable or text in the DISPLAY window.

To retrieve the name of the last function key pressed by a user, use FKEYNAME.

LASTKEY is used in conjunction with CONTROL ENTER, ALWAYS, and ALLCMDS. LASTKEY does not retrieve the number of a function key that has a global command assigned to it.

## Example

Return the number of the last function key that a user pressed. (This example requires a window with at least one window variable.)

```
INIT:
    control enter;
return;

MAIN:
    keynum=lastkey();
```

```
      if (keynum ne 0) then
         put 'Last function key is ' keynum;
      else
         put 'Last function key is not defined
              or the ENTER key was pressed';
   return;
```

### See Also

"FKEYNAME" on page 413

"GETFKEY" on page 440

"SETFKEY" on page 649

"CONTROL" on page 302

# LEAVE

**Stops processing the current DO group or DO loop and resumes with the next statement in sequence**

**Category:**   Control Flow

**Comparisons:**   SAS Statement with limitations in SCL

### Syntax

**LEAVE** < *label*>;

*label*

> is the name of a program label that is associated with the DO group.
>     Type: Character

**Details**    The LEAVE statement is provided in SCL to control the execution of DO groups. When you need to force the statements in a DO group to stop executing, you can use the LEAVE statement to stop executing statements in a DO group and to start executing a statement that is outside of that DO group.

*Note:*   In DATA step code, the LEAVE statement stops processing only the current DO loop. In SCL code, the LEAVE statement stops processing the current DO loop *or DO group*, whichever is closest. For example, suppose your code contains a DO loop that contains DO groups:

```
do n=1 to 5;     /* DO loop */
   if n=3 then do; leave; end;        /* DO group */
  put n=;
end;
```

When this code is compiled and run as part of an SCL program, the output is:

```
n=1
n=2
n=3
n=4
n=5
```

When this code is submitted as part of a DATA step, the output is:

```
n=1
n=2
n=3
```

See "DO" on page 356 for more information on DO groups and DO loops. △

For details about the LEAVE statement in the base SAS language, see *SAS Language Reference: Dictionary.*

## Examples

**Example 1: LEAVE Statements Without Label Names**    If a LEAVE statement does not contain the name of a program label, the program stops executing the statements in the DO group and starts executing the first statement after the DO group's END statement. For example, when the condition in the IF statement in the following program is true (that is, when the value of SUM > 10), the program jumps immediately to the statement following the END statement (in this case, the PUT statement).

```
INIT:
return;

MAIN:
 do while(i<5);
   sum+i;
   i=i+2;
   if (sum>10) then
     do;
        leave;
     end;
   put sum=;
   end;
totalsum=sum;
return;
TERM:
return;
```

**Example 2: LEAVE Statements With Label Names**    In this example, when the condition SUM > 50 is true, the program leaves the LAB1 DO group and returns to the next statement following the DO group (in this case, the PUT statement).

```
INIT:
    sum=45;
return;
MAIN:
    link LAB1;
return;
LAB1:
    do i=1 to 10;
        if (sum>10) then do;
            k=0;
            do until (k>=20);
                sum+k;
                if (sum>50) then leave LAB1;
                k+2;
            end;
```

```
        end;
    end;
    put 'LEAVE LAB1, sum >50 ' sum=;
return;
TERM:
return;
```

## See Also

"CONTINUE" on page 300

"DO" on page 356

---

# LEFT

### Returns a left-aligned character string

**Category:** Character

---

## Syntax

*lstring*=**LEFT**(*string<,length>*);

### *lstring*

contains the left-aligned character string. If *lstring* already exists, then specifying a length in the LEFT function affects the current length of *lstring* only if the specified length is less than the trimmed length of the string.
   Type: Character

### *string*

is the character string to be left-justified.
   Type: Character

### *length*

is the length in which the character string is to be left-justified. The default is the maximum length of *lstring*.
   Type: Numeric

**Details**    Any leading blanks in the string are removed so that the first character in the string is nonblank. The default length of the returned value is the trimmed length of the left-aligned string. Use *length* to specify a different maximum length for the returned string.

   In order for LEFT to work properly when *lstring* is a window variable, set the justification field (**JUST**) in the field attribute window for *lstring* to **NONE**.

   To right-justify a character string, use RIGHT. To center a character string, use CENTER.

## See Also

"RIGHT" on page 620

"CENTER" on page 275

# LEGEND

**Displays a legend window or refreshes the current LEGEND window**

**Category:**  Legend

## Syntax

**CALL LEGEND**(< *window-name*< ,*back-color*
  < ,*border-color*< ,*border-attr*> > > >);

***window-name***

is the name that is displayed in the window border. Once assigned, a window name is displayed on subsequent legend windows until it is changed by another LEGEND routine that assigns a different name or that assigns a null string (*' '*) to delete the name from the current legend window.
    Type: Character

***back-color***

is a background color name, or *' '* for the default color. Available colors are BLACK, BLUE, BROWN, CYAN, GRAY, GREEN, MAGENTA, ORANGE, PINK, RED, WHITE, and YELLOW. SASCOLOR window elements can also be used.
    The default background color is the SASCOLOR window element "Secondary Background."
    Type: Character

***border-color***

is a border color name, or *' '* for the default color. Available colors are listed under *back-color*. SASCOLOR window elements can also be used for *border-color*.
    The default border color is the SASCOLOR window element "Secondary Border."
    Type: Character

***border-attr***

is a border attribute, or *' '* for the default attribute. Attributes are NONE, BLINKING, HIGHLIGHT, HIREV, REVERSE, and UNDERLINE. If you specify a SASCOLOR window element for *border-color*, then *border-attr* is ignored, because the SASCOLOR window element contains a display attribute.
    The default border attribute is the SASCOLOR window element "Secondary Border".
    Type: Character

**Details**    The LEGEND routine displays legend text that has been previously specified with the PUTLEGEND routine. You can specify any combination of optional arguments for LEGEND.
    By default, the LEGEND window has the following characteristics:

- ☐ The window occupies rows 1 through 6 and columns 1 through the width of the display device.

☐ The window name is either the name that was specified by the last LEGEND routine or the name of the current legend window.

Before invoking the LEGEND routine, you may need to resize the associated application window so that it does not obscure the LEGEND window. To do this, either use the WDEF routine or assign a new size to the window.

Additionally, you can specify a size for a legend window by using the WREGION routine before calling the legend.

## Example

Suppose you have two FRAME entries, X and Y. Assume that X.FRAME contains two pushbuttons named PUSHPOP and ENDLGND, and that X.SCL contains the corresponding control labels. When the PUSHPOP button is activated, the PUSHLEGEND call will save X's legend, and the Y.FRAME will be displayed. Y will then set up and display its own legend. After the return from Y, the POPLEGEND call will restore X's legend.

If the ENDLGND button is activated, ENDLEGEND will close the LEGEND window, and the application window will be restored to its original size.

X.SCL contains the following program:

```
INIT:
      /* Get the number of rows and columns for later */
      /* use.                                         */
   nr = winfo('numrows');
   nc = winfo('numcols');
      /* Resize the application window to */
      /* start at row 10. */
   call wdef(10, 1, nr-9, nc);

      /* Set the size of the LEGEND window - row 1  */
      /* through row 9.  Pass a null string */
      /* as the fifth parameter to indicate */
      /* that the LEGEND window has no      */
      /* command area.                      */
   call wregion(1, 1, 9, nc, '');

      /* Set up the legend text and display it. */
   call putlegend(1,'This is line one of the legend for X',
               'yellow','none');
   call putlegend(2,'This is line two of the legend for X',
               'yellow','none');
   call legend('Sample LEGEND Window for X',
            'gray','blue');
   return;

MAIN:
   return;

      /* PUSHPOP label.  If this is executed, */
      /* we'll save the current  */
      /* legend and call y, */
      /* which will display its own legend. */
PUSHPOP:
```

```
        /* Push and call. */
    call pushlegend();
    call display('y.frame');

        /* Restore the original legend. */
    call poplegend();
return;

    /* ENDLGND label. If this is executed,  */
    /* the LEGEND window will be             */
    /* closed, and the application window    */
    /* will be restored to its original size. */
ENDLGND:
    call endlegend();
    call wdef(1, 1, nr, nc);
return;


TERM:
return;
```

Y.SCL contains the following program:

```
INIT:
        /* Set up and display Y's own */
        /* LEGEND window. */
    nr = winfo('numrows');
    nc = winfo('numcols');
    call wdef(10, 1, nr-9, nc);
    call wregion(1, 1, 9, nc, '');
    call putlegend(1,'This is line one of the legend for Y',
                   'yellow', 'none');
    call putlegend(2,'This is line two of the legend for Y',
                   'yellow', 'none');
    call legend('Sample LEGEND Window for Y',
               'gray', 'blue');
return;
MAIN:
TERM:
return;
```

## See Also

"ENDLEGEND" on page 366

"POPLEGEND" on page 596

"PUSHLEGEND" on page 603

"PUTLEGEND" on page 606

# LENGTH

**Returns the length of a trimmed character string**

**Category:** Character

## Syntax

*length*=**LENGTH**(*cval*,<'NOTRIM'>);

***length***
    contains the length of the trimmed character string.
        Type: Numeric

***cval***
    is the character value whose length is to be determined.
        Type: Character

**'NOTRIM'**
    specifies that trailing blanks should be counted as part of the string length.
        Type: Character

**Details**     The resulting value is the position of the right-most nonblank character in the specified string *cval*.

When NOTRIM is specified, LENGTH returns the length of a string, including trailing blanks.

By default, variables automatically remove leading blanks when values are assigned to them. The $CHAR format and informat must be assigned to a variable in order for leading blanks to be considered in determining the length of a variable.

## Examples

**Example 1: Using the LENGTH Function**     Return the length of the character variable S:

```
length s $ 5;
s='ab ';
l=length(s);
put 'L='l;
```

This program produces the following output:

```
L=2
```

**Example 2: Using the LENGTH Function with NOTRIM**     Return the length of the character variable S, using the NOTRIM option:

```
s = 'xy ';
l = length(s, 'notrim');
put 'L='l;
```

This program produces the following output:

```
L=4
```

## See Also

"MLENGTH" on page 549

---

# LENGTH

**Declares variables and specifies their length and whether their data type is numeric or character**

**Category:** Declarative Statement

**Comparisons:** SAS Statement with limitations in SCL

## Syntax

**LENGTH**< *variable-list*><DEFAULT=*n*>;

*variable-list*
> is one or more variables, specified as *variable-1* <. . . *variable-n*> <$> *length*, where

> *variable*
>> names a variable to be assigned a length.

> $
>> designates that the preceding variable or variables are character type.

> *length*
>> is the length of the preceding variable or variables. *Length* can range from 1 to 32,767 for character variables. All numeric variables have a length of 8. If you specify a different length for a numeric variable, SCL still reserves 8 bytes for it. Type: Character

**DEFAULT=*n***
> is the maximum length of character variables that are not defined by a LENGTH statement. If this option is not used, the default length for character variables is 200. Type: Numeric

**Details**    In SCL, LENGTH is a declarative statement and can be used only to set the lengths of nonwindow variables. If you attempt to specify a length for a window variable, a compile error occurs.

You typically place LENGTH statements at the beginning of a program, before the first labeled section. A compiler error occurs if you attempt to place a LENGTH statement within a DO group or within a conditional clause.

You can use the LENGTH statement to reduce the amount of memory required for storing character-type nonwindow variables. For example, if your program assigns only single-character values to the variable CODE, and if the default length of character variables is 200, then you can save 199 bytes of storage space by defining the length of the variable explicitly in the SCL program. To do so, use a statement like the following:

```
length code $ 1;
```

For details about the LENGTH statement in the base SAS language, see *SAS Language Reference: Dictionary* .

## Example

Set the maximum length of all character variables that are not defined by a LENGTH statement to 150:

```
length default=150;
length a $ 8;
INIT:
   b='';
   max_a=mlength(a);
   max_b=mlength(b);
   put max_a= max_b=;
```

```
return;
```

The output is:

```
max_a=8 max_b=150
```

## See Also

"DECLARE" on page 330

# LETTER

**Displays the FSLETTER window or sends a letter that was created with the FSLETTER procedure**

**Category:**   Utility

## Syntax

**CALL LETTER**(*letter-entry<,open-mode<,table-name>>*);

*letter-entry*
:   is a catalog containing one or more LETTER, FORM, or EDPARMS entries. A one- or two-level name is assumed to be *catalog* or *libref.catalog*. The catalog is created if it does not already exist.
    Type: Character

*open-mode*
:   specifies the type of access to the FSLETTER window:

    **'BROWSE'**
    :   opens the catalog or letter-entry for browsing.

    **'EDIT'**
    :   opens the catalog or letter-entry for editing. (This is the default.)

    **'PRINT'**
    :   prints a letter for each row in the SAS table specified by *table-name*. The SEND window is not displayed for the items that are printed. **PRINT** mode is valid only when the specified entry is a letter.

    **'SEND'**
    :   displays the FSLETTER SEND window for one row (or letter), enabling a user to customize the letter. To use this option, you do not have to specify a value for *table-name*. If a table name is provided, the letter is displayed in the SEND window with the fields filled with values from the first row in the table. This mode is valid only when the specified entry is a letter.
        Type: Character

*table-name*
:   is the SAS table containing values for the fill-in fields. Use the syntax *<libref.>member-name<(SAS-data-set-options)>*. If you omit *libref*, the default SAS data library, WORK, is used.
    Specify ' ' to use the _LAST_ table. If no _LAST_ table exists, the program halts.
    You can add a list of SAS data set options following the table name. The list must be enclosed in parentheses. Valid data set options include DROP, KEEP, RENAME,

WHERE, and CNTLLEV. See *SAS Language Reference: Dictionary* for a list of data set options and their descriptions.
Type: Character

**Details**   The LETTER routine displays the FSLETTER window or sends a letter.

*Note:*   The FSLETTER window is not displayed if a PRINT argument is used. △

If the value supplied for *letter-entry* is a three- or four-level name, the user is returned to the calling application when the FSLETTER window is closed. If a one- or two-level name is supplied, the user is returned directly to the calling application when the SAS Explorer window is closed.

SAS data set options can be specified by enclosing them within parentheses immediately following the *table-name* argument, as in the following example:

```
call letter('my.letters.subscrib','print',
    'personal(where=(name="John"))');
```

## Examples

☐ Open the FSLETTER window to edit a document named SUBSCRIB:

```
call letter('my.letters.subscrib');
```

☐ Send a copy of the SUBSCRIB letter for each row in the SAS table SUBSCRIB.DATA. Direct FSLETTER output to a print file when you use CALL LETTER.

```
rc=filename ('myfile',fname);
call execcmdi('prtfile myfile');
call letter('my.letters.subscrib','print','subscrib.data');
```

☐ Send a copy of the SUBSCRIB letter for the first row in the SAS table SUBSCRIB.DATA:

```
call letter('my.letters.subscrib','send','subscrib.data');
```

**SEND** mode for the letter SUBSCRIB accepts user input.

## See Also

"FSEDIT" on page 433

# LIBLIST

**Displays a host selection window that lists the currently assigned librefs, and returns user's selections**

**Category:**  SAS Table

## Syntax

*selections*=**LIBLIST**(< *sel-excl*< ,*engine*< ,*message* <,*autoclose*<,*num-sel*>>>>>);

**selections**

contains one or more librefs from the list, or blank if no selection is made. Multiple selections are separated by blanks. By default, *selections* is 200 bytes long. To

accommodate values longer than 200 bytes, explicitly declare *selections* with a longer length.
   Type: Character

**sel-excl**

is one or more librefs to include or exclude from the selection list window. Specify names using a style described in "Styles of Name Specification" on page 514.
   Type: Character

**engine**

is one or more engines to use as criteria for determining which librefs are displayed. Specify names using a style described in "Styles of Name Specification" on page 514.
   Type: Character

**message**

is the text for a message to display above the selection list. The default message tells users to make up to the number of selections in *num-sel*.
   Type: Character

**autoclose**

is an obsolete argument but is retained for compatibility with earlier releases. If you want to specify a value for *num-sel*, then specify ʹ ʹ as a placeholder for this argument.
   Type: Character

**num-sel**

specifies the maximum number of items a user can select from the list. To display the list for information purposes only (no selections allowed), specify 0. To specify unlimited selections, use a value such as 9999 that is larger than the number of available selections. A user cannot make a number of selections that exceeds the number of items in the list.
   Type: Numeric

## Styles of Name Specification

To specify more than one name, separate the names with a space — for example, `MYLIB1 MYLIB2`.

To specify all names, use an asterisk (ʹ*ʹ) or a null string (ʹ ʹ).

To specify all names *except* those listed after the NOT sign, use a NOT sign (¬ or ^) followed by one or more names. For example, `^MYLIB1` displays all defined librefs except `MYLIB1`.

**Details**   LIBLIST opens the Library Selector window, which lists librefs, engines, and the physical names of the operating system files. However, only the selected libref is returned. The window contains a `Browse` button which a user can select to display the SAS Explorer window and select from the librefs that are currently assigned and their contents. After browsing data libraries, a user can select

to return to the Library Selector window.

If you omit all the arguments for LIBLIST (for example, `selections=liblist();`), the selection list window lists all librefs that have been assigned in the current SAS session.

You can provide a default value that will be initially selected when the libref selection list is displayed. To do this, assign the value to the *selections* variable before calling LIBLIST.

If a user closes the selection list window without making a selection, LIBLIST returns a blank value unless there was an initial value for *selections* before LIBLIST was called.

Selections from the window can be returned in the current result list, if one is available. The current result list is a special SCL list that is automatically filled with the values that are selected from a selection list. To use a current result list, use the MAKELIST function to create the list, and use the CURLIST function to designate it as the current result list. The current result list must exist before you call the LIBLIST function.

When LIBLIST is invoked, the current result list is cleared. After LIBLIST is invoked, the result list contains the following named items:

TAG
> identifies the list as one that was created by the LIBLIST function.
> Type: Character

COUNT
> contains the number of selected librefs, or 0 if a user makes no selections or issues a CANCEL command in the list window.
> Type: Numeric

LIBREF
> contains the name of each selected libref. There is one LIBREF element for each selected libref name.
> Type: Character

LIBNAME
> contains the physical name of the operating system file for each selected libref. There is one LIBNAME element for each selected libref.
> Type: Character

## Examples

- Create a selection list that displays all librefs except MYLIB1 and MYLIB2, and display the message **'Choose a libref'**.

  ```
  select=liblist('^mylib mylib2','*',Choose a libref');
  ```

- Create a selection list that displays all librefs associated with the V609 engine, and exclude the librefs SASHELP and MAPS. Allow users to make up to three selections.

  ```
  select=liblist('^sashelp maps','v609',
  'Choose up to 3 librefs','',3);
  ```

- Create a current result list to receive user selections. Use MAKELIST to create the list and CURLIST to define it as the current result list. Display all librefs except MYLIB1 and MYLIB2, and allow users to make up to five selections. Use a DO loop to retrieve the selections from the current result list.

  ```
  listid=makelist();
  rc=curlist(listid);
  select=liblist('^ mylib1 mylib2',' ',
  'Choose up to 5 librefs','', 5);
  n=getnitemn(listid,'COUNT');
  do i=1 to n;
     libref=getnitemc(listid,'LIBREF',i);
     physname=getnitemc(listid,'LIBNAME',i);
     put libref= physname=;
  end;
  ```

## See Also

"CATLIST" on page 269

"DIRLIST" on page 347

"FILELIST" on page 401

---

# LIBNAME

**Assigns or deassigns a libref for a SAS data library**

**Category:** SAS Table

---

## Syntax

*sysrc=***LIBNAME**(*libref<,SAS-data-library<,engine <,options>>>*);


***sysrc***
    contains the return code for the operation:

| | |
|---|---|
| 0 | The operation was successful. |
| >0 | The operation was not successful. |
| <0 | The operation was completed, but a warning or a note was generated. |

        Type: Numeric

***libref***
    is the libref to assign.
        Type: Character

***SAS-data-library***
    is the physical name of the SAS data library to be associated with the libref. This name can be up to 32K characters long. Specify this name as required by the host operating system.
        Type: Character

***engine***
    is the engine to use for accessing the SAS files in the data library. If you are specifying a SAS/SHARE server, the engine should be REMOTE.
        Type: Character

***options***
    are options that are used by the specified engine. For information about engines and options, see the SAS documentation for your operating environment.
        Type: Character

**Details**    The LIBNAME function follows the rules for the LIBNAME statement in base SAS software.

*Operating Environment Information:*  Some operating systems allow a *SAS-data-library* value of ' ' (with a space) and some allow ' . ' to assign a libref to the current directory. The behavior of LIBNAME when a single space or a period is specified for *SAS-data-library* is host dependent. Under some operating systems, librefs can be assigned using system commands outside the SAS session. △

## Examples

**Example 1: Assigning a Libref**    Assign the libref NEW to the SAS data library
TEST.DATA. If an error or warning occurs, display the message on the message line.

```
if (libname('new','test.data'))then
   _msg_=sysmsg();
```

**Example 2: Deassigning a Libref**    Deassign the libref NEW. If an error or warning
occurs, display the message on the message line.

```
if (libname('new')) then
   _msg_=sysmsg();
```

**Example 3: Using a List to Assign a Libref to Multiple SAS Data Libraries**    Assign the
libref DEF to several PC files whose names are stored in an SCL list:

```
lid=makelist();
rc=insertc(lid,''('',-1);
rc=insertc(lid,'''M:\SAS\MAPS''',-1);
rc=insertc(lid,'''C:\CATALOGS\sasuser''',-1);
rc=insertc(lid,'')'',-1);
rc=libname('DEF',' ','','',lid);
```

Assign the libref DEF to several UNIX files whose names are stored in an SCL list:

```
v1=''(/mylib/store/data/facilities''';
v2='''/mylib/store/data/hresorces''';
v3='''/mylib/store/data/supplies')''';
lid = makelist ();
rc =insertc(lid,v1,-1);
rc =insertc(lid,v2,-1);
rc =insertc(lid,v3,-1);
RC =LIBNAME('DEF',' ','','',lid);
```

## See Also

"LIBREF" on page 517

---

# LIBREF

**Verifies that a libref has been assigned**

**Category:**  SAS Table and Utility

---

## Syntax

*sysrc*=**LIBREF**(*libref*);

***sysrc***
   contains the return code for the operation:

   =0                          The operation was successful.

|  |  |
|---|---|
| <0 | The operation was completed, but a warning or a note was generated. |
| >0 | The operation was not successful. |

Type: Numeric

**libref**
is the libref to be verified.
Type: Character

## Example

Verify a libref. If an error or warning occurs, the message is displayed on the application window's message line.

```
if (libref('sashelp'))
then _msg_=sysmsg();
```

## See Also

"LIBNAME" on page 516

---

# LISTC and LISTN

**Display a selection list window containing values stored in a catalog entry**

**Category:**   Selection List

---

## Syntax

*selections*=**LISTC**(*entry<,message<,autoclose<,num-sel>>>*);

*selections*=**LISTN**(*entry<,message<,autoclose<,num-sel>>>*);

**selections**
contains one or more character values that have been selected by the user.
For LISTC, if a selection is not made, *selections* will be blank. Multiple selections are separated by blanks. By default, *selections* is 200 bytes long. To accommodate values longer than 200 bytes, explicitly declare *selections* with a longer length.
For LISTN, *selections* is the first value that the user selected. The value is numeric.
Type: Character or Numeric

**entry**
is a LIST entry (for LISTN) or a HELP, LIST, or MENU entry (for LISTC). The entry must be specified as *entry.type* for an entry in the current catalog or as *libref.catalog.entry.type* for an entry in a different catalog.
Type: Character

**message**
is text for a message to be displayed above the selection list. The default message tells users to make up to the number of selections specified by *num-sel*, or 1 if *num-sel* is not provided. The default is 1.
Type: Character

*autoclose*

specifies whether the selection list window closes automatically after a user makes a selection when only one choice is allowed:

'Y'                    closes the window automatically. (This is the default.)

'N'                    leaves the window open until the user explicitly closes it.

This option is ignored when *num-sel* is not 1. However, use ' ' as a placeholder if you are also specifying a value for *num-sel*.

Type: Character

*num-sel*

specifies the maximum number of items a user can select from the list. To display the list for information purposes only (no selections allowed), specify 0. To specify an unlimited number of selections, use a value such as 9999 that is larger than the number of available selections. The default is one selection.

Type: Numeric

**Details**    LISTC automatically displays a selection list containing character values that are stored in a LIST, HELP, or MENU entry. A LIST entry that is used with LISTC must be of character type. Typically, a LIST entry is used if the selections in the LIST entry are self-explanatory. A HELP or MENU entry is used if a definition is needed next to the selection.

LISTN automatically displays a selection list containing numeric values stored in a LIST entry, which must be of numeric type. The numeric values are displayed using the format that was specified for the LIST entry. If no format was specified, the values are displayed using the BEST. format.

For a selection list that is produced with a LIST entry, you can provide a default or initial selected value by specifying a value for *selections* before calling LISTC. If *selections* contains valid values when LISTC is invoked, those values are automatically designated as selected when the selection list is displayed.

When multiple selections are allowed in LISTN, *selections* contains the first value selected from the list. However, the values for all selections can be returned in the current result list, if one is available. The current result list is a special SCL list that is automatically filled with the values selected from a selection list. To use a current result list, use the MAKELIST function to create the list, and use the CURLIST function to designate it as the current result list. The current result list must exist before you call LISTC. You can use GETITEMC to retrieve values from the list.

## Examples

### Example 1: Using LISTC with a LIST Entry
Open the entry MYLIST.LIST in the current catalog, and then display it as a selection list. Users can make up to four selections. The selected values are retrieved from the current environment list.

```
listid=makelist();
rc=curlist(listid);
selections=listc('mylist.list','','n',4);
n=listlen(listid);
do i=1 to n;
   item=getitemc(listid,i);
   put item=;
end;
```

### Example 2: Using LISTC with the Current Result List
Create LIST_C and make it the current list. Use LISTC to display a selection list containing the values ABC, DEF,

GHI, and JLK, which are stored in MYCHAR.LIST, and allow a user to make up to 4 selections.

```
list_c=makelist();
cur_list=curlist(list_c);
   /* Display the list and put the user      */
   /* selection in SELECTIONS.               */
   /* Then print the number of selections.   */
selections=listc('mychar.list',' ',' ',4);
put 'User selected' selections;
   /*  Find out the number of items          */
   /*  in LIST_C and print the number.       */
num_selected=listlen(list_c);
put 'Total number selected is' num_selected;
   /* Get the selections from                */
   /* the current list                       */
   /* and print each one.                    */
do i=1 to num_selected;
   item=getitemc(list_c,i);
   put 'Item' i 'is ' item;
end;
```

Testing the program and selecting GHI, DEF, JKL, and then ABC produces the following output:

```
User selected GHI DEF JKL ABC
Total number selected is 4
Item 1 is GHI
Item 2 is DEF
Item 3 is JKL
Item 4 is ABC
```

**Example 3: Using LISTN with the Current Result List**   Create LIST_N and make it the current list. Use LISTN to display a selection list containing the numbers 1, 2, 3, and 4, which are stored in MYLIST.LIST, and allow a user to make up to 4 selections.

```
list_n=makelist();
cur_list=curlist(list_n);
   /* Display the list and put the first user */
   /* selection in SELECTED_FIRST,            */
   /* then print the number of user selections. */
selected_first=listn('mylist.list',' ',' ',4);
put 'First selection is ' selected_first;
   /*  Find out the number of items in LIST-N */
   /* and print the number.                   */
num_selected=listlen(list_n);
put 'Total number selected is ' num_selected;
   /* Get any other selections from           */
   /* the current list                        */
   /* and print each number.                  */
do i=1 to num_selected;
   item=getitemn(list_n,i);
   put 'Item ' i 'is ' item;
end;
```

Testing the program and selecting 3, 2, 4, and 1, produces the following output:

```
First selection is 3
Total number selected is 4
Item 1 is 3
Item 2 is 2
Item 3 is 4
Item 4 is 1
```

## See Also

"DATALISTC and DATALISTN" on page 326

# LISTLEN

**Reports the length of an SCL list**

**Category:** List

## Syntax

*n*=**LISTLEN**(*list-id* );

*n*

contains either the length of an SCL list or status information:

| | |
|---|---|
| >0 | the length of a non-empty list |
| 0 | the list is empty |
| −1 | the list identifier is invalid. |

Type: Numeric

*list-id*

is the identifier of the list whose length is being queried, or any other number.

Type: Numeric or List

**Details**  The length of a list is the number of items in the list, excluding the contents of sublists. Because LISTLEN returns -1 if *list-id* is an invalid list identifier, you can use LISTLEN to determine whether a list exists. For example:

```
listid=getniteml(envlist('G'),'MYLIST');
invalid=(listlen(listid)=-1);
if invalid then
do;
   put 'MYLIST in the global environment has been deleted.';
   stop;
end;
```

## Example

Create the empty list LISTA, and then insert LISTA into a copy of itself, LISTB. The lengths of the two lists are then computed and are stored in the variables LEN_A and LEN_B.

```
lista=makelist();
listb=copylist(lista);
listb=insertl(listb,lista);
len_a=listlen(lista);
len_b=listlen(listb);
_msg_='The length of LISTA is '||len_a||' and '||
      'the length of LISTB is '||len_b;
```

This example shows that the length of LISTA is 0, whereas the length of LISTB is 1.

## See Also

"MAKELIST" on page 535

"MAKENLIST" on page 536

---

# LNAMECHK

**Validates a path string**

**Category:**  Image

---

## Syntax

*rc*= **LNAMECHK**(*path-string*);


**rc**
    contains the return code for the operation:

| | |
|---|---|
| 0 | The path string is a valid path to a file. |
| >0 | The path string is not a valid path to a file. |

   Type: Numeric

**path-string**
    is the string generated by LNAMEMK.
       Type: Character

**Details**    LNAMECHK validates that the specified path string refers to an external file that exists. It does not determine whether the file contains a readable image.

## Example

Test whether a file exists:

```
imgpath=lnamemk(2,fromdir,file)
rc=lnamechk(2,imgpath);
if (rc ne 0) then
   do;
       _msg_="File does not exist.";
   end;
```

# LNAMEGET

**Decodes a path string**

**Category:** Image

## Syntax

*rc=***LNAMEGET**(*path-string,type,< name-string1<,name-string2><,options>>*);

***rc***
contains the return code for the operation:

| 0 | successful |
|---|---|
| >0 | not successful |

Type: Numeric

***path-string***
is the string generated by LNAMEMK.
Type: Character

***type***
is the type of the path. See "LNAMEMK" on page 524 for more information. If no other arguments are specified, the function returns only the type.
Type: Numeric

***name-string***
is the *name-string* provided in LNAMEMK. Specify enough *name-string* arguments for the *type*. See "LNAMEMK" on page 524 for more information.
Type: Character

***options***
are any options used with LNAMEMK.
Type: Character

**Details**    Path strings that are created by LNAMEMK are not readable, and their internal format may change from release to release. The *only* way to decode a path string is to use LNAMEGET.

You may find it useful to encode an image filename with LNAMEMK and to store that path string in a SAS data set. Then, later retrieve the path string and use LNAMEGET to find the arguments that were originally specified in LNAMEMK.

If you use the *type, name-string,* and *options* arguments, they are filled with the corresponding arguments specified in LNAMEMK (such as the libref/member name, physical pathname, and so on). The number of optional arguments that you specify must match the number specified in LNAMEMK.

## Examples

☐ Encode and decode a pathname. Store the type of path in TYPE, and store the pathname in IMGFILE.

```
imgpath=lnamemk(1,filename);
rc=lnameget(imgpath,type,imgfile);
```

□ Encode and decode the location of an image file. Store the directory that contains the image file in DIR, and store the filename in IMGFILE.

```
imgpath=lnamemk(2,dirname,filename);
rc=lnameget(imgpath,type,dir,imgfile);
```

## See Also

"LNAMECHK" on page 522

"LNAMEMK" on page 524

# LNAMEMK

**Makes a path string for an image file**

**Category:**   Image

## Syntax

*path-string*=**LNAMEMK**(*type*,< *name-string1*< ,*name-string2*>< ,*attributes*>>);

***path-string***
contains a packed string containing information about the file path and format. Declare a length of at least 300 characters.
Type: Character

***type***
is a number from 1 through 5 that specifies the type of path used to read the external file.
Type: Numeric

***name-string***
is the string that identifies the location of the image. The specification depends on the value specified for *type*.

| For type | use name-string1 | and name-string2 |
|----------|------------------|------------------|
| 1 | physical-pathname | |
| 2 | directory-pathname | filename |
| 3 | fileref | |
| 4 | fileref | filename |
| 5 | libref.catalog.member | |

Type: Character

***attributes***
specify file-specific attributes. See Table A2.1 on page 773and Table A2.2 on page 775 for possible choices. The FORMAT= attribute must be specified for Targa images, for images residing in SAS catalogs, and for host-specific formats. FORMAT is not required in other cases, but it is always more efficient to specify it.
Type: Character

**Details**    LNAMEMK creates a character variable that contains information about the location of the image as well as other image attributes.

The path string can be used with the READ and WRITE commands in IMGOP or with the image object. The path string contains binary data and can be decoded only with the LNAMEGET and LNAMECHK functions.

## Example

Create path strings for image files:

```
length file $ 200;

file=lnamemk(1,filename,'format=gif');
file=lnamemk(2,directory,filename,'format=gif');
file=lnamemk(3,fileref,'format=gif');
file=lnamemk(4,fileref,filename,'format=gif');

imgentry=libref||"."||catalog||"."||member;
file=lnamemk(5,imgentry,'format=cat');
```

## See Also

"IMGOP" on page 472

"LNAMECHK" on page 522

"LNAMEGET" on page 523

# LOADCLASS

**Loads a class and returns its identifier number**

**Category:**   Object Oriented

## Syntax

*class-id*=**LOADCLASS**(*class-name*);

***class-id***

contains the identifier that has been assigned to the class. If the class is not loaded, *class-id* contains 0.

   Type: Numeric

***class-name***

is the one- to four-level name of the CLASS catalog entry to load. If *class-name* is a one- or two-level name, then the current search path is used to find the CLASS entry. If the CLASS entry was previously loaded, then the same class identifier is returned. Otherwise, the CLASS entry is loaded from the catalog into the application class list, and the class identifier is returned in *class-id*.

   Type: Character

**Details**    LOADCLASS loads a class definition from a CLASS catalog entry. The identifier number that LOADCLASS returns can be used to create an instance of the class with the INSTANCE function.

## Example

Load SASUSER.CLASSES.TIMER.CLASS and use the INSTANCE function to create an instance of the TIMER class:

```
timerclass=loadclass('sasuser.classes.timer');
timer=instance(timerclass);
```

## See Also

"APPLY" on page 252

"INSTANCE" on page 485

"LOADRES" on page 526

"_NEO_" on page 559

"NOTIFY" on page 572

"SEND" on page 644

"SUPAPPLY" on page 679

"SUPER" on page 681

# LOADRES

**Loads a RESOURCE entry**

**Category:** Object Oriented

## Syntax

*resource-id*=**LOADRES**(*resource-name*);

**resource-id**
contains the identifier that is assigned to the resource list.
Type: Numeric

**resource-name**
is the RESOURCE catalog entry to load. If *resource-name* is a one- or two-level name, the current search path is used to find the RESOURCE entry.
Type: Character

**Details**    LOADRES loads a list of classes from a RESOURCE entry. This list is called a resource list. RESOURCE entries are used primarily by FRAME entries, although you can create RESOURCE entries for component classes as well. This function is useful for loading several classes or even entire class hierarchies at one time instead of having to load several CLASS entries.

If a class contained in the resource list has already been loaded, the existing class replaces the class in the resource list (although the RESOURCE entry is not modified). This prevents duplicate class lists for the same class name.

## Example

Load a resource list that is stored in APPQR.HIER1.GROUPS.RESOURCE, then load several classes contained in the RESOURCE entry. After the LOADRES call, the LOADCLASS calls do not have to read the classes from the catalog.

```
groups = loadres('appqr.hier1.groups.resource');
   c1=loadclass('appqr.hier1.c1.class');
   c2=loadclass('appqr.hier1.c2.class');
   c3=loadclass('appqr.hier1.c3.class');
```

## See Also

"APPLY" on page 252

"INSTANCE" on page 485

"LOADCLASS" on page 525

"_NEO_" on page 559

"NOTIFY" on page 572

"SEND" on page 644

"SUPAPPLY" on page 679

"SUPER" on page 681

# LOCATEC and LOCATEN

**Search a SAS table for a row that contains a specified value**

**Category:**  SAS Table

## Syntax

*rc*=**LOCATEC**(*table-id,col-num,cval<,sort<,direction>>*);

*rc*=**LOCATEN**(*table-id, col-num,nval <,sort<,direction>>*);

*rc*
>    contains information about the search:

| | |
|---|---|
| >0 | the number of rows read before a match is found |
| 0 | no row with a matching value was found |

>    Type: Numeric

*table-id*
>    is the identifier that was assigned when the SAS table was opened. If *table-id* is invalid, the program halts.
>    Type: Numeric

*col-num*
>    is the number of the column to search for. This number can be returned by the VARNUM function. If the number is invalid, the program halts and sends a message to the log.
>    Type: Numeric

*cval*
> is the character value for LOCATEC to search for. If *cval* is not a character value, the program halts and sends a message to the log.
> Type: Character

*nval*
> is the numeric value for LOCATEN to search for. If *nval* is not a numeric value, the program halts and sends a message to the log.
> Type: Numeric

*sort*
> indicates whether the SAS table is sorted:

> | | |
> |---|---|
> | **'A'** | The table is sorted in ascending order. |
> | **'D'** | The table is sorted in descending order. |
> | **'U'** | The table is not sorted. (This is the default.) |

> Type: Character

*direction*
> specifies the direction in which to search the SAS table:

> | | |
> |---|---|
> | **'A'** | searches all rows, starting with the first row. (This is the default.) |
> | **'B'** | searches from the previous row backward. |
> | **'F'** | searches from the next row forward. |

> Type: Character

**Details**   LOCATEC and LOCATEN do not search for partial values. For LOCATEC, preceding blanks are part of *cval* but trailing blanks are not. Therefore, you can facilitate searching for LOCATEC by using the LEFT function to left-justify character values.

LOCATEC and LOCATEN search all rows, starting with the first row by default and skipping rows marked for deletion. When a WHERE clause is active, these functions search the rows that meet the WHERE condition for a match. If a matching row is found, it is loaded into the Table Data Vector (TDV). Otherwise, the current row remains in the TDV.

LOCATEC and LOCATEN return the number of rows read before a match is found. This number may not correspond to the row number where the match is found because these functions skip deleted rows. Moreover, if a WHERE clause is active, they read only the rows, including any appended rows, that meet the WHERE condition. Also, if *direction* is supplied, the number returned is the number of rows read from the previous row where the search began. By default, the search direction is forward, starting with the first row in the table.

If the table is sorted, then specifying **'A'** or **'D'** for *sort* uses the more efficient binary search algorithm. Perform a binary search only when you have member-level access so that no one else can be editing the table concurrently. With a binary search, LOCATEC and LOCATEN make assumptions about how the data is sorted, and they assume that they can identify the first and last rows. If the table is being edited concurrently, rows could be appended so that the table is no longer in sorted order. As a result, the binary search might not find the correct values.

## Examples

**Example 1: Using the LOCATEC Function**   Locate a customer named SMITH in the PAYROLL table. The table is opened with a *table-id* of TABLEID and is sorted by NAME. The customer's name is specified in the CUSTOMER column.

```
customer='SMITH';
rc=locatec(tableid,varnum(tableid,'name'),customer,'a');
if (rc=0) then _msg_=
   'There is no customer named '||customer||'.';
else do;
     ...more SCL statements...
   end;
return;
```

**Example 2: Using the LOCATEN Function**    Locate a house whose price is $94,000 in the SASUSER.HOUSES table, which is opened with a *table-id* of HOUSEID. The price is specified in the window variable PRICE.

```
houseid=open('sasuser.houses');
price=94000;
rc=locaten(houseid,varnum(houseid,'price'),price);
if (rc=0) then
   _msg_='No house is priced at '||
         putn(price,'dollar9.2')||'.';
else do;
   rows=curobs(houseid);
   _msg_=
      'The specified price was found in row '||rows;
   end;
return;
```

## See Also

"FETCH" on page 389

"FETCHOBS" on page 390

"GETVARC and GETVARN" on page 450

"SET" on page 646

# LOCK

**Locks or unlocks a SAS table or a SAS catalog entry**

**Category:** SAS Table

## Syntax

*sysrc*=**LOCK**(*member*<,*action*>);

***sysrc***
contains the return code for the operation:

| | |
|---|---|
| 0 | successful |
| >0 | not successful |
| <0 | the operation was completed, but a warning or a note was generated. |

### member

is a member of a SAS data library or a SAS catalog entry. The value that you specify can be a one-, two-, three-, or four-level name. A one-level name is presumed to be a libref, whereas a two-level name defaults to the SAS table type DATA.

Type: Character

### action

specifies an action to be performed on the SAS table or catalog entry:

**'CLEAR'**

unlocks the specified SAS table(s) or SAS catalog entry.

**'LOCK'**

locks the specified SAS table(s) or SAS catalog entry. (This is the default.)

**'QUERY'**

queries the lock status of a SAS table or a SAS catalog entry.

_SWNOLKH

not currently locked. SYSRC of -630099.

_SWLKUSR

locked by another user. SYSRC of -630097.

_SWLKYOU

locked or in use by the caller. SYSRC of -630098.

Type: Character

**Details**    If *action* is not provided, the action defaults to LOCK.

## Example

Lock the data library that is associated with a libref of A, unlock data view LIB.A, and lock LIB.A.B.PROGRAM. Then, query the lock state of the FOO.ONE table:

```
rc=lock('a');
rc=lock('lib.a.view','clear');
rc=lock('lib.a.b.program');
rc=lock('foo.one.data','query');
if (rc=%sysrc(_SWLKUSR)) then
  _msg_='Table foo.one is currently locked.';
```

# LOOKUPC

**Searches for a string among a list of valid tokens**

**Category:**  Command

## Syntax

*rc*=**LOOKUPC**(*string,token-1*<, . . .,*token-12*>);

### rc

contains the return code for the operation:

0                              indicates that no match was found.

>0         is the position in the token list if a unique match was found.

<0         is the negative of the position in the token list if a duplicate token was found.

       Type: Numeric

***string***

     is the character value to search for.

       Type: Character

***token***

     is up to 12 character values, separated by commas.

       Type: Character

**Details**     A *token* can be a name, a literal, digits, or special characters. This function is useful for looking up valid commands.

The function accepts abbreviations as valid commands. That is, the function reports a match if the search string matches the starting characters of a token.

LOOKUPC does not search the token list for embedded strings. For example, the search string LIST would not be found in the token NEWLIST.

## Example

Get the command (SURVEY, NEWLIST, or ADDNAME) that the user issued from the command line, and execute code accordingly:

```
array cmds{*} $8 ('SURVEY','NEWLIST','ADDNAME');
INIT:
   control always;
return;
MAIN:
cmdword=WORD(1,'u');
cmdnum=lookupc(cmdword,cmds{1},cmds{2},cmds{3});
select;
when (cmdnum=1)
     ...SCL statements to process SURVEY command...
when (cmdnum=2)
     ...SCL statements to process NEWLIST command...
when (cmdnum=3)
   ...SCL statements to process ADDNAME command...
otherwise _msg_='Command conflict';
   end;
```

In this example, SUR, NEWL, and ADDN are considered valid commands.

# LVARLEVEL

**Fills an SCL list with the unique values of a column from a SAS table**

**Category:** List

## Syntax

*rc*=**LVARLEVEL**(*dsid,varname,n-level*< *,list-id*>);

***rc***

contains the return code for the operation:

0                        successful

≠0                       not successful
   Type: Numeric

***dsid***

is the identifier that was assigned when the table was opened. An invalid *dsid* produces an error condition.
   Type: Numeric

***varname***

is the column whose unique formatted values are to be reported.
   Type: Character

***n-level***

is the name of the column in which the function stores the number of unique values, or levels. This column must be initialized to a nonmissing value before its value is set by LVARLEVEL.

   *Note:*   This parameter is an update parameter. See "Input, Output, and Update Parameters" on page 34 for more information. △
   Type: Numeric

***list-id***

is the identifier of the list to fill with the unique formatted values. If *list-id* is not provided, the values are placed in the current result list. An invalid *list-id* produces an error condition.
   Type: Numeric or List

**Details**   The values are placed in the list identified by *list-id*, or in the current result list identified by CURLIST (if *list-id* is not specified). The values placed in the list are always character values. It is an error if *list-id* is omitted and you have not created a current result list with the CURLIST function. *n-level* must be a column, because LVARLEVEL uses it to store the number of unique values it finds. *n-level* must be initialized to any value except missing before LVARLEVEL executes.

## Examples

**Example 1: Placing Values in the Current List**   Get the unique formatted values for the table column NAME from SASUSER.CLASS, place the values in the current list, and print them:

```
dsid=open('sasuser.class');
nlevels=0;
rc=curlist(makelist());
rc=lvarlevel(dsid,'name',nlevels);
put nlevels=;
call putlist(curlist(),'levels',0);
rc=close(dsid);
```

**Example 2: Placing Values in a Specified List**   Get the unique formatted values for the table column NAME from SASUSER.CLASS, place the values in the specified list, and print them:

```
dsid=open('sasuser.class');
nlevels=0;
listid=makelist();
rc=lvarlevel(dsid,'name',nlevels,listid);
put nlevels=;
call putlist(listid,'levels',0);
rc=close(dsid);
rc=dellist(listid);
```

### See Also

"CURLIST" on page 320

"OPEN" on page 576

"VARLEVEL" on page 708

"VARSTAT" on page 714

# MAKEARRAY

**Creates an array of the given size with all elements in the array initialized to missing for numeric values or blank for character values**

**Category:**  Array

## Syntax

*array*=**MAKEARRAY**(*dim1*<,...,*dimN*>);

***array***

> is the dynamic array to be created. A non-dynamic array causes an error condition.
> Type: Array

***dim1,...,dimN***

> is the size of each specified dimension. If you specify negative sizes or an invalid
> number of dimensions, an error condition occurs.
> Type: Numeric

**Details**    Unlike static arrays, whose bounds must be set at compile time, you can
create and resize (change the bounds of) dynamic arrays at run time. The low bound of
the dynamic array will always be 1, and the high bound will be determined as given at
run time. If you create a one-dimensional dynamic array with 5 elements, then the low
bound and high bound will be 1 and 5, respectively. The array must be declared using
an asterisk (*) for the array dimensions with no array elements or initial values
specified. The syntax is the same as for a reference array. For example, the following
lines declare a one-dimensional numeric dynamic array named A and a
two-dimensional character dynamic array named B:

```
DCL num A(*);
DCL char B(*,*);
```

The MAKEARRAY function creates an array of the given size. All elements in the array
initialized to missing for numeric values or blank for character values. The number of
dimensions must be the same as what was specified in the DECLARE statement.

If you use the MAKEARRAY function to resize a dynamic array, all the data is lost and becomes garbage. If you try to reference an array element without first creating the array, an error occurs.

Dynamic arrays can be used with the other existing array functions (DIM, HBOUND, LBOUND) as long as the array has been created with MAKEARRAY. If you try to use these other functions without first creating the array, a program halt occurs.

## Examples

**Example 1: Create a One–Dimensional Array**   This example creates a one-dimensional array of 5 elements.

```
DCL num a(*);
a = makearray(5);
```

**Example 2: Create a Two–Dimensional Array**   This example creates a two-dimensional 5x5 array.

```
DCL num a(*,*);
a = makearray(5,5);
```

**Example 3: Create an Array from a Table**   This example uses table **work.a**, which has only numerical variables. The data from all the table rows is placed into a two-dimensional array. The dimensions and size of the array are determined by the number of rows and columns in the table.

```
init:

/* Open the table and create the array. */

DCL num arr(*,*) rc;
dsid = open('work.a');
nlobs = attrn(dsid, 'NLOBS');
nvars = attrn(dsid, 'NVARS');
arr = makearray(nlobs,nvars);

/* Move the contents of the table into the array. */

do i = 1 to dim(arr, 1);
 rc = fetch(dsid);
   do j = 1 to dim(arr, 2);
     arr[i,j] = getvarn(dsid, j);
   end;
 end;

/* Close the table and delete the array. */
call close(dsid);
rc = delarray(arr);
return;
```

## See Also

"DECLARE" on page 330

"DELARRAY" on page 332

"REDIM" on page 610

DIM, HBOUND, and LBOUND in *SAS Language Reference: Dictionary*

Chapter 4, "SCL Arrays," on page 37

# MAKELIST

**Creates an SCL list**

**Category:** List

## Syntax

*list-id*=**MAKELIST**(<*n*<, *visibility*>>);

### list-id

contains the identifier of the new list, or 0 if the list could not be created.
Type: Numeric or List

### n

is the number of items to place in the list initially. By default, *n* is 0.
Type: Numeric

### visibility

specifies whether the list is global or local:

| | |
|---|---|
| **'G'** | The list is global and can be shared by all applications executing in the same SAS session. A global list is deleted when the SAS session ends. |
| **'L'** | The list is local to the current SAS application. A local list is deleted when the application ends. (This is the default.) |

Type: Character

**Details**    MAKELIST creates either an empty list or a list with the number of items specified in *n*. Each item contains a missing value. Use the list identifier returned by MAKELIST with all other SCL list functions that use the list.

SCL lists can contain numeric items, character items, other list items, or object items. Each item can have a name. Both lists and list items have attributes. See Chapter 5, "SCL Lists," on page 47 for complete information about using SCL lists.

## Example

Create lists in the local and global environments:

```
n = 12;
   /*  Make an empty local list.  */
list1=makelist();
   /*  Make a local list with 24 items.  */
```

```
list2=makelist(2*n);
   /*  Make an empty global list.  */
list3=makelist(0,'G');
```

## See Also

"CLEARLIST" on page 290

"COPYLIST" on page 311

"DELLIST" on page 336

"LISTLEN" on page 521

"MAKENLIST" on page 536

"PUTLIST" on page 607

"SAVELIST" on page 629

# MAKENLIST

**Creates an SCL list that contains named items**

**Category:**  List

## Syntax

*list-id*=**MAKENLIST**(*visibility,name-1<, . . . ,name-n>*);

**list-id**
>   contains the identifier of the new list, or 0 if the list could not be created.
>>   Type: Numeric or List

**visibility**
>   specifies whether the list is global or local:

| | |
|---|---|
| **'G'** | The list is global and can be shared by all applications executing in the same SAS session. A global list is deleted when the SAS session ends. |
| **'L'** | The list is local to the current SAS application. A local list is deleted when the application ends. (This is the default.) |

>>   Type: Character

**name**
>   is one or more list item names, separated by commas. Item names are converted to uppercase, and trailing blanks are removed. Each name can be any SCL string. The same name can be used more than once.
>>   Type: Character

**Details**    MAKENLIST creates a list that contains an item for each name that you specify. Each item contains a missing value. Use the list identifier returned by MAKENLIST with all remaining functions that manipulate the list. When you create a list of named items, you can assign or access list values by their names as well as by their positions. However, it is more efficient to access items by position rather than by name.

You can use MAKENLIST to create structures that group related information into one list. For example, a row in a SAS table can be placed in a named list where each named item corresponds to the table column of the same name.

Note that the *visibility* argument (L or G) is required and is the first argument, unlike the MAKELIST function. Note also that this function does not use an *n* argument.

Using MAKENLIST is simpler than using MAKELIST and then naming each item independently.

### Example

The following statement creates a list of four named items:

```
mylist=makenlist('L','A','B','C');
```

It is equivalent to these four statements:

```
mylist=makelist(3,'L');
rc=nameitem(mylist,1,'A');
rc=nameitem(mylist,2,'B');
rc=nameitem(mylist,3,'C');
```

### See Also

"LISTLEN" on page 521

"MAKELIST" on page 535

"NAMEDITEM" on page 555

"NAMEITEM" on page 558

# MESSAGEBOX

**Displays a host message window with a specified text and icon**

**Category:** Utility

## Syntax

*text*=**MESSAGEBOX**(*textlist-id*<,*icon*<,*buttons*
    <,*caption*<,*default*<,*right*>>>>>);

**text**
    contains the text of the button that a user pressed in the message dialog window. This text can be OK, CANCEL, ABORT, RETRY, IGNORE, YES, or NO. When a user presses **Enter** instead of selecting a button, either *default* is returned (if specified) or the text of the first button in the message window is returned.
    Type: Character

**textlist-id**
    contains the identifier for the SCL list that contains the lines of text to display in the message window. Lines that are too long are wrapped. For example, if there are two lines and the first is too long, the text displays as three lines.
    Type: List

***icon***
>    specifies the icon to display in the message window:

>    `'I'`                Information or note icon (default)

>    `'?'`                Query icon

>    `'!'`                Warning icon

>    `'S'`                Error icon (stop sign/hand)

>    Type: Character

***buttons***
>    specifies the set of command buttons to display in the message window:

>    `'O'`                Ok (default)

>    `'OC'`               Ok Cancel

>    `'YN'`               Yes No

>    `'YNC'`              Yes No Cancel

>    `'ARI'`              Abort Retry Ignore

>    `'RC'`               Retry Cancel

>    Type: Character

***caption***
>    is the title for the message window.
>        Type: Character

***default***
>    is a single character that corresponds to one of the characters specified in *buttons*. *Default* specifies the value that is returned when a user presses **Enter** in the message window instead of selecting a button. If *default* is not supplied, the default selection is the text of the first button in the message window.
>        Type: Character

***right***
>    specifies whether the text in the message window is right- or left- justified:

>    `'N'`                Left justify the text. (default)

>    `'Y'`                Right justify the text.

>    Type: Character

**Details**    MESSAGEBOX calls a host message window and specifies text to be displayed there. It can also specify an icon, one or more buttons, and a title to display in the window.

If the message window cannot open, or if *textlist-id* is invalid, the program halts. Otherwise, MESSAGEBOX returns OK, CANCEL, ABORT, RETRY, IGNORE, YES, or NO. On hosts that allow users to close the message window without selecting a button, CANCEL is returned even if it is not one of the button choices.

## Example

Create a requestor window to prompt users to save the latest changes when they close an application window. If no button is selected to close the window, NO is returned to the variable COMMAND.

```
commandlist=makelist();
commandlist=insertc(commandlist,
   'You have not saved the latest changes.',1);
commandlist=insertc(commandlist,
   'Do you want to save your changes?',2);
...more SCL statements...
command=messagebox(commandlist,'!','YN','','N','');
commandlist=dellist(commandlist);
```

# METHOD

### Executes a method block that is defined in an SCL entry

**Category:** Modular Programming and Object Oriented

## Syntax

**CALL METHOD**(*entry,label< ,parameters>*);

*return-value=***METHOD**(*entry,label< ,parameters>*);

*entry*
> is a catalog entry of type SCL. To specify an entry in the current catalog, use *entry* or *entry.type*. To specify an entry in a different catalog, use *libref.catalog.entry.type*. If *type* is not specified, it defaults to SCL.
> Type: Character

*label*
> is the name of the method block in the SCL entry.
> Type: Character

*parameters*
> are parameters to pass to the method block. The SCL entry that receives these parameters must declare each of them in a METHOD statement.
>
> *Note:* These parameters are update parameters. See "Input, Output, and Update Parameters" on page 34 for more information. △
> Type: Character

*return-value*
> contains the value that is returned by the method block.
> Type: Numeric, Character, List, Object, Class, or Interface

**Details** METHOD can pass parameter values to the called method, and it can receive a value when it is used as a function. In order to return a value, the associated METHOD statement must contain the RETURN= option, and the RETURN statement must specify the variable or literal value to return.

Parameters that are passed must agree with the number of arguments, relative positions, and data types in the corresponding method block unless the REST= or ARGLIST= options are used in the method block. The parameter names in METHOD do not have to match the argument names in the method block.

A method block, which contains a sequence of SCL statements, can be defined either in the current SCL entry or in another, external SCL entry. If the method block is defined in the current entry, it is more efficient to use a LINK statement instead of a METHOD routine.

Parameters are passed in the following ways:

call-by-reference
  passes variables and enables values to be returned to CALL METHOD. This approach enables the called method block to modify values and then to return them.

  An example of a call-by-reference is

```
call method('b.scl','abc',var1,name,field2);
```

  If you do not want to return the values, use the NOCHANGE() routine in the method block. Or, you can assign the INPUT, OUTPUT, and UPDATE options to the variables listed in the METHOD statement to determine which variables can receive and return values. For example:

```
abc: method var1 :input :num
             name :update :char
             field1 :output :num;
```

call-by-value
  is used for all numeric constants, character constants, and expressions. It does not return values to the calling METHOD routine. An example of a call-by-value is

```
call method('b.scl','abc',100,'hello',x+y);
```

## Example

Call the method block that is labeled ABC in the SCL entry CODE. The following three parameters are passed: the contents of the variable A, the literal value 3, and the contents of the variable C.

```
call method('code.scl','abc',a,3,c);
```

The method block can return modified values to the variables A and C unless the NOCHANGE routine is specified in the method block or unless A and C are not specified in the METHOD statement as input parameters.

## See Also

"DISPLAY" on page 350

"NOCHANGE" on page 569

"METHOD" on page 540

# METHOD

**Defines a method that can be called by the METHOD routine**

**Category:**   Modular Programming and Object Oriented

## Syntax

*method-name-label*:< *method-access-scope* > **METHOD** < *argument-list*>
    <OPTIONAL=*argument-list*> <ARGLIST=*arg-list-id* |
    REST=*rest-list-id*><RETURN=*data-type*>;

**method-name-label**

specifies the method name label, which can be up to 32 characters in length. Method labels have the same syntax as SCL labels.

> **CAUTION:**
>
> **Leading underscores in method names typically identify methods that are supplied with the SAS System.** It is recommended that you do not define method names that have leading underscores unless the underscores are required. For example, you may need to create a new component that supports an interface, such as the staticStringList interface, that has methods that are defined with leading underscores. △

**method-access-scope**

species how the method can be accessed. If the *method-access-scope* is not provided, a method has **PUBLIC** scope. *Method-access-scope* is valid only for METHOD statements in a CLASS or USECLASS block.

**PUBLIC**

specifies that the method can be accessed by any SCL program.

**PRIVATE**

specifies that the method can be accessed only by methods in the same class in which the method is defined. Private methods are not inherited by subclasses of the class.

**PROTECTED**

specifies that the method can be accessed only by subclasses of the class in which the method is defined. Because a class can be considered a subclass of itself, a protected method can also be accessed from the class in which it is defined.

**argument-list**

list one or more sets of arguments, with each set specified as follows:
*var-list*:**<INPUT|UPDATE|OUTPUT>**:*data-type(length)*

*var-list*

lists one or more variables to contain values that are passed in from a method call using either dot notation or the METHOD, SEND, SUPER, APPLY or SUPAPPLY routine or function. Variables can also be a reference array. Reference array's dimensions are specified by '*'. Comma delimiters are required to separate '*' for multiple dimensions. The actual size of the reference array will be determined at run-time based on the dimensions specified in the array parameter of the calling method. For more information, see "ARRAY" on page 254 and Example 3 on page 546.

**INPUT | I**

specifies that, at run-time, the variable contains the value that is copied from the corresponding parameter of the calling method. However, when the program finishes, the value is not copied back to the calling method. This is equivalent to using CALL NOCHANGE() inside the METHOD block.

**UPDATE | U**

specifies that, at run-time, the variable contains the value that is copied from the corresponding parameter of the calling method. When the program finishes, the value is copied back to that parameter. All the Version 6 SCL method parameters are UPDATE parameter.

**OUTPUT | O**

specifies that, when the program finishes, the value is copied back to the corresponding parameter in the calling program (unless CALL NOCHANGE is specified). An error condition results if the corresponding parameter in the calling program is a constant, because a constant cannot receive a value.

*data-type*

specifies the type of data that the variable will contain. A named data type (for example, CHAR or LIST) must be preceded by the **:** delimiter. The delimiter is optional for unnamed data types (for example, $).

**CHAR**<(*length*)>

specifies that the variable will contain character data. *Length* can be 1 to 32,767 characters. If *length* is not provided, the default length is 200.

*Note:*  You cannot specify *length* for the **CHAR** *data-type* within the RETURN option. △

**LIST**

specifies that the variable will contain an SCL list identifier.

**NUM**

specifies that the variable will contain a numeric value.

**OBJECT**

specifies that the variable will contain the identifier for an object when it is defined at run time.

This type causes the SCL compiler to generate extra conversion instructions. Consequently, you should use it only when necessary so as to achieve optimal run-time performance.

*class-name*

specifies that the variable will contain the identifier for an object of the class specified in *class-name*. This type of object is defined at compile time. *Class-name* must be a three- or four-level name unless an IMPORT statement has specified the libref and catalog. In that case, the name can be a one- to four-level name. If the entry type is not specified, it is assumed to be CLASS.

*interface-name*

specifies that the variable will contain the identifier for an object of the class that supports the interface specified in *interface-name*. *Interface-name* must be a three- or four-level name unless an IMPORT statement has been used to specify the libref and catalog. In that case, the name can be a one- to four-level name.

If the entry type is not specified and a class with that name does not exist, the default entry type of INTERFACE is assumed.

To be compatible with the applications built in earlier releases of SAS software, the **:** delimiter is optional for variables that are declared with unnamed data types (for example, $), but it is required for variables that are assigned named data types. The following example shows a variety of data type declarations including the reference arrays using * as the dimensions:

```
mymethod: method
   char1  : Char(20)
   char2  : Char(10)
   char3  :input :char(50)
   charArr(*):u:char /* a reference array */
   num1   : Num
   num2   : Num
   num3   : num
   numArr(*):num      /* a reference array */
   myList :list
   myObj  :object
```

```
      myCol :sashelp.fsp.Collection.class ;
```
Type: Character

*length*
> is a numeric constant that specifies the length of the preceding variable or variables. The length of a character variable does not have to match the length of the corresponding passed parameter. SCL pads or truncates as necessary. When a length is specified for a variable that is declared as CHAR, the length specification must be enclosed in parentheses.
> Type: Character

**arg-list-id**
> contains the identifier for the SCL list that will contain all the arguments passed to the method. This includes all optional arguments.
> Type: List

**rest-list-id**
> contains the identifier for the SCL list that will contain all arguments that are passed to the method but are not explicitly specified in *argument-list* for either METHOD or OPTIONAL=.
> Type: List

**data-type**
> specifies the type of data that the method can return. The valid data types are Num, Char, List , Object , Array, and Class types.

## Details

The METHOD statement enables you to create method blocks and methods for SAS/AF classes. A method block is a feature for defining methods or for making a frequently used routine available to other programs. Methods define the actions for a class. A method block starts with the METHOD labels and ends with an ENDMETHOD statement. Only SCL entries can contain method blocks. Each method block contains additional SCL statements.

RETURN=*data-type* enables you to return a value to the calling method. An error condition is produced if *data-type* is not the same as the type of data to be returned to the calling program. Use a RETURN statement in the method to specify the value to return.

In SCL CLASS statement block or USECLASS statement block, each METHOD statement starts a new local variable scope just like an SCL DO/END block. Parameters with the same name but with the different types can be used across different method statements.

The METHOD statement receives parameters from the calling routine. When there are no optional arguments in the METHOD statement, a strict correspondence is required between the parameters that are passed by the calling routine and the arguments for the METHOD statement. The arguments and parameters must agree in number, data type, and relative position. If the calling program passes an incorrect number of parameters or a parameter of an incorrect type, SCL stops executing the program. The argument-parameter correspondence is less restrictive when you use the options OPTIONAL=, ARGLIST=, and REST= in the METHOD statement:

OPTIONAL=
> enables you to specify one or more optional arguments that are used only if the calling program supplies the corresponding parameters in the parameter list of the calling routine. If corresponding parameters are not supplied, then the optional arguments are initialized to missing values.

ARGLIST= and REST=
  enable you to pass a variable number of parameters to the METHOD statement. You determine the types and order of the variable arguments. The lists identified by *arg-list-id* and *rest-list-id* are created automatically when the entry is called, and they are deleted automatically when the entry ends. When an array is passed as a parameter, the array is expanded into individual items and these items are inserted into the *arg-list-id* and *rest-list-id* lists. ARGLIST= and REST= are mutually exclusive, so you can use only one or the other.

**Calling and Executing Method Blocks**    Other SCL programs call a method block by specifying its label in a dot notation statement or in a METHOD, APPLY, SUPER, SUPAPPLY, or SEND routine or function. Execution of the method block starts at the METHOD statement and ends with the ENDMETHOD statement. After a method block is executed, control returns either to the calling program statement or to the command line. A method block can be tested individually by invoking a TESTAF command with the label=*method-name* option with the SCL debugger. For example, the following statement tests the COMBINE method:

```
testaf label=combine
```

**Scope of Method Block Variables**    All variables that are declared using the DECLARE statement in a method block are local to that method. You cannot use a GOTO statement to jump into a method block in the current entry. All the method parameters are also local to that method if method blocks are written inside a CLASS statement block or a USECLASS statement block.

**Passing Parameters to Method Blocks**    The METHOD statement can receive parameter values for variables that are declared as UPDATE or INPUT. By default, all parameters declared in a METHOD statement are UPDATE parameters.
  The parameter-receiving mechanism for the METHOD statement is very similar to that mechanism for the ENTRY statement. The METHOD statement receives parameters from the third argument of the calling METHOD routine. The calling METHOD routine must agree with the corresponding METHOD statement in the following ways (unless OPTIONAL=, ARGLIST=, or REST= are specified):

  □ The number of arguments received must be the same as the number of parameters passed.
  □ The relative positions of the arguments passed must match the parameters in the corresponding METHOD statement.
  □ The data types of both sets of variables must agree.

  Otherwise, SCL stops executing the calling METHOD routine and prints an error message.

**Returning Modified Parameters to the Calling Routine**    The METHOD statement can return values to parameters from variables that are declared as UPDATE or OUTPUT. A called method block can modify any argument it receives. However, it cannot return new values to calling routine parameters that are numeric literals, character literals, or expressions. By default, values for variables are returned to the calling routine. If you want a called method block to receive values but not to return values to its calling routine, declare the variables as INPUT. If you want variables in the method to only return values, then declare the method's variables as OUTPUT.
  For more information, see "What Happens When Attribute Values Are Set or Queried" on page 122.

**Returning a Value to the Calling Routine**    A METHOD statement can return a value to the calling routine when the METHOD statement uses the RETURN= option to declare the data type of the returned value. A RETURN statement in the method specifies either the variable or expression that contains the value or the literal value to return.

## Examples

### Example 1: METHOD Statement Declarations
Method M1 contains a variety of argument specifications.

```
IMPORT work.myclass.collection.class;
Class Example1;
M1: PUBLIC  METHOD
      /* usenum is UPDATE (default) numeric     */
    usenum :NUM
      /* usechar is UPDATE (default) character */
    usechar :CHAR
      /* mylist is UPDATE (default) list        */
    mylist :LIST
      /* myobject is UPDATE (default) object    */
    myobject :OBJECT
      /* mycoll is UPDATE (default) collection */
    mycoll :COLLECTION
      /* innum is INPUT   numeric               */
    innum :INPUT :NUM
      /* state is OUTPUT character              */
    state :OUTPUT :CHAR
      /* namelist is UPDATE list                */
    namelist :UPDATE :LIST
      /* outputobj is OUTPUT object             */
    outputobj :OUTPUT :OBJECT
      /* amountin is INPUT   numeric            */
    amountin :I :NUM
      /* c3 is OUTPUT character                 */
    c3 :O :CHAR
      /* l3 is UPDATE list                      */
    l3 :U :LIST
      /* numarr is a numeric UPDATE array       */
    numarr(5) : NUM
      /* states is a character reference array */
    states(*) : CHAR
      /* return a numeric value                 */
    RETURN=NUM;

    ...SCL statements that define the method...
    RETURN(0);

ENDMETHOD;
EndClass;
```

### Example 2: Using the RETURN= Option
Define an ADD method to add the numbers stored in N1 and N2, and return the sum in the variable TOTAL:

```
Class Example2;
add: public method n1:num n2:num return=num;
   total=n1+n2;
   return(total);
```

```
endmethod;
EndClass;
```

**Example 3: Reference Array Whose Size Is Determined at Run Time**   The following Sort class contains two overloaded methods that are named SORT. Each method contains an array parameter that is a reference array. The size of the reference array will be determined at run time based on the associated array parameters in the calling methods.

```
Class Sort;
/* Generic sort routine for any size of */
/* 1-dimensional numeric array           */
sort: method narr(*):Num;
      /* Find dimensions from the calling program */
   DCL Num temp;
   DCL Num size = dim(narr);
     /* --- Bubble Sort --- */
   do i = 1 to size - 1;
      do j = i+1 to size;
         if narr(i) > narr(j) then
            do;
              temp = narr(i);
              narr(i) = narr(j);
              narr(j) = temp;
            end;
      end;
   end;
   /* Array narr is now sorted in ascending order */
endmethod;

    /* Generic sort routine for any size of */
    /* 1-dimensional  character array        */
sort: method carr(*):Char;
      /* Find dimensions from the calling program */
   DCL Char tempc;
   DCL Num size = dim(carr);
     /* --- Bubble Sort --- */
   do i = 1 to size - 1;
      do j = i+1 to size;
         if carr(i) > carr(j) then
            do;
               tempc = carr(i);
              carr(i) = carr(j);
              carr(j) = tempc;
            end;
      end;
   end;
   /* Array carr is now sorted in ascending order */
endmethod;
EndClass;
```

**Example 4: Calling a Method**   This example creates a new instance of the Sort class and sends a message to the sort method to sort the order of the existing arrays CARR and NARR.

```
Init:
DCL Char(20) carr(3)=('c','b','a');
DCL Num narr(3)={3, 2, 1};
DCL Sort obj = _NEW_ Sort();
obj.sort(carr);
obj.sort(narr);
put carr= narr=;
```

The output is

```
carr=
carr[1]='a'
carr[2]='b'
carr[3]='c'
narr[1] = 1
narr[2] = 2
narr[3] = 3
```

### Example 5: Using the REST= Argument

Add a variable number of numbers, and print out the sum. The method ignores any character types that are passed in.

```
Class Varying;

SUMPRINT: method msg:Char REST=rest_list;
    DCL num totsum;
    if rest_list = . then
        do;
            put 'No numbers to add were passed in!';
            return;
        end;
    totsum = 0;
    do i = 1 to listlen( rest_list );
        type = itemtype( rest_list, i );
        if ( type = 'N' ) then
            do;
                valn = getitemn( rest_list, i );
                totsum = totsum + valn;
            end;
    end;

    put msg totsum;
endmethod;
EndClass;
```

Use the following program to invoke the SUMPRINT method:

```
Init:
    DCL Varying obj = _NEW_ Varying();
    obj.SUMPRINT('The total is:', 15, 30, 1);
```

The output of this example is

```
The total is: 46
```

### Example 6: Parameter Scope and Method Variable Scope

This program shows the parameters of the same name and different types being used across different method statements.

```
Class ReUseName;
   m1: Method n:Num c:Char;
         DCL  Num  localN;
         DCL  Char localC;
       EndMethod;
   m2: Method n:Char c:num;
         DCL Char localN;
         DCL Num  localC;
       EndMethod;
EndClass;
```

## See Also

"IMPORT" on page 475

## _METHOD_

**Contains the name of the method that is currently executing**

**Category:** System Variable

**Details** _METHOD_ is a character system variable that is provided automatically by the FRAME entry in SAS/AF. However, the SCL compiler does not automatically create a space for it in the SCL data vector. As a result, you get a warning when you compile a FRAME or SCL entry that uses _METHOD_, because the variable is being referenced at compile time but is not assigned a value until run time. You can safely ignore this warning. If you prefer to prevent the warning message from being generated, use the following assignment statement at the top of your program:

```
_method_ = _method_;
```

_METHOD_ is useful when you have one or more methods that share the same section of code but which require a CALL SUPER.

In order to use _METHOD_, you must use the DECLARE or LENGTH statement to declare it as a character variable.

_METHOD_ has a valid value only when a method is executing.

## Example

For a window control, you may define the _update and _bupdate methods to execute the same section of code if they perform similar functions:

```
length _method_ $40;
BUPDATE:
UPDATE:
   method;
   ...code for _update and _bupdate methods...
   call super(_self_, _method_);
endmethod;
```

Without _METHOD_, you would not know which method to do a CALL SUPER on, so you would have to code the above as

```
BUPDATE:
   method;
   methodName = '_bupdate';
   link update1;
endmethod;
UPDATE:
   method;
   methodName = '_update';
   link update1;
endmethod;

UPDATE1:
   ...code for _update and _bupdate goes here...

   call super(_self_, methodName);
return;
```

## See Also

"_SELF_" on page 643

"SUPER" on page 681

"_VALUE_" on page 704

---

# MLENGTH

**Returns the maximum length of a variable**

**Category:** Character

---

## Syntax

*length*=**MLENGTH**(*var*);

**length**
    contains the maximum length of a variable.
        Type: Numeric

**var**
    is the variable whose maximum length you want to determine.
        Type: Character

**Details**    MLENGTH is different from LENGTH, which returns the trimmed length. For window variables, MLENGTH returns the length of the variable in the display.

    If a numeric variable is passed to MLENGTH, MLENGTH always returns a length of 8 for the variable. For non-window variables, MLENGTH returns the declared length of the variable.

## Example

In this example, MLENGTH returns the value 5, which is the declared length of variable S. However, LENGTH returns the value 2, because S contains **ab**.

```
length s $ 5;
s='ab';
l=length(s);
m=mlength(s);
```

## See Also

"LENGTH" on page 509

# MODIFIED

**Reports whether a field or FRAME entry control has been modified**

**Category:**   Control or Field

## Syntax

*rc*=**MODIFIED**(*wcol-name*);

***rc***
contains the return code for the operation:

1                    modified

0                    not modified
     Type: Numeric

***wcol-name***
is the name of the field or FRAME entry control in the window. This name cannot be an element of an array nor an expression. If *wcol-name* is invalid, the program halts.
     Type: Character

**Details**    A field's state changes to modified when a user types any character in the field and presses ENTER or a function key or selects a FRAME entry control.
     The field or FRAME entry control cannot be an element of an array. To report this information for an array element, use FIELD instead.
     The ERRORON statement causes MODIFIED to return a value of 1.
     FRAME entry controls can also use the _isModified method.

## Examples

**Example 1: Opening an FSEDIT Window**    Open an FSEDIT window for the SAS table specified in the TBLNAME variable. The FSEDIT function displays the table for interactive editing.

```
if (modified(tblname) and tblname ne ' ' ) then
   call fsedit(tblname);
else
   _msg_='Please enter a valid table name.';
```

**Example 2: Invalid Syntax for MODIFIED**    The following are examples of invalid syntax that will not compile:

```
      /* A literal string is used. */
   rc=modified('xyz');
      /* Concatenation of two columns. */
   rc=modified(a||b);
      /* An array element is used. */
   rc=modified(a{i});
```

## See Also

"DISPLAYED" on page 353

"ERROR" on page 375

"ERROROFF" on page 376

"ERRORON" on page 377

"FIELD" on page 394

"OBSINFO" on page 575

# MODVAR

**Changes the name, label, format, or informat of a column in a SAS table**

**Category:**  Variable

## Syntax

*sysrc=***MODVAR**(*table-id,var-name,new-name<,label <,format<,informat>>>*);

*sysrc*
  contains the return code for the operation:

  0                              successful

  ≠0                             not successful
     Type: Numeric

*table-id*
  is the identifier that was assigned when the table was opened. If *table-id* is invalid,
  the program halts.
     Type: Numeric

*var-name*
  is the column whose attribute or attributes you want to change. The column must
  already exist in the SAS table.
     Type: Character

*new-name*
  is the new name to assign to the column. The value must be a valid SAS name and
  cannot already exist in the SAS table.
     Type: Character

*label*
  is the label to assign to the column.
     Type: Character

*format*
> is the format to assign to the column.
> > Type: Character

*informat*
> is the informat to assign to the column.
> > Type: Character

**Details**    The table must be opened in UTILITY (V) mode, or the function halts.
If you do not want to change an argument, insert a null string ( ′ ′)as a placeholder.

## Example

Change only the label for the column PHONENUM in the SAS table CUSTOMR:

```
dsid=open('customr','v');
if dsid then
   do;
      rc=modvar(dsid,'phonenum','','Office Phone');
      rc=close(dsid);
   end;
```

## See Also

"OPEN" on page 576

"VARFMT" on page 705

"VARINFMT" on page 706

"VARLABEL" on page 706

"VARLEN" on page 707

"VARNAME" on page 712

"VARNUM" on page 713

"VARTYPE" on page 716

# MOPEN

**Opens a member file in a directory**

**Category:**    Directory

## Syntax

*file-id*=**MOPEN**(*directory-id,member-name< open-mode*
   *<,record-length<,record-format>>>*);

*file-id*
> contains the identifier for the file, or 0 if the file could not be opened. You can use a
> *file-id* that is returned by the MOPEN function just as you would use a *file-id*
> returned by the FOPEN function.
> > Type: Numeric

**directory-id**
> is the identifier that was returned by DOPEN when the directory was opened. If *directory-id* is invalid, the program halts.
> Type: Numeric

**member-name**
> is the name of a file in the directory that is identified by *directory-id*.
> Type: Character

**open-mode**
> is the type of access to the file:

> | | |
> |---|---|
> | **'A'** | APPEND mode, which allows writing new records after the current end of the file. |
> | **'I'** | INPUT mode, which allows reading only. (This is the default.) |
> | **'O'** | OUTPUT mode, which defaults to the OPEN mode that was specified in *host-options* in the FILENAME statement or function. If no host option was specified, then OUTPUT mode allows writing new records at the beginning of the file. |
> | **'S'** | Sequential input mode, which is used for pipes and other sequential devices such as hardware ports. |
> | **'U'** | UPDATE mode, which allows both reading and writing. |

> Type: Character

**record-length**
> is the logical record length of the file. To use the existing record length for the file, specify a length of 0 or do not provide a value here.
> Type: Numeric

**record-format**
> is the record format of the file:

> | | |
> |---|---|
> | **'B'** | Interpret data as binary data. |
> | **'D'** | Use the default record format. |
> | **'E'** | Use an editable record format. |
> | **'F'** | The file contains fixed-length records. |
> | **'P'** | The file contains printer carriage-control characters in a host-dependent record format. |
> | **'V'** | The file contains variable-length records. |

> To use the existing record format, do not specify a value here.
> Type: Character

## Details

***CAUTION:***
> **Use OUTPUT mode with care.** Opening an existing file for output may overwrite the current contents of the file without warning. △

The member file is identified by *directory-id* and *member-name* instead of by a fileref. You can also open a directory member by using FILENAME to assign a fileref to the member, followed by a call to FOPEN. However, using MOPEN saves you from having to use a separate fileref for each member.

If the file already exists and is opened with an *open-mode* of O, then the output mode defaults to either APPEND or REPLACE, based on *host-options* that were specified in the FILENAME function or statement. For example:

```
rc=filename('file',filename,' ','mod');
fid=fopen('file','o');
rc=fput(fid,'This is a test.');
rc=fwrite(fid);
rc=fclose(fid);
```

If FILE already exists, then FWRITE appends a new record. However, if no host option was specified with the FILENAME function, then FWRITE writes the value at the beginning of the file, which could replace an existing value.

If the open fails, use SYSMSG to retrieve the message text.

*Operating Environment Information:*   The term *directory* in this description refers to an aggregate grouping of files managed by the host operating system. Different host operating systems identify such groupings with different names, such as directory, subdirectory, MACLIB, or partitioned data set. See the SAS documentation for your operating environment for details.

Opening a directory member for output is not possible on some operating systems. △

## Example

Assign the fileref MYDIR to a directory. Then open the directory, determine the number of members, retrieve the name of the first member, and open that member. The last three arguments to MOPEN are the defaults.

```
rc=filename('mydir','filename');
did=dopen('mydir');
frstname=' ';
memcount=dnum(did);
if (memcount>0) then
    do;
        frstname=dread(did,1);
        fid=mopen(did,frstname,'i',0,'d');
        ...SCL statements to process the member...
        rc=fclose(fid);
    end;
else
    _msg_=sysmsg();
rc=dclose(did);
```

## See Also

"DOPEN" on page 357

"FCLOSE" on page 386

"FOPEN" on page 420

# _MSG_

**Contains the text to display on the window's message line the next time the window is refreshed**

**Category:**  System Variable

**Details**      _MSG_ is a system variable that is created for every SCL program you compile. The compiler creates a space for _MSG_ in the SCL data vector.

Typically an application displays error and warning messages on the window's message line. The text for system error and warning messages can be obtained by using the SYSMSG or STDMSG functions. You can also assign your own text to the _MSG_ variable. Messages are displayed when the window is refreshed.

FRAME entries can also use the _getMsg and _setMsg methods to query and update the _MSG_ variable.

On some operating systems, _MSG_ is not displayed if the window has BANNER set to NONE.

## Example

Display a message if a table cannot be opened:

```
INIT:
   dsid = open('sasuser.class');
   if dsid eq 0 then
      _msg_ = sysmsg();
return;
```

## See Also

"SYSMSG" on page 686

# NAMEDITEM

**Returns the index of a named item in a list**

**Category:** List

## Syntax

*index*=**NAMEDITEM**(*list-id*,*name*< ,*occurrence*
  <,*start-index*<,*forceup*>>>);

**index**
> contains the position of the item in the list, or 0 if the named item is not found.
> Type: Numeric

**list-id**
> is the identifier of the list that NAMEDITEM searches. An invalid *list-id* produces an error condition.
> Type: Numeric or List

**name**
> is the name of the item to search for. If *name* is specified, then trailing blanks are removed before the search. If *name* is blank, the first unnamed item is returned.
> Type: Character

**occurrence**
> specifies which occurrence of the named item to search for. The default, 1, specifies the first occurrence of the item.
> Type: Numeric

### start-index

specifies where in the list to begin searching for the item. By default, *start-index* is 1 (the first item). If *start-index* is positive, then the search begins at position *start-index* items from the beginning of the list. If *start-index* is negative, then the search begins at the item specified by ABS(*start-index*) items from the end of the list. An error condition results if the absolute value of *start-index* is zero or if it is greater than the number of items in the list.

Type: Numeric

### forceup

can have one of the following values:

| | |
|---|---|
| **'Y'** | specifies a case-insensitive search, which overrides the HONORCASE or NOHONORCASE list attribute. |
| **'N'** | specifies a search that uses the HONORCASE or NOHONORCASE list attribute and is the default action for lists when FORCEUP is not specified. |
| IGNORECASE | is an alias for NOHONORCASE. |

**Details**    NAMEDITEM searches only the top level of the list specified by *list-id*. That is, it does not search sublists. Several functions that access items in a list by position have counterparts that access items by their names such as GETITEMC versus GETNITEMC. Because it is more efficient to retrieve an item by its position rather than by its name, you can use NAMEDITEM to find the position and then use the functions that access items by position rather than by name.

If *occurrence* and *start-index* are both positive or both negative, the search proceeds forward from the *start-index* item. For forward searches, the search continues only to the end of the list and does not wrap back to the front of the list. If *occurrence* or *start-index* is negative, the search is backwards. For backward searches, the search continues only to the beginning of the list and does not wrap back to the end of the list.

## Example

Swap the numeric values associated with the first and last occurrence of the item named **x**:

```
/*  Return first occurrence of X.  */
first=getnitemn(listid,'X');
/*  Return last occurrence of X.   */
last=getnitemn(listid,'X',1,-1);
list=setnitemn(listid,last,'X');
list=setnitemn(listid,first,'X',1 -1);
```

The following example shows a slightly more efficient way to perform the swap operation. This method does not require a second search for the item, and it can also detect when item **x** does not exist in the list.

```
/*  Return the position number of the */
/* first item X. */
ifirst=nameditem(listid,'X');
if (ifirst>0) then
   do;
      first=getitemn(listid,ifirst);
/* Return the position of the last item X.*/
      ilast=nameditem(listid,'X',1,-1);
      list=setitemn(listid,getitemn(listid,ilast),
```

```
                                ifirst);
          list=setitemn(listid,first,ilast);
      end;
```

*Note:* This example checks to see whether there is at least one item named **x** but never checks to see whether there is another item named **x**. It assumes that there is at least one more item named **x** △

## See Also

"DELNITEM" on page 337

"NAMEITEM" on page 558

"SEARCH" on page 635

# NAMEDIVIDE

**Returns the number of parts of a compound name as well as the values of each part**

**Category:** Utility

## Syntax

*rc*=**NAMEDIVIDE**(*name,num-parts, part-1, . . . part-4*);

**rc**

contains the return code for the operation:

| | |
|---|---|
| 0 | successful |
| ≠0 | not successful |

Type: Numeric

**name**

is the name of a two- to four-part compound name to be separated.
Type: Character

**num-parts**

returns the number of parts in *name*.

*Note:* This parameter is an update parameter. See "Input, Output, and Update Parameters" on page 34 for more information. △
Type: Numeric

**part-1. . . part-4**

contains the values of the first through fourth parts of *name*.

*Note:* These parameters are an update parameters. See "Input, Output, and Update Parameters" on page 34 for more information. △
Type: Character

**Details**  NAMEDIVIDE divides a compound name into parts and returns the number of parts as well as the value of each part.

*Note:* NAMEDIVIDE does not validate individual parts of the name. △

## Example

Divide NAME into parts and invoke DIALOG if NAME is a FRAME entry. If NAME is not a FRAME entry, CALL DISPLAY.

```
rc=namedivide(name,parts,part1,part2,part3,part4);
   /* Was NAMEDIVIDE successful? */
if (rc^=0) then do;
   put 'Error: Invalid name ' name;
   return;

type=upcase(part4);
if (part4='FRAME') then
   call dialog(name);
else
   call display(name);
```

## See Also

"NAMEMERGE" on page 559

# NAMEITEM

**Returns and optionally replaces the name of an item in an SCL list**

**Category:**   List

## Syntax

*item-name*=**NAMEITEM**(*list-id*<,*index*<,*new-name*>>);

***item-name***
   contains the name of the specified list item, or a blank if the item does not have a name.
   Type: Character

***list-id***
   is the identifier of the list that contains the indexed item. An invalid *list-id* produces an error condition.
   Type: Numeric or List

***index***
   is the position of the item in the list. The position can be specified as a positive or negative number. By default, *index* is 1 (the first item). If *index* is a positive number, then the item is at position *index* from the beginning of the list. If *index* is a negative number, then the item is at position ABS(*index*) from the end of the list. An error condition results if the absolute value for *index* is zero or if it is greater than the number of items in the list.
   Type: Numeric

***new-name***
   is the new name to assign to the list item.
   Type: Character

**Details** NAMEITEM returns the name of the item at the list position specified by *index*. If a value for *new-name* is also provided, then NAMEITEM assigns that name to the item, replacing the old name.

An error condition results if the value for *new-name* is provided and the list has any of the following attributes:

- □ NOUPDATE
- □ SASNAMES, and *new-name* is not a valid SAS name
- □ NODUPNAMES, and *new-name* duplicates the name of another item in the list.

To check the attributes of a list or list item, use HASATTR. To change attributes, use SETLATTR.

## See Also

"DELNITEM" on page 337

"NAMEDITEM" on page 555

---

# NAMEMERGE

**Returns a compound name by merging name parts**

**Category:** Utility

---

## Syntax

*name=***NAMEMERGE**(*part-1*,*part-2*< ,*part-3*< ,*part–4*>>);

**name**
   contains a two- to four-part compound name. Name is blank if any error is detected.

**part-1 . . . part-4**
   contain the name segments to be merged. Both *part-1* and *part-2* must be specified.

**Details** NAMEMERGE creates a SAS name by merging the values that are stored as two to four parts. If four parts are specified, then *part-1* and *part-4* can be blank.

## Example

Create a CATALOG entry name, using the values stored in the variables LIBREF, CATALOG, NAME, and TYPE. Then run the CATALOG entry through DISPLAY.

```
entry=namemerge(libref,catalog,name,type);
if (entry^=' ') and (cexist(entry)) then
    call display(entry);
```

## See Also

"NAMEDIVIDE" on page 557

---

# _NEO_

**Creates an object**

**Category:**   Object Oriented

## Syntax

*object-id*=**_NEO_** *class-name(< init-arg<,new-arg-1<, . . . ,new-arg-n>>>);*

**object-id**
   contains the identifier for the new object.
      Type: Numeric or Object

**class-name**
   is the name of the class from which to create the object. This can be a one- to
   four-level name. If *class-name* is a one- or two-level name, and if the CLASS entry
   that defines *class-name* is not in the application catalog, then *class-name* must exist
   in one of the catalogs defined by the IMPORT statement. Otherwise, the compiler
   produces an error message.

**init-arg**
   is the argument to pass to the _init method for the new object.
      Type: Character

**new-arg**
   are additional arguments to pass to the _new method of the new object.
      Type: Character

**Details**    The _NEO_ operator provides a faster and more direct way to create an
object. It combines the actions of loading a class with LOADCLASS and initializing the
object with the _new method, which invokes the object's _init method.

## Example

Create a frame and enter the following source code:

```
import sashelp.classes;

init:
  dcl list AttrList RegionList;
  dcl checkbox_c c;

  AttrList   = makelist();
  RegionList = makelist();

  startcol=10;  startrow=10;
  rc = setniteml(AttrList, RegionList, '_region_');
  rc = setnitemn(AttrList, -1, 'num');
  rc = setnitemn(RegionList, startcol, 'ulx');
  rc = setnitemn(RegionList, startrow, 'uly');
  rc = setnitemc(RegionList, 'simple', 'border_style');
  rc = setnitemn(RegionList, 5, 'border_width');
  rc = setnitemc(RegionList, 'red', 'border_color');

  c = _neo_ checkbox_c(attrlist);
  return;
```

Note that you cannot use the _NEW_ operator to do this, because _NEW_ passes its
arguments to a constructor, whereas _NEO_ passes them to the _new method (which is

what you want in this case). Even if you created a constructor for the checkbox, it would not work with the _NEW_ operator because the checkbox will be displayed before the constructor has a chance to run. Therefore, you must either resort to the old behavior using CALL SEND, or use the _NEO_ operator as shown above.

## See Also

"DECLARE" on page 330

"IMPORT" on page 475

"INSTANCE" on page 485

"LOADCLASS" on page 525

# NEW

**Defines a new SAS table interactively**

**Category:**  SAS Table

## Syntax

**CALL NEW**(*table-name,model-table,num-row, display-window*);

*table-name*
is the SAS table to be created, specified as *<libref.>member*. The default library, USER, is used if *libref* is omitted. If a null string (*' '*) is specified for *table-name*, then the DATA*n* naming convention is used to create a table in the USER library.
Type: Character

*model-table*
is an existing SAS table after which the new SAS table is to be modeled. Use a null string (*' '*) as a placeholder if you do not want to specify a model table.
Type: Character

*num-row*
is the number of initial rows for the new SAS table. This value must be equal to or greater than 0. If the default is set to *'0'*, then the value is a negative number. All columns in all rows initially contain missing values. The value for *num-row* cannot be a missing value.
Type: Character

*display-window*
specifies whether the NEW window is displayed so that column definitions for the new SAS table can be edited before the table is created:

*'Y'*
displays the NEW window to allow editing of the column names and attributes before the new SAS table is created. (This is the default.)

*'N'*
does not display the NEW window. The column definitions in the new SAS table will be an exact replica of those in the model table. A value must also be supplied for *model-table*.
Type: Character

**Details** NEW creates a new blank SAS table. However, it does not replace an existing table.

*CAUTION:*

**Specifying an existing SAS table for *table-name* causes a program halt.** To prevent the program halt, use EXIST to determine whether the table already exists, DELETE to delete the table, and CALL NEW to create a new table with the same name. △

By default, the routine opens the NEW window to enable a user to interactively define the names and attributes of the columns in the new SAS table. The NEW window that this routine opens is the same as the window that is displayed when the NEW= option is used with the PROC FSEDIT or PROC FSVIEW statement.

You can specify *model-table* so that all the names and attributes of the model are automatically copied to the new table. (Only the column names and column attributes of the model table are copied, not the values that it contains.) When you specify a model table, you can use *display-window* to bypass the NEW window and create the new table with the same column names and attributes as the model table. Open the NEW window only if you want to enable users to alter the column names and attributes before the new table is created.

Use *num-row* to specify how many blank rows to create for the new SAS table. All columns in all rows of the new table initially contain missing values.

## Examples

**Example 1: Creating a SAS Table from a Model Table** Create a new SAS table with a name that the user supplies in the field for the window variable TABLE. Before attempting to create the table, determine whether a SAS table with the specified name already exists. If so, issue a message on the application window's message line. The new table is modeled after the existing table MODEL.A, and the user is not given the opportunity to modify the column definitions (the NEW window is not opened). The new table is created with ten blank rows.

```
if (exist(table)) then
 _msg_='SAS table '||table||' already exists.';
else
   do;
      call new(table,'model.a',10,'n');
      _msg_='SAS table '||table||' has been created.';
   end;
```

**Example 2: Creating a SAS Table from a User Definition** Create a new SAS table with a name that the user supplies in the field for the window variable TABLE. These statements display the NEW window for the user to define the columns in the table. No model table is used.

```
if (exist(table)) then
 _msg_='SAS table '||table||' already exists.';
else
   do;
      call new(table,' ',1,'y');
      _msg_='SAS table '||table||' has been created.';
   end;
```

## See Also

"FSEDIT" on page 433

"FSVIEW" on page 437

"NEWVAR" on page 565

"OPEN" on page 576

# _NEW_

**Creates an object and runs an associated class constructor**

**Category:** Object Oriented

## Syntax

*object-id=*__NEW_ *class-name*(< *arg1, arg2, . . . , argn>*);

**object-id**
> contains the identifier for the new object.
>> Type: Numeric, Classes, and Object

**class-name**
> is the name of the class from which to create the object. This can be a one- to four-level name. If *class-name* is a one- or two-level name, and if the CLASS entry that defines *class-name* is not in the application catalog, then *class-name* must exist in one of the catalogs defined by the IMPORT statement. Otherwise, the compiler produces an error message.

**arg1, arg2, . . . , argn**
> are the arguments that are passed to the class constructor.
>> Type: Character

## Examples

**Example 1: Creating an Instance of an Object and Running a Class Constructor**   The _NEW_ operator enables you to create an instance of an object and run a class constructor all in one step.

```
X.SCL
class Complex;
  private num x y;

  Complex: method a1: num a2: num;
          x = c.x;
          y = c.y;
  endmethod;
endclass;

Y.SCL
init:
  dcl Complex c = _new_ Complex(1,2);
```

```
    dcl Complex c2 = _new_ Complex(c);
    return;
```

### Example 2: Using a Class That Has an Overloaded Constructor    Where you have a class, Complex, that has an overloaded constructor, one version takes two numeric arguments, and the other takes a complex number.

In the first _NEW_ statement, you create a complex number, **1 + 2i**, by passing in the real and imaginary parts (1 and 2) as arguments to the _NEW_ operator. _NEW_ first creates an instance of the Complex class, and then calls the appropriate constructor based on its argument list. In this case, it calls the constructor that takes two numeric arguments.

In the second _NEW_ statement, you create a complex number by passing in another complex number (in this case, the first one you created, **1 + 2i**). _NEW_ calls the second constructor in the Complex class — the one that takes a complex number as an argument.

Constructors must always have the same name as the class in which they are located, and they must always be void methods (that is, they do not return a value). Constructors provide a convenient way to initialize a class before you begin using it.

For example, if you didn't use constructors in the above example, you would have to create another set of methods to initialize the complex number and call those separately, as in the following example:

```
X.SCL
class Complex;
  private num x y;

  set: method a1: num a2: num;
          x = a1;
          y = a2;
  endmethod;

  set: method c: Complex;
          x = c.x;
          y = c.y;
  endmethod;
endclass;

Y.SCl
init:
 dcl Complex c = _new_ Complex();
 dcl Complex c2 = _new_ Complex();
 c.set(1,2);
 c2.set(c);
 return;
```

You can overload constructors as shown above, or you can have only one constructor, or you can have none. If you don't supply a constructor in a class, the _NEW_ operator still attempts to run a parent class constructor. In the following example, the _NEW_ operator for the class Y calls the constructor in X, since X is the parent of Y.

```
X.SCL
class x;
 x: method n: num;
    put n=;
 endmethod;
```

```
endclass;

Y.SCL
class y extends x;
endclass;

Y.SCL
init:
 dcl y y = _new_ y(100);
 return;
```

This behavior applies to all classes that are instantiated by using _NEW_ — even those that have no explicit constructors.

If you do not supply a constructor for your classes, you can still use _NEW_ with no arguments because OBJECT.CLASS (which all classes extend) contains a constructor that takes no arguments and performs no actions. This "dummy" constructor needs to be overridden if you want to supply a constructor that does not take an argument by using the following:

```
class x;
 x: method /(state='0');
    put 'in x constructor';
 endmethod;
endclass;
```

Constructors can be used only in conjunction with the _NEW_ operator. They are not called if the object is instantiated in some other way, such as by using the _NEW_ method in CALL SEND, or by dropping the object in a frame. In particular, in the case of a visual object, you cannot run a constructor after the object is instantiated, but only before it is displayed. Therefore, you cannot use a constructor to initialize the object. For these types of objects, you must either use the _NEO_ operator or use the _NEW_ method with CALL SEND.

## See Also

"DECLARE" on page 330

"IMPORT" on page 475

"LOADCLASS" on page 525

"_NEO_" on page 559

# NEWVAR

**Adds a column to a new SAS table**

**Category:**  SAS Table

## Syntax

*sysrc*=**NEWVAR**(*table-id,col-name,type<,length<,label*
    *<,format<,informat>>>*);

*sysrc*
contains the return code for the operation:

| 0 | successful |
|---|---|
| ≠0 | not successful |

Type: Numeric

*table-id*
is the identifier that was assigned when the table was opened. If *table-id* is invalid, the program halts. The SAS table must be opened with an open mode of NEW.
Type: Numeric

*col-name*
is the name to assign to the new column. The name must be a valid SAS name.
Type: Character

*type*
specifies the data type of the new column:

| 'C' | character |
|---|---|
| 'N' | numeric |

Type: Character

*length*
is the length of the new column. For a character column, this value can be between 1 and 32,767. For a numeric column, it can be between 3 and 8. On some systems, the minimum length can be 2.
Type: Numeric

*label*
is the label for the new column. This is a character string from 1 to 40 characters. If the label contains single quotes, use two single quotes for each of these internal single quotes, or surround the label with double quotes. Each set of two single quotes counts as one character.
Type: Character

*format*
is the format for the new column. This must be a valid SAS format name. Formats can be either defined by the user or supplied by SAS software. If not specified, SAS assigns a default format. If *type* is **c**, then a character format should be specified. Otherwise, a numeric format should be specified.
Type: Character

*informat*
is the informat for the new column. This must be a valid SAS informat name. Informats can be either defined by the user or supplied by SAS software. If not specified, SAS assigns a default informat. If *type* is **c**, then a character informat should be specified. Otherwise, a numeric informat should be specified.
Type: Character

## Details

### *CAUTION:*
**The table must be opened in NEW mode, or SCL halts the program.** Opening an existing SAS table in NEW mode creates a new table that overwrites the old table. When the table is closed after using NEWVAR, the SAS table is created with zero rows. If the column name matches a column name that was defined for the table by a previous NEWVAR function, the new definition overrides the previous definition. △

## Example

Open a new SAS table, MYDATA, in NEW mode, and then add the column AGE, which is numeric, and NAME, which is character. AGE has a length of 8, and NAME has a length of 20. The label of NAME is set to **Last Name**.

```
dsid=open('mydata','n');
rc=newvar(dsid,'num','n',8);
rc=newvar(dsid,'char','c',20,'Last Name');
rc=close(dsid);
```

## See Also

"OPEN" on page 576

---

# NEXTCMD

**Discards the current command on the command line**

**Category:** Command

---

## Syntax

**CALL NEXTCMD();**

**Details**    NEXTCMD deletes the words up to the next semicolon or up to the end of the command. If a semicolon is not found, the entire contents of the command line are deleted.

Ordinarily, you clear the command line after reading a command or a series of commands. NEXTCMD is usually used in conjunction with CONTROL ENTER, ALWAYS, or ALLCMDS.

If the command line contains two or more commands separated by semicolons, then only the first command on the command line is executed during the current execution of the MAIN section. The next command is executed when control is returned to the program or when another entry is displayed, as in the use of the DISPLAY routine.

## Example

Suppose you have an FSEDIT application and you want to prevent everyone but one user from deleting rows. You can use NEXTCMD to remove all commands that start with DEL for users other than USERAA.

```
FSEINIT:
    control always;
return;

INIT:
return;

MAIN:
if word(1,'u') =: 'DEL' and
```

```
      symget('sysjobid') ne 'USERAA' then
         do;
            call nextcmd();
            _msg_ =
            'You are not authorized to delete rows';
         end;
      return;

      TERM:
      return;
```

Issue the command **AXX BXX; CXX DXX**. After NEXTCMD is called, only **CXX DXX** remains in the command buffer. After NEXTCMD is called a second time, no commands remain to be processed.

## See Also

"NEXTWORD" on page 568

"WORD" on page 725

# NEXTWORD

**Deletes the current word and advances to the next word in the current command**

**Category:**   Command

## Syntax

**CALL NEXTWORD();**

**Details**    A *word* is the text at the current position up to the next blank or semicolon. A semicolon denotes the end of a command in addition to the end of a word. NEXTWORD is used with WORD and is usually used in conjunction with CONTROL ENTER, CONTROL ALWAYS, or CONTROL ALLCMDS.

If the command line contains two or more commands separated by semicolons, then only the first command on the command line is executed during the current execution of the MAIN section. The next command is executed when control is returned to the program or when another entry is displayed, as in the use of the DISPLAY routine.

## Example

If a user issues the command **AXX BXX CXX DXX**, the succession of words is as follows:

| | Initial | After 1st NEXTWORD | After 2nd NEXTWORD |
|---|---|---|---|
| word(1) | AXX | BXX | CXX |
| word(2) | BXX | CXX | DXX |
| word(3) | CXX | DXX | *blank* |

## See Also

"NEXTCMD" on page 567

"WORD" on page 725

"WORDTYPE" on page 726

# NOCHANGE

**Causes the called program to return the original values for the variables that it received as parameters in an ENTRY statement**

**Category:** Modular Programming and Object Oriented

## Syntax

**CALL NOCHANGE();**

**Details** The NOCHANGE routine causes a called program to return the original values for the variables that it received as parameters in an ENTRY statement, disregarding any changes that subsequently may have been made to those variables. This routine is used in the called program that contains the ENTRY statement.

NOCHANGE has no effect on reference arrays. See "ARRAY" on page 254 for more information about reference arrays. NOCHANGE overrides the I/O/U mode that was specified for parameters in the ENTRY and METHOD statements.

## Example

Suppose that A.SCL calls B.SCL and passes to it the parameters X, Y, and Z. B.SCL tests the _STATUS_ variable for the value C (indicating that a CANCEL command has been issued). If a user exits B.SCL with a CANCEL command, then no updated values are returned to A.SCL.

Here is the A.SCL program:

```
INIT:
return;

MAIN:
call display('mylib.test.b.scl',x,y,z);
return;

TERM:
```

```
      return;
```

Here is the B.SCL program:

```
entry a b c 8;
INIT:
return;

MAIN:
   ...SCL statements...
return;

TERM:
   if _STATUS_='C' then call nochange();
return;
```

## See Also

"APPLY" on page 252

"DISPLAY" on page 350

"ENTRY" on page 369

"METHOD" on page 540

"NOTIFY" on page 572

"SEND" on page 644

"SUPAPPLY" on page 679

"SUPER" on page 681

# NOTE

**Returns an identifier for the current row of a SAS table**

**Category:**  SAS Table

## Syntax

*note-id*=**NOTE**(*table-id*);

**note-id**
> contains the identifier that is assigned to the row.
>    Type: Numeric

**table-id**
> is the identifier that was assigned when the table was opened. If *table-id* is invalid,
> the program halts.
>    Type: Numeric

**Details**    You can use *note-id* in the POINT function to return to the current row. (Use NOTE to mark a row, then use POINT to return to the row.) Each *note-id* is a unique numeric value. There can be up to 1,000 *note-ids* per open table.

To free the memory that is associated with a row ID, use DROPNOTE.

## Example

Use NOTE to return the identifier for the 10th row. Then use POINT to point to the row that corresponds to NOTEID.

```
INIT:
   tableid=open('sasuser.fitness','i');
return;
MAIN:
   /* Read row 10 */
rc=fetchobs(tableid,10);
if (abs(rc) ne 0) then
   do;
      put "Read operation failed";
      return;
   end;
   /* Display the row number in the LOG window */
cur=curobs(tableid);
put "CUROBS=" cur;
   /* Mark row 10 */
noteid=note(tableid);
   /* Rewind the pointer to the beginning of the table */
rc=rewind(tableid);
   /* Read first row */
rc=fetch(tableid);
   /* Display the row number */
cur=curobs(tableid);
put "CUROBS=" cur;
   /* POINT to row 10 marked earlier by NOTE */
rc=point(tableid,noteid);
   /* Read the row */
rc=fetch(tableid);
   /* Display the row number to confirm it is 10 */
cur=curobs(tableid);
put "CUROBS=" cur;
return;

TERM:
   if (tableid >0) then rc=close(tableid);
return;
```

The output produced by this program is

```
CUROBS=10
CUROBS=1
CUROBS=10
```

### See Also

"DROPNOTE" on page 361

"POINT" on page 592

"REWIND" on page 618

---

# NOTIFY

**Sends a method to a control that is identified by its name**

**Category:** Object Oriented
**Valid:** FRAME programs only

---

## Syntax

**CALL NOTIFY**(*control-name,method-name< ,parameters>*);

*control-name*
    is the control to send the method to, or `'.'` (a string containing a period) to send the method to the FRAME entry component.
        Type: Character

*method-name*
    is the method to invoke.
        Type: Character

*parameters*
    specify additional numeric or character arguments, separated by commas, that are required by the method.

       *Note:* These parameters are update parameters. See "Input, Output, and Update Parameters" on page 34 for more information. △
        Type: Numeric, Character

**Details**    NOTIFY sends a method to a control in a FRAME entry by specifying the control's name. NOTIFY may be called only from the SCL program for the FRAME entry to which the control belongs, because that is the only code in which the control's name is not ambiguous. You can also use NOTIFY as a function if the called method returns a value with a RETURN statement in the program that defines the method.

*Note:* As with DISPLAY, the SCL compiler cannot determine which data types are expected for each of the parameters passed to a method. When the application executes, SAS/AF software verifies that each parameter is correct. If there is a type error, the SCL program halts. △

In most cases, put quotation marks around the control name so that the value of the control is not passed to NOTIFY. For example, the following code hides the Version 6 control named BUTTON:

```
CALL NOTIFY('button','_hide');
```

However, if BUTTON has a value of **OK**, the following code hides the control named OK:

```
CALL NOTIFY(button,'_hide');
```

If the value of BUTTON is not the name of a control, the program halts.

Similarly, be sure to put quotation marks around *method-name* unless *method-name* is an expression.

For more information about dot notation, see "Accessing Object Attributes and Methods With Dot Notation" on page 119.

## Example

Suppose you have a FRAME entry with two Version 6 pushbuttons, **OK** and **NOT_OK**. The following code causes **OK** to be grayed when a user clicks on **NOT_OK**:

```
NOT_OK:
   call notify('ok','_gray');
return;
```

The following example fills a list with the set of controls in the FRAME entry:

```
controls=makelist();
call notify('.','_getWidgets',controls);
```

## See Also

"APPLY" on page 252

"INSTANCE" on page 485

"LOADCLASS" on page 525

"LOADRES" on page 526

"SEND" on page 644

"SUPAPPLY" on page 679

"SUPER" on page 681

# NSELECT

**Returns the number of rows that have been selected in a selection list**

**Category:** Extended Table

## Syntax

*num-rows*=**NSELECT**();

**num-rows**
contains the number of selected rows.
   Type: Numeric

**Details**     Because you can define extended tables only in SAS/AF software, you cannot use NSELECT in FSEDIT or FSVIEW programs. NSELECT is valid only for PROGRAM entries. FRAME entry controls must use the _getNselect method.

In order for an extended table to be considered a selection list, you must specify a number of selections in the SETROW routine.

## Example

Return the number of selected rows:

```
nsel = nselect();
_msg_ ='You have selected ' || nsel || ' rows.';
```

## See Also

"ISSEL" on page 495

"SELECT" on page 639

"SELECTED" on page 642

"UNSELECT" on page 696

# NUMFKEYS

**Returns the number of function keys that are available for the device**

**Category:**  Keys

## Syntax

*fkeynum*=**NUMFKEYS**();

**fkeynum**
  contains the number of function keys that are available for the device.
    Type: Numeric

**Details**    You can use this function only in entries that have a window variable or text
in the DISPLAY window.

  You can use NUMFKEYS when you want to use SCL to return the number of
function keys, then disable procedure-specific commands and SAS windowing
commands and redefine the function keys while a window is open. When you redefine
the function keys, you can limit the commands that can be used in an application
window. (If you do this, you may want to restore the settings with SETFKEY before the
application window closes.)

## Example

Assign a custom PMENU. Then use NUMFKEYS to find out how many function keys
a user's device has. Use SETFKEY first to disable them and then again to restore the
settings when the window closes.

```
dcl char command(30);

INIT:
/* Assign the PMENU entry to the window.  */
   rc=pmenu('editdata.pmenu');
/* Turn the PMENU facility on.  */
   call execcmd('pmenu on');
```

```
/* Execute the MAIN section even if a user makes */
/* an error or issues an unknown command.  */
  control enter;
/* Determine the number of function keys */
/* on a user's keyboard.  */
  numkeys=numfkeys();
  do n=1 to numkeys;
    command{n}=getfkey (fkeyname(n));
 /* Disable function key assignments.  */
    call setfkey(fkeyname(n),'');
  end;
return;
MAIN:
  ...Statements to process custom commands...
return;
TERM:
/* Restore command assignments to function keys.*/
  do n=1 to numkeys;
    call setfkey(fkeyname(n),command{n});
  end;
/* Turn the PMENU facility off.  */
  call execcmd('pmenu off');
return;
```

## See Also

"FKEYNAME" on page 413

"GETFKEY" on page 440

"SETFKEY" on page 649

# OBSINFO

**Returns information about the current row in an FSEDIT application**

**Category:** SAS Table
**Valid:** FSEDIT programs only

## Syntax

*rc*=**OBSINFO**(*info-item*);

**rc**
   contains the return code for the operation.
      Type: Numeric

**info-item**
   is one information item from the following list:

   **'ALTER'**
      reports whether the currently displayed row can be edited:

      0            The row cannot be edited. If ALTER=0 and LOCKED=0, the
                   row is open in FSBROWSE. If ALTER=0 and LOCKED=1, the
                   row is open in FSEDIT, but the row is locked.

| 1 | The row can be edited. If ALTER=1 and LOCKED=0, then the row is open in FSEDIT. |

**'CUROBS'**

reports the number of the current row:

| *n* | The number of the row. |
| −1 | The table is accessed using an engine that does not support row numbers. |

CUROBS returns a missing value (.) when there are no rows in the table, when no rows meet the specified WHERE condition, and when you are on a deleted row.

**'DELETED'**

reports whether the currently displayed row is marked for deletion:

| 1 | The row is marked for deletion. |
| 0 | The row is not marked for deletion. |

**'LOCKED'**

reports whether the currently displayed row is locked by another user:

| 1 | The row is locked. |
| 0 | The row is not locked. |

**'MODIFIED'**

reports whether a value has been changed in any table column in the currently displayed row or the row is new:

| 1 | Either column has been changed or the row is new. |
| 0 | No table columns have been changed. |

**'NEW'**

Reports whether the currently displayed row is a new row:

| 1 | The row is new. |
| 0 | The row already exists in the table. |

Type: Character

## Example

Return information for the row that is currently displayed in the FSEDIT window:

```
rc=obsinfo('curobs');
rc=obsinfo('deleted');
rc=obsinfo('locked');
rc=obsinfo('new');
rc=obsinfo('modified');
```

## See Also

"CUROBS" on page 321

# OPEN

**Opens a SAS table**

**Category:** SAS Table

## Syntax

*table-id*=**OPEN**(< *table-name*< >,*mode*>);

**table-id**
　contains the table identifier, or 0 if the table could not be opened.
　　Type: Numeric

**table-name**
　is the SAS table or SAS/ACCESS view descriptor to open, specified as
　< *libref.*>*member-name*<(*data-set-options*)>. The default value for *table-name* is
　_LAST_, which is the last table created in the current SAS session. A one-level name
　is assumed to be USER.*member-name*.
　　All SAS data set options are valid except the FIRSTOBS= and OBS= options,
　which are ignored.
　　Type: Character

**mode**
　specifies the type of access to the table:

| | |
|---|---|
| **'I'** | an INPUT mode in which values can be read but cannot be modified. (This is the default.) Rows are read in random order. |
| **'IN'** | an INPUT mode in which rows can be read sequentially and can also be revisited. |
| **'IS'** | an INPUT mode in which rows can be read sequentially but cannot be revisited. |
| **'N'** | NEW mode, which creates a new table. If *table-name* already exists, the table is replaced without warning. |
| **'U'** | an UPDATE mode in which values in the table can be modified and rows can be read in random order. |
| **'UN'** | an UPDATE mode in which values in the table can be modified, rows can be read sequentially, and rows can be revisited. |
| **'US'** | an UPDATE mode in which values in the table can be modified and rows can be read sequentially. However, rows cannot be revisited. |
| **'V'** | UTILITY mode, which must be used in order to change any column attributes or to manipulate any associated table indexes. |

　　Type: Character

**Details**　OPEN opens a SAS table or a SAS/ACCESS view descriptor and returns a
unique numeric table identifier, which is used in most other SCL functions that
manipulate tables.
　　If *mode* is I or U , then OPEN defaults to the strongest access mode available in the
engine. That is, if the engine supports random access, OPEN defaults to random access.
Otherwise, the file is opened in IN or UN mode automatically. Files are opened with
sequential access, and a system level warning is set. For example, opening a DB2 SAS/
ACCESS view descriptor in INPUT (I) mode opens the file but produces the warning
"This task requires reading rows in a random order, but the engine allows only

sequential access." To enable the file to be read multiple times and to prevent this warning, use an open mode of IN instead.

Note that both IS and IN (as well as US and UN )refer to sequential access. However, IN allows revisiting a row, whereas IS does not.

*Note:*  If sequential access is too restrictive but random access is too slow, try specifying the TOBSONO= data set option. See *SAS Language Reference: Dictionary* for more information. △

By default, a SAS table is opened with a control level of RECORD. See *SAS Language Reference: Dictionary* for details about the CNTLLEV (control level) SAS data set option.

A table that is already opened can be opened again, subject to the following restrictions:

□ If the table is already opened in UPDATE or INPUT mode, it cannot be opened again in UTILITY mode.

□ If the table is already opened in UTILITY mode (so that columns can be dropped, inserted, or changed), it can only be opened again in NEW mode.

A table that is already open in any mode can be opened again in NEW mode, because that replaces everything in the old table.

An open SAS table should be closed when it is no longer needed.

## Example

Open the table PRICES in the library MASTER, using INPUT mode:

```
tableid=open('master.prices','i');
if (tableid=0) then _msg_=sysmsg();
else _msg_='PRICES table has been opened';
```

You can pass values from SCL variables to be used in data set options. Open the table MYDATA, and use the WHERE= data set option to apply a permanent WHERE clause, using the value from the numeric variable SCRNUM:

```
tableid=
open('mydata(where=(num='||put(scrnum,5.)||'))');
```

Open the table MYDATA, and use the WHERE= data set option to apply a permanent WHERE clause, using the value from the character variable SCRNAME:

```
tableid=
open('mydata(where=(name='||quote(scrname)||'))');
```

## See Also

"CLOSE" on page 292

"MODVAR" on page 551

"NEWVAR" on page 565

---

# OPENENTRYDIALOG

**Displays a dialog window that lists catalog entries, and returns the user's selection**

**Category:**  Selection List

## Syntax

*selection-item*=**OPENENTRYDIALOG**(< *type* <,*entry-name*<,*list-id*>>>);

**selection-item**
> contains the four-level name of the selected SAS file, or a blank if nothing is selected.
> Type: Character

**type**
> specifies the member types to list in the dialog window, such as CLASS, SCL, or FRAME. This can reduce the length of the list in the dialog window. If *type* is not used, the names of all catalog entry types in the data library are listed.
> Type: Character

**entry-name**
> is a two- or four-level name of a catalog entry to call when a user selects the [Advanced] button in the dialog window. The entry can be any of the following types: FRAME, SCL, PROGRAM, HELP, CBT, or MENU.
> If *entry-name* is not specified, then the window does not contain [Advanced].
> Type: Character

**list-id**
> contains the identifier of an SCL list that is passed to *entry-name*.
> Type: Numeric or List

**Details**    OPENENTRYDIALOG displays a list of SAS catalog entries from which a user can make a selection. You can pass that selection to code that opens the catalog entry.

If *entry-name* is supplied and [Advanced] is selected, the item selected in the dialog window is passed to *entry-name* through the following variables, which are created automatically:

USERDATA
> contains the list that is passed in the call to the OPENENTRYDIALOG and SAVEENTRYDIALOG functions.

LIBREF
> contains the libref of the selected item.

MEMBER
> contains the member name of the selected item.

ENTRY
> contains the entry name of the selected item.

TYPE
> contains the member type of the selected item.

*List-id* enables information to be passed between the calling entry and *entry-name*. It is passed to *entry-name* through the USERDATA variable.

## Examples

**Example 1: Opening a Catalog Entry**    Select a catalog entry of type FRAME to open and display the selected entry.

```
selection=openentrydialog('frame');
call display(selection);
```

**Example 2: Using the Advanced Button with an SCL List**   Specify an entry to call when a user selects Advanced, as well as an SCL list that contains values to pass to the entry. The entry can be any of the following types: FRAME, SCL, PROGRAM, HELP, CBT, or MENU. If *entry-name* is not specified, then the window does not contain Advanced.

```
dcl list mydata;
mydata=makelist();
rc=insertc(mydata,'test');
selection=openentrydialog('frame',
    'mylib.mycat.myentry.frame',mydata);
if sysrc(1)=-1 then do;
    ...SCL statements to execute when
    the user cancels from the window...
    end;
else do;
    ...SCL statements to handle selections...
end;
```

The SCL entry for MYLIB.MYCAT.MYENTRY.FRAME contains the following program:

```
dcl char(8)  libref type;
dcl char(32) catalog entry;
dcl list userdata;
init:
put libref=;
put catalog=;
put entry=;
put type=;
call putlist(userdata);
return;
```

*Note:*   The SCL entry must declare these exact variables, in the order specified, to properly reference the selected entry. △

If the user selects MYLIB2.MYCAT2.MYENTRY2.FRAME in the dialog window and then selects Advanced, the output for this program is

```
libref=Mylib2
catalog=Mycat2
entry=Myentry2
type=Frame
('test')[1]
```

### See Also

"SAVEENTRYDIALOG" on page 627

## OPENSASFILEDIALOG

**Displays a dialog window that lists SAS files, and returns the user's selection**

**Category:**   Selection List

## Syntax

*selection*=**OPENSASFILEDIALOG**(< *type*< ,*level-count*< ,*entry-name*< ,*list-id*>>>>);

### *selection*

contains the two- or three-level name of the selected SAS file, or a blank if nothing is selected.
Type: Character

### *type*

specifies one or more member types to list in the dialog window, such as DATA, VIEW, MDDB, and CATALOG. This can reduce the length of the list in the dialog window. If *type* is not used, the names of all SAS files in the data library are listed. Multiple types should be separated by blanks.
Type: Character

### *level-count*

specifies whether the function returns a two- or three-level name. The only valid choices are 2 and 3. The default is 2.
Type: Numeric

### *entry-name*

is a two- or four-level name of a catalog entry to call when a user selects the Advanced button in the dialog window. The entry can be any of the following types: FRAME, SCL, PROGRAM, HELP, CBT, or MENU.
If *entry-name* is not specified, then the window does not contain Advanced .
Type: Character

### *list-id*

contains the identifier of an SCL list that is passed to *entry-name*.
Type: Numeric or List

**Details**    OPENSASFILEDIALOG displays a list of SAS files from which a user can make a selection. You can pass that selection to code that opens the SAS file.

If *entry-name* is supplied and Advanced is selected, the item selected in the dialog window is passed to *entry-name* through the following variables, which are created automatically:

USERDATA
contains the list that is passed in the call to OPENSASFILEDIALOG.

LIBREF
contains the libref of the selected item.

MEMBER
contains the member name of the selected item.

TYPE
contains the member type of the selected item.

*List-id* enables information to be passed between the calling entry and *entry-name*. It is passed to *entry-name* through the USERDATA variable.

## Examples

**Example 1: Opening a SAS File**    Select a SAS file of type DATA to open and display the table.

```
selection=opensasfiledialog('data');
call fsview(selection);
```

**Example 2: Returning a Two-Level Name**    Open a SAS file of type DATA that returns a two-level name.

```
selection=opensasfiledialog('data view',2'work.a.a.scl',listid);
```

**Example 3: Using the Advanced Button with an SCL List**    Specify an entry to be called when a user selects ⟨Advanced⟩ as well as an SCL list that contains values to pass to the entry. The entry can be any of the following types: FRAME, SCL, PROGRAM, HELP, CBT, or MENU. If *entry-name* is not specified, then the window does not contain ⟨Advanced⟩.

```
dcl list mydata;
mydata=makelist();
rc=insertc(mydata,'test');
selection = opensasfiledialog('data',
    'mylib.mycat.myentry.frame',mydata);
if sysrc(1)=-1 then do;
    ...SCL statements to execute when
    the user cancels from the window...
end;
else do;
    ...SCL statements to handle selections...
end;
```

The SCL entry for MYLIB.MYCAT.MYENTRY.FRAME contains the following program:

```
dcl char(8) libref type;
dcl char(32) member;
dcl list userdata;
init:
put libref=;
put member=;
put type=;
call putlist(userdata);
return;
```

*Note:*    The SCL entry must declare these exact variables, in the order specified, to properly reference the selected entry. △

If the user selects MYLIB2.MYMEMBER2.DATA in the dialog window and then selects ⟨Advanced⟩, the output for this program is

```
libref=Mylib2
member=Mymember2
type=Data
('test')[1]
```

### See Also

"SAVESASFILEDIALOG" on page 631

# OPTGETC and OPTGETN

**Return the current setting of a SAS system option**

**Category:** SAS System Option

### Syntax

*cval*=**OPTGETC**(*option-name*);

*nval*=**OPTGETN**(*option-name*);

**cval**

contains the setting of the SAS system option returned by OPTGETC, or a blank if *option-name* is invalid.
Type: Character

**nval**

contains the setting of the SAS system option returned by OPTGETN, or a missing value if *option-name* is invalid. For options with binary settings of ON or OFF, the function returns 1 if the setting is on, and 0 if the setting is off.
Type: Numeric

**option-name**

is the name of the SAS system option to retrieve.
Type: Character

**Details**    If you try to use OPTGETC to get information about a numeric option or OPTGETN to get information about a character option, an error message is generated. To determine whether a SAS system option has a numeric or character setting, see the SAS documentation for your operating environment or *SAS Language Reference: Dictionary*.

For options that have ON/OFF settings (for example, DATE/NODATE), use OPTGETN, because these options have the numeric value 1 for ON and 0 for OFF.

You can view current option settings by using the OPTIONS procedure in the SAS session or by using the OPTIONS command.

### Examples

**Example 1: Using the OPTGETC Function**    Check to see whether new SAS tables will be compressed:

```
if optgetc('compress')='YES' then
    _msg_='Observations are compressed.';
else _msg_='Observations are not compressed.';
```

**Example 2: Using the OPTGETN Function**    Return the setting of the CAPS option and place it in the column CAPS. The value returned is 0 if the NOCAPS form of the option is in effect, or 1 if CAPS is in effect.

```
caps=optgetn('caps');
```

## See Also

"OPTSETC and OPTSETN" on page 584

---

# OPTSETC and OPTSETN

**Assign a value to a SAS system option**

**Category:**  SAS System Option

---

## Syntax

*rc*=**OPTSETC**(*option-name,cval*);

*rc*=**OPTSETN**(*option-name,nval*);

**rc**
> contains the return code for the operation:

> 0                              successful

> ≠0                            not successful
>     Type:  Numeric

**option-name**
> is the name of the character SAS system option to set.
>     Type:  Character

**cval**
> is the new character setting for the option.
>     Type:  Character

**nval**
> is the new numeric setting for the option. For options with binary settings of ON and
> OFF, specify an *nval* of 1 to turn the option on and 0 to turn it off.
>     Type:  Numeric

**Details**    If you try to use OPTSETC to assign a value to a numeric option or
OPTSETN to assign a value to a character option, an error message is generated. To
determine whether a SAS system option has a numeric or character setting, see the SAS
documentation for your operating environment or *SAS Language Reference: Dictionary*.
    For options that have ON/OFF settings (for example, DATE/NODATE), use
OPTSETN, because the options have the numeric values 1 for ON and 0 for OFF.
    You can view current option settings by using the OPTIONS procedure in the SAS
session or by using the OPTIONS command.

## Examples

**Example 1: Using the OPTSETC Function**    Set the COMPRESS option to allow
compression of new SAS tables:

```
rc=optsetc('compress','yes');
```

**Example 2: Using the OPTSETN Function**    Turn on the CAPS option:

```
rc=optsetn('caps',1);
```

## See Also

"OPTGETC and OPTGETN" on page 583

---

# PACKAGE

**Defines a group of classes whose metadata must be recognized by objects defined on the client**

**Category:**  Object Oriented

---

## Syntax

**PACKAGE** *package-name*<EXTENDS *parent-package-name*>;
  <*ITEM-statements*>
  **ENDPACKAGE**;

*package-name*
>  is the name that you want to assign to the class package. You can specify a name as a one- to four-level name.

*parent-package-name*
>  specifies the parent class package of *package-name*. *Parent-package-name* can be specified as a one- to four- level name.

*ITEM-statements*
>  are the ITEM statements that define the classes need by client objects. See "ITEM" on page 496 for more information.

## Details

To build client/server applications, class information such as methods and attributes that are defined on the server must be recognized by objects that are defined on the client. The class package block defines a set of classes that are defined by the server. These classes can then be translated (by the WEB/AF proxy wizard or the CREATESCL function, for example) to interface formats and used by client objects to invoke methods and access attributes defined in these classes.

When you compile the entry that contains the PACKAGE block, SCL generates a CLASSPKG entry with the name that you specified in the PACKAGE statement.

No SCL statements, except for the IMPORT statement, are allowed within the SCL entry that contains the PACKAGE block.

Unlike RESOURCE entries, which directly embed class information in the entry, CLASSPKG entries use a reference (or link) to the class name of each of the classes that are defined in the class package block. Therefore, the class package will automatically pick up any changes that are made to the classes.

## Example

If you enter the following code into an SCL entry, then issue the SAVECLASS command, SCL generates the entry **work.a.a.classpkg**.

```
package work.a.a.classpkg;
   item sashelp.classes.scllist.class;
   item sashelp.classes.format_c.class;
endpackage;
```

You can use the IMPORT statement to define the searchpath for CLASS references:

```
import sashelp.classes;
package work.a.a.classpkg;
   item scllist.class;
   item format_c.class;
endpackage;
```

## See Also

"ITEM" on page 496

"ENDPACKAGE" on page 367

# PATHNAME

**Returns the physical name of a SAS data library or an external file**

**Category:**   External File

## Syntax

*filename*=**PATHNAME**(*fileref*);

**fileref**
    contains the physical name of an external file or a SAS data library, or a blank if
    *fileref* is invalid.
      Type: Character

**fileref**
    is the fileref assigned to an external file or a SAS data library.
      Type: Character

## Examples

**Example 1: Using PATHNAME with the FILEREF Function**   Use the FILEREF function to
verify that the fileref MYFILE is associated with an external file, and then use
PATHNAME to retrieve the name of the external file:

```
rc=fileref('myfile');
if (rc=0) then do;
    fname=pathname('myfile');
    put "Path = " fname;
end;
```

**Example 2: Appending to a Pathname**   This example assigns the fileref F1 to
**/u/sasssf**, and then uses F1 in a second call to FILENAME. The second call to
FILENAME defines the fileref F2 by appending **/temp** to the path for F1.

```
rc=filename('f1','/u/sasssf');
path=pathname('f1');
put path=;
rc=filename('f2','temp','','','f1');
path=pathname('f2');
put path=;
```

The output would be

```
path=/u/sasccf
path=/u/sasccf/temp
```

**Example 3: Concatenating Pathname**    In this example, FILENAME concatenates the directories **/u/sasccf** and **/u/sasshh** and assigns the concatenated list of names to the fileref F1. The second call to FILENAME is the same as the second call to FILENAME in Example 2. However, in this example, because F1 is assigned to a concatenated list of directory names instead of to a single directory, FILENAME does not append **/temp** to the paths.

```
rc=filename('f1','''/u/sasccf','/u/sasshh''');
path=pathname('f1');
put path=;
rc=filename('f2','temp','','','f1');
path=pathname('f2');
put path=;
```

The output would be

```
path=('/u/sasccf','/u/sasshh')
path=('/u/sasccf','/u/sasshh')
```

## See Also

"FILENAME" on page 403

"FILEREF" on page 406

"FEXIST" on page 392

"FILEEXIST" on page 400

# PICCLOSE

**Closes the graphics environment**

**Category:**  Image

## Syntax

*rc*=**PICCLOSE**(*graphenv-id*);

*rc*

contains the return code for the operation:

0                    successful

>0                    not successful
    Type: Numeric

***graphenv-id***
contains the graphics environment identifier that was returned by PICOPEN.
    Type: Numeric

**Details**    PICCLOSE closes the graphic environment that was initialized by PICOPEN.

## Example

Close the graphics environment that was opened by a previous PICOPEN:

```
fseterm:
   rc=picclose(graphenv_id);
return;
```

# PICDELETE

**Deletes a region**

**Category:**  Image

## Syntax

*rc=***PICDELETE**(*graphenv-id,region-id*);

***rc***
contains the return code for the operation:

0                    successful

>0                    not successful
    Type: Numeric

***graphenv-id***
contains the graphics environment identifier that was returned by PICOPEN.
    Type: Numeric

***region-id***
contains the region identifier that was returned by PICFILL
    Type: Numeric

## Example

Delete a region:

```
term:
   if (region_id ne 0 and graphenv_id ne 0) then
      rc=picdelete(graphenv_id,region_id);
return;
```

# PICFILL

**Defines a region and fills it with an image**

**Category:** Image

## Syntax

*region-id=***PICFILL***(graphenv-id,type,ulr,ulc,lrr,lrc, source,< command< ,arguments>>);*

*rc*
    contains the return code for the operation:

    0           indicates that an error condition occurred.

    >0         is the number identifying the region that was just defined.
        Type: Numeric

*graphenv-id*
    contains the graphics environment identifier that was returned by PICOPEN.
        Type: Numeric

*type*
    is the type of item to be displayed: IMAGE, GRSEG, or BITMAP.
        Type: Character

*ulr*
    is the upper left row of the screen area in which to display the image or graphics segment.
        Type: Numeric

*ulc*
    is the upper left column of the screen area in which to display the image or graphics segment.
        Type: Numeric

*lrr*
    is the lower right row of the screen area in which to display the image or graphics segment.
        Type: Numeric

*lrc*
    is the lower right column of the screen area in which to display the image or graphics segment.
        Type: Numeric

*source*
    specifies the location of the image.
    For *type* BITMAP, specify the numeric value of a bitmap in a host-dependent resource file.
    For *type* GRAPH, specify the four-level name of the graphic segment to be displayed.
    For *type* IMAGE, specify either the name of an external file to be loaded or the path string from the LNAMEMK function.
    Type: Numeric or Character

***commands***

lists commands that are used with *type* IMAGE to manipulate the image before displaying it. Valid commands are listed in "Commands Used with PICFILL" on page 590.

Type: Character

***arguments***

are arguments for the specified command.

Type: Numeric

## Commands Used with PICFILL

For detailed information about these commands, see Appendix 1, "Commands Used with the IMGCTRL, IMGOP and PICFILL Functions," on page 735 .

CROP

crops the selected image.

DITHER

dithers an image to a color map.

DITHER_BW

dithers the selected image to a monochrome black and white image.

EXECLIST

executes a list of commands.

GAMMA

applies a gamma value to the selected image.

MAP_COLORS

maps colors to the closest color in the selected color map.

MIRROR

mirrors an image.

NEGATE

changes the image to a negative.

QUANTIZE

reduces the number of colors used for an image.

ROTATE

rotates an image clockwise by 90, 180, or 270 degrees.

SCALE

scales an image.

**Details**    PICFILL performs two functions:

□ It defines the four corners of the region in which the image is to be displayed.

□ It fills the region with the specified image.

If you specify a *command*, the PICFILL manipulates the image before displaying it.

## Example

Display an image when the window opens:

```
init:
    imgfile=lnamemk(2,location,file);
    region_id=picfill(graphenv_id,"IMAGE",
```

```
                    15,12,40,78,imgfile);
  return;
```

# PICOPEN

**Initializes the graphics environment**

**Category:** Image

## Syntax

*graphenv-id*=**PICOPEN**(*pane-number*);

***graphenv-id***
  contains the identifier for the graphics environment:

  0                    indicates that an error condition occurred.

  >0                   is the graphics environment identifier for use in other PIC
                       functions.

    Type: Numeric

***pane-number***
  is the number of the pane to contain the graphics environment:

  1                    the main portion of a SAS/AF window, or the first screen in an
                       FSEDIT window.

  2                    the extended table portion of a SAS/AF window, or the second
                       screen in an FSEDIT window.

  *n*                  the *n*th screen in an FSEDIT window.
    Type: Numeric

**Details**   The PICOPEN function initializes the graphics environment within a
window. *Panes* are the physical areas of the screen in which text can be displayed. In
SAS/AF software, there can be two panes per window, numbered 1 and 2. An FSEDIT
window can have up to 101 screens.
  A graphic environment must be opened for each pane in which an image or a graph
is to be displayed.

## Example

Initialize the graphics environment in the main portion of the FSEDIT window:

```
fseinit:
  graphenv_id=picopen(1);
return;
```

# PMENU

**Changes the PMENU for an application**

**Category:** Window

## Syntax

*rc*=**PMENU**(*pmenu*);

*rc*
> contains the return code for the operation:

| | |
|---|---|
| 0 | The PMENU entry was assigned successfully. However, the PMENU function does not verify that *pmenu* exists. |
| ≠0 | The operation was not successful. |

> Type: Numeric

*pmenu*
> is the PMENU entry to assign. If the PMENU entry resides in a different catalog, then specify a value of the form *libref.catalog.pmenu*. If a one-level name is specified, then SCL searches for the PMENU entry first in the current catalog, then in SASUSER.PROFILE, and then in SASHELP.FSP.
> Type: Character

**Details**   The PMENU function only changes the pull-down menu that is associated with the window. It does not turn on the pull-down menus. If the pull-down menus are on, the new pull-down menu is displayed immediately.

See *SAS Procedures Guide* for more information about creating custom PMENU entries. FRAME entries can also use the _setPmenu method.

## Example

Change the default PMENU that is associated with an application to MYPMENU in the catalog NEWLIB.TESTS:

```
rc=pmenu('newlib.tests.mypmenu');
```

# POINT

**Locates a row that is identified by the NOTE function**

**Category:**   SAS Table

## Syntax

*sysrc*=**POINT**(*table-id,note-id*);

*sysrc*
> contains the return code for the operation:

| | |
|---|---|
| 0 | successful |

≠0                                      not successful
   Type: Numeric

**table-id**

   is the identifier that was assigned when the table was opened. If *table-id* is invalid,
   the program halts.
      Type: Numeric

**note-id**

   is the identifier that was assigned to the row by the NOTE function, or −1 to go to
   the previous non-deleted row in the table. If *note-id* is invalid, the program halts and
   sends a message to the log.
      Type: Numeric

**Details**     POINT locates the row identified by *note-id*, which is a value that is returned
from NOTE. The Table Data Vector is not updated until a "read" is performed by
FETCH or FETCHOBS.

## Example

   Call NOTE to obtain a row ID for the last row that was read in the SAS table
MYDATA. Call POINT to point to the row that corresponds to *note-id*. Call FETCH to
return the row that is marked by the pointer.

```
dsid=open('mydata','i');
rc=fetch(dsid);
noteid=note(dsid);
    ...more SCL statements...
rc=point(dsid,noteid);
rc=fetch(dsid);
    ...more SCL statements...
rc=close(dsid);
```

## See Also

"DROPNOTE" on page 361

"NOTE" on page 570

# POPC, POPL, POPN, and POPO

**Removes an item from an SCL list and returns the value of the item**

**Category:**  List

## Syntax

*cval*=**POPC**(*list-id*<,*index*>);

*sublist-id*=**POPL**(*list-id*<,*index*>);

*nval*=**POPN**(*list-id*<,*index*>);

*obj-id*=**POPO**(*list-id*<,*index*>);

*cval*
> contains the character value that was removed from the list by POPC.
> > Type: Character

*sublist-id*
> contains the identifier of the sublist that was removed from the list by POPL.
> > Type: List

*nval*
> contains the numeric value that was removed from the list by POPN.
> > Type: Numeric

*obj-id*
> contains the identifier of the object item that was removed from the list by POPO.
> > Type: Object

*list-id*
> contains the identifier of the list from which the value or sublist is removed. An invalid *list-id* produces an error condition.
> > Type: List

*index*
> is the position of the item in the list. The position can be specified as a positive or negative number. By default, *index* is 1 (the first item). If *index* is a positive number, then the item is at position *index* from the beginning of the list. If *index* is a negative number, then the item is at position ABS(*index*) from the end of the list. An error condition results if the absolute value for *index* is zero or if it is greater than the number of items in the list.
> > Type: Numeric or List

**Details**    These functions are useful for implementing stacks and queues of values. An error condition results if

☐ the item has the NODELETE attribute

☐ the list has the FIXEDLENGTH or NOUPDATE attribute

☐ the list is empty

☐ the specified item is not a character item and you use POPC, the item is not a sublist and you use POPL, the item is not numeric and you use POPN, or the item is not an object and you use POPO.

To check the attributes of a list or list item, use HASATTR. To change attributes, use SETLATTR. Use ITEMTYPE to test the type of an item when the list contains items with types other than the one for which you are searching.

## Examples

These examples assume that all list items are character. Programs A and B are equivalent. Both remove the last item in an SCL list.

```
A:  cval1=popc(listid,-1);
    put cval1=;
B:  cval2=getitemc(listid,-1);
    put cval2=;
    listid=delitem(listid,-1);
```

**Example 1: Using the POPC Function**    This example creates an SCL list called TODOQ, which represents a queue of tasks to do. A SAS/AF FRAME entry has a text entry named NEWTASK for entering a new task into the TODOQ queue. A second text entry, TODO, displays the first task in the to-do queue. A DONE button removes the top task from the TODOQ queue.

```
INIT:
   todoq = makelist();
   done._gray();
return;


NEWTASK:
   todoq = insertc(todoq, newtask.text, -1);
      /* Enqueue */
   newtask.text = '';
   cursor newtask;
return;


DONE:
      /* Dequeue */
   finished = popc(todoq);
return;


MAIN:
   if listlen(todoq) then do;
      done._ungray();
      todo.text = getitemc(todoq);
   end;
   else do;
      done._gray();
      todo.text = '';
   end;
return;


TERM:
   rc = dellist(todoq);
return;
```

**Example 2: Using the POPL Function**   This program searches for, retrieves, and deletes the first sublist item from the list LISTID:

```
LOOP:
   do i=1 to listlen(listid);
      if itemtype(listid,i)='L' then
         do;
            list=popl(listid,i);
            leave loop;
         end;
   end;
   ...other SCL statements...
```

**Example 3: Using the POPN Function**   This example creates a new list called DATETIMES and treats it as a stack. The entry displays SAS datetime values when the button PUSH is pressed. The text entry pops and displays SAS datetime values from the DATETIMES stack when the button POP is pressed.

```
INIT:
   datetimes = makelist();
   pop._gray();
```

```
return;

PUSH:
   datetime.value = datetime();
   datetimes = insertn(datetimes, datetime.value);
   pop._ungray();
return;

POP:
   datetime.value = popn(datetimes);
   if listlen(datetimes) = 0 then
       pop._gray();
return;

TERM:
   rc = dellist(datetimes);
return;
```

**Example 4: Using the POPO Function**    This example inserts an object into an SCL list and then removes the object from the list:

```
DCL sashelp.fsp.object.class obj1;
DCL object obj2;
init:
   obj1=_new_ sashelp.fsp.object.class();
   ll = makelist();
   ll = inserto(ll,obj1);
     /* Insert object as first item of list */
   obj2 = popo(ll);
     /* Remove object from the list into obj2 */
return;
```

## See Also

"DELITEM" on page 335

"GETITEMC, GETITEML, GETITEMN, and GETITEMO" on page 442

"INSERTC, INSERTL, INSERTN, and INSERTO" on page 482

# POPLEGEND

**Restores to the LEGEND window the last contents saved with the PUSHLEGEND routine**

**Category:**  Legend

## Syntax

**CALL POPLEGEND**();

**Details** POPLEGEND is useful if several entries in a CALL DISPLAY nested sequence have their own legends and you want to restore the original legend of each calling entry when a called entry ends.

If no legend contents have been saved, then this function is ignored.

To save the contents of the LEGEND window, use PUSHLEGEND.

For an example that includes POPLEGEND as well as other functions that manipulate a legend window, see "LEGEND" on page 507.

### See Also

"ENDLEGEND" on page 366

"LEGEND" on page 507

"PUSHLEGEND" on page 603

"PUTLEGEND" on page 606

# POPMENU

**Displays a pop-up menu that contains character items from an SCL list**

**Category:** List

## Syntax

*index*=**POPMENU**(*list-id*<,*max-popup*<,*row,column*>>);

### *index*

specifies the *index* of the item to be selected by default when the pop-up menu appears. On return, *index* will be set to the index of the selected pop-up menu item.
   Type: Numeric

### *list-id*

is the identifier of the list that contains the character or list items to display in the pop-up menu. An invalid *list-id* produces an error condition.
   Type: Numeric or List

   Lists may contain sublists as items. These list items must include one or more of the following named items to be valid:

Text

specifies the menu text (required).
   Type: Character

Checked

specifies whether a check should appear to the left of the item. Valid values are Yes|No (Default).
   Type: Character

Classifier

specifies the numeric representation of an icon to be associated with the menu item.
   Type: Numeric

Grayed
> specifies whether the menu item should be grayed. Valid values are Yes|No (Default).
>> Type: Character

HelpText
> is the text to display on the status line.
>> Type: Character

Mnemonic
> specifies the character that is used as a keyboard shortcut. The character must be one of the characters of the menu text.
>> Type: Character

*max-popup*
> is the maximum number of items to display in a pop-up menu window. If the list is longer than *max-popup*, the menu is displayed in a window with a scrollable listbox.
>> Type: Numeric

*row*
> is the starting row of the pop-up menu.
>> Type: Numeric

*column*
> is the starting column of the pop-up menu.
>> Type: Numeric

**Details**    If the list contains too many items to fit in a pop-up menu, POPMENU displays the choices in a list box that includes scrollbars. If no display window is available, POPMENU always puts the menu in a list box.

An item in the list that has the INACTIVE attribute cannot be selected and is grayed on devices that support graying. However, it is still displayed in the menu. You can use SETLATTR to assign the INACTIVE attribute to an item or to restore the item to an ACTIVE state.

If the pop-up menu is displayed in a list box, inactive items are marked with a dash, indicating that they may not be selected.

To display a separator on the pop-up menu, insert a dash as a character item in the list where you would like the separator to appear.

To display a dash, add a space before or after the dash to prevent the text from being interpreted as a separator.

POPMENU returns 0 if

□ the user cancelled the pop-up menu or closed it without making a selection

□ the list is empty

□ the list contains numeric or sublist items

□ there is insufficient memory to create the pop-up.

In the last three cases, the pop-up menu is not displayed.

If *row* and *column* are specified and either is outside the boundaries of the current window, the pop-up menu is positioned elsewhere on the window.

*Note:*  Some window systems do not allow row and column positioning of pop-up menus. They may appear at the position where the pointing device was last clicked. △

## Example

Display a pop-up menu when the user presses enter. Initialize the pop-up menu with three menu items: **Select 1**, **Numeric**, and **Character**. Define a separator between **Select 1** and **Numeric**.

```
init:
  dcl list ;
  control enter;
  list = { {text='Select 1',
            helpText='This is a selection.',
            mnemonic='S',
            classifier = 107},
          ''_'',
          ''Numeric'',
          ''Character''};

    return;
main:
 rc= popmenu (list);
 put rc=;
 return;

term:
/* Delete the list recursively to avoid memory leak */
rc = dellist ( list, 'y;);
return;
```

## See Also

"FILLIST" on page 407

"SETLATTR" on page 656

# PREVIEW

**Manipulates an application's preview buffer**

**Category:**  Submit Block

## Syntax

*rc*=**PREVIEW**(*action<,argument-1<,argument-2<,argument-3>>>*);

**rc**

contains the return code for the operation:

| | |
|---|---|
| 0 | The operation was successful. |
| −1 | For actions that open the PREVIEW window, the CANCEL command was used to exit the PREVIEW window. For other actions, the requested operation was not performed successfully. |

   Type: Numeric

**action**

is an action from "Actions for the PREVIEW Function" on page 600.

   Type: Character

**argument**

specifies up to three arguments for the specified action from "Actions for the PREVIEW Function" on page 600.

   Type: Character

## Actions for the PREVIEW Function

### 'BROWSE'

opens the PREVIEW window for browsing only. You can optionally specify a window title as *argument-1*.

### 'CLEAR'

clears the preview buffer. Any statements that were generated previously by SUBMIT statements or that were included by COPY or INCLUDE actions are lost. No optional arguments are used with this action.

### 'CLOSE'

closes the PREVIEW window. No optional arguments are used with this action.

### 'COPY'

copies a catalog entry of type SOURCE, OUTPUT, LOG, or SCL into the preview buffer. You must specify the name of the entry to be copied as *argument-1*. For the syntax for *argument-1*, see the description of the SAVE action.

*Note:* If you copy an SCL entry to the PREVIEWwindow, you should CLEAR the window before closing it. Otherwise, the SCL code that was copied will be submitted to SAS. △

### 'DISPLAY | EDIT'

opens the PREVIEW window to display the contents of the preview buffer for editing. All standard text editor commands are valid in this window. Control stays with the PREVIEW window until the PREVIEW window is exited. Issue the END command to exit the window and return to the SAS/AF program. Changes that a user makes to the statements in the window are not reversed by issuing a CANCEL command. However, the SCL program can check for the return code of −1 from the PREVIEW function, indicating that a CANCEL command was issued in the PREVIEW window, and can then specify not to save the contents of the PREVIEW window.

You can optionally specify a window title as *argument-1*.

### 'FILE'

saves the current contents of the PREVIEW window to an external file. With this action, you must specify the fileref for the external file as *argument-1*. You must specify a fileref; physical filenames are not allowed.

You can specify APPEND for *argument-2* to append the contents of the preview buffer to the contents of the external file.

### 'HISTORY'

saves or appends the statements submitted from SCL programs to a catalog member. You must specify the name of an entry as *argument-1*, in one of the following forms:

*entry*
saves the submitted statements in SASUSER.PROFILE.*entry*.SOURCE.

*entry*.SOURCE
saves the submitted statements in SASUSER.PROFILE.*entry*.SOURCE.

*libref.catalog.entry*
saves the submitted statements in *libref.catalog.entry*.SOURCE.

*libref.catalog.entry*.SOURCE
saves the submitted statements in *libref.catalog.entry*.SOURCE.

Once a history destination is set, it remains in effect for the application until a reset is performed. To clear the destination, invoke PREVIEW again by passing the HISTORY action without any subsequent argument. The application stops appending the submitted statements to the previously specified SOURCE entry.

You can also optionally specify a description of up to 40 characters for the entry as *argument-2*.

**'INCLUDE'**

copies into the PREVIEW window the contents of an external file. With this action, you must specify the fileref for the external file as *argument-1*. A physical filename is not allowed.

**'LINES'**

returns the number of the last non-blank line in the PREVIEW window.

**'MODIFIED'**

returns 1 if the PREVIEW window was modified and 0 if it was not modified.

**'OPEN'**

displays the PREVIEW window and immediately returns control to the SCL program. New SAS statements are displayed continually as they are generated.

This window is displayed until the application closes or until you use the PREVIEW function and specify the CLOSE action. Thus, specifying OPEN enables you to keep the window open throughout an application by allowing control to return to the procedure while the window is open. With OPEN, you can optionally specify a window title as *argument-1*.

**'PRINT'**

prints the contents of the PREVIEW window. This action accepts three arguments:

- ☐ You can optionally use *argument-1* to specify a form to use for controlling printing. Use *name* or *name*.FORM to specify a form in the current catalog. Use *libref.catalog.name* or *libref.catalog.name*.FORM to specify a form in a different catalog. If you do not specify a form, SASHELP.FSP.DEFAULT.FORM is used. For more information about forms, see *SAS Language Reference: Dictionary*.
- ☐ You can optionally use *argument-2* to specify a fileref for a print file. If this argument is blank or missing, the printout is sent to the default system printer.
- ☐ You can optionally use *argument-3* to specify append mode. Use **A** to append the output to the print file. If this argument is blank or missing, each new PRINT option replaces the contents of the print file.

**'SAVE'**

copies the contents of the PREVIEW window to a catalog member. With this action, you must specify the name of an entry as *argument-1*, in one of the following forms:

*entry*
    saves the contents in SASUSER.PROFILE.*entry*.SOURCE.

*entry.type*
    saves the contents in SASUSER.PROFILE.*entry.type*. Entry types can be SOURCE, LOG, OUTPUT, or SCL.

*libref.catalog.entry*
    saves the contents in *libref.catalog.entry*.SOURCE.

*libref.catalog.entry.type*
    saves the contents in *libref.catalog.entry.type*.

You can also optionally specify a description for the entry as *argument-2*. The first 256 characters of the description are saved.

You can also optionally specify **APPEND** as *argument-3* to append the contents of the PREVIEW window to the specified catalog entry.

**Details**    The preview buffer is where statements that are generated by SUBMIT blocks are stored before they are submitted for execution.

## Example

Manipulate the PREVIEW window. The user enters values in text entry controls TABLENAME (the name of a SAS table to be created), MIMIC (the name of an existing SAS table after which the new table is modeled), and FNAME (the fileref of a file in which submitted SAS statements will be stored). If the user does not issue a CANCEL command from the application window, then PREVIEW displays the statements in the PREVIEW window. If the user does not issue a CANCEL command from the PREVIEW window, then the statements are submitted for execution. If a user issues a CANCEL command from the application or from the PREVIEW window, the PREVIEW window is cleared of all statements. When a user presses the RUN button, the statements are submitted.

```
INIT:
   control label;
return;
RUN:
 submit;
    data &tablename;
       set &mimic;
    run;
  endsubmit;
 if (_status_ ne 'C') then
     do;
       if (preview('EDIT') = -1) then
          rc=preview('clear');
         else
          do;
             rc=preview('FILE',FNAME);
               submit continue;
                 endsubmit;
               end;
        end;
     else
        rc=preview('clear');
return;
```

## See Also

"ENDCLASS" on page 366

"SUBMIT" on page 676

"WREGION" on page 730

# PROTECT

**Assigns protection to a FRAME entry control or field**

**Category:**    Control or Field

## Syntax

**PROTECT** *wcol-names* | _ALL_;

**wcol-names**

> lists one or more window columns to protect, or **_ALL_** to protect all window columns. To specify multiple window columns, separate the names with blanks.
>
> Type: Character

**Details**    Protecting a window column prevents the cursor from tabbing to the associated control or field. You can use the PROTECT statement to temporarily override a PROTECT attribute that has been specified for a window column. The column to be protected cannot be an element of an array. To protect an array element, use the FIELD function.

If you protect a field column with the PROTECT statement in FSEDIT applications and issue the MODIFY command to edit the custom screen, the PROTECT attribute is saved for that field column in the PROTECT window.

Window controls can also use the _protect method. Protecting some window controls (block, check box, icon, list box, pushbutton, radio box, scroll bar, and slider) is the same as calling the GRAY function or the _gray method.

The protection status remains in effect until the UNPROTECT statement is used.

The following statements are incorrect because they do not name window columns:

```
protect a{i};
protect a||b;
```

## Example

Prevent the user from changing the value of the window column TABLENAME after the value has been entered:

```
if (modified(tablename) and ERROR(tablename)=0)
then protect tablename;
```

## See Also

"DISPLAYED" on page 353

"ERROR" on page 375

"ERROROFF" on page 376

"ERRORON" on page 377

"FIELD" on page 394

"MODIFIED" on page 550

"UNPROTECT" on page 695

# PUSHLEGEND

**Saves the contents of the LEGEND window**

**Category:** Legend

## Syntax

**CALL PUSHLEGEND**();

**Details** PUSHLEGEND is useful if several entries in a CALL DISPLAY nested sequence have their own legends and you want to restore the original legend of each calling entry when a called entry ends.

To restore a pushed legend to the LEGEND window, use POPLEGEND.

For an example that includes PUSHLEGEND as well as other functions that manipulate a legend window, see "LEGEND" on page 507.

## See Also

"ENDLEGEND" on page 366

"LEGEND" on page 507

"POPLEGEND" on page 596

"PUTLEGEND" on page 606

# PUT

**Writes text to the LOG window**

**Category:** Utility

**Comparisons:** SAS Statement with limitations in SCL

## Syntax

**PUT** <<'*character-string*'> < *variable-name*<=>>< *object.attribute*<=>>> | _ALL_;

***character-string***
is the literal text to write to the LOG window.
Type: Character

***variable-name***
lists one or more variables whose name and value are to be written to the LOG window.
Type: Character

**_ALL_**
specifies that all variables and their values are to be written to the LOG window.
Type: Character

## Details

PUT supports dot notation for returning the value of an object. Use the form **put object.attribute=;**. For more information about dot notation, see "Accessing Object Attributes and Methods With Dot Notation" on page 119.

## Differences in PUT Statement Execution

SCL supports only the forms of the PUT statement shown in "Syntax." You can combine these forms. For example:

```
PUT 'character-string' variable-name=;
```

For details about the PUT statement in the base SAS language, see *SAS Language Reference: Dictionary* .

---

# PUTC and PUTN

**Return a formatted value, using the specified format**

**Category:** Formatting

---

## Syntax

*formatted-val*=**PUTC**(*char-val,format*);

*formatted-val*=**PUTN**(*num-val,format*);

**formatted-val**
> contains the value with the specified format applied.
> > Type: Character

**char-val**
> is the character value to be formatted by PUTC.
> > Type: Character

**num-val**
> is the numeric value to be formatted by PUTN.
> > Type: Numeric

**format**
> is the character format to apply with PUTC or the numeric format to apply with PUTN. *Format* can be an SCL variable or a character literal.
> > Type: Character

**Details**    Dot notation cannot be used with the PUTC or PUTN functions. This restriction is necessary to allow proper parsing of the *char-val* and *num-val* parameters.

For more information about using a format to return a value, see the PUT function in *SAS Language Reference: Dictionary* .

## Examples

**Example 1: Using the PUTC Function**    Format the value that a user enters into the text entry control named VALUE:

```
MAIN:
   value=putc(value,'$QUOTE.');
   put value=;
return;
```

Entering SAS into the field displays "SAS" in the field and produces the following output:

```
VALUE="SAS"
```

**Example 2: Using the PUTN Function**     Format the variable NETPD using the DOLLAR12.2 format, and store the value in the variable SALARY.

```
INIT:
   netpd=20000;
   put netpd=;
   fmt='dollar12.2';
   salary=putn(netpd,fmt);
   put salary=;
return;
```

This program produces the following output:

```
NETPD=20000
SALARY=   $20,000.00
```

## See Also

"INPUTC and INPUTN" on page 481

# PUTLEGEND

**Specifies the contents of one line in the LEGEND window**

**Category:**  Legend

## Syntax

**CALL PUTLEGEND**(*line,text<,color<,attribute>>*);

*line*
> is the number for the line on which to display the text. If this value is larger than the MAXROW returned from the WINFO function, the line number is ignored.
> Type: Numeric

*text*
> is the text to display on one line of the LEGEND window. Once you specify text for a legend line, that text is redisplayed each time the LEGEND routine is called. To delete the text for a line, you can specify either new text or a null string ( ' ')for that line number.
> Type: Character

*color*
> is a color name, or ' 'for the default color. Colors are BLACK, BLUE, BROWN, CYAN, GRAY, GREEN, MAGENTA, ORANGE, PINK, RED, WHITE, and YELLOW. SASCOLOR window elements can also be used for *color*.
> The default color is the SASCOLOR window element "Informational Text."
> Type: Character

> **attribute**
>> is a display attribute, or ' ' for the default attribute. Attributes are: NONE, BLINKING, HIGHLIGHT, HIREV, REVERSE, and UNDERLINE. If you specify a SASCOLOR window element for *color*, then *attribute* is ignored, because the SASCOLOR window element contains a display attribute.
>> The default attribute is the SASCOLOR window element "Informational Text."
>> Type: Character

**Details**    Use multiple PUTLEGEND routines to display multiple lines. The default legend window size allows four lines of text. You can change the LEGEND window size by using WREGION. To display the legend window, use LEGEND.

For an example that includes PUTLEGEND as well as other functions that manipulate a legend window, see "LEGEND" on page 507.

## See Also

"ENDLEGEND" on page 366

"LEGEND" on page 507

"POPLEGEND" on page 596

"PUSHLEGEND" on page 603

# PUTLIST

**Displays the contents of an SCL list in the LOG window**

**Category:**   List

## Syntax

**CALL PUTLIST**(*list-id<,label<,indent>>*);

> **list-id**
>> is the identifier returned by the function that created the list.
>> Type: Numeric or List

> **label**
>> specifies the label for the printed output.
>> Type: Character

> **indent**
>> is the number of characters to indent list items in the printed list.
>> Type: Numeric

**Details**    After printing the optional label, PUTLIST prints a left parenthesis '(' to mark the beginning of the list, followed by the list of items separated by blanks. Each named item is preceded by its name and an equal sign (=), but nothing is printed before items that do not have names. PUTLIST ends the list with a right parenthesis ')', followed by the list's identifier number within square brackets.

If the value for *indent* is greater than or equal to 0, the list is printed in a vertical format where each list item is printed on its own line. Sublists are indented the number of spaces to the right that is specified by *indent*.

If the list contains sublists that have been deleted, PUTLIST identifies each invalid list identifier with the text **<invalid list id>[listid]**.

## Examples

The following examples are based on an SCL list whose list identifier is stored in the variable A. This list contains the numbers 17 and 328 plus the character value "Any characters". These examples display the list in several ways:

- □ in its simplest form
- □ with values indented
- □ after a numeric item is replaced with a sublist item
- □ after the list has been added to itself as a sublist.

**Example 1: Displaying a List with Indented Values**    Print a list and indent the list items:

```
call putlist(a,'A=',2);
```

The above statement produces the following output:

```
A=(   17
      328
      'Any characters'
    )[7]
```

**Example 2: Replacing a Numeric Item with a Sublist Item**    Replace the second item in the list A with the list identifier for sublist B, which contains the values -4.75 and 12.875:

```
/*  Assign the second item to list B.  */
   a=setiteml(a,b,2);
   name=nameitem(a,1,'MIN');
   name=nameitem(a,2,'B');
   call putlist(a,'A=',2);
```

These statements produce the following output:

```
A=(   MIN=17
   B=(   -4.75
         12.875
     )[5]
   'Any characters'
   )[7]
```

**Example 3: Adding a List to Itself as a Sublist**    If a sublist appears more than once in the list that is being printed, PUTLIST prints only the following for the second and subsequent occurrences of the list:

```
(...) [listid-number]
```

To view the full contents of the list, scan the output of PUTLIST for other occurrences of [*listid-number*]. This prevents infinite loops if a list contains itself.
Create and display a recursive list:

```
r1=makelist();
   r1=setnitemn(r1,1,'X');
   r1=setniteml(r1,r1,'SELF');
   call putlist(r1,'R1=',2);
```

These statements display the following information in the LOG window. Note that the full contents of the list that has the identifier 7 are printed only once. The other occurrence is represented as (...)[7].

```
R1=(   X=1
       SELF=(...)[7]
    )[7]
```

## See Also

"MAKELIST" on page 535

"MAKENLIST" on page 536

# PUTVARC and PUTVARN

**Write a value to the Table Data Vector (TDV) for a SAS table**

**Category:** SAS Table

## Syntax

**CALL PUTVARC**(*table-id,col-num,cval*);

**CALL PUTVARN**(*table-id,col-num,nval*);

***table-id***
   is the identifier that was assigned when the table was opened. If *table-id* is invalid, the program halts.
   Type: Numeric

***col-num***
   is the number of the column in the SAS table. This is the number that is adjacent to the column when the CONTENTS procedure lists the columns in the SAS table. You can use the VARNUM function to obtain this value.
   Type: Numeric

***cval***
   is the character value to be written to the TDV.
   Type: Character

***nval***
   is the numeric value to be written to the TDV.
   Type: Numeric

**Details**    After PUTVARC writes a character value to a table column, use UPDATE to update the row in the SAS table.

If the SCL program uses CALL SET to link columns in the SCL data vector (SDV) with columns in the Table Data Vector (TDV), do not use the PUTVARN and PUTVARC routines for any columns that are linked by SET. UPDATE and APPEND automatically copy the data from the SDV to the TDV before writing a row to a physical file. Therefore, the value that is copied from the SDV will overwrite the value written to the TDV by PUTVARC or PUTVARN, and the value of the corresponding table column will not be updated with the value specified by PUTVARC or PUTVARN.

## Examples

**Example 1: Using the PUTVARC Routine**    Change an employee's last name from **SMITH** to **UPDIKE** in the column NAME in the table referenced by the table identifier PAYID:

```
vnum=varnum(payid,'name');
rc=locatec(payid,vnum,'SMITH','u');
if (rc>0) then
    do;
        call putvarc(payid,vnum,'UPDIKE');
        rc=update(payid);
    end;
```

**Example 2: Using the PUTVARN Routine**    Change an item's price from 1.99 to 2.99 in the table referenced by the table identifier PAYID:

```
vnum=varnum(payid,'price');
rc=locaten(payid,vnum,1.99,'u');
if (rc>0) then
    do;
        call putvarn(payid,vnum,2.99);
        rc=update(payid);
    end;
```

## See Also

"APPEND" on page 251

"FETCH" on page 389

"FETCHOBS" on page 390

"GETVARC and GETVARN" on page 450

"INITROW" on page 480

"UPDATE" on page 697

"VARNUM" on page 713

# REDIM

**Resizes a dynamic array**

**Category:** Array

## Syntax

*rc=***REDIM**(*array,dim1<,dim2<,dim3....<,dimN>...>>*);

**rc**

    indicates whether the operation was successful.

| | |
|---|---|
| 0 | successful |
| ≠0 | not successful |

      Type: Numeric

*array*
> is the dynamic array to be resized. A non-dynamic array causes an error condition.
> Type: Array

*dim1...dimN*
> is the size of each specified dimension. If you specify negative sizes or an invalid number of dimensions, an error condition occurs.
> Type: Numeric

**Details**    You can use the REDIM function to resize a dynamic array. You cannot change the numbers of dimensions or type of the array, only the bounds. The REDIM function will preserve the data in the array. However, if you resize the array to a smaller size, you will lose the data in the eliminated elements. There is no limit to the number of times that you can resize an array.

## Examples

**Example 1: Create an Array and Resize It Preserving the Data**    The example creates a one-dimensional array of 5 elements and resizes it, preserving the data, to 10 elements.

```
DCL num a(*);
rc = makearray(a,3);
do i=1 to dim(a);
    a[i]=i;
end;
rc = redim(a,5);
put a=;
rc=delarray(a);
```

The output would be:

```
a=
a[1]=1
a[2]=2
a[3]=3
a[4]=.
a[5]=.
```

**Example 2: Create an Array and Resize it Without Preserving the Data**    The example creates a two-dimensional 5x5 array, resizes it to a 10x10 array and does not preserve the data.

```
DCL num a(*);
rc = makearray(a,3);
do i=1 to dim(a);
    a[i]=i;
end;
rc = makearray(a,5);
put a=;
rc = delarray(a);
```

The output would be:

```
a=
a[1]=.
a[2]=.
a[3]=.
a[4]=.
```

```
a[5]=.
```

## See Also

"DELARRAY" on page 332

"MAKEARRAY" on page 533

Chapter 4, "SCL Arrays," on page 37

---

# REFRESH

**Redisplays a window using current field or control values**

**Category:**   Window

## Syntax

**REFRESH**;

**Details**    Refreshing a window can result in updating window variable values. FRAME entries can also use the _refresh method.

## Example

Suppose the field NAME is displayed on the left side of a PROGRAM entry and that NEW.PROGRAM is sized so that it is displayed on the right side of the window. When the following code runs, NAME changes to red and then NEW.PROGRAM is displayed. If the REFRESH statement were not present, NAME would not appear red until NEW.PROGRAM is closed and control is returned to the application.

```
rc=field('color red','name');
refresh;
call display('new.program');
```

---

# RENAME

**Renames a member of a SAS data library, an external file, or a directory**

**Category:**   Utility

## Syntax

*sysrc=***RENAME**(*old-name,new-name< ,type< ,description< ,generation< ,password>>>>*);

*sysrc*
  contains the return code for the operation:
    Type: Numeric

| 0 | successful |
|---|---|
| ≠0 | not successful |

*old-name*
  is the current name of a member of a SAS data library, an external file, or an external directory. For a member, this can be a one-, two-, or four-level name. For an external file or a directory, *old-name* must be the full pathname of the file or a directory; otherwise, the current directory is used.
    Type: Character

*new-name*
  is the new one-level name for the library member, external file, or directory.
    Type: Character

*type*
  specifies the type of element to rename:
    Type: Character

  **'ACCESS'**
    an access descriptor that was created using SAS/ACCESS software

  **'CATALOG'**
    a SAS catalog or catalog entry

  **'DATA'**
    a SAS table (This is the default.)

  **'VIEW'**
    a SAS table view

  **'FILE'**
    an external file or a directory.

*description*
  is the description of a catalog entry. You can specify *description* only when *type* is CATALOG.
    Type: Character

*password*
  is the password for the file that is being renamed.
    Type: Character

*generation*
  is the generation number of the data set that is being renamed.
    Type: Numeric

**Details**   You can use RENAME to rename files or directories that are external to a SAS session as well as members of a SAS data library.

To rename an entry in a catalog, specify the four-level name for *old-name* and a one-level name for *new-name*. You must specify CATALOG for type when renaming an entry in a catalog.

## Examples

**Example 1: Renaming Tables and Catalog Entries**   Rename a SAS table from DATA1 to DATA2. Also rename a catalog entry from A.SCL to B.SCL.

```
rc1=rename('mylib.data1','data2');
rc2=rename('mylib.mycat.a.scl','b','catalog');
```

**Example 2: Renaming an External File**   Rename an external file:

```
    /* rename a file that is in another directory */
rc=rename('/local/u/testdir/first',
         '/local/u/second','file');
    /* rename a PC file */
rc=rename('d:\temp','d:\testfile','file');
```

**Example 3: Renaming a Directory**   Rename a directory:

```
rc=rename('/local/u/testdir/','/local/u/oldtestdir','file');
```

**Example 4: Renaming a Data Set Generation**   Rename a generation of the data set **work.one** to **work.two**, where the password for **work.one#003** is "blahblah":

```
rc=rename('work.one','two','data','','blahblah',3);
```

## See Also

"DELETE" on page 334

---

# REPLACE

**Substitutes a replacement string for a reference to an SCL variable in the SUBMIT block**

**Category:**   Submit Block

---

## Syntax

**REPLACE** *variable replacement-string*;

*variable*
    is the variable whose value the replacement value is substituted for.
      Type: Character

*replacement-string*
    is the text to substitute for the variable's value. This text can include a variable's
    value, but that is not mandatory.
      Type: Character

**Details**   REPLACE substitutes a replacement string for a reference to an SCL variable in the SUBMIT block only if the variable is not blank. It functions as an implicit IF statement, determining when to substitute the string in the SUBMIT block. Using the REPLACE statement reduces the amount of code needed to generate statements to be submitted.

The REPLACE statement is evaluated when the program is compiled. Different replacement strings cannot be substituted based on conditions that exist at execution time. For example, the following statements cause errors when you compile the program:

```
if (x) then
    replace y '&y';
  else
    replace y '&z';
```

If you use multiple REPLACE statements for the same variable, the last REPLACE statement is used and a warning is generated by the compiler to that effect.

A good programming practice is to collect all the REPLACE statements in one place in your SCL program.

You can also use the REPLACE option in the ATTR window of a PROGRAM entry to specify the replacement string. However, this can be overridden by REPLACE statements in the SCL program.

SCL performs substitution according to the following rules:

□ If the value of the SCL variable is blank (or _BLANK_), no substitution is performed.

□ If the value of the SCL variable is not blank, SCL performs substitution into the replacement string for the variable and substitutes the resulting string into the SUBMIT block.

The replacement string can reference other SCL variables.

*Note:* Replacement strings are not recursive. When you refer to another variable in the replacement string, the program uses the current value of the variable, not the value that is based on its replacement string. △

### Example

```
replace tablename 'data=&tablename';
   ...more SCL statements...
submit continue;
   proc print &tablename;
   run;
endsubmit;
```

If TABLENAME contains ''(or _BLANK_), the submitted statements are

```
submit continue;
   proc print;
   run;
endsubmit;
```

However, if TABLENAME contains **work.sample**, the submitted statements are

```
submit continue;
   proc print data=work.sample;
   run;
endsubmit;
```

# RETURN

**Stops executing statements in the program section that is currently executing and may return a value to the caller**

**Category:**  Control Flow

**Comparisons:**  SAS statement with limitations in SCL

## Syntax

**RETURN**< (*value*)>;

*value*

is a value to be returned by the current method. *Value* can be an SCL variable, a numeric or character constant, or an expression (except for an array). Use *value* only for RETURN statements that end METHOD and ENTRY statements.

Type: Character, Numeric, List, Object

**Details**    When RETURN stops executing statements in the current section of an SCL program, control passes to the next section in the program execution cycle.

The RETURN statement for an ENTRY or METHOD statement block can return *value* if the ENTRY or METHOD statement contains RETURN=*data type*. The returned value from the RETURN statement has no effect if the statement does not immediately return the program control back to the calling program.

For details about the RETURN statement in the base SAS language, see *SAS Language Reference: Dictionary.*

## Example

Define a method for LIB.CAT.MYCLASS.CLASS that compares two lists, L1 and L2. Return 1 if the strings are identical and 0 if the strings are not identical.

```
useclass lib.cat.myclass.class;
compare: method l1 l2:list return=num;
  dcl num len1 len2 i;
  len1=listlen(l1);
  len2=listlen(l2);
  if (len1 ^= len2) then return 0;

  do i=1 to len1;
    dcl char(1) type;
    type=itemtype(l1,i);
    if (type ^= itemtype(l2,i)) then
      return 0;

    select type;
      when ('O') do;
        if (getitemo(l1,i) ^= getitemo(l2,i)) then
          return 0;
      end;
      when ('N') do;
        if (getitemn(l1,i) ^= getitemn(l2,i)) then
          return 0;
      end;
      when ('L') do;
        if (getiteml(l1,i) ^= getiteml(l2,i)) then
          return 0;
      end;
      when ('C') do;
        if (getitemc(l1,i) ^= getitemc(l2,i)) then
```

```
            return 0;
        end;
        otherwise return 0;
    end;
  end;
  return(1);
endmethod;
enduseclass;
```

## See Also

"ENTRY" on page 369

"METHOD" on page 540

"RUN" on page 625

"STOP" on page 674

# REVLIST

**Reverses the order of the items in an SCL list**

**Category:** List

## Syntax

*list-id*=**REVLIST**(*list-id*);

**list-id**
> is the identifier of the list to reverse. The function returns the list identifier that is passed in. An invalid *list-id* produces an error condition.
>
> Type: Numeric or List

**Details**   Any names and attributes that are assigned to list items remain with the items when the items are reversed.

REVLIST does not make a copy of the list before reversing the order of the list items. The list is modified in place. To keep a copy of the original list, use COPYLIST before REVLIST.

An error condition results if the list has the NOUPDATE attribute.

To check attributes, use HASATTR. To change attributes, use SETLATTR.

## Example

Make a nonrecursive copy of the list identified by MYLISTID, reverse the items in the copied list, and assign the new list identifier to the variable REVLISTID:

```
revlistid = revlist(copylist(mylistid));
```

## See Also

"HASATTR" on page 458

"ROTLIST" on page 622

"SETLATTR" on page 656

"SORTLIST" on page 669

# REWIND

**Positions the table pointer at the beginning of a SAS table**

**Category:**   SAS Table

## Syntax

*sysrc*=**REWIND**(*table-id*);

**sysrc**
contains the return code for the operation:

| | |
|---|---|
| 0 | successful |
| ≠0 | not successful |

Type: Numeric

**table-id**
is the identifier that was assigned when the table was opened in any mode except IS, US, or N. If *table-id* is invalid, the program halts.
Type: Numeric

**Details**    After a call to REWIND, a call to FETCH reads the first row in the table.
If there is an active WHERE clause, REWIND moves the table pointer to the first row that satisfies the WHERE condition.

## Example

Call FETCHOBS to fetch the tenth row in the table MYDATA. Then call REWIND to return to the first row and fetch the first row:

```
dsid=open('mydata','i');
rc=fetchobs(dsid,10);
rc=rewind(dsid);
rc=fetch(dsid);
```

### See Also

"FETCH" on page 389

"FETCHOBS" on page 390

"FREWIND" on page 431

"NOTE" on page 570

"POINT" on page 592

# RGBDM

**Returns the name supported by the SAS windowing environment for a color**

**Category:** Utility

## Syntax

*DM-color-name*=**RGBDM**(*color-name*<,*RGB-color*>);

*DM-color-name*
> contains the name of the SAS windowing environment color that is closest to *color-name*.
>
> Type: Character

*color-name*
> is a color name to look up: BLACK, BLUE, BROWN, CYAN, GRAY, GREEN, MAGENTA, ORANGE, PINK, RED, WHITE, or YELLOW. Any SAS/GRAPH color name is allowed, as well as SASCOLOR window elements. Arbitrary RGB colors can be specified using the CX*rrggbb* convention.
>
> Type: Character

*RGB-color*
> returns *color-name* in the CX*rrggbb* format.
>
> *Note:* This parameter is an update parameter. See "Input, Output, and Update Parameters" on page 34 for more information. △
>
> Type: Character

**Details**    The RGBDM function provides a way to determine both the closest color that is supported by the SAS windowing environment for a specified color and the RGB values for a color name. If *color-name* is a variable and the specified color is a valid color abbreviation, the variable is updated with the complete color name. For example, the color "R" would be translated to "RED" and the *RGB-color* would be "CXFF0000". The value for *RGB-color* may be different depending on the host operating system.

For more information about the CX*rrggbb* format, see *SAS/GRAPH Software: Reference*.

## Example

Display the color components of several different colors:

```
length rgbclr $ 8;
INIT:
```

```
        /* display txtclr=red */
        /* rgbclr=cxff0000    */
    txtclr = rgbdm("RED", rgbclr);
    put txtclr= rgbclr=;

        /* display txtclr=red */
    txtclr = rgbdm("cxf00000");
    put txtclr=;

        /* display txtclr=red clr=red */
    clr='r';
    txtclr = rgbdm(clr);
    put txtclr= clr= ;

        /* display the foreground */
        /* color in rgb values    */
    txtclr = rgbdm("FOREGROUND", rgbclr);
    put txtclr= rgbclr=;
return;
```

In some operating environments, this example produces the following output:

```
txtclr=RED rgbclr=CXFF0000
txtclr=RED
txtclr=RED clr=RED
txtclr=WHITE rgbclr=CXF2F2F2
```

# RIGHT

### Returns a right-aligned character value

**Category:**   Character

## Syntax

*rstring*=**RIGHT**(*string*< ,*length*>);

**rstring**
> contains the right-aligned character string. If *rstring* already exists, then specifying a length in the RIGHT function changes the current length of *rstring* to *length*. If the length has not been defined with a DECLARE or LENGTH statement, and if *rstring* is not a window variable, then the default SCL variable length is 200 characters.
> Type: Character

**string**
> is the character string to be right-justified.
> Type: Character

**length**
> is the length in which the character string is to be right-justified. The default is the maximum length of *rstring*.
> Type: Numeric

**Details**    The string is justified by padding with leading spaces. The default length is the maximum length of *rstring* characters.

In order for RIGHT to work properly when *rstring* is a window variable, set the justification attribute (**JUST**) for *rstring* to **NONE** when you define the window variables.

To left-justify a character string, use the LEFT function when you define the window variable. To center a character string, use CENTER.

## See Also

"CENTER" on page 275

"LEFT" on page 506

# RLINK

**Reports whether a link exists between the current SAS session and a remote SAS session**

**Category:**   Interface to SAS Software

**Requires SAS/CONNECT software**

## Syntax

*rc*=**RLINK**(*remote-session-id*);

**rc**

contains the return code for the operation:

| 1 | The link exists. |
|---|---|
| 0 | The link does not exist. |

Type: Numeric

**remote-session-id**

is the name of the remote session (REMOTE= value) that is being tested.
Type: Character

**Details**    See *SAS/CONNECT User's Guide* for details about accessing remote hosts from SAS software.

To get the name of the last remote host that was linked to during the current SAS session, use OPTGETC, specifying 'REMOTE' as *option-name*.

## Example

Check to see whether the link is active:

```
REMSESS=optgetc('remote');
msg=sysmsg();
put msg REMSESS;
rc=rlink(REMSESS);
   if (rc=0) then
      msg='No link exists.';
   else
      msg='A link exists.';
```

```
put msg;
```

## See Also

"OPTGETC and OPTGETN" on page 583

"RSESSION" on page 623

"RSTITLE" on page 624

---

# ROTLIST

**Rotates the items in an SCL list**

**Category:** List

---

## Syntax

*list-id*=**ROTLIST**(*list-id*<,*n*>);

**list-id**
> is the identifier of the list to rotate. The function returns the list identifier that is passed in. An invalid *list-id* produces an error condition.
> Type: Numeric or List

**n**
> is the number of times to rotate the list. The default is 1.
> Type: Numeric

**Details** The items are rotated the number of times specified by *n*. If the value for *n* is positive, the items are rotated from right to left. This means that each rotation moves the item at the front of the list to the end of the list (that is, from position 1 to position -1). If the value for *n* is negative, the items are rotated from left to right. This moves the item at the end of the list to the front of the list (that is, from position -1 to position 1).

When a list is rotated, item names and attributes are moved along with the elements.

Fetching a named item from a list that has more than one item of the same name may return a different item from the list after rotating than was returned before rotating.

ROTLIST does not make a copy of the list before rotating the items in the list. The list is modified in place. To keep a copy of the original list, use COPYLIST before ROTLIST.

An error condition results if the list has the NOUPDATE attribute.

To check a list's attributes, use HASATTR. To change these attributes, use SETLATTR.

## Example

Manipulate the list identified by LISTID, which contains the five character values A, B, C, D, and E. Display the list, rotate it right to left one time and display that list, and then rotate it left to right twice and display that list.

```
call putlist(listid,'Input list=');
listid = rotlist(listid); /* Rotate 1 time */
call putlist(listid,'Rotated  1=');
```

```
listid = rotlist(listid,-2);
call putlist(listid,'Rotated -2=');
```

The preceding statements produce the following changes. The net result is that the list is rotated backwards one time.

```
Input list=('A' 'B' 'C' 'D' 'E')[3]
Rotated  1=('B' 'C' 'D' 'E' 'A')[3]
Rotated -2=('E' 'A' 'B' 'C' 'D')[3]
```

*Note:* [3] is the list identifier that was assigned when this example was run and may be different each time the example is run. △

## See Also

"HASATTR" on page 458

"REVLIST" on page 617

"SETLATTR" on page 656

"SORTLIST" on page 669

# RSESSION

**Returns the name, description, and SAS software version of a remote session**

**Category:** Interface to SAS Software

**Requires SAS/CONNECT software**

## Syntax

*cval*=**RSESSION**(*n*);

**cval**
    contains up to 48 characters of information identifying a remote session. Characters 1 through 8 contain the session identifier (the REMOTE= value). Characters 9 through 48 contain the description.
        Type: Character

**n**
    is the number of the remote session to identify.
        Type: Numeric

**Details**    RSESSION returns the session identifier and the corresponding description for a remote session that has been established with SAS/CONNECT software. You must have previously defined the description using RSTITLE.

If no remote link exists, the returned value is blank. If a link exists but no description has been specified, then characters 9 through 48 in the returned value are blanks.

See *SAS/CONNECT User's Guide* for more information about establishing a link between local and remote hosts.

## Example

Retrieve the name and description of remote session number 1:

```
value=rsession(1);
```

## See Also

"RLINK" on page 621
"RSTITLE" on page 624

---

# RSTITLE

**Defines a description for an existing connection to a remote session**

**Category:**   Interface to SAS Software

**Requires SAS/CONNECT software**

---

## Syntax

*sysrc*=**RSTITLE**(*session-id,description*);


*sysrc*
  contains the return code for the operation:

  0                    successful

  ≠0                   not successful
     Type: Numeric

*session-id*
  is one to eight characters that identify the remote session (the REMOTE= value).
     Type: Character

*description*
  is one to 40 characters to associate with the remote session.
     Type: Character

**Details**    You can retrieve the information that RSTITLE saves by using RSESSION to build a list of connections. You can then use the list to select a connection when submitting statements to a remote host.
   In order to use this function, Release 6.07 or later of SAS software must be running on both the local and remote host systems.
   See *SAS/CONNECT User's Guide* for more information about establishing a link between local and remote hosts.

## Example

Define the description **MVS Payroll Data** for the remote session that has the identifier **A**:

```
session='A';
   description='MVS Payroll Data';
```

```
rc=rstitle(session,description);
```

### See Also

"RLINK" on page 621

"RSESSION" on page 623

---

# RUN

**Stops executing statements in the program section that is currently executing**

**Category:** Control Flow

**Comparisons:** SAS Statement with limitations in SCL

**Alias:** RETURN

### Syntax

**RUN**;

**Details** In SCL, RUN is treated as an alias for RETURN.

For details about the RUN statement in the base SAS language, see *SAS Language Reference: Dictionary*.

### See Also

"RETURN" on page 615

"STOP" on page 674

---

# SASNAME

**Verifies that a name is a valid SAS name**

**Category:** Utility

### Syntax

*rc*=**SASNAME**(*name*);

***rc***

contains the return code for the operation:

| | |
|---|---|
| 1 | The name is a valid SAS name. |
| 0 | The name is not a valid SAS name. |

Type: Numeric

*name*
>   is the name to be verified as a valid SAS name.
>       Type: Character

**Details**    SASNAME verifies that a specified name is a valid SAS name. SAS names can be up to 32 characters long. The first character must be a letter (A, B, C, . . . , Z) or underscore (_). Other characters can be letters, numbers (0, 1, . . . , 9), or underscores. Blanks cannot appear in SAS names, and special characters (for example, $, @, #), except underscores, are not allowed.

## Example

```
erroroff catalogname;
rc=sasname('catalogname');
if (rc=0) then do;
   erroron 'catalogname';
   _msg_ = 'Catalog name is invalid.';
   end;
```

*Note:*   In this example, the value for CATALOGNAME must be a one-level SAS name. SASNAME considers a two-level name of the form *libref.catalog-name* invalid because it contains the dot (.) character. △

# SASTASK

**Determines whether a SAS procedure is running**

**Category:**   Interface to SAS Software

## Syntax

*rc*=**SASTASK**();

*rc*
>   contains the return code for the operation:
>
>   1                   A SAS procedure is active.
>
>   0                   No SAS procedure is active.
>       Type: Numeric

## Example

Determine whether a SAS procedure is currently running before attempting to submit code to SAS software. If so, display a message to inform the user why the code cannot be submitted.

```
if (sastask()) then
 _msg_='Another procedure is currently active.';
else
   do;
       submit continue;
```

```
        data a;
           x=1;
        run;
     endsubmit;
  end;
```

# SAVEENTRYDIALOG

**Opens a dialog window that lists catalog entries, and returns the name of the selected entry**

**Category:** Selection List

## Syntax

*selection*=**SAVEENTRYDIALOG**(< *type*< ,*initial*< ,*entry-name*< ,*list-id*< ,*description*>>>>>);

**selection**
contains the four-level name of the selected SAS file, or a blank if nothing is selected.
  Type: Character

**type**
specifies member types to list in the dialog window, such as CLASS, SCL, or FRAME. This can reduce the length of the list in the dialog window. If *type* is not used, names of all catalog entry types in the data library are listed.
  Type: Character

**initial**
is the four-level name of the catalog entry to be the initially selected item in the dialog window when it opens.
  Type: Character

**entry-name**
is a two- or four-level name of a catalog entry to call when a user selects the Advanced button in the dialog window. The entry can be any of the following types: FRAME, SCL, PROGRAM, HELP, CBT, or MENU.
  If *entry-name* is not specified, then the window does not contain Advanced .
  Type: Character

**list-id**
contains the identifier of an SCL list that is passed to *entry-name*.
  Type: Numeric or List

**description**
contains the description of the returned *selection*.

  *Note:* This parameter is an update parameter. See "Input, Output, and Update Parameters" on page 34 for more information. △
  Type: Character

**Details**  SAVEENTRYDIALOG enables you to implement a **Save As** choice by displaying a dialog window that lists entries in SAS catalogs. SAVEENTRYDIALOG returns a user's selection, which enables you to create code that performs the save action. The entry can be saved under a different name or the same name.

If *entry-name* is supplied, the item selected in the dialog window is passed to *entry-name* through the following variables, which are created automatically:

USERDATA
: contains the list passed in the call to the OPENENTRYDIALOG and SAVEENTRYDIALOG functions.

LIBREF
: contains the libref of the selected item.

CATALOG
: contains the catalog name of the selected item.

ENTRY
: contains the entry name of the selected item.

TYPE
: contains the member type of the selected item.

*List-id* enables information to be passed between the calling entry and *entry-name*. It is passed to *entry-name* through the USERDATA variable.

## Examples

**Example 1: Saving a Catalog Entry**   Select a catalog entry of type FRAME to save and display the selected entry.

```
selection=saveentrydialog('frame');
call display(selection);
```

**Example 2: Using the Advanced Button with an SCL List**   Specify an entry to call when a user selects Advanced, as well as an SCL list that contains values to pass to the entry.

```
dcl list mydata;
mydata=makelist();
rc=insertc(mydata,'test');
selection=saveentrydialog('frame','mylib.mycat.inital.frame',
   'mylib.mycat.myentry.frame',mydata, description);
if sysrc(1)=-1 then do;
   ...SCL statements to execute when
   the user cancels from the window...
   rc=dellist(mydata);
end;
else do;
   ...SCL statements to handle selections...
end;
```

The SCL entry for MYLIB.MYCAT.MYENTRY.FRAME contains the following program:

```
dcl char(8)  libref;
dcl char(8)  type;
dcl char(32) catalog;
dcl char(32) entry
dcl list userdata;

init:
put libref=;
put catalog=;
put entry=;
```

```
put type=;
call putlist(userdata);
return;
```

*Note:* The SCL entry must declare these exact variables, in the order specified, to properly reference the selected entry. △

If the user selects MYLIB2.MYCAT2.MYENTRY2.FRAME in the dialog window and then selects Advanced , the output for this program is

```
libref=Mylib2
catalog=Mycat2
entry=Myentry2
type=Frame
('test')[1]
```

# SAVELIST

**Stores SCL list items in a SAS catalog entry or in an external file**

**Category:** List

## Syntax

*sysrc=***SAVELIST**(*type,target,list-id<,attr-list-id<,description>>*);

**sysrc**
contains the return code for the operation:

| | |
|---|---|
| 0 | successful |
| ≠0 | not successful |

Type: Numeric

**type**
specifies the type of file or data source named in *source* and one or more options to use:

'**CATALOG**<(*options*)>'
saves text in a SAS catalog entry.

'**FILE**<(*options*)>'
saves text in an external file that is named in *target*.

'**FILEREF**<(*options*)>'
saves text in an external file that is identified by a fileref named in *target*.
Type: Character

The available options are described in "*Type* Options" on page 630. Separate multiple options with blanks. For example, when you save a list to a catalog entry, the first character of each item is assumed to be a carriage-control character, because FILLIST puts a carriage control in the first character of each item when it fills a list. If a list was not filled with FILLIST and does not have a carriage-control character as the first character, the first character of text is lost in each item of the list saved with SAVELIST. For lists of this type, use CATALOG(ADDCC) to add a carriage-control character as the first character in each list item.

*target*
> is the name of the catalog entry, external file, or fileref in which the list items are stored. For catalog entries, this must be a four-level name (*libref.catalog.entry-name.entry-type*).
> Type: Character

*list-id*
> contains the identifier of the list that contains the items to be stored in a SAS file or external file. An invalid *list-id* produces an error condition. For text catalog entries, the first character in each item in the list contains the FORTRAN carriage-control character: 1 means that a new page starts with this line.
> Type: Numeric or List

*attr-list-id*
> contains the identifier of the list to fill with text attribute information when *type* is **CATALOG**. An error condition results if *attr-list-id* is not a valid list identifier.
> Type: Numeric

*description*
> is the text of a catalog entry description. This argument is ignored if the value for *type* is **FILE** or **FILEREF**. (The description is displayed in the catalog directory.)
> Type: Character

## *Type* Options

**ADDCC**
> adds a default carriage-control character. Used with *type* **FILE**, **FILEREF**, and **CATALOG** and with catalog entry types **LOG**, **OUTPUT**, and **SOURCE**. If you use **ADDCC** and **STRIPCC** together, then both options are ignored.

**APPEND**
> attempts to open the external file in APPEND mode and appends text from the list to the external file. Used with *type* **FILE** or **FILEREF**.

**PRINT**
> designates an external file as a PRINT file (uses host carriage-control characters). Used with *type* **FILE** or **FILEREF**.

**STRIPCC**
> removes carriage-control characters. Used with *type* **FILE**, **FILEREF**, and **CATALOG** and with catalog entry types **LOG**, **OUTPUT**, and **SOURCE**. If you specify **STRIPCC**, then carriage-control characters are ignored and default carriage control is used. If you use both **STRIPCC** and **ADDCC**, then both options are ignored.

**TRIM**
> trims trailing blanks. Used with *type* **FILE**, **FILEREF**, and **CATALOG** and with catalog entry types **LOG**, **OUTPUT**, and **SOURCE**.

**Details** SAVELIST stores the items from an SCL list into a SAS catalog entry or an external file.

When *type* is **CATALOG** and you specify LOG, SOURCE, or OUTPUT as the *entry-type* of *target*, SAVELIST assumes that the first character of each item is a carriage-control character, because the default behavior of FILLIST for these entry types is to put a carriage-control character in the first item of list items when it creates a list. Therefore, if the items in the list identified by *list-id* do not have a carriage-control character as the first character, then save the list to a SOURCE entry using the ADDCC option. That will add a default (' ')carriage-control character as the first character in each line of text that is written to the SOURCE entry.

When *type* is **CATALOG** and you specify SLIST as the *entry-type* of *target*, the list — including names, list attributes, and item attributes — can be re-created with the FILLIST function, although the list identifiers will be different. The lists that you save with SAVELIST can persist across SAS sessions if you save them in a permanent catalog.

When a list is stored into any file type other than an SLIST entry, each item in the list identified by *list-id* must be a character string. Each string is stored as a separate line of text. When *type* is **CATALOG** and the entry type of *target* is LOG, OUTPUT, or SOURCE and a value is specified for *attr-list-id*, the attribute list items must also contain text. See the description of FILLIST for a description of the text attribute specifications. If the value for *attr-list-id* is omitted or is 0, then no attributes are stored with the catalog entry. Any value specified for *attr-list-id* is ignored when a list is stored in an external file or in an SLIST catalog entry.

When SAVELIST writes a list, an item that has the NOWRITE attribute is not written to the file. This is useful for placing temporary run-time values into a list that should not be written to the file because of its transient nature. For example, if you place table identifiers in lists to be saved with SAVELIST and restored with FILLIST in another task or another SAS session, the table identifiers become invalid. Thus, use SETLATTR to set the NOWRITE attribute on that list item.

(Do not confuse text attributes such as color and highlight with list attributes as specified with SETLATTR.) To check the attributes of a list or list item, use HASATTR. To change attributes, use SETLATTR.

## Example

Perform operations similar to copying a list recursively with COPYLIST(mylistid,'Y'):

```
/* Assume that the catalog WORK.TEMP exists: */
rc=savelist('catalog','work.temp.mylist.slist',
    mylistid);
newlistid=makelist();
rc=fillist('catalog','work.temp.mylist.slist',
    newlistid);
rc=delete('work.temp.mylist.slist','catalog');
```

## See Also

"FILLIST" on page 407

# SAVESASFILEDIALOG

**Displays a dialog window that lists SAS files, and returns the name of the selected file**

**Category:** Selection List

## Syntax

*selection*=**SAVESASFILEDIALOG**(< *type*< ,*level–count*< ,*initial*< ,*entry-name*< ,*list-id*>>>>>);

*selection*
> contains the two- or three-level name of the selected SAS file, or a blank if nothing is selected.
> Type: Character

*type*
> specifies a member type to list in the dialog window, such as DATA, VIEW, MDDB, and CATALOG. This can reduce the length of the list in the dialog window. If *type* is not used, the names of all SAS files in the data library are listed.
> Type: Character

*level-count*
> specifies whether the function returns a two- or three-level name. The only valid choices are 2 and 3. The default is two.
> Type: Numeric

*initial*
> is the name of the SAS file to be the initially selected item in the dialog window when it opens.

*entry-name*
> is a two- or four-level name of a catalog entry that is called when a user selects the [Advanced] button in the dialog window. The entry can be any of the following types: FRAME, SCL, PROGRAM, HELP, CBT, or MENU.
> If *entry-name* is not specified, then the window does not contain [Advanced].

*list-id*
> contains the identifier for an SCL list that you can pass when *entry-name* is specified. The items in this list are the items to be displayed in the application's Advanced window for selection by application users.

**Details**   SAVESASFILEDIALOG enables you to implement a **Save As** choice by displaying a dialog window that lists SAS files. SAVESASFILEDIALOG returns a user's selection, which enables you to create code that performs the save action. The SAS file can be saved under a different name or the same name.

If *entry-name* is supplied and [Advanced] is selected, the item selected in the dialog window is passed to *entry-name* through the following variables:

USERDATA
> contains the list that is passed in the call to SAVESASFILEDIALOG.

LIBREF
> contains the libref of the selected item.

MEMBER
> contains the member name of the selected item.

TYPE
> contains the member type of the selected item.

*List-id* enables information to be passed between the calling entry and *entry-name*. It is passed to *entry-name* through the USERDATA variable.

## Examples

**Example 1: Saving a SAS File**   Select a SAS file of type DATA to save and display the table.

```
selection=savesasfieldialog('data view',3,'work.one');
```

**Example 2: Using the Advanced Button with an SCL List**　Specify an entry of type DATA to be called when a user selects the ⬚Advanced⬚ button, as well as an SCL list that contains values to pass to the entry. The entry can be any of the following types: FRAME, SCL, PROGRAM, HELP, CBT, or MENU. If *entry-name* is not specified, then the window does not contain ⬚Advanced⬚.

```
dcl list mydata;
mydata=makelist();
rc=insertc(mydata,'test');
selection = savesasfiledialog('data', 2','mylib.mycat.initial.frame',
    'mylib.mycat.myentry.frame',mydata);
if (sysrc(1)=-1) then do;
    ...SCL statements to handle when the user
    cancels from window...
end;
else do;
    ...SCL statements to handle selections...
end;
```

The SCL entry for MYLIB.MYCAT.MYENTRY.FRAME contains the following program:

```
dcl char(8) libref;
dcl char(32) member;
dcl char(8) type;
dcl list userdata;

init:
put libref=;
put member=;
put type=;
call putlist(userdata);
return;
```

*Note:*　The SCL entry must declare these exact variables, in the order specified, to properly reference the selected entry. △

If the user selects MYLIB2.MYMEMBER2.DATA in the dialog window and then selects ⬚Advanced⬚, the output for this program is

```
libref=Mylib2
member=Mymember2
type=Data
('test')[1]
```

**Example 3: Using the LEVEL Parameter**　Select a SAS file to save and return different levels.

```
selection=savesasfiledialog ('data'',2);
put selection=
selection=savesasfiledialog('data',3);
put selection=
```

If the user selects MYLIB.MYMEMBER.DATA for both selections, the output would be

```
selection=mylib.mymember
selection=mylib.mymember.data
```

### See Also

"OPENSASFILEDIALOG" on page 580

# SAVESCREEN

**Saves the values of data entry fields without exiting from the window**

**Category:**  Window

## Syntax

**CALL SAVESCREEN();**

**Details**     SAVESCREEN copies the current values of all window variables in a PROGRAM entry into the user's profile for later restoration. The values are stored for recall across invocations of SAS software in a catalog entry named SASUSER.PROFILE.*entry*.AFPGM, where *entry* is the name of the SAS/AF entry whose values are saved. This is similar to the SAVE command in the SAS/AF program window.

The saved values can be reloaded either with the RECALL command in the application window, or with the AUTORECALL=YES option in the AF command that invokes the application.

SAVESCREEN is valid only for PROGRAM entries.

## Example

Save the final contents of the fields in an application window:

```
TERM:
   call savescreen();
return;
```

# SCREENNAME

**Returns the name of the current window**

**Category:**  Window

## Syntax

*name*=**SCREENNAME();**

**name**
     contains the four-level name of the current window.
          Type: Character

**Details**    The SCREENNAME function returns the name of the current window. For example, assume that there are two PROGRAM entries named SURVEY and NEWMAP in a catalog named MYLIB.TESTS. When SURVEY is executing, SCREENNAME returns MYLIB.TESTS.SURVEY.PROGRAM. When NEWMAP is executing, SCREENNAME returns MYLIB.TESTS.NEWMAP.PROGRAM.

In the FSEDIT and FSVIEW procedures, SCREENNAME returns the name of the SCREEN or FORMULA entry that the application is currently using.

### Example

Display the window name on the message line:

```
_msg_=screenname();
```

# SEARCH

**Creates or manipulates the current catalog search path**

**Category:**   Catalog

## Syntax

*rc*=**SEARCH**(*cat-name* | *special-argument*);

**rc**
contains the return code for the operation:

| | |
|---|---|
| 0 | successful |
| −1 | not successful |

Type: Numeric

**cat-name**
is the catalog to push to the front of the current search list.
Type: Character

**special-argument**
are any of the following:

**'-DISABLE'**
to disable the current search list.

**'-ENABLE'**
to enable the current search list. If there is no disabled list, then the current search list remains empty.

**'-POP'**
to remove the first name from the current search list.

**'-POPALL'**
to clear the current search list.

*Note:*  You must include the hyphen (-) as the first character in each of these argument values. Otherwise, the value will be treated as a catalog name in the WORK library. △
Type: Character

**Details**    You do not need to know the exact location of a catalog member, only that it is in one of the catalogs in the current search path.

When a function that uses the current search path is called, the catalogs in the search path are searched from first to last until the specified entry is found or until the end of the search path is reached.

If there is no current search path, or if the current search path has been disabled or overridden, then the search is limited to the current catalog.

## Example

Set up a search list with MYLIB1.CAT1, MYLIB1.CAT2 and MYLIB1.CAT3. Each time SEARCH is called, the new value of the argument is pushed to the front of the list. Therefore, MYLIB1.CAT3 is searched first. If MYPROG.PROGRAM exists only in MYLIB1.CAT1, it still executes correctly, because MYLIB1.CAT1 is also in the search path.

```
rc=search('mylib1.cat1');
rc=search('mylib1.cat2');
rc=search('mylib1.cat3');
call display('myprog.program');
```

## See Also

"CEXIST" on page 276

"DISPLAY" on page 350

"SEARCHPATH" on page 638

# SEARCHC, SEARCHL, SEARCHN, and SEARCHO

**Search for a value in an SCL list and return its position number**

**Category:**  List

## Syntax

*index=***SEARCHC**(*list-id,cval<,start-index*
     *<,occurrence<,ignore-case<,prefix>>>>*);

*index=***SEARCHL**(*list-id,sublist-id<,occurrence*
     *<,start-index>>*);

*index=***SEARCHN***list-id,nval(<,occurrence*
     *<,start-index>>*);

*index=***SEARCHO**(*list-id,object-id<,occurrence*
     *<,start-index>>*);

*index*
     contains the index from the SCL list of the item that has the specified character value, or 0 if the value was not found.
     Type: Numeric

**list-id**
: is the identifier of the list to search. An invalid *list-id* produces an error condition.
  Type: Numeric or List

**cval**
: is the character value for SEARCHC to search for. *Cval* is compared only to the character values in the list.
  Type: Character

**sublist-id**
: contains the identifier of the sublist for SEARCHL to search for. *Sublist-id* is compared only to the list identifiers in the list.
  Type: Numeric

**nval**
: is the numeric value for SEARCHN to search for. *Nval* is compared only to numeric values in the list.
  Type: Numeric

**object-id**
: contains the identifier of the object for SEARCHO to search for. *Object-id* is compared only to the object identifiers in the list.
  Type: Numeric or Object

**occurrence**
: is the occurrence of the value to search for. The default, 1, indicates the first occurrence of the item.
  Type: Numeric

**start-index**
: is the position in the list at which to start the search for the item. By default, *start-index* is 1 (the first item). If *start-index* is positive, then the search begins at position *start-index* items from the beginning of the list. If *start-index* is negative, then the search begins at the item specified by ABS(*start-index*) items from the end of the list. An error condition results if the absolute value of *start-index* is zero or if it is greater than the number of items in the list.
  Type: Numeric

**ignore-case**
: specifies how SEARCHC should compare string values:

| | |
|---|---|
| **'Y'** | ignores the case of the character strings. |
| **'N'** | does a case-sensitive comparison of the character strings. (This is the default.) |

  Type: Character

**prefix**
: specifies whether the value should be treated as a prefix:

| | |
|---|---|
| **'Y'** | does a prefix comparison and searches for any items that have *cval* as a prefix. SEARCHC compares only the first *m* characters, where *m* is the length of *cval*. |
| **'N'** | does not do a prefix search but compares all characters to *cval*. (This is the default.) |

  Type: Character

**Details**    SEARCHC, SEARCHL, SEARCHN, and SEARCHO do not search for a value in any sublists of the list identified by *list-id*.

If *occurrence* and *start-index* are both positive or both negative, then the search proceeds forward from the *start-index* item. For forward searches, the search continues only to the end of the list and does not wrap back to the front of the list. If either *occurrence* or *start-index* is negative, then the search proceeds from the last item toward the beginning of the list. For backward searches, the search continues only to the beginning of the list and does not wrap back to the end of the list.

To search for an item by name rather than by value, use NAMEDITEM.

## Examples

**Example 1: Using the SEARCHC Function**     Find the position of the next-to-last occurrence of a string that begins with **SAS**, ignoring case:

```
last2=searchc(mylistid,'sas',2,-1,'Y','Y');
```

**Example 2: Using the SEARCHL Function**     Search the list identified by MYLISTID for the third occurrence of the identifier for the sublist item identified by the value of NAMELISTID:

```
third=searchl(mylistid,namelistid,3);
```

**Example 3: Using the SEARCHN Function**     Search for the third occurrence of the number 46 in the list identified by MYLISTID:

```
third=searchn(mylistid,46,3);
```

**Example 4: Using the SEARCHO Function**     Search the list identified by MYLISTID for the third occurrence of the identifier for the object BUTTON:

```
third=searcho(mylistid,objectid,3);
```

## See Also

"NAMEDITEM" on page 555

---

# SEARCHPATH

### Reports the complete pathname of a SAS catalog entry

**Category:**   Catalog

---

## Syntax

*path-name*=**SEARCHPATH**(*entry-name*< ,*description*>);

**path-name**
>   contains the path (four-level name) for the specified entry if it was found in the current catalog or in the search path. If the entry was not found, then the value is blank.
>      Type: Character

**entry-name**
>   is the SAS catalog entry to search for.
>      Type: Character

### description

specifies whether to return the description of the entry and the date the entry was last updated. Specify **Y** to return the description and the date.

Type: Character

**Details**   SEARCHPATH returns the full four-level SAS library member name for a catalog entry if the entry is found in one of the catalogs that are in the current search path. It also returns the description that is stored with the entry in *description*.

If an entry that has the specified name appears in more than one catalog in the search path, then only the path to the first entry found is returned. If no search path is defined, the search is limited to the current catalog (the catalog in which the executing entry is stored).

To define the search path for your application, use SEARCH.

*Note:*   To get the pathname and description of an entry, you can use the method interface of the Catalog entry class. △

## Example

Load a stored list from a catalog entry if the entry is found in the current search path:

```
init:
   DCL num desclen
   rc=rc;
   rc=search('sashelp.afclass');
   rc=search('sashelp.aftools');
   rc=search<'sashelp.assist');

   path=searchpath('listed.frame','y');
   pathlen=length(path);
   name=scan(path,1,'');
   namelen=length(name) + 1;
   desclen = pathlen - (namelen) - 10;
   desc = substr(path, namelen + 1, desclen);
   date = substr(path, pathlen - 9, 10);
   put name=;
   put desc=;
   put date=;
return;
```

This program produces the following output:

```
name=sashelp.aftools.LISTED.FRAME
desc=   Generic list editor
date=10/09/1996
```

## See Also

"SEARCH" on page 635

# SELECT

**Selects a specified row of a selection list**

**Category:**   Extended Table

## Syntax

*rc*=**SELECT**(*row*);

**rc**

contains the return code for the operation:

0                     successful

≠0                    not successful

    Type: Numeric

**row**

is the number of the row to select.

    Type: Numeric

**Details**    The selection highlights the specified row. SELECT is useful for forcing the selection of a row. For example, you can use this function to set initial values or default values. Ordinarily, a user selects a row by pressing ENTER or clicking on the row with the mouse.

You can use SELECT only for selection lists that were built with extended tables in PROGRAM entries. FRAME entry controls must use the _selectRow method. Because you can define extended tables only in SAS/AF software, you cannot use SELECT in FSEDIT or FSVIEW programs.

In order for an extended table to be considered a selection list, you must specify a number of selections in the SETROW routine.

## Example

Select row 5 of the selection list:

```
INIT:
   call setrow(10,2);
   rc=select(5);
return;
```

## See Also

  "ISSEL" on page 495

  "NSELECT" on page 573

  "SELECTED" on page 642

  "SETROW" on page 664

  "UNSELECT" on page 696

# SELECT

**Executes one of several statements or groups of statements**

**Category:**   Control Flow

**Comparisons:**   SAS Statement with limitations in SCL

## Syntax

**SELECT**< *(select-expression)* >;
  **WHEN**-*1* < *(when-expression)* >*statement(s)*;
  <. . .**WHEN**-*n* < *(when-expression)* >*statement(s)*;>
  <**OTHERWISE** < *statement(s)* >;>
**END**;

*select-expression*
> is an expression that evaluates to a single value. This argument is optional. If used, *select-expression* must be in parentheses.
> Type: Character

*when-expression*
> is a constant or an expression that evaluates to a single value.
> Type: Character

*statement(s)*
> are one or more executable SAS statements, including DO, SELECT, and null statements. When used in a WHEN statement, a null statement causes SAS to recognize a condition as true without taking further action. In OTHERWISE statements, null statements prevent SAS from issuing an error message when all WHEN conditions are false.
> Type: Character

## Differences in SELECT Statement Execution

For SELECT groups in SCL, WHEN statements of the form WHEN(*a1, a2, a3*) are not supported. However, the following forms are supported:

- ☐ WHEN(*constant*)
- ☐ WHEN(*expression*).

OTHERWISE is an optional statement. If OTHERWISE is omitted, and if no WHEN conditions are met, the program halts.

Each WHEN statement implies a DO group of all statements until the next WHEN or OTHERWISE statement. Therefore, the following program is valid:

```
select(x);
   when(1)  call display('a');
     ...optionally, more SCL statements...
   when(2)  call display('b');
     ...optionally, more SCL statements...
   otherwise call display('bad');
     ...optionally, more SCL statements...
end;
```

For details about the SELECT statement in the base SAS language, see *SAS Language Reference: Dictionary*.

## Example

This example shows how to use expressions with the SELECT statement:

```
select;
    when(x=1)   put 'one';
    when(2<x<5) put 'between two and five';
    when(x>5 or x<0) put 'other';
end;
```

# SELECTED

**Returns the number of the row that corresponds to a user's choice in a selection list**

**Category:** Extended Table

## Syntax

*row*=**SELECTED**(*nval*);

*row*

> contains the number of the selected row, or −1 if the value specified for *nval* is greater than the total number of selections.
> Type: Numeric

*nval*

> is the number of the selection.
> Type: Numeric

**Details**    You can use SELECTED only for selection lists that were built with extended tables in PROGRAM entries. FRAME entry controls must use the _selected method. Because you can define extended tables only in SAS/AF software, you cannot use SELECTED in FSEDIT or FSVIEW programs.

In order for an extended table to be considered a selection list, you must specify a number of selections in the SETROW routine.

## Example

Suppose the application displays a selection list that contains ten rows and that the user selects first row 3 and then row 5. If SELECTED is called with the value 2 specified for *nval* (as in the following statement), then the value returned in the variable ROW is 5, because row 5 was the second selection.

```
row=selected(2);
```

### See Also

"ISSEL" on page 495

"NSELECT" on page 573

"SELECT" on page 639

"SETROW" on page 664

"UNSELECT" on page 696

# SELECTICON

**Displays a dialog window that contains a list of icons, and returns the value of the selected icon**

**Category:** Selection List

### Syntax

*selected-icon*=**SELECTICON**(< *initial-icon*>);

*selected-icon*
    contains the value of the icon that is selected.
      Type: Numeric

*initial-icon*
    is the value of the icon that is active when the selector window opens. If *initial-icon*
    is not supplied, or if *initial-icon* is not a valid icon, then no icon is active when the
    selector window opens.
      Type: Numeric

**Details**    SELECTICON enables a user to select a SAS icon from a selection list.

# _SELF_

**Contains the identifier of the control for the currently executing method, or the identifier of the FRAME entry if the FRAME entry is not running as a method**

**Category:** System Variable

**Details**    _SELF_ is a system variable that is provided automatically by the FRAME
entry in SAS/AF. The SCL compiler automatically creates a space for it in the SCL data
vector.

    _SELF_ has a valid value only when the FRAME entry's SCL code is running or
when a method is running.

    See "USECLASS" on page 698 for information on bypassing _SELF_ references in a
USECLASS block.

## Example

Suppose a FRAME entry contains an icon. The icon's _select method is defined as follows:

```
SELECT:
   method;
      /* If the icon is a Version 8 icon,  */
      /* the following statement could be  */
      /*         _self_.icon=2;            */
   _self._setIcon(2);
endmethod;
```

When a user selects the icon, the _select method executes, and _SELF_ contains the identifier of the icon. In a FRAME entry, _SELF_ contains the identifier of the FRAME entry if the FRAME entry is not running as a method. For example, you can use _SELF_ to send a method to the FRAME entry from the INIT section.

```
INIT:
   _self_._setMsg_('in init section');
return;
```

## See Also

"_METHOD_" on page 548

"SEND" on page 644

"SUPER" on page 681

"USECLASS" on page 698

"_VALUE_" on page 704

# SEND

**Sends a method to an object using its identifier and can return a value from a called method**

**Category:**   Object Oriented

## Syntax

**CALL SEND**(*object-id,method-name<,parameters>*);

*object-id*
   contains the identifier that is associated with the object for which the method is invoked.
      Type: Numeric or Object

*method-name*
   is the name of the method to send. The method must be defined for the object's class or for one of the classes from which the object inherits methods. Case and trailing blanks are ignored in method names.
      Type: Character

***parameters***
> specifies one or more numeric or character parameters that are required by the method. Use commas to separate multiple parameters.
>
> *Note:* These parameters are update parameters. See "Input, Output, and Update Parameters" on page 34 for more information. △
> Type: Numeric, Character

**Details** SEND passes one or more arguments to a method in the form of parameters to the routine. The method may modify any of these parameters and pass values back to the calling program via the parameters, or the method may modify the object's automatic system variables. You can use the _getWidget method to return the *object-id* for a control.

You can also use SEND as a function if the called method returns a value with a RETURN statement.

The classes provided with SAS/AF software include a set of predefined methods. Subclasses that you define from these classes inherit those methods. You can also define your own methods. Methods are defined with the METHOD statement in an SCL entry, or they may be entire SAS/AF entries. (SCL, PROGRAM, FRAME, HELP, and MENU entries are allowed.) A METHOD statement uses the syntax of an ENTRY statement to declare the types and names of the parameters that the method expects.

The parameters that are passed to SEND must match the parameter definitions of the METHOD or ENTRY statement of the method. You can specify optional parameters, using the OPTIONAL= option for the METHOD or ENTRY statement of the method. You can specify variable lengths and types for parameters, using the ARGLIST= and REST= options in the METHOD or ENTRY statement of the called method.

The same method may be defined for one or more classes; each class has its own definition of the method. Therefore, when a method is invoked, the appropriate method definition is determined based on the object's class. If the specified method is not defined for the object's class, SAS/AF searches the hierarchy of parent classes for the method definition.

When a method executes, the SCL variable _SELF_ is automatically initialized to the object identifier *object-id*, enabling the method to invoke other methods for the same object. Also, any of the object's automatic system variables are initialized if the SCL program uses a variable of the same name and type as the automatic system variable. If a character variable named _METHOD_ is declared, it will be initialized with the method name.

If an SCL method executes a SEND or otherwise invokes a method, the values of all automatic SCL variables in the calling method are copied into the object. After the called method executes, the automatic SCL variables are re-initialized with the values of the caller's system variables. Other routines that execute methods are APPLY, NOTIFY, SUPAPPLY, and SUPER.

To send methods to Version 8 objects, you should use dot notation instead of CALL SEND. Dot notation provides compiler time checking and better performance at run time. For more information about dot notation, see "Accessing Object Attributes and Methods With Dot Notation" on page 119.

Using dot notation is the only way to call overloaded methods, because the compiler must be able to check method signatures in order to call the correct method.

For example, to send a message to an object using dot notation, you could use

```
_frame_._setMsg('Table '||tablename||
    ' does not exist');
```

(The system variable _FRAME_ contains the identifier for the frame.)

*Note:* If a component is a control in an extended table, then you can invoke methods only during the getrow and putrow sequences or for _init and _term methods. Also, in a

FRAME SCL entry, to send methods to controls in an extended table, you can use NOTIFY rather than SEND. △

## Example

Send a _term method to an icon whose name is ICON1 and whose identifier is stored in the variable ICON1ID:

```
call send(_frame_,'_getWidget','icon1',icon1id);
call send(icon1id,'_term');
```

## See Also

"APPLY" on page 252

"ENTRY" on page 369

"INSTANCE" on page 485

"LOADCLASS" on page 525

"LOADRES" on page 526

"METHOD" on page 540

"NOTIFY" on page 572

"SUPAPPLY" on page 679

"SUPER" on page 681

# SET

**Links SAS table columns to SCL variables of the same name and data type**

**Category:** SAS Table

## Syntax

**CALL SET**(*table-id*);

*table-id*
    contains the identifier that was assigned when the table was opened. If *table-id* is invalid, the program halts.
      Type: Numeric

**Details**    Using the SET routine can significantly reduce the coding required for accessing the values of variables for modification or verification. After a CALL SET, whenever a read operation is performed from the SAS table, the values of the SCL variables are set to the values of the corresponding SAS table columns. If the lengths do not match, then the values are truncated or padded as needed. When UPDATE or APPEND is called, the values that are written to the SAS table are the values of the SCL variables. If you do not use SET, then you must use GETVARC, GETVARN, PUTVARC, and PUTVARN to explicitly move values between table columns and SCL variables.

For each read/write operation that is performed on a SET SAS table, SCL loops through all the SAS table columns and updates the corresponding SCL variables. If the mapped SCL variables are only a small subset of the total SAS table columns, the looping could slow the process and prevent optimal performance. To enhance the performance of the application, you could open a SAS table as follows, using an option that limits the columns to only those to be set:

```
dsid=open('sasuser.employee (keep=age name)');
call set(dsid);
```

SET links only SCL variables that are accessible to the entire SCL program. SET does not link local variables, and using SET to link local variables in CLASS and USECLASS blocks may cause compilation errors.

As a general rule, use SET immediately following OPEN if you want to link table columns and SCL variables. Character variables that are associated with table columns must be declared with a DECLARE or LENGTH statement. Otherwise, the SCL compiler considers these variables to be numeric and thus sets them to missing instead of copying the appropriate character value from the table column.

If you use SET, do not use PUTVARN and PUTVARC for any variables that would be linked by SET. UPDATE and APPEND automatically move the data from the SCL data vector to the table data vector before writing the row to the physical file.

If a table column and a Version 8 frame control have the same name, and if the table column has the same data type as the frame control's default attribute, SET links the frame control's default attribute with the table column.

### Example

Automatically set the values of the SCL variables NAME and SALARY when a row is fetched for a window that contains the fields NAME and SALARY. The SAS table PERSONEL has three columns: NAME, SALARY and DEPT.

```
tableid=open('personel','i');
call set(tableid);
rc=fetchobs(tableid,10);
```

### See Also

"APPEND" on page 251

"FETCH" on page 389

"FETCHOBS" on page 390

"GETVARC and GETVARN" on page 450

"LOCATEC and LOCATEN" on page 527

"PUTVARC and PUTVARN" on page 609

"UPDATE" on page 697

# SETCR

**Controls the cursor's response to the carriage-return key**

**Category:** Control or Field

## Syntax

**CALL SETCR**(*advance,return< ,modify>*);

*advance*
: specifies how the cursor moves when a user presses the carriage-return key:

  **'STAY'**
  : The cursor does not move.

  **'HTAB'**
  : The cursor moves to the next field in the same row. This option makes the carriage-return key work like a horizontal tab key. When the last field in the current row is reached, the cursor moves to the first field in the next row.

  **'NEWL'**
  : The cursor moves to the first field in the next line. This option makes the carriage-return key work like a new-line key. When the last line is reached, the cursor moves to the first field in the first line.

  **'VTAB'**
  : The cursor moves to the first field in the next line in the current column. This option makes the carriage-return key work like a vertical tab key. When the last field in the current column is reached, the cursor moves to the top of the next column.

  **'HOME'**
  : The cursor moves to the command line, or to the first field in the window if the window has no command line.
  : Type: Character

*return*
: specifies whether a carriage return passes control back to the application:

  **'RETURN'**
  : A carriage return passes control to the application, whether or not a field is modified. That is, the MAIN section of an SCL program is executed.

  **'NORETURN'**
  : A carriage return does not pass control to the application unless a field is modified.
  : Type: Character

*modify*
: specifies whether the field should be marked as modified:

  **'MODIFY'**
  : A carriage return on a field is considered a modification of the field unless the field is protected.

  **'NOMODIFY'**
  : A carriage return on a field is not considered a modification of the field.
  : Type: Character

**Details**     SETCR works like a more powerful version of CONTROL ENTER for defining the behavior of the carriage-return key. This routine overrides the ENTER or NOENTER option of the CONTROL statement.

FRAME entries ignore SETCR.

## Example

Move the cursor vertically to the first field in the next line in the current column when the user presses the carriage-return key. Control does not pass to the application, and the field is not modified by a carriage return.

```
call setcr('vtab','noreturn','nomodify');
```

## See Also

"CONTROL" on page 302

# SETFKEY

**Assigns a command to a function key**

**Category:**  Keys

## Syntax

**CALL SETFKEY**(*key-name,command*);

*key-name*
> is the function key name, as listed in the KEYS window. Function key names vary depending on the device that is being used.
> Type: Character

*command*
> is the command to assign to the key.
> Type: Character

**Details**  You can use SETFKEY only in entries that have a DISPLAY window containing fields or text. You cannot use it to assign function key settings in windows that use BLOCK to display block menus.

## Example

Use FKEYNAME to return the name of a particular function key and GETFKEY to return the command that is assigned to the function key. If the command is not CANCEL, then SETFKEY assigns the CANCEL command to the function key.

```
INIT:
   keyname=fkeyname(1);
   command=getfkey(keyname);
   if (command ne 'CANCEL') then
      call setfkey(keyname,'CANCEL');
return;
```

### See Also

"FKEYNAME" on page 413

"GETFKEY" on page 440

"NUMFKEYS" on page 574

## SETFLD

**Assigns a value to up to ten blank variables**

**Category:**   Control or Field

### Syntax

**CALL SETFLD**(*value*,*variable-1*<, . . . ,*variable-10*>);

*value*
> is the character value to assign.
> > Type: Character

*variable-1*, . . . ,*variable-10*
> are up to ten character variables whose values you want to change from blank to *value*.
> > Type: Character

**Details**   If the variable is blank, *value* is assigned to the variable. No values are changed for variables that are not blank.

This function is useful for setting the default values for a series of fields.

### Example

Set each of the variables SYM1 through SYM5 to the value **-REQUIRED-** for each variable that is blank:

```
call setfld ('-REQUIRED-',sym1,sym2,sym3,sym4,sym5);
```

The above statement is equivalent to the following statements:

```
if (sym1=' ') then sym1='-REQUIRED-';
if (sym2=' ') then sym2='-REQUIRED-';
if (sym3=' ') then sym3='-REQUIRED-';
if (sym4=' ') then sym4='-REQUIRED-';
if (sym5=' ') then sym5='-REQUIRED-';
```

### See Also

"CLRFLD" on page 293

## SETFOOT

**Sets the text of a footnote definition**

**Category:** SAS System Option

## Syntax

**CALL SETFOOT**(*foot-num,foot-text*);

*foot-num*
>is the number (1 to 10) of the footnote definition to create or modify.
>>Type: Numeric

*foot-text*
>is the text for the footnote definition.
>>Type: Character

**Details**    SETFOOT works just like the FOOTNOTE statement. It clears all footnote definitions that are numbered higher than the one created. You cannot use SETFOOT to set graphic options such as color, tint, and position.

You can view footnote definitions in the FOOTNOTES window by using the FOOTNOTE command. Changing any text in the FOOTNOTES window, however, resets all graphically defined footnote options such as color, font, and position.

For more information about footnotes, see *SAS Language Reference: Dictionary*. For more information about graphical footnotes, see *SAS/GRAPH Software: Reference*.

## Example

Create a footnote numbered 5. The statement deletes all footnotes with numbers greater than 5.

```
call setfoot(5,'This is the Fifth Footnote');
```

## See Also

"GETFOOT" on page 441

"GETTITLE" on page 449

"SETTITLE" on page 666

# SETITEMC, SETITEML, SETITEMN, and SETITEMO

**Store a value at an indexed position in an SCL list**

**Category:** List

## Syntax

*rc*=**SETITEMC**(*list-id,cval*< ,*index*< ,*autogrow*>>);

*rc*=**SETITEML**(*list-id,sublist-id*< ,*index*< *autogrow*>>);

*rc*=**SETITEMN**(*list-id,nval*< ,*index*< ,*autogrow*>>);

*rc*=**SETITEMO**(*list-id,object-id*< ,*index*< ,*autogrow*>>);

**rc**

is the *list-id*, which is the identifier of the modified list.
Type: Numeric

***list-id***

is the identifier of the list into which the value is stored. An invalid *list-id* produces an error condition.
Type: Numeric or List

***cval***

is the character value for SETITEMC to store in the list.
Type: Character

***sublist-id***

is the identifier of the sublist for SETITEML to store in the list. An invalid *sublist-id* produces an error condition.

***nval***

is the numeric value for SETITEMN to store in the list.
Type: Numeric

***object-id***

is the identifier of the object for SETITEMO to store in the list. An invalid *object-id* produces an error condition.
Type: Numeric or Object

***index***

is the position of the item in the list. The position can be specified as a positive or negative number. By default, *index* is 1 (the first item). If *index* is a positive number, then the item is at position *index* from the beginning of the list. If *index* is a negative number, then the item is at position ABS(*index*) from the end of the list. An error condition results if the absolute value for *index* is zero or if it is greater than the number of items in the list.
Type: Numeric

***autogrow***

specifies whether the list can expand to accommodate a new item:

'**N**'        The size of the list cannot change. (This is the default.)

'**Y**'        The size of the list can increase to accommodate a new item that is being added to the list. The list expands only if *index* is greater than the current number of items in the list and the list does not have the FIXEDLENGTH attribute.
Type: Character

**Details**    Using SETITEMC, SETITEML, SETITEMN, or SETITEMO is analogous to assigning a character, a sublist identifier, a numeric value, or an object identifier, respectively, to an indexed item in an array. *Index* specifies the position in the list of the item whose value is assigned. If *autogrow* is Y , then *index* can be greater than the length of the list. These functions then expand the list to a total of *index* items. They also set all other new items to missing values, and they place the new value into the list. These functions can add items only to the end of a list. Use INSERTC, INSERTL, INSERTN, or INSERTO to insert values elsewhere in a list.

SETITEMC, SETITEML, SETITEMN, and SETITEMO replace an existing item in a list and even change its type unless the item or the list has the FIXEDTYPE attribute.

SETITEMC, SETITEML, SETITEMN, and SETITEMO do not make a copy of the list before assigning the new item. The list is modified in place.

*Note:* The return value of these functions is not used to indicate whether an error has been detected. When an error occurs, the program simply halts. △

An error condition results

☐ if the absolute value of *index* is zero, or if it is greater than the number of items in the list and *autogrow* is N.

☐ if the absolute value of *index* is greater than the length of the list and the list has the FIXEDLENGTH attribute (even if *autogrow* is Y).

☐ if the list or item has the NOUPDATE attribute.

☐ if the list or item has the FIXEDTYPE attribute and the function attempts to set the item to a different type. For example, if item 4 is numeric and has the FIXEDTYPE attribute, then the following statement fails:

```
list=setitemc(list,'abc',4);
```

☐ with SETITEMC or SETITEML, if the list has the NUMONLY attribute.

☐ with SETITEMN or SETITEML, if the list has the CHARONLY attribute.

☐ with SETITEML, if *sublist-id* identifies a local list and *list-id* identifies a global list. (You cannot place local lists into global lists.)

To check the attributes of a list or list item, use HASATTR. To change attributes, use SETLATTR.

## See Also

"GETITEMC, GETITEML, GETITEMN, and GETITEMO" on page 442

"INSERTC, INSERTL, INSERTN, and INSERTO" on page 482

"NAMEITEM" on page 558

"SETNITEMC, SETNITEML, SETNITEMN, and SETNITEMO" on page 661

# SETKEY

**Defines an index key for retrieving rows from a SAS table**

**Category:** SAS Table

## Syntax

*nval*=**SETKEY**(*table-id*<,*key-name*<,*condition*< ,*scroll-option*<,*list-id*>>>>);

**nval**
contains the return code for the operation:

| 0 | An active key was successfully set or cleared. |
| ≠0 | An error or warning condition occurred. |

Type: Numeric

***table-id***
> is the identifier that was assigned when the table was opened. If *table-id* is invalid, the program halts.
> Type: Numeric

***key-name***
> is the index key to be used for retrieval.
> Type: Character

***condition***
> specifies comparison criteria for the key value:

> | | |
> |---|---|
> | **'EQ'** | equal to the key value (This is the default.) |
> | **'GE'** | greater than or equal to the key value |
> | **'GT'** | greater than the key value |
> | **'LE'** | less than or equal to the key value |
> | **'LT'** | less than the key value. |

> Type: Character

***scroll-option***
> specifies whether rows can be randomly retrieved:

> **'SCROLL'**
> Rows can be retrieved in random order. (This is the default.)

> **'NOSCROLL'**
> Rows can only be retrieved sequentially. This option improves performance when the table is accessed via the REMOTE engine and the IS mode is specified for the second argument of the OPEN function. Those options reduce the number of data transfer operations that are required when the table is read.
> Type: Character

***list-id***
> is the identifier for the list that contains values for the index key variables. You must use SETNITEMC and SETNITEMN to assign the values to the corresponding key variables in the list. An invalid *list-id* produces an error condition.
> Type: Numeric or List

**Details**    SETKEY enables you to set an active key in an open table to a simple or composite key. It establishes a set of criteria for reading SAS table rows by comparing the value of the columns from the SDV to the key value in the rows.

Using a composite key with SETKEY operates the same way as the WHERE function only when the condition is 'EQ'. The value returned when the condition is 'EQ' is the same as if the columns specified in the composite key are connected by WHERE conditions using AND or ALSO.

For all other conditions (GT, GE, LT, or LE) specified with SETKEY for a composite key, the composite key columns are concatenated to form the index key. The number returned by the KEYCOUNT function is the number of rows in the table that satisfy the composite key. For example, if the composite index consists of columns SEX and AGE and the condition is GT (greater than), the values to search for are concatenated such that key values of F for SEX and 13 for AGE yield an index key of F13. Because the search is performed on the concatenated values, some values that you did not expect may meet a search condition. For example, key values of M for SEX and 11 for AGE meet the search condition, because the string M11 is considered greater than the string F13. If the active key is a composite key and the *condition* parameter is set to GT, GE, LT, or LE, the table subsets into rows whose primary key column values meet the specified criteria. Consequently, you still have to check the values of other key parts against the data vector to narrow down the subset of rows.

SETKEY works only after SET is called in the SCL program or when a list identifier is passed. The list identifier must point to a list that contains the values of the index key columns. Once an active key is set through SETKEY, it remains active until

□ the table is closed

□ another key is set

□ the current setting is cleared by passing the table identifier alone to SETKEY.

The table is automatically positioned at the first row that meets the specified criteria. Use FETCH or FETCHOBS to read the row.

SETKEY returns an error code if a WHERE clause is in effect. Index keys cannot be used in conjunction with WHERE clauses.

## Examples

**Example 1: Defining an Index Key That Was Created Previously**    Define an index key for the table MYDATA, which subsets the table into only those rows where the value of the AGE column is greater than or equal to 20:

```
/* Assuming a simple key, AGE, has been defined */
age=20;
dsid=open('MYDATA','I');
call set(dsid);
rc=setkey(dsid,'age','ge');
do while(fetch(dsid) ne -1);
   name=getvarc(dsid,1);
   put name=;
end;
```

**Example 2: Using a Composite Index Key with GE**    Search the table CHILDREN for all boys who are 5 years old or older. The composite key ATTR, which is created by ICREATE, is used for retrieval. The values of the composite key columns are concatenated, and the search is performed on the combined value. In this example, the key selects rows where AGE||GENDER ≥ 5M. The FETCH function within the DO-loop returns all rows where AGE>=5. Because some of the rows may not have a matched concatenated key part, you need an additional check on the value of the GENDER column in order to skip unmatched rows.

```
dsid=open('children','v');
   /* Create a composite key ATTR with AGE */
   /* as primary key column              */
rc=icreate(dsid,'attr','age gender');
call set(dsid);
age=5;
gender='M';
rc=setkey(dsid,'attr','ge');
do while(rc=0);
      /* FETCH function applies the retrieval */
      /* criteria and retrieves all rows      */
      /* for which AGE >=5                     */
   rc=fetch(dsid);
   if (rc) then leave;
      /* Filter out rows with gender ne 'M' */
   if (upcase (gender) ne 'M') then continue;
```

```
      child=getvarc(dsid,varnum(dsid,'name'));
      put child=;
   end;
rc = close (dsid);
```

**Example 3: Using an SCL List Instead of CALL SET**   Using an SCL list avoids possible name collisions. Also, it enables you to set the retrieval criteria for rows at run time instead of at compile time.

```
dsid = open ( 'children','v');
rc = icreate( dsid, 'attr','age gender');
list = makelist();
list = setnitemc (list,cval,'gender');
   /* cval contains the value of 'M' */
list = setnitemn (list,nval,'age');
   /* nval contains the value of 5 */
rc = setkey (dsid,'attr','ge','',list);
   /* Print out all names with */
   /* age >= 5 and gender= 'M'     */
do while ( rc= 0 );
rc = fetch (dsid);
if (rc) then leave;
   sex1 = getvarc (dsid, varnum(dsid, 'gender'));
   if (upcase (gender) ne 'M') then continue;
   child = getvarc (dsid, varnum(dsid, 'name'));
      put child=;
end;
rc = close (dsid);
```

## See Also

"ICREATE" on page 464

"IDELETE" on page 468

"IOPTION" on page 490

"IVARLIST" on page 498

"KEYCOUNT" on page 499

"SET" on page 646

"WHERE" on page 718

# SETLATTR

**Sets the attributes of an SCL list or an item in a list**

**Category:**   List

## Syntax

*rc*=**SETLATTR**(*list-id,attributes<,index>*);

*rc*

contains the return code for the operation:

0                      successful

≠0                    not successful

Type: Character

*list-id*

is the identifier of the list whose attributes or item attributes are set. An invalid *list-id* produces an error condition.
    Type: Numeric or List

*attributes*

lists one or more attributes of the list or list item as shown in "Attribute Values for Lists and List Items" on page 657 and "Attribute Values for Lists Only" on page 658. Use blanks to separate multiple attributes. Attributes for lists are ignored when you are setting list item attributes, and attributes for list items are ignored when you are setting list attributes. This enables you to create a single attribute string that you can apply both to lists and to list items.
    Type: Character

*index*

is the position of the list item whose attributes are being modified. The position can be specified as a positive or negative number. By default, *index* is 1 (the first item). If *index* is a positive number, then the item is at position *index* from the beginning of the list. If *index* is a negative number, then the item is at position ABS(*index*) from the end of the list. If *index* is zero or omitted, then SETLATTR sets list attributes. An error condition results if the absolute value for *index* is zero or if it is greater than the number of items in the list.
    Type: Numeric

## Attribute Values for Lists and List Items

**'DEFAULT'**

combines all the default attributes.

**'DELETE'**

allows the list or item to be deleted. (This is a default.)

**'FIXEDTYPE'**

prevents changes in the type of the item. See also NUMONLY and CHARONLY. For a list, prevents changes in the type of all individual items.

**'NODELETE'**

prevents a list or list item from being deleted. List items that do not have the NODELETE attribute can be deleted from a list with this attribute. A list without this attribute can be deleted even though it contains items that have the NODELETE attribute.

**'NOFIXEDTYPE'**

allows the type of an item to change. For a list, allows the type of each item to change as long as the list does not have the CHARONLY or NUMONLY attribute and the item does not have the FIXEDTYPE attribute. (This is a default.)

**'NOUPDATE'**

prevents updates to the value for a list item. For a list, updates are not allowed to any item, even those with the UPDATE attribute. This enables you to make a list read-only in one step without having to make each individual item read-only.

**'UPDATE'**

allows updates to the value of a list item. For a list, UPDATE allows updates to all items that do not have the NOUPDATE attribute. (This is a default.)

## Attribute Values for Lists Only

**'ANYNAMES'**

allows item names to be any character string, although names are always converted to uppercase and trailing blanks are removed. (This is a default.)

**'CHARONLY'**

requires all items to have character values.

**'COPY'**

copies the list during a recursive copy operation if the list is a sublist. (This is a default.)

**'DUPNAMES'**

allows duplicate names in the list. (This is a default.)

**'FIXEDLENGTH'**

prevents the list length from changing.

**'HONORCASE'**

specifies that searches must be case-sensitive and that values for successful searches must match the case of the list item value.

**'NOCHARONLY'**

allows items to have numeric values and list identifier values. (This is a default.)

**'NOCOPY'**

prevents the list from being copied during a recursive copy operation if the list is a sublist. Instead, only the list identifier is copied to the target list. No recursion takes place for the list.

**'NODUPNAMES'**

requires all item names to be unique.

**'NOFIXEDLENGTH'**

allows the list length to change. (This is a default.)

**'NOHONORCASE'**

allows a search of list items to match values, regardless of the case in which they are stored. (This is a default.)

**'NONUMONLY'**

allows the list to contain character values and list identifier values. (This is a default.)

**'NUMONLY'**

requires all items to have numeric values.

**'SASNAMES'**

requires all items in the list to be named, and requires all names to be valid SAS names with no leading or trailing blanks.

## Attribute Values for List Items Only

**'ACTIVE'**

makes the item active in a pop-up menu that is opened by the POPMENU function. (This is a default.)

**'INACTIVE'**
> prevents the item from being active in a pop-up menu that is opened by the POPMENU function. (Users cannot select it.)

**'AUTO'**
> specifies that the item is an automatic instance variable. Refer to *SAS/AF Software: FRAME Entry Usage and Reference, Version 6, First Edition* for more information on automatic instance variables.

**'NOAUTO'**
> specifies that the item is not an automatic instance variable.

**'NOWRITE'**
> prevents the item from being written by the SAVELIST function.

**'WRITE'**
> allows the item to be written when the list is stored via SAVELIST. (This is a default.)

**Details**    If *index* is omitted or zero, the attributes are assigned to the list. Otherwise, the attributes are assigned to the item at the position specified by *index*. Item attributes are attached to the items in the list, not to the position in the list, so that an item keeps its attributes after the list is rotated or reversed or after other items are inserted or deleted. That is, if you assign the NODELETE attribute to the fourth item in the list and then delete the item at position 2, the item still has the NODELETE attribute even though it is now at position 3.

If a list has the NOCOPY attribute, it is not copied if it is a sublist in a recursive call of COPYLIST. Instead, only the list identifier is copied to the target list, and no recursion takes place on the list. You can still copy a list with NOCOPY if it is the source (top-level) list.

## Attribute Pairs

The attributes for lists and list items come in mutually exclusive pairs. For example, NOUPDATE designates that UPDATE is off. Setting one attribute of a mutually exclusive pair automatically turns off the other. The attribute pairs are shown in the following table.

| Attribute | Complement Attribute | Applies To |
|---|---|---|
| ACTIVE | INACTIVE | Items |
| ANYNAMES | SASNAMES | Lists |
| COPY | NOCOPY | Lists |
| DELETE | NODELETE | Items and Lists |
| DUPNAMES | NODUPNAMES | Lists |
| HONORCASE | NOHONORCASE | Lists |
| NOCHARONLY | CHARONLY | Lists |
| NOFIXEDLENGTH | FIXEDLENGTH | Lists |
| NOFIXEDTYPE | FIXEDTYPE | Items and Lists |
| NONUMONLY | NUMONLY | Lists |

| Attribute | Complement Attribute | Applies To |
|---|---|---|
| UPDATE | NOUPDATE | Items and Lists |
| WRITE | NOWRITE | Items and Lists |

The attributes of a list (such as CHARONLY, NUMONLY, FIXEDTYPE, and NOUPDATE) do not apply to sublists that the list contains. You must assign these attributes to the sublists if you want them to have these attributes.

Both list and item attributes are copied by COPYLIST. However, COPYLIST does not copy passwords.

Most of the list functions that alter lists or their contents are affected in some way by list attributes and item attributes. See the documentation for the individual functions to see how they are affected.

## Using Passwords to Protect List Attributes from Modification

You can assign a password to list attributes, which enables you to protect them. The password is stored with the list and must be supplied in subsequent SETLATTR statements in order to modify either list attributes or item attributes. The password is specified as PASSWORD=*password* in the attribute string. The password may not contain any blanks, but case is significant. For example, the passwords frobble and FROBBLE are different.

The following statements show how to assign a password:

```
pwd='password=grombaq';
myattr='nodelete noupdate';
rc=setlattr(mylist,myattr||' '||pwd);
```

If an SCL program attempts to modify the value of one item in MYLIST, the program halts, because the list has the NOUPDATE attribute. If you want to permit updates of the list again, you can execute SETLATTR as follows:

```
rc=setlattr(mylist,pwd ||'update');
```

*Note:* An error condition results if you attempt to alter list attributes without specifying the PASSWORD= option and password. △

You can remove the password from a list with NOPASSWORD=. Thereafter, any SCL program can change attributes or set the password. Either of the following statements removes the previously set password from the list identified by MYLIST:

```
rc=setlattr(mylist,'no'||pwd);
```

```
rc=setlattr(mylist,'nopassword=grombaq');
```

You must supply the correct password in order to remove a password that was previously set.

## Example

The NODELETE list attribute means that the list itself cannot be deleted with DELLIST. The NODELETE item attribute indicates that an item cannot be deleted from the list regardless of the item's type. The following statements show this distinction:

```
a=makelist(3);
b=makelist();
```

```
   /*  Set 3rd item in A to B.  */
a=setiteml(a,b,3);
   /* Give list B the NODELETE attribute. */
   /* DELLIST(b) will be an error.         */
rc=setlattr(b,'NODELETE');
   /* Give the 3rd item in A the      */
   /* NODELETE attribute.             */
   /* DELITEM(a, 3) will be an error.  */
rc=setlattr(a,'NODELETE',3);
   /* Move B to the second item in the list */
   /* and set the third item with 0.        */
a=setiteml(a,b,2);
a=setitemn(a,0,3);
   /* Remove B from list A,         */
   /* but B still exists.           */
   /* DELITEM(a,2) will be an error now. */
a=delitem(a,2);
```

See "CLEARLIST" on page 290 and "DELLIST" on page 336 for more information about the DELETE and NODELETE attributes.

## See Also

"GETLATTR" on page 443

"HASATTR" on page 458

# SETNITEMC, SETNITEML, SETNITEMN, and SETNITEMO

**Assign a value to a named item in an SCL list**

**Category:** List

## Syntax

*rc*=**SETNITEMC**(*list-id,cval,name,< occurrence*
   *<,start-index <,index<,forceup>>>>*);

*rc*=**SETNITEML**(*list-id,sublist-id,name,< occurrence*
   *<,start-index<,index<,forceup>>>>*);

*rc*=**SETNITEMN**(*list-id,nval,name ,< occurrence*
   *<,start-index<,index<,forceup>>>>*);

*rc*=**SETNITEMO**(*list-id,object-id,name, < occurrence*
   *<,start-index<,index<,forceup>>>>*);

**rc**
   is the *list-id*, which is the identifier of the modified list.
      Type: Numeric

**list-id**
   is the identifier of the list that contains the named item. An invalid *list-id* produces an error condition.
      Type: Numeric or List

***cval***
is the character value for SETNITEMC to assign.
Type: Character

***sublist-id***
is the identifier of the sublist for SETNITEML to assign. An error condition results if *sublist-id* is not a valid identifier.
Type: Numeric

***nval***
is the numeric value for SETNITEMN to assign.
Type: Numeric

***object-id***
is the identifier of the object for SETNITEMO to assign. An error condition results if *object-id* is not a valid identifier.
Type: Numeric or Object

***name***
is the name of the item. If the named item is not found in the list, it is inserted into the list.
Type: Character

***occurrence***
specifies which occurrence of the named item to assign the specified value to, starting from the position specified in *start-index*. The default, 1, indicates the first occurrence of the item.
Type: Numeric

***start-index***
specifies where in the list to begin searching for the item. By default, *start-index* is 1 (the first item). If *start-index* is positive, then the search begins at position *start-index* items from the beginning of the list. If *start-index* is negative, then the search begins at the item specified by ABS(*start-index*) items from the end of the list. An error condition results if the absolute value of *start-index* is zero or if it is greater than the number of items in the list.
Type: Numeric

***index***
is a variable to contain the index of the modified or inserted item.

   *Note:*   This parameter is an update parameter. See "Input, Output, and Update Parameters" on page 34 for more information. △
Type: Numeric

***forceup***
specifies whether to conduct the name search in uppercase.

| | |
|---|---|
| **'N'** | searches according to the list attributes HONORCASE and NOHONORCASE, which are specified with SETLATTR. (This is the default.) |
| **'Y'** | conducts the name search in uppercase regardless of the list attributes that are specified with SETLATTR. The HONORCASE and IGNORECASE attributes are ignored. |

IGNORECASE is an alias for NOHONORCASE.
Type: Character

**Details**    SETNITEMC, SETNITEML, SETNITEMN, and SETNITEMO do not make a copy of the list before modifying or inserting an item. The list is modified in place. If the named item is not found in the list (and if the list does not have the FIXEDLENGTH attribute), the item is inserted into the list.

If you specify a variable name for *index*, then these functions return the index number in the list of the modified or inserted item. You can reference this index to access the same item with these functions and other SCL list functions, as long as the items do not change positions (for example, as a result of an insert or delete operation). If the position of items in a list is stable, then using the *index* argument and subsequent index-based functions such as SETITEMC rather than name-based functions improves performance, because the list does not have to be searched multiple times to find a name match.

If *occurrence* and *start-index* are both positive or both negative, then the search proceeds forward from the *start-index* item. For forward searches, the search continues only to the end of the list and does not wrap back to the front of the list. If the named item is not found, it is inserted at the end of the list. If *occurrence* or *start-index* is negative, the search proceeds backwards from the end to the beginning of the list. For backward searches, the search continues only to the beginning of the list and does not wrap back to the end of the list. If the named item is not found, it is inserted at the beginning of the list.

The result of using SETNITEMC, SETNITEML, SETNITEMN, and SETNITEMO is similar to combining NAMEDITEM and SETITEM, SETITEML, SETITEMN, and SETITEMO, respectively. For example, consider the following statement:

```
mylist=setnitemc(mylist,'Jones','NAMES',1,1,i);
```

This statement performs the same operations as the following statements:

```
i=nameditem(mylist,'NAMES');
   /* If NAMES isn't found, insert it */
   /* at the end of the list. */
if i=0
then mylist=insertc(mylist,'Jones',-1,'NAMES');
else mylist=setitemc(mylist,'Jones',i);
```

*Note:* The return value of these functions is not used to indicate whether an error has been detected. When an error occurs, the program simply halts. △

An error condition results

☐ if either the item or the list has the NOUPDATE attribute.

☐ if either the item or the list has the FIXEDTYPE attribute and the new value is being assigned to an item that has a different type.

☐ if the named item was not found and the list has the FIXEDLENGTH attribute.

☐ with SETNITEMC and SETNITEML, if the list has the NUMONLY attribute.

☐ with SETNITEMN and SETNITEML, if the list has the CHARONLY attribute.

☐ with SETNITEML, if *list-id* identifies a global list and *sublist-id* identifies a local list. (Local lists cannot be placed into global lists.)

To check the attributes of a list or list item, use HASATTR. To change attributes, use SETLATTR.

### See Also

# SETPARMID

**Makes the value of an SCL numeric variable available between SCL programs**

**Category:**   Object Oriented

### Syntax

**CALL SETPARMID**(*nval*);

*nval*
>   is the numeric value to store for retrieval by GETPARMID.
>       Type: Numeric

**Details**      SETPARMID stores a number that can then be retrieved by calling GETPARMID. One program can use SETPARMID to store a value and another program can use GETPARMID to retrieve the value.

SETPARMID and GETPARMID allow only one value to be passed. To pass multiple values between entries, use the ENTRY statement. Other ways of making values available to other SCL programs include using macro variables and SCL lists.

### Example

Open the SAS table MYDATA. Then use SETPARMID to store the table identifier value so that other programs can use GETPARMID to access the table:

```
dsid=open('mydata','i');
call setparmid(dsid);
```

### See Also

# SETROW

**Determines the characteristics of extended tables**

**Category:** Extended Table

## Syntax

**CALL SETROW**(*num-rows*<,*num-sel*<,*sel-order*<,*dynamic*>>>);

***num-rows***
　　is the maximum number of rows for the table. If the table is dynamic, *num-rows* can be 0.
　　　Type: Numeric

***num-sel***
　　is the number of items a user can select from the list. To display the list for information purposes only (no selections allowed), specify 0. To specify unlimited selections, use a value such as 9999 that is larger than the number of available selections. If *num-sel* is 1, then selecting one row deselects any previously selected row.
　　　Type: Numeric

***sel-order***
　　specifies the selection order:

'Y'　　　　Selected items are highlighted and are moved to the top of the list in the order in which they are selected.

'N'　　　　Selected items are highlighted, but they are not moved to the top of the list. (This is the default.)

'A'　　　　The selection list window automatically closes when the user makes a selection if only one selection is allowed. This option is valid only if *num-sel* is 1.

'B'　　　　Combines Y and A.
　　　Type: Character

***dynamic***
　　specifies whether the table is dynamic:

'Y'　　　　specifies that the extended table is a dynamic table. Use the ENDTABLE routine in the getrow section to specify that no more rows are available.
　　　Type: Character

**Details**　　In PROGRAM entries, a regular extended table has a specified number of rows, and a dynamic extended table has an unspecified number of rows. You cannot use the SETROW statement in the getrow or putrow section of an SCL program. In order to use SETROW, you must have specified the EXTENDED TABLE attribute from the GATTR window.

You can also use both regular and dynamic extended tables as selection lists. The second and third arguments, *num-sel* and *sel-order*, define a selection list. Making an extended table a selection list automatically turns on the block cursor. Use FIELD to turn off the block cursor.

To define a dynamic table that is not a selection list, specify 0 for *num-sel* and " for *sel-order*.

You can use SETROW only on extended tables. Because you can define extended tables only in SAS/AF software, you cannot use SETROW in FSEDIT or FSVIEW programs. FRAME entries must use the _setMaxrow method.

## Examples

**Example 1: Specifying an Extended Table**    Specify an extended table that has 20 rows:

```
call setrow(20);
```

**Example 2: Using an Extended Table as a Selection List**    Specify a selection list that has 20 rows. Three selections are allowed, and the selections are moved to the top of the table.

```
call setrow(20,3,'y');
```

**Example 3: Specifying a Dynamic Extended Table**    Specify a dynamic table:

```
call setrow(0,0,'','y');
```

**Example 4: Using a Dynamic Extended Table as a Selection List**    Specify a dynamic table to be used as a selection list. Three selections are allowed, and the selections are not moved to the top of the table.

```
call setrow(0,3,'n','y');
```

## See Also

"CURTOP" on page 324

"ENDTABLE" on page 368

"TOPROW" on page 689

---

# SETTITLE

Sets the text of a title definition

**Category:**   SAS System Option

---

## Syntax

**CALL SETTITLE**(*title-num,title-text*);

*title-num*
>   is the number (1 to 10) of the title definition to create or modify.
>     Type: Numeric

*title-text*
>   is the text for the title definition.
>     Type: Character

**Details**    SETTITLE works just like the TITLE statement. It clears all title definitions that are numbered higher than the one created. You cannot use SETTITLE to set graphic options such as color, font, and position.

You can view title definitions in the TITLES window by using the TITLE command. However, changing any text in the TITLES window resets all graphically defined title options such as color, font, and position.

For more information about titles, see *SAS Language Reference: Dictionary.* For more information about graphical titles, see *SAS/GRAPH Software: Reference.*

## Example

Create a title numbered 2. The statement deletes all titles with numbers greater than 2.

```
call settitle(2,'This is the Second Title');
```

## See Also

"GETFOOT" on page 441

"GETTITLE" on page 449

"SETFOOT" on page 650

# SHOWLIST

**Displays a selection list window that contains up to 13 items, and returns the user's selections**

**Category:** Selection List

## Syntax

*selection=***SHOWLIST**(*item-1*<, . . . ,*item-13*>,*message*);

**selection**
contains the selected items, or a blank if no selection is made. By default, *selection* is 200 bytes long. To accomodate values longer than 200 bytes, explicitly declare *selection* with a longer length.
Type: Character

**item**
lists up to 13 items, separated by commas, for the selection list.
Type: Character

**message**
is the text for a message to display above the selection list. Regardless of how many *item* values are supplied, the last argument is assumed to be the message. Use a null string ( ' ')to specify the default message, which instructs users to make one selection.
Type: Character

**Details**     SHOWLIST automatically displays a custom selection list and returns the user's selections. Only one user selection is allowed, and the selection list window closes automatically after the user makes a selection.

You can provide a default or initial selected value in the list by assigning a value to *selection* before executing SHOWLIST. If *selection* contains a value that corresponds to one of the *item* arguments when SHOWLIST executes, then that selection is designated as selected when the selection list is displayed.

If a user closes the selection list window without making a selection, SHOWLIST returns a blank value unless there was an initial value for *selection* before SHOWLIST was called.

## Example

Open a selection list window that displays a list of three colors:

```
color='BLUE';
color=showlist
('RED','BLUE','GREEN','Please select a color.');
```

Because a value is assigned to the variable COLOR before SHOWLIST executes, and the value **BLUE** is one of the arguments for SHOWLIST, the item BLUE in the list is highlighted with an asterisk when the list is displayed.

## See Also

"DATALISTC and DATALISTN" on page 326

"LISTC and LISTN" on page 518

# SORT

**Sorts a SAS table by one or more columns**

**Category:** SAS Table

## Syntax

*sysrc=***SORT**(*table-id,col-list-1<. . .col-list-4>*);

*sysrc*
contains the return code for the operation:

| 0 | successful |
|---|---|
| ≠0 | not successful |

    Type: Numeric

*table-id*
contains the identifier that was assigned when the table was opened. The table must be open in UPDATE mode. If *table-id* is invalid, the program halts.
    Type: Numeric

*col-list*
is one to four quoted strings of columns or options, separated by blanks. For a list of options, the first character in the list must be a forward slash (/). Columns and options cannot be mixed in the same list.
    Type: Character

**Details**     SORT uses the sorting program that SAS supports on your operating system. If a column list contains more than one column, the table is sorted by those columns in the order in which they are specified.

You can use the following options for *col-list*, depending on your operating system:

```
DATECOPY
DIAG
EQUALS
FORCE
LEAVE
LIST
MESSAGE
NODUPKEY
NODUPLICATES
NOEQUALS
OUT
REVERSE
SORTSEQ=ASCII|EBCDIC|DANISH|FINNISH
    |NATIONAL|NORWEGIAN|SWEDISH
SORTSIZE
SORTWKNO
TAGSORT
TRANTAB
```

SAS views cannot be sorted in place. To sort views, you must specify an output SAS table.

If a SAS table is already in sorted order, then you must use the FORCE option.

*Note:* Unless you specify the FORCE option, the SORT function and PROC SORT do not sort and replace an indexed SAS table, because sorting destroys indexes for the table. △

## Example

Use the SORT function with the options NODUPKEY, NODUPLICATES, and TAGSORT to sort the SAS table MYDATA by column A in ascending order and by column B in descending order:

```
rc=sort(mydataid,'a descending b',
'/ nodupkey noduplicates tagsort');
```

# SORTLIST

**Sorts the items in an SCL list by value or by name**

**Category:** List

## Syntax

*rc*=**SORTLIST**(*list-id*<,*options*<,*start-index*<,*n-items*>>>);

*rc*

contains the identifier of the sorted list. The value passed as *list-id* is returned unless there is an error. The value 0 means out of memory.
Type: Numeric

**list-id**

is the identifier of the list to sort. An invalid *list-id* produces an error condition.
Type: Numeric or List

*options*

specify how the sort operation is performed. Multiple options can be specified, separated by blanks. Each option can be abbreviated to a unique substring. The substring can be as short as the first character for all options except **'NAME'** and **'NODUP'**, which may be abbreviated to two characters, **'NA'** or **'NO'**, respectively. Later keywords override previous keywords.

**'ASCENDING'**

Sort the list in ascending order. (This is a default.)

**'DESCENDING'**

Sort the list in descending order.

**'NOHONORCASE'**

Ignore case when comparing string values. Case is always ignored when sorting by name, because names are always converted to uppercase.

**'NAME'**

Sort the list by item name. Unnamed items appear before named items in an ascending sort.

**'NODUP'**

Delete duplicate items when sorting. All but the first item in the sort range that have the same value (or the same name, if sorting by name) are deleted. The default is not to delete duplicates.

**'OBEYCASE'**

Obey case when comparing string values. This is the default when sorting by value.

**'VALUE'**

Sort the list by item value. In an ascending sort, character items precede list identifiers, which precede numeric missing values, followed by non-missing numeric values. (This is a default.)
Type: Character

**start-index**

specifies the starting position for sorting a range of items in the list. By default, *start-index* is 1 (the first item). If *start-index* is positive, then the range begins *start-index* items from the beginning of the list. If *start-index* is negative, then the range begins at the item specified by ABS(*start-index*) items from the end of the list. An error condition results if the absolute value of *start-index* is zero or if it is greater than the number of items in the list.
Type: Numeric

**n-items**

specifies the number of items in the list to sort. The default is all items between *start-index* and the opposite end of the list. To explicitly specify all items, specify −1.
Type: Numeric

**Details**    SORTLIST does not make a copy of the list before it is sorted. The list is modified in place.

Sublists that are contained in the sorted list are not sorted recursively.

When you specify the **'NODUP'** and **'NOHONORCASE'** options, the character list items or names that are spelled the same but differ only in case are considered duplicates, and all but the first occurrence are removed from the sorted list.

An error occurs if the list has the NOUPDATE attribute or if an item to be removed has the NODELETE attribute, if NODUP is specified. Use HASATTR to check the attributes of a list or item. To change attributes, use SETLATTR.

## Examples

- Sort the first 10 items in a list in descending order:

  ```
  list=sortlist(list,'D',1,10);
  ```

- Sort the last 16 items in a list in ascending order:

  ```
  list=sortlist(list,'',-1,16);
  ```

- Sort the second ten items in a list in ascending name order, deleting items that have duplicate names:

  ```
  list=sortlist(list,'NODUP ASCENDING NAME',11,10);
  ```

## See Also

"HASATTR" on page 458

"REVLIST" on page 617

"ROTLIST" on page 622

"SETLATTR" on page 656

# _STATUS_

**Contains the status of program execution or overrides the normal flow of control**

**Category:** System Variable

**Details** _STATUS_ is a system variable that is created for every SCL program that is compiled. The compiler creates a space for _STATUS_ in the SCL data vector. _STATUS_ is maintained as a single-character string variable.

When an SCL program executes, _STATUS_ can have one of the following values:

| | |
|---|---|
| ' ' (blank) | A control or field was modified or selected. |
| E | An END or equivalent command was issued. |
| C | A CANCEL or equivalent command was issued. |
| P | A pop-up menu event occurred. |
| G | The getrow section was called for the top row of an extended table. |
| K | A command other than an END or CANCEL, or their equivalents, was issued. Valid only for FRAME entries. |

D                                  A control was selected with a double click. Valid only for FRAME
                                   entries.

In addition to the execution values, you can assign the following values to _STATUS_:

'**H**'                            Terminate the current window without further input from the user.
                                   Control returns to the program or window that invoked the
                                   application. Note that the TERM section of the program is not
                                   executed in this case. In FSEDIT, if a user modified a table variable
                                   value in the current row, the modified values are not written to the
                                   SAS table.

'**R**'                            Resume execution of the SCL program without exiting the
                                   application in SAS/AF or the current row in FSEDIT. When you set
                                   the value of the _STATUS_ variable to 'R', the procedure ignores the
                                   END or CANCEL command that the user just issued. This value is
                                   useful only when set in the TERM section of your program or in the
                                   _preterm method of a FRAME entry control, because the specified
                                   action (not allowing an exit from the program or the current row)
                                   occurs after the user has issued an END or CANCEL command in
                                   SAS/AF or after a user has attempted to leave a row in FSEDIT.

Assigning a value to _STATUS_ does not imply an immediate return. The value of
_STATUS_ is queried only after the SCL program returns control to the application. To
return control to the application after assigning a value to _STATUS_, use the STOP or
RETURN statement.

FRAME entries can also use the _getStatus and _setStatus methods to query and
update the _STATUS_ variable.

## Example

The following program calls OKTOEND.FRAME to display a confirmation window
that allows the user to select 'ok' or 'cancel' in response to the END command.
OKTOEND returns a 1 if it is OK to end or a 0 if it is not.

```
TERM:
 /* Check whether the END command was issued */
  if _status_ eq 'E' then
     do;
     call display( 'oktoend.frame', ok );
 /* Check whether the user wants to cancel the */
 /* END command */
        if ok eq 0 then
           do;
              _status_ = 'R';
             return;
        end;
   end;
   ...The rest of the TERM section...
return;
```

## See Also

"_EVENT_" on page 379

# STDMSG

**Displays the text of the SAS software message that is generated by an unknown command**

**Category:** Message

## Syntax

*cval*=**STDMSG**();

**cval**

> contains the message text. A blank means that no window exists in which to display the message.
>
> > Type: Character

## Example

Use WORD to read a command from the command line in a PROGRAM entry and check the command for validity. If the command is not valid, the standard message is displayed. Valid commands in this case are PRINTIT and FILEIT. Any other commands produce the standard error message for invalid commands.

```
INIT:
   control always;
return;
MAIN:
   if _status_ in ('C' 'E') then return;
   command=word(1);
   call nextcmd();
   select(upcase(command));
      when('PRINTIT') _msg_='PRINTIT is specified';
      when('FILEIT') _msg_='FILEIT is specified';
      otherwise do;
         call execcmdi(command);
         stdmsg=stdmsg();
         if stdmsg ne _blank_ then _msg_=stdmsg;
         return;
         end;
   end;
return;
TERM:
return;
```

### See Also

"NEXTCMD" on page 567

"NEXTWORD" on page 568

"SYSMSG" on page 686

"WORD" on page 725

# STOP

**Stops executing statements in the program section that is currently executing**

**Category:**   Control Flow

**Comparisons:**   SAS Statement with limitations in SCL

## Syntax

**STOP**;

## Example

The chain of execution is begun by executing OBJ1 and includes LAB1 and LAB2. When the STOP statement is executed, the chain of execution ends, and the two PUT statements are never executed. Control is passed to MAIN.

```
INIT:
   control label;
return;
MAIN:
   put 'in MAIN';
return;

OBJ1:
   link LAB1;
   put 'after link to LAB1';
return;

LAB1:
   link LAB2;
   put 'after link to LAB2';
return;

LAB2:
   stop;
return;

TERM:
return;
```

## See Also
"_STATUS_" on page 671

# STRATTR

**Defines a string for color and display attributes**

**Category:** Widget or Field

## Syntax

*cval*=**STRATTR**(*color,attribute,start,length*);

**cval**
is a string that contains the specified color and display attributes.
Type: Character

**color**
is a color name, or ' ' to retain the current color. Colors are BLACK, BLUE, BROWN, CYAN, GRAY, GREEN, MAGENTA, ORANGE, PINK, RED, WHITE, and YELLOW. SASCOLOR window elements can also be used for *color*.
Type: Character

**attribute**
is a display attribute, or ' ' to retain the current attribute. Attributes are NONE, BLINKING, HIGHLIGHT, HIREV, REVERSE, and UNDERLINE. If you specify a SASCOLOR window element for *color*, then *attribute* is ignored, because the SASCOLOR window element contains a display attribute. However, you must specify a placeholder (' ') for *attribute* when you specify arguments after it.
Type: Character

**start**
is the starting character position to store in the attribute string.
Type: Numeric

**length**
is the number of character positions to store in the attribute string.
Type: Numeric

**Details** STRATTR defines a string that you can use with FLDATTR to change the color and display attributes of fields or portions of fields in an application window. STRATTR can be called multiple times to create a string with multiple attributes in it.

Characters whose positions are after *start* + *length* - 1 do not change color or attributes. Characters whose positions are before the start position must be initialized to the special hexadecimal character 'FF'x in order to maintain their current color and attribute. For more information about using hexadecimal characters, see "FLDATTR" on page 414.

To change the color for an entire text entry widget or field, use the FIELD function.

## Example

Define an attribute string named STR that contains red reverse in the first half of the string and blue highlight in the second half. Apply the attribute string to the field ABC.

```
half=mlength(abc)/2;
str=strattr('red','reverse',1,half);
str=strattr('blue','highlight',half+1,half);
rc=fldattr('abc',str);
```

## See Also

"FLDATTR" on page 414

"FLDCOLOR" on page 416

# SUBMIT

**Submits statements or commands to SAS for execution**

**Category:** Submit Block

## Syntax

**SUBMIT**< *when* < *where*>>< *host*> <'STATUS'>;

*when*
specifies when to submit the generated statements or commands for execution and what action, if any, the procedure must take. If an option is not specified, the SUBMIT block statements are collected by SCL in a PREVIEW buffer. Options are

CONTINUE
specifies that at the end of the current submit block, the procedure submits all statements stored in the PREVIEW window and returns control to the SCL program. Execution of the program continues with the statement that follows ENDSUBMIT.

IMMEDIATE
specifies that at the end of the current submit block, the procedure submits all statements stored in the PREVIEW window and returns control to the procedure. You cannot use this option with FRAME entries, because its action could prevent the execution of other labeled sections.

*Note:* This means that any statements following ENDSUBMIT are not executed on this pass through the SCL program. To execute the statements following ENDSUBMIT, use conditional logic to branch around the SUBMIT IMMEDIATE statement. △

PRIMARY
specifies that at the end of the current submit block, the procedure submits all SAS statements stored in the PREVIEW window, and the user is returned to the primary window (the entry specified with the CATALOG= option in the AF command). If the current entry is the primary entry for the application, then this option restarts the current entry.

*Note:* This means that any statements following ENDSUBMIT are not executed on this pass through the SCL program. To execute the statements following ENDSUBMIT, use conditional logic to branch around the SUBMIT PRIMARY statement. △

TERMINATE
> specifies that at the end of the current submit block, the procedure submits all SAS statements stored in the PREVIEW window and closes the AF window.

> *Note:* The IMMEDIATE, PRIMARY, and TERMINATE options are honored only if the *where* option is not specified, that is, only if statements are to be submitted to the SAS system for execution. △
> Type: Character

**where**

determines where statements are submitted for execution. If this option is omitted, the statements are submitted to SAS for execution. Options are

COMMAND
> submits command line commands to SAS for execution. You can specify multiple commands by separating them with semicolons. You must specify the CONTINUE option along with the COMMAND option.

EDIT
> submits the statements to the Program Editor window.

> *Note:* In Version 8, using the RECALL command from the Program Editor window does not recall code that was submitted from SCL to the Program Editor. △

SQL
> submits the statements to SQL for processing from both TESTAF and AF modes.

> *Note:* The COMMAND, EDIT, and SQL options work only with the CONTINUE option. △
> Type: Character

**host**

provides instructions for submitting the code on a particular operating system. Options are

LOCAL
> executes on the current system. (This is the default.)

REMOTE
> executes on a remote host. Use this option with the CONTINUE option.
> Type: Character

**'STATUS'**

is the instruction to display the status window at all times. Use this option with the CONTINUE option.
> Type: Character

**Details**   SUBMIT labels the beginning of a block of SAS statements or commands to submit to SAS software. When SUBMIT is encountered, SCL collects all the text between SUBMIT and ENDSUBMIT and places it in the PREVIEW buffer. Based on the value of the *when* option, SCL submits the statements to SAS for execution at the appropriate time.

The *where* and *host* options are valid only if the *when* option is specified. Regardless of the value of the *where* option, all submit block text can be buffered in the PREVIEW window. You need to make certain that the CONTINUE option is specified when you want the statements to be submitted.

By default, when control returns to SCL, the program continues to execute the statements that follow ENDSUBMIT.

You can use the REMOTE command to override the *host* option of a SUBMIT statement. That is, in the SUBMIT statement, you can choose not to use the *host* option

**REMOTE** and can instead use the REMOTE command to control whether the generated code is executed on the local or remote host. For more information about the REMOTE command, see "Submitting Statements to a Remote Host" on page 84.

The ASIS option in the CONTROL statement allows a submit block to be submitted without formatting. Use CONTROL ASIS before the SUBMIT block to submit code that contains a DATALINES statement.

When an AF application that is invoked from an autoexec file uses both SUBMIT CONTINUE REMOTE and LOCAL blocks, the order of execution may not be correct. In this situation, you can avoid problems by using the following in place of the SUBMIT CONTINUE REMOTE blocks:

```
submit continue;
   rsubmit;
   ...SCL statements...
   endrsubmit;
endsubmit;
```

*Note:* If CONTROL LABEL is specified, a window variable section must not contain a SUBMIT IMMEDIATE block. △

## Examples

□ Submit a simple SAS program that invokes the PRINT procedure for a previously referenced SAS table:

```
submit continue;
   proc print;
   run;
endsubmit;
```

□ Submit the LIBNAME command:

```
main:
   submit command continue;
      libname;
   endsubmit;
return;
```

## See Also

"ENDCLASS" on page 366

"PREVIEW" on page 599

# SUBMITCLEAR

**Aborts a pending submit transaction**

**Category:** Submit Block

## Syntax

*sysrc=***SUBMITCLEAR**();

*sysrc*
> contains the return code for the operation:

| | |
|---|---|
| 0 | successful |
| !0 | not successful |

> Type: Numeric

**Details** SUMBITCLEAR aborts a pending submit transaction. A submit transaction may be pending if the submitted DATA steps or procedure statements are not complete, or if the submitted text contains an open quoted string or other syntax errors. SUBMITCLEAR is particularly useful for terminating programs that are waiting on input because of unmatched quotes or other syntax errors.

A submit transaction starts as SAS/AF sends submitted text in the PREVIEW buffer to SAS for execution (usually through the SUBMIT CONTINUE option). If SUBMIT requests were queued up, they would be flushed out without being executed. The currently running step is aborted, and as a result, the log will not be updated with any specific status information relating to the step that is being terminated.

## Examples

### Example 1: Abort a Pending Transaction
Submit code to SAS for execution, then call SUBMITCLEAR to ensure there is no hanging transaction due to mismatched quoted string or other syntax errors.

```
SUBUMIT CONTINUE;
  data test;
    . . .
ENDSUBMIT;

rc = SUBMITCLEAR();
```

## See Also

"PREVIEW" on page 599

"SUBMIT" on page 676

---

# SUPAPPLY

**Invokes the inherited definition of a method and passes the method's arguments in an SCL list**

**Category:** Object Oriented

---

## Syntax

**CALL SUPAPPLY**(*object-id,method-name,arg-list-id*);

*return-value*=**SUPAPPLY**(*object-id,method-name,arg-list-id*);

*object-id*
> contains the identifier of the object for which the method is invoked.
> Type: Numeric or Object

**method-name**
> is the name of the method to invoke.
>> Type: Character

**arg-list-id**
> is the identifier of a list of arguments that are required by the method. An invalid *arg-list-id* produces an error condition.
>> Type: Numeric

**return-value**
> contains the value returned by *method-name*. The data type for *return-value* should match the data type for the called method.
>> Type: Numeric, Character, List, Object-name, Class, or Interface

**Details**    SUPAPPLY provides the same functionality as SUPER except that you can pass arguments to inherited methods in an SCL list. You use SUPAPPLY to execute an inherited method when you define another method that performs additional actions. A method that calls an inherited method and includes additional actions is called an overloaded method. See "Overloading Methods" on page 108 for more information.

In Version 8, you must use dot notation to call overloaded methods. Dot notation provides compiler time checking and better performance at run time. With overloaded methods, the compiler must be able to check method signatures in order to call the correct method. For details about dot notation, see "Accessing Object Attributes and Methods With Dot Notation" on page 119.

You can use SUPAPPLY as a function if the called method returns a value with a RETURN statement in the program that defines the method.

Although the method name is typically the name of the currently executing method, which is stored in the system variable _METHOD_, any other method name can be used.

The object identified by *object-id* must be the same object whose method is currently executing. The identifier for this object is stored in the system variable _SELF_. In methods defined in a CLASS or USECLASS statement block, all references to the class methods and attributes can bypass references to _SELF_.*attribute* and _SELF_.*method*(...). For example, to call a super method with dot notation in a method definition, you can use **supapply();** , which is equivalent to **call supapply(_self_,'m1');**.

## Example

Consider an Object class in which a Transaction method receives a variable-length parameter list of transactions to record in a table. A subclass of this class records the transactions in an audit trail table that contains two numeric variables, DATETIME and TCOUNT. These variables record the date/time and the number of transactions processed. This example shows the Transaction method, which invokes the inherited Transaction method and then records the size of the transaction (the number of items in the argument list) for a table. The object has the attributes **audit**, **tc_vnum**, and **dt_vnum**. **Audit** is a table ID for an audit table. **Tc_vnum** is the variable number for the TCOUNT variable. **Dt_vnum** is the variable number for the DATETIME variable.

```
useclass lib.cat.myclass.class;

/* TRANSACT.SCL: TRANSACTION method */
Transaction: method arglist= transactions;
   call supapply(_self_,'Transaction',transactions);
   if audit then do;
      nTransactions=listlen(transactions);
      call putvarn(audit,tc_vnum,nTransactions);
```

```
        call putvarn(audit,dt_vnum,datetime());
        rc=update(audit);
    end;
endmethod;
enduseclass;
```

This method can be invoked with an arbitrary number of transactions using dot notation, where the SCL variable **listOftransactions** is an SCL list that contains one or more transaction objects.

```
dcl lib.cat.myclass.class obj=_NEW_lib.cat.myclass();

obj.Transaction(t1,t2,t3,t4,t5);
obj.Transaction(t1,t2);
obj.Transaction(listOftransactions);
```

## See Also

"APPLY" on page 252

"INSTANCE" on page 485

"METHOD" on page 540

"NOTIFY" on page 572

"SEND" on page 644

"SUPER" on page 681

---

# SUPER

**Invokes the inherited definition of a method**

**Category:** Object Oriented

---

## Syntax

**CALL SUPER**(*object-id,method-name< ,parameters>*);

*< return-value=>*_**SUPER**<*.method-name>*(*< parameters>*);

*object-id*
> contains the identifier of the object for which the method is invoked.
> > Type: Numeric or Object

*method-name*
> is the name of the method to invoke.
> > Type: Character

*parameters*
> are additional numeric or character arguments that are required by the method. Use commas to separate multiple options.
>
> *Note:* These parameters are update parameters. See "Input, Output, and Update Parameters" on page 34 for more information. △
> > Type: Numeric, Character

***return-value***
    contains the value returned by the inherited method.
        Type: Numeric, Character, List, Object-name, Class, or Interface

**Details**    SUPER provides a convenient way of calling a method in the parent class from a method in the child class. In particular, it is useful for calling the corresponding parent method from an overridden method in the child.

Although *method-name* is typically the name of the currently executing method, which is stored in the system variable _METHOD_, any other method name can be used.

The object identified by *object-id* must be the same object whose method is currently executing. The identifier for this object is stored in the system variable _SELF_.

For more information about system variables, see "System Variables" on page 24.

SUPER can also be used with CLASS blocks, USECLASS blocks and dot notation by using _SUPER. If you are specifying the same method in the parent and child classes, you do not need to specify the method name.

## Examples

**Example 1: Calling the Parent Method of an Overridden Method**    In this example, _SUPER is used to call the parent method of an overridden method in class X.

```
Y.SCL
  class y;
    m: method;
      ...SCL statements...
    endmethod;
  endclass;

X.SCL
  class x extends y;
    m: method;
      _super();
      /* _super invokes method M in class Y */
    endmethod;
  endclass;
```

**Example 2: Calling a Different Method in the Parent Class**    To call a different method in the parent class, specify the method name after _SUPER using dot notation. The following example invokes the M2 method in class Y using _SUPER:

```
Y.SCL
  class y;
    m2: method;
      ...SCL statements...
    endmethod;
  endclass;

X.SCL
  class x extends y;
    m: method;
      _super.m2();
    endmethod;
  endclass;
```

**Example 3: Calling a Method in the Parent of a Parent Class** This example demonstrates how you can use inheritance to invoke a method in the parent of a parent class.

```
S.SCL
  class s;
    m: method n: num return=num;
      dcl num x;
      x=n+199;
      return x;
    endmethod;
  endclass;
```

```
S2.SCL
  class s2 extends s;
    m: method n: num return=num/(state='O');
      dcl num x;
      x=n+_super(1);
      return x;
    endmethod;
  endclass;
```

```
S3.SCL
  class s3 extends s2;
    n: method return=num;
      dcl num x;
      x=_super.m(-10);
      return x;
    endmethod;
  endclass;
```

```
DRS.SCL
init:
  dcl s3 sobj=_new_ s3();
  dcl num x;
  dcl string s;
  x=sobj.n();
  put x=;
return;
```

This example results in the following output:

`x=190`

The calling sequence for the above example is as follows:

**1** Method N in class S3 is invoked in DRS.SCL.

**2** In N, method M is invoked in class S2 via _SUPER. The parameter is **-10**.

**3** Method M, which is within S2, invokes method M in class S via _SUPER. The parameter is **1**.

**4** In S, **1** is added to **199** and returned to S2.

**5** In S2, **200** is added to **-10** and returned to S3.

**6** In S3, **190** is returned to DRS.SCL.

## See Also

"APPLY" on page 252

"INSTANCE" on page 485

"METHOD" on page 540

"NOTIFY" on page 572

"SEND" on page 644

"SUPAPPLY" on page 679

# SYMGET and SYMGETN

**Return the value stored in a macro variable**

**Category:** Macro

## Syntax

*cval*=**SYMGET**(*macro-var*);

*nval*=**SYMGETN**(*macro-var*);

### cval

contains the character value returned by SYMGET.
Type: Character

### nval

contains the numeric value returned by SYMGETN.
Type: Numeric

### macro-var

is the macro variable.
Type: Character

**Details**   SYMGET and SYMGETN return values of macro variables when the program executes, whereas "&*macro-var*" returns values when the program compiles. SYMGET returns the value of a SAS macro variable as a character value and SYMGETN returns the value as a numeric value.

## Examples

**Example 1: Using the SYMGET Function**   Execute commands if the operating system is Windows:

```
if symget('SYSSCP') = 'WIN' then do;
   rc = optsetn('xwait',0);
   rc = optsetn('xsync',0);
end;
```

**Example 2: Using the SYMGETN Function**   Return the value of the macro variable UNIT at program execution time:

```
nval=symgetn('unit');
```

**Example 3: Returning Macro Values at Program Compile Time**    Return the values of the macro variables UNIT and SYSJOBID at program compile time:

```
nval=&unit;
cval="&sysjobid";
```

## See Also

"SYMPUT and SYMPUTN" on page 685

# SYMPUT and SYMPUTN

**Store a value in a SAS macro variable**

**Category:**  Macro

## Syntax

**CALL SYMPUT**(*macro-var,cval*);

**CALL SYMPUTN**(*macro-var,nval*);

*macro-var*
> is the macro variable to store a value in.
> > Type: Character

*cval*
> is the character value for SYMPUT to store in *macro-var*.
> > Type: Character

*nval*
> is the numeric value for SYMPUTN to store in *macro-var*.
> > Type: Numeric

**Details**    SYMPUT stores a character value in a SAS macro variable, whereas SYMPUTN stores a numeric value in a SAS macro variable. If *macro-variable* does not exist, SYMPUT and SYMPUTN create it. SYMPUT and SYMPUTN make a macro variable assignment when the program executes.

## Examples

**Example 1: Using the SYMPUT Routine**    Store the value of the SCL variable SCLVAR in the macro variable TBL:

```
call symput('tbl',sclvar);
```

**Example 2: Using the SYMPUTN Routine**    Store the numeric value 1000 in the macro variable UNIT:

```
call symputn('unit',1000);
```

## See Also

"SYMGET and SYMGETN" on page 684

# SYSMSG

**Returns the text of SCL error messages or warning messages**

**Category:**   Message

## Syntax

*cval*=**SYSMSG**();

**cval**

contains the text of the SCL error message.
Type: Character

**Details**   SYSMSG returns the text of error messages or warning messages that are produced when SCL encounters an error condition. If no error message is available, the returned value is blank. The internally stored error message is reset to blank after a call to SYSMSG. Therefore, if you subsequently call SYSMSG before another error condition occurs, it returns a blank value.

## Example

Display the system error message that is generated if FETCH cannot copy the next row into the Table Data Vector for the SAS table identified by the value stored in DSID. The return code is 0 only when a next record is successfully fetched.

```
rc=fetch(dsid);
if rc ne 0 then _msg_=sysmsg();
```

## See Also

"SYSRC" on page 686

"_MSG_" on page 554

# SYSRC

**Returns a system error number or the exit status of the most recently called entry**

**Category:**   Message

## Syntax

*rc*=**SYSRC**(< *display-stat*>);

*rc*

contains the return code for the most recent error or warning condition, if *display-stat* is omitted. Otherwise, returns the exit status of CALL DISPLAY:

0 A user used an END command.

−1 A user used a CANCEL command.
Type: Numeric

*display-stat*

causes the SYSRC function to return the most recent exit status of CALL DISPLAY. The value of the argument does not matter, only whether any value is specified.
Type: Numeric

**Details** If you pass an argument to SYSRC, the function returns the exit status of the most recently called execution of CALL DISPLAY rather than the SAS system return code for the most recent error or warning condition. Thus, you can use SYSRC to determine how a user terminated an entry that was called with CALL DISPLAY.

To return the SAS system return code, do not specify any value for *display-stat*. See Chapter 14, "SAS System Return Codes," on page 227 for more information about how to use return code values.

## Example

Determine how a user exited from another entry that was called within the current application:

```
call display('test.scl');
if sysrc(1)=-1 then
 _msg_=
    'User exited TEST.SCL with a CANCEL command';
else
 _msg_=
    'User exited TEST.SCL with an END command';
```

## See Also

"SYSMSG" on page 686

# SYSTEM

**Issues a host system command**

**Category:** Command

## Syntax

*rc*=**SYSTEM**(*cval*);

*rc*

contains the host system return code for the operation.
Type: Numeric

*cval*
> is the host command to be executed. To enter the host command processor for your system, specify a blank string (' ').
> Type: Character

**Details**    Using SYSTEM is equivalent to using the X command for issuing a system command. The action that takes place depends on which command you specify. The window may be temporarily overwritten due to the actions of the command. The commands that can be issued are operating-system dependent.

## Example

Issue the DIR command to the host operating system:

```
rc=system('dir');
if (rc) then _msg_ =
    'Failed to execute the DIR command.';
```

# THROW

**Raises an exception**

**Category:**   Control Flow

## Syntax

**THROW** *exception*;

*exception*
> is the local variable for the exception that you want to process.

## Details

All exceptions are subclasses of the SCLException class. You can use the CLASS statement to define your own exception classes, and then use THROW statements to raise the exceptions.

When an exception is thrown, normal execution of the SCL entry stops, and SCL begins looking for a CATCH block to process the exception.

*Note:*   You must always declare a variable to hold the thrown exception. △

## Example

The following class defines a subclass of SCLException called NewException, which defines an attribute named SecondaryMessage:

```
Class NewException extends SCLException
    dcl string SecondaryMessage;
endclass;
```

You can create a new instance of NewException and raise this exception with the THROW statement, as shown here in the ThrowIt class:

```
Class ThrowIt;
  m: method;
  dcl NewException NE = _new_ NewException('Exception in method m');
  NE.SecondaryMessage = "There's no code in m!";
  throw NE;
  endmethod;
endclass;
```

### See Also

"CATCH" on page 268

Chapter 10, "Handling Exceptions," on page 157

# TOPROW

**Scrolls a row to the top of an extended table**

**Category:** Extended Table

## Syntax

**CALL TOPROW**(*row*);

*row*

> is the number of the table row to be scrolled to the top of the table.
> Type: Numeric

**Details**    The TOPROW routine cannot be called in the getrow or putrow section of an SCL program.

You can use TOPROW only on extended tables in PROGRAM entries. Because you can define extended tables only in SAS/AF software, you cannot use TOPROW in FSEDIT or FSVIEW programs.

## Examples

### Example 1: Specifying Which Row to Scroll

Scroll the fifth row to the top of the table:

```
call toprow(5);
```

### Example 2: Letting the Program Determine Which Row to Scroll

Suppose you have a PROGRAM entry window that contains three character fields:

1 VALUE, in the non-scrollable area of the window. Turn the CAPS attribute off for VALUE.

2 NAME, the first field in the extended table's logical row. Turn the CAPS attribute off for NAME.

**3** GENDER, the second field in the extended table's logical row.

When a user enters a name in **VALUE**, the table scrolls so that the corresponding row is at the top of the table.

This program controls the window:

```
INIT:
  dsid=open('sasuser.class');
  call set(dsid);
  call setrow(0,0,'','y');
  vnum=varnum(dsid,'name');
return;
MAIN:
rc=
where(dsid,"name contains '"||value|| "'");
 any=attrn(dsid,'any');
   if any then do;
     rc=fetch(dsid);
     firstmatch=getvarc(dsid,vnum);
     rc=where(dsid);
     recnum=locatec(dsid,vnum, firstmatch);
     call toprow(recnum);
   end;
return;

TERM:
  if dsid then dsid=close(dsid);
return;

getrow:
  if fetchobs(dsid,_currow_)=-1
    then call endtable();
return;
```

## See Also

"CURTOP" on page 324

"ENDTABLE" on page 368

"SETROW" on page 664

# TRACEBACK

**Displays traceback information for an SCL execution stack**

**Category:** Utility

## Syntax

**CALL TRACEBACK**(< *list-id*><,'_ALL_'>;

***list-id***
> contains the identifier of the SCL list to store traceback information in. You must create the list before passing it to TRACEBACK. An invalid *list-id* produces an error condition.
>
> Type: Numeric or List

**_ALL_**
> is the instruction to display the link stack in addition to the SCL execution stack.
>
> Type: Character

**Details**    The execution stack consists of the program that is currently being executed, plus all programs that were called to display the current program. TRACEBACK displays the execution stack as a list of entry names and associated line numbers. The _ALL_ argument displays the *link stack*, which lists the labeled sections that are called within the program. The link stack does not include labeled sections that are called with a GOTO statement. The line number for an entry indicates where the entry transferred control to the next entry in the list.

## Examples

The following examples use three SCL entries, START.SCL, ANALYZE.SCL, and REPORT.SCL. START.SCL contains a link at line 5 and calls ANALYZE.SCL at line 9. ANALYZE.SCL contains links at line 5, 11, and 16 and calls REPORT.FRAME at line 21.

**Example 1: Tracing Program Execution**    The TRACEBACK routine is executed at line 6 of REPORT.SCL.

```
call traceback();
```

The following traceback list is printed in the LOG window:

```
In routine: LIB.TEST.REPORT.SCL line 6
Called from LIB.TEST.ANALYZE.SCL line 21
Arguments passed to DISPLAY:
  1 (Character Literal) = 'report.scl'
Called from LIB.TEST.START.SCL line 9
Arguments passed to DISPLAY:
  1 (Character Literal) = 'analyze.scl'
```

**Example 2: Saving Traceback Information in an SCL List**    Change REPORT.SCL to save traceback information in an SCL list, and then display the traceback list:

```
tb = makelist();
call traceback(tb);     /* line 7 */
call putlist(tb, 'Traceback:', 0);
tb = dellist(tb);
```

This program produces the following output:

```
Traceback:(LIB.TEST.REPORT.SCL=7
          LIB.TEST.ANALYZE.SCL=21
          LIB.TEST.START.SCL=9
          )[1905]
```

**Example 3: Tracing the Execution Stack and Program Links**    Change REPORT.SCL to execute a traceback, using the _ALL_ argument on line 6:

```
call traceback(0,'_all_');
```

The following traceback list is printed in the LOG window:

```
In routine: LIB.TEST.REPORT.SCL line 6
Called from LIB.TEST.ANALYZE.SCL line 21
Arguments passed to DISPLAY:
  (Character Literal) = 'report.scl'
Linked from LIB.TEST.ANALYZE.SCL line 16
Linked from LIB.TEST.ANALYZE.SCL line 11
Linked from LIB.TEST.ANALYZE.SCL line 5
Called from LIB.TEST.START.SCL line 9
Arguments passed to DISPLAY:
  1 (Character Literal) = 'analyze.scl'
  Linked from LIB.TEST.START.SCL line 5
```

**Example 4: Comparing Tracebacks With and Without _ALL_**    Change REPORT.SCL to execute the traceback without the _ALL_ option at line 8 and to execute the traceback with the _ALL_ option at line 9:

```
listid1=makelist();
listid2=makelist();
call traceback(listid1);
call traceback(listid2,'_ALL_');
call putlist(listid1,
   'Traceback without LINK stack=',0);
call putlist(listid2,
   'Traceback with LINK stack=',0);
listid1=dellist(listid1);
listid2=dellist(listid2);
```

This program produces the following output:

```
Traceback without LINK stack=(LIB.TEST.REPORT.SCL=8
LIB.TEST.ANALYZE.SCL=21
LIB.TEST.START.SCL=9
                              )[1905]
Traceback with LINK stack=(
 LIB.TEST.REPORT.SCL=9
 LIB.TEST.ANALYZE.SCL=21
 LIB.TEST.ANALYZE.SCL=16
 LIB.TEST.ANALYZE.SCL=11
 LIB.TEST.ANALYZE.SCL=5
 LIB.TEST.START.SCL=9
 LIB.TEST.START.SCL=5
                    )[1907]
```

*Note:* 541, 1905, and 1907 are the list identifiers that were assigned when these examples were run and may be different each time the examples are run. △

### See Also

"MAKELIST" on page 535

"TRACEBACK" on page 223

# UNGRAY

**Ungrays a window element**

**Category:** Control or Field

## Syntax

*rc*=**UNGRAY**(*var-name*<,*station*<,*row*>>);

**rc**

contains the return code for the operation:

| | |
|---|---|
| 0 | successful |
| ≠0 | unsuccessful |

Type: Numeric

**var-name**

is the control or choice group to be ungrayed.
Type: Character

**station**

is the number of a field within the choice group or the number of a button within the radio box.
Type: Numeric

**row**

is the number of a row when the choice group is in the scrollable section of an extended table. The *row* parameter is valid for PROGRAM entries but not for FRAME entries. Specify *row* only when you want to ungray a station from outside the extended table's getrow or putrow section.
Type: Numeric

**Details** You can use UNGRAY along with GRAY to control the availability of a choice group, a station, or a window element, based on the program flow.

When a window element is ungrayed, it becomes unprotected and reverts to its normal color. An ungrayed window element can once again receive input such as mouse clicks. FRAME entry controls can also use the _ungray method.

## Example

Make a station available only when the value of variable DEPT is ADMIN:

```
if (dept='ADMIN') then
    rc=ungray('personal',3);
  else
    rc=gray('personal',3);
```

### See Also

"ACTIVATE" on page 249

"GRAY" on page 457

"ISACTIVE" on page 492

"ISGRAY" on page 493

# UNIQUENUM

**Returns a unique number**

**Category:**   Utility

## Syntax

*num*=**UNIQUENUM**();

**num**
>   contains the unique number that is returned by the function.
>   Type: Numeric

**Details**   UNIQUENUM returns a number that is unique for each call to the function during a SAS session.

## Example

```
num=uniquenum();
put num=;
```

# UNLOCK

**Releases a lock on the current row**

**Category:**   SAS Table

## Syntax

*sysrc*=**UNLOCK**(*table-id*);

**sysrc**
>   contains the return code for the operation:

>   0                          successful

>   ≠0                         not successful
>      Type: Numeric

***table-id***
> is the identifier that was assigned when the table was opened. If *table-id* is invalid, the program halts.
>
> Type: Numeric

**Details**  A table that is opened in UPDATE mode receives RECORD-level locking by default. Whenever an application reads a row from a table that was opened in UPDATE mode, it attempts to obtain a lock on the row. All of the following functions lock a row when the table is opened in UPDATE mode:

> DATALISTC
>
> DATALISTN
>
> FETCH
>
> FETCHOBS
>
> LOCATEC
>
> LOCATEN

Row locks are implicitly released when a different row is read. However, when a user is finished with a row but has not read another row, you can use UNLOCK to explicitly release a lock on the row.

This function is useful when rows from a secondary SAS table are read to obtain values.

*Note:*  UNLOCK is not directly related to the LOCK function, which locks SAS catalogs, catalog members, and SAS tables. However, if the table in question is accessed through SAS/SHARE software using the REMOTE engine, then UNLOCK can be used to enable other applications to access individual rows. See *SAS Language Reference: Dictionary* for more information. △

## Example

Call FETCH to read a new row from the SAS table MYDATA, which is opened in UPDATE mode. After data from the row is processed, call UNLOCK to release the lock on the row.

```
dsid=open('mydata','u');
rc=fetch(dsid);
     ...more SCL statements...
rc=unlock(dsid);
```

## See Also

"CLOSE" on page 292

"DATALISTC and DATALISTN" on page 326

"FETCH" on page 389

"FETCHOBS" on page 390

"LOCATEC and LOCATEN" on page 527

"OPEN" on page 576

# UNPROTECT

**Removes protection from a FRAME entry control or a field**

**Category:**   Control or Field

## Syntax

**UNPROTECT** *wvar-names* | _ALL_;

*wvar-names*

lists one or more window variables to unprotect, or **_ALL_** to unprotect all window variables. To specify multiple names, use blanks to separate the names.
    Type: Character

**Details**    Use UNPROTECT to temporarily override the PROTECT attribute. The variable to be unprotected cannot be an element of an array. To unprotect an array element, use FIELD.

When used with PROTECT, UNPROTECT enables you to unprotect and protect controls and fields selectively. Thus, you can force the user to enter values in a predetermined order.

If you unprotect a window variable with the UNPROTECT statement in FSEDIT applications and then issue the MODIFY command to edit the custom screen, the PROTECT attribute is removed for this variable in the PROTECT window.

FRAME entry controls can also use the _unprotect method. Unprotecting some FRAME entry controls (block, check box, icon, list box, pushbutton, radio box, scroll bar, and slider) is the same as calling the UNGRAY function or the _ungray method.

## Example

Enable users to enter values for fields that were previously protected:

```
if (modified(tablename)) then
    do;
        protect tablename;
        unprotect vars;
        cursor vars;
        _msg_=
'Enter the names of the variables to be printed.';
    end;
```

## See Also

"DISPLAYED" on page 353

"ERROR" on page 375

"ERROROFF" on page 376

"ERRORON" on page 377

"FIELD" on page 394

"MODIFIED" on page 550

"PROTECT" on page 602

# UNSELECT

**Deselects a specified row of a selection list**

**Category:** Extended Table

## Syntax

*rc*=**UNSELECT**(*row*);

***rc***

contains the return code for the operation:

0                          successful

≠0                        not successful

Type: Numeric

***row***

is the row number to deselect. If an invalid row number is specified, no action is taken.

Type: Numeric

**Details**     UNSELECT is useful for forcing the deselection of a row. Normally a user selects and deselects a row by pressing ENTER or by clicking on the row with the mouse.

You can use UNSELECT only for selection lists that were built with extended tables in PROGRAM entries. Window controls must use the _unselectRow method. Because you can define extended tables only in SAS/AF software, you cannot use UNSELECT in FSEDIT or FSVIEW programs.

In order for an extended table to be considered a selection list, you must specify the number of selections in the SETROW routine.

## Example

Force row 5 to be deselected:

```
rc=unselect(5);
```

## See Also

"ISSEL" on page 495

"NSELECT" on page 573

"SELECT" on page 639

"SELECTED" on page 642

# UPDATE

**Writes values from the Table Data Vector (TDV) to the current row in a SAS table**

**Category:** SAS Table

## Syntax

*sysrc*=**UPDATE**(*table-id*);

*sysrc*
contains the return code for the operation:

0                         successful

≠0                        not successful
   Type: Numeric

*table-id*
is the identifier that was assigned when the table was opened. If *table-id* is invalid, the program halts.
   Type: Numeric

**Details**   The table must be opened in UPDATE mode. The row to be updated is the current row. To place values in the TDV, use PUTVARC, PUTVARN, or SET.

## Example

Update the current row in the open SAS table whose table identifier value is stored in the column MYDATAID. If the return code, RC, is nonzero, the system error message is displayed on the message line.

```
rc=update(mydataid);
if rc then _msg_=sysmsg();
```

## See Also

"APPEND" on page 251

"FETCH" on page 389

"FETCHOBS" on page 390

"GETVARC and GETVARN" on page 450

"PUTVARC and PUTVARN" on page 609

"SET" on page 646

# USECLASS

**Implements methods for a class and binds them to the class definition**

**Category:**   Object Oriented

## Syntax

**USECLASS** *class-name*;
   <(*method-implementation-blocks*)>

**ENDUSECLASS**;

*class-name*
is the name of a class entry that has been defined either with an SCL CLASS statement or with the AF Class Editor.

**method-implementation-blocks**
> are SCL method implementation blocks. For detailed information, see "METHOD" on page 540 or "CLASS" on page 277.

**Details** The USECLASS statement binds methods that are implemented within it to a class definition. USECLASS blocks are especially useful for defining method implementations in a separate SCL entry from the one that contains the CLASS statement that defines the class. This feature enables group development of classes, because multiple people can work on class methods implementations simultaneously.

USECLASS labels the beginning of a program block that implements methods for *class-name*. The USECLASS statement block ends with the ENDUSECLASS statement. *Class-name* must be already defined in an existing CLASS entry.

The only SCL statements allowed in USECLASS blocks are METHOD implementation blocks. The signature (parameter types) of methods must match the associated method definitions in the CLASS entry. If a return type is defined, it must also match the associated method definition in the CLASS entry. If the parameter storage (INPUT/OUTPUT/UPDATE) is omitted, the SCL compiler will assume that it has the same storage specification as the associated method definition in the CLASS entry.

Method implementations inside a USECLASS block can include any SCL statements (except CLASS, USECLASS, or INTERFACE statements), or SCL functions and routines, including DECLARE to declare local variables. If you want to define a local variable that can be used across the class, you must define it as a private attribute either inside the CLASS statement or in the Class Editor. METHOD blocks can include labeled sections. However, labeled sections that are outside a method block must be re-coded as PRIVATE methods, and the LINK statements that call them must be changed to method calls. For more information, see "METHOD" on page 540.

If a local variable that is defined in a METHOD block has the same name as a class attribute, SCL gives precedence to the local variable. If a class method has the same name as any SCL-supported function, SCL gives precedence to the function. If an attribute array has the same name as a class method, SCL gives precedence to the method.

Do not declare the _SELF_, _FRAME_, _CFRAME_, _METHOD_, or _EVENT_ system variables inside a CLASS or USECLASS block. SCL automatically sets these values when it is running methods that are defined in CLASS or USECLASS blocks. Redefining any of these system variables can introduce unexpected behavior.

Because USECLASS binds the methods that it contains to the class that is defined in a CLASS entry, all references to the methods and the attributes of the class can bypass references to _SELF_.*attribute* and _SELF_.*method*(...). Because the binding occurs at compile time, the SCL compiler can detect whether an undefined variable is a local variable or a class attribute.

You can also use the _super method in method code that is inside a USECLASS statement block without having to specify either an object identifier or the method whose super method you are calling. You can use the _super method to call any method. For example, to invoke the super ADD method, you would use

```
_super.add();
```

To override the _init method, you must first call the super _init method. The _init method can be short-cut. For example:

```
_super();
```

The USECLASS statement also enables you to define implementations for overloading methods, which means that multiple methods have the same name. Methods that have the same name are allowed in a USECLASS block only if the signatures, or parameter numbers or types, are different. For example, a class can have a COMBINE method that has numeric parameters and that adds parameter values. It can also contain another COMBINE method that has character parameters and that concatenates parameter values.

## Examples

**Example 1: Group Development Using a USECLASS Block**　　USECLASS can be used for group development. Suppose a group with three members ONE, TWO and THREE was assigned to develop WORK.A.GROUP.CLASS. This class is defined as follows:

```
Class work.a.group.class;
   Public  Num  nAttr;
   Public  Char cAttr;
   m1: Method n:Num / (scl='work.a.one.scl');
   m1: Method c:Char / (scl='work.a.one.scl');
   m2: Method n:num / (scl='work.a.two.scl');
   m3: Method Return=Num / (scl='work.a.two.scl');
   m4: Method Return=Char / (scl='work.a.three.scl');
EndClass;
```

Issue the SAVECLASS command to create this class. After the class is created, programmer ONE starts to create method implementations in WORK.A.ONE.SCL as follows:

```
UseClass work.a.group.class;
   m1: Method m:Num;
           nAttr = m;
       EndMethod;
   m1: Method c:Char;
           cAttr = c;
       EndMethod;
EndUseClass; +
```

Programmer ONE is also responsible for compiling and testing this method implementation before the final system integrations.

Programmer TWO creates method implementations in WORK.A.TWO.SCL as follows:

```
UseClass work.a.group.class;
   m2: Method n:Num;
           put n=;
       EndMethod;
   m3: Method Return=Num;
            return(nAttr);
       EndMethod;
EndUseClass;
```

Programmer TWO is also responsible for compiling and testing this method implementation before the final system integrations.

Programmer THREE creates method implementations in WORK.A.THREE.SCL as follows:

```
UseClass work.a.group.class;
   m4: Method return=Char;
```

```
            Return(cAttr);
        EndMethod;
    EndUseClass;
```

Programmer THREE is also responsible for compiling and testing this method implementation before the final system integrations. From this example, we found that a USECLASS block can be used to simplify group development in an object-oriented development environment.

**Example 2: Valid SCL Statements in a USECLASS Block**    This example shows that a method implementation block is the only SCL statement allowed in a USECLASS block. Other SCL statements such as the DECLARE statement are not allowed in a USECLASS block. However, these SCL statements can be written inside the method implementation block.

```
USECLASS work.classes.myclass.class;
     /* Method M1 without a signature */
   M1:  method;
       ...more SCL statements...
   endmethod;
     /* The next statements are invalid because  */
     /* they are not in a METHOD statement. They */
     /* will produce a compiler warning message. */
   DCL num n = 1; /* Invalid statement */
   n=10;    /* Invalid statement */
     /* Method M1 has a numeric parameter. */
   M1:  method n: num;
       /* Any SCL statement can be applied in the */
       /* method implementation block. */
       DCL num n;
       n = n + 1;
       ...more SCL statements...
   endmethod;
     /* Method M1 has a character parameter. */
   M1:  method s: char;
       DCL Char arr(3);
       DCL num i;
       DO i = 1 to dim(arr);
          arr(i) = s;
       END;
       ...more SCL statements...
   endmethod;
     /* The next statement is invalid because */
     /* it is not in a METHOD statement.      */
   if s=1 then
      put 'pass';
      /* Other methods */
   M2:  method return=num;
       ...more SCL statements...
       return(1);
   endmethod;
 ENDUSECLASS;
```

**Example 3: Bypassing _SELF_ References in a USECLASS Block**    Assume that there are four class attributes defined for a class: N1 and N2 are numeric attributes, and C1 and C2 are character string attributes. Both M1 methods are class methods. One of the M1 methods takes no parameter. The other M1 method takes one numeric parameter. The private method M2 is used as a debugging routine. If the variables or methods are class attributes or class methods, short-cut syntax (see also "Referencing Class Methods or Attributes" on page 99) can be used to bypass dot notation.

```
Import Sashelp.Fsp.Colleciton.Class;
Useclass work.classes.another.class;

    _init: method / (State='O');
        /* Equivalent of _super._init();   */
        /* or call super(_self_,'_init'); */
    _super();
        /* Equivalent to _self_.n1=1  */
    n1=1;
        /* Local variable n2 dominates */
        /* class attribute n2           */
    n2=1;
        /* Use SAS function ABS  */
    n3(1)=abs(n2);
        /* Equivalent to _self_.c1='a' */
    c1='a';
        /* Local variable c2 dominates */
        /* class attribute c2           */
    c2='a';
    endmethod;

m1: method;
        /* Equivalent to if _self_.n1>0 then */
    if n1>0 then
        /* Equivalent to _self_.n1 + 1     */
        n1+1;
    else
            /* Equivalent to           */
            /* _self_.m1(_self_.n1);   */
        m1(n1);
    endmethod;

    /* Method m1 with numeric parameter */
m1: method n: num;
        if (n < 0) then
            n = ---n;
        /* - Invoke M1 method --- */
        m1(n);
        m2(n+n);
        DCL Collection col = _NEW_ Collection();
        /* -- Must use the dot notation here - */
        col.add(3);
    endMethod;

    /* - Private Debugging method --- */
m2: Private Method n:Num;
        put 'Debugging ' n=;
```

```
        endMethod;

endUseClass;
```

## Example 4: Subclassing TextEntry_c for FRAME Programming

The class Mywidget is defined using SCL class syntax. First, edit WORK.A.MYWIDGET.SCL and include the following source:

```
Import Sashelp.Classes;
Class work.a.Mywidget.class Extends textEntry_c;
    m1: Public Method c: char / (scl='work.a.myClass.scl');
EndClass;
```

Issue the SAVECLASS command to compile this program and create the CLASS entry WORK.A.MYWIDGET.CLASS.

Edit WORK.A.MYCLASS.SCL, using USECLASS to include the method implementations.

```
Useclass work.a.Mywidget.class;
    m1: Method c:char;
        text = c; /* Equivalent to _SELF_.text = c; */
                  /* Text is an class attribute    */
        EndMethod;
EndUseClass;
```

Compile this program.

Now edit WORK.A.B.FRAME, and in the component window add the Mywidget class to the list (via the AddClasses button on the pop-up menu). Drag the Mywidget class to the frame and in the frame's SCL source, enter

```
Init:
    Mywidget1.m1('Hello! ');
    Return;
Main;
    Return;
```

Compile and TESTAF this program. You should see Mywidget with "Hello!" in the text field. This example could also be done using only the CLASS block (without USECLASS). Just put the method implementation directly in the CLASS block.

```
Import Sashelp.Classes;
Class Mywidget Extends TextEntry_C;
    m1: Method c:Char;
        Text = c;
        EndMethod;
EndClass;
```

## See Also

"ARRAY" on page 254

"CLASS" on page 277

"CREATESCL" on page 316

"DECLARE" on page 330

"ENDCLASS" on page 366

"METHOD" on page 540

# _VALUE_

**Contains the value of a FRAME entry component**

**Category:** System Variable

**Details** _VALUE_ is a system variable. It is provided automatically by the FRAME entry in SAS/AF, but the SCL compiler does not automatically create a space for it in the SCL data vector. As a result, you get a warning when you compile a FRAME or SCL entry that uses _VALUE_. The warning is generated because _VALUE_ is being referenced at compile time, but no value is assigned to it until run time. You can safely ignore this warning. If you prefer to prevent the warning message from being generated, use the following assignment statement at the top of your program:

```
_value_ = _value_;
```

If the FRAME entry component has a character value, then you must declare _VALUE_ as a character variable using the DECLARE or LENGTH statement.

Numeric FRAME entry components and character FRAME entry components cannot share the same methods if the methods use _VALUE_, because _VALUE_ cannot be declared as both a numeric and character variable in the same SCL entry. Doing so results in one of the following execution errors:

```
ERROR: Expecting string ($),
       received SCL number (symbol '_VALUE_').
ERROR: Expecting number (#),
       received SCL string (symbol '_VALUE_').
```

_VALUE_ has a valid value only when a FRAME entry or a method for a FRAME entry component is running.

## Example

Suppose a FRAME entry contains two Version 6 text entry controls, OBJ1 and OBJ2. OBJ1 is subclassed, and its _select method is defined as follows:

```
length _value_ text $20;
SELECT: method;
   _frame_._getWidgets('obj2',obj2);
   obj2._getText(text);
   _value_ = text;
endmethod;
```

When OBJ1 is modified, the _select method queries the object identifier for OBJ2 and retrieves its value. It then assigns that value to OBJ1 by assigning TEXT to _VALUE_.

## See Also

"_SELF_" on page 643

"_METHOD_" on page 548

# VARFMT

**Returns the format that is assigned to a SAS table column**

**Category:**  Variable

## Syntax

*format=***VARFMT**(*table-id,var-num*);

**format**
> contains the format that was assigned to the specified column.
>> Type: Character

**table-id**
> is the identifier that was assigned when the table was opened. If *table-id* is invalid, the program halts.
>> Type: Numeric

**var-num**
> is the number of the column's position in the SAS table. This number is adjacent to the column in the list that is produced by the CONTENTS procedure. The VARNUM function returns this number.
>> Type: Numeric

**Details**    If no format has been assigned to the column, a blank string is returned.

## Example

Obtain the format of the column NAME in the SAS table MYDATA:

```
length fmt $ 12;
dsid=open('mydata','i');
if dsid then
   do;
      fmt=varfmt(dsid,varnum(dsid,'name'));
      rc=close(dsid);
   end;
```

## See Also

"VARINFMT" on page 706

"VARNUM" on page 713

# VARINFMT

**Returns the informat that is assigned to a SAS table column**

**Category:**  Variable

## Syntax

*informat*=**VARINFMT**(*table-id*,*var-num*);

**informat**
>    contains the informat that is assigned to the column.
>       Type: Character

**table-id**
>    is the identifier that was assigned when the table was opened. If *table-id* is invalid, the program halts.
>       Type: Numeric

**var-num**
>    is the number of the column in the SAS table. This number is adjacent to the column in the list that is produced by the CONTENTS procedure. The VARNUM function returns this number.
>       Type: Numeric

**Details**    If no informat has been assigned to the column, a blank string is returned.

## Example

Obtain the informat of the column NAME in the SAS table MYDATA:

```
length infmt $ 12;
tableid=open('mydata','i');
if tableid then
    do;
        infmt=varinfmt(tableid,varnum(tableid,'name'));
        rc=close(tableid);
    end;
```

## See Also

"VARFMT" on page 705

"VARNUM" on page 713

# VARLABEL

**Returns the label that is assigned to a SAS table column**

Category:   Variable

## Syntax

*cval*=**VARLABEL**(*table-id*,*var-num*);

*cval*

    contains the label that is assigned to the specified column.
      Type:  Character

*table-id*

    is the identifier that was assigned when the table was opened. If *table-id* is invalid,
    the program halts.
      Type:  Numeric

*var-num*

    is the number of the column in the SAS table. This number is adjacent to the column
    in the list that is produced by the CONTENTS procedure. The VARNUM function
    returns this number.
      Type:  Numeric

**Details**    If no label has been assigned to the column, a blank string is returned.

## Example

Obtain the label of the column NAME in the SAS table MYDATA:

```
length lab $ 40;
dsid=open('mydata','i');
if dsid then
    do;
        lab=varlabel(dsid,varnum(dsid,'name'));
        rc=close(dsid);
    end;
```

## See Also

"VARNUM" on page 713

# VARLEN

**Returns the length of a SAS table column**

Category:   Variable

## Syntax

*length*=**VARLEN**(*table-id*,*var-num*);

*length*

    contains the length of the column.
      Type:  Numeric

*table-id*
is the identifier that was assigned when the table was opened. If *table-id* is invalid, the program halts.
Type: Numeric

*var-num*
is the number of the column in the SAS table. This number is adjacent to the column in the list that is produced by the CONTENTS procedure. The VARNUM function returns this number.
Type: Numeric

## Example

Obtain the length of the column ADDRESS in the SAS table MYDATA:

```
dsid=open('mydata','i');
if dsid then
   do;
       namelen=varlen(dsid,varnum(dsid,'address'));
       rc=close(dsid);
   end;
```

## See Also

"VARNUM" on page 713

# VARLEVEL

**Reports the unique values of a SAS table column**

**Category:** Variable

## Syntax

*rc=***VARLEVEL**(*array-name,n-level,table-id,var-name*);

*rc*
contains the return code for the operation:

| | |
|---|---|
| 0 | successful |
| ≠0 | not successful |

Type: Numeric

*array-name*
is the array that will contain the unique column values. This should be a character array with an element size that is large enough to hold the longest value. VARLEVEL assigns to array items the unique values of the SAS table column *var-name*.
Type: Character

*n-level*
is the name of the variable in which the function stores the number of unique values (or levels). This variable must be initialized to a nonmissing value before its value is set by the VARLEVEL function.

*Note:* This parameter is an update parameter. See "Input, Output, and Update Parameters" on page 34 for more information. △
Type: Numeric

**table-id**
is the identifier that was assigned when the table was opened. If *table-id* is invalid, the program halts.
Type: Numeric

**var-name**
is the column for which unique values are to be returned.
Type: Character

**Details** VARLEVEL fills the array *array-name* with the unique values of the SAS table column *var-name*.

This function returns values to the specified array. It also returns the total number of unique values in the *n-level* argument. Therefore, the second argument to this function cannot be a literal. If the number of unique values found exceeds the dimension of the array, the function returns only DIM(*array-name*) levels. That is, VARLEVEL requires the static allocation of an array that is big enough to hold all the unique values.

LVARLEVEL provides the same functionality, but it stores the unique values in an SCL list rather than an array. Because an SCL list can grow dynamically, you should consider using it rather than VARLEVEL.

### Example

Get the unique formatted values for the table column X. Use ASORT to sort those values in ascending order. If NLEVELS is greater than 25, then only the first 25 values are written to the array.

```
array values {25} $ 20;
tableid=open('mylib.data','i');
nlevels=0;
rc=varlevel(values,nlevels,tableid,'x');
rc=asort(values);
do i=1 to dim(values);
   put values(i);
end;
rc=close(tableid);
```

### See Also

"LVARLEVEL" on page 531

"VARNAME" on page 712

"VARSTAT" on page 714

# VARLIST

**Displays a dialog window that lists the columns in a SAS table, and returns the user's selections**
**Category:** SAS Table

## Syntax

*selections*=**VARLIST**(*table-id,var-type,num-sel<,message
<,autoclose<,sel-order<,exclude<,select>>>>>);*

**selections**
> contains one or more user selections from the list, or a blank if no selection is made. Multiple selections are separated by blanks. By default, *selections* is 200 bytes long. To accomodate values longer than 200 bytes, explicitly declare *selections* with a longer length.
> Type: Character

**table-id**
> is the identifier that was assigned when the table was opened. If *table-id* is invalid, the program halts.
> Type: Numeric

**var-type**
> specifies the data type of the columns to display in the list:

> | `'C'` | The list contains only character columns. |
> |---|---|
> | `'N'` | The list contains only numeric columns. |
> | `'A'` | The list contains all of the columns. (This is the default.) |

> Type: Character

**num-sel**
> is the maximum number of items a user can select from the list. The default is 1. To display the list for information purposes only (no selections allowed), specify **0**. To specify an unlimited number of selections, use a value such as 9999 that is larger than the number of available selections. A user cannot make a number of selections that exceeds the number of items in the list.
> Type: Numeric

**message**
> is the text for a message to display above the selection list. The default message tells users to make up to the number of selections specified in *num-sel.*
> Type: Character

**autoclose**
> is an obsolete argument but is retained for compatibility with earlier releases. If you want to specify a value for *sel-order, exclude,* or *select,* then specify ' ' as a placeholder for this argument.
> Type: Character

**sel-order**
> is an obsolete argument but is retained for compatibility with earlier releases. If you want to specify a value for *exclude* or *select,* then you must specify ' ' as a placeholder.
> Type: Character

**exclude**
> lists one or more columns to exclude from the selection list. Separate multiple columns with at least one blank.
> Type: Character

*select*

lists one or more columns to select for the selection list. Separate multiple columns with at least one blank.

Type: Character

**Details** VARLIST opens a dialog window in which a user can select columns from a SAS table. The columns specified in the VARLIST function are listed in the **Available** list. To make a selection, a user selects one or more columns and then presses the arrow control that points to the **Selected** list. The selected values move to the **Selected** list and are removed from the **Available** list. The **Variable Details** fields display the type, length, and description of a selected column.

For each column in the table, VARLIST uses the following steps to determine which columns to display:

- □ If one or more column names are specified in the *select* argument, VARLIST includes those columns in the selection list. Columns that are not in the *select* argument list do not appear in the selection list.

- □ If one or more column names are specified in the *exclude* argument, VARLIST excludes those columns from the selection list.

- □ If a value is specified for the *var-type* argument, VARLIST excludes all columns that are not of the specified type.

You can provide default values that will be initially selected when the column selection list is displayed. To do this, assign the column name to the *selections* variable before calling VARLIST. When the window opens, the column name appears in the **Selected** list.

If a user closes the dialog window without making a selection, VARLIST returns a blank value unless there was an initial value for the *selections* column before VARLIST was called.

The values for all selections can be returned in the current result list, if one is available. The current result list is a special SCL list that is automatically filled with the values selected from a selection list. To use a current result list, use the MAKELIST function to create the list, and use the CURLIST function to designate it as the current result list. The current result list must exist before you call the VARLIST function. You can use GETITEMC to retrieve these selections.

## Examples

- □ Display all columns and allow the user to select only one:

  ```
  select=varlist(dsid,'a',1);
  ```

- □ This next statement displays only character columns, allows two selections, uses a custom message, moves the selections to the top of the list when they are selected, and excludes the columns NAME and ADDRESS:

  ```
  select=varlist(dsid,'c',2,'Choose a column',
                 '','','name address');
  ```

- □ Display a dialog window that contains the character columns from an open SAS table, excluding the columns NAME and ADDRESS. Users can make two selections. The selected column names are retrieved from the current result list. LISTLEN returns the number of selections because there is only one element in the list for each selection made.

  ```
  listid=makelist();
  rc=curlist(listid);
  select=varlist(dsid,'c',2,
  ```

```
            'Choose a column','','','name address');
        n=listlen(listid);
        do i=1 to n;
            varname=getitemc(listid,i);
            put varname=;
        end;
```

## See Also

"DATALISTC and DATALISTN" on page 326

"LISTC and LISTN" on page 518

"SHOWLIST" on page 667

---

# VARNAME

**Returns the name of a SAS table column**

**Category:**  Variable

---

## Syntax

*var-name*=**VARNAME**(*table-id*,*var-num*);

**var-name**
> contains the name of the column.
>> Type: Character

**table-id**
> is the identifier that was assigned when the table was opened. If *table-id* is invalid, the program halts.
>> Type: Numeric

**var-num**
> is the number of the column in the SAS table. This is the number that is adjacent to the column in the list that is produced by the CONTENTS procedure. The VARNUM function returns this number.
>> Type: Numeric

## Example

Copy the names of the first five columns in the SAS table CITY into an SCL variable. The column names are separated by blanks.

```
length varlist $ 80;

tableid=open('city','i');
varlist=' ';
do i=1 to min(5,attrn(tableid,'nvars'));
    j=9*(i-1)+1;
    substr(varlist,j,8)=varname(tableid,i);
end;
```

```
put varlist=;
rc=close(tableid);
```

## See Also

"VARNUM" on page 713

# VARNUM

**Returns the number of a SAS table column**

**Category:** Variable

## Syntax

*var-num*=**VARNUM**(*table-id*,*var-name*);

**var-num**
contains the position number of the column in the SAS table, or 0 if the column is not in the SAS table.
Type: Numeric

**table-id**
is the identifier that was assigned when the table was opened. If *table-id* is invalid, the program halts.
Type: Numeric

**var-name**
is the name of the column.
Type: Character

**Details** VARNUM returns the number of a SAS table column.

## Example

Obtain the number of a column in the SAS table MYDATA, using the value of the NAME variable:

```
tableid=open('mydata','i');
if (sasname(name)) then do;
   citynum=varnum(tableid,name);
   if (citynum=0) then
      _msg_='The column is not in the table.';
   else
      _msg_='The column number is '|| citynum;
end;
else
   _msg_='Invalid SAS name--please reenter.';
```

### See Also

"VARNAME" on page 712

---

# VARSTAT

**Calculates simple statistics for SAS table columns**

**Category:**  Variable

---

## Syntax

*rc*=**VARSTAT**(*table-id,varlist-1,statistics,varlist-2*);

***rc***
contains the return code for the operation:

0                    successful

≠0                   not successful
   Type: Numeric

***table-id***
is the identifier that was assigned when the table was opened. If *table-id* is invalid, the program halts.
   Type: Numeric

***varlist-1***
specifies one or more numeric columns for which to create the statistics.
   Type: Character

***statistics***
specifies one or more statistics, separated by blanks, from the table below. For more information about these statistics, see the *SAS/STAT User's Guide.*
   Type: Character

***varlist-2***
specifies one or more output variables to contain the values produced by the specified statistics. The number of output variables must equal the number of columns in *varlist-1* multiplied by the number of *statistics*.

   *Note:*   These parameters are update parameters. See "Input, Output, and Update Parameters" on page 34 for more information. △
   Type: Numeric

| Statistic | Description |
|-----------|-------------|
| CSS | sum of squares of a column's values, corrected for the mean |
| CV | coefficient of variation of a column's values |
| KURTOSIS | kurtosis of a column's values |
| MAX | largest value for a column |
| MEAN | mean of a nonmissing column's values |

| Statistic | Description |
| --- | --- |
| MEDIAN | median value for a column |
| MIN | smallest value for a column |
| MODE | value with the most rows for a column |
| N | number of rows on which calculations are based |
| NMISS | number of rows with missing values |
| NUNIQUE | number of rows having a unique value for a column |
| RANGE | range of values for a column |
| SKEWNESS | skewness of a column's values |
| STD | standard deviation of a column's values |
| STDERR | standard error of the mean |
| SUM | sum of nonmissing column values |
| USS | uncorrected sum of squares for a column |
| VAR | variance of a column's values |

**Details**  If more than one input column is specified with more than one statistic, then each statistic is calculated on all columns before the next statistic is calculated.

## Example

Calculate the maximum, mean, and minimum values for the columns I and X from the table MY.NUMBERS:

```
tablename='my.numbers';
length imax xmax imean xmean xmin imin 8;
 /* Declare the results as numeric. */
varname='i x';
numberid=open(tablename);
if (numberid=z0) then
    do;
        _msg_='Cannot open '||tablename;
        return;
    end;
statcode=varstat(numberid,varname,
    'max mean min',imax,xmax,imean,xmean,imin,xmin);
put 'Column X';
put xmax= xmean= xmin=;
put 'Column I';
put imax= imean= imin=;
rc=close(numberid);
return;
```

## See Also

"LVARLEVEL" on page 531

"VARLEVEL" on page 708

---

# VARTYPE

**Returns the data type of a SAS table column**

**Category:** Variable

## Syntax

*type*=**VARTYPE**(*table-id*,*var-num*);

*type*
  contains the data type of the column:

  C                    character column

  N                    numeric column
      Type: Character

*table-id*
  is the identifier that was assigned when the table was opened. If *table-id* is invalid, the program halts.
      Type: Numeric

*var-num*
  is the position number of the column in the SAS table. This is the number that is adjacent to the column in the list that is produced by the CONTENTS procedure. VARNUM function returns this number.
      Type: Numeric

## Example

Place the first five numeric columns of the SAS table MYDATA into an SCL variable:

```
length varlist $ 44;
dsid=open('mydata','i');
varlist=' ';
j=0;
do i=1 to nvar(dsid) while (j<5);
if (vartype(dsid,i)='N') then
   do;
      varlist=varlist||' '||varname(dsid,i);
      j+1;
   end;
end;
rc=close(dsid);
```

### See Also

"MODVAR" on page 551

"VARNUM" on page 713

---

# WAIT

**Suspends execution of the next program statement**

**Category:** Control Flow and Utility

---

## Syntax

**CALL WAIT**(*seconds*);

***seconds***
is the number of seconds before execution resumes.
Type: Numeric

**Details**    You can also use WAIT to allow the screen to refresh before performing another task.

## Example

Wait for 4.5 seconds between the times stored in TIME1 and TIME2, and then display those values in the LOG window:

```
time1 = datetime();
call wait( 4.5 );
time2 = datetime();
diff=putn((time2-time1),'4.1');
put time1= time2= diff=;
```

Take the last three digits before and after the decimal point from the two times: TIME1=872.229 and TIME2=876.749. Subtracting TIME2 from TIME1 results in 4.52 seconds total wait time.

```
time1=1069234872.22999
time2=1069234876.74999
diff=4.5
```

Create numeric text entry controls named START and FINISH and assign the format DATETIME20.2 to them. Enter the following program in the frame's SCL entry:

```
init:
   start.text=datetime();
   call wait(3.1);
   finish.text=datetime();
return;
```

# WDEF

**Resizes the active window**

**Category:** Window

## Syntax

**CALL WDEF**(*start-row,start-col,num-rows,num-cols*);

*start-row*
    is the starting row for the window.
        Type: Numeric

*start-col*
    is the starting column for the window.
        Type: Numeric

*num-rows*
    is the number of rows for the window.
        Type: Numeric

*num-cols*
    is the number of columns for the window.
        Type: Numeric

**Details**    The active window is redefined and displayed in the area specified by WDEF. The WDEF routine performs the same function as the WDEF command. See the SAS online Help for more information about the WDEF command.

For windows that are not of type STANDARD, you must call WDEF before the window is displayed.

WDEF is frequently used to define a smaller size for a window that will be displayed along with a legend window.

## Example

Use WDEF to resize the current window to occupy the bottom half of the window before calling another program. The other program is sized to display in the top half of the window. Then, return the window back to its original size.

```
call wdef(13,1,12,80);
call wregion(1,1,11,80);
call display('tophalf.program');
call wdef(1,1,24,80);
```

## See Also

"WINFO" on page 721

"WREGION" on page 730

# WHERE

**Applies a WHERE clause to a SAS table**

**Category:** SAS Table

## Syntax

*sysrc*=**WHERE**(*table-id*<,*clause-1*<, . . . ,*clause-5*>>);

**sysrc**
 contains the return code for the operation:

| 0 | successful |
| >0 | not successful |
| 0< | the operation was completed, but a warning or a note was generated. If the row is locked, it is still fetched (read in), but a *sysrc* of **_SWNOUPD** is returned. |

 Type: Numeric

**table-id**
 is the identifier that was assigned when the table was opened. If *table-id* is invalid, the program halts.
 Type: Numeric

**clause-1, . . . , clause-5**
 is the condition for the search, expressed as a WHERE clause but without the keyword WHERE. The arguments *clause-1*, *clause-2*, *clause-3*, *clause-4*, and *clause-5* are treated as multiple lines of the WHERE clause.

 Each of the clauses, *clause-1* through *clause-5*, can contain multiple conditions separated by the AND operator. Each clause cannot exceed 200 bytes.

 If the clause starts with the keyword ALSO, then the new WHERE clause is considered to be a subclause of the current WHERE clause. Specifying no clauses undoes all current temporary WHERE clauses that have been applied to the SAS table.
 Type: Character

**Details**  The WHERE function may take advantage of indexing. The syntax of the WHERE clause is the same as for the WHERE statement in base SAS software. Any WHERE clause that is applied by the WHERE function is only temporary and is considered to be a subclause of any WHERE clause that was issued when the table was opened. To apply a permanent WHERE clause to a SAS table, use the WHERE= data set option following the table name in OPEN.

The WHERE clause subsets the rows to which you have access. You must then issue a function such as FETCH or FETCHOBS to read rows from the subset. When a WHERE clause is active, FETCHOBS fetches the specified row by counting only rows that meet the WHERE condition.

To create views with more complicated WHERE clauses, use the SQL procedure or the SUBMIT CONTINUE SQL statement.

To remove only the last WHERE condition, use

```
rc=WHERE(tableid,'undo');
```

To remove all WHERE conditions, use either of the following:

```
rc=WHERE(tableid);
rc=WHERE(tableid,'clear');
```

# Examples

**Example 1: Applying a Compound WHERE Clause**    Apply a WHERE clause to the SAS table MYDATA, which subsets the table into only those rows in which column X is equal to 1 and column Z is less than 0:

```
tableid=open('mydata','i');'
rc=where(tableid,'x=1 and z<0');
```

You can separate the WHERE clause into two clauses as follows. This is equivalent to the previous example.

```
tableid=open('mydata','i');
rc=where(tableid,'x=1','and z<0');
```

**Example 2: Applying a WHERE Clause in Separate SCL Statements**    Instead of using one WHERE clause, you can separate the WHERE clause into two statements. The following statements are equivalent to Example 1:

```
tableid=open('mydata','i');
rc=where(tableid,'x=1');
    ...more SCL statements...
rc=where(tableid,'also z<0');
```

**Example 3: Using a Numeric Variable in a WHERE Clause**    You can pass values from SCL variables to the WHERE clause. Subset the table referenced by TABLEID, based on the value that was entered for the numeric variable SCRNUM.

```
rc=where(tableid,'num= '||put(scrnum,5.));
```

**Example 4: Using a Character Variable in a WHERE Clause**    To subset a table based on a character value, you can use the quote function to return the quoted value. (Otherwise, you must use double quotation marks around the WHERE condition, because the quoted value itself must be enclosed in quotation marks.) Subset the table referenced by TABLEID based on the value that was entered for the character column SCRNAME. Use the QUOTE function to return the quoted value.

```
rc=where(tableid,'name= '||quote(scrname));
```

**Example 5: Combining WHERE Conditions into One Statement**    Combine the previous two WHERE conditions into one statement:

```
rc=where(tableid,'num= '||put(scrnum,5.)||'
    and name='||quote(scrname));
```

**Example 6: Determining Whether Any Rows Meet the WHERE Condition**    You can use the ATTRN function with the NLOBSF argument to check for rows that meet a WHERE condition, and then conditionally execute SCL code. Apply a WHERE clause to the SAS table MYDATA, which subsets the table into only those rows in which the column X is equal to 1. Use ATTRN with NLOBSF before fetching the first row of the subset.

```
tableid=open('mydata', 'i');
rc=where(tableid,'x=1');
if attrn(tableid,'nlobsf')>0 then
    rc=fetch(tableid);
```

### See Also

"ATTRC and ATTRN" on page 258

"OPEN" on page 576

"FETCH" on page 389

"FETCHOBS" on page 390

"SETKEY" on page 653

# WINFO

**Returns information about the current window**

**Category:** Window

## Syntax

*rc*=**WINFO**(*info-item*< ,*aux-info*>);

**rc**

contains the return code for the operation.
Type: Numeric

**info-item**

specifies either a characteristic of the window or an action. See "Values for *Info-item*" on page 722.
Type: Character

**aux-info**

specifies an additional argument that is required by some *info-item* actions:

*pane-number* (for **PANECOL**, **PANECCOL**, **PANECROW**, and **PANEROW**)
is the number of the pane to be queried. For example, in an extended table the non-scrollable section is pane 1 and the scrollable portion is pane 2.

*item-id* (for **PMENUGRAY**)
is the item identifier that you specified with the ID= option for the ITEM statement in PROC PMENU when you built the menu. Use the negative of the ID number to gray a selection, and use the positive ID number to ungray a selection.

*item-id* (for **PMENUSTATE**)
is the item identifier that you specified with the ID= option for the ITEM statement in PROC PMENU when you built the menu. Use the negative of the ID number to turn off the check mark or radio button for the selection, and use the positive ID number to turn on the check mark or radio button. Whether the menu selection gets a check mark or radio button depends on the value of the STATE= option when the menu was built.

*flag* (for **POPUP**)
can have the following values:

| | |
|---|---|
| 0 | disables pop-up events. |
| 1 | enables pop-up events. |

Type: Numeric

## Values for *Info-item*

The following list explains the meaning of the return code, *rc*, for each value that you can specify for *info-item*:

**BACKCOLOR**
WINFO returns 1 if the device supports background colors.

**BATCH**
WINFO returns 1 if the application is running in batch mode.

**COMMAND**
WINFO returns 1 if the window has a command line.

**CURSCREEN**
WINFO returns the number of the SCREEN or FRAME entry in which the cursor is located.

**CURSORCOL**
WINFO returns the column number of the cursor position.

**CURSORROW**
WINFO returns the row number of the cursor position.

**GRAPHICS**
WINFO returns 1 if the user's output device supports graphics.

**ICON**
WINFO returns the number of Institute-supplied icons available under the user's host operating system. See the SAS documentation for your operating system for information about whether SAS software supports icons under your host operating system.

**LOGON**
WINFO returns 1 if a logon was specified when the SAS/AF application was invoked.

**MAXCOL**
WINFO returns the maximum number of columns to which the window can grow, excluding the command and border areas.

**MAXROW**
WINFO returns the maximum number of rows to which the window can grow, excluding the command and border areas.

**MONO**
WINFO returns 1 if the device is monochrome.

**NSCREEN**
WINFO returns information about the windows currently open in an application:
FSEDIT applications return the number of screens that are defined for the current FSEDIT window.
FSVIEW applications return 4 to indicate the four parts of the FSVIEW window: the column title area, the row number or ID column area, the data area, and the area above the column titles.
SAS/AF applications return 1 or 2 if you used ^^^ or ¬ ¬ ¬ to divide the entry's window into two or more frames.

**NUMCOLS**
WINFO returns the current number of columns in the window.

**NUMROWS**
WINFO returns the current number of rows in the window.

**NUMXINCH**
>   WINFO returns the number of pixels per horizontal inch of the window (valid only for FRAME entries).

**NUMYINCH**
>   WINFO returns the number of pixels per vertical inch of the window (valid only for FRAME entries).

**NUMXPIXEL**
>   WINFO returns the window width in pixels (valid only for FRAME entries).

**NUMYPIXEL**
>   WINFO returns the window height in pixels (valid only for FRAME entries).

**PANECCOL**
>   WINFO returns the column position of the cursor relative to the pane of the window in which it resides. Use *aux-info* to specify the pane.

**PANECROW**
>   WINFO returns the row position of the cursor relative to the pane of the window in which it resides. Use *aux-info* to specify the pane.

**PANECOL**
>   WINFO returns the number of columns in a specified pane. Use *aux-info* to specify the pane.

**PANEROW**
>   WINFO returns the number of rows in a specified pane. Use *aux-info* to specify the pane.

**PMENU**
>   WINFO returns 1 if a PMENU entry has been specified for this program regardless of whether the PMENU facility is currently active for the window.

**PMENUGRAY**
>   WINFO returns 0 when it grays or ungrays selections in the window's pull-down menus. Use *aux-info* to specify which selection to gray or ungray.

**PMENUSTATE**
>   WINFO returns 0 when it enables or disables the state of a selection in the window's pull-down menus. Use *aux-info* to specify the state.

**POPUP**
>   WINFO returns 0 when it enables or disables pop-up events in the window. Use the *aux-info* argument to specify whether events are to be enabled or disabled.

**STARTCOL**
>   WINFO returns the current column on which the window starts.

**STARTROW**
>   WINFO returns the current row on which the window starts.

**UICON**
>   WINFO returns the number of user-defined icons available under the user's host operating system.

**XPIXCELL**
>   WINFO returns the width (in pixels) of the font used in the SAS windowing environment.

**XPIXEL**
>   WINFO returns the horizontal location (in pixels) of the most recent mouse event.

**YPIXCELL**
WINFO returns the height (in pixels) of the font used in the SAS windowing environment.

**YPIXEL**
WINFO returns the vertical location (in pixels) of the most recent mouse event.

## Example

Store the current size of the window, and then resize it back to its original size:

```
sr=winfo('startrow');
sc=winfo('startcol');
nr=winfo('numrows');
nc=winfo('numcols');
call display('top half');
call wdef(sr,sc,nr,nc);
```

## See Also

"WDEF" on page 718

"WREGION" on page 730

# WNAME

**Specifies a name for the active window**

**Category:**   Window

## Syntax

**CALL WNAME**(*window-name*);

***window-name***
is up to 80 characters for the window's name.
Type: Character

## Example

Use WNAME to change the window name to "TimeData Application":

```
call wname('TimeData Application');
```

### See Also

"WDEF" on page 718

"WINFO" on page 721

"WREGION" on page 730

# WORD

**Returns a word from a command that was issued with the command line, function keys, command processing, or a control**

**Category:** Command

## Syntax

*word-text*=**WORD**(*word-pos<,case>*);

**word-text**

contains the text of the word.
Type: Character

**word-pos**

is the position of the word to be retrieved from the command line. Specify either 1, 2, or 3 for the first, second, or third word.
Type: Numeric

**case**

is the type of case conversion to be performed:

`'L'`                    converts the word to all lowercase characters

`'U'`                    converts the word to all uppercase characters.
By default, SAS leaves all commands in the case in which they are entered.
Type: Character

**Details**     WORD returns the first, second, or third word of the command that was issued. A *word* is the text from the current position up to the next token, such as the end of a leading number, a blank, an operator, or a semicolon.

*Note:*  To retrieve more than three words, use NEXTWORD. △

To support custom commands in your application, you must use a CONTROL statement with either the ENTER, ALWAYS, or ALLCMDS option specified. When one of these options is specified in the CONTROL statement and when multiple commands are specified on the command line (separated by semicolons), the MAIN section is executed for each command. MAIN is executed only once if only one command is entered.

When CONTROL ALWAYS is specified, words entered on the command line that are not valid SAS commands are not flagged in error. See "CONTROL" on page 302 for information about the advantages of each CONTROL statement option before deciding which is best for your application.

WORD cannot capture windowing environment global commands, because the SCL program is not executed when a SAS windowing environment command is issued.

## Examples

**Example 1: Using WORD to Return the Value of the Command**    Suppose a user types the command **AXX BXX CXX DXX** on the command line. Use WORD to return the value of the command.

```
word1=word(1); put ''word1 is '' word1;
word2=word(2); put ''word2 is '' word2;
word3=word(3); put ''word3 is '' word3;
/* to retrieve more than three words, use NEXTWORD. */
call nextword();
word4=word(3); put ''word4 is '' word4;
```

The following output is produced:

```
word1 is AXX
word2 is BXX
word3 is CXX
word4 is DXX
```

**Example 2: Using WORD to Return an Alphanumeric Value**    Suppose the user enters **123abc** on the command line of the frame. Use WORD to return the value of the command.

```
init:
control enter;
return;

main:
dcl char word1 word2;
word1=word(1);
word2=word(2);
put word1= word2=;
return;
```

The following output is produced:

```
word1=123 word2=abc
```

## See Also

"CONTROL" on page 302

"NEXTCMD" on page 567

"NEXTWORD" on page 568

# WORDTYPE

**Identifies the word type of a word on the command line**

**Category:**  Command

## Syntax

*type*=**WORDTYPE**(*word-pos*);

*type*
contains one of the following word types:

DATE
The word is a SAS date constant such as 25AUG98.

DATETIME
The word is a SAS datetime constant such as 25AUG98:08:15:39.30.

EOD
There are no more words on the command line (end of command).

INTEGER
The word is an integer such as 6.

LABEL
The word type is unknown to the SAS tokenizer.

NAME
The word is a SAS name such as DATA.

NUMBER
The word is a numeric constant that contains a decimal point '.', or a scientific notation 'E' for example, 6.5.

SEMI
The word is a semicolon.

SPECIAL
The word is a special operator such as '=', '+', and so on.

STRING
The word is a character string such as MYDATA.

TIME
The word is a SAS time constant such as 08:16:30.

UNKNOWN
The word type is unknown to the SAS tokenizer.
Type: Character

*word-pos*
is the position of the word to be retrieved from the command line. Specify either 1, 2, or 3 for the first, second, or third word.
Type: Numeric

**Details**    WORDTYPE returns the type of the first, second, or third word that is currently on the command line. A word is the text at the current position and up to the end of a leading number or the next blank or semicolon. You can use this function with WORD.

To support custom commands in your application, you must use a CONTROL statement with either the ENTER, ALWAYS, or ALLCMDS option specified. When CONTROL ALWAYS is specified, words entered on the command line that are not valid SAS commands are not flagged in error. See "CONTROL" on page 302 for information about the advantages of each CONTROL statement option before deciding which is best for your application.

## Example

Return the type of the four words that are currently on the command line:

```
wl=word(1); wltype=wordtype(1); put wl= wltype=;
w2=word(2); w2type=wordtype(2); put w2= w2type=;
w3=word(3); w3type=wordtype(3); put w3= w3type=;
CALL NEXTWORD();
w4=word(3); w4type=wordtype(4); put w4= w4type=;
```

If a user types **ABC = 3  9** on the command line, then this program produces the following output:

```
wl=ABC wltype=NAME
w2==w2type=SPECIAL
w3=3 w3type=INTEGER
w4=9 w4type=INTEGER
```

## See Also

"CONTROL" on page 302

"NEXTWORD" on page 568

"WORD" on page 725

# WOUTPUT

### Manipulates the OUTPUT window

**Category:** Window

## Syntax

*sysrc*=**WOUTPUT**(*action*< ,*argument-1*<, . . . ,*argument-3*>>);

**sysrc**
  contains the return code for the operation:

  0                          successful

  ≠0                         not successful
    Type: Numeric

**action**
  is an action to perform, from the list below.
    Type: Character

**argument-1, . . . , argument-3**
  are additional arguments that can be specified for some of the actions, as indicated in the following list.
    Type: Character

**'CLEAR'**
  clears the OUTPUT window. There are no additional arguments for this action.

**'DROPNOTE'**
  clears the note marked with the 'NOTE' and causes it to use its default behavior to write only the last output.

**'FILE'**

writes the current contents of the OUTPUT window to an external file. This action allows two additional arguments:

*argument-1*

is the fileref for the external file to which the window contents are to be written. This argument is required.

*argument-2*

optionally specifies append mode. By default, each new output replaces any current contents of the external file. Specify the value **'A'** to append the output to the external file instead.

**'NOTE'**

puts the pointer at the end of the current output. The NOTE action has a direct effect on the FILE, PRINT and SAVE actions. When the output is written via WOUTPUT, the pointer is reset to get the next output.

**'POPOFF'**

turns off the AUTOPOP option of the OUTPUT window.

**'POPON'**

turns on the AUTOPOP option of the OUTPUT window.

**'PRINT'**

prints the current contents of the OUTPUT window. This action allows three additional arguments, all of which are optional:

*argument-1*

is the name of a form to use to control printing. Use *name*.FORM or simply *name* to specify a form in the current catalog. Use *libref.catalog.name*.FORM or *libref.catalog.name* to specify a form in a different catalog. The default form is the one specified in the FORMNAME option.

*argument-2*

is the fileref for a print file. If this argument is blank or if it is not specified, the output is sent to the default system printer.

*argument-3*

specifies append mode. Use the value **'A'** to append the output to the current contents of the print file. If this argument is blank or if it is not specified, then each new output replaces the previous contents of the print file.

**'SAVE'**

saves the current contents of the OUTPUT window in a catalog entry of type SOURCE, LOG, or OUTPUT. This action allows three additional arguments:

*argument-1*

is the name of the entry in which the window contents are saved. The name can be a one- or three-level name. A one-level name saves the entry in SASUSER.PROFILE.*name*.OUTPUT. A three-level name saves the entry in *libref.catalog.name*.OUTPUT. You can also use a four-level name of the form *libref.catalog.entry.type*, where *type* is SOURCE, LOG, or OUTPUT. This argument is required.

*argument-2*

is an optional description of up to 40 characters.

*argument-3*

optionally specifies append mode. Specify the value **'A'** to append the output to the current contents of the entry. By default, each new output replaces the previous contents of the entry.

**Details**    The list of options varies depending on the action specified.

## Example

Print the OUTPUT window and append it to the file to which the fileref EXTERN has previously been assigned. Use the form specified in a previous FORMNAME option:

```
rc=woutput('print','','extern','a');
```

# WREGION

**Defines the boundaries for the next window that is displayed**

**Category:**   Window

## Syntax

**CALL WREGION**(*start-row,start-col,num-rows,num-cols,options*);

*start-row*
> is the starting row for the next window.
> > Type: Numeric

*start-col*
> is the starting column for the next window.
> > Type: Numeric

*num-rows*
> is the number of rows for the next window.
> > Type: Numeric

*num-cols*
> is the number of columns for the next window.
> > Type: Numeric

*options*
> are one or more window attributes that the window's size needs to accommodate:
>
> ''
> > no command line, command menu, or scroll bars
>
> '**CMDLINE**'
> > a command area
>
> '**HSBAR**'
> > a horizontal scroll bar
>
> '**INNERSIZE**'
> > interior size is determined by the values of *num-rows* and *num-cols*
>
> '**PMENU**'
> > a command menu
>
> '**VSBAR**'
> > a vertical scroll bar
> > Type: Character

**Details**    The size of the next window depends on whether it has a command area, a pmenu, and scroll bars. (The command area includes the message line.) By default, WREGION assumes that the next window will have all of these attributes. You can use *options* to change this assumption. Note that *options* does not cause the next window to have these attributes. Rather, it helps WREGION determine the correct size.

'INNERSIZE' specifies that the values of *num-rows* and *num-cols* will control the interior size of the window. Normally, the *num-rows* and *num-cols* control the exterior size of the window (including the borders).

WREGION does not affect the size of subsequent FSEDIT windows that are opened by using CALL FSEDIT. The function cannot resize windows when a SAS/AF or FSEDIT application is called with the NOBORDER option.

## Examples

□ Specify a WREGION for the LEGEND window. Notice that the *options* argument to WREGION is a null string, designating that none of the display options are used in the LEGEND window. The window size is four rows long: two lines of text plus the top and bottom borders.

```
call wregion(1,1,4,80,'');
call putlegend
   (1,'This is legend line 1','yellow','none');
call putlegend
   (2,'This is legend line 2','yellow','none');
call legend
   ('mylegend window name','','white','reverse');
```

□ Execute a WREGION function and invoke a PROGRAM entry. The application window for the entry has a command line. However, because scrolling is not necessary, the HBAR and VBAR options are not specified. Only the CMDLINE option is specified.

```
call wregion(1,1,20,80,'cmdline');
call display('another.program',a,b,c);
```

## See Also

"WDEF" on page 718

"WINFO" on page 721

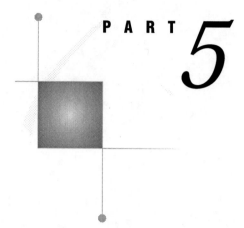

P A R T 5

# Appendices

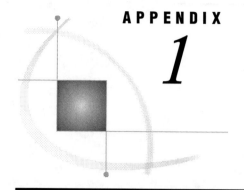

# APPENDIX

## 1

# Commands Used with the IMGCTRL, IMGOP and PICFILL Functions

## CONVERT

Converts an image to the specified image type and depth

### Syntax

*rc*=**IMGOP**(*task-id*, 'CONVERT', *type*);

*type*
   specifies the type of image to convert to:

'**GRAY**'
   a monochrome (black and white) image

'**CMAP**'
   a color-mapped image

'**RGBA**'
   an RGB image
   Type: Character

**Details**   CONVERT performs dithering, quantizing, and other operations in order to reduce an image to a simpler form. It can also create a two-color (black and white) RGB image by converting a monochrome image to an RGBA image. Images that are originally gray-scale or black and white cannot be colorized. CONVERT acts on the currently selected image.

### Example

Convert an RGB image to a dithered monochrome image:

```
rc=imgop(task-id,'READ','rgb.tif');
rc=imgop(task-id,'CONVERT','GRAY');
rc=imgop(task-id,'WRITE','gray.tif');
```

Convert the GRAY image back to RGB. Because all color information is lost, the final RGB image has only two colors:

```
rc=imgop(task-id,'READ','gray.tif');
rc=imgop(task-id,'CONVERT','RGBA');
```

```
        rc=imgop(task-id,'WRITE','rgb.tif');
```

# COPY

**Copies an image**

## Syntax

*rc*=**IMGOP**(*task-id*, 'COPY', *source-image-id*< , *destination-image-id*>);

***source-image-id***
    is the identifier of the image to copy.
        Type: Numeric

***destination-image-id***
    is the new identifier of the copied image.
        Type: Numeric

**Details**    COPY copies an image from *source-image-id* to *destination-image-id*. That is, it assigns another image identifier to an image. If *destination-image-id* is not specified, it copies to the currently selected image. The copied image is not automatically displayed.

## Example

Simulate zooming and unzooming an image:

```
path=lnamemk(5,'sashelp.imagapp.gkids','format=cat');
rc=imgop(task-id,'SELECT',1);
rc=imgop(task-id,'READ_PASTE',1,1,path);

if (zoom eq 1) then
    do;
        rc=imgop(task-id,'SELECT',2);
        rc=imgop(task-id,'COPY',1,2);
        rc=imgop(task-id,'SCALE',width,height);
        rc=imgop(task-id,'PASTE',1,1);

        if (unzoom=1) then
            do;
                rc=imgop(task-id,'UNPASTE');
            end;

    end;
```

# CREATE_IMAGE

**Creates a new image that is stored in memory**

## Syntax

*rc=**IMGOP**(task-id, 'CREATE_IMAGE', width, height, type, depth<, color-map-len>);*

**width**
   is the width of the new image in pixels.
      Type: Numeric

**height**
   is the height of new image in pixels.
      Type: Numeric

**type**
   is the type of the image. These values match the values that QUERYN returns for type:

   | | |
   |---|---|
   | 1 | specifies a GRAY image (1–bit depth) |
   | 2 | specifies a CMAP image 8–bit depth) |
   | 3 | specifies an RGB image (24–bit depth) |

      Type: Numeric

**depth**
   is the depth of the new image. The depth must match the value given for *type*, above.
      Type: Numeric

**color-map-len**
   is the number of colors in the color map. This value is used only with a *type* of 2 (CMAP). If not specified, it defaults to 256.
      Type: Numeric

**Details**    CREATE_IMAGE creates an "empty" image in which all data and color map values are set to 0 (black). You must use SET_COLORS to set the color map and use SET_PIXEL to set the pixel values. Note that processing an entire image in this manner can be very slow.

## Example

   Copy an image. Note that the COPY command is a much faster way of doing this, and this example is here to show how to use the commands.

```
COPY:
   width=0; height=0; type=0; depth=0; cmaplen=0;
   r=0; g=0; b=0; pixel=0; pixel2=0; pixel3=0;

   task-id=imginit(0,'nodisplay');
   task-id2=imginit(0,'nodisplay');
```

```
    /* read and query original image */
rc=imgop(task-id,'READ','first.tif');
rc=imgop(task-id,'QUERYN','WIDTH',width);
rc=imgop(task-id,'QUERYN','HEIGHT',height);
rc=imgop(task-id,'QUERYN','TYPE',type);
rc=imgop(task-id,'QUERYN','DEPTH',depth);
rc=imgop(task-id,'QUERYN','COLORMAP_LEN',
        cmaplen);

    /* Create the new image */
rc=imgop(task-id2,'CREATE_IMAGE',width,height,
        type,depth);

    /* Copy the color map */
do i=0 to cmaplen-1;
   rc=imgop(task-id,'GET_COLORS',i,r,g,b);
   rc=imgop(task-id2,'SET_COLORS',i,r,g,b);
end;

    /* Copy the pixels */
do h=0 to height-1;
   do w=0 to width-1;
     rc=imgop(task-id,'GET_PIXEL',w,h,pixel,
            pixel2,pixel3);
     rc=imgop(task-id2,'SET_PIXEL',w,h,pixel,
            pixel2,pixel3);
   end;
end;

    /* Write out the new image */
rc=imgop(task-id2,'WRITE','second.tif',
        'format=tif');
rc=imgterm(task-id);
rc=imgterm(task-id2);
return;
```

# CROP

### Crops the selected image

## Syntax

*rc*=**IMGOP**(*task-id*, 'CROP', *start-x, start-y, end-x, end-y*);

*region-id*=**PICFILL**(*graphenv-id, type, ulr, ulc,*
    *lrr, lrc, source*<, 'CROP'<, *arguments*>>);

*start-x*
    is the row number of the upper corner.
    Type: Numeric

*start-y*
is the column number of the upper corner.
Type: Numeric

*end-x*
is the row number of the lower corner.
Type: Numeric

*end-y*
is the column number of the lower corner.
Type: Numeric

**Details**    The *start-x*, *start-y*, *end-x*, and *end-y* points use units of pixels and are included in the new image. The top left corner of the image is (0,0).

## Example

Display an image and then crop it:

```
name=lnamemk(1,path);
rc=imgop(task-id,'SELECT',1);
rc=imgop(task-id,'READ_PASTE',1,1,name);

if (crop eq 1) then
   do;
        rc=imgop(task-id,'CROP',ucx,ucy,lcx,lcy);
        rc=imgop(task-id,'PASTE',1,1);
   end;
```

# DESTROY

**Removes an image from memory and from the display**

## Syntax

*rc=**IMGOP**(task-id,* 'DESTROY'<, *image-id>*);

*image-id*
contains the identifier of the image to remove.
Type: Numeric

**Details**    DESTROY removes an image from memory and from the display. Unless *image-id* is specified, this command acts on the currently selected image. The command does not affect the image that is stored in the external file or catalog.

## Example

Remove an image from the display:

```
if (remove=1 and imgnum > 0)
then
```

```
rc=imgop(task-id,'DESTROY',imgnum);
```

# DESTROY_ALL

**Removes all images from memory and from the display**

---

## Syntax

*rc*=**IMGOP**(*task-id*, 'DESTROY_ALL');

**Details**    DESTROY_ALL runs the DESTROY command for all images in memory. The external image files are not affected.

## Example

Remove all images:

```
if (clear=1) then
    rc=imgop(task-id,'DESTROY_ALL');
```

# DITHER

**Dithers an image to a color map**

---

## Syntax

*rc*=**IMGOP**(*task-id*, 'DITHER'<, *option*>);

*region-id*=**PICFILL**(*graphenv-id*, *type*, *ulr*, *ulc*,
    *lrr*, *lrc*, *source*<, 'DITHER'<, *arguments*>>);

***option***
    specifies which color searching algorithm to use. Each algorithm searches the color map at a different speed. You can specify FS_NORMAL, FS_FAST, FS_FASTER, or FS_FASTEST. If you specify FS_NORMAL, then SCL exhaustively searches the color map for the closest match. FS_FAST, FS_FASTER, and FS_FASTEST each use a progressively faster searching algorithm. These algorithms will find a close color match but not the closest. Usually, a close match is sufficient. The faster the search, the less accurate the color match might be. The default option is FS_FASTEST.

**Details**    DITHER acts on the currently selected image. It dithers an image to the current color map: the one specified by a previous GENERATE_CMAP, STANDARD_CMAP, or GRAB_CMAP command.

Like the MAP_COLORS command, DITHER reduces the number of colors in an image. Unlike the MAP_COLORS command, DITHER attempts to choose colors by looking at pixels in groups, not as single pixels, and tries to choose groups that will result in the appropriate color. This is similar to the half-toning algorithm that print vendors use to show multiple colors with the use of only four ink colors. This command is much more computationally expensive than the other color-reduction commands, but it handles continuous-tone images much better.

## Example

Dither an image:

```
if (dither=1) then
   do;
       rc=imgop(task-id,'GENERATE_CMAP','COLORRAMP',
                5,5,4);
       rc=imgop(task-id,'DITHER');
       rc=imgop(task-id,'PASTE');
   end;
```

# DITHER_BW

**Dithers the selected image to a monochrome black and white image**

## Syntax

*rc=***IMGOP**(*task-id*, 'DITHER_BW');

*region-id=***PICFILL**(*graphenv-id, type, ulr, ulc,*
      *lrr, lrc, source<*, 'DITHER_BW'*<, arguments>>*);

**Details**    This command reduces an image to a black-and-white image. DITHER_BW is much more efficient for this task than the general purpose DITHER command.

## Example

Dither an image either to black and white or to a color map:

```
if
(dither=1) then
   do;
       rc=imgop(task-id,'DITHER_BW');
       rc=imgop(task-id,'PASTE');
   end;
if (dither=2) then
   do;
       rc=imgop(task-id,'GENERATE_CMAP',
          'COLORRAMP',5,5,4);
       rc=imgop(task-id,'DITHER');
```

```
        rc=imgop(task-id,'PASTE');
      end;
```

# EXECLIST

### Executes a list of commands

### Syntax

*rc*=**IMGOP**(*task-id*, 'EXECLIST', *commandlist-id*);

*region-id*=**PICFILL**(*graphenv-id*, *type*, *ulr*, *ulc*,
    *lrr*, *lrc*, *source*<, 'EXECLIST'<, *arguments*>>);

***commandlist-id***
    contains the identifier of the SCL list of commands to pass and execute. The
    commands are processed as the task starts. A value of zero means that no list is
    passed.
    Type: Numeric

**Details**    EXECLIST provides a mechanism for sending multiple commands to be
processed at one time. If your program includes the same set of commands several
times, you can fill an SCL list with those commands and then use EXECLIST to
execute the commands.

### Example

Create an SCL list that consists of two sublists. Each sublist contains one item for a
command name and one item for each command argument.

```
length rc 8;
init:
   task-id=imginit(0);
   main_list=makelist(0, 'G');

   sub_list1=makelist(0, 'G');
   main_list=setiteml(main_list, sub_list1, 1, 'Y');
   sub_list1=setitemc(sub_list1, 'WSIZE', 1, 'Y');
   sub_list1=setitemn(sub_list1, 500, 2 , 'Y');
   sub_list1=setitemn(sub_list1, 500, 3 , 'Y');

   sub_list2=makelist(0, 'G');
   main_list=setiteml(main_list, sub_list2, 2, 'Y');
   sub_list2=setitemc(sub_list2, 'WTITLE', 1, 'Y');
   sub_list2=setitemc(sub_list2, 'EXECLIST example',
       2, 'Y');
   rc=imgop(task-id, 'EXECLIST', main_list);
return;

main:
```

```
    return;
term:
    rc=imgterm(task-id);
    return;
```

# FILTER

**Applies a filter to an image**

## Syntax

*rc*=**IMGOP**(*task-id*, 'FILTER', *filter-type*, *matrix*);

***filter-type***
> must be specified as `'CONVOLUTION'`. Other filter types will be added in the future.
>   Type: Character

***matrix***
> contains the matrix size, the filter matrix, the divisor, the bias, and 1 if you want to use the absolute value of the resulting value. If not specified, the defaults are 1 for divisor, 0 for bias, and 0 for not using the absolute value. Separate each number with a space.
>   Type: Character

**Details**   The FILTER command supports convolution filters that are provided by users. A filter matrix is moved along the pixels in an image, and a new pixel value is calculated and replaced at the pixel that is at the center point of the filter matrix. The new value is determined by weighting nearby pixels according to the values in the filter matrix.

A detailed explanation of the concept and theory behind filtering is beyond the scope of this document. However, it is explained in many textbooks. For example, see *Digital Image Processing*, by Rafael Gonzalez and Paul Wintz, and *The Image Processing Handbook*, by John C. Russ.

The equation that FILTER uses is shown in Figure A1.1 on page 744.

**Figure A1.1**   Calculating New Pixel Values

matrixsize

$$N = \left( \left\{ \sum_{i=1} P_i M_i \right\} \,/\, \text{Divisor} \right) + \text{Bias}$$

Where:
 N is the new pixel value (replaced in center of matrix).
 P is the pixel value in the matrix area.
 M is the filter matrix.
 Divisor is the divisor value provided.
 Bias is the bias value provided.
 Matrixsize is the sized of the filter matrix (e.g. in a 3x3 filter,  matrixsize is 9)

EXAMPLE:

| Image Pixels (P) | | | | Filter Matrix (M) | | | | Products | | | | Sums |
|---|---|---|---|---|---|---|---|---|---|---|---|---|
| 25 | 10 | 100 | | -1 | -1 | -1 | | -25 | -10 | -100 | = | -135 |
| 10 | 35 | 25 | x | -1 | 9 | -1 | = | -10 | 315 | -25 | = | 280 |
| 25 | 0 | 100 | | -1 | -1 | -1 | | -25 | 0 | -100 | = | -125 |

| | |
|---|---|
| Sum of sums | 20 |
| | / |
| Divisor | 1 |
| | + |
| Bias | 1 |
| New Pixel (N) | 21 |

## Example

Consider the following 3x3 matrix:

```
-1 -2 -3
 4  5  6
-7  8 -9
```

Design the matrix with a divisor of 1 and a zero bias, and use the absolute value of the answer:

```
matrix="3 -1 -2 -3 4 5 6 -7 8 -9 1 0 1";
rc=imgop(tid,'FILTER',"CONVOLUTION",matrix);
```

*Note:*   Calculated values that are larger than 255 are normalized to 255, and calculated values that are smaller than zero are normalized to zero. If 1 is set for 'absolute value', then negative numbers are converted to positive numbers before normalization.

   A filter selection and creation window is available. An example of using it is in the image sample catalog (imagedmo) named FILTEXAM.FRAME. It is essentially the same window that is used in the Image Editor. It accesses the filters that are shipped with the Image Editor. △

# GAMMA

**Applies a gamma value to the selected image**

## Syntax

*rc*=**IMGOP**(*task-id*, 'GAMMA', *gamma-value*);

*region-id*=**PICFILL**(*graphenv-id*, *type*, *ulr*, *ulc*,
        *lrr*, *lrc*, *source*<, 'GAMMA' <, *arguments*>>);

**gamma-value**
   is the gamma value to apply to the image.
      Type: Numeric

**Details**    GAMMA corrects the image by either darkening or lightening it. Gamma values must be positive, with the most useful values ranging between 0.5 and 3.0. A gamma value of 1.0 results in no change to the image. Values less than 1.0 darken the image, and values greater than 1.0 lighten it.

## Example

Apply a gamma value that has previously been stored in GAMNUM:

```
if
(gamma eq 1) then
   do;
      rc=imgop(task-id,'GAMMA',gamnum);
      if (rc ne 0) then _msg_='gamma error';
      rc=imgop(task-id,'PASTE');
   end;
```

# GENERATE_CMAP

**Generates a color map for the selected image**

## Syntax

*rc*=**IMGOP**(*task-id*, 'GENERATE_CMAP', COLORRAMP, *reds*, *greens*, *blues*);

*rc*=**IMGOP**(*task-id*, 'GENERATE_CMAP', GRAYRAMP, *n*);

*reds*
>   is the number of red colors to generate.
>   Type: Numeric

*greens*
>   is the number of green colors to generate.
>   Type: Numeric

*blues*
>   is the number of blue colors to generate.
>   Type: Numeric

*n*
>   is the number of gray colors to generate.
>   Type: Numeric

**Details**    GENERATE_CMAP generates two kinds of color maps:

COLORRAMP
>   is a color ramp of RGB colors that fill the RGB color spectrum, given the desired number of red, green, and blue shades to use. This command generates a color map of *reds× greens× blues* colors, with a maximum of 256 colors allowed. It is possible to generate a color map that consists only of reds, greens, or blues by specifying that only one shade be used for the other two colors.

GRAYRAMP
>   is a color map that consists only of grays. The number of shades of gray is limited to 256.

After the color map is generated, it can be applied to an image with either the DITHER command or the MAP_COLORS command.

## Example

Use the GENERATE_CMAP command to generate a color ramp and a gray ramp, each containing 100 color map entries:

```
gray:
   rc=imgop(task-id,'GENERATE_CMAP','GRAYRAMP',100);
return;

color:
   rc=imgop(task-id,'GENERATE_CMAP','COLORRAMP',5,5,4);
return;
```

# GET_BARCODE

**Returns the value of the specified bar code**

## Syntax

*rc*=**IMGOP**(*task-id*, 'GET_BARCODE', *bar-code-type*,
  *return-string*<, *x1, y1, x2, y2*>);

***bar-code-type***
> is a character string that contains one value from the following list:
>
> **'CODE39'**          code 39 bar codes
>
> **'CODE39X'**         extended code 39 bar codes
>
> **'CODE128'**         code 128 bar codes.
> > Type: Character

***return-string***
> contains the returned value. Remember to make this variable long enough to hold the longest value that could be returned.
> > Type: Character

***x1,y2***
> are the upper coordinates of the area in the image to search for the bar code. The default is 0,0.

***x2,y2***
> are the lower coordinates of the area in the image to search for the bar code. The default is the width and height of the image. Note that the area specified for the bar-code location can be larger than the bar code. This area should be relatively free of things like other text.

**Details**   Given an image with a bar code, the GET_BARCODE command attempts to decode the bar code and then returns the value of the bar code. The bar code can be decoded only if it is clear in the image. The DPI resolution that is used when the image is scanned determines how clearly the bar code appears in the image. Below 200 DPI, recognition is very poor.

## Example

Return the value of the bar code that is located in the 10,10,300,200 area of the image:

```
rc=imgop(taskid,'GET_BARCODE','CODE39',retstring,
        10,10,300,200);
```

# GET_COLORS

**Returns the RGB values of the index positions of a color map for the selected image**

## Syntax

*rc=***IMGOP**(*task-id*, 'GET_COLORS', *index, red, green, blue*);

***index***
> contains the identifier for the color map index.
> > Type: Numeric

*red*
    is the red value for the index.
        Type: Numeric

*green*
    is the green value for the index.
        Type: Numeric

*blue*
    is the blue value for the index.
        Type: Numeric

**Details**    The color values must be between 0 and 255. If *index* is outside the valid range for the color map, an error is returned.

## Example

See the example for "CREATE_IMAGE" on page 737.

---

# GET_PIXEL

**Returns the pixel value of a specified position in the selected image**

---

## Syntax

*rc*=**IMGOP**(*task-id*, 'GET_PIXEL', *x, y, red*<, *green, blue*>);

*x*
    is the row location in the image.
        Type: Numeric

*y*
    is the column location in the image.
        Type: Numeric

*red*
    is either the red value of an RGB image or the pixel value for a CMAP or GRAY image.
        Type: Numeric

*green*
    is the green value for an RGB image and is ignored for all others.
        Type: Numeric

*blue*
    is the blue value for an RGB image and is ignored for all others.
        Type: Numeric

**Details**    The color values for a CMAP image or an RGB image must be between 0 and 255. If any value is out of range, an error is returned. For a GRAY image, GET_PIXEL returns a red value of either 0 or 1.

## Example

See the example for "CREATE_IMAGE" on page 737.

---

# GRAB_CMAP

**Grabs the color map from the selected image**

---

## Syntax

*rc*=**IMGOP**(*task-id*, 'GRAB_CMAP');

**Details**    After the color map is grabbed, it can be applied to another image with either the DITHER command or the MAP_COLORS command.

## Example

Grab the color map of one image and then apply it to another image with the DITHER command:

```
rc=imgop(task-id,'READ','image-1');
   rc=imgop(task-id,'GRAB_CMAP');
   rc=imgop(task-id,'READ','image-2');
   rc=imgop(task-id,'DITHER');
```

---

# MAP_COLORS

**Maps colors to the closest colors in the selected color map**

---

## Syntax

*rc*=**IMGOP**(*task-id*, 'MAP_COLORS'<, *option*>);

*region-id*=**PICFILL**(*graphenv-id*, *type*, *ulr*, *ulc*,
    *lrr*, *lrc*, *source*<, 'MAP_COLORS' <, *arguments*>>);

### option

specifies the order in which the colors are to be mapped. By default, the colors are mapped in an order that is defined by an internal algorithm. Specify 'SAME_ORDER' to force the color map of the image to be in the same order as the selected color map.
Type: Character

**Details**    MAP_COLORS acts on the currently selected image. Like the DITHER and QUANTIZE commands, MAP_COLORS reduces the number of colors in a color image.

Unlike DITHER, MAP_COLORS attempts to choose colors by looking at pixels individually, not in groups. This technique is much less computationally expensive than DITHER, although it does not handle continuous-tone images as well.

Continuous-tone images contain many shades of colors. Because MAP_COLORS maps the colors in an image to their closest colors in the color map, many of the shades of a color re-map to the same color in the color map. This can reduce the detail in the image. For example, a continuous-tone, black-and-white image would contain several shades of gray in addition to black and white. When MAP_COLORS re-maps the colors in the image, the shades of gray are mapped to either black or white, and much of the detail in the image is lost.

Unlike the QUANTIZE command, MAP_COLORS is passed a particular color map to use. Therefore, multiple images can be reduced to the same color map, further reducing the number of colors used in a frame that contains multiple images. The algorithm looks at each pixel in the image and determines the closest color in the color map. This type of algorithm works best for images that are not continuous-tone images, such as charts, cartoon images, and so on.

Specify the option 'SAME_ORDER' if you are mapping several images and you want the color map to be identical for all of them.

## Example

Grab the color map of one image and then apply it to another image with the MAP_COLORS command:

```
rc=imgop(task-id,'READ',image1);
   rc=imgop(task-id,'GRAB_CMAP');
   rc=imgop(task-id,'READ',image2);
   rc=imgop(task-id,'MAP_COLORS');
```

# MIRROR

**Mirrors an image**

## Syntax

*rc*=**IMGOP**(*task-id*, 'MIRROR');

**Details**     MIRROR acts on the currently selected image. It flips an image on its vertical axis, resulting in a "mirror" copy of the original image.

## Example

Mirror an image:

```
if (mirror=1) then
    rc=imgop(task-id,'MIRROR');
```

# NEGATE

**Changes an image to a negative**

## Syntax

*rc*=**IMGOP**(*task-id*, 'NEGATE');

*region-id*=**PICFILL**(*graphenv-id, type, ulr, ulc,*
    *lrr, lrc, source*<, 'NEGATE'<, *arguments*>>);

**Details**    NEGATE acts on the currently selected image. It creates a photographic negative of the image by reversing the use of dark/light colors. The negative is created by replacing each color with its complement.

## Example

Create a negative of an image:

```
if (negative=1) then
   rc=imgop(task-id,'NEGATE');
```

# PASTE

**Displays an image at a specified location**

## Syntax

*rc*=**IMGOP**(*task-id*, 'PASTE'<, *x, y*>);

*x*

is the X coordinate of the top left corner of the image.
    Type: Numeric

*y*

is the Y coordinate of the top left corner of the image.
    Type: Numeric

**Details**    PASTE acts on the currently selected image. If no coordinates are specified, the selected image is displayed either at location 0,0 or at the coordinates that were set by a previous PASTE. To set new coordinators, you can use a PASTE command with no image specified. Coordinates that are specified by a new PASTE override previous settings.

## Example

Display an image with its upper left corner at 200, 200:

```
if (display=1) then
    rc=imgop(task-id,'PASTE',200,200);
```

# PASTE_AUTO

**Displays an image automatically**

## Syntax

*rc*=**IMGOP**(*task-id*, 'PASTE_AUTO'<, *x*, *y*>);

**x**

is the X coordinate (on the display) of the top left corner of the image.
    Type: Numeric

**y**

is the Y coordinate (on the display) of the top left corner of the image.
    Type: Numeric

**Details**    PASTE_AUTO acts on the currently selected image. It provides the same basic function as PASTE. In addition, PASTE_AUTO modifies an image by dithering it (changing the color map) or quantizing it (reducing the number of colors it uses), so that you can display it on the current device. It also attempts to prevent switching to false colors or to a private color map.

## Example

Automatically display an image with its upper left corner at 200, 200:

```
if (display=1) then
    rc=imgop(task-id,'PASTE_AUTO',200,200);
```

# PRINT

**Prints an image**

## Syntax

*rc* = **IMGOP**(*task-id*, 'PRINT'<, *x*, *y*<, *width*, *height*<, *type*>>>);

**x**

is the X coordinate (on the page) of the top left corner of the image.
    Type: Numeric

*y*

is the Y coordinate (on the page) of the top left corner of the image.
Type: Numeric

### width

specifies either the actual width in pixels or a scaling factor for the width.
Type: Numeric

### height

specifies either the actual height in pixels or a scaling factor for the height.
Type: Numeric

### type

specifies the type to convert the image to before the image is printed. You can specify one of the following:

| | |
|---|---|
| CMAP | color mapped image (maximum of 256 colors) |
| GRAY | gray-scale image |
| MONOCHROME | two-color (black and white) image |
| RGBA | true-color image. |

Type: Character

**Details**    By default, PRINT centers the image. If you do not specify the width and height, PRINT fills the page.

If you want to specify either *x* or *y*, you must specify both. Also, if you want to specify either *width* or *height*, you must specify both. If you specify only one option in either of these pairs, PRINT uses the default values for both options in the pair. For example, if you specify the *width* but not the *height*, PRINT uses the default values for both the width and the height.

Use options *x* and *y* to position the image on the page. To center an image, specify **-1** for the dimension in which you want to center the image (either *x* or *y*, or both). For example, if *x* is **0** and *y* is **999999**, then the image will be printed in the lower left corner. If both *x* and *y* are **0**, then the image will be printed in the upper left corner. If both *x* and *y* are **-1**, then the image will be printed in the center of the page.

To specify the actual *width* or *height* that you want to use to print the image, specify a positive number. To use the actual image size, specify **0** for both *width* and *height*. To scale the image, specify the scaling factor as a negative number. A scaling factor of **-100** prints the image without scaling it up or down. A scaling factor of **-150** is a scaling factor of 150 percent, and **-50** is a scaling factor of 50 percent.

To keep the same aspect ratio, specify **0** for either *width* or *height*. For example, if you specify **-75** for one option and **0** for the other, PRINT scales the image by 75 percent while keeping the same aspect ratio. You cannot specify **0** for both *width* and *height*.

If the scaling factor that you specify is larger than the easel, PRINT reduces the factor to the size of the easel. If the combination of options that you specify would postion the image off the page, then the width and height options take priority, and the position is adjusted so that the image fits on the page.

## Examples

☐ Position the image in the lower right corner:

```
rc=imgop(task-id,'PRINT',999999,999999);
```

☐ Print the image in the center of the page and use the actual pixel size:

```
rc=imgop(task-id,'PRINT',-1,-1,-100,-100);
```

☐ Scale the image up to fill the whole page:

```
            rc=imgop(task-id,'PRINT',0,0,-99999,-99999);
```
□  Scale the image up by 150 percent:

```
            rc=imgop(task-id,'PRINT',0,0,-150,-150);
```
□  Scale the width to 200 percent and keep the same aspect ratio:

```
            rc=imgop(task-id,'PRINT',0,0,-200,0 );
```
□  Print the image with a width of 200 and keep the same aspect ratio:

```
            rc=imgop(task-id,'PRINT',0,0,200,0);
```
□  Scale the width by 150 percent and use a height of 99:

```
            rc=imgop(task-id,'PRINT',0,0,-150,99);
```
□  Fill in one direction and keep the same aspect ratio:

```
            rc=imgop(task-id,'PRINT',0,0,99999,0);
```
□  Fill the page with the image:

```
            rc=imgop(task-id,'PRINT',0,0,99999,99999);
```

# QUANTIZE

**Reduces the number of colors used for an image**

## Syntax

*rc* = **IMGOP**(*task-id*, 'QUANTIZE', *colors*);

*region-id*=**PICFILL**(*graphenv-id*, *type*, *ulr*, *ulc*,
    *lrr*, *lrc*, *source*<, 'QUANTIZE'<, *arguments*>>);

*colors*
> is the number of colors to use for the image. The value of the *colors* variable must be between 2 through 256.
> Type: Numeric

**Details**    QUANTIZE acts on the currently selected image. It generates a color-mapped image for which the command assigns the values in the color map. QUANTIZE results in a very good approximation of the image, with the possible negative effect that two or more images that are quantized to the same number of colors might still use different colors for each image. (The algorithm is an adaptation of the Xiaolin Wu algorithm, as described in *Graphics Gems II*.*)

## Example

Reduce the number of colors for an image to the number stored in NUMCOLOR:

---

* Wu, Xiaolin (1991), " Efficient Statistical Computations for Optimal Color Quantization," in *Graphics Gems II*, ed. J. Arvo, Boston: Academic Press, 126–133.

```
if (quantize eq 1) then
    rc=imgop(task-id,'QUANTIZE',numcolor);
```

# QUERYC, QUERYL, and QUERYN

**Query information about images**

## Syntax

*rc=***IMGOP**(*task-id*, 'QUERYC', *attribute*, *information*);

*rc=***IMGOP**(*task-id*, 'QUERYL', *attribute*, *list-id*);

*rc=***IMGOP**(*task-id*, 'QUERYN', *attribute*, *information*);

*attribute*
is the value to report. Attributes for QUERYC are listed in "Attributes for the QUERYC Command" on page 755. Attributes for QUERYL are listed in "Attributes for the QUERYL Command" on page 755. Attributes for QUERYN are listed in "Attributes for the QUERYN Command" on page 756.
Type: Character

*information*
contains the information that is returned by QUERYC and QUERYN. QUERYC returns a character value, and QUERYN returns a numeric value.
Type: Character or Numeric

*list-id*
contains the identifier for the SCL list of information items that are returned by QUERYL. See *attribute* for details.
Type: List

## Attributes for the QUERYC Command

The values for *attribute* for QUERYC are:

DESCRIPT
returns information about the image size and color map. The information can be up to 45 characters long.

FILENAME
returns the image-path string.

FORMAT
returns the original file format, such as GIF.

TYPE
returns the IMAGE type, which can be 'CMAP', 'GRAY', or 'RGBA'.

## Attributes for the QUERYL Command

The values for *attribute* for QUERYL are:

ACTIVE_LIST
> returns an SCL list that contains the identifiers for all active images (images that are being used but that are not necessarily visible).

GLOBAL_INFO
> returns a named list that contains the following items:

> > NUM_ACTIVE
> > > is the number of active images that are used but not necessarily visible.

> > SELECT
> > > is the identifier of the currently selected image.

> > WSIZE_WIDTH
> > > is the window width in pixels.

> > WSIZE_HEIGHT
> > > is the window height in pixels.

SELECT_INFO
> returns a named SCL list that contains the numeric values for the currently selected image:

> > IS_ACTIVE
> > > has a value of 1 if the image is being used and if data is associated with it. If IS_ACTIVE=1, the following items are also returned:

> > > | | |
> > > |---|---|
> > > | WIDTH | the image width in pixels |
> > > | HEIGHT | the image height in pixels |
> > > | DEPTH | the image depth |
> > > | TYPE | the image type: 'CMAP', 'GRAY', 'RGBA' |

> > IS_VISIBLE
> > > has a value of 1 if the image is being displayed.

> > XPOSN
> > > is the x position.

> > YPOSN
> > > is the y position.

> > NCOLORS
> > > is the number of colors, if TYPE='CMAP' (color mapped)

> > RDEPTH
> > > is the red depth, if TYPE='RGBA'

> > GDEPTH
> > > is the green depth, if TYPE='RGBA'

> > BDEPTH
> > > is the blue depth, if TYPE='RGBA'

> > ADEPTH
> > > is the alpha depth (degree of transparency), if TYPE='RGBA'

VISIBLE_LIST
> returns an SCL list that contains the identifiers for all currently displayed images.

## Attributes for the QUERYN Command

The values for *attribute* for QUERYN are:

ADEPTH
:   returns the alpha depth (degree of transparency), if TYPE=3 (RGBA).

BDEPTH
:   returns the blue depth, if TYPE=3 (RGBA).

COLORMAP-LEN
:   returns the size of the color map.

DEPTH
:   returns the image depth.

GDEPTH
:   returns the green depth, if TYPE=3 (RGBA).

HEIGHT
:   returns the image height in pixels.

IS_BLANK
:   returns a value that indicates whether the current page is blank:

| | |
|---|---|
| 1 | blank |
| 0 | not blank (valid for monochrome images only). |

NCOLORS
:   returns the number of colors.

RDEPTH
:   returns the red depth, if TYPE=3 (RGBA).

SELECT
:   returns the identifier of the currently selected image.

TYPE
:   returns the image type:

| | |
|---|---|
| 1 | GRAY (gray-scale) |
| 2 | CMAP (color mapped) |
| 3 | RGBA. |

WIDTH
:   returns the image width in pixels.

**Details**   The QUERYC, QUERYL, and QUERYN commands return information about all images as well as about the Image window. QUERYC returns the values of character attributes. QUERYL returns the values of attributes that are stored in an SCL list. QUERYN returns the values of numeric attributes. These commands act on the currently selected image.

## Examples

**Example 1: Using QUERYC**   Display the description, filename, format, and type of an image:

```
rc=imgop(task-id,'READ',
          '/usr/local/images/color/misc/canoe.gif');
rc=imgop(task-id,'QUERYC','DESCRIPT',idescr);
put idescr=;
```

```
rc=imgop(task-id,'QUERYC','FILENAME',ifile);
put ifile=;
rc=imgop(task-id,'QUERYC','FORMAT',iformat);
put iformat=;
rc=imgop(task-id,'QUERYC','TYPE',itype);
put itype=;
```

This program writes the following lines to the LOG window:

```
IDESCR=640x480 8-bit CMAP, 256 colormap entries
IFILE=/usr/local/images/color/misc/canoe.gif
IFORMAT=GIF
ITYPE=CMAP
```

## Example 2: Using QUERYL

☐ Display the number of active images:

```
qlist=0;
rc=imgop(task-id,'SELECT',1);
rc=imgop(task-id,'READ',path1);
rc=imgop(task-id,'SELECT',2);
rc=imgop(task-id,'READ',path2);
rc=imgop(task-id,'PASTE');
rc=imgop(task-id,'QUERYL','ACTIVE_LIST',qlist);
images=listlen(qlist);
put images=;
```

This program writes the following line to the LOG window:

```
images=2
```

☐ Display an SCL list of information about the current image:

```
qlist=makelist();
rc=imgop(task-id,'SELECT',1);
rc=imgop(task-id,'READ',path);
rc=imgop(task-id,'QUERYL','SELECT_INFO',qlist);
call putlist(qlist);
```

This program writes the following information to the LOG window:

```
(IS_ACTIVE=1 IS_VISIBLE=0 XPOSN=0 YPOSN=0 WIDTH=1024
HEIGHT=768 DEPTH=8 TYPE='CMAP' NCOLORS=253 )[18]
```

☐ Display an SCL list of information about the Image window:

```
qlist=makelist();
rc=imgop(task-id,'SELECT',1);
rc=imgop(task-id,'READ',path);
rc=imgop(task-id,'QUERYL','GLOBAL_INFO',qlist);
call putlist(qlist);
```

This program writes the following lines to the LOG window:

```
(NUM_ACTIVE=1 SELECT=1 WSIZE_WIDTH=682
WSIZE_HEIGHT=475 )[20]
```

## Example 3: Using QUERYN   Display information about the Image window. (Assume that all variables have been initialized before they are used.)

```
rc=imgop(task-id,'READ',path);
rc=imgop(task-id,'QUERYN','SELECT',select);
rc=imgop(task-id,'QUERYN','HEIGHT',height);
rc=imgop(task-id,'QUERYN','WIDTH',width);
rc=imgop(task-id,'QUERYN','DEPTH',depth);
rc=imgop(task-id,'QUERYN','RDEPTH',rdepth);
rc=imgop(task-id,'QUERYN','GDEPTH',gdepth);
rc=imgop(task-id,'QUERYN','BDEPTH',bdepth);
rc=imgop(task-id,'QUERYN','ADEPTH',adepth);
rc=imgop(task-id,'QUERYN','NCOLORS',ncolors);
rc=imgop(task-id,'QUERYN','TYPE',type);
put select= height= width= depth= rdepth= gdepth=;
put bdepth= adepth= ncolors= type= ;
```

This program writes the following values to the LOG window:

```
SELECT=1 HEIGHT=470 WIDTH=625 DEPTH=8 RDEPTH=0
GDEPTH=0 BDEPTH=0 ADEPTH=0 NCOLORS=229 TYPE=2
```

# READ

**Reads an image from an external file, a SAS catalog, or a device**

## Syntax

*rc*=**IMGOP**(*task-id*, 'READ', *image-path*<, *attributes* >);

*rc*=**IMGOP**(*task-id*, 'READ', *device-name*,
    'DEVICE=CAMERA | SCANNER <*attributes*>');

***image-path***
   is either the pathname of the external file that contains the image or the path string
   that is returned by the LNAMEMK function.
      Type: Character

***device-name***
   specifies the name of a camera or scanner:

   'KODAKDC40'
      Kodak DC 40 camera (available only in the Windows 95 operating environment)

   'HPSCAN'
      HP Scanjet scanners (available only in the Windows and HP/UX operating
      environments)

   'TWAIN'
      TWAIN scanners and cameras (available only in the Windows operating
      environment)
      If you specify a device name, then you must use the DEVICE= attribute to
   indicate the type of device.
      Type: Character

> ***attributes***
> are file- or device-specific attributes. See "Attributes for Reading Image Files" on
> page 774 for possible choices.
>      Type: Character

**Details**    READ acts on the currently selected image. You can specify the file directly
(using its physical filename path), or use the information returned by a previous
LNAMEMK function call. The LNAMEMK function creates a single character variable
that contains information about the location of the image (even if it resides in a SAS
catalog), as well as other image attributes.

The FORMAT= attribute must be specified for Targa images, for images that reside
in SAS catalogs, and for host-specific formats. FORMAT is not required in other cases,
but it is always more efficient to specify it.

## Examples

- ☐ Read an image that is stored in a SAS catalog:

  ```
  path=lnamemk(5,'sashelp.imagapp.gfkids','format=cat');
  rc=imgop(task-id,'READ',path);
  ```

- ☐ Specify a file in the READ command:

  ```
  rc=imgop(task-id,'READ','/usr/images/color/sign.gif');
  ```

- ☐ Read from a scanner:

  ```
  rc=imgop(task-id,'READ','hpscan','device=scanner dpi=100');
  ```

- ☐ Take a picture with a camera:

  ```
  rc=imgop(task-id,'READ','kodakdc40','device=camera takepic');
  ```

- ☐ Read a Portable Networks Graphics image:

  ```
  rc=imgop(taskid,'READ','/images/test.png','format=PNG');
  ```

- ☐ Read an image and wait 5 seconds before displaying the image after each PASTE
  command:

  ```
  rc=imgop(taskid,'READ',path);
  rc=imgop(taskid,'PASTE');
  rc=imgctrl(taskid,'WAIT',5);
  rc=imgop(taskid,'READ',path2);
  rc=imgop(taskid,'PASTE');
  rc=imgctrl(taskid,'WAIT',5);
  ```

# READ_CLIPBOARD

**Reads an image from the host clipboard**

## Syntax

*rc*=**IMGOP**(*task-id*, 'READ_CLIPBOARD');

**Details**    READ_CLIPBOARD acts on the currently selected image. On some hosts, the clipboard can be read only after you use the WRITE_CLIPBOARD command.

### Example

Read an image from the clipboard and display it:

```
rc=imgop(task-id,'READ_CLIPBOARD');
rc=imgop(task-id,'PASTE');
```

# READ_PASTE

**Reads and displays an image**

### Syntax

*rc=***IMGOP**(*task-id*, 'READ_PASTE', *x*, *y*, *image-path*<, *attributes*>);

*x*
    is the X coordinate of the top left corner of the image.
      Type: Numeric

*y*
    is the Y coordinate of the top left corner of the image.
      Type: Numeric

*image-path*
    contains either the pathname of the external file that contains the image or the path string that is returned by the LNAMEMK function.
      Type: Character

*attributes*
    are file-specific attributes. See "Attributes for Reading Image Files" on page 774 for possible choices.
      Type: Character

**Details**    READ_PASTE acts on the currently selected image. It provides the same functionality as READ plus PASTE. Notice that *x* and *y* are required.

### Example

Read and paste an image that is stored in a SAS catalog:

```
path=lnamemk(5,'sashelp.imagapp.gfkids',
    'format=cat');
rc=imgop(task-id,'READ_PASTE',1,1,path);
```

# READ_PASTE_AUTO

**Reads and automatically displays an image**

## Syntax

*rc*=**IMGOP**(*task-id*, 'READ_PASTE_AUTO', *x*, *y*, *image-path*<, *attributes*>);

**x**
is the X coordinate of the top left corner of the image.
Type: Numeric

**y**
is the Y coordinate of the top left corner of the image.
Type: Numeric

***image-path***
contains either the pathname of the external file that contains the image or the path string that is returned by the LNAMEMK function.
Type: Character

***attributes***
are file-specific attributes. See "Attributes for Reading Image Files" on page 774 for possible choices.
Type: Character

**Details**    READ_PASTE_AUTO acts on the currently selected image. It provides the same functionality as READ plus PASTE_AUTO. Notice that *x* and *y* are required.

## Example

Read and automatically paste an image that is stored in a SAS catalog:

```
path=lnamemk(5,'sashelp.imagapp.gfkids','format=cat');
rc=imgop(task-id,'READ_PASTE_AUTO',1,1,path);
```

# ROTATE

**Rotates an image clockwise by 90, 180, or 270 degrees**

## Syntax

*rc*=**IMGOP**(*task-id*, 'ROTATE', *degrees*);

*region-id*=**PICFILL**(*graphenv-id*, *type*, *ulr*, *ulc*, *lrr*, *lrc*, *source*<, 'ROTATE'<, *arguments*>>);

*degrees*
>   is the number of degrees to rotate the image: 90, 180, or 270.
>   Type: Numeric

**Details**    ROTATE acts on the currently selected image.

## Example

>   Rotate an image the number of degrees stored in RV:

```
main:
    rc=imgop(task-id,'READ',path);
    if (rv ge 90) then
        do;
            rc=imgop(task-id,'ROTATE',rv);
            rc=imgop(task-id,'PASTE');
        end;
return;
```

# SCALE

**Scales an image**

## Syntax

*rc*=**IMGOP**(*task-id*, 'SCALE', *width, height<, algorithm>*);

*region-id*=**PICFILL**(*graphenv-id, type, ulr, ulc,*
>   *lrr, lrc, source<, 'SCALE'<, arguments>>*);

*width*
>   is the new width of the image (in pixels).
>   Type: Numeric

*height*
>   is the new height of the image (in pixels).
>   Type: Numeric

*algorithm*
>   specifies which scaling algorithm to use:

>   BILINEAR
>>   computes each new pixel in the final image by averaging four pixels in the source image and using that value. The BILINEAR algorithm is more computationally expensive than LINEAR, but it preserves details in the image better.

>   LINEAR
>>   replicates pixels when the image is scaled up and discards pixels when the image is scaled down. The LINEAR algorithm yields good results on most images. However, it does not work very well when you are scaling down an image that

contains small, but important, features such as lines that are only one pixel wide. LINEAR is the default.
Type: Character

**Details**    SCALE acts on the currently selected image. It scales the image to a new image. If you specify **-1** for either *width* or *height*, then SCALE preserves the image's aspect ratio.

## Example

Double the size of an image:

```
main:
    rc=imgop(task-id,'READ',path);
    rc=imgop(task-id,'QUERYN','WIDTH',width);
    rc=imgop(task-id,'SCALE',2*width,-1);
    rc=imgop(task-id,'PASTE');
return;
```

# SELECT

**Selects the image identifier to be used in other commands**

## Syntax

*rc*=**IMGOP**(*task-id*, 'SELECT'<, *image-id*>);

*image-id*
    contains the identifier of the image to select. The value of *image-id* must be between 1 and 999. The default is 1. Using a value of 32 or less is more efficient.
    Type: Numeric

**Details**    The SELECT command enables you to work with more than one image. The command specifies the image identifier to be used in all subsequent commands until another SELECT command is issued.
    Only the COPY, DESTROY, and UNPASTE commands can act on either the currently selected image or on a specified image identifier.

## Example

Display two images at once:

```
rc=imgop(task-id,'SELECT',1);
rc=imgop(task-id,'READ_PASTE',1,1,path1);
rc=imgop(task-id,'SELECT',2);
rc=imgop(task-id,'READ_PASTE',200,200,path2);
```

# SET_COLORS

**Assigns the RGB values for the index positions of a color map for the current image**

## Syntax

*rc*=**IMGOP**(*task-id*, 'SET_COLORS', *index, red, green, blue*);

**index**
  contains the identifier for the color map index.
    Type: Numeric

**red**
  is the red value for the index.
    Type: Numeric

**green**
  is the green value for the index.
    Type: Numeric

**blue**
  is the blue value for the index.
    Type: Numeric

**Details**    SET_COLORS acts on the currently selected image. It can be used with either a new image or an existing image. If *index* is outside the valid range for the color map, an error is returned. The color values must be between 0 and 255.

## Example

See the example for "CREATE_IMAGE" on page 737.

# SET_PIXEL

**Assigns the pixel value in an image at the specified position**

## Syntax

*rc*=**IMGOP**(*task-id*, 'SET_PIXEL', *x, y, red<, green, blue>*);

**x**
  is the row location in the image.
    Type: Numeric

**y**
  is the column location in the image.
    Type: Numeric

***red***
>     is either the red value of an RGB image or the pixel value for a CMAP or GRAY
>     image.
>         Type: Numeric

***green***
>     is the green value for an RGB image and is ignored for all other image types.
>         Type: Numeric

***blue***
>     is the blue value for an RGB image and is ignored for all other image types.
>         Type: Numeric

**Details**    SET_PIXEL acts on the currently selected image. It can be used with either
a new image or an existing image. The colors for a CMAP and an RGB image must be
between 0 and 255. If any value is out of range, an error is returned. For a GRAY
image, SET_PIXEL returns either 0 or 1 for *red*.

**CAUTION:**
>     **Image data can be destroyed.** Use this function carefully, or you can destroy your
>     image data. SET_PIXEL overwrites the image data in memory and thus destroys the
>     original image. △

## Example

See the example for "CREATE_IMAGE" on page 737.

---

# STANDARD_CMAP

Selects a color map

---

## Syntax

*rc=***IMGOP**(*task-id*, 'STANDARD_CMAP', *color-map*);

***color-map***
>     is the color map to designate as the current color map.

>     BEST
>>         is a special, dynamic color map that can contain up to 129 colors. The color map
>>         contains the 16 personal computer colors, a set of grays, and an even distribution of
>>         colors. The colors are dynamically selected, based on the capabilities of the display
>>         and on the number of available colors. The best set of colors is chosen accordingly.

>     COLORMIX_CGA
>>         is the 16-color personal computer color map.

>     COLORMIX_192
>>         is a 192-color blend.

DEFAULT
is an initial set of colors that is chosen by default. The available colors may vary between releases of the SAS System.

SYSTEM
is the color map for the currently installed device or system. The color map that STANDARD_CMAP obtains is a "snapshot" of the color map for the current device and does not change when the device's color map changes.
Type: Character

**Details**     STANDARD_CMAP specifies that the current color map should be filled with one of the "standard" image color maps. This new color map can be applied to any image by using either the DITHER command or the MAP_COLORS command.

## Example

Select a new color map and use the DITHER command to apply it to an image:

```
rc=imgop(task-id,'STANDARD_CMAP','COLORMIX_CGA');
   rc=imgop(task-id,'READ',path);
   rc=imgop(task-id,'DITHER');
```

# THRESHOLD

Converts a color image to black and white, using a *threshold* value

## Syntax

*rc*=**IMGOP**(*task-id*, 'THRESHOLD', *value*);

**value**
is a threshold value for converting standard RGB values to monochrome. *Value* can be:

| | |
|---|---|
| 1...255 | sets the threshold that determines whether a color maps to black or white |
| 0 | defaults to 128 |
| -1 | calculates the threshold value by averaging all pixels in the image. |

Type: Numeric

## Details

The THRESHOLD command acts on either the currently selected image or on the image specified by *task-id*. It enables documents that are scanned in color to be converted to monochrome for applying optical character recognition (OCR) and for other purposes. Dithering is not a good technique for converting images when OCR is used.

The *threshold* is a color value that acts as a cut-off point for converting colors to black and white. All colors greater than the *threshold* value map to white, and all colors less than or equal to the *threshold* value map to black.

The algorithm weights the RGB values, using standard intensity calculations for converting color to gray scale.

# TILE

**Replicates the current image**

## Syntax

*rc*=**IMGOP**(*task-id*, 'TILE', *new-width*, *new-height*);

**new-width**
> is the width (in pixels) for the tiled images to fill.
>> Type: Numeric

**new-height**
> is the height (in pixels) for the tiled images to fill.
>> Type: Numeric

## Details

TILE acts on the currently selected image. The area defined by *new-width*× *new-height* is filled beginning in the upper left corner. The current image is placed there. Copies of the current image are added to the right until the row is filled. This process then starts over on the next row until the area defined by *new-width*× *new-height* is filled. For example, if the current image is 40×40 and *new-width*× *new-height* is 200×140, then the current image is replicated 5 times in width and 3.5 times in height. This technique is useful for creating tiled backdrops.

*Note:* Before tiling an image, you must turn off the SCALE option for the image. △

## Example

Create a 480×480 tiled image from a 48×48 image:

```
rc=imgop(task-id,'READ','sashelp.c0c0c.access','format=cat');
rc=imgop(task-id,'TILE',480,480);
```

# UNPASTE

**Removes an image from the display**

## Syntax

*rc*=**IMGOP**(*task-id*, 'UNPASTE'<, *image-id*>);

*image-id*
   contains the identifier of the image to remove from the display.
      Type: Numeric

**Details**   UNPASTE acts either on the currently selected image or on the image specified by *image-id*. The image is removed from the display, but it is not removed from memory. UNPASTE enables you to remove an image from the display and to later paste it without re-reading it.

## Example

Display two images at once and then remove one of them:

```
rc=imgop(task-id,'SELECT',1);
rc=imgop(task-id,'READ_PASTE',1,1,name1);
rc=imgop(task-id,'SELECT',2);
rc=imgop(task-id,'READ_PASTE',200,200,name2);
...more SCL statements...
if (omit=1) then
   rc=imgop(task-id,'UNPASTE',1);
```

# WRAISE

**Raises the Image window**

## Syntax

*rc=***IMGCTRL**(*task-id*, 'WRAISE');

**Details**   WRAISE attempts to force the Image window to the top of the display as long as the IMGOP or IMGCTRL commands are executing. This command might not be executed by some window managers. Note that when you start the image task with the IMGINIT function, you can specify the TOPWINDOW option to force the window to always be on top.

## Example

Raise the Image window to the top of the display:

```
pop:
   rc = imgctrl(task-id,'WRAISE');
return;
```

# WRITE

**Writes an image to a file or to a SAS catalog**

## Syntax

*rc*=**IMGOP**(*task-id*, 'WRITE', *image-path*<, *attributes*>);

**image-path**
> contains either the pathname of the external file that contains the image or the path string that is returned by the LNAMEMK function.
>> Type: Character

**attributes**
> lists attributes that are specific to the file type. See "Attributes for Reading Image Files" on page 774.
>> Type: Character

**Details**   WRITE writes the currently selected image to an external file. The file can be specified either directly (using its physical filename path) or by using the information that was returned by a previous LNAMEMK function call. The LNAMEMK function creates a character variable that contains information about the location of the image (even if it is to reside in a SAS catalog), as well as information about other image attributes.

The FORMAT= attribute (described in "Attributes for Writing Image Files" on page 776) must be specified if *image-path* does not include that information.

## Examples

□ Write an image to a SAS catalog:

```
path=lnamemk
(5,'mine.images.sign','FORMAT=CAT');
rc=imgop(task-id,'WRITE',path);
```

□ Specify a file in the WRITE command. (Notice that file attributes are included.)

```
rc=imgop(task-id,'WRITE','/user/images/sign.tif',
    'FORMAT=TIFF COMPRESS=G3FAX');
```

# WRITE_CLIPBOARD

**Writes an image to the host clipboard**

## Syntax

*rc*=**IMGOP**(*task-id*, 'WRITE_CLIPBOARD');

**Details**   WRITE_CLIPBOARD acts on the currently selected image. The image must be pasted before it can be written to the system clipboard.

## Example

Read in an image and then write it to the clipboard:

```
rc=imgop(task-id,'READ',path);
rc=imgop(task-id,'WRITE_CLIPBOARD');
```

# WSIZE

**Sets the size of the Image window**

## Syntax

*rc*=**IMGCTRL**(*task-id*, 'WSIZE', *width*, *height*<, *x*, *y*>);

**width**
  is the width of the window (in pixels).
    Type: Numeric

**height**
  is the height of the window (in pixels).
    Type: Numeric

**x**
  is the X coordinate of the top left corner.
    Type: Numeric

**y**
  is the Y coordinate of the top left corner.
    Type: Numeric

**Details**    WSIZE sets the size of the Image window. Optionally, it positions the window at *x* and *y*. Some window managers might not support positioning.

## Example

Make the Image window match the size of the image that is being displayed:

```
main:
   height=0;
   width=0;
   rc=imgop(task-id,'READ',path);
   rc=imgop(task-id,'QUERYN','WIDTH',iwidth);
   rc=imgop(task-id,'QUERYN','HEIGHT',iheight);
   rc=imgctrl(task-id,'WSIZE',iwidth,iheight);
   rc=imgop(task-id,'PASTE',1,1);
return;
```

# WTITLE

Specifies a title for the Image window

## Syntax

*rc*=**IMGCTRL**(*task-id*, 'WTITLE', *title*);

*title*
   is the text to display as the window title.
      Type: Character

**Details**     The specified title appears in parentheses after SAS: IMAGE in the title bar
of the window.

## Example

Specify *gname* as the title of the Image window:

```
path=lnamemk(5,catname,'format=cat');
rc=lnameget(path,type,name,form);
gname=scan(name,3,'.');
rc=imgctrl(tid,'wtitle',gname);
```

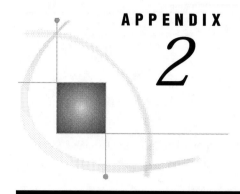

APPENDIX

*2*

# Image File Types and Associated Attributes

## File Types

The file types that are supported by the IMGOP function and by the Image Data Model class are described in Table A2.1 on page 773. The file type of the image determines which attributes can be used in reading or writing the image. The attributes that you can specify for each file type are described in the following sections:

"Attributes for Reading Image Files" on page 774

"Attributes for Writing Image Files" on page 776

"Attributes for Reading Images from Kodak DC40 Cameras" on page 778

"Attributes for Reading Images from HP ScanJet and TWAIN Scanners" on page 779

"Attributes for Reading Images from TWAIN Scanners and Cameras" on page 780

**Table A2.1**  Supported Image File Types

| File Type | Description |
|---|---|
| BMP (Microsoft Windows Device Independent Bitmap) | Supports color-mapped and true color images that are stored as uncompressed or run-length encoded data. BMP was developed by Microsoft Corporation. |
| CAT (SAS Catalog IMAGE entry) | |
| DIB (Microsoft Windows Device Independent Bitmap) | See the description of BMP. DIB is supported only under the Windows 95, Windows 98, Windows NT, and OS/2 operating systems. |
| EMF (Microsoft NT Enhanced Metafile) | Supported only under Windows 95, Windows 98, and Windows NT. |
| EPSI (Encapsulated PostScript Interchange) | An extended version of the standard PostScript (PS) format. Files that use this format can be printed on PostScript printers and can also be imported into other applications. Notice that EPSI files can be read, but PS files cannot be. |

| File Type | Description |
|---|---|
| GIF (Graphics Interchange Format) | Supports only color-mapped images. GIF is owned by CompuServe, Inc. (available if licensed). |
| JFIF (JPEG File Interchange Format) | Supports JPEG image compression. JFIF software is developed by the Independent JPEG Group. |
| MET (OS/2 Metafile) | Supported only under OS/2. |
| PBM (Portable Bitmap Utilities) | Supports gray, color, RGB, and bitmap files. The Portable Bitmap Utilities are a set of free utility programs that were developed primarily by Jef Poskanzer. |
| PCD (Photo CD reader) | Photo CD is owned by and licensed from Eastman Kodak Company. |
| PCX (PC Paintbrush) | Supports bitmapped, color-mapped, and true color images. PCX and PC Paintbrush are owned by Zsoft Corporation. |
| PICT (The QuickDraw Picture Format) | Supports 256-color images and bitmaps. The QuickDraw Picture Format is owned by Apple Computer, Inc. and is supported only in the Macintosh environment. |
| PNG (Portable Networks Graphics) | The PNG Reader and Writer use 'libpng' in their implementations. Permission to use is freely granted. Copyright (c) 1995, 1996 Guy Eric Schalnat, Group 42, Inc. |
| PS (PostScript Image File Format) | The Image classes use only PostScript image operators. A level II PS printer is required for color images. PostScript was developed by Adobe Systems, Inc. |
| TGA (Targa) | Supports both true color images and color-mapped images; however, the current release of the Image classes supports only true color TGA files. Targa is owned by Truevision, Inc. |
| TIFF (Tagged Image File Format) | Internally supports a number of compression types and image types, including bitmapped, color-mapped, gray-scaled, and true color. TIFF was developed by Aldus Corporation and Microsoft Corporation and is used by a wide variety of applications. (available if licensed) |
| WMF (Microsoft Windows Metafile) | Supported only under MicroSoft Windows operating systems. |
| XBM (X Window Bitmaps) | Supports bitmapped images only. XBM is owned by MIT X Consortium. |
| XPM (X Window Pixmap) | Is an extended version of XBM that supports color bitmaps; supported only under UNIX operating systems. |
| XWD (X Window Dump) | Supports all X visual types (bitmapped, color-mapped, and true color). XWD is owned by MIT X Consortium. |

# Attributes for Reading Image Files

Table A2.2 on page 775 describes the attributes that you can specify for the image readers.

When you are reading images, include the FORMAT= attribute in the method if any of the following conditions are true:

□ You are reading a format that is supported only on certain hosts.

□ The images reside in SAS catalogs.

□ The images are being read from a system pipe.

FORMAT= is not required in other cases, but it is always more efficient to specify it.

**Table A2.2** Reader Attributes for Supported File Types

| File Type | Reader Attributes | Comment |
|---|---|---|
| BMP | FORMAT=BMP | |
| | COMPRESS=NONE | Default. |
| | COMPRESS=RLE | Run-length encoded data. |
| CAT | FORMAT=CAT | |
| DIB | FORMAT=DIB | Supported only under the Windows 95, Windows 98, Windows NT, and OS/2 operating systems. |
| EMF | FORMAT=EMF | Supported only under Windows 95, Windows 98, and Windows NT. |
| EPSI | FORMAT=EPSI | |
| | DPI=*num* | Number of dots per inch specified when the output file was created. |
| GIF | FORMAT=GIF | |
| JFIF | FORMAT=JFIF | Required for reading JPEG files that use the JPEG File Interchange Format (JFIF). |
| | DCT=*mode* | Specifies which type of Discrete Cosine Transform (DCT) to use when processing the image. *Mode* can be |
| | | INT          an integer DCT |
| | | FAST        a faster and less accurate integer DCT |
| | | FLOAT      a slightly more accurate method that can be much slower unless the host has very fast floating-point hardware. |
| | | The results of the floating-point method can vary across host machines, whereas the integer methods should give the same results on all hosts. |
| | GRAYSCALE | Produces a gray-scale image even if the JPEG file is in color. This is useful for viewing on monochrome displays. The reader runs noticeably faster in this mode. |
| | VERSION | Writes to the SAS log the version number and copyright messages for the Independent JPEG Group's JFIF software. |
| | FAST | Enables certain recommended processing options for fast, low quality output. Specifying FAST is equivalent to enabling ONEPASS, DITHER=ORDERED, COLORS=216, NOSMOOTH, and DCT=FAST. |
| | NOSMOOTH | Uses a faster, lower quality, upsampling routine. |
| | ONEPASS | Uses a one-pass color quantization instead of the standard two-pass quantization. The one-pass method is faster and requires less memory, but it produces a lower-quality image. This attribute is ignored unless you also specify the COLORS attribute. ONEPASS is always enabled for gray-scale output. |
| | COLORS=*n* | Reduces the number of colors in the image to at most *n* colors; *n* must be between 2 and 256, inclusive. |
| | SCALE_RATIO=*n* | Scales the output image by a factor of $1/n$. Currently the scale factor must be 1/1, 1/2, 1/4, or 1/8. This is useful when you are processing a large image and only a smaller version is needed, because the reader is much faster when the output is scaled down. |
| | DITHER=*mode* | Specifies which type of dithering to use for color quantization. *Mode* can be |
| | | FS             Floyd-Steinberg dithering |

| File Type | Reader Attributes | Comment |
|---|---|---|
| | | ORDERED    ordered dithering |
| | | NONE    no dithering. |
| MET | FORMAT=MET | Supported only under OS/2. |
| PBM | FORMAT=PBM | |
| PCD | FORMAT=PCD | RES= specifies the image resolution to be read. Photo CD images have multiple resolution images in each image. Values are |
| | | BASE/64    64x96 |
| | | BASE/16    128x192 |
| | | BASE/4    256x384 |
| | | BASE    512x768 (default) |
| | | 4BASE    1024x1536 |
| | | 16BASE    2048x3072 |
| PCX | FORMAT=PCX | |
| PICT | FORMAT=PICT | Supported only in the Macintosh environment. |
| PNG | FORMAT=PNG | |
| TGA | FORMAT=TGA | |
| TIFF | FORMAT=TIFF | |
| WMF | FORMAT=WMF | Supported only under MicroSoft Windows operating systems. |
| XBM | FORMAT=XBM | |
| XPM | FORMAT=XPM | Supported only by the X Window System under UNIX. |
| XWD | FORMAT=XWD | |

# Attributes for Writing Image Files

Table A2.3 on page 777 describes the attributes that you can specify for the image writers.

When you are writing images, you must specify the FORMAT= attribute. You can specify this attribute either directly as an argument for the WRITE command or as part of the *image-path* (if you use the LNAMEMK function to specify the pathname). For example:

```
/* Specify the FORMAT= attribute directly */
/* as an argument to the WRITE command.   */
rc=imgop(task-id,'WRITE','/user/images/sign.tif', 'format=tiff');

/* Use the LNAMEMK function to specify the image-path, */
/* and include the FORMAT= attribute as part of the path. */
path=lnamemk(5,'mine.images.sign','format=cat');
rc = imgop(task-id,'WRITE',path);
```

**Table A2.3**  Writer Attributes for Supported File Types

| File Type | Writer Attributes | Comment |
|---|---|---|
| BMP | FORMAT=BMP | |
| CAT | FORMAT=CAT | |
| | COMPRESS=G3FAX | FAX CCITT Group 3 for monochrome black-and-white images (depth of 1) only. |
| | COMPRESS=G4FAX | FAX CCITT Group 4 for monochrome black-and-white images (depth of 1) only. |
| | DESC=*desc* | *Desc* is a catalog description. |
| DIB | FORMAT=DIB | Supported only under the Windows 95, Windows 98, Windows NT, and OS/2 operating systems. |
| EMF | FORMAT=EMF | Supported only under Windows 95, Windows 98, and Windows NT. |
| EPSI | FORMAT=EPSI | |
| GIF | FORMAT=GIF | |
| JFIF | FORMAT=JFIF | Required for writing JPEG files that use the JPEG File Interchange Format. |
| | DCT=*mode* | Specifies which type of Discrete Cosine Transform (DCT) to use when processing the image. *Mode* can be |
| | | INT　　　　an integer DCT |
| | | FAST　　　a faster and less accurate integer DCT |
| | | FLOAT　　a slightly more accurate method that can be much slower unless the host has very fast floating-point hardware. |
| | | The results of the floating-point method can vary across host machines, whereas the integer methods should give the same results on all hosts. |
| | GRAYSCALE | Produces a gray-scale image even if the JPEG file is in color. This option is useful for viewing on monochrome displays. The reader runs noticeably faster in this mode. |
| | VERSION | Writes to the SAS log the version number and copyright messages for the Independent JPEG Group's JFIF software. |
| | BASELINE | Generates a baseline JPEG file even for low-quality settings. |
| | OPTIMIZE | Optimizes the entropy encoding parameters. This usually results in a smaller JPEG file, but writer processing is longer and more memory is needed. Image quality and speed of decompression are not affected. |
| | PROGRESSIVE | Produces a progressive JPEG file in which the data is stored in multiple scans of increasing quality. This option is useful if the file is being transmitted over a slow communications link and the decoder can display each scan as it is received. |
| | QUALITY=*n* | Scales the quantization tables to adjust for image quality. *N* must be in the range 0...100. 0 is worst; 100 is best; the default is 75. This option lets you trade file size for quality of the reconstructed image. Normally, you want to use the lowest quality setting that results in an image that is visually indistinguishable from the original image. The optimal value will vary from image to image. |
| | SMOOTH=*n* | Specifies the strength of the smoothing filter to eliminate dithering noise. *N* must be in the range 0...100. The default is 0, which disables smoothing. A smoothing factor that is too large blurs the image. |
| MET | FORMAT=MET | Supported only under OS/2. |

| File Type | Writer Attributes | Comment |
|---|---|---|
| PBM | FORMAT=PBM | |
| | COMPRESS=NONE | Text PBM file (default). |
| | COMPRESS=BINARY | Binary PBM file. |
| | COMPRESS=RAW | Binary PBM file. |
| PCL | FORMAT=PCL | |
| | DPI=*num* | Number of dots per inch to be used in the output file. |
| | EPS | Does not reset the printer margins. You can use this option to embed an image into another PCL document. |
| PICT | FORMAT=PICT | Supported only in the Macintosh environment. |
| PNG | FORMAT=PNG | |
| PS | FORMAT=PS | |
| | COMPRESS=NONE | Default for color images. |
| | COMPRESS=RLE | Run-length encoded; default for gray-scale images. |
| | DPI=*num* | Number of dots per inch to be used in the output file. |
| | EPS | Does not reset the printer margins. You can use this option to embed an image in another PCL document. |
| | PREVIEW | Specifies whether a scaled-down, 1-bit, black-and-white preview image is written into the encapsulation header. The preview image enables this file to be read by software (such as SAS) that does not support a real PostScript reader. |
| | PREWIDTH=*x*PREHEIGHT=*y* | Size of the preview image in pixels if PREVIEW is specified (default: 25% of original size). |
| | XSCALE | Directly sets width scaling (default: calculate it). |
| | YSCALE | Directly sets height scaling (default: calculate it). |
| | PAGEX | Sets the output page width in pixels (default: 612, typical 8.5-inch page). |
| | PAGEY | Sets the output page height in pixels (default: 792, typical 11-inch page). |
| | NOFIT | Turns off the default of scaling down an oversized image to fit the page. Must be used with XSCALE and YSCALE. |
| TIFF | FORMAT=TIFF | |
| | COMPRESS=NONE | Default. |
| | COMPRESS=G3FAX | FAX CCITT Group 3 for monochrome black-and-white (depth of 1) images only. |
| | COMPRESS=G4FAX | FAX CCITT Group 4 for monochrome black-and-white (depth of 1) images only. |
| WMF | FORMAT=WMF | Supported only under MicroSoft Windows operating systems. |
| XBM | FORMAT=XBM | Supported for writing only from interactive windows under UNIX. |
| XPM | FORMAT=XPM | Supported only on the X Window System under UNIX. |

# Attributes for Reading Images from Kodak DC40 Cameras

The image command READ supports reading from Kodak DC 40 digital cameras only under Windows 95 and Windows 98 cameras and scanners. When you read images from these devices, you must include the DEVICE= attribute with the command.When you use DEVICE=CAMERA, you must also specify either TAKEPIC or PICNUM=. For example:

```
rc=imgop(taskid,'READ','kodakdc40','device=camera takepic');
```

The TAKEPIC and PICNUM commands are mutually exclusive. The DELLAST and DELALL commands are also mutually exclusive.

You can specify the RESET or RES command only if the camera is empty. Use the DELALL command to empty the camera.

You can use the FLASH and EXPOSE options to control the flash unit and exposure. You can also change the flash and exposure settings manually on the camera itself.

Any changes that you make by specifying the RES, FLASH, and EXPOSE commands will be in effect until you change them again.

**Table A2.4**  Attributes for Reading Images from Kodak DC40 Cameras

| Attribute | Description |
|---|---|
| DELLAST | Deletes the last image as the picture is returned from the camera. Specifying this option limits the number of images the camera can hold. |
| DELALL | Deletes all of the images in the camera (empties the camera). |
| EXPOSE=*shift* | Shifts the exposure under or over the automatic exposure setting. You can specify **+1**, **+.5**, **0**, **–.5**, or **–1**. |
| FLASH=*setting* | Sets the flash unit to **AUTO**, **ON**, or **OFF**. |
| PICNUM=*n* | Gets picture number *n*. |
| PORT=*n* | Specifies the serial port number of the camera. The default is to search for and automatically detect the camera. |
| RES=*resolution* | Sets the resolution. You can specify **HIGH** or **LOW**. You cannot change the resolution after pictures have been taken. |
| RESET | Resets the camera to default values. |
| TAKEPIC | Takes a photo and returns it. |
| THUMB | Returns a thumbnail-sized image instead of a full-sized image. |

# Attributes for Reading Images from HP ScanJet and TWAIN Scanners

Table A2.5 on page 779 describes the attributes that are supported the under Windows 95, Windows 98, and Windows NT operating systems for the HP ScanJet scanners and TWAIN scanners. They are supported under HP/UX operating systems for HP ScanJet scanners only. You must specify DEVICE=SCANNER. For example:

```
rc=imgop(taskid,'READ','hpscan','device=scanner dpi=100');
```

**Table A2.5**  Device Attributes for HP ScanJet and TWAIN Scanners

| Attribute | Description | Default |
|---|---|---|
| BRIGHT=*n* | Sets the brightness setting. | 0 |
| CONTRAST=*n* | Sets the contrast setting. This option is ignored with bi-tonal images. | 0 |

| Attribute | Description | Default |
|---|---|---|
| DPI=*n* | Sets the number of dots per inch. | 200 |
| FEEDER \| NOFEEDER | Specifies how the document is scanned. FEEDER assumes that there is a document feeder and produces an error if there is no document feeder. NOFEEDER scans from the bed and ignores the feeder if one is attached. | Use the feeder if it is attached; otherwise, use scan from the bed. |
| TYPE=*type* | Sets the type of image to generate. You can specify BITONAL, RGB, or GRAY. For HP/UX scanners, you can also specify CMAP. | For HP/UX scanners, BITONAL; for TWAIN scanners, the highest resolution (bits/pixel) that is supported by the device. |
| UNITS=*units* | Sets the size units for the SIZE and START options. You can specify IN, CM, MM, or PIXEL. | IN |
| XDPI=*n* | Sets the dots per inch for the width only. | 200 |
| XSIZE=*d* | Sets the width to scan (decimal value). | 8.5 inches |
| XSTART=*d* | Sets the starting point of the scan along the width. | 0 |
| YDPI=*n* | sets DPI for height only | 200 |
| YSIZE=*d* | Sets the height to scan (decimal value). | 11 inches |
| YSTART=*d* | Sets the starting point of the scan along the height. | 0 |

# Attributes for Reading Images from TWAIN Scanners and Cameras

Table A2.6 on page 780 describes the attributes that are supported for TWAIN scanners and cameras under the Windows 95, Windows 98, and Windows NT operating systems.

**Table A2.6**   Device Attributes for TWAIN Scanners and Cameras

| Attribute | Description |
|---|---|
| SELSRC | Displays the TWAIN Select Source window. The default source is highlighted, but you can select a different source. If you do not specify SELSRC, then the application uses the default source. |
| SETCAP | Displays the data source's capability window. |
| SCNAME=*product* | Sets the default source. Specify the product name (as displayed in the TWAIN Select Source window) of the scanner. (This product name may not be the same as the name of the scanner.) If *product* matches more than one scanner's product name, then the first match is selected.<br><br>If you do not specify SCNAME, then the source defaults either to the last source used or to the first source in the list (if the application has not been run yet). |

# Index

# Your Turn

If you have comments or suggestions about *SAS® Component Language: Reference, Version 8*, please send them to us on a photocopy of this page or send us electronic mail.

Send comments about this book to

SAS Institute
Publications Division
SAS Campus Drive
Cary, NC 27513
**email:** yourturn@sas.com

Send suggestions about the software to

SAS Institute
Technical Support Division
SAS Campus Drive
Cary, NC 27513
**email:** suggest@sas.com

*Welcome * Bienvenue * Willkommen * Yohkoso * Bienvenido*

# SAS Publishing Is Easy to Reach

## Visit our Web page located at www.sas.com/pubs

You will find product and service details, including

- **sample chapters**
- **tables of contents**
- **author biographies**
- **book reviews**

Learn about

- **regional user-group conferences**
- **trade-show sites and dates**
- **authoring opportunities**
- **custom textbooks**

## Explore all the services that SAS Publishing has to offer!

### Your Listserv Subscription Automatically Brings the News to You

Do you want to be among the first to learn about the latest books and services available from SAS Publishing? Subscribe to our listserv **newdocnews-l** and, once each month, you will automatically receive a description of the newest books and which environments or operating systems and SAS® release(s) that each book addresses.

To subscribe,

1. Send an e-mail message to **listserv@vm.sas.com**.

2. Leave the "Subject" line blank.

3. Use the following text for your message:

   subscribe **NEWDOCNEWS-L** *your-first-name your-last-name*

   For example: subscribe NEWDOCNEWS-L John Doe

SAS Publishing